CORNELL STUDIES IN CIVIL LIBERTY

ROBERT E. CUSHMAN, *Advisory Editor*

Conscription of Conscience

THE AMERICAN STATE AND THE CONSCIENTIOUS OBJECTOR

1940-1947

CONSCRIPTION
of CONSCIENCE

The American State and the

Conscientious Objector, 1940-1947

BY MULFORD Q. SIBLEY

University of Minnesota

AND PHILIP E. JACOB

University of Pennsylvania

Cornell University Press

ITHACA, NEW YORK, 1952

PRINTED IN THE UNITED STATES OF AMERICA BY THE

VAIL-BALLOU PRESS, INC., BINGHAMTON, NEW YORK

Editor's Preface

O<small>N</small> J<small>UNE</small> 8, 1789, James Madison introduced in the House of Representatives his proposals for a federal Bill of Rights. There were twenty clauses in Madison's draft and one of them read as follows:

> The right of the people to keep and bear arms shall not be infringed; a well armed and well regulated militia being the best security of a free country; but *no person religiously scrupulous of bearing arms shall be compelled to render military service in person* [italics added].

The concession to the "conscientious objector" in the last clause was retained in two later committee drafts of the proposed amendments and was seriously debated by Congress, but it was dropped out before the Bill of Rights took its final form. We may conclude that the Founding Fathers were unwilling to extend to those "religiously scrupulous of bearing arms" any specific constitutional exemption.

The problem of the conscientious objector was not solved, however, by failing to mention it in the Constitution. It was merely dumped, as a problem of policy rather than of constitutional law, into the lap of Congress, whose delegated power to "raise and support armies" carried with it the authority to deal with men whose religious scruples prevented them from performing military service. It was, of course, not necessary to deal with the problem at all so long as we could fight our wars with volunteer armies. But when in World War I we resorted to universal selective conscription into the armed forces, the difficulties and complexities of the conscientious objector problem were brought home to us for the first time. While it was perhaps not a problem of major proportions, viewed relatively, it was by its nature a persistent one; and there grew up a fairly general opinion that it had not been handled as wisely and humanely as it should have been, in spite of the fact that the Selective Service Act of 1917 did recognize certain forms of conscientious objection and made concessions to them.

With a second world war raging in Europe, Congress passed the Selective Training and Service Act of 1940. In the enactment and implementing of this statute very serious thought was given to the problem of how the conscientious objector might be most fairly dealt with conformably to the demands of military security. Advice and co-operation were sought by the government from the old and respected pacifist churches and societies, and a number of novel policies and procedures were set in motion in an effort to avoid or correct the mistakes of World War I.

In 1944 the Rockefeller Foundation made a grant to Cornell University to be used under my direction for making studies which would record our management of civil liberties during World War II. It seemed to me that the conscientious objector presented a problem in civil liberty, for while, as we have seen, he is without any special constitutional protection, it is clear that the national conscience cannot condone unfair or inhumane treatment extended to those who, as Mr. Justice Holmes put it, "believe more than some of us do in the teachings of the Sermon on the Mount."

I persuaded Mulford Q. Sibley and Philip E. Jacob to undertake jointly this laborious study. I did this in full knowledge of the fact that both men are sympathetic to the viewpoint of the conscientious objector. I felt that this predisposition was an asset rather than a disqualification, for it enabled them to bring to this study a keenness of interest, a sympathetic understanding, and an acuteness of perception which could hardly be possessed by one who was indifferent or perhaps even hostile to the conscientious objector's position. Their high reputations for sound scholarship provided an adequate guarantee that the problem would be treated with objective honesty and the facts presented with scrupulous integrity. As one who is not a conscientious objector, I wish to pay tribute to the scholarly neutrality with which the two authors have handled this controversial problem.

This book was written to tell the story and analyze the problem of the conscientious objector in World War II. That is what it does. The story stops with 1947. Unforeseen circumstances prevented the earlier publication of this book, but it has seemed neither feasible nor desirable to try to bring the record down to date by discussing what has happened to the conscientious objector since the authors, some three years ago, completed the work as it was originally planned.

I wish to associate myself with Professors Jacob and Sibley in expressing gratitude to those who were generous enough to contribute the information, suggestions, and criticism which added to the value and reliability of this book.

ROBERT E. CUSHMAN

Ithaca, New York
May, 1952

ACKNOWLEDGMENTS

THE AUTHORS are grateful for assistance and counsel rendered by many persons and organizations.

The manuscript, in whole or in part, was read by Roger N. Baldwin, Purnell Benson, Stephen Carey, Edgar Crane, Harrop Freeman, Paul C. French, Richard W. Taylor, Norman Thomas, and Walter W. Van Kirk.

General Lewis Hershey, A. S. Imirie, and the late Dr. Clarence Dykstra extended many courtesies and made available some of the records of the Selective Service headquarters. James V. Bennett, Director of the Bureau of Prisons, and his staff also placed valuable data at the disposal of the authors. None of these officials ventured any appraisal or criticism of the book.

The authors acknowledge the generous and steady co-operation of the officers and staffs of the American Friends Service Committee, the Mennonite Service Committee, the Brethren Service Committee, the War Resisters League, the American Civil Liberties Union (in New York, San Francisco, and Los Angeles), Northern California Service Board for Conscientious Objectors, and the National Service Board for Religious Objectors. The Pacifist Research Bureau made a major contribution in the form of staff assistance in assembling data.

Mary Ogilvie, Harvey Cochran, Ada Wardlaw, Genevieve Walther, and William Wardlaw served as research associates; Melvin Gingerich and Leslie Eisan aided in providing and checking material; John W. Hastie helped prepare the manuscript for the printer.

George Houser and Winslowe Ames allowed the use of correspondence with conscientious objectors.

THE AUTHORS

Contents

PART 4. OBJECTORS AS LAW VIOLATORS

PART 5. DILEMMAS AND PROSPECTS

Conscription of Conscience

THE AMERICAN STATE AND THE CONSCIENTIOUS OBJECTOR

1940-1947

1: The Problem of Conscience in the Modern State

CONSCIENTIOUS objection need not refer to war. Indeed, the term was used originally to designate scruples about many things—vaccination, for example. But the overwhelming impact of war on the modern world; the compulsion which the state has increasingly felt called upon to use to recruit its armed servants; the "totalitarian" character of war itself; the persistence of individuals who somehow believe that war is immoral—all these factors have combined to narrow the application of "conscientious objector" primarily to those who refuse in various degrees to conform to the state's and society's requirements with respect to warmaking and military service. The conscientious objector is thus an individual whose scruples will not allow him to assist in the waging of war, and his refusal to assist inevitably leads to a clash between the conscientious claims that he supports and the demands of the state that professes to believe that it is fighting to protect social values and ideals.

Conscientious objection to war is very old in human history. The Chinese philosopher Lao-tze, more than 500 years before Christ, evolved a social theory that could easily be used to justify refusal of military service. Although we do not read of them in history, there were probably conscientious objectors in Europe prior to the rise of Christianity. During the first two and a half centuries of the Christian era, Christians were almost without exception conscientious objectors, not only because they objected to the shedding of blood, but also because service in the army was connected with worship

1

of idols and sacrifices to the emperor. When the Church, after the conversion of Constantine, decreed the excommunication of Christians who threw away their arms in time of peace, religious objection to war in Europe became a minority current. In most generations, however, it was held by small groups—in the twelfth century, for example, by the Albigensians and in the sixteenth by many Anabaptists. With the breakup of medieval Christianity, the sects that at one time or another held to the principles of war objection became relatively numerous; there were the Mennonites of various kinds, the Quakers, the Christadelphians, the Church of the Brethren. And to the religious objectors were added those who, on "rational" grounds, took a similar position.

Conscientious objection in the modern world is closely related to the phenomenon of modern military conscription. There had been examples of forced military service before the eighteenth century, it is true, but never had the systems been as universal and as effectively administered as the conscription patterned after French revolutionary legislation. French conscription was copied throughout Continental Europe in the nineteenth century and in the United States and Great Britain during the twentieth. Modern conscription arises with the modern "democratic" state, or, perhaps more accurately, with the "mass" state. Against the claims of the "mass" state the objector sets his own principles of moral obligation; and in opposing the "mass" state, he is made by legal and moral pressures to feel that he is attacking not merely a small ruling class but the vast majority of his right-minded fellow citizens.

How the modern state has dealt with conscientious objectors becomes an important chapter in intellectual, legal, and general history alike. Here a few examples from British and American experience will illustrate the modern problem.

In Great Britain

On the whole, Great Britain made more serious efforts to establish legal provision for conscientious objectors than any other state in the world. During the First World War, the law set up a scheme of alternative civilian service. There were approximately 16,000 objectors of various types. Of these, 5,000 accepted alternative civilian service, 1,200 worked in the Friends' Ambulance Unit overseas,

3,400 entered noncombatant work in the army and navy. But the tribunals that passed on objector cases denied the claims of about 6,000. These were tried and sent to prison. Later on, the government worked out a scheme whereby those sent to prison would be offered civilian work outside prison but under penal regulations. About 4,500 of the 6,000 whose claims had been denied were willing to undertake work under this "Home Office" plan, as it was called. The remaining 1,500, however, continued as absolutists, and some suffered severe privations. About 900 served prison sentences of two years or more, and 10 died in prison. Thirty-one of the absolutists became insane as a direct result of their experiences. Several objectors were sent to France with the army where, under military law, they could be sentenced to death for refusal to serve. Thirty-four actually received the death sentence and were saved only because many in Great Britain had heard of their plight and petitioned for commutation. At the beginning of 1919, 1,359 objectors still remained in prison, of whom 147 had received sentences after Armistice Day.[1]

Conscientious objectors increased in numbers between the wars. With able spokesmen in Parliament and press, they developed a widespread and evangelical following. They were influential in the Labor Party. When in 1935 Anglican Canon H. R. L. Sheppard invited men of military age to sign a pledge renouncing war and promising never to support another, 80,000 responded within a short time; by the opening stages of the Second World War, the Peace Pledge Union, as Sheppard's organization came to be called, claimed well over 100,000 members. Both the War Resisters International and the International Fellowship of Reconciliation—the two most prominent international organizations of pacifists and objectors—had their headquarters in London. The pacifist movement in Great Britain was criticized from time to time on the ground that its ideas had led to the supposedly defenseless position in which Great Britain found itself at the opening of World War II. On the other hand, when it became clear that the Labor Party was abandoning its opposition to "rearmament," its leader in the House of Commons, George Lansbury—an out-and-out pacifist—resigned. Lord Ponsonby, leader in the House of Lords, gave up his position for the same reason and later left the Labor Party altogether. As in the United States, pacifism

and conscientious objection had a considerable influence among
university students.

When in 1939 Great Britain established conscription, it was clear
that opinion would insist on more liberal provisions for conscientious
objectors than those in force during World War I days. The National
Service Act of 1939 established a separate Register for Conscientious
Objectors and independent civilian tribunals to pass upon the claims
of those seeking status as objectors. Objection could be for any
reason, and the objector could declare scruples about being registered on the Military Service Register, performing military service,
or engaging in combatant duties. If an individual could convince a
tribunal that he objected to all three, the tribunal, taking all the facts
into consideration, could exempt him either conditionally or unconditionally. If he was placed in the former category, he would be excused from any military service on condition that he take up the kind
of civilian work specified by the tribunal, which might be with or
without pay. If placed in the "unconditional exemption" class, the
objector's name remained on the Register of Conscientious Objectors, but he could not be required to perform either military or
alternative civilian service. Thus Great Britain provided for noncombatant, alternative civilian service, and absolutist objection.

Tribunals had relatively wide discretion with respect to assignments of conditionally exempted objectors: some were simply ordered to remain in the occupations they then held; others were
instructed to perform agricultural service or to obtain employment in
another occupation, for which they might have to train. The labor
might be either part or full time, paid or unpaid. It had, however,
to be civilian labor under civil direction.[2]

Despite these seemingly liberal provisions, considerable numbers
became entangled in the meshes of the law. If one refused to register
as an objector, for example (and some did take the position that
even registration as an objector was a part of military service or a
recognition of the right of conscription), one could be fined up to £5.
If the tribunal, local or appellate, did not recognize one's claims,
one could be imprisoned for refusal to obey the order to report for
medical examination. However, the law after December 18, 1941,
provided a procedure whereby those sentenced to prison for refus-

ing medical examination could have their cases reviewed. If the objector had previously been registered on the Register of Objectors, either voluntarily or involuntarily, if he was undergoing or had undergone imprisonment for three months or more for failure to obey a court order instructing him to take a medical examination for service in the army, and if he claimed that his disobedience was due to conscientious objection to military service or combatant duties, he could petition the Appellate Tribunal to reconsider his case. If the Tribunal ruled favorably, the objector could be assigned to one of the usual categories and thus have his claims recognized. A similar provision existed for those who disobeyed military orders on conscientious grounds and who had been sentenced to imprisonment for three months or more by a court-martial. Even if one had not originally registered as an objector, there was provision for an advisory tribunal to review the cases of any persons who had committed military offenses on allegedly conscientious grounds. The advisory tribunal had the power to recommend transfer to noncombatant service in the army or outright discharge from the service.

In sum, the laws and regulations developed for conscientious objectors in Great Britain during World War II were the most elaborate and far-reaching (in terms of their concern and sensitivity for the individual conscience) in the world.

There were approximately four times as many objectors as in World War I. Their numbers in relation to total registration under the National Service Acts tended to fall in successive registrations. In October, 1939, 222 men out of every 10,000 registered claimed conscientious objection; by 1942, the number had fallen to 36 per 10,000.[3] On the whole, the percentages of those given unconditional exemption, conditional exemption, noncombatant military service, and full military service by local tribunals remained roughly the same throughout the war. Thus, up to July, 1941, 41,313 cases had been heard by local tribunals. Of these, 2,389 (6%) were granted total exemption; 15,310 (37%), conditional exemption; 12,168 (29%) were assigned to noncombatant service; and 11,446 (28%) had their claims denied. By July, 1943, tribunals had heard 56,902 cases and the figures in the respective categories were 2,760 (4.9%); 21,423 (37.60%); 16,194 (28.5%); and 16,525 (29%). By the beginning of

1945, the corresponding figures were 59,836 cases heard and divided into 2,865 (4.8%); 22,568 (37.7%); 16,753 (28%); and 17,650 (29.5%).[4]

By the time the war with Japan was concluded, 2,337 male objectors had been sent to prison for refusal of medical examinations and 1,013 had been court-martialed.[5]

There was no provision for conscientious objection to such legal requirements as fire-watching, civil defense, and industrial conscription, and many objectors were prosecuted because of conscientious scruples respecting such occupations. For example, down to the end of hostilities with Japan, 479 men and 80 women had been prosecuted for refusal, on conscientious grounds, to watch fires.

The problem of "cat-and-mouse" treatment—repeated prosecutions of objectors for essentially the same offense—was not the issue in the Second World War that it had been during World War I. However, the problem did arise. For example, of all objectors court-martialed down to the end of hostilities, 328 had been prosecuted more than once, often because of the technical requirement of the regulation that the sentence of a court-martial must be three months' imprisonment in a civil prison (not detention in military confinement) to qualify for review by an appellate tribunal. Some objectors, too, were sentenced several times for refusal of medical examinations. Cat-and-mouse procedures also arose in relation to the power of the government to direct men and women into any civil work it believed essential. As a matter of concession, objectors were not assigned to work directly connected with the war effort. But some objectors felt they could not perform even nonmilitary work to which they were directed, either because they were absolutists or because they believed that the work they were already performing was more important than that to which they had been directed. In fire-watching, too, cat-and-mouse treatment occurred. The classic case was that of George Elphick, who was prosecuted no fewer than eight times for continuing to refuse. No sooner would he be released from jail than he would be ordered to fire-guard work, would refuse, and would then again face either a fine or prison.[6]

On the whole, however, British practice seems to have been remarkably liberal. Not only was there a much better public understanding of the position of the objector, but administrative authorities having to do with his problems were much more carefully selected than during World War I. All during the war there continued to be men prominent in the literary world and in Parliament who spoke out for the objector's rights.[7] Even at the time of the most severe bombing raids on London and Coventry, there were members of both houses of Parliament who took the trouble to ask questions of Cabinet Ministers and to voice appeals on behalf of objectors. There was nothing comparable in the United States during the Second World War. The tolerance which Great Britain showed to objectors was as remarkable in the annals of civil liberties as its military resistance to Germany was in the history of war.

New Zealand. Compulsory military training began in New Zealand in 1911. During World War I the law exempted only those who were members of a religious body having as one of its tenets objection to arms-bearing; and even then noncombatant service in the army was required. Altogether, about 400 were sentenced to prison, for terms ranging up to two years. Finally, in December, 1918, with two members of the House of Representatives dissenting,[8] all those whose claims as objectors had not been recognized were by act of Parliament deprived of their civil rights for ten years.

Compulsory military training was highly unpopular between wars, so much so that virtually a general strike against it was carried on by schoolboys subject to its demands. Encouraged in many cases by their parents, the young men simply failed to show up for training. All together, some 40,000 were punished for refusing training. These tactics were apparently successful, for in 1931 operation of the conscription law was formally suspended.

During the Second World War, all those who held "a genuine belief that it is wrong to engage in warfare in any circumstances" were exempt; and provision was made for alternative civilian service. However, those who confined their objection to the Second World War (without necessarily being opposed to all wars) went unrecognized, as did the absolutists.

While the law was relatively liberal, its administration was less so. To illustrate: more than 3,000 claims involving conscientious objection had been heard down to the beginning of 1944; of these, 1,800 were allowed and 1,200 disallowed (about 40 per cent of the total).[9] Since there was no appeal from the classification board (unlike both Great Britain and the United States), this meant that the 1,200 whose claims had been dismissed would either go to prison or be rejected on medical or other grounds for service in the army.

Those who were granted conditional exemption could choose their own work, provided that it was in the public interest and that the income was no higher than that of a private soldier. Any income in excess of a private soldier's salary would be taken by a special tribunal and turned over to the New Zealand Social Security Fund. All together, about 700 had been granted alternative civilian service at the conclusion of hostilities with Japan.

More than 800 objectors were serving in prison or "defaulters' camps" at the beginning of 1945. The practice was that a conscientious objector who had been denied his claim and who still refused to accept military service would be sentenced to up to three months in prison, after which he would be confined to a defaulters' camp for the duration of the war. By 1945 there were nine such camps, operated with unusual strictness. Some camps were surrounded by barbed-wire fences ten feet high and floodlighted at night to prevent escape. The objector in defaulters' camp was not allowed to receive visits from friends unless he had no relatives in New Zealand. When visits did occur, an attendant was usually listening. Objectors lived in huts that were not heated. Much of the work done was of the "made work" variety, and when objectors asked to be allowed to contribute their services to mental hospitals, where facilities were grossly inadequate, they were not only refused but were threatened with disciplinary action should they renew their requests. "Agitators" in defaulters' camps were often disciplined by means of solitary confinement in their own huts. Appeals to the Prime Minister (himself an objector in the First World War) to modify this system were largely in vain, until on June 8, 1945, a scheme was worked out whereby those in defaulters' camps could be paroled. But by then the war was nearly over.

Canada. Canadian conscription differed from most compulsory service laws during the Second World War in that no one could be conscripted for service outside Canada—a concession to strong French-Canadian opposition. Conscientious objection was, then, to military service at home. Regulations provided "postponement" of service for those who conscientiously objected "by reason of religious training and belief, to war in any form and to participation in combatant military service." As a matter of practice "religious training and belief" was interpreted broadly, even atheists being included within its terms. Mennonites and Doukhobors were automatically granted postponement on certificate of a pastor or leader.[10]

As in New Zealand during World War II, there was no appeal from the decisions of the mobilization boards that classified objectors. Those whose claims were denied would be escorted to a military barracks and if they persisted in refusing to join the army would be court-martialed. After one, two, or three courts-martial, the military authorities would usually recommend to the Mobilization Board that the objector's claims be recognized. Some three hundred objectors were thus court-martialed, and another four hundred were prosecuted for failure to obey the orders of Alternative Service officers.

Those granted postponement as objectors were offered the opportunity to serve in the medical corps of the army, and some two hundred chose to do so. The others (there were about eleven thousand objectors granted postponement, all together) came under the authority of the Alternative Service system, headed by the Chief Alternative Service Officer in Ottawa. Originally, the Alternative Service system was under administration of the Selective Service system (hence under military direction), but on April 7, 1943, it was transferred to the Ministry of Labor. Up to 1943, objectors were assigned to work camps engaged in forestry and road-building labor. After the transfer of alternative service from Selective Service, however, individual assignments of objectors became the practice, although in the last year of the war there were still nearly five hundred men working in alternative-service camps. In camps, men were entitled to fifty cents per day plus board and room and medical care. Dependents of men in camps were cared for by the province or municipality involved, which was then compensated by the Ministry of Labor. Walkouts from camp would be sentenced to jail for terms ranging from thirty days to six months.

Those who were assigned to individual labor, as contrasted with camp work, might be given any type of employment. The Alternative Service system would make a contract with the employer, who would pay prevailing wages. The objector kept twenty-five dollars a month and thirty-eight dollars for room and board, with ten to twenty dollars for his dependents. The balance would be turned over to the Canadian Red Cross, which used the money to care for Canadian prisoners of war and dependents of men in the army and navy. Some of the Jehovah's Witnesses and Doukhobors raised objections to this use of the money, but the system was not changed. The Alternative Service system was reluctant to assign objectors to social service work or to educational positions where they might have, from the government's point of view, a "pernicious" influence. Some, however, were allowed to serve as teachers in Eskimo schools and a few in the Japanese-Canadian relocation centers.

In the United States Prior to World War II

American experience with conscription began with the Civil War and hence it can be said that the issue of conscience against the state dates from that period; for while local pressures and militia laws had created difficulties for objectors in the Revolutionary War and during the War of 1812, it was not until the Civil War that anything resembling the modern type of conscription was adopted.

Both the Union and the Confederacy accepted the principle of compulsory military service. The law in the North permitted the hiring of substitutes and some objectors took advantage of this provision, despite the fact that pacifist religious organizations generally discouraged the practice. If an objector had scruples about hiring a substitute, his friends and family might do it for him, and there was very little he could do about it. Some objectors who refused to compromise their position found themselves mishandled by the military. Some were paroled for hospital work, and others were given indefinite paroles by the President. Then, too, the generally lax enforcement of the law, vigorous opposition to it in certain districts, and other similar factors lightened the burdens of the objector in the North.[11]

In the South, conscription was adopted early in the war and until 1864, under certain circumstances, members of pacifist sects could secure exemption on payment of five hundred dollars. Some objectors could not or would not take advantage of this loophole and thus clashed with the military. Objectors in the South were in a peculiarly difficult position, because they were not only opposed to war but also on the whole sympathized with the Union and with the conception of freedom for which it was presumably fighting. They were thus looked upon in many districts as "fifth-column" agents for the Yankees. Some hid out in the woods to escape the wrath of their neighbors and the demands of conscription, and many were eventually sent to prison. Some were forced into the front lines of the army, where they generally refused to aim their weapons at the enemy. In general, the lot of the objector in the South was much harder than that of his brother in the North.[12]

During the Spanish-American War, of course, the problem of conscientious objection did not arise in a legal sense, as there was no conscription law.

When World War I broke out in 1914, opinion in the United States seems to have been virtually unanimous in demanding neutrality. General "pacifist" sentiment—opposition to war, without any explicit statement as to what one would do in case of a specific war—was strong. The President seemed to reflect this general view in his neutrality proclamation, when he spoke of neutrality in thought as well as in deed; later he talked of "peace without victory."

But public opinion changed sharply after the declaration of war on Germany in 1917. The tendency for Americans to demand uniformity and to be suspicious of eccentricity now became apparent in treatment of the conscientious objector. The conscription law itself was passed on May 18, 1917, with rather narrow provisions for conscientious objection, although the Friends, the American Union Against Militarism, and such individuals as Jane Addams, Lillian Wald, and Norman Thomas had argued strenuously for more liberal treatment. As finally approved, the law, in Section 4, provided:

Nothing in this act contained shall be construed to require or compel any person to serve in any of the forces herein provided for who is found to be a member of any well recognized religious sect or organization at present organized and existing and whose existing creed or principles forbid its members to participate in war in any form and whose religious convictions are against war or participation therein in accordance with the creed or principles of said religious organizations, but no person so exempted shall be exempted from service in any capacity that the President shall declare to be noncombatant.

Thus exemption was provided only for those who were members of "well recognized" religious organizations whose creeds forbade participation in war; even then, the exemption extended only to combatant military service, thus making no provision whatsoever for those who might have conscientious scruples against service in both combatant and noncombatant military service. And this rather clumsily worded "exemption" provision, which excluded "political" and "philosophical" objectors and even "religious" objectors unaffiliated with a Peace Church, was not changed during the course of World War I.

According to War Department figures, 64,693 claims for noncombatant status under the law were made, and 56,830 of these claims were recognized as valid by the local Selective Service boards. Only 29,679 objectors, however, were found physically fit for military service and only 20,873 were actually inducted into service. Of these 20,000, 3,989 continued to maintain their position after reaching camp; some 16,000 were persuaded by the pressures of the time to abandon the status that had been granted them. The nearly 4,000 who persisted in their views actually included a number whose claims had not been recognized by local boards but who continued to maintain their position even in military camp. There were also a number of absolutists who refused even to register under the terms of the law or to appear for medical examinations. How many fell within this category is uncertain. Thus objectors were not numerous, especially when it is remembered that there were some 171,000 "draft evaders" and 2,810,296 men inducted into the armed forces, all together.[13]

What happened to the 4,000 objectors who refused to modify their views? The answer to this question is complex. In the first place, it should be noted that selection for service by a local board led immediately to induction into the Army, whether one was an objector or not. Thus those objectors whose claims were not recognized, as well as those who were given c.o. status, found themselves in a military organization. If one objected both to noncombatant and to combatant military service, there were only two alternatives: either to refuse to register, or to apply for c.o. classification and then refuse to serve in the only c.o. category recognized by law—that of noncombatant military service. If the first alternative were chosen, a prison sentence awaited the objector; if the second avenue were selected, one would have to enter the Army and there await whatever decision the military authorities—ultimately the President—made with respect to one's refusal to join the noncombatant branches.

A problem that immediately arose for objectors was whether to wear the uniform. Some saw no objection, but many refused. On September 25, 1917, the Secretary of War directed that Mennonites not be compelled to wear the uniform in camp, since they had religious scruples about doing so. Gradually, this ruling was applied to other objectors, although until the end of the war certain camp commanders clashed with objectors on the issue.

Even more serious was the fact that many months elapsed before the President finally designated which branches of the armed forces should be regarded as noncombatant and hence open to conscientious objectors. Some objectors were gradually assigned informally to work that they were willing to do, but it was not until March 20, 1918—ten months after the passage of the Selective Service Act—that the President issued an executive order declaring service in the Medical Corps, the Quartermaster Corps, and the Engineer Service as noncombatant. The same executive order directed camp commanders to recognize as objectors those whose claims had not been recognized by local boards but who appeared to the commanders to be sincere.

This order, however, did not solve the problem of what to do with those who objected to both combatant and noncombatant military service, nor did it say anything about the small group of absolutists in camps who objected to all conscripted service. With respect to the first group, however, it did direct that they be "segregated" under officers of tact and treated with consideration, until the Secretary of War should decide what to do with them. But the War Department was slow in making up its mind. For a time it argued that it lacked Congressional authority to assign to civilian work those objecting to noncombatant military service. Indeed, the Attorney General supported this contention. Then, in March, 1918, Congress passed the Farm Furlough Act, which gave the Secretary of War authority to furlough soldiers to farms in order to increase agricultural production. Even after the passage of this act, however—and it was a law that did not have the objectors particularly in mind—the War Department was slow to move. It was June 1 before the first of a series of executive orders was issued which provided a par-

tial solution for the problem—more than a year after the passage of
the Selective Service Act.

These orders permitted the War Department to furlough men for
farm service, for Quaker relief work in France, and for certain types
of industrial labor. But the granting of furloughs in any particular
case was to depend upon personal examinations conducted by a
Board of Inquiry appointed by the Secretary of War. Those whom
the Board held to be "sincere" could be given furloughs for civilian
work, while those adjudged "insincere" and those who rejected both
noncombatant military work and alternative civilian service were
to be court-martialed.

The Board of Inquiry was composed, during most of its existence,
of Major Walter G. Kellogg of the United States Army, United States
Circuit Judge Julian W. Mack, and Dean Harlan F. Stone of the
Columbia University Law School. Moving about from camp to
camp, these men heard the cases of men held as conscientious objectors and decided, often after a hearing of only a few minutes,
which were "sincere" and which "insincere." The Board undoubtedly
made mistakes, and, despite the fact that its hearings were often
rather summary, it had not concluded its labors when the armistice
was signed. Of the approximately 4,000 objectors, some 1,300 eventually entered noncombatant military service (some before the Board
had begun its hearings); about 1,200 were given furloughs to do
farm work; 100, after much discussion and investigation, were assigned to Quaker war relief work in France; 500 were court-martialed
and sentenced to prison (of these, 50 had their convictions reversed
by higher authorities); and at the time of the armistice some 900
were still held in the various military camps throughout the country.

The original sentences of the court-martialed were severe. To
illustrate: 17 were sentenced to death, 142 to life imprisonment, 3
to fifty years, 4 to forty years, and 57 to twenty-five years. None of the
death sentences were actually carried out, and most of the more
severe prison sentences were modified on review. On the whole,
however, the sentences were more severe than those imposed for
comparable offenses in Great Britain and Germany and far more
harsh than sentences given for profiteering or graft in the United
States.

Besides those sentenced by courts-martial, some 100 to 150 objectors who refused to register, or otherwise violated the law for conscientious reasons prior to induction, were sentenced by civil courts.

In military camp and prison alike, objectors were often subjected to indignities and to physical cruelty. Some were beaten; others were hung by their fingers to the doors of their cells in such a way that their feet barely touched the floor. In one case, an objector who refused to don the army uniform was kept in a damp cell, where he contracted pneumonia and died. His dead body was then dressed in the uniform that in life he had spurned, and, thus attired, was sent home to his family. A number of objectors among the absolutists went on hunger strikes and had to be fed forcibly.[14]

On the whole, there was a great deal of bungling by officials in handling objectors during the First World War. Not that the President and Secretary of War were hostile: their intentions seem to have been of the best. But what seemed to them the more pressing concerns of military victory tended to obscure their vision of such civil-liberties issues as conscientious objection. Most of the Army officers concerned apparently tried to be fair in their administration of the law and regulations, although some officers undoubtedly allowed their sadistic tendencies to be expressed against the objectors. The chief difficulties during World War I centered on the narrowness of the law, the slowness and indecision exhibited by the War Department in providing for noncombatant military service, and the rather tardy recognition of the need for some form of alternative civilian service. As for the absolutists, they were never given a place in the legal scheme, either by the original legislation or by executive orders; indeed, few of those in authority seemed even to attempt to understand them.

In addition to the problem of objectors drafted into the Army, there was the issue of treatment of pacifist citizens in civil society. Here the American record during World War I was bad. Many who opposed the war found their houses defaced by irate and "superpatriotic" citizens, often with the connivance of local authorities. One group of Hutterites found its life made so miserable by "patriots" that it eventually migrated to Canada. Some of those who, on grounds of conscience, refused to buy Liberty bonds were threatened with tarring and feathering. In fact, the whole problem of treatment of objectors during World War I was intimately related to the precarious status of civil liberties in general, to the arrest and trial of individuals simply for expressing political opinions, to denial of mailing privileges to newspapers, and to the general spirit of intolerance so characteristic of the period.

That intolerance continued to haunt the American scene between the wars. With criminal syndicalism statutes, "anti-Communist" crusades, and imprisonment for labor organizers, it is not surprising that conscientious objectors had to wait until 1933 before the last of their number who had been imprisoned in World War I were given full and free pardon by the President of the United States. This came none too soon, for, when President Roosevelt issued his proclamation of pardon in 1933, only seven years remained before the problem of conscientious objection in World War II would arise.

Significance of Comparative Study

As we proceed to investigate the whole problem of American conscientious objection during World War II, it is well to keep in mind certain conclusions that emerge from a survey of comparative conscientious objection. The most startling, perhaps, is the fact that conscription should meet so little real opposition. Everywhere during the First and Second World Wars there was but little organized attack on the claims of the state. Most citizens were docile and accepted with only nominal complaints the orders of the drill sergeant and the commands of the military. The fact that the number of conscientious objectors was so infinitesimal is a partial indication of this docility.

Although we have not dealt with the issue here, it is remarkable that hardly any provision for conscientious objectors existed in the laws of Continental Europe's major nations. True, limited recognition of some objectors was granted by Czarist Russia, and similar regulations existed during the early period of Communist rule. However, by the beginning of World War II, formal recognition of objection on the Continent seems to have been confined to Scandinavia and the Netherlands.

Equally remarkable is the relatively large place that pacifism and conscientious objection occupied in the public life of Great Britain. While still a minority current, pacifism in Great Britain was at least understood by a larger percentage of the population than elsewhere in Europe, and the eccentricities and scruples of conscientious objectors were generally respected, particularly during the Second World War.

Finally, one cannot help being impressed by the difficulty, if not the impossibility, of reconciling the claims of the conscientious objector with those of the warmaking and war-preparing state, even where, as in Great Britain during the Second World War, a relatively elaborate and sensitive framework was developed. The imperatives and claims of conscience can assume such a wide variety of forms—not only objection to war and conscription, we should remember—and the cultural monism and centralization of the modern state are increasingly such jealous deities, that the gulf between the varieties of conscience and the uniformities of a state-dominated culture would seem to be unbridgeable. It has often been said that the problem of church in relation to state is an eternal one. The same can be said of conscience and the state.

II: The Community of Conscientious Objectors

A MAJOR clue to the understanding of American—indeed, of all—conscientious objectors is the observation that they came from extremely diverse backgrounds of religious and political belief. The teaching and traditions of the Wengerite Mennonites led them to take one position with reference to the state, while a radically different background constituted the setting for objectors belonging to the Socialist Labor Party. Yet both the Wengerite Mennonite and the Socialist Laborite were opposed to war for reasons of conscience.

Conscientious objectors during the Second World War can be somewhat arbitrarily divided into eight major groups: (1) the Mennonites of various denominations; (2) the Church of the Brethren; (3) the Friends (Quakers); (4) Protestants outside the so-called Peace Churches; (5) Roman Catholics; (6) Jehovah's Witnesses; (7) minor religious groups; and (8) philosophical and political objectors. It is obvious that classifications of this kind are unsatisfactory in many respects, particularly since it can be seen that, in terms of religious and political philosophy, there will be considerable overlapping. But on the whole it seems best to treat the subject in this way, examining the significant teaching of each group, pointing out the relationship of the group and its members to the wider society, and particularly inquiring into grounds for conscientious objection and pacifism.[1]

The Mennonites

The Mennonites were the major inheritors of the great Anabaptist tradition which, flowering for a brief period during the early part of the sixteenth century, was suppressed by the Christian powers of Europe, only to be revived and restated by Menno Simons.[2] The disciples of Menno Simons were often persecuted, and many sought refuge during the seventeenth century in Pennsylvania, where they found congenial fellow colonists in the Quaker followers of William Penn.[3] Later, fellow religionists from Russia emigrated to the United States, so that by the twentieth century more than one hundred thousand Mennonites lived and worked in the United States and Canada. They remained predominantly an agricultural people, usually isolated from the major currents of society, and in their family and church life tended to follow a rather authoritarian type of organization. The father of the household and the bishop or pastor of the church were given wide powers of supervision and direction; the religious and social creeds of the younger generation, it was assumed, would be determined by their elders.

While American Mennonites came to be divided into several denominations—from the conservative Amish to the more "modern" General Conference Mennonites—and adhered with varying degrees of strictness to the main body of traditional Mennonite social and political teaching, it is not impossible to state in broad terms what they believed.

Their position was rooted basically in a sharp dichotomy between the kingdom of the world and the community of the saved. The fall of man, said this conception, has laid the burden of sin on all mankind. Sin implied the absence of a true sense of fellowship among men and hence the necessity for the use of force to maintain some semblance of order in human society. Now the characteristic quality of the state is the use of force for the maintenance of order and for the settlement of disputes among men. Controversies regarding property rights and personal liberty are legitimate concerns of the state, and in settling such questions it is fully justified morally in the use of force. Even war might be necessary in the unregenerate world, since it is the result of sin and the punishment for sin.

But some men have been saved from the blight of inherited sin, said Mennonite doctrine. Through the grace of Christ they have been lifted into that community where love alone is the binding tie. As members of the community of the saved they must, therefore, use only those methods compatible with the New Testament conception of love. Now the New Testament excludes force in any form as an instrumentality for settlement of controversies—physical force, suits at law, administration of justice, participation in the affairs of state (defined, it will be remembered, as being essentially an instrument of force), and, above all, war. Hence members of the community of the saved must rigorously abstain from such means and must, moreover, never ask for protection by "worldly" methods. Even nonviolent "pressure politics" are excluded as a permissible means to members of the community of the saved.[4]

But if the saved are called upon by Mennonite teaching to renounce the methods of the "world," they are equally called upon to obey the laws. The first letter of Peter speaks of the necessity of obedience.[5] Obedience, however, does not mean administration. Thus, while the good Mennonite will meekly obey the law, he will not administer it, for administration implies active participation in the affairs of the world, which for the saved would constitute sin.

Mennonite theory referred to its doctrine on war and the use of force as "nonresistance," the term itself being based upon the sixth chapter of Matthew.[6] Nonresistance, Mennonites were careful to point out, had nothing to do with the "nonviolent resistance" so often associated with modern pacifism; there was no affinity between nonresistance and the techniques used by Gandhi's movement in India.[7] The latter were "political"—power-seeking and power-using—while "nonresistance" meant the refusal to use force or pressure of any kind in human relations. Nonresistance did not mean acquiescence in every case, of course, but if the nonresister found he could not conscientiously do what the state commanded him to do, he would simply refuse and take the consequences, without any attempt to use concerted action in opposition. Nonresistance ruled out both strikes and lockouts in labor disputes; indeed, since pressures of various kinds seemed inevitable in industrial society, it virtually required agrarian communities and modes of life for its full observance.[8] Repudiation of war was thus only one facet of Mennonite social doctrine, for conscientious objection itself was but one expression of a way of life which, consistently and rigorously applied, clashed at almost every point with modern industrialism and with the state that was so largely associated with industrialism.

When the problem of applying this political philosophy to the Second World War became a matter for action, Mennonites generally had no objection to alternative civilian service in lieu of Army service. They rejected, on the one hand, the possibility of noncombatant service in the Army, and, on the other, any course of action that would repudiate civilian service under conscription. The primary objection of most Mennonites was to war, not to conscription.

Mennonites also found it compatible with their general position to administer the Civilian Public Service to which their conscripted members were sent, even though the over-all supervision of Civilian Public Service camps was vested in a government agency (the Selective Service System) which was administered by a general. It is probable that the authoritarian pattern of Mennonite church and home life made it easier for Mennonite objectors to accept without great overt protest the somewhat rigid organization of alternative service.

Any analysis of Mennonite social theory would be incomplete without mention of its position on relief of human suffering. While holding that they were not "of the world," Mennonites also taught that it was incumbent on them to relieve the world's suffering. Hence, like the Friends, they were active in relief enterprises in several parts of the world; in such activities no attempt was made to differentiate between potential recipients who lived in the kingdom of the world and those who dwelt in the community of the saved.

The Brethren

The basic position of the Church of the Brethren was originally not unlike that of the Mennonites. Founded in Germany by Alexander Mack in 1708, the Brethren professed a doctrine of "nonresistance" and found themselves persecuted, in many cases, for their self-separation from the state churches of the time. Like the Mennonites, they found the invitation of William Penn to Pennsylvania attractive and in 1719 began their emigration from Europe. In 1723 their first church was founded, and by the Revolution there were about eight hundred Brethren in the United States.[9]

After the Revolutionary War, during which they were persecuted because of their views on war, the Brethren tended to move westward and to live in isolated communities without adequate educational opportunities. This was their general condition until shortly before the Civil War, when a general revival of learning began which was to restate and reinterpret the position of the church with respect to war and the state.

During this long period of semi-isolation, however, there were occasions when the position of the church was defined. On the whole, the official attitude followed the Mennonite argument that participation in public affairs was tantamount to having relationship with war.

After the end of the pre-Civil War period, while the church continued to maintain its general view of nonresistance, it was undecided about the exact application of the doctrine. On the one hand were the traditional forces within the church which took a Mennonitelike position with respect to participation in general politics, looking upon "pressures" of any kind, including "peace organization," as violative of the spirit of nonresistance. On the other hand, there was a segment of the church which was influenced by the Social Gospel movement of Protestant Christianity and which believed that the church should make its weight felt in the "political" realm.

The latter tendency grew in the period between the First and Second World Wars. Opposition by the church to war was conceived to be not only a negative refusal to bear arms but also an active struggle for reduction of armaments and opposition to conscription. "The church," says Rufus Bowman of this period, "became more of a pressure group endeavoring to influence legislation." [10] Insofar as it moved in that direction, it was, of course, departing from its traditional interpretation of nonresistance and taking on the character of what certain modern pacifists call "nonviolent resistance."

This change should not be exaggerated, nor did it proceed without opposition; even during the period of the Second World War there is evident the clash of the two principles within the church. While the Brethren during the Second World War could hardly be called pure "nonresistants" in the Mennonite sense, they were certainly much closer to that position than any other non-Mennonite religious denomination. While most Brethren young men entered the Army rather than C.P.S. (unlike most Mennonites), those who did accept the traditional "peace" position of the church tended for the most part to give it a semi-Mennonite interpretation. In any reading of the story of American conscientious objection during the Second World War, this must be constantly kept in mind, for on nonresistant assumptions many actions might be logical which on other grounds might appear contradictory and illogical.

The Friends

Quaker tradition in the United States is so long and so comparatively well known that a few words will perhaps suffice to call it to mind. Tracing Quaker origins back to the experiences of George Fox, the seventeenth-century religious genius, modern Quaker insights exhibited all the variations in emphasis which were characteristic of the founders.

There was, however, a common core. Friends judged all matters by what they called the "Inner Light." The "Light" was the spirit of God working through an informed mind and a sensitive conscience. It was neither the mind nor the conscience, but rather that which illumined both mind and conscience.[11] The ethical quality of an individual's action depended upon the quality of the Light Within. While other religious bodies—including even the Mennonites and the Brethren—tended to exalt the authority of the Bible on the subjects of war and the state, the tradition of the Friends made it imperative that they read their Bibles according to judgments pronounced by the Inner Light. Thus, while Quakers were far from rejecting the Bible, its teaching could at best but confirm the insights of the Inner Light, whose pronouncements were independent of any Biblical texts.

Was the Inner Light wholly individual or was it both individual and corporate? The history of the Friends is filled with controversies revolving about these questions. Here we need only remark that the predominant interpretation has been that the Inner Light reveals itself completely only in corporate experience. Against those Friends who would have interpreted the guidance of the Inner Light in purely individualistic terms, Robert Barclay, the great Quaker theologian and writer on church government, developed the theory that one's religious experiences were subject to correction and testing by the experiences of others as revealed in a meeting; that out of the corporate guidance of the Inner Light the authority of church government arose; and that individual Friends, once the sense of the meeting was discovered, were bound by its deliverances—not because they were "coerced" by external authority but because they had come to see that the corporate decision was a more complete manifestation of the Inner Light.[12] While there have always been individualistic interpretations of the Inner Light, the Barclay interpretation can probably be called the predominant one throughout the three centuries of Quakerism.[13]

Yet the modern period of American Quakerism witnesses a gradual breakdown of any real application of the corporate theory of the Inner Light. This can be illustrated by reference to the traditional hostility of the Friends to war. Originally this hostility was taken as a matter of course. No convert could remain long within the Society of Friends without giving up his sword; and in the history of American Friends, it was the rule down to the nineteenth century that those members of the Society who joined the Army or Navy were automatically expelled from the Society. By the First and Second World Wars, however, corporate control in so significant a matter had completely vanished. In this respect, the Inner Light seemed to be interpreted in a purely individualistic sense, and, while the official position of Friends' Meetings was still opposed to war, persons who joined the Army or Navy were still considered in good standing. As a matter of fact, there were more Quakers who accepted service in the Army and Navy during the Second World War than there were conscientious objectors; this statement, incidentally, is applicable to the Brethren as well.[14]

With the tendency to accept a more individualistic interpretation of the Inner Light in the twentieth century, it is not difficult to understand why Quakers differed so radically from one another, even when they accepted the traditional Friends' testimony against war under any circumstances. Some Friends found it compatible with the Inner Light to enter noncombatant service in the Army and Navy; others spurned the Army and Navy completely but were content to operate fully within the framework of alternative civilian service; a very few Friends could not comply with the terms of the Selective Service Act in any way, declining even to register.

On the problem of the state, Friends throughout history took varying positions. On the whole, however, the Quaker "testimony" did not interpret antiwar principles as implying renunciation of "the world" or refusal under any circumstances to administer affairs of state. Indeed, the great hero of the American Friends, William Penn, was himself the founder of a state and for several years its chief administrator. Penn believed it was possible for the antiwar views of the Friends gradually to become predominant in society and to infuse themselves throughout even the structure of the state. Pennsylvania under his leadership, and even for many years after he had given up control, was not armed for defense against the Indians, and it was only when the colony ceased to be predominantly Quaker that this disarmament policy was abrogated.[15] While Mennonites tended to argue that "the world" would always remain within history and that the saved should under no circumstances help in its administration, Friends in general maintained that whether they could participate actively in public affairs depended on the circumstances.

Thus it was that Friends often made a distinction between force applied in a purely police sense and force used in war. In Pennsylvania under Quaker control there was a police force and even provision for capital punishment. Indeed, the celebrated plan for world peace which William Penn drew up included a scheme for coercion of those states which refused to abide by the law.[16] Principles such as these were utterly at variance with the major stream of Mennonite tradition and, indeed, with a large part of the Brethren tradition as well. For these ideas implied "resistance" at some points and under certain circumstances. The tradition of the Friends was, then, not "nonresistant" in the Mennonite sense.

Indeed, the Quaker belief which held that "the world" might be made more peaceful, hence more Christian, as a result of participation by Friends themselves in political affairs led to actions and ideas at many other points out of harmony with "nonresistance." Many Friends were receptive to Gandhi's *satyagraha* conceptions. It was a Quaker lawyer, Richard Gregg, who wrote what some regarded as an American classic on the subject.[17] But Gandhi's conceptions embraced the idea of a struggle for political power, the use of such devices as the boycott and civil disobedience, and the establishment of a "parallel government." All Friends, it is true, did not accept these conceptions of "nonviolent coercion," but they were sufficiently

understood by many Quakers to be seriously considered. To the
Mennonites, such beliefs were only less heterodox than the acceptance
of war itself.

To imply, of course, that all American Friends, or, indeed, the
bulk of them, accepted this "political" version of pacifism would be
glaringly untrue. There were modified versions of Mennonite "nonresistance" among the Quakers. While several young Friends during
the Second World War, for example, refused to register for the draft,
there were many Friends who had but little criticism to offer with
respect to alternative civilian service. Many believed that their social
principles could best be expressed by relief of suffering, without any
attempt to challenge the principle of conscription. This segment,
then, quite naturally, clashed with the nonregistrant group and with
all those who, for whatever reason, withdrew from support of alternative civilian service.

So difficult, in fact, is it to generalize about the Friends, that about
all one can say in summary is that the general principle of the Inner
Light, when interpreted wholly individualistically, might quite conceivably and honestly justify *any* position, from acceptance of war
to anarchism. And the variation among Friends was indeed that
great. Complicating the picture still further was the clash between
"liberals" and "conservatives" and the tension between rural and
urban groups. Generally speaking, theologically conservative Friends
maintained the historic "peace" testimony of the Society to a greater
degree than did the theological "liberals," the bulk of whose members tended to enter the Army. Urban Friends tended to take on the
colorings of twentieth-century "liberal" Protestantism, while the
rural groups to a greater extent remained conservative in dress and
theology alike.

Whatever may have been their individual social and political philosophies, however, Friends were seemingly united with respect to
one aspect of their "testimony," and that was their support of relief
and social welfare ventures. Activities of this kind were by Quaker
tradition supposed to exemplify the spirit that "takes away the occasion for wars." Between the First and Second World Wars, for
example, the American Friends Service Committee continued its
efforts in famine relief, distribution of food and clothing to those in

need on both sides of the Spanish Civil War, and, before the United States entered the Second World War, shipment of supplies to children in German-occupied France. The Friends also conducted summer camps where young people could assist in health projects for low-income families, guide the recreation of children, study co-operatives, and engage in discussion of international questions. Various institutes of international relations were developed, usually in connection with certain colleges; here men and women could examine issues directly related to the problems of war and peace. Activities of this kind were an integral part of Quaker tradition as expressed in the twentieth century.

Protestants outside the Peace Churches

Mennonites, Brethren, and Friends came to be called the Historic Peace Churches because their corporate beliefs for so long a period had embraced the principle of conscientious objection to war, however different the interpretations of that principle might be. Down to the twentieth century, the major Protestant denominations in the United States had remained, at least in their corporate capacities, largely indifferent to the questions involved in conscientious objection.

Toward the end of the nineteenth century, this indifference began slowly to change. The impact of the Social Gospel theology in Protestantism was one factor in the change. Under the leadership of Walter Rauschenbusch and others,[18] Protestant theology turned away from the predominant interest in individual salvation which had hitherto so largely characterized it. The Social Gospel taught that individual salvation could not be complete in the absence of social salvation: that the life of the individual was so bound up with institutions, so determined by forces outside his own control, that unless what were deemed to be the principles of the Gospel could be infused into the collective life of mankind, individual salvation became meaningless. The Social Gospel often called for a radical change in the distribution of economic goods and looked upon war as the result of an un-co-operative social order—an order which, however, with political insight and determination, could be transformed into a co-operative scheme of things. War, the Social Gospel taught, was indeed the fruit of "sin," but it was the "sin" of an unintelligent social organization as much as any inherited tendency to wrong doing.

With this general outlook penetrating in some degree most of the major Protestant denominations, it was not surprising that individual members of the churches should in increasing numbers proclaim themselves "pacifists" or that the denominations themselves should feel called upon to make pronouncements that would clarify their positions on the church and war. Generally speaking, the pacifist views of individual Protestants resembled Quaker views of the world rather than Mennonite conceptions. The state, it was argued, could be "redeemed" and infused with the Christian ethic; to achieve this end political agitation and propaganda and personal refusal to engage in the act of war would constitute legitimate means. Protestant young people's societies like the Methodist Epworth League stimulated discussions of war, and it was through such groups, usually with Social Gospel overtones, that many young people during the 1920's and early 1930's were undoubtedly influenced to take pacifist positions. It was during this epoch also that the so-called Oxford Oath—a vow that one would never support the state in another war —played its part in formulating the terms of pacifism for individual action.[19]

As for Protestant denominations themselves, their public resolutions were usually twofold in nature, consisting of a condemnation of war as an institution and an assertion of the denomination's protection for any of its members who might take the position of conscientious objection. The Methodist Episcopal General Conference of 1928 condemned war as "the supreme enemy of mankind." [20] And this was reiterated in slightly different terms by the General Conferences of 1932 and 1936. On the eve of American entry into the Second World War, the General Conference of the recently unified Methodist Church thus summarized the position of this largest of Protestant denominations:

The Methodist Church, although making no attempt to bind the consciences of its individual members, will not officially endorse, support, or participate in war. . . .

Believing that "in the long run any people have far more to gain by cherishing freedom of conscience than by any regimentation that takes away that freedom" and that conscientious objection to war is a natural outgrowth of Christian desire for peace on earth, we ask and claim exemption from all forms of military preparation or service for all conscientious objectors who may be members of the Methodist Church. Those of our members who, as conscientious objectors, seek exemption from military training in schools and colleges or from military service anywhere or at any time have the authority and support of their church.[21]

Similar statements were issued by other denominations in the decade between 1930 and 1940. Summarizing these tendencies in the larger Protestant denominations only a few years before the beginning of the Second World War, Dr. Walter Van Kirk said:

It should be made clear that the churches believe that the consummation of the peace ideal depends on bringing into the political, economic, and social relations of governments and peoples the teachings of our Lord. . . . The churches, more than any other single institution, can educate the millions to understand and appreciate the signs of the times. . . . It is in this spirit that the churches are going forward in their efforts for a warless world. They will not be intimidated; they will not be stopped. They will be heard.[22]

Roman Catholics

Roman Catholic moral philosophy was used by a small group of Catholics to support their position of pacifism and conscientious objection. In general, that position was defended along two broad lines—the vocational doctrine and the just-war theory, although it is true, of course, that elements of both might be discovered in the personal positions of any one Catholic pacifist.[23]

The vocational view was rooted in the belief that some men were called to an "unworldly" life by God and that for the state to require them to engage in acts essentially worldly would be to violate their higher call to duty. Thus, monks in taking the vows of chastity, poverty, obedience, and abstention from "lusts of the flesh" in general, could, because of their vocation, claim moral exemption from any political obligation to go to war; for warmaking, in light of their general withdrawal from "the world," would be totally out of harmony with their general position. Similarly, men and women who were neither monks nor nuns but who sought a limited withdrawal from "the world" by means of simple food, voluntary poverty, and other acts, could claim exemption from any obligation to aid the state in time of war. Like the Mennonite view, this particular Roman Catholic position did not deny the necessity at times of the state's warmaking—indeed, in conformity with general Catholic teaching, it agreed that some types of war were "just"—but it did argue that those who endeavored to follow the "counsels of perfection" of the Gospel could regard themselves as absolved of any obligation to participate and that the state was obliged morally to recognize their vocational objection. Among the Catholic Worker group in the United States were many who took this vocational view of conscientious objection. Those who took this particular view were often among the most devoted when they were assigned to work in general or mental hospitals.

The "just-war" theory of Catholic conscientious objection was based on an entirely different section of Catholic moral philosophy. The great doctors of the Church had evolved a doctrine which had laid it down that some wars were "just," and hence to be supported by good Catholics, while others were "unjust" and to be repudiated. The doctors went on to define a "just" war as one which was declared by a public authority, which was waged by methods capable of making distinctions between combatants and noncombatants, which gave reasonable promise of creating a situation morally better after the war than before the war, and which promised success at a cost not disproportionate to the results expected. The individual Roman Catholic was to interpret in each instance whether any particular war was "just." [24]

Many Roman Catholics who became conscientious objectors took these criteria of a "just war," laid them beside modern wars, and reached the conclusion that probably no modern war could be just. Thus, beginning with an ethical standard that certainly did not condemn all wars, Roman Catholics of this persuasion ended with a practical position not unlike that of the Friends. Personal participation in war was for them un-Catholic, holding as they did that the conditions of a just war could not exist with modern methods of warfare, undeclared wars, and great uncertainty about the possibility of creating a social situation after the war ethically better than that which existed before the conflict.

It is true that this application of the "just-war" theory was not widespread among Roman Catholics, but neither did outright pacifism, of whatever kind, attract more than an infinitesimal proportion of Methodists, Presbyterians, or Congregationalists. And whatever may have been the private feelings or beliefs of Roman Catholic officials, the pacifist application of the "just-war" doctrine was never condemned by the Roman Catholic hierarchy.

Jehovah's Witnesses

From the viewpoint of the state, Jehovah's Witnesses were to prove perhaps the most troublesome of all those groups that could, broadly speaking, be called "conscientious objector" during the Second World War. Organized during the last quarter of the nineteenth century, the Witnesses during the First World War were known variously as the Russellites (after their leader, Pastor Russell) or the International Bible Students' Association. Later, under the leadership of Judge Rutherford, their missionary activities were extended. During the twenties and thirties of the twentieth century they often clashed with groups like the American Legion and with public officials attempting to enforce local ordinances that not infrequently were directed specifically against Witnesses' activities. To get into difficulties with the state was quite normal for the Witnesses, whether in British Africa, where they attacked "British imperialism," or in Quebec, where their diatribes were directed against the Roman Catholic Church, or in the United States and elsewhere, where their criticism of other religious bodies aroused bitter hostility. In part, however, the difficulties of the Witnesses were due to a popular misunderstanding of their theology and social philosophy, particularly as these affected their views on the state and on war.[25]

Witness theory discovered the first Jehovah's Witness in Abel. Between the time of Abel and that of Noah, Satan and the Lord were contesting against each other for the souls of men—so much so that eventually God seemed to be defeated, having only one man of integrity left upon the earth, Noah. Great giants strode about the earth, personifications of demons, and the people were deluded into severing all actual connections with the Lord Jehovah.[26] Then came the Flood, through which it was demonstrated that even one man of integrity with the help of the Lord could subdue the spirits of evil—a demonstration of the power of those who witness for Jehovah. The Flood represented the world coming to an end, and Noah was symbolical of a greater Witness who would eventually destroy all evil.

But evil was not eliminated after the great inundation; it only took different shape following upon a reorganization of the kingdom of Satan. At the same time God continued to give forth prophecies of a new heaven and a new earth. The reorganization of the kingdom of Satan was reflected in the establishment of human government under Nimrod, the great hunter. The "earth" was now to be identified with the political state in which priestcraft and "religion"—really demonism—are in the saddle and in firm alliance. Abraham, it is true, carried on the witness for Jehovah, but at the same time Satan, through the "great powers" of the world—Egypt, Assyria, Babylonia, Persia, Greece, and Rome, both pagan and papal—extended his dominion over the earth. Papal Rome became a connecting link between ancient empires and the modern imperial struggle. As a matter of fact, seven empires of the devil—totalitarian, and constantly battling against the witnesses of Jehovah—constituted steppingstones from ancient to modern times. The seventh empire was the Anglo-American combination which, wounding the papal-German alliance of 1914–1918, became the "professed champion of democracy" in the Second World War [27] against the renewed alliance of the papacy with Germany.

In the meantime, symbols of the future ideal order arose to antagonize the kingdom of the earth and typify the coming of the kingdom of the Lord. Thus such men as David, Moses, and Solomon represented, however imperfectly, the great Theocracy which God, co-operating with his witnesses, will set up in the new world. But the Israelites failed to heed the word of the Lord—they became corrupted by religion, and God punished them for their misdeeds. After the overthrow of Nineveh, the "times of the Gentiles" were initiated.[28] Known also as the "seven times"—each "time" being equivalent in prophecy to 360 years—it was apparent that this period would expire 2,520 years after the fall of Nineveh, or by 1914. In that year, the beginning of the First World War, Satan's rule began to be interrupted and the "time of the end" was established. The final judgment had not come, but was on its way. The year 1918 was significant for Jehovah's Witnesses because it marked the entry of Jesus into the Temple, where he began to judge which servants of

Jehovah should be the leaders in finally ridding the earth of Satan. Jesus Christ was the chief Theocratic Servant, and when he entered the Temple the widespread propagation of Jehovah's word was assured throughout the earth. This universal evangelization was foretold in the New Testament,[29] where witnessing was viewed as the harbinger of the end.[30] The climax of the process will be reached at the battle of Armageddon, where the Witnesses of Jehovah will triumph at last over the hosts of Satan—a victory which will not be temporary, like that of the Flood, but permanent.

The Witnesses predicted that history just before the end would be exciting.[31] After Christ Jesus came into the Temple, there seemed to be a brief respite in the violent political struggles of the world. This was not because the end of Satan had come—indeed, he was girding his loins for another blow. The "King of the North" mentioned in the prophecy of Daniel was the Papacy, which, with its German and Central European allies, was defeated in the First World War by the King of the South (symbolically, Egypt; on the scene of twentieth-century struggle, the alliance of the United States and Great Britain). But no sooner had the defeat come about than the Northern King began to scheme to regain his power. He aided in the destruction of the democracies of Germany and Spain and supported the bloody dictator of the latter country. He established diplomatic relations with the United States in 1939. Finally, when the time was ripe, he struck through his Fascist allies—in Ethiopia, Spain, Austria, and Czechoslovakia, and the King of the South gave way in each case. In the end, however, the King of the South counterattacked and the Second World War was waged.

It was a war in which one power symbolized the totalitarian order in the world and another the democratic principle. But democracy is government by creatures, not rule by God the Creator. So the Second World War was not to be interpreted as a struggle between a man-idolizing power and a God-exalting regime. Rather was it a search for power and dominion on both sides. The Witnesses were at first endangered by the King of the North, who persecuted them unmercifully because they declined to submit to the Papacy and Fascism. But the King of the South, ostensibly democratic and "liberal," soon followed his northern rival in the practice of persecution. Certain religious groups supposedly resisted the demands of the King of the North, but their pretences were belied, for they supported the King of the South, whose purpose, too, was world domination and opposition to the Witnesses of Jehovah.[32]

In the meantime it becomes evident that, fulfilling prophecy,[33] the King of the South (the alliance of Great Britain and the United States) has disappeared. This does not mean that he has been defeated in battle, but it does mean that his rule has become totalitarian, like that of his rival, and that he has discarded his "liberal" pretences. In fact, the end of the process will see the establishment of a "World Federation" in which the Northern and Southern kings pool their resources. Thus both will achieve the goal of world domination, and, with their combined strength, will be able to harry and persecute the Witnesses of Jehovah. Overwhelmingly victorious, the new World Federation will think it is secure.

But its supremacy will be only apparent. Soon afterward, fulfilling Daniel's prophecy,[34] Christ Jesus will announce in a loud voice that the end is at hand. The battle of Armageddon will be fought, Jehovah's Witnesses will emerge triumphant with the Lord, and the New World will be born. The Theocracy of the Lord will then reign supreme throughout the earth and all man's domination will have withered away and died.

Intensely believed, this world outlook produced in the Witnesses a firm conviction that they should preach the gospel of the imminent end of the world and look upon the political struggles of the twentieth century as secondary in importance. Rejecting the designations "pacifist" and "conscientious objector," they tended, nevertheless, to feel that the only battle in which they could directly participate was that of Armageddon. Until that final struggle, they maintained that their basic vocation was to preach the gospel openly and freely. Since they had been set apart to proclaim the gospel, they argued, the state had no moral right to conscript them either for the Army or for alternative civilian service; for in either the military forces or alternative service, they maintained, their freedom of preaching would be restricted. Hence their "covenant" with God to preach would be broken. Thus, like some Catholic and Protestant objectors, they based their objection primarily on vocational grounds, and they tended to ask not for recognition as conscientious objectors, in the technical sense of the law, but for full exemption as ministers of the gospel.

It should be emphasized that the official doctrine of the Watchtower Society, the publishing and directing group of Jehovah's Witnesses, was that each individual Witness interpreted what general Witness doctrine meant for his own personal action. Thus, the president of the Watchtower Society, H. N. Knorr, denied that there was any instruction or command from the central organization to take any particular course of action with respect to conscription and war. Each Witness decided for himself whether he would claim conscientious objection or exemption as a minister or go into the Army. It was a matter of individual conscience. Nevertheless, there seems to have been fairly widespread agreement among followers of the Watchtower Society as to what the basic doctrine of Jehovah's Witnesses meant for individual conduct.

Unlike the Mennonites, they did not hold to the doctrine of non-resistance; indeed, in personal matters they did not hesitate to use physical force, and in questions involving civil rights they filled the courts with their protests, carrying many an issue to the Supreme Court of the United States.[35] Nor could they be said, with the Friends, to believe in the Inner Light or, with Friends, Mennonites, and Brethren, to emphasize the necessity for relief activities. Their whole world was, of course, antagonistic to the Social Gospel that so conditioned Protestant pacifism and conscientious objection. With respect to Roman Catholic objection, their antagonism to the Roman Catholic Church in general and to its social doctrine in particular gave their views a cast that could hardly fit easily into the world view of Catholicism, although, curiously enough, their strong sense of vocation brought them very close in a practical sense to one aspect of the Catholic position.

Other Religious Groups

Any survey of American pacifism and conscientious objection immediately before and during the Second World War would be incomplete without at least mentioning the many other religious bodies which were either pacifist in a corporate sense or many of whose members took the pacifist position. In the first category were the Christadelphians, a semi-premillennial group; the Seventh-Day Adventists, whose social and political doctrine permitted them to serve as noncombatants in the Army and Navy; and the Molokans, a group that originated in Russia during the eighteenth century. In the second category might be included the Negro Moslems, a rather mysterious organization, many of whose members contended they could not participate in the Second World War because it did not constitute a "holy war" as defined by the Koran; Mankind United, one of the many religious organizations which grew up in California during the twenties of the twentieth century; [36] and Hopi Indian religionists whose creed apparently made a place for non-violence, although their objections were probably as much "political" as "religious." [37] Some Jews were also pacifists on religious grounds.

To elaborate the beliefs of all religious bodies as they related to pacifism and conscientious objection would require much more space than is available. For the most part, however, those doctrines could be characterized as "more or less Mennonite" or "more or less Friend" or "more or less Protestant Social Gospel," with admixtures of the three tendencies perhaps predominating.

Political and Philosophical Objection

Political and philosophical objection consisted of no one set of well-articulated beliefs, but rather was highly individualistic in its expression. Often it could not be differentiated from so-called "religious" objection; for it is evident that all religious objection has political implications and that statements of political belief assume conceptions of the universe which others might call "religious." During the Second World War, due partly to the phraseology of the law, much was to be made of the supposed distinction between "religious" and merely "political and philosophical" objection, but such distinctions were frequently highly artificial and tended often to be utterly unrealistic.

A keynote of that objection which some called "political and philosophical" was the absence, or near absence, of such terms as the Bible, Christ, God, the Church, and the Inner Light. Often objection of this type stemmed from some form of socialist doctrine. The American Socialist Labor Party was resolutely opposed to the Second

World War on grounds of what it regarded as strict Marxist doctrine
—that the war was essentially imperialist and that it would tend to
place the worker in an even more subordinate position than he occupied in ordinary times. The Workers' Socialist Party, a very small
group that also professed to expound the pure Marxist gospel, actually expelled any member who accepted military service—the only
political party and one of the few groups of any kind which adopted
such an attitude.[38]

The largest socialist group, the American Socialist Party, had before the war experienced much lively discussion on the problem of
its attitude toward war. The Party vigorously opposed the entrance
of the United States into the war, and even after the Pearl Harbor
incident, there were many within its ranks who wished it to take
an open and belligerent stand against the waging of the war. There
would have been ample precedent for such action, for, in the First
World War, the 1917 convention of the Socialist Party had committed
it to a clear-cut antiwar position; its leader, Eugene V. Debs, had
been sentenced to prison for a speech opposing the conflict.

The Party's position during the Second World War certainly could
not be construed as support of the war. But the position finally
adopted by its 1942 biennial convention was not as clear as the 1917
declaration had been. The Party recognized "that within the framework of the present capitalist-imperialist set-up and the circumstances which it creates, capitalist governments have no alternative
other than the pursuit of war." This fact, however, did not mean that
the Party was reconciled to war, but rather that it recognized even
more emphatically its mission to fight capitalism. "Capitalism, which
is destroying democracy, will not and cannot conduct a war for democratic ends." The statement concluded:

The Socialist Party does not give its blessing to this war—or any war—
as the proper method for attaining social objectives, national or international. Nor does it give its support to the economic system or political administration that is responsible for the war and its conduct.

The defeat of fascism demands that the peoples of the democracies
create their own independent international front against Hitlerism; that
they appeal directly to the oppressed people of the Axis powers, the conquered countries and the colonies to join with them in that front with
every means at their command. . . .[39]

Declarations of this kind certainly did not discourage those Socialists who became conscientious objectors, and the fact that a substantial section of the Socialist Party was fully pacifist in its viewpoint re-enforced the Party's support of those who took the stand of war objection. Several strong Socialist locals were organized in Civilian Public Service camps during the war.

Other "political and philosophical" objectors were unattached to any group. There were anarchist conscientious objectors who found their way into prison and some of near-anarchist tendencies who went to Civilian Public Service camps. There were spiritual disciples of Henry David Thoreau and followers of Mohandas K. Gandhi. Other "philosophical" objectors could hardly be associated with any leader, and often their opinions might be composed of seemingly contradictory views.

One characteristic of conscientious objectors outside the Mennonite and Jehovah's Witness groups was their tendency to atomize —to split into minuscule segments having no particular ties with other groups save their common war objection; this was particularly true of political and philosophical objectors, even where they might be members of the same political party. This tendency, of course, was characteristic of general social and political radicalism in the twentieth century, and its reflection in the ranks of conscientious objectors was perhaps to be expected. It tended, however, to minimize their political effectiveness and to strengthen the position of those who were conducting the war.

Currents and Crosscurrents

The Second World War itself made apparent certain tendencies in American pacifism and conscientious objection which cut across any formal religious and political demarcations. While these currents were for the most part present before the actual entry of the United States into the war, they were sharply delineated during the course of the war and their principles questioned, defined, and redefined by the intellectual leaders of pacifists and conscientious objectors.

Conscientious Objection, Pacifism, and "War Resistance." It had long been apparent that terminology was none too exact, but during the war itself the problem of classifying "objectors" took on new urgency, for the obviously great ideological gulf between a Mennonite, on the one hand, and a political anarchist, or even a Friend, on the other hand, made accurate classification extremely difficult. The general tendency was, however, to make "conscientious objector" the more inclusive term, applying it broadly to all those who opposed the war and who expressed their opposition by any action, from refusal to serve as a combatant in the Army to refusal to register. Many, however, including the Department of Justice, did not include Jehovah's Witnesses in this category. It should also be pointed out that, from the viewpoint of the government, such groups as the Puerto Rican Nationalists, who did not profess to oppose all war but only the Second World War, could not be looked upon as "conscientious objectors," since the government tended to think of an objector as one who opposed *all* war, and not one who opposed merely the Second World War while reserving judgment regarding possible future conflicts.

"Pacifist" was more narrow in its connotations than "conscientious objector." All pacifists were conscientious objectors, but not all conscientious objectors were pacifists. Most Mennonites repudiated "pacifism" because they associated it with the conception of nonviolent resistance to tyranny and war—a conception which, as we have seen, they regarded as directly contrary to their own principle of nonresistance. Jehovah's Witnesses likewise tended to avoid the term when describing themselves, for to them it implied the complete renunciation of physical force, and the Witnesses not only accepted the utilization of force in personal matters but seemingly believed that the final battle of Armageddon would be a physical conflict, in which, of course, they would be called upon to participate.

What "pacifism" was in concrete and positive terms is difficult to say. For the most part it tended to accept the necessity for political struggle (which the Mennonites repudiated) but rejected its "violent" forms. Pacifists voted, wrote letters to congressmen, and even, in some cases, advocated a world state—all of which activities were frowned upon by orthodox Mennonites. Some pacifists were Socialists, while others were more orthodox in their party affiliations. Some were anarchists. Some were "religious"; others repudiated "religious" interpretations of life.[40]

The term "war resister" was sometimes used to designate the more "radical" of the pacifists. The name itself, intimately associated with such organizations as the War Resisters League, was often taken to imply a break with the more orthodox of the pacifists and conscientious objectors. A conscientious objector, in stating his social and political views, might remark, "I'm not a pacifist; I'm a war resister," implying thereby that he looked upon "pacifist" as too mild a term. Those in the ranks of conscientious objectors who thought of themselves as anarchists or near-anarchists often described themselves as "war resisters." But the term itself was not an exact expression, sometimes being used, in fact, to designate conscientious objectors in general.

Influence of Gandhian Conceptions. No analysis of the social and political thought of conscientious objectors, especially during the Second World War, could omit specific reference to the impact of Mohandas K. Gandhi's ideas and actions on the theory and practice of pacifism and war resistance. This influence was both negative and positive: negative, in that it stimulated groups like the Mennonites to restate and elaborate their counterdoctrine of nonresistance; positive, in that it furnished much of the inspiration for the abstract theory of pacifism, as well as the stimulus for such actions as hunger strikes, work strikes, protests, and civil disobedience.[41]

For Gandhi's conceptions of social struggle encouraged what one writer has called "war without violence."[42] And it was precisely this peculiar species of war which some conscientious objectors conceived themselves to be waging. When they "slowed down" their work in Civilian Public Service camp, it was "war" against Selective Service or against the principles upon which alternative civilian service was erected. When they refused to work in prison, it was a kind of war against those who administered racial segregation or censored letters.

The key to an understanding of Gandhi's influence on American conscientious objection is to remember that it was revolutionary in its implications. Among the principles of Gandhi's *satyagraha* (soul force) was one proposing the eventual establishment of an alternative government which, with support of those who engaged in acts of nonviolent resistance, would ultimately take over control from the existing government. While it is obvious that the few hundreds of American conscientious objectors who fully believed in *satyagraha* were in no position to establish an alternative government during the Second World War, it is well to keep in mind this frame of reference, for it sharply differentiates all those who accepted it from

Mennonites and other objectors who did not conceive conscientious objection in terms of political revolution.

The Impact of the Social Action Movement. During the course of the war, the experiences of objectors in Civilian Public Service and in prison brought to the forefront the problem of co-ordinating the energies of all those who looked upon objection as something more than a personal ethical problem and who saw it as integral to a social and political program. There is no one name which is adequate to describe this current in wartime pacifist thought, but "social action movement" is perhaps as adequate as any other.

The social action movement is represented in terms of the two conferences so often associated with it. The first, in 1943, was composed of representatives from the various Civilian Public Service camps who defied an order of Selective Service and attended the meeting in Chicago.[43] The conference was concerned with bettering types of alternative civilian service and examining the relationship between conscientious objection and general objectives in politics.

The second conference, held in Chicago in February, 1946—after hostilities had ceased but before Civilian Public Service camps had been abandoned or large numbers of conscientious objectors had been released from prison—came to be known as the Conference on Non-Violent Revolution. It was composed mainly of the "radical" wing of those who had seen service in Civilian Public Service or in prison and was called specifically to formulate a program of postwar action. On the whole, the conference was dominated by groups which were virtually anarchist in political outlook. The outcome was a series of resolutions which advocated nonviolent "direct action" (like seizure of factories, boycotting of business establishments which practice racial discrimination, and mass demonstrations of civil disobedience) as the primary technique of achieving what the conference regarded as its goal—a co-operative, nonviolent world. A Continuation Committee was appointed, and after the conference had adjourned, various local Committees of Non-Violent Revolution were established in some parts of the country.

The significance of the Conference on Non-Violent Revolution lay in the fact that for the first time an attempt was made to organize the "left wing" of the American pacifist movement for purposes beyond those of direct war resistance. Committees on Non-Violent Revolution, as the name implied, were supposed to initiate and sustain attempts to reorganize the economic and political orders and were to use methods which might conceivably violate the law. In saying this, one should, of course, remember that the Second Chicago Conference could be said to represent only a very small segment of the entire number of conscientious objectors.

"Service" Motif and "Resistance" Motif. In considerable degree, the conflicts which developed in conscientious-objector thought and action had their origin in two different emphases. The first can be termed the "service," and the second the "resistance," motif.

The "service motif" saw war and conscription as part of the basic pattern of society as it actually existed—some said, with the Mennonites, of all "worldly" society, while others said of the society of the 1940's—so that the problem of the conscientious objector was how he could do those kinds of work which his conscience would allow within the framework of such a society. A parallel problem had to do with the possibility of his rendering those services which would best reflect his own religious impulses. To this type of conscientious objector, then, the issue was twofold: (1) How can I confine my activities to non-military work in an increasingly militaristic society? and (2) How can I evidence religious sincerity and good will by rendering "service" to others over and above what they might be led to expect?

To those whose main emphasis was the "service motif," relief activities, conservation, medical experimentation, hospital work—and, indeed, almost any type of civilian work—were proper expressions of the religious impulse, which, while it declined one type of service (the military), was supposed to make up for its negative attitude in that respect by offering to labor without stint and even without pay on projects which could not be regarded as military. Even when such work was performed under compulsion (as in Civilian Public Service camps), the supporter of the "service motif" argued that the individual could overcome its compulsory nature—counteract it—by doing more than was required and thus make the work his own. For some objectors, this "service without stint" was their payment for their share of the guilt in bringing on war. The "service motif" thus exalted work, partly to evidence sincerity, partly to atone for guilt, and partly to be of service to humanity in its time of need. What one was paid for such work was a secondary matter, as was also the issue of whether the work was performed under a conscription law.

To those who supported the "service motif," this conception followed the commands of the New Testament to "go the second mile" and "turn the other cheek." Often implicit in it was the belief that man's institutions must necessarily be fundamentally evil. The ethical person would not attempt the hopeless task of changing institutions —the very attempt would, indeed, corrupt him—but rather try to transform himself through labor and service to others. This inward transformation would neutralize even the most oppressive of institutions.

By contrast, the "resistance motif" emphasized liberty, civil rights, transformation of social and political institutions, and, in some cases, social and political revolution. To those who grounded their beliefs on the "resistance motif," institutions were transformable, opposition to war was a method of transformation, and the state had no moral right to deny the right of conscientious objection or to condition it by requirement of any particular type of service. Currents like those of the social action movement and, to a considerable extent, Gandhian influences, exalted the "resistance" motif. Many "resisters" came to look upon "service motif" conscientious objectors as slavish in mentality and uninterested in human liberty. Religious groups which exalted "service" as the dominating theme of conscientious objection were held by "resistance" objectors to be agents of the warmaking state and aiders and abettors of conscription. On the other hand, "service motif" objectors could often see but little affinity between themselves and their "resistant" fellow objectors.

The conflict between the two approaches provoked considerable pamphleteering during the war, and the bitterness engendered produced deep sores on the pacifist and conscientious-objector movement as a whole. Many a "resistance motif" objector, for example, felt that he had more in common with certain nonpacifists than with his fellow "service motif" conscientious objectors.

It is true, of course, that the distinction between "service" and "resistant" conscientious objectors was not absolute. No objector was pure "service" and no one simple "resister." There were gradations in emphasis. But even with these qualifications, the contrast between the two approaches remained a division of primary significance.

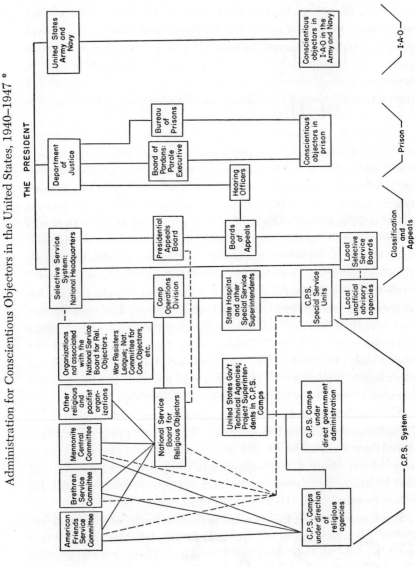

Administration for Conscientious Objectors in the United States, 1940–1947 *

* Solid lines indicate direct responsibility or connections; broken lines indicate sponsorship or unofficial liaison.

PART 2. CONSCRIPTING THE OBJECTOR

III: *Protecting Conscience*
in the Act of 1940

B Y THE early part of 1940 it became evident to many that the United States was moving rapidly into a prewar period. Those interested in the problem of the conscientious objector saw the period of American neutrality drawing to a close and the issues of conscription and protection of conscience arising. The President was calling for stronger armaments, and "preparedness" became the watchword of many politicians. On January 10, 1940, seven representatives of the so-called Historic Peace Churches visited President Roosevelt and handed him a letter in which they expressed their concern at the trend of events and their hope that if war should come adequate provision would be made for conscience.[1] They proposed a scheme of alternative civilian service and complete exemption for absolutists. Other religious bodies, antiwar groups, and civil-liberties organizations also began to consider the problem.

After the fall of France, in June, 1940, it became evident that the Roosevelt Administration was eager to press for a conscription act as soon as possible. Henry L. Stimson, a leading Republican proponent of conscription, was appointed Secretary of War, and official statements made it clear to those who were not naïve about politics that the United States no longer considered itself neutral. A Gallup poll in the summer of 1940 indicated that 67 per cent of those polled favored some form of military conscription.

Between the two World Wars the Army War College and General Staff had, of course, worked out plans for future conscription, so the matter of formulating the general provisions of the proposal was relatively simple. The original draft of the proposed law was the work of Grenville Clark, a New York attorney. It was introduced in the Senate by Senator Edward R. Burke of Nebraska and in the House by Representative James W. Wadsworth of New York. Known as the Burke-Wadsworth bill, it included a provision—Section 7(d) —for conscientious objectors; this section merely repeated the language of the Act of 1917 by providing objector status only for those who were members of religious groups having as a part of their creeds objection to war. The proposal, moreover, made provision only for those objectors who could not conscientiously serve in the combatant branches of the Army and Navy; it did not protect in any way those who might object to both combatant and noncombatant service. Still less did it recognize the fact, highlighted by experience in the First World War and in Great Britain, that some could not conscientiously perform even civilian work if that work was part of a conscription program.

The Military Affairs Committees of the House and Senate held hearings on the Burke-Wadsworth bill during July and August of 1940. A large number of civil-liberties, religious, and antiwar groups testified through their representatives before the committees. The concern of most was to defeat the conscription bill itself, and only secondarily—if it became evident that the bill would pass—to argue for more liberal provisions for objectors. A partial list of those who testified will indicate the variety of sources of opposition to the bill and concern for freedom of conscience: Harold Evans, Paul Comly French, and E. Raymond Wilson, for the Friends; Dorothy Day, of the *Catholic Worker;* John Nevin Sayre, representing the Fellowship of Reconciliation; Norman Thomas for the Socialist Party; Catherine FitzGibbon of the Women's International League for Peace and Freedom; Frederick J. Libby of the National Council for the Prevention of War; Abraham Kaufman of the War Registers League; Charles S. Longacre of the Seventh Day Adventists; Amos Horst of the Mennonites; Paul H. Bowman for the Church of the Brethren; Howard K. Beale for the American Civil Liberties Union; Harry Emerson Fosdick of Riverside Church, New York City; James A. Crain, of the Disciples of Christ; Charles Boss, of the Methodist Commission on World Peace; and Roswell P. Barnes for the Federal

Council of the Churches of Christ in America. It was the general feeling of those who testified that the provisions for conscientious objectors were inadequate.[2]

On the whole, the inadequacies of the proposed law were felt to include failure to make provision for those who objected to both combatant and noncombatant service; the confining of exemption to those who were members of the Historic Peace Churches; unsatisfactory provisions for civilian direction and administration; failure to provide for nonreligious objectors; and absence of protection for absolutists—that is, for those who objected to combatant, noncombatant, and alternative civilian service alike. Witnesses emphasized different aspects of these issues, but hardly anyone deemed the provision in the original bill satisfactory. On the other hand, there were some witnesses who thought that no provision whatsoever should be made for objectors.

The story of the objector provisions of the Act of 1940 is largely that of the efforts of those concerned to obtain provisions as closely like those of the British Act as possible. This endeavor involved conferences with Army officers, with members of Congress, and with representatives of public opinion. Rightly or wrongly, those who originally began by advocating provisions similar to those of the British Act reached the conclusion, long before final passage of the Burke-Wadsworth bill, that a clause somewhat less sweeping than the British, but more liberal than that originally proposed in the bill, would be all that would be acceptable to Congress. Hence the religious groups concerned gradually retreated before the hostility of congressmen and executive officials, presumably actuated by the belief that if they did not fall back in time they might get something less than even half a loaf.

Among the religious groups, the Friends were the most active in pressing for provisions modeled on those of the British law. On July 22, the Friends War Problems Committee drew up a substitute for Section 7(d) of the Burke-Wadsworth bill. The substitute exempted all who were "conscientiously opposed to participation in war in any form." All such persons were to be listed provisionally on a register of conscientious objectors to be established in the Department of Justice, and the provisions were to be administered by a bureau of conscientious objectors in that Department. Final determination of claims for conscientious objection was to be vested in civilian boards of inquiry in each state and territory. Membership in a church or religious organization whose creed opposed participation in war was to be prima-facie evidence of conscientious objection if supported by oath or affirmation of the individual that he agreed with the creed. The boards of inquiry, after determining that a person was an objector within the meaning of the law, would then be obliged to classify him in one of three categories: as a noncombatant in Army service, as one willing to do work of national importance under civilian direction, or as one opposed to combatant, noncombatant, and conscripted civilian service alike, in which event he would be exempted from any type of service. The bureau of conscientious objectors was to establish a national board of appeal with power of review. These provisions, it will be seen, resembled very closely those of the British law during the Second World War.

The Friends War Problems Committee provided at the same time a shorter substitute which was substantially the same as the longer proposal, except that it left more to administrative discretion.[3]

A little later E. Raymond Wilson and Paul French, of the Friends, spent three hours with Colonel O'Keliher at the Army War College and attempted to secure his aid in drafting a liberal substitute, as he was then engaged in revising the proposed conscientious-objector provisions. Colonel O'Keliher's substitute amendment, drawn up after his conference with French and Wilson, greatly narrowed the original Friends proposals. It granted exemption only to those opposed to war "by reason of religious training and belief." It retained provision for a register of conscientious objectors and for investigation by the Department of Justice before classification. Separate boards of inquiry, however, were dropped, and classification of objectors was left to the regular Local Selective Service Boards, which were to act on recommendations of the Department of Justice.[4]

About the same time, Senator Sherman Minton of Indiana, one of the sharpest questioners of objectors appearing before the Senate Military Affairs Committee, proposed a substitute very much resembling that of Colonel O'Keliher. The Minton proposal, however, confined statutory recognition to those who objected only to combatant service.

On August 5, 1940, the Senate Committee on Military Affairs reported out the Burke-Wadsworth bill with the Committee's own version of protection for conscientious objectors. Granted exemption were those who objected to combatant or both combatant and noncombatant service and whose objection was derived from "religious training." The register of conscientious objectors was retained and the O'Keliher provision for classification by regular Local Boards was adopted. Initial classification was to be a recommendation of the Department of Justice, however, and if the Department did not hold in favor of the objector, the Local Board or the objector could appeal to the Board of Appeals. Apparently the local board could not appeal if the claims of the objector were sustained by the Department of Justice. Those whose claims of objection to both combatant and noncombatant service were sustained were to be assigned to "work of national importance under civilian direction." [5]

On August 28, the Senate passed the Burke-Wadsworth bill with these provisions; efforts of the defenders of conscientious objectors were now concentrated on the attempt to broaden the provisions of the Senate bill as passed.

The Friends War Problems Committee now sent a new substitute to members of the House Military Affairs Committee, somewhat liberalizing the Senate provisions but not going nearly as far as the original proposals of the Friends. The substitute used the expression "by reason of religious training and/or belief" and included provision for exemption of absolutists.

In the meantime, the bill had come up for consideration before the House of Representatives. There, toward the end of debate on September 6, Representative Francis Walter of Pennsylvania proposed that administration of the provisions for conscientious objectors be shifted from the Department of Justice to the Local Selective Service Boards set up by the Act.[6] Without debate, the Walter amendment was adopted; and although Representative Jerry Voorhis protested this hasty action the next day, the House allowed its decision to stand.

House and Senate representatives now met in conference to iron out differences. They were told by a staff member of the Department of Justice that the number of conscientious objectors was likely to be large and that the Department did not have facilities and personnel for investigating all the claims of those asking for objector status. He suggested that the function of initial investigation and weighing of claims be turned over to the Local Boards, as in the House version, but that the Department of Justice be given the task of investigating appeals. The conference accepted this recommendation, and on September 13 the final section on conscientious objectors —now called 5(g)—was reported back to the Senate and House as part of the revised Selective Training and Service bill. The conference report was accepted by Senate and House on September 14 and on September 16 the President's signature made the bill a law.

The Act as thus finally passed provided that it should not be construed to require any person to be "subject to combatant training and service in the land or naval forces of the United States, who, by reason of religious training and belief, is conscientiously opposed to participation in war in any form." Local boards as established by the act for general classification purposes were also to pass upon the claim of objectors; if the claims were sustained, the boards were to place the individuals involved either in noncombatant Army training and service or assign them to "work of national importance under civilian direction." The Department of Justice was to investigate appeals of objectors and to recommend a decision to one of the regular Boards of Appeals set up throughout the country. The register of conscientious objectors, which had occupied a very important place in the original Friends proposal, was now reduced to minor significance; instead of being a provisional list of objectors drawn up by the Department of Justice and from which names would be stricken only after due investigation by the Department, it was now to come into existence as a kind of afterthought, only when the local board had finally determined whether the objector's claims should be sustained. The register, moreover, was now to be kept by the local board, not by the Department of Justice. Nothing was said in the final version about the character of "work of national importance under civilian direction," and it is to be noted that the Act did not even guarantee that the objector would not be assigned to do work connected with the war effort.[7]

Throughout the formulation of the provision which eventually emerged as Section 5(g), it is evident from the record that congressmen were only vaguely aware of many of the problems involved. Most congressmen knew nothing of American experience in the

First World War or of the history of British conscientious objection in World War II. Unlike the membership of the British Parliament, which included several, there were no pacifists in the American Congress. There was hardly any debate on the floor of the House or Senate, and questioning of witnesses before the Military Affairs Committees was often concerned, not with an examination of the problem of how to protect the objector, assuming him to exist, but rather with barbed questions from congressmen seeking to show the invalidity of the objector's theoretical position. On the record, no sympathy whatsoever was shown by the overwhelming majority of members of Congress for the position of the absolutist, although Friends, War Resisters League and American Civil Liberties Union representatives, among others, asked that recognition be given to the absolutist and pointed out that without such recognition serious difficulties would arise.

Congress, moreover, gave no serious thought to the problem of the objector whose views were not based on "religion." Here again the position of the Friends, Mennonites, War Resisters League, American Civil Liberties Union, and others was clear and emphatic. British experience seemed to show that no serious administrative problems would arise should "nonreligious" objection also be recognized. Congressmen claimed that dropping the "religious" test would open up the floodgates to Communists seeking to evade their responsibilities, but this attitude merely emphasized the fact that most congressmen were simply not conversant with problems of conscience and illustrated a curious logic which seemed to hold that while Communists ought not to be objectors, they should be in the Army.

Later on, after the United States had formally entered the war, it was asserted by some that had religious and civil-liberties agencies been more aggressive and clever, they might have induced Congress to pass a more liberal provision for conscientious objectors. Some even asserted that groups like the Mennonites and the Friends had not even tried to secure exemption for absolutists and nonreligious objectors. This latter assertion, as we have seen, was without warrant. Had the original Friends proposal been written into the law, some, at least, of the difficulties that later developed would undoubtedly have been averted: it is difficult to see how legislative provision for objectors could have been more liberal than the first

Friends amendment. Whether religious and civil-liberties organizations were aggressive, persistent, and clever enough in pushing their proposals is another matter. It must be remembered in any evaluation that they labored under formidable difficulties: indifference and hostility of congressmen; the fact that the drafting of the conscientious-objector provision was largely in the hands of the military; pressure by the Administration to rush the conscription bill through Congress; inability of congressmen to brief themselves within a short time on the problems of conscientious objection; and political inexperience of some who represented the cause of the objector. Whether under these circumstances church and civil liberties representatives did less than their best is almost anybody's guess.

When all is said, moreover, Section 5(g) *was* more liberal than the First World War provision in that it did provide a status for those objecting to noncombatant military service and also did not make "religious training and belief" dependent on membership in any church.

A Note on Section 5(d)

In the Act as finally passed by Congress was Section 5(d), which exempted ministers of religion and theological students. Catholic Church representatives were particularly insistent that Congress provide complete exemption for ministers, arguing, with Monsignor Michael J. Ready, that "this immunity from military service is inseparable from the right of a people to religious liberty. It is not a privilege conceded unfairly to ministers as a class." Whatever the reasons, Congress agreed to complete exemption for ministers. Unfortunately, however, it did not define in any detail what it meant by "minister," and this absence of definition was to cause difficulties with respect to one great body of conscientious objectors, the Jehovah's Witnesses. Hence, throughout the story of conscientious objection Sections 5(g) and 5(d) are intimately interrelated.

IV: *Separating the Sheep from the Goats: The Classification of Objectors*

The Selective Training and Service Act of 1940 provided that, with one exception, the administrative machinery used for classifying other registrants should also be utilized for the purpose of determining the claims of conscientious objectors.

At the base of the classification structure stood the local Selective Service board. There were some sixty-seven hundred such boards in the United States, and the official theory was that they were composed of the neighbors of registrants about to be classified. It was the local board which determined initially whether the claims of the registrant for objector status would be recognized.

If either the objector or the government was not satisfied with the classification of the local board, an appeal might be taken to the Regional Board of Appeals, which was charged with the task of hearing all classification appeals within a given territory.

But before an objector's adverse classification could be reviewed by the Board of Appeals, the matter had to be referred to the Department of Justice for investigation. As a part of that investigation, a Hearing Officer named by the Department interviewed the registrant claiming objection, and, after reading the report of the Federal Bureau of Investigation, reported his recommendation to the Regional Board of Appeals. That Board was not bound to follow the recommendation of the Hearing Officer, although, as we shall see a little later, it usually did.

Under certain circumstances a final appeal could be taken from the Regional Board of Appeals to the President of the United States. If the appeal was allowed, it was referred to a presidential appeal board that recommended the final action to be taken.

This, in general, was the system. The details of each step in the process bring it to life.

Filling Out the Forms

The young man who was called up under the Selective Training and Service Act of 1940 did not need to decide at registration whether he was a conscientious objector. He could, however, indicate his objection on his registration card, although his notation would have no legal effect. Many objectors did, in fact, explain their objection at this stage, feeling no doubt that there should be no question about their position.

Another test came, however, when the registrant received the questionnaire sent out by the local board to all registrants, whether they were conscientious objectors or not. The questionnaire went into great detail with respect to family status, ancestry, occupation, and general availability for service. Known as D.S.S. Form 40, it contained a "Series X" in which the objector could indicate his position on war and through which he could request D.S.S. Form 47, which was the special form for conscientious objectors.[1] The burden of requesting Form 47 was placed squarely upon the shoulders of the objector, and if through some oversight or through ignorance he failed to ask for it in Series X, he often found it difficult later on to sustain his claim for conscientious objection before the local board. On the other hand, if he clearly requested Form 47, the local board was obliged to send it to him.

The real test came when Form 47 arrived and its detailed questions involving the registrant's beliefs about war had to be answered. Since the Act required than an objector, to receive legal recognition, must be opposed to war "in any form," Form 47 included questions as to the sources of his beliefs, how long he had held his opinion regarding war, and what persons could offer comment on his position. He was asked in the questionnaire to submit any documents or letters which might tend to support his claim for objection and to indicate with what religious groups, if any, he had been associated. The

Act, it will be remembered, gave objector status only to those who were opposed to war by reason of "religious training and belief"; while this did not mean that one had to belong to a religious organization, evidence that one was in fact associated with some type of "religious" association might help to sustain a claim. It was particularly important that the objector indicate how he was related to pacifist organizations or churches, for, again, although there was no legal requirement to that effect, those who administered the Act often gave great weight to facts of that kind.

In answering the questions on Form 47, it might frequently be found necessary to consult advisers, and during the war various types of advisory bodies developed whose purpose it was, not only to help the conscript answer the questions on Form 47, but also to aid him should he fail to get the classification he requested or decided he could not accept any conscientious-objector category. Thus, in the metropolitan area of New York City, the Metropolitan Board for Conscientious Objectors, supported by many groups interested in the problems of the c.o., performed this function. The National Service Board for Religious Objectors (the N.S.B.R.O., as it came to be called)—a co-operative organization supported by the Historic Peace Churches and other religious organizations to aid objectors and assist in the administration of alternative service—had an elaborate advisory service with designated representatives in many communities. The National Service Board had several able persons on its advisory staff throughout the course of the war, and it undoubtedly did much to assist the objector at every stage of his Selective Service "processing."

Groups like the Fellowship of Reconciliation, the War Resisters' League, Friends, Brethren, Mennonites, Methodist Commission on World Peace, American Civil Liberties Union, Northern California Board for Conscientious Objectors, Los Angeles County Committee for Conscientious Objectors, and many others acted in a similar capacity. But none of them had facilities as elaborate as those of the National Service Board for Religious Objectors.

Despite the existence of this network of advisory agencies, however, a number of objectors were without organized help, especially in the rural areas. This accounts for many of the failures to answer questionnaires and to fill out forms properly and in some instances for what were cases of obvious misclassification by local boards. Failures on the part of objectors to understand the law and regulations also played a role in the imprisonment of a relatively large number of men who did not receive the classifications they requested.

It should be emphasized that by no means all objectors were certain about what classifications they should request on Form 47; this statement applies not only to those who were ignorant of the law and regulations but also to those who were thoroughly familiar with legal classifications. The latter not infrequently found it difficult to decide whether to ask for the noncombatant category of military service (I-A-O) or to request classification IV-E, which meant that one was willing to serve in alternative civilian service (Civilian Public Service). Similarly, there were ministers of religion who, under the law, were entitled to complete exemption (Classification IV-D), but who were also conscientious objectors. Not a few ministers who found themselves in this position waived their ministerial exemption, stood squarely on their position as conscientious objectors, and requested IV-E. The great majority of Jehovah's Witnesses asked for IV-D rather than IV-E or I-A-O, primarily because they conceived their "witnessing" to be ministerial in character and their vocations as ministers as taking precedence over any claims of the state. Nevertheless, as their general social philosophy showed, Jehovah's Witnesses also objected to serving in the wars of man-made states, while reserving full freedom to fight in the final battle of Armageddon, when God's Theocracy would overturn all earthly powers.[2]

General Rules of Classification

In acting upon requests for conscientious-objector status, local boards throughout the war were instructed by the Director of Selective Service to treat the objector according to the same principles applicable to the nonobjector. Form 47 was not supposed to be examined until all possible claims to other deferment had been exhausted. If the objector was beyond the age of military service, for example, he was supposed, in 1944, to be placed in category IV-A (deferred by reason of age—over 45). If he could claim deferment by reason of dependency, the local board was required to place him in classification III-C. If induction would work extreme hardship on his dependents, the board was instructed to put him in III-D. Only if all possible deferred categories were exhausted in his case was the local board supposed to act upon his request for classification as a conscientious objector opposed only to combatant military service (I-A-O) or his statement that he was opposed to both combatant and noncombatant military service (IV-E). Needless to say, it was the failure of some local boards to observe this general principle which led to many classification difficulties.

As in classification, so in general rules of procedure, the objector was in theory granted the same rights as the nonobjector. Thus his failure to return the general questionnaire constituted a delinquency; his failure to return Form 47, when he had requested it, while not in itself a violation of the regulations, might jeopardize any future claims to objector status. The general regulation that a local board might grant extension of time for fulfilling any obligation was applicable to objector and nonobjector alike. All registrants likewise had the right to request personal hearings before the local board, providing that the request was written and that it was received by the local board within ten days of mailing notice of classification. The right of appeal was also guaranteed by law and regulations. Again, of course, law and regulations said one thing and the practice of local boards, in many cases, another.

Character of Local Boards

The discretion of local boards was, in fact, so wide that the manner in which regulations were applied, and with what exactitude, depended in considerable degree upon the personnel and social background of the local board itself. Each local board was to consist of three or more members to be appointed by the President on recommendation of the state governor.[3] By the time the United States had entered the war, 6,422 local boards had been appointed; there was at least one board of three to five members in each of the 3,070 counties of the United States.[4] Attached to each local board was a government appeal agent, who was always a lawyer, and whose duties were to protect the interests of registrants by assisting them in providing information for the local board and to protect the interests of the government or registrants by taking appeals when either the government or the registrant requested them.[5] In addition, physicians and dentists were attached to each board; their services, like those of the appeal agents, were uncompensated.

For the most part, local Selective Service boards were composed of business and professional men and fairly comfortably fixed farmers, and in this sense could be said to be middle-class institutions. To find a manual laborer or even a clerical white-collar worker among their membership was indeed unusual. In a questionnaire sent to men in Civilian Public Service and to noncombatant conscientious objectors in the Army, the Pacifist Research Bureau and Mulford Sibley tried to gain some understanding of the social and occupational composition of local boards, and, while there were fewer than five hundred responses to the questionnaire, its results tally fairly well with other information regarding board memberships. Occupations like oil-company executive, haberdasher, college professor, retail merchant, small businessman, insurance agent, sales manager, and other similar businesses and professions appear often. Lawyers and farmers also show up with great frequency, especially lawyers. In a great many communities former officers of the American Legion were to be found on the local board; in any event, ex-servicemen were deliberately selected, where possible. Local political leaders were usually good candidates for the board, and this was particularly true where the individual involved was not only a leading personality in the dominant political party but was also prominent in business and an ex-serviceman besides. It is true that in some areas manual laborers appear—we hear of a "railroad machinist" representing labor, for example—but by and large, even where "labor" men are appointed, control of the board is in the hands of other occupational groups. This is not to say that the viewpoint of labor men necessarily differed from that of others, but simply to indicate broadly the classes from which boards were, in the main, drawn.

The theory that local boards were "neighbors" of registrants seems to have been only partially achieved in practice. One of the most obvious conclusions to be drawn from the Pacifist Research Bureau's local-board poll of Civilian Public Service men is the fact that relatively few conscientious objectors knew very much about the members of their own local boards. Some, it is true, knew all the members fairly well, others knew one or two, and yet others had some slight indirect knowledge, but approximately 40 per cent of those who replied to the questionnaire either ignored the question completely or said that they knew none of the board members personally.[6] Whether this ignorance of their board members was peculiar to conscientious objectors or applicable to all registrants we do not, of course, know. It may have been that objectors were in many cases so hostile to the whole Selective Service System that they tried to keep their relations with it at a minimum. Or it might be suggested that objectors naturally moved in circles which could not be expected to have much knowledge of those groups from which local boards were so predominantly drawn. Whatever the explanation, however, the fact remains that objectors were, on the whole, not very well acquainted with their local boards.

Examinations and Hearings before the Local Board

When the local board received the completed Form 47 from the objector, the document was added to the registrant's file and when all other categories had been considered and rejected (dependency claims, industrial and farm deferments, overage), the problem of accepting the request for classification as a conscientious objector came before the board. If the board accepted the claim, it sent a classification notice to the objector informing him that he had been put in either IV-E or I-A-O, as the case might be. Prior to the spring of 1943, this classification would be made definite for IV-E's (although not for those in I-A-O, who still had to pass the rigid Army examinations) after a rather cursory physical examination conducted by local-board doctors; the superficiality of the examination resulted in a great many unfit men being sent to C.P.S. camps, from which, sooner or later, they would have to be discharged. This was a situation against which objectors vigorously protested. After the reforms of 1943, the objector was given a regular Army-type physical examination to determine whether he should be placed in IV-F (unavailable by reason of physical or mental defect) or retain his objector classification.

It is impossible to say what proportion of objectors, as contrasted with nonobjectors, failed their physical examinations. We do hear of cases where objectors were passed under circumstances in which nonobjectors would almost certainly have failed. On the other hand, we also know of instances where I-A registrants otherwise fit were placed in IV-F (on grounds of mental unfitness) when, under examination by Army psychiatrists, they denounced the war.[7]

If the board decided that the applicant for objector status should not be granted the desired classification, it informed him of the category into which he was placed and of the fact that he had the right, under Selective Service regulations,[8] to ask the board for a personal hearing on his application. If the objector applied for a personal hearing within ten days, the board was required under the regulations to grant it. The board was also authorized, of course, to require a personal hearing on its own initiative, and this was sometimes done.

How frequently personal hearings were held is not exactly known. Evidence accumulated in the Pacifist Research Bureau questionnaire indicates that there were oral hearings in approximately 25 per cent of the cases of all those who were eventually classified as conscientious objectors. In a number of local boards, hardly any oral hearings were given, due to the fact that the board approved virtually all requests for IV-E or I-A-O status almost automatically. This was sometimes true, for example, where the overwhelming majority of applicants for c.o. status were Mennonites, whose position on war was well known. Likewise, in some communities, where boards were relatively well informed about the theory and practice of conscientious objection, mere request for classification as IV-E or I-A-O was in most instances sufficient to secure the classification.

On the other hand, it is well established that there were local boards which refused to give any applicant IV-E, either because the boards were ignorant of the regulations or because they wished to shift the responsibility of judgment to the appeals bodies. Thus, in one Midwest community of eight thousand inhabitants, it was notorious that the board automatically denied all requests for IV-E, thus forcing the Department of Justice Hearing Officer to assume a responsibility which was by law and regulations vested in the local board.[9] Examples like this were by no means difficult to find. In such cases, of course, oral hearings could not affect the decision of the board one way or the other: a I-A classification was inevitable; the appeals machinery was then burdened with cases which, had the local board observed the law, would never have developed.

When oral hearings were granted or ordered by the board, they might be long or short, superficial or searching, depending upon the composition of the board and its acquaintance with conscientious objection. Since types of questions asked by board members might give us a clue as to the mental attitudes of local boards where serious issues of classification were raised, an attempt was made in this study to determine the questions most frequently asked in oral hearings. It is felt that the questions listed here, while they by no means embrace all the queries which board members might ask the objector, nevertheless give a fairly accurate insight into the exchanges which took place at oral hearings.[10]

The objector was usually questioned regarding religion and the church, since conscientious objection was associated both in law and in popular opinion with "religious" belief. Typical questions were: To what church do you belong? How long have you been a member? Do you attend regularly? What is the position of your church in regard to conscientious objection? How can you be a conscientious objector when your church is backing the war? What are your religious beliefs? Are you a minister? Do you think an atheist can be a conscientious objector? How do you explain God's command (in some passage of the Old Testament) to smite the enemy? Are you a genuine Quaker (Methodist, Christian, Catholic, etc.) in the light of your actions? How can you reconcile dancing and folk games with the religious attitude to life which you profess?

Often the objector was queried about issues of an ethical-political character, some of which were presumably meant to cast doubt on his consistency or sincerity. What is the reasoning on which you base conscientious objection? Who influenced you to take this stand? How long have you held these ideas? What is your home background? You have received benefits from your country—why shouldn't you defend it? Do you owe any obligation to your country? Why should other men fight for you? What are your political affiliations? What is your social philosophy? How can you be a member of society with your views? How can you honestly take the teacher's oath [to teachers, of course]? What about your other activities which have a bearing on the war (such as farming)? What do you think of the Constitution? Was the United States justified in fighting the Revolutionary War? Why should you oppose noncombatant service, especially helping the wounded?

Frequently there were questions involving practical applications of beliefs. While a few of the queries were put to trip or confuse the applicant, the bulk seem to have represented a genuine attempt to understand his position. By way of illustration, boards would ask: What would you do if your sister (wife, mother, child, grandmother, self, house, town, etc.) were attacked? Would it be all right if the Japs just came here and took over? What if everyone took your point of view? What would you advise in case of invasion? Do you really think nonviolence would work against such people as the Germans (or Japanese)? Do you think we can trust Hitler? Under what conditions would you use force? Did you have any fights in school? How explain taking ROTC, or ground-school training? Do you drink, or frequent gambling places? Explain the work you do. Are you willing to go to C.P.S. camp? Is your wife able to support herself (since you will get no pay in C.P.S.)? Do you refuse to enter the Army?

It might have been expected that the "What-would-you-do-if-your-sister-were-attacked?" type of question would have been avoided, since in the years between the First and Second World Wars it had been so often ridiculed. But it appears that many boards still used it and in some cases pressed it to extreme lengths. It is not surprising that some objectors waxed sarcastic or turned the "attack type" of question off with a quip. Thus one applicant was asked at his oral hearing: "What would you do if a Jap suddenly began to attack your sister?" The reply was immediate: "I'd tell him to go ahead. That's what's wrong with my sister—she's been needing a man for a long time."

On another occasion and before a different board, the fact that one member of the board was a lawyer was credited with saving the situation. "The chief question asked me was what I would do if my wife were being raped by an enemy. Mr. Brown, a professor of law, had enough pride in that profession to see that my case was decided on the basis of fact rather than of personal prejudice." [11]

Boards often found it easier to make decisions in favor of the applicant if he clearly belonged to one of the so-called Historic Peace Churches—those which had taken the antiwar position for years. In such cases, the board did not find it necessary to inquire into the applicant's personal views, but assumed that because he was a member of one of the Historic Peace Churches he was therefore opposed to all war "by reason of religious training and belief"—and that despite the fact that a large percentage of the Friends and Brethren were no longer conscientious objectors. The experience of one objector is illustrative: "I was asked what I had to say in support of my request for a IV-E. I started to tell them how I understood the teachings of Jesus, but was interrupted before I had got four words out by the brusque question: 'Never mind all that; are you a Quaker or not?' . . . I admitted that I was. . . . The members of the Board nodded to each other, saying "OK, IV-E." [12]

Where boards were definitely hostile to objectors—and such boards were by no means rare, although certainly a minority of the whole— literalistic interpretations of the Bible could often be used to point up their hostility and sometimes Biblical texts would be quoted out of context to confuse the objector. After all, God *is* represented as having instructed the Israelites to make war.[13] Jesus *did* say, according to the New Testament, "I came not to bring peace but a sword"; while that saying, when read in context, clearly had nothing to do with war,[14] an embarrassed, sometimes timid, and often uncertain objector might easily be nonplused by it. One case will illustrate. A young objector just about to graduate from the college of agriculture of a large university came up for a personal hearing before his local board. The board was located in a farming area, and the applicant had been planning (before the coming of war) an agricultural career in that very community. During the course of the oral hearing, the following colloquy occurred: "I understand you plan to farm when you graduate from college." "Yes, sir." "You have been studying agriculture at the University." "Yes, sir." "Now when you prepare to farm you have to plan, don't you—plan your planting, plowing, harvests, and so on?" "Yes." "You have to look ahead to the future?" "Yes." "Now in the Bible we are commanded to 'Take no thought for the morrow,' [15] aren't we?" "Yes, I believe so." "Now you profess to be religious, don't you? You say that you are opposed to war by reason of your religion, don't you?" "Yes." "But how can you be religious when you propose to plan for your farm? The Bible says 'Take no thought for the morrow' and yet here you are planning for the morrow. That would seem to make you insincere in your religion." The applicant could not convince the board on this point, with the result that he was classified I-A and had to take an appeal before he eventually obtained his IV-E.[16]

All this is not to say that badgering of the type illustrated here was typical of oral hearings. It was sufficiently common so that we are safe in saying that it was not rare. On the other hand, many boards were eminently fair in conducting the hearing, so much so that objectors were sometimes surprised. Comments like "courteous," "fair," and "kind" are not uncommon in the replies of those who indicated that they had had oral hearings. Hearings of this kind ought, of course, to have been universal, since local boards had been instructed by Selective Service authorities to make hearings "dignified." But so great was variation among local boards that this sometimes remained an ideal observed only in the breach.

Misclassification, Discrimination, and Inadequate Law and Regulations

That there were many cases in which local boards discriminated against conscientious objectors is clear from the testimony of conscientious objectors themselves as well as from investigation of particular local-board situations. Three major areas can be discerned in which local boards either misinterpreted regulations (by design or through ignorance) or applied with seeming correctness Selective Service regulations which were themselves too narrow to cover adequately all possible cases of genuine conscientious objection.

Discrimination and Occupational Deferments. The most detailed, extreme, and best-corroborated examples of gross discrimination against conscientious objectors in connection with occupational deferments occurred in Oklahoma, where, in a community which included many Mennonites and members of the Church of the Brethren, the local board for many months gave virtually every person who applied for Form 47 an immediate classification of IV-E, despite the fact that the individuals involved were in most instances clearly entitled to occupational deferment under Selective Service regulations. These cases will serve to illustrate the general problem, although they are admittedly extreme and not typical examples.

The board involved was the Washita County, Oklahoma, Selective Service Board, located in Cordell, county seat of the county. Many Mennonites and Brethren had settled in the county when it was opened for settlement in 1892 and 1893; because of their views on war, as well as, apparently, because of their widespread use of the German language, they were opposed by a small but articulate group of "patriots" in the community. During the First World War, a very small coterie in Cordell had demanded that the German language be prohibited, and because of this agitation and other acts of social pressure, many farmers had refused any longer to trade in the county seat, transferring their patronage elsewhere. This only added to the tension, which still existed on the eve of the Second World War. Certain "patriotic" groups desired to "drive the Dutchmen out."

During the first two years of the Washita Board's existence, there was apparently but little trouble. Few complaints were heard regarding the Board's treatment of either objectors or nonobjectors. Then two members of the Board resigned, and their successors were violently prejudiced against Mennonites and Brethren, or, if they were not themselves violently prejudiced (testimony differed somewhat at this point), were at least unable to resist organized pressures in the community.

From this point on, the Board became emphatically hostile to all applicants for Form 47. They were referred to by Board members as "un-American yellow dogs" and "demn conscientious objectors." The local board made available to the Department of Agriculture's War Labor Board and to the local ration board the names of all those who had applied for conscientious objector status. These bodies then proceeded to certify conscientious objectors as "nonessential" in farm occupations and to deny their applications for tires, tractor gas, farm implements, and so on—all solely because they were conscientious objectors. There seems to have been a close working agreement between the three boards. The Selective Service Board furnished names and the War Labor Board certified applicants to be "nonessential" farmers. Once this certification was received by the Selective Service Board, all pleas of conscientious objectors for deferment as "essential" farmers, or as men with several dependents, were vain.

In an interview, the Secretary of the War Labor Board defended practices of the Board with respect to conscientious objectors in this way: "Men who file Form 47 state that they do not want to aid the war effort. The USDA has declared that the production of food is as essential to the war effort as munitions. Therefore, these men who do not want to aid the war effort cannot be declared essential to farming. Thus the Board must declare them non-essential."

These practices were called to the attention of the State Director of Selective Service on several occasions, and the state Selective Service System would respond by sending investigators. After commenting briefly on the local situation, the state investigators would almost always end by saying: "Now you, after all, make the decisions in this county and you can count on the state office to back you up." Statements of this kind were hardly designed to enhance respect for regulations or to eliminate discriminatory practices.

With such obvious discrimination, it is not surprising that appeals from the local board's decisions were numerous nor that the local board was reversed in a very high percentage of cases so appealed. In fact, one member of the Board told several men that he had voted against them because he could not resist community pressure. He then proceeded to advise them to appeal, remarking that he was sure they could obtain the proper classification from the Appeal Board. It seemed to be assumed by conscientious objectors in this area that the only way to obtain a classification in conformity with regulations was not to rely on the local board but to put one's entire faith in the Board of Appeals.

Concrete cases make more vivid the curious situation which had developed by 1944. A—— A—— G——, thirty-five years old and the father of two children, operated a four-hundred-acre farm. In 1940 he had been deferred by the local Board. In 1943 he was suddenly placed in IV-E, at a time when regulations provided deferments for men who were without dependents and who farmed fewer acres than he. In August, 1943, on appeal, he was placed in III-C—deferment by reason of dependency and agricultural occupation.

J—— E—— R—— was thirty-seven years old and had nine children, ranging in age from two to fifteen years. He operated a four-hundred-acre farm. Originally he was deferred. His dependency situation alone would seem to have called for deferment. Then, only a few weeks later, he was suddenly placed in IV-E. The Appeal Board restored him to deferred status. Twice he applied for tractor tires, but was rejected on both occasions, on the ground that tires were not available. He was, however, told by a neighbor (not a conscientious objector) that the county agent had stated that no conscientious objector need fill out farm unit blanks, as the claims of objectors would not be allowed.

It is true that in many cases like those above, the appellate machinery served to correct injustice. But in others it failed to do so; the result was that men went to Civilian Public Service camps who under fair local Board conditions would have remained at work on their farms.[17] So notorious did the discrimination become that the situation was not substantially altered until, on instructions from National Headquarters of the Selective Service System, the Selective Service machinery in Washita County was radically overhauled.

"Religious Training and Belief." This expression in the Selective Training and Service Act was given widely different interpretations by local boards. Could an atheist be given objector status under the Act? Some boards said he could and proceeded to classify him IV-E. What about a "humanitarian" objector—one who professed no religion, attended no church, claimed no "religious" training in his family? Again, the answer varied enormously. In one case, an objector defined "religion" in these terms:

We must look *within,* and we must look for ourselves; no one else can do the job for us. This is the point at which the concept of "conscience" enters in; a "conscientious objector" to anything which he considers to be of an evil nature or fundamentally wrong is a person who has looked within, and who is determined to be guided by the light which he finds there. For that force, or light, to which I am constantly referring, is within each person; we may see it or ignore it, but it is there just the same; you have it, I have it, and so have Chancellor Hitler and Comrade Stalin.[18]

In this case, as it turned out, the local board found the applicant to be not "religious" within the meaning of the Act and denied him his IV-E. Yet the belief he expressed strongly resembles in tone that of the great Quaker mystics of all centuries, and Quakers were usually looked upon as objectors "by reason of religious training and belief."

If the local board, then, defined religion in formalistic terms and made the evidences of "religious belief" church attendance or other outward manifestations, it was likely to reject the claims of an objector who had a purely personal belief formed as a result of his own inward experience. If, on the other hand, the local board looked upon religion as simply a deep and profound belief in a particular ideal, it could, and did, make room for "philosophical, humanitarian, and political" objectors, as well as for those who were "religious" in the more orthodox sense. Few local boards, however, had read William James's *Varieties of Religious Experience*.[19]

In their interpretations of the meaning of "religious training and belief," local boards were guided to some extent by directives from the National Headquarters of the Selective Service System and by significant court decisions. As early as December, 1940, for example, Clarence A. Dykstra, first Director of Selective Service, stated in a memorandum that to qualify as an objector under the terms of the Act an applicant did not have to show "membership in a religious organization or sect." And he went on: "Any and all influences which have contributed to the consistent endeavor to live the good life may be classed as 'religious training.' Belief signifies sincere conviction. Religious belief signifies sincere conviction as to the supreme worth of that to which one gives his supreme allegiance." [20]

While this definition of "religion," if consistently applied, might have embraced almost all objectors to "all war," it was superseded by a new instruction drawn up by General Hershey, Mr. Dykstra's successor. In March, 1942, the General defined "religion" in these terms: "I must be satisfied that the objection is based on 'religious training and belief' which contemplates recognition of some source of all existence, which, whatever the type of conception, is Divine because it is the Source of all things." [21] It is obvious that this interpretation virtually required belief in a transcendent God to qualify as a "religious objector"; to the degree that boards observed the new ruling their decisions consequently became less liberal. Many objectors sincerely believed that all war was morally wrong and held their beliefs with a conviction which Dykstra's memorandum would have called "religious," but under the Hershey ruling they could not obtain classification as objectors if they did not also profess belief in a Divine Creator. The General did not say whether a pantheistic outlook would qualify under his ruling, but presumably it would not.

Guidance from the courts came in a number of decisions. In the case of Mathias Kauten, for example, the Second Circuit Court of Appeals had this to say: "A conscientious objection to participation in war under any circumstances . . . may justly be regarded as a response of the individual to an inward mentor, call it conscience or

God, that is for many persons at the present time the equivalent of what has always been thought a religious impulse." [22] And in the case of Randolph Phillips, this statement equating conscientious objection with religious conscientious objection was reiterated.[23]

Although the Kauten and Phillips cases were decided after the Hershey statement was issued and apparently contradicted the General's memorandum, the Selective Service System seemed to think that there was no serious conflict. Local boards, then, continued to be under the guidance of definitions of "religion" which to the average observer could not be reconciled, while the official administrators of the law seemed to see no incompatibility. Small wonder, then, that local boards should continue to be confused, even after 1943 (when both the Hershey and Kauten decisions had been publicized). It may well be doubted whether the debate on religion within the ranks of the Selective Service colonels and in the judiciary actually clarified the issue.

Closely associated with the problem of religion was the issue of the conscientious objector who was opposed to some wars but not necessarily to all wars. Here local boards sometimes found themselves in extremely difficult situations. A Roman Catholic, for example, might appear before a local board and ask for IV-E status, explaining that the Second World War was not a "just" war within the meaning of Catholic moral philosophy.[24] There might be no doubt regarding his religious character, yet because he did not repudiate "all war," as required by the Act, he might find his application rejected. Or a Socialist might appear, whose "religious" character might fulfill all the requirements of the Kauten decision but whose objection was primarily to the Second World War, not to all wars. In cases of this kind, some boards might, and did, overlook the technical requirements of the Act, and, despite absence of opposition to "all war," grant objector status. But more meticulous boards would deny the application and the objector would eventually be imprisoned.

The Problem of Jehovah's Witnesses. The Witnesses have been treated elsewhere from the viewpoint of their theology and social philosophy.[25] Here we need only emphasize the classification issues they raised before the local board. It will be remembered that, for the most part, they did not seek IV-E, but rather sought exemption as ministers of the gospel (in IV-D). Many of them, however, also took a position very close to that of conscientious objection in the ordinary sense. Thus, one Witness told the writer that to go into the Army would mean not only a breaking of his covenant to preach but would also be participation in the act of killing and destroying human beings. All wars since those of the Old Testament (many of which were commanded by God), he remarked, have been selfish, and the true Witness of Jehovah can have nothing to do with them. The Witness will defend himself and his family, but such defense is far removed from what is called war. He personally would not serve in a munitions factory or navy yard and had rejected a civil service position in an arsenal.[26]

While all did not take this position—some, indeed, were willing to serve in shipyards and munitions plants—it was this combination of opposition to war and emphasis on the request for IV-D which put squarely before many local boards the issue of whether to grant IV-E or IV-D. Since the Witness was not a minister in the orthodox sense of the term (he often earned his livelihood in a factory or in some other "secular" occupation), many boards concluded that his proper classification was IV-E. But the Witness, who thought of work in alternative civilian service as "acquiescing" in the curtailment of his ministerial powers, usually chose to go to prison rather than serve in Civilian Public Service.

A similar situation arose when the Witness was not a pronounced objector to war in the usual sense of the term. He might actually have worked in a navy yard or munitions plant. But even then he would ask for IV-D, since his primary responsibility was still, he thought, to God and his ministry. In such cases the local board usually classified the witness I-A, or, in some instances, in I-A-O. But the classification would frequently not be accepted, and, if it was upheld on appeal, the Witness usually chose to go to prison rather than accept service in the Army in any capacity.

Local boards often denied IV-D classifications to Jehovah's Witnesses, even when they could prove that they were "pioneers"—that is, when they spent at least 150 hours a month in ministerial duties. This would seem to have been virtually full-time work. But despite a ruling of General Hershey in 1942 that persons who were engaged in ministerial work more than 80 hours a month could claim IV-D status,[27] local boards persisted in giving IV-E or I-A classifications to "pioneers" and to others whose monthly time devoted to Jehovah's Witness work exceeded 80 hours. Sometimes this discrimination was due to local prejudice against Jehovah's Witnesses; in other cases it was undoubtedly attributable to the ignorance of the board; in yet other instances influential Roman Catholics on the board might be responsible (the bitter hostility of Jehovah's Witnesses to the Roman Catholic Church was well known).[28] It is true that some Witnesses were given IV-D by local boards, but the number was far fewer than those who were denied the classification.

The experiences of Jehovah's Witnesses before local boards illustrated the difficulty of framing law and regulations in such a manner as to provide for all the idiosyncrasies of conscientious objection. They also re-emphasized the decentralized character of the Selective Service System as a whole, when, despite an endeavor on the part of the head of the system to secure some uniformity in ministerial classifications, local boards continued to interpret law and regulations in widely differing ways. Finally, it was in the classification of Jehovah's Witnesses that local prejudice was probably most pronounced.

Appeals

Before June 20, 1941, five days (after notice of classification had been mailed) were allowed for taking an appeal from the local board to one of the approximately three hundred regional Boards of Appeals.[29] After that date, ten days became the limit.[30] To appeal from the local board to a regional Board of Appeals was a matter of right, and it was not within the province of the local board to refuse to transmit the necessary papers to the appellate body. The local board could, of course—and sometimes did—change its classification to the satisfaction of the objector and thus remove the necessity for the latter's appeal.

Once the appeal had been taken, the first task of the Board of Appeals was to decide whether the objector belonged in any deferred category, such as essential agricultural worker. If it found that he could not legitimately be deferred, the Board was then obliged to turn his file over to the Department of Justice for investigation of his claim to be recognized as an objector. This was the only point at which classification procedure for objectors differed from that used for other registrants—there was no investigation by the Department of Justice in the nonobjector's appeal.

The first stage in the Department of Justice's investigation was an inquiry by the Federal Bureau of Investigation. The FBI assigned an agent to interview any references given by the objector. The agent interviewed his employer and sometimes his parents, teachers, and pastor. This testimony was summarized, evaluation by the investigator was noted, and the file was then ready for the Hearing Officer. It would seem from such evidence as we have and from relative absence of complaints by objectors themselves that FBI agents were usually conscientious, considerate, and genuinely interested in getting an accurate picture of the objector's personal, religious, and political background. Of course, many such investigators knew very little about the pacifist movement and were often astonishingly ignorant of general social trends; their lack of knowledge, perspective, and experience sometimes led them to make blunders.

Hearing Officers were lawyers appointed by the Department of Justice to inquire into the claims of conscientious objectors on appeal. They were concerned solely with objectors and not with other appellants under the Selective Training and Service Act. After an oral hearing of the objector, during which the latter was supposed to be afforded an opportunity to answer charges made against him in the FBI evidence, the Hearing Officer made his report, recommending that the objector either be placed in IV-E or I-A-O or that his claims be denied. After approval of his report by the Department of Justice, the recommendation of the Hearing Officer was submitted to the Board of Appeals, which then classified the appellant. It should be emphasized that the report of the Hearing Officer was wholly recommendatory. The Board of Appeals was not bound by it and could, indeed, reverse it.

The Hearing Officer's interview with the objector was usually rather informal, and to it the latter might bring friends or advisers who might be given an opportunity to testify. As likely as not, the Officer's first comments might be for the purpose of putting the appellant at ease. Questions would concern past life, religious affiliations, basis for objection, and social and political views. Frequently, the Officer would inquire into any alleged inconsistencies in the conduct of the objector: for example, how could he reconcile his service in the National Guard (at one period in his life) with his present position? Or, to illustrate more particularly: in one case the objector, shortly after Pearl Harbor, had applied for service with Naval Intelligence, wrongly thinking that it would be noncombatant service. Denied employment, he had then returned to his earlier beliefs, which had rejected both combatant and noncombatant service. The Hearing Officer tried to determine, by a series of questions, whether his return to pacifist views of the more extreme kind was sincere. The applicant convinced the Hearing Officer that his change in outlook was genuine, and the Officer thereupon recommended IV-E.[31]

The applicant was entitled to know the general charges which had been made against him by persons whom the FBI had interviewed. Prior to October 10, 1942, he could ask for such a statement before his hearing. After that date, the request had to be made at the hearing. This change was criticized by many advisers of conscientious objectors, on the ground that it left the applicant in the dark until the time of the hearing.[32] On the other hand, the Department of Justice claimed that clerical help was not available to make the earlier procedure practicable; that under the new rule, the Hearing Officer could (to afford the applicant time to rebut contentions in the FBI file) postpone the hearing until a later date or invite the applicant to submit written material; and that in 80 per cent of the cases before Hearing Officers, objectors did not utilize their right to ask for unfavorable testimony in FBI reports.[33]

As in the case of local boards, Hearing Officers found one of their greatest difficulties to be interpretation of "religious training and belief." Some officers were exceedingly narrow, as in the case of one, a strict Methodist, who seemed to require evidence of Sunday-school attendance and rather formal church activity.[34] On the other hand, some seemingly went even further than the Kauten decision in their interpretations.

A selection of difficult cases will perhaps illustrate the problems with which Hearing Officers found themselves confronted. One objector was a member of the Society for Ethical Culture, which professed no particular belief in God but which the objector termed a "religious fellowship." The Hearing Officer decided that the applicant should be given IV-E.[35]

Another objector was brought up in the Jewish faith, confirmed at the age of thirteen, but at the time of the hearing professed no belief in God or in Judaism. The Hearing Officer recommended I-A in this language:

The Hearing Officer finds the registrant on his own personal observation and the record, to be one of those young men who, fed on the postwar literature which he describes, made many doubt how young America would answer a call to arms. This is one of the youthful philosophers who, without any religious basis for their attitude, are unwilling to serve the country where their parents took refuge from persecution. Fortunately they constitute a minority.[36]

In another case, the Hearing Officer found the objector to be "sincere" in his objection to all war but not to be "religious." "Registrant does not believe in any Divine Providence." The recommendation was I-A.[37]

A few Hearing Officers were attacked by objectors for gross incompetency and at least one, apparently with good reason and on good authority, for "immorality" as well as incompetency. In the latter case, the individual involved was a roadhouse proprietor in his spare time, and liquor flowed freely in his establishment. Objectors also criticized his connection with organized vice. But they were even more critical of his frequently brusque five- or six-minute hearings, during which he was often quite rude.[38] On the whole, however, Hearing Officers seem to have been men respected in their communities for moral integrity and professional competence, whatever one may say about the often narrow basis for some of their recommendations.

The Department of Justice was not bound to concur in the reports of its Hearing Officers, but in only a few cases did it refuse to do so (24 out of 8,126 cases for which complete statistics were available down to June 30, 1944). Up to June 30, 1944, 11,313 cases were referred to the Department of Justice for investigation. Departmental recommendations for these cases are indicated in Table I.

Complete statistics were available on 8,126 cases which eventually found their way to the Department of Justice. An analysis of these cases in Table II shows the classifications requested on Form 47,

TABLE I. DEPARTMENT OF JUSTICE RECOMMENDATIONS ON OBJECTORS' APPEALS *

IV-E	3,362
I-A-O	2,014
Claims denied	3,071
Withdrew claims (mostly Jehovah's Witnesses)	1,217
Returned for administrative reasons or because of change in law and regulations to Appeal Boards or Local Boards	1,295
Pending	354
TOTAL	11,313

* *Report* of Linton Collins, Special Assistant to the Attorney General, to the Attorney General, July, 1944.

TABLE II. REQUESTED CLASSIFICATIONS BEFORE LOCAL BOARDS AND LOCAL BOARD DECISIONS IN 8,126 CASES *

Requested:		
IV-E	6,121	75.33% of total
I-A-O	1,883	23.17% of total
No objection indicated	122	1.50% of total
Decisions of Local Boards:		
Objector claims denied	6,228	76.64%
I-A-O	1,146	14.10%
IV-E	383	4.71%
Other disposition	369	4.55%

* *Report* of Linton Collins, Special Assistant to the Attorney General, to the Attorney General, July, 1944.

before the local boards, and the categories in which the objectors were placed.

After reference to the FBI, subsequent hearings by Hearing Officers, and review by the Assistant to the Attorney General on behalf of the Department of Justice, the recommendations by the Department of Justice and subsequent decisions by the Boards of Appeals in the same cases took the form indicated in Table III.

TABLE III. DEPARTMENT OF JUSTICE RECOMMENDATIONS AND BOARD OF APPEALS DECISIONS IN 8,126 CASES *

Department Recommendations:

Objector claims denied	2,997	36.71%
I-A-O	1,964	24.05%
IV-E	3,160	38.70%
Reversal of Hearing Officer	24	

Boards of Appeals Disposition of Recommendations:

I-A	3,222	39.47%
I-A-O	1,828	22.39%
IV-E	2,772	33.96%
Other deferred classifications	341	

* *Report* of Linton Collins, Special Assistant to the Attorney General, to the Attorney General, July, 1944.

These figures clearly show that Department of Justice recommendations reduced the number of "claims denied" by more than 50 per cent; and that, while Boards of Appeals were not nearly as liberal in granting IV-E and I-A-O as the Department of Justice was in recommending them, the regional Boards of Appeals nevertheless granted objector status in more than 50 per cent of the cases. This is the average for the bulk of the war period.

Boards of Appeals did not follow the recommendations of the Department of Justice in about one case out of seventeen—in 5.82 per cent of the cases, to be exact. As the statistics indicate, Boards were more severe on objectors than the Department of Justice, and often the failure of the Board to follow the advice of the Department was considered a weighty ground for reversal by the President. And "presidential appeal" was the highest administrative recourse open to the objector as to other registrants.

Originally appeals to the President from the Board of Appeals were severely restricted, the only ground which was allowed being dependency, and then only if there had been a dissenting vote in the Board of Appeals.[39] On March 30, 1941, however, the grounds were liberalized. According to the regulation of that date the National Director or State Director of Selective Service could take appeals to the President whenever either one of them believed such appeals to be in the national interest or to prevent an injustice.[40]

Actually, of course, the President did not hear the appeals personally, but delegated his power in that respect to the Director of Selective Service. The Director, in turn, assigned the task to several panels, or committees, in his office, composed for the most part of Army officers. When the Director was asked to take an "appeal to the President," the decision as to whether the appeal should be taken depended in considerable degree upon the advice of those in the Director's office who handled appeals, although General Hershey, the Director, seemed to take an active interest in administering presidential appeals.

If the objector's Appeals Board was not unanimous, his right to have his case reviewed by the President was unqualified. If, however, the Board was unanimous, the objector was obliged to ask either the National Director or the State Director to take an appeal in his behalf. This involved sending letters to one of the Directors, making out a case for the appeal, and rebutting contentions of FBI investigators and others. The objector was entitled, under Selective Service regulations,[41] to examine his file at the local board and to copy the Hearing Officer's report. Often local boards through ignorance—or, in some cases, it seems, through prejudice—refused to allow inspection; in such cases it was sometimes necessary to ask the State Director to instruct the local board to obey the regulations.[42]

In appealing to the President, it was particularly important for the objector to indicate whether the Appeals Board had overruled the recommendations of the Hearing Officer. If it had done so, it was often much less difficult to secure presidential appeal, and the chances of securing a favorable decision on review were enhanced.

The advisory section of the National Service Board for Religious Objectors was active in presenting appeals to the President and in aiding objectors. Members of the advisory section would confer directly with the Selective Service committees which recommended whether appeals should be taken and would then present cases before the review committees. There was always a lawyer attached to the advisory section of the National Service Board, and his assistance, in doubtful cases particularly, could prove invaluable. Anyone going through the files of the National Service Board must be impressed with the care given by the advisory section to each case. Correspondence with the objector and his friends was sometimes voluminous, and details which to outsiders might appear petty were carefully noted if it seemed they could aid the appeal.

Similar advisory functions were performed by the National Committee on Conscientious Objectors of the American Civil Liberties Union, although the scope of its activities never became as wide with respect to appeals as that of the National Service Board. Some objectors looked upon the National Committee with greater favor, however, since they thought it could be more independent of Selective Service than the National Service Board, which was so closely connected with Selective Service in the administration of alternative civilian service.

A question which agitated conscientious objectors and their friends during the first three years of the Selective Training and Service Act was the composition of the committees which reviewed presidential appeals cases in National Headquarters of Selective Service. The Selective Service Act in its original form provided that the President should "establish within the Selective Service System civilian local boards and other civilian agencies, including appeal boards and agencies of appeal, as may be necessary to carry out the provisions of this act." [43] In pursuance of this provision, civilian local boards and Boards of Appeals had been established; but presidential appeals were heard, as has been noted above, by committees composed of Army officers. Was this not in clear violation of the law?

To many conscientious objectors it seemed to be an obvious breach, and they sought to have it declared such by the courts. But they were unable to get a judicial condemnation. In the meantime, lawyers for the Selective Service System themselves began to question the legality of the presidential appeals committees. Instead of transforming those bodies into civilian agencies, however, the Selective Service System began to press for legislation which would legalize the practice of staffing the committees with Army officers. Congress complied on December 5, 1943, amending the Selective Training and Service Act to provide that the President "shall establish within the Selective Service System civilian local boards, civilian appeal boards, and such other agencies, including agencies of appeal, as may be necessary to carry out the provisions of this Act." [44] This, of course, removed the legal objections to review by committees of Army officers but did not at all answer the question as to whether the law had not been violated by their establishment in the beginning. It seems clear that both the letter and the spirit of the original provision in the Selective Service Act had been violated down to December 5, 1943. While after that date military review committees became legal, they did not become any more desirable from the objector's point of view. The whole controversy about composition of appeals committees illustrated the degree to which the Selective Service System was dominated by Army officers and, equally, the extent to which even Congress was overshadowed by the military group.

Presidential review raised substantially the same issues as those brought before local and appellate boards. During the early period of presidential review, before the review committees were swamped by appeals, the committees attempted to render written opinions in cases coming before them. While written opinions were later discarded, the decisions of the early days constitute an interesting study in the thinking of the Army officers composing the committees. One of the most surprising conclusions of such a study is that some "presidential" decisions went far beyond General Hershey's definition of religion and certainly far beyond the often narrow constructions of Hearing Officers. Yet General Hershey approved these wider constructions and they were made the subject of a memorandum of the Department of Justice to all district attorneys and Hearing Officers.[45]

Thus, in the case of J—— W—— H——, a member of the Humanist Society of Friends, the Hearing Officer, while admitting that the registrant was sincere, denied that he was an objector "by reason of religious training and belief." He doubted that the principles of the Humanist Society of Friends constituted a "religion" and held that the registrant objected to war not because of religious belief but because of his "ideas of social organization." He was therefore denied IV-E. The presidential appeals committee, in overruling the Board of Appeals, remarked: "If a man's experience in the world leads him to a sincere conviction that he may not and must not participate in war, it cannot be maintained that his conviction is invalid because he arrived at it along other than accepted and defined paths of religious training." [46]

In a presidential appeal from Massachusetts, the registrant was

on record as having once been a member of the Presbyterian church
and having attended a Christian Science Sunday school. However,
he had begun to question his early beliefs, was now frankly an agnostic, and was searching for something in which he might believe.
The Board of Appeals had classified him I-A, despite a Hearing
Officer's recommendation of IV-E. The presidential appeals committee concluded that the Hearing Officer was right, in these words:
"He is revealed as one passing through a common religious experience, seeking for the rock to which he may anchor. . . . The variety
of religious experience and belief is almost infinite." [47]

The statistics on presidential appeals shown in Table IV indicate
the degree to which I-A, III-A and III-B, and I-A-O classifications
were diminished and the extent to which presidential appeal en-
larged IV-D and IV-E categories.

TABLE IV. PRESIDENTIAL APPEALS, OCTOBER, 1940, TO JUNE 1, 1944 *

Classification	Local Board	Board of Appeals	Presidential Appeal
I-A	36,593	24,705	19,942
I-A-O	198	349	96
IV-E	232	104	278
IV-D	18	63	619
III-A and III-B	547	4,655	3,535

Presidential appeal changed

168 from I-A to IV-E	4 from II-C to I-A-O
46 from I-A-O to IV-E	4 from III-D to I-A-O
3 from II-A to IV-E	3 from III-A and III-B to I-A-O
6 from II-C to IV-E	3 from other classes to I-A-O
1 from IV-D to IV-E	3 from IV-E to I-A
1 from III-C to IV-E	10 from IV-E to II-A
1 from III-A and III-B to IV-E	2 from IV-E to II-B
46 from I-A to I-A-O	2 from IV-E to II-C
3 from IV-E to I-A-O	17 from IV-E to IV-D
4 from II-A to I-A-O	4 from IV-E to III-A and III-B
2 from II-B to I-A-O	

52 confirmed in IV-E
27 confirmed in I-A-O

* Selective Service as the Tide of War Turns, Appendix 121, 560.

From the viewpoint of the objector, the weakest links in the appellate system seem to have been:

(1) Unwillingness of some local boards to observe the regulations with respect to inspection of files by the objector.

(2) Inexperience of FBI agents investigating c.o. claims. This often led the agents to commit blunders which had the effect of creating injustice.

(3) Hearing Officers of narrow outlook.

(4) Military domination of the appellate scheme, particularly with respect to the presidential appeals committees. This military domination was reflected in the fact that National and State Directors of Selective Service were military officers as well as in the military composition of the appeals panels. Throughout the war religious and civil-liberties organizations attempted to make the appellate system civilian in fact as well as in theory, but to no avail. At one period, indeed, General Hershey indicated that he would seriously consider the appointment of a civilian presidential appeals board, and on December 7, 1942, a list of names was submitted for his consideration by Paul C. French, Executive Secretary of the National Service Board for Religious Objectors. But nothing ever came of the proposal.

To the end of hostilities, the organization responsible for forcing men *into* the Army—an organization dominated by regular Army officers—was also responsible for passing on the claims of conscientious objectors for exemption *from* the Army.

Illustrative Classification Stories

A more nearly complete insight into issues of classifying conscientious objectors can only be obtained by examining illustrative case histories which treat the problems of classification from the viewpoint of individuals.

Case of H—— S—— B——. B—— was classified I-A by his local board, despite the fact that he came from a Quaker family, his parents, grandparents, and great-grandparents having been Friends. On April 14, 1943, the Board of Appeals confirmed his local-board classification by a vote of 5 to 0.

After learning the decision of the Appeals Board, B—— talked to

a Sergeant J—— at the State Selective Service headquarters. J——
told him that he had no further right of appeal, that he could not
talk to the State Selective Service Director, that he could not see the
appeal record, and that his only chance was to ask the government
appeal agent to ask the State Director to appeal for him. This advice was, of course, in large degree incorrect, but B—— proceeded
to interview the appeal agent. That official lectured him on patriotism,
informing B—— that any man who would not take noncombatant
service in the armed forces would not get any help from him. The
appeal agent also said he could not see the appeal record—advice
which clearly violated Selective Service regulations.

Somehow, by accident, it would appear, B—— finally discovered
that he could ask the National Director of Selective Service to take
an appeal to the President. The appeal was granted, the presidential
appeals committee reversed the Board of Appeals, and B—— was
eventually assigned to a C.P.S. camp.

Case of B—— M——. M——'s history is illustrative of the reclassification process. He was assigned to C.P.S. and worked in a
camp for ten months in 1942. The camp director thought he had great
mental instability. He seemed to be uncertain of his position. Once
he thought of entering the armed forces; then he suddenly changed
his mind. After medical examination, Selective Service approved his
release from camp on psychiatric grounds.

He was now given a I-A classification by his local board. M——
appealed, but his plea was rejected by the Board of Appeals, 5 to 0.
On July 14, 1943, the National Service Board for Religious Objectors
asked General Hershey to appeal to the President, but this request
was denied on the ground that M—— had worked in a defense plant
until after Pearl Harbor and had requested information on the Medical Corps. These facts, General Hershey argued, demonstrated his
insincerity in asking for IV-E.

Despite the fact that he had requested classification as a c.o.,
M—— went to the Army induction station on July 28, 1943. There,
after examination, he was turned down on psychiatric grounds, and
his local board at last classified him IV-F.[48]

How Many Conscientious Objectors?

How many men were officially classified as conscientious objectors during the course of the war? Unfortunately, we lack this information, at least in exact terms. Selective Service records were not available for inspection to determine how many applications for Form 47 had been filed. Even had the records been available, it is doubtful whether they would have provided an accurate accounting. Many local boards were careless about their filing systems, and while all were supposed to keep "registers" of conscientious objectors, many of them failed to do so. The National Headquarters of the Selective Service System apparently did not wish to interfere too much with local board autonomy or was not sufficiently concerned about statistics of this kind to press for any uniform system. Officials of the Selective Service System were frank to confess their inability to provide accurate statistics.[49]

We do know, however, that 11,868 objectors actually reported for alternative service work under Civilian Public Service.[50] Official sources estimated that approximately 25,000 reported for service in the Army and Navy as I-A-O objectors.[51] Actually, competent observers believed that the number of I-A-O men was considerably larger—perhaps 50,000.[52]

Such official statistics as we have will be found in the Selective Service System's report on conscientious objectors.[53] Table V gives these figures.

TABLE V. SELECTIVE SERVICE SYSTEM'S ESTIMATE OF TOTAL NUMBER OF LIABLE SELECTIVE SERVICE REGISTRANTS CLAIMING CONSCIENTIOUS OBJECTION, 1940–1947

Inducted into armed forces for noncombatant service (estimate)	25,000
Assigned to camp for work of national importance	11,950
Convicted for failing to report to camp	1,624
Reclassified from I-A-0 or IV-E as not available	13,780
Claimants never classified in I-A-0 or IV-E	20,000

There is reason to believe that these figures do not give an entirely accurate picture of the numbers of registrants who are regarded by this study as conscientious objectors. In the first place, it may well be doubted whether the local board figures (52,354) of those who were at any time classified as I-A-O or IV-E, upon which the above statistics are in part based, are high enough. Local board records, as has been remarked, were rather defective on conscientious objectors. Secondly, the 25,000 estimate for objectors in the armed forces is probably too low, as has been suggested elsewhere. There are no records, of course, to corroborate this guess. Thirdly, the official figures take no account (and on legal grounds this was entirely justified) of Jehovah's Witnesses, who from the viewpoint of this study are regarded as conscientious objectors. Approximately 5,000 Jehovah's Witnesses served time in prison, and there were many other Witness objectors among the registrants who for various reasons did not go to prison. Finally, the Selective Service report itself tells us that the figure of 20,000 claimants who were never classified in I-A-O or IV-E is merely an estimate.

Partly, then, because our definition of "conscientious objector" is broader than that of the law and Selective Service, and partly because we believe some of the official figures can be questioned, we suggest that the total figure of 72,000 is too low. How far it should be revised upward we do not know. We are willing to hazard the guess, however, that there were possibly as many as 100,000 objectors, as we use the term. This figure, of course, like the Selective Service statistics themselves, embraces only men of military age, 19 through 44. If one were to include those outside these age limits who claimed to be objectors, the figure would have to be greater.

The incompleteness of statistics on conscientious objectors is itself a fact of considerable significance. But whatever may be thought of this, even a generous estimate of their numbers makes them an infinitesimal part of the more than 34,000,000 registrants—probably not more than 0.30 of 1 per cent.

Who Were the C.O.'s?

The men classified or conscripted as conscientious objectors or who unsuccessfully claimed such status came from a diverse geographical, occupational, and social background. Geographically, large numbers were concentrated in eastern Pennsylvania, Ohio, Indiana, Kansas, and California, although no part of the United States was without representation. All occupations were to be found, but due to the fact that Mennonites and Brethren tended to be rural, a far higher percentage of c.o.'s than in the general population were farmers. Teachers seem also to have constituted a disproportionately large occupational group. As for social status, the c.o. contingent was a mirror of the country as a whole. However, the so-called upper classes were but poorly reflected.

In terms of religious affiliation, the largest single group of c.o.'s who entered the Army and Navy as noncombatants were the Seventh-Day Adventists. Among those who rendered alternative civilian service (C.P.S.), members of the Historic Peace Churches constituted about 60 per cent of the total. As for the objectors who on various grounds were imprisoned, more than three-quarters were Jehovah's Witnesses.

But no general statement can express adequately the variety of personality types and experiences which characterized the c.o. population. More detailed accounts given in subsequent chapters bring out the humor, tragedy, conflict, and achievement which, more than formal statistics, reveal the essential character of the c.o.'s who were drafted into the armed forces and C.P.S. or who were imprisoned.[54]

v: The Conscientious Objector
in the Armed Forces

How many conscientious objectors entered the Army and Navy for noncombatant service? Unfortunately, we do not know. The Selective Service System kept no central records and there was no practicable way in which the records of more than 6,500 local Selective Service boards could be examined. Even if this had been possible, local board records were often inaccurate and incomplete. Nor did the War Department keep records of those classified as I-A-O, although estimates were from time to time made.

Numbers

At best, then, any estimate of numbers of conscientious objectors who served in the Army and Navy must be a guess, and a very rough guess at that. We do know that some 12,000 Seventh-Day Adventists entered the Army as noncombatants,[1] and by 1945, according to church authorities, at least 1,382 members of the Church of the Brethren had gone into the armed services as I-A-O.[2] Rough guesses could also be made after considerable correspondence with known conscientious objectors in the Army and Navy, whose estimates should be considered of some value.

Even the official figures are admitted to be only estimates. According to the Selective Service System's report on conscientious objection, 25,000 I-A-O objectors are said to have served in the armed forces.[3] But these figures are almost certainly too low. Correspondence by Winslowe Ames with objectors in the Army indicated that their numbers were much more numerous than these figures would indicate. Fifty thousand has been suggested as a more nearly accurate figure. From the viewpoint of this study, it is probably safe to guess that the number of conscientious objectors in the armed services was some figure between 25,000 and 50,000. The very fact that the figure must be a guess indicates the woeful lack of records with respect to certain important phases of the war.

In addition to those who were officially recognized as c.o.'s when they entered the Army and Navy, there were others who were objectors without official recognition. Local boards had refused to give them I-A-O classifications and they had reported to Army induction stations without surrendering their convictions about war. In some cases, they refused to take the induction oath or to put on the uniform. In others, they conformed outwardly to Army induction requirements but, once in the Army, refused to obey military orders. How many were included in this category of unrecognized c.o.'s is not known; but they constituted in many instances the most difficult disciplinary problems from the viewpoint of the military and naval authorities.

A third broad division of conscientious objectors in the armed services was composed of those who entered as straight I-A conscripts but developed conscientious scruples after a period of service. Again, it is utterly impossible to obtain figures on the numbers in this group. They were probably relatively few, however.

This enumeration takes no account, of course, of those members of the armed services who, while not classified as conscientious objectors or claiming conscientious objection at some point during their service, yet sympathized with the general outlook of those opposed on principle to combatant military service. This latter group, from all accounts, was fairly large.

Why Objectors Entered Army and Navy

In inquiring into the reasons which led objectors to choose service in the Army and Navy, rather than go to Civilian Public Service, or, perhaps, to prison, it should be emphasized that the nature of those beliefs and motivations differed considerably. No one pattern fits all, and in many cases the individual himself was not aware, at least not fully aware, of all the factors leading to his decision. In some instances the objector was so uncertain as to how his conscientious objection could best be expressed that he found himself in the armed forces almost by default. Family and group pressures were undoubtedly important in many decisions; in others, the armed services were chosen because they were looked upon as lesser evils than Civilian Public Service or prison.

With respect to one large group, the Seventh-Day Adventists, the objector who chose Army or Navy had the official blessing and encouragement of his church. Before American entrance into the war, the church had organized and trained its young men to be stretcher-bearers and Medical Corps assistants.[4] The official position of the church was that noncombatant work in the armed services was the best expression of conscientious objection and simultaneous loyalty to the state. "Thou shalt not kill" was taken in a sense which would not bar co-operation with the military machine so long as the individual was not required to participate in direct killing. Thus it was estimated in 1944 that more than 80 per cent of all Seventh-Day Adventists in the armed services were enrolled in noncombatant branches, either as officially recognized conscientious objectors or because they requested such assignment.[5] With this official support, then, it was small wonder that it was the exception rather than the rule for Seventh-Day Adventists to choose regular Army service or Civilian Public Service in preference to I-A-O.

Other objectors who entered the Army and Navy did not have such group support. Indeed, the Christadelphians "dis-fellowshipped"—expelled—members who joined the Army or Navy as c.o.'s.[6] The only recognized position for the Christadelphian was rejection of both combatant and noncombatant military service. As for groups like the Friends, Brethren, Roman Catholics, Methodists, Presbyterians, Socialists, and Socialist Laborites, choice of the Army and Navy as the expression of conscientious objection was an individual matter—the group neither expelled the member who entered noncombatant service nor commended him for doing so.

One factor which led conscientious objectors to enter the armed forces rather than go to Civilian Public Service, and which induced them to leave Civilian Public Service for the armed forces, was the feeling that work in the Army and Navy constituted a more direct relief of human suffering than was possible in most Civilian Public Service camps and units. This was particularly true after January 21, 1943, when "noncombatant" work in the Army, after having included service in several different branches, including the Quartermaster Corps, was confined to the Medical Corps.[7] The saving of human life was a magnet which was particularly attractive to c.o.'s—especially those who believed that they had an obligation to share in the suffering of those who had been forced into the combatant branches of the armed services.

Closely associated with desire to relieve human suffering was the belief that I-A-O service offered greater opportunity for generally constructive service than did Civilian Public Service. A large percentage of those who asked for reclassification from Civilian Public Service into I-A-O—and they constituted about 5 per cent of all those who served in Civilian Public Service during the course of the war—were apparently determined in their choice by this appeal.[8] Thus C—— M—— remarked: "I thought giving medical aid to wounded soldiers more 'work of national importance' than most anything in C.P.S."[9] And another believed that 60 per cent of the work in West Campton Civilian Public Service camp was merely "made" work, from which he wished to be transferred to the supposedly more constructive work of the Army Medical Corps.[10] Similar reasons were given by others.

It is impossible to determine just how large a role financial considerations played in decisions. That they were important we cannot doubt. In Civilian Public Service one had to pay one's own way or rely upon what one might regard as the charitable contributions of others. In the Army and Navy one received a private's pay and allowances for dependents, as well as cheap insurance. In these respects there was no distinction between the regular soldier and the conscientious objector in the Army.

That lack of pay in Civilian Public Service was definitely a factor in pushing would-be alternative service objectors into the Army was admitted by General Hershey, Director of Selective Service, before a Congressional committee: "They get no pay, and . . . they have to be financed. I do not want to impugn the motive of anybody, but it has been a factor in not only keeping them from going, but once they get there, they leave, and take I-A-O, in the army, when they find out." [11] And General Hershey consistently refused, throughout the course of the war, to propose that objectors in Civilian Public Service be paid.

It is certainly not exaggerating to say that if Civilian Public Service men had been paid at Army rates, the number of objectors choosing I-A-O would have been considerably diminished. In evaluating the treatment of conscience during World War II, the loading of the scales financially in favor of Army service must play a considerable role.

There were, of course, many other factors, conscious and sub-conscious, which entered into one's choice. There was pressure from family and friends, who looked upon I-A-O service as somehow more "respectable" and less likely to interfere with a future career than a record in Civilian Public Service. There were classification irregu-larities which might almost willy-nilly place the objector in I-A-O. In one instance a man left Civilian Public Service for I-A-O to take advantage of the Army course in mechanics.[12] A Jehovah's Witness who had gone to Civilian Public Service camp gave up his religious beliefs after association with other campers. After that, he found he was not really against the "government of the devil" any longer and was willing to go I-A-O.[13] The Selective Service System was, of course, eager to facilitate a change of classification from IV-E to I-A-O; and General Hershey himself spoke of "reclaiming" men from Civilian Public Service for the Army.[14] The General made no dis-tinction between those who transferred to regular combatant duty and those who requested I-A-O. From his point of view, apparently, either was better than C.P.S.

Activities in the Army and Observations on Army Life

Prior to January 21, 1943, an objector in the Army might be as-signed to diverse tasks. He might assist in the movement of food to the front lines, play a role in the Army communications system, or act as a clerk in the services of supply. After 1943, however, he served only in the Medical Corps, although even there he might be assigned a wide variety of tasks, including clerical work as well as the more dramatic medical service on or near the battlefield. One reason for confining objectors to the Medical Corps was undoubtedly the belief of Army and Selective Service authorities that such action would result in a larger number of objectors abandoning the IV-E position and taking up noncombatant military service.

In general, objectors were indistinguishable from noncombatant nonobjectors as to types of work performed. When in the Medical Corps, for example, they received the same training as nonobjectors —about seventeen weeks of basic training without the use of guns. The training was supposed to consist of two weeks' basic instruction, which included military courtesy, personal hygiene, and first aid; care of equipment, clothing, and tents; physical training; interior guard and drill without use of arms; marches; and personal defense measures, including defense against hostile chemical agents. The trainee was then assigned to Medical Corps courses: elementary anatomy and physiology; nomenclature and care of organization equipment; field medical records; treatment of gas casualties; litter drill; field sanitation and sanitary appliances; materia medica and pharmacy; medical and surgical nursing; medical organization; medical aid; bandages and dressings.[15]

Broadly speaking, it seems, with important exceptions to be noted later, the military conscientious objector adjusted himself about as well or as poorly as the ordinary soldier. He was subject to the same officer system, ate the same service "mess," and slept in the same kind of bunk. When about to be sent overseas, he was gripped by the same fears (often called "gangplank fever"), and, once abroad, he welcomed news from home with as much avidity as his combatant fellow soldier. If perchance he was assigned to front-line service under fire, he was as likely to be killed or mangled as his nonobjector comrade.

In many cases the objector was not known by his fellow soldiers to be a conscientious objector, both because he sometimes made no endeavor to state his position and because he wore no distinctive badge that would indicate his religious and political beliefs. Some objectors deliberately tried not to reveal their position in any way, either because they regarded it as purely a personal matter or because they believed they could make their influence felt to a greater degree if they were not tagged beforehand with a term that was to many an epithet of opprobrium. As one put it in a letter:

I have found it wiser not to permit the average soldier to think of me as a C.O. To them, a C.O. (I quote) ". . . is a fellow who does not *wish* to fight." They are not aware that the C.O. has a POSITIVE program (of world co-operation); only the NEGATIVE (refusing to fight because of religious fanaticism or personal meekness). As "one of the boys," I have been able to suggest a different outlook on present world issues.[16]

On the whole, when they did reveal their position, they seem to have been respected, or at least not discriminated against, by both officers and men. There were exceptions, of course, as when one's noncommissioned officer happened to be prejudiced. Then one might expect all kinds of extra chores, like additional K.P. In rare cases, it was probably true that objectors on the front lines were assigned to extraordinarily dangerous positions by hostile commanders. On the other hand, it was not uncommon to find nonobjectors expressing considerable sympathy for the I-A-O position.[17] And in this connection it should be pointed out that some nonobjectors who requested assignment to the Medical Corps did so because they were doubtful, however ambiguously and subconsciously, about the ethics of combatant service.

Data are utterly lacking for any comprehensive discussion of the reactions of conscientious objectors to military life. It would probably be fair to maintain that as a group the objectors found even more to criticize in Army life than the average soldier. But there is no conclusive proof for this statement. Even with respect to men who had been in Civilian Public Service, there seemed to be no agreement on comparisons of military living with existence in Civilian Public Service. One group—how large it was we cannot know—agreed with Private M—— H—— S—— that, on the whole, and from the viewpoint of the war objector, service in the Army was far more significant socially than work in C.P.S. "To compare this ward work in hospitals and assistance at operating tables near the front lines to manicuring Crabtree Meadows," he wrote, "is absurd. Naturally, there was training, grief and boredom and the whole affair stinks. So did C.P.S., despite its weekly spray of perfume and holy water." [18]

On the other hand, Private E—— T—— S—— undoubtedly spoke for others as well as himself:

I believe that I could have accomplished more good in actual duty hour work, and in working for improvement of the world's sorry plight in various ways in C.P.S. than I have been able to do in the army. Actually, a small percentage of medical corps men get the chance to relieve suffering on the battle field, and those medics who desire to do this work rather than do a "gravy job" similar to my own are looked upon by their companions as a little queer.[19]

From the viewpoint of the conscientious objector, disillusionment regarding the possibilities of peace "testimony" in the Army must have been a not infrequent experience. One objector put it well when he said that the military life did not afford much opportunity for genuine discussion. The trivial tasks at which one was kept busy crowded out intellectual ambition. The inaction and boredom that were the plague of all men in military service, leading to deterioration of character and cynical attitudes to life, were not without their effects on objectors. Heroic living, which some had been led to expect, was not easy in the regimented atmosphere of military service.

Of course, another side was also reflected. One objector called attention to the fact that Army service as a I-A-O enabled him to prepare for postwar foreign relief work, while alternative civilian service afforded no such opportunity. Another thought that, despite frustrations and disillusionment, the possibility of direct contact with a large number of men gave him invaluable insights into human nature. Yet another pointed out that the respect in which the Medical Corps was held by most men gave him an opportunity for teaching by example such as he could hardly ever hope to have in the future. Among those who based their objection on a somewhat literal interpretation of biblical injunctions, many felt that the very frustrations and "temptations" of military life drew out one's best in terms of personal living.

An extraordinarily thoughtful statement of a discriminating I-A-O summarized his position in weighing noncombatant military service against other forms of protest:

It is practically impossible to avoid complicity with the war effort altogether, even the man in prison probably contributes thru the products of his work; there are two scales to be balanced—the degree of participation in the destruction and the degree of activity in constructive work; in prison and in C.P.S., while there is little of the former, there is also very little opportunity for significant alternative service; in I-A-O there is closer participation in the warfare, but the opportunities for a ministry of goodwill are much greater and more needed.[20]

The vast bulk of I-A-O's, like the great bulk of I-A servicemen, lived unheroic lives. Army routine surrounded them and Army authority controlled them, and the opportunities for individual heroism were rarer than many had anticipated. But for the front-line medical corpsmen, of course, both danger and dramatic opportunities were great. Congress eventually recognized the extraordinary danger of front-line medical service when it provided a ten-dollar-a-month bonus for front-line medical corpsmen. No distinction was made between I-A and I-A-O soldiers.[21]

Several objectors received wide publicity during and immediately after the war. Some, like Lew Ayres, the moving-picture actor, became known because they had been prominent in civilian life. Their very assertion of the objector position led some newspapers to follow their noncombatant careers. Thus, in the case of Ayres, there were occasional references to his activities in the Pacific; and although his army life resembled that of most I-A-O's, he was never quite on their plane.

On the other hand, several objectors came to be well known because of their Medical Corps activities. There was, for example, Private Orville Cox, a Seventh-Day Adventist, who was cited for bravery on Guadalcanal. Under heavy Japanese machine gun and rifle fire, he crawled forward to tend the wounds of two infantrymen who might otherwise have died.[22] There was, above all, Desmond Doss, another Seventh-Day Adventist, who achieved the distinction of being the only conscientious objector to receive the Congressional Medal of Honor.

Doss's story was dramatic and well documented. It was so appealing that it even "made" the colored cartoon books.[23] Doss became famous in the 77th Division for the serenity with which he faced danger and his recklessness when death seemed near. The actions which led to the award were thus described in a press dispatch:

First Lt. Cecil L. Gornto, . . . to whose platoon Doss was attached, recalled on the morning of April 29 someone called for a medic from an area under heavy mortar fire.

"Doss left his hole and climbed to the top of the hill," Gornto said. "He found the wounded man in total darkness and gave him first aid. As soon as it was light enough I observed him lowering the wounded man over the cliff on a rope. This man had both legs blown off."

On May 5, during an intense grenade battle near Kakazu, four men were badly wounded trying to blow up a cave. They lay amidst vicious grenade and mortar fire.

Second Lt. Kenneth L. Phillips, Lexington, N.C., reported that Doss, with total disregard for himself, went into the area four times and pulled the men to safety.

On May 2, according to Pfc. Carl B. Bentley, . . . Doss went out in the front lines between American and Japanese positions, and brought in a wounded man under rifle and mortar fire.

Doss was wounded May 21 by a grenade. He did not call for help but treated his wounds and gave himself a shot of morphine.

"Litter bearers reached him in the morning, almost six hours later," related T/5 Ralph E. Baker, of the 1st Battalion medics.

"After they carried him 50 yards, the litter bearers were halted momentarily by bursts of mortar fire. Doss crawled off the litter and told the aid men to take more seriously wounded men in first.

"He was wounded a second time while he lay there. He bound a rifle stock to his shattered arm to form a splint and crawled to the aid station despite his wounds." [24]

During one day in April, 1945, Doss lowered seventy-five wounded men down a four-hundred-foot escarpment. This took several hours and was accomplished despite continuous Japanese artillery, mortar, and rifle fire.

But few objectors were placed in positions where dramatic heroism was possible. They worked or died as part and parcel of the generally humdrum and ironclad army and navy system.

Objectors and the Use of Firearms

One of the issues which created considerable difficulty and misunderstanding between objectors and the military administration was the question of the use of firearms and the degree to which the official exemption from their use extended to so-called "indirect" combatant activities. In the Medical Corps of the Army, objectors were not to be trained in the use of firearms. But suppose, as was the case with Private D—— N——, that they were commanded to set up targets on the rifle range. Private N—— refused to do so, on the ground that to obey would be to assist the "killing" side of the war effort. For this disobedience Private N—— was punished by a summary court-martial, and the National Service Board for Religious Objectors took up his case with the War Department. The Department, through Major General J. A. Ulio, adjutant general, decided that the command was legitimate. War Department regulations, he ruled, exempted objectors from the bearing of arms or training in their use, but did not go beyond that. The General concluded:

It is not considered to be practicable or desirable for the Department to go further and provide that individuals who are inducted into the Army with I-A-O classifications will be assigned to no duties connected, even remotely, with the use of firearms and other weapons. Such provision would impose unwarranted restrictions on commanding officers in their efforts to utilize this personnel effectively.[25]

This did not mean, of course, that particular officers might not make individual adjustments which removed the danger of clashes between the objector's scruples and army administration. Indeed, such adjustments on an individual basis were often made, the general policy remaining the same.

In the early part of 1944, it was rumored that the Army was about to reverse its policy on rifle training for the Medical Corps by requiring every member of the corps to take six weeks' basic training, including rifle training. On May 1, 1944, the new policy began, and immediately there were reports that objectors were being forced to train with arms. Investigation seemed to show that this was not generally true. Potential medical corpsmen were now, indeed, to get the additional six weeks' training, but objectors continued to be exempted. It is true that some objectors ran into difficulties, especially where Army records were not clear as to their objector status, but such difficulties with respect to training with rifles seem to have been relatively rare.

A closely related issue was the arming of Medical Corps units actually serving in the Pacific theater of operations. Toward the close of 1943, it began to be rumored that the Army was furnishing rifles to members of the Medical Corps facing battle in the Pacific. This rumor was later confirmed.[26] Although the Geneva Convention of 1929 forbade military sanitary formations to commit acts "injurious" to the enemy,[27] the military authorities justified arming the Medical Corps by citing another article of the Geneva Convention which permitted formations to use arms in "self-defense" or in defense of their wounded and sick. The Army contended that the Japanese had deliberately fired on medical corpsmen and that therefore it was legitimate for Americans to resist.[28] Hence the modification of training was begun in May, 1944, and medical units were armed, even though this ran counter to previous practice.

But were objectors serving in the Pacific compelled to carry rifles? The answer is again, apparently, "No." If the I-A-O insisted, he was not forced to bear firearms. "Firearms," however, was interpreted in a literal sense. Objectors could, for example, be compelled to carry clubs while on guard duty, as the War Department ruled that a club was not an "arm." [29] The pressure on objectors to bear all types of "arms" was great, and some I-A-O's undoubtedly succumbed. But often a whole Medical Corps unit would be armed with the exception of the few objectors serving in it. It is not difficult to imagine how isolated and curious the objectors must have seemed, both to themselves and to the nonobjector members of their unit. But men like Desmond Doss, who won the Congressional Medal of Honor, remained unarmed throughout the severe Pacific fighting, even though medical corpsmen were frequently fired upon; and Winslowe Osborne tells us specifically of one instance where all the members of a Medical Corps unit with the exception of its lone objector were armed. Despite social pressure on this objector to do so, he remained adamant in his refusal to carry arms of any kind.[30]

But it was not always possible to find easy solutions. This was particularly true of medical corpsmen in the Navy who were assigned to operate with combatant troops in the Pacific theater. One illustration will perhaps point up the kind of difficulty which might arise. Lieutenant C—— S—— W——, a member of the Church of the Brethren, had originally registered as a conscientious objector, but on the advice of his local board appeal agent he postponed filling in Form 47. For a time he was in a deferred category. Then he was offered a commission in the Navy, which he accepted reluctantly. He was not, of course, officially in I-A-O but was assured that all doctors in the Navy were noncombatant and therefore unarmed. He was assigned to duty with combatant troops operating in the amphibious forces.

Once in the Navy, he was told that he must be armed with an automatic pistol and rifle and that all medical corpsmen under his command would carry the same weapons, in addition to hand grenades. This created a disturbing problem of conscience for him and he sought the counsel of the National Service Board for Religious Objectors. The Board suggested that he might apply for release to Civilian Public Service or might ask for assignment to work with the United States Public Health Service.

In the meantime, Lieutenant C—— S—— W—— had become ill and was hospitalized in California. There he talked to a medical officer about his problem and found the officer sympathetic. The lieutenant was taken before a board of medical surgery, which recommended discharge from the Navy. This recommendation, however, was modified by the Navy's Bureau of Medicine and Surgery, which placed him in a group of Navy officers who were to be assigned for duty within the continental limits of the United States. The work was to be noncombatant. Thus for him the problem of accepting armed service in the Pacific was solved.[31]

Misclassified Conscientious Objectors

Thus far we have been considering mainly conscientious objectors classified in I-A-O and accepting such classification. Whatever their difficulties in the Army and Navy, they at least could cite Army and Navy regulations to secure protection for many of their scruples. If they were commanded to train with rifles, they could plead the official regulation exempting them from such training. If they were asked to bear arms in the Pacific zone of operations, they could cite chapter and verse in official rules to support their refusal to do so. But suppose a man wished IV-E and was given I-A-O instead; or, requesting I-A-O, he was put in I-A; or, placed in I-A and accepting it, he became convinced after Army experience that he was a conscientious objector either to combatant service alone or to both combatant and noncombatant service; or, placed in I-A-O, he decided that he really objected to both combatant and noncombatant service. How, in these cases, would he fare in the Army and Navy?

Broadly speaking, the Army and Navy never met these issues

squarely and consistently. Gradually, through modification of service regulations, by means of co-operation with the Selective Service system, or under the impetus of rulings by the civil courts, certain procedures were worked out which were supposed to solve these problems. Nevertheless, the cessation of hostilities in the late summer of 1945 still found a large number of conscientious objectors in guardhouses or serving long sentences in prison for military offenses.

The best way to show the types of cases which could arise is to select representative samples.

The Case of R—— J—— J——. J—— was drafted in New York City on October 15, 1943. He refused to sign his induction papers, was fingerprinted forcibly by three shore patrolmen (whose clubs were held in threatening positions throughout), and was locked up when he declared he was a conscientious objector. Next day he refused to take the oath of office. Returning home for four days, he reported back to the Navy, was locked up in the train's toilet while being transported to Providence, Rhode Island, and was met by the provost marshal when he arrived in Providence. He was sent to the commandant, reported, on orders, to the psychiatrist, and for seventeen days was interviewed by eighteen doctors. Eventually he was found fit for duty and was held not to be a mental case.

Once this decision was made, he was ordered to put on the uniform. This he refused to do, constantly maintaining that he was a conscientious objector. Thereupon he was placed in a dark prison room, subsisting three days on bread and water. Again he was asked to put on the uniform and again he refused. The result was another five days in the dark room on bread and water. Then over a period of eighteen days he was examined by another psychiatrist and once more found fit for duty.

But he continued to refuse the uniform, stating that he would be a disgrace to it because of his beliefs. He was brought up before a court-martial, and his sentence of eight years and a dishonorable discharge was subsequently approved.[32]

The Case of J—— A——. A—— was a Southern Baptist who claimed that he had never handled arms of any kind. Unacquainted with Selective Service procedure, he never made any claim to be a conscientious objector. The Army psychiatrist diagnosed him as "neurotic." From the induction center, A—— was sent to the Medical Corps. This was after the Medical Corps had begun to train with arms, and along with other members of his unit he was ordered to take the training. He refused, claiming conscientious objection. His commander was apparently understanding, however, and A—— was excused from drill. A little later, however, for reasons which are not clear, he was transferred to the Signal Corps at Camp Enoch Crowder, Missouri.

Enrolled in the Signal Corps, he was again ordered to train with arms and once more refused. Over a period of time the order was repeated some four or five times. Remaining adamant in his refusal, on January 25, 1945, A—— was summoned before a court-martial.

The record of the court-martial is of interest because it indicates the line of questioning that was frequently resorted to in cases of this kind. The defense of A—— is worth noting, too, for while it perhaps indicates a lack of clarity at many points, it also demonstrates how objectors of but slight education were willing and able to resist official efforts to change their beliefs. Excerpts from the trial record follow: [33]

Defense Question: Private A——, you have chosen to make a sworn statement about the case now in hearing. Will you tell the court what you wish to tell them in this case?

A. Well, sir, it has always been my beliefs of not killing and the reason I have never been in a combat outfit and I have never had to use arms until I was in the Medics and the Medics started training, sir, and I was excused and then I was transferred from the Medics to Camp Crowder, Missouri, and I was working in a carpenter shop on special duty and I have never went hunting, never used my guns at all, sir. I don't believe in it. I have felt that way ever since I can remember and from Camp Crowder they transferred me here to the infantry. I don't claim to be a conscientious objector because I am willing to serve my country in any way except by using arms and killing, sir. I am willing to serve and I have understood that a conscientious objector is one who doesn't serve his country at all and I am willing to serve, sir. . . .

Q. (by court) Are you a married man?

A. Yes, sir, I am.

Q. Have you any children?

A. Yes, sir, I have a little girl, two years old.

Q. Let me ask you this question. Suppose a drunken man seized your child and was about to dash its brains out and the only way that you could save the child would be by killing this man, what would you do?

A. Well, sir, there is always a way that you can stop a man without killing him.

Q. I have set up the question that way. The question is if this man was about to dash its brains out and the only way you could prevent that was to kill the man, what would you do?

A. I'd just let him kill me and my child too. The Bible says, "Do not take what you cannot give" and you cannot give anyone life.

Q. Do you recall the chapter and verse?

A. The Bible says "Do not take what you cannot give" and you cannot give anyone life.

Q. Do you recall the chapter and verse in the Bible?

A. No, sir, I do not remember. . . .

Q. (by court) Private A——, when you were told to draw a rifle and fall out to drill or words to that effect, did you understand by that that you were ordered to go out and kill somebody?

A. No, sir, I didn't understand it that way.

Q. Your objection is to killing, is it not?

A. My objection is to carrying arms or killing with them, sir.

Q. But you would use a rock or some other missile?

A. If I had to, yes, sir.[34]

The upshot of the court-martial was a sentence of ten years and a dishonorable discharge. On review, however, the sentence was reduced to seven years and the dishonorable discharge was eliminated.

The Case of Henry Weber. Weber's was probably the most publicized of all court-martial cases involving conscientious objectors. It was also the only case during the Second World War in which a conscientious objector was sentenced to death.

Weber had at various times worked as a logger and shipyard employee. He had joined the Socialist Labor Party and absorbed its anticapitalist, Marxist philosophy. Although other members of the Party had received IV-E classifications from their local boards despite absence of "religious" training and belief, the Vancouver, Washington, local board declined to classify Weber as an objector. Instead of refusing to report for induction, however, Weber decided to appear at the induction station and then to refuse to obey orders so long as he remained in I-A. As a matter of fact, an Army officer at the induction station is reported to have told him: "There doesn't seem to be much we can do. If I were you, I'd object every place you can. . . . When they order you to carry a gun, object." [35]

He soon had an opportunity to follow this advice and, when he remained adamant, was sentenced to the stockade for six months. Released from the stockade after serving part of his sentence, he stated clearly that he was willing to accept a classification as I-A-O. But the officer told him that "he would be a disgrace to the medical corps." Again he was ordered to shoulder a gun, and when he refused once more he was directed to appear before a general court-martial.

The court-martial was held at Camp Roberts, California. In his statement to the court, Weber said:

I do not mind being in the medics or any place just as long as I don't have to learn to hate and kill other people. . . . I am interested in building a new world in which we can live in peace and pursuit of happiness and I cannot do that, I cannot do any good toward building this world in the Army if I have to learn to hate and to kill which is the object of Camp Roberts when you go through this training. . . .

That is why I preferred arrest to learning to hate and kill, because my means are peaceful means only. [36]

But Weber was convicted of violating the 64th Article of War (willfully disobeying a superior officer—in Weber's case, refusal to drill) and was sentenced to death by hanging.

The sentence aroused critical comment in many different quarters. Pacifist organizations, naturally, protested in vigorous terms. Congressional mail for a time was flooded, the overwhelming majority of letters opposing the death sentence. Senator Burton K. Wheeler demanded an investigation and stated publicly: "It is inconceivable to me that an army court martial would sentence a man to be hanged because of the fact that he refused to drill."

In the meantime, the officer who had appointed the court-martial, Major General Thompson Lawrence, asked the court to reconsider its sentence. This was done and the new sentence was life imprisonment and a dishonorable discharge. The protests continued, and, on automatic review of the sentence, it was first reduced to twenty years and finally to five. The dishonorable discharge remained, as did total forfeiture of Army benefits.

The final public act in the drama of Private Weber was denial by the Under Secretary of War in August, 1945, of petitions for clemency and assignment to a Civilian Public Service camp. The Under Secretary's decision was based on the advice of his clemency board, which said that, since Weber was not a conscientious objector "by reason of religious training and belief" he should not be assigned to an alternative service camp. This decision ignored, of course, the plain fact that many objectors with Weber's beliefs *had* been given IV-E classifications by the Selective Service System itself.[37]

Cases of "Conversion" in the Army. That some were "converted" to the objector position in the Army and Navy there can be no doubt. One or two examples have already been cited. Their number was probably larger than one would suspect. But Army and Navy authorities remained highly suspicious of individuals who had not claimed some form of objection when entering the armed forces. Sudden conversions were, therefore, among the most difficult types with which to deal. Thus in the case of one sailor, his wife wrote: "At the time he was drafted into the Navy, my husband was not a true Christian—but since being in the service he has repented of his sins, been baptized in the name of the Lord and is now trying very hard to live a Christian life—which isn't possible now since he is having to take part in this war." [38] But it was difficult to persuade the Navy that he had had a change of mind. To cite another case, a Friend had given up his scruples after Pearl Harbor and had requested that he be placed in I-A. He came to believe that the war was indeed being fought for the "four freedoms." After he had been inducted into the Army, however, the conflict within his personality became fierce, and fifteen months after induction he was writing to the National Service Board for Religious Objectors: "I am completely convinced that my actions are wrong and have been wrong. I feel that I can no longer live or work under military law or participate in war or war efforts. Therefore, regardless of the price I have to pay, I feel that I must stop." [39] But under such circumstances, the advisory agencies of pacifist groups could hold out but little hope.

The Armed Services and Misclassified Objectors

Thus far, we have been examining individual cases of misclassified objectors. Most of these resulted in court-martial sentences, despite the fact that the sincerity of many of the individuals was patent.

This fact alone would be enough to indicate that the armed services had not worked out beforehand procedures which could deal adequately with problems of conscience in the Army and Navy. But gradually, during the course of the war, and in unsystematic fashion, the military authorities attempted more positive solutions. Sometimes they were compelled to do so by the courts. In other instances, they were undoubtedly influenced by considerations of administrative expediency: obstreperous objectors were useless to the Army and it might be the best policy to discharge them or at least to give them work which they could perform without violating conscience. On the other hand, one can detect in Army and Navy policy a fear lest objection, and especially conversion to objection in the armed services, be made too attractive.

Aside from punishment through courts-martial, three major "solutions" developed: assignment to noncombatant branches without classification as I-A-O, "Billings" discharges, and discharges through armed services administrative action.

Assignment to Noncombatant Branches. Where the objector would accept it, individual officers frequently assigned those claiming conscientious scruples to noncombatant branches of the Army and Navy. Of course, where there had been no formal classification of I-A-O such assignments were of limited value only, for if one officer could assign to noncombatant work, another could reverse the assignment and return the objector to a combatant branch. There was no notation indicating the basis of the original transfer and the reassignment to combatant work might, and indeed frequently did, lead to a court-martial, due to the objector's disobedience of orders while in a combatant unit. Thus Private W—— O—— was transferred to the Medical Corps and later reassigned to combatant service. Since he could not conscientiously serve, he disobeyed orders and was court-martialed. In the spring of 1946 he had served more than eighteen months of his sentence and was trying desperately to be reassigned to noncombatant duty.[40] His case was not unique; yet, despite a great deal of correspondence between responsible War Department officials and the National Service Board for Religious Objectors, the Army consistently refused to enter on the service record of the objector a notation as to reason for transfer to noncombatant work.

Nor did the Army explain its refusal. Had such record notations been made, much difficulty might have been avoided.

Both Army and Navy insisted on secrecy in the formal procedures they worked out for transfer to noncombatant units. Thus the Navy regulations, dated October 20, 1944, warned objector advisory groups not to publicize the procedure; it was to be applied only when individual cases actually arose. The regulations went on to require that all petitions for transfer be in writing and that the application be accompanied by a certificate from the pastor of a church "stating that at the time of induction, he [that is, the objector] was a member of such church and that the religious convictions of the church, or the man himself, do not permit him to be assigned to combat service." [41]

It is impossible to determine how many individuals were transferred to noncombatant branches because of their conscientious scruples, but there is some indication that, relative to the number of officially recognized I-A-O objectors, it was surprisingly large. Of course, as the distinction between "combatant" and "noncombatant" branches tended to be wiped out during the course of the war, especially with reference to units assigned to the Far East, the significance of noncombatant transfers was lessened.

Billings Discharges. Where an individual refused to take the oath, it was originally assumed by the Army that he was nevertheless subject to military law and that court-martial sentences given in punishment could stand. Thus, down to 1944, many objectors languished in guardhouses and disciplinary barracks because, although they argued that they were not a part of the Army, since they had refused to take the oath, the Army contended that they were subject to military discipline by virtue of their classifications and the fact that they had reported for induction. The Billings decision, however, whose legal ramifications will be discussed elsewhere,[42] made it possible for men in this category to petition a civil court for a writ of habeas corpus which, if granted, freed them from military jurisdiction and military prisons and subjected them to civil trial instead. The Supreme Court said in substance that if an objector refused to take the Army oath he was not under Army jurisdiction. The armed services refused, however, even after the Billings decision, to free automatically all those objectors who had declined to take the oath. It insisted that each individual objector held by the Army must petition separately for the habeas corpus that would free him.

Discharge Through Armed Forces Administrative Action. Sometimes it was possible for conscientious objectors to get armed services discharges directly, and during the course of the war the procedure was formalized. Thus, if a I-A-O or I-A decided that his beliefs really necessitated a IV-E, he might apply to his commanding officer for a discharge. Under Army regulations, the discharge might read "for convenience of the Government," [43] "inadaptness, lack of ability for military service, or enuresis," [44] or "undesirable habits or traits of character." [45] Decision as to whether discharge on these grounds would be granted rested largely with the commanding officer to whom the application was made. Some commanding officers were willing to give discharges of this type to conscientious objectors, while others were not. In some cases the commanding officer might be overruled by superior authority in the War Department,[46] although this was apparently rare. In other cases, the Director of Selective Service might request the discharge [47] (acting usually, of course, on pressure from objector and pacifist advisory agencies).

The discharge itself might be either "honorable," "dishonorable," or "without honor" (usually called a "blue" discharge, from the color of the paper on which it was printed). If one got either an honorable or a without-honor discharge, he went again before his local board, which might then reclassify him to IV-E and order him to report to a Civilian Public Service camp. The Army, of course, was required to keep the Selective Service System informed with respect to discharges of conscientious objectors, and Selective Service could then proceed to reopen the question of classification. Dishonorable discharges required further permission from Washington, in the form of a waiver, before the objector could be sent to a C.P.S. camp.

Release from the Army after conviction by a general court-martial (and objectors who disobeyed orders more than once usually went before a general court-martial, the highest in the military court hierarchy) was more difficult. The procedure included application by the prisoner to the commandant of the disciplinary barracks for either a "blue" or a dishonorable discharge, investigation by the commandant and report by him to the adjutant general, a statement by the prisoner agreeing to accept transportation to his local Selective Service board in place of transportation to his home, transmission of these documents to the Director of Selective Service, recommendations by the adjutant general to the Under Secretary of War, and final decision by the Under Secretary.[48]

If discharge in any form was granted by the Under Secretary of War, the next step was for the Director of Selective Service to reclassify the ex-prisoner under Selective Service regulations.[49] After the final action taken by the commandant, the objector was released from military prison, ready for the characteristic "reprocessing" of Selective Service.

The whole procedure for release of conscientious objectors after court-martial was supposed to be highly confidential. There was no general publication of the rules for discharge, even after these had been stated in written form. The War Department apparently feared that a general knowledge might increase the number of conscientious objectors or at least make spurious objectors more numerous.[50]

Discharges after court-martial were very few indeed.

The Army Clemency Board

The unsatisfactory disposition of court-martial cases, examples of apparently obvious injustice (as in the case of Henry Weber), and the belief that genuine objectors should not be in the Army at all led pacifist, civil-liberties, and objectors' organizations [51] in the spring of 1945 to ask for the creation of a civilian board to review court-martial sentences, as well as to consider other difficulties of objectors in the Army.

At first the Army declined to consider such suggestions, but finally, on June 17, 1945, the War Department announced the creation of the Advisory Board on Clemency to aid the Under Secretary of War in reviewing court-martial sentences. While the Board's objectives were more limited than many would have liked, objectors generally welcomed the willingness of the War Department to provide civilian, rather than military, review. Judge Sherman Minton of the Circuit Court of Appeals was made chairman of the Board, and among the members was Austin H. MacCormick, a well-known student of prisons.[52] On November 28, former Justice Owen J. Roberts of the

United States Supreme Court succeeded Judge Minton as chairman
of the Board.

The Board recommended a number of modifications in sentences
of objectors in the Army, and some few succeeded in securing their
release as a result of its advice. But on the whole its performance was
disappointing to civil-liberties and objector groups. It denied clemency to Henry Weber, for example, because Selective Service deemed
him not to be an objector "by reason of religious training and belief." [53] In general, it seemed to give great weight to the opinions
of Selective Service whenever questions of this kind arose.

Military Prisons

How many conscientious objectors in the Army and Navy were
actually court-martialed for offenses growing out of their beliefs,
and where did they serve "time" once they were sentenced? To the
first question, apparently, there is only one answer: "We don't know."
The Judge Advocate General of the Army kept no separate record
of objectors sentenced by courts-martial.[54]

As for the second question, where objectors served their "time"
depended upon the character of the court-martial to which they were
subjected and the nature of the offense. Men refusing to obey orders
for the first time were usually given a special court-martial,[55] with
sentences up to six months to be served in the camp stockade. If they
again refused to obey, they were in most instances ordered to appear
before a general court-martial. Here punishment varied, but common sentences for objectors were five to ten years, although these
were not infrequently reduced on review by Washington. Sentences
on the whole were much lighter than those imposed by courts-martial
during the First World War but more severe, on the average, than
those meted out by civil courts during the Second World War.[56]
Sentences of general courts-martial were served in the several disciplinary barracks of the Army, but in some instances objectors were
first sent to a "rehabilitation center," where the Army gave prisoners
a second chance to "reform"; if "reformation" did not take place, they
served out their sentences in the disciplinary barracks. Army regulations provided for periodic and automatic clemency reviews, the first
during the initial six months of the sentence and subsequent reviews
once each year.

What conditions obtained in guardhouses, camp stockades, and disciplinary barracks? In detail, accurate information is difficult to obtain. We do know enough, however, to make certain general observations. On the whole, the guard's authority in military prisons was much greater than in civil institutions; he was more often poorly trained; his word, as against that of a prisoner, was more frequently accepted as final; and in practice he was less subject to effective supervision by higher authorities. It is fairly certain that there was more actual physical brutality in military than in civil prisons—beatings of Jehovah's Witnesses, for example, and long periods in "solitary" on bread and water. Even before imprisonment, an objector might suffer violence at the hands of his fellow soldiers, as in the case of Bertram Silber, who was beaten severely by twelve privates on March 26, 1943, presumably because he refused to co-operate (for conscientious reasons) in cleaning the barracks. Even the Assistant Secretary of War admitted that the beatings had taken place and also granted that one factor in the physical violence was Silber's openly expressed antiwar views.[57] The brutalities later revealed at the Army's Lichfield, England, prisoners' camp—brutalities which included striking of prisoners with clubs—fall into the pattern indicated by the experiences of several conscientious objectors serving "time" in military prisons.[58]

On the other hand, the higher officers as a rule undoubtedly attempted to prevent mistreatment in cases where they had some knowledge of the situation. The difficulty was that their knowledge was often inaccurate and frequently based upon the testimony of guards, which was notoriously unreliable.

Such direct evidence as we have indicates that there was nothing comparable to the physical mistreatment suffered by objectors in the Army during the First World War. Where men were beaten or forced, while physically unfit, to drill with brick-loaded packs (a practice in some disciplinary barracks), there seemed to be no general discrimination against conscientious objectors. Army prisons at best were hardly pleasant places, but the unpleasantness and arbitrary controls were experienced by ordinary prisoners as well as by conscientious objectors.

VI: The American Concession to Conscience: Civilian Public Service

IN THE Second World War, conscientious objectors in the United States who relished neither military service nor the solitude of prison found an alternative in Civilian Public Service. Here they could perform "work of national importance under civilian direction," provided they were properly qualified under the Selective Training and Service Act.

This program was launched as a deliberate experiment to discover how far a nation dedicated to democracy would tolerate freedom of conscience under the stress of bitter ideological and military conflict. Before Pearl Harbor, government and public alike were indulgent toward those who wanted to abstain from war. The Director of Selective Service aptly expressed the mood in affirming that "the judgment of individual conscience opposed to the national will should be given consideration and allowed a form of co-operation consistent with its judgments if they are the results of religious training and belief." But the limits of American tolerance narrowed as the country plunged into war and the conflict grew desperate. On the premise that objectors should enjoy no favors while men were losing their lives in battle, the conditions of alternative service were progressively restricted and the men assigned to it in effect penalized for their beliefs.

Success of the Civilian Public Service experiment depended upon close co-operation between government, church, and conscientious objector. At first each of these appeared to support the program as a practical compromise between national necessity and religious freedom. Time showed, however, that the three groups did not at heart share the same conception of tolerance for conscience. This lack of unity in underlying assumptions led to bitter disagreement over the policies of administration. Holding the whip of legislative authority, the Selective Service System generally insisted that its definition of tolerance should prevail, but many conscientious objectors vehemently opposed the government's directives as a denial of fundamental liberty. Between the men in Civilian Public Service and the administrators of Selective Service, the Historic Peace Churches unexpectedly found themselves serving in an unfamiliar and uneasy role as mediator and go-between.

What began as an experiment in tolerance ultimately demonstrated in unmistakable terms the deep and inherent contradiction between the American demand for national security and the claims of individuals for personal liberty of conscience.

The Pattern of Civilian Public Service

In Civilian Public Service drafted c.o.'s were required to render national service, but of an essentially nonmilitary character. This program was designed neither to afford an easy berth to the c.o. for the duration of the war nor to subject him to the arduous labors of a chain gang. The fundamental conception of C.P.S. was rather that of a religious order whose members, though under legal compulsion, were moved primarily by their personal ideals to perform a sacrificial service. The c.o. was expected to demonstrate by the superior quality of his work the integrity and constructive nature of his faith. While the program fell short of this goal, it did succeed in mobilizing the effort of a great number of c.o.'s for services of public benefit outside of the direct prosecution of the war.

A second striking characteristic of the American alternative service pattern was the unprecedented partnership of the government and of organized religious agencies in a public enterprise. With full legal authority to run the entire program itself, the Selective Service System nevertheless assigned to committees representing the Brethren, Friends, Mennonites, and other denominations a major responsibility for the administration of Civilian Public Service.[1] Responsibility was deliberately divided. What is more, the government granted public authority to private agencies that were without official status.

Such an arrangement was even more startling when viewed through the eyes of religious organizations whose centuries-old stand against the encroachment of government upon the province of the church was now modified. Here certain church groups voluntarily assumed a public responsibility and entered an understanding with the United States government binding them to perform functions of administration essentially governmental in character.

Another unique feature of Civilian Public Service was that over a period of six years a total of almost twelve thousand men worked from forty to ninety-six hours a week without receiving a cent of pay, either from the government which conscripted them, the institution or agency which benefited from their service, or the religious organizations which sponsored or administered their work. Congress made no appropriation for compensation to conscientious objectors. Instead, many of the men in Civilian Public Service, or their families, themselves contributed toward the cost of their maintenance. This pattern of payless service did not by any means enjoy the support of the whole body of conscientious objectors or of all the religious groups responsible for the program. Established at the very beginning of C.P.S., however, the practice of exacting service from conscientious objectors without remuneration persisted to the end of the program. Upon discharge each conscientious objector could think, with whatever satisfaction he might derive, "I gave my service without charge."

Roots of the Idea

Civilian Public Service grew out of four experiences: the Mennonites' historic performance of alternative service under Russian conscription from 1881–1917; the scheme of alternative service ultimately improvised for American c.o.'s drafted during World War I; the voluntary work camps privately organized in Europe and the United States during the interwar period to aid in reconstruction and demonstrate good will through service; and the Civilian Conservation

Corps, developed by the United States government during the depression to aid jobless youth.

The Mennonite experience set a precedent of church-supported, state-directed civilian service for conscripted c.o.'s, which the Mennonite churches in the United States (largest source of American c.o.'s) were strongly disposed to accept as a proper arrangement for the recognition of conscience.[2]

The experience with American c.o.'s in World War I implanted the pattern of alternative service in the United States. Persistent efforts by the Historic Peace Churches in 1917–1918 were finally successful in securing the "furlough" of thirteen hundred c.o.'s from the Army to farms, and of ninety-nine to engage in relief work in Europe under the American Friends Service Committee.[3]

This scheme did not involve the same element of compulsion which later characterized Civilian Public Service. A man had to work on a prescribed project if he left the Army, but in comparison with the disciplinary barracks, the opportunity to serve persons in need, or to farm, inevitably appeared as a release from compulsion. Neither the individual c.o.'s nor the religious committees under whose supervision the men worked were continually accountable to an organ of the government. The men were "furloughed," not "assigned," and the administering organizations thereupon assumed full responsibility for what the c.o.'s did. Furthermore, the men on farms were allowed to keep the equivalent of a soldier's pay—thirty dollars a month—in addition to subsistence.

Shortly after the conclusion of the armistice the third precursor of Civilian Public Service emerged—the voluntary work camp. In 1920, the International Voluntary Service was formed by the International Fellowship of Reconciliation under the leadership of Pierre Ceresole, a Swiss pacifist. Young Germans, Swiss, Dutch, Americans, English, and youth of other nationalities labored without remuneration to repair war-devastated French communities. They hoped their service together in good will would overcome some of the war-bred hatred between nations. "IVS" teams later helped in emergencies caused by floods, earthquakes, and other civil disasters, all with the same purpose of building international brotherhood.

The idea of a *voluntary* work camp as an instrument of peacemaking spread far beyond the rather small and largely pacifist movement led by Ceresole. International Student Service on the Continent and the Student Christian Movement in England conducted international service camps. During the depression similar projects were undertaken to help needy communities secure social services and develop a spirit of co-operative self-help. In the United States, the American Friends Service Committee brought college students into summer work camps in depressed industrial areas where they gained firsthand knowledge of acute social tension while building a playground, repairing a community center, or rendering some other service to the neighborhood.

As the Second World War approached, pacifist leaders again began to think of the voluntary work camp as a means through which conscientious objectors could demonstrate their readiness to serve without becoming involved in military training. Before the draft law was passed, a group of volunteers of both sexes were recruited for a camp started in 1939 in Cooperstown, New York, by the A.F.S.C. and the Fellowship of Reconciliation. The volunteers worked six months to a year without pay on the reforestation and conservation program of the Oswego County Farmers' Co-operative.

The fourth forerunner of C.P.S. was the Civilian Conservation Corps, organized in the early days of the New Deal as a partial answer to the double problems of unemployed youth and the wastage of natural resources. This experience convinced the government, from the President down, of the practical values of a nationally organized civilian work corps for youth, and paved the way for it to consider a similar plan for conscripted c.o.'s.[4]

Government officials were confident that the C.C.C. program could be adapted to form the basic pattern of alternative service for c.o.'s. As war industries picked up momentum and economic conditions improved, many C.C.C. camps lacked workers. The Department of Agriculture and the Department of the Interior faced the necessity of curtailing important aspects of their conservation programs unless a substitute for the C.C.C. could quickly be found. C.o.'s would be likely replacements for the C.C.C. "boys." Furthermore, the C.C.C. system of semimilitary discipline and control would meet the demand for adequate supervision of drafted men. Equipment, administrative personnel, and work projects were on hand, and the C.C.C. record of service was so definitely established that a good case could be made for the value of the work the c.o.'s would be doing.[5]

Birth of the Experiment

No one has accepted full parental responsibility for the C.P.S. experiment. Throughout its life, even to its burial, vehement argument raged over who was guilty of creating its deformities, in particular the obligation of the conscientious objector to work without pay.

Congress, of course, authorized the alternative-service program for conscientious objectors, in passing Section 5(g) of the Selective Training and Service Act of 1940.[6] It did not, however, specify the character or the conditions of service, beyond requiring the work to be "of national importance" and conducted "under civilian direction." The President received final power to implement the Act and determine the fate of the c.o. within the broad design sketched by Congress and the limits which might later be set by appropriations.

According to one view (advanced both by Selective Service and by extreme pacifist critics of the program), the Historic Peace Churches took the critical step which actually shaped the character of the C.P.S. system.[7] On their own initiative they asked to run the service program for their own members. They ultimately agreed to pay a "purchase price" for this privilege—assuming the cost of maintenance and the responsibility of administration for *any* c.o.'s who might be drafted, regardless of affiliation, and, of greater import, relinquishing on behalf of all c.o.'s any claim to pay. Thus, according to this interpretation, the Peace Churches had an overpowering resolve to run the camps which overshadowed all other factors.

This interpretation of their responsibility was disputed by the Historic Peace Churches. They did offer to administer an alternative service program; but they insisted that President Roosevelt himself, at a crucial stage of the negotiations, threw out the conditions they originally advocated—which included government responsibility *and pay for all c.o.'s except those who specifically and voluntarily chose to serve under private religious agencies.* The President wanted sterner treatment for conscientious objectors. The churches accepted the final pattern of C.P.S. as the best which could be gotten, but consistently disclaimed any part in bringing about either the denial of pay to all c.o.'s or a private religious monopoly of alternative service.

The evidence available does not conclusively prove who actually laid which portion of the egg. No stenographic minutes were kept of conferences from October to December, 1940, between government officials and the representatives of the religious bodies. Other records clearly show, however, that the creation of C.P.S. was a composite work—by Selective Service officials, Historic Peace Church representatives, a wide variety of denominational and pacifist organizations, many individual conscientious objectors, and, in a negative but tremendously critical way, by President Roosevelt.[8]

Hershey's Initiative. The real initiative for church administration of C.P.S. appears to have come from Selective Service. On September 30, 1940, two weeks after the passage of the Selective Service Act, Colonel Lewis E. Hershey of Selective Service headquarters suggested that the Historic Peace Churches prepare concrete proposals for a program of service which they would administer, and indicate how much responsibility they would assume. On October 15 he renewed his proposition.

To the Historic Peace Churches this request had a double importance. They interpreted Colonel Hershey's proposal as a friendly recognition of the line beyond which most c.o.'s would not co-operate —military control.

Second, the Historic Peace Churches realized that the suggestion of Colonel Hershey would involve obligations much greater than they had ever before assumed. They would be responsible not only for their own members but for conscientious objectors belonging to other denominations and perhaps to no denomination at all. The National Service Board for Religious Objectors was immediately created to consider the proposal of Selective Service and facilitate joint action on behalf of the c.o.[9]

Within three weeks the National Service Board submitted a detailed proposal for the administration of work of "national importance," following recommendations of the Historic Peace Church Committees.[10] It provided that *both* governmental and private agencies administer services by conscientious objectors. A c.o. would have the alternative of working either for a government agency—in which case the government would pay maintenance and wages—or under the direct control of private agencies such as the Historic Peace

Churches. The private agencies would then pay all the costs connected with the service but would assume responsibility only for those c.o.'s who expressed a preference to work under the particular agency and who were individually acceptable to it. This plan for alternative conditions of service was unanimously supported by all representatives on the National Service Board.

Dr. Clarence Dykstra, newly appointed Director of Selective Service, Colonel Hershey, and other officials of Selective Service considered this proposal and approved a program substantially in line with it.

The President Objects. This plan was acceptable to the Selective Service System, to the Historic Peace Churches, to representatives of the larger religious denominations, and, as far as could be discovered, to the great majority of conscientious objectors who would be involved, but not to the President of the United States.[11]

On November 29, Dr. Dykstra informally discussed the proposed program with President Roosevelt. The President expressed "instant and aggressive opposition to the plan," as Dr. Dykstra reported the conversation to the National Service Board. He quoted the President as saying the boys should not even be sent to C.C.C. camps because that would be too easy for them. Instead, an Army officer should drill them.[12] Finding the President's mood so antagonistic, Dr. Dykstra dropped the matter temporarily and hastened to call together representatives of the religious agencies to discuss with Selective Service officials and Lowell Mellett (one of the President's confidential secretaries) what solution might be satisfactory to the President.

At this time, Dr. Dykstra asked whether the church agencies would be willing, on an experimental basis, to administer all of the projects for conscientious objectors and pay the entire cost except transportation. He suggested that this was probably the only means of providing an opportunity for c.o.'s to serve under private auspices, for otherwise he would have to ask Congress for a specific appropriation to finance the work, and, in the light of the President's attitude, this would entail full government control and direction of the program. It was in effect an all-or-nothing alternative.[13]

The churches faced a problem as serious as it was unexpected.

They had counted on the government to carry the main financial responsibility for c.o.'s. They assumed that only a few men other than their own members would forego maintenance and pay at government expense in order to work under religious auspices or because they were conscientiously opposed to accepting government support. Now the possibility of parallel programs, government- and church-administered, was ruled out. Every c.o. would have to work without pay on projects completely government-administered unless the churches accepted Dr. Dykstra's suggestion and shouldered the entire financial and administrative responsibility—not only for their own members but for every person accepted by Selective Service as a conscientious objector.

The Standing Committee of the Church of the Brethren, the Mennonites' Central Committee, the American Friends Service Committee, the Fellowship of Reconciliation, the Methodist Commission on World Peace, and other groups wrestled with the grave issue.

Decision. The decision was to accept the main responsibility of administering and financing work of national importance for all c.o.'s for an experimental period of six months and within the limits of the financial ability of the co-operating groups.[14]

Dr. Dykstra welcomed the decision and agreed that if the financing became too hard the Selective Service administration would stand ready to ask for an appropriation. The arrangement would in any case be reconsidered prior to July 1, 1941, the beginning of the government's fiscal year. After clearing the revised proposal with Cabinet officers and the Director of the Budget, Dr. Dykstra formally presented it to the President and on December 20, 1940, the President approved it.[15] The program was legally initiated when the President signed an executive order on February 6, 1941, authorizing the Director of Selective Service to "establish or designate work of national importance under civilian direction for persons opposed to combatant and non-combatant service in the land or naval forces of the United States." [16] On the same day camp regulations for c.o.'s were prescribed by the Director of Selective Service. Various administrative delays prevented the actual opening of a camp until May 15, 1941. Once launched, the unpredictable experiment of Civilian Public Service lasted until March 29, 1947, through a year of uneasy peace, four years of total war, and almost two years of "reconversion."

Terms of Partnership

The plan, as finally approved, provided that c.o.'s drafted for service under civilian direction be assigned to camps for soil-conservation and reforestation work. The Departments of Agriculture and the Interior would provide technical supervision for the work projects, as well as tools and other necessary equipment. The Federal Security Agency would make available abandoned C.C.C. camp sites. The War Department would furnish or loan cots, bedding, and other items of camp equipment. Selective Service would furnish general administrative and policy supervision and inspection and pay the men's transportation costs to the camps, as permitted under the Selective Service appropriation.

The co-operating church groups "agreed for a temporary period to undertake the task of financing and furnishing all other necessary parts of the program, including actual day-to-day supervision and control of the camps (under such rules and regulations and administrative supervision as were laid down by Selective Service), to supply subsistence, necessary buildings, hospital care, and generally all things necessary for the care and maintenance of the men." Admission to the camps would not be dependent on membership in the particular church groups undertaking the work. Should the church groups prove unable to finance their part permanently, or should other difficulties develop, the government "could at any time modify the program or take it over in its entirety." [17]

The precise relationship of the religious agencies to the Selective Service Administration was not clearly defined in a written agreement—a fact which led later to interminable dispute and misunderstanding. Were the church committees "agents" of Selective Service, or were they "independent contractors" having full responsibility for their prescribed functions? The Historic Peace Churches had in the course of negotiations declared their determination to retain an independent status. For instance, the American Friends Service Committee Board of Directors insisted that they would be willing to take administrative responsibility only on condition that they continue as "an independent private agency . . . not under the control of the Selective Service administration."

Dr. Dykstra appreciated the desire of the churches for a large measure of freedom to plan and administer the program for which they were assuming such a heavy financial responsibility. He suggested, however, and the church representatives agreed, that a formal, contractlike statement delimiting the churches' administrative responsibilities might hamper their freedom to act more than it would protect them against unwelcome governmental interference. He asked the churches and Selective Service to go ahead on the basis of a gentlemen's agreement, granting to the private agencies full discretion in their methods of administration, in the choice of service projects, in the internal discipline and management of the camps, and in providing for educational and religious activities. He emphasized the experimental nature of the whole program and the possibility of reviewing the relationship at the end of the first six months' trial.

The Civilian Public Service agreement failed to meet several of the conditions which had originally been considered essential for a satisfactory alternative-service program. The c.o. could not choose whether to serve under the government or under a religious body. He had only the alternative of a church-administered camp, unless he was willing to accept military service or take the consequences of violating the Selective Service Act. Furthermore, public funds were not made available either to pay the c.o.'s for their work or to meet the bulk of the operating and maintenance expenses. This saddled an untold financial burden upon that small segment of the community which was sufficiently concerned about freedom of conscience to pay for it. Third, the co-operating private agencies had not received an explicit and binding assurance of full control over their part of the program. This confronted the c.o.'s and the churches of which many of them were members with the possibility of paying the major costs of the service but having little real choice over its conditions.

The Seal of Approval

Although the program fell short of the full desires of those concerned with the conscientious objector, Civilian Public Service was generally accepted as the best alternative which could be secured.

Most pacifist leaders, even those on the "absolutist" fringe, were ready to support the compromise because they expected it to assure a better chance for the c.o. to express his convictions than if the government had sole control. A. J. Muste, Executive Secretary of the Fellowship of Reconciliation and a publicly declared nonregistrant, was convinced that "the pattern of compulsory government-managed service is in the present historic context a fascist one." C.P.S. on the other hand afforded "an important opportunity for pacifist service, witness against war and conscription, growth in the pacifist way of life, and preparation for future volunteer services including nonviolent direct action to achieve basic social change." [18] The Chairman of the War Resisters' League, Frank Olmstead, acclaimed the C.P.S. program as "the most effective argument for pacifism which the anti-war forces of the country can offer . . . a sermon on peace preached in terms of life itself . . . a reservoir of liberty." [19]

On the other hand, Dr. Evan Thomas, chairman of the War Resisters League and a leading conscientious objector in World War I, opposed the C.P.S. program from the start, at least insofar as it involved the responsibility of pacifist groups.

The conscientious objectors who went to C.P.S. camps never expressed a common opinion. As will be seen, the longer the program continued, the more divergent became the points of view of those who served in it. In the beginning, however, almost all who entered C.P.S. were agreeably relieved to find themselves in a setup far different from that of an army or a concentration camp. By and large, the conscientious objector found little to disturb him during his first months of service, aside from the confusion and uncertainty of a new type of life. He quickly discovered that he was in the company of friends who shared his point of view, whether they were fellow "assignees" or his camp administrators. His normal response was enthusiasm, with a determination to do his work well. C.P.S. men were grateful and proud that they were to live and serve as they believed.

The Historic Peace Churches, despite some misgiving, were not too unhappy about their Civilian Public Service bargain. They were surprised and challenged by the confidence of the government in their capacity for effective public service. They were reassured about the fate of their members and of other c.o.'s under the draft. The C.P.S. program gave them, they were convinced, effective control over the conditions of alternative service and an opportunity to "shepherd the young men." [20]

Leaders in the Historic Peace Churches also envisioned Civilian

Public Service as an opportunity to demonstrate the positive nature of their pacifist beliefs. Here they could build a "good community," the model of a peaceful world, instead of simply protesting the war-like actions of their countrymen.

While the Historic Peace Churches took the lead in assuming direct administrative responsibilities, other religious bodies approved and encouraged their action. The Federal Council of the Churches of Christ in America took part in the negotiations for Civilian Public Service and the Council's special committee on c.o.'s formally asked the Historic Peace Churches to take members of other denominations into their camps and promised to make every effort to cover the financial costs of these additional men if they were accepted.[21] During the first months of C.P.S. other denominational groups indicated their willingness to co-operate. Fifteen denominations were represented at the first meeting of the Consultative Council of the National Service Board. These church leaders approved Civilian Public Service as a satisfactory answer for the c.o.'s of their denominations. Some argued that the government should assume the responsibility for all those willing to work under government administration—as originally advocated by the Historic Peace Churches themselves. When they understood the reasons why this possibility had been ruled out, most of the denominational leaders consulted were glad for their members to go into the Peace Church camps and agreed to secure funds for the expenses involved.[22]

The strongest defender of Civilian Public Service was the Selective Service Administration. Some officials, recalling the Army's troubles with the c.o.'s in World War I, were glad to have the churches shoulder responsibility for the conduct of persons who could, with infinite firmness, say "No" to every military demand. Dr. Dykstra reminded President Roosevelt that "during the World War, conscientious objectors presented difficulties to both the armed forces and the law enforcement agencies far out of proportion to the numbers involved," and advocated the C.P.S. program as an experimental solution, designed "to avoid so far as possible a recurrence of such difficulties." [23] Later, Dr. Dykstra told the churches responsible for C.P.S. that "here is an experiment in which the Government and voluntary groups share a responsibility and a burden in a very unique way. Maybe we are going to learn something about how these two agencies will work together in national service, how when we get young people together we can develop a pattern of civic education, materials in that field, local leadership, project leadership. It is going to be significant to us for many years to come. Others with evident sincerity accepted C.P.S. as a fair expression of democratic tolerance for a minority. Lieutenant-Colonel Franklin A. McLean, a shrewd and often sharply critical field inspector for the Camp Operations Section of Selective Service, told conscientious objectors at a Mennonite-administered camp, "It is a good thing under our system of government to grant privileges to the minority, for thus are the principles of democracy kept alive. It is therefore beneficial for the future of our country to have such groups as are in Civilian Public Service Camps." [24] General Hershey, appointed Director of Selective Service after the resignation of Clarence Dykstra, strongly championed the pattern of Civilian Public Service. He labeled it an "experiment in democracy"—an experiment "such as no nation has ever made before . . . to find out whether our democracy is big enough to preserve minority rights in a time of national emergency." To Congress, he pointed out the amount of work extracted from the conscientious objectors on government projects and the number of men "salvaged" for the Army after a term in C.P.S. [25] To the conscientious objectors, he outlined the fine reputation they could secure through exemplary work in C.P.S. He claimed that Selective Service had thrown a protective mantle about them which immunized them from the sting of public criticism. To the churches, General Hershey presented Civilian Public Service as an instrument by which they could throughout the war guide the religious and educational development of their members, at the same time earning public respect by engaging in a congenial task of national service.

The Civilian Public Service compromise thus received the support of most pacifist organizations, of the first conscientious objectors to be drafted, of the Historic Peace Churches and a great body of other religious organizations, and of responsible officials of the government. The compromise did not meet the ideal favored by some, but it appeared to offer the basis for united action by government, c.o., and church in the assurance of tolerance.

VII: *The Service Record*

of the Conscientious Objector

On MAY 15, 1941, twenty-six conscientious objectors and fifty-four photographers and reporters opened the first Civilian Public Service camp in the Patapsco State Forest, outside of Baltimore, Maryland. It was promptly dubbed the "gold fish bowl." At first the spotlight of publicity focused on the peculiarity of the c.o.'s beliefs. But six years later, after the last C.P.S. camp had closed, conscientious objectors were distinguished primarily by their record of service.

In sheer physical terms, 11,950 men gave over eight million man-days of work to their country.[1] They served in conservation and forestry camps, in hospitals and state training schools, at university laboratories and agricultural experiment stations, on individual farms and government survey crews. They made roads, cleared truck and foot trails, fought forest fires, dug irrigation ditches, constructed dams, built fence, planted trees, pulled weeds, conducted soil-conservation experiments, acted as "guinea pigs" for medical and scientific research, tended dairy cattle, tilled the soil, built sanitary facilities for hookworm-ridden communities, cared for the mentally ill, the feeble-minded, and the juvenile delinquent.[2]

If the United States Government had paid for this work at the same rate as for its army, it would have spent over $18,000,000 in addition to its actual expenditure of $4,731,000 for Selective Service administration and the expenses of technical supervision. As it was, the c.o.'s were obliged to work for nothing, while they, their families, and the churches voluntarily contributed or raised $7,202,000 for

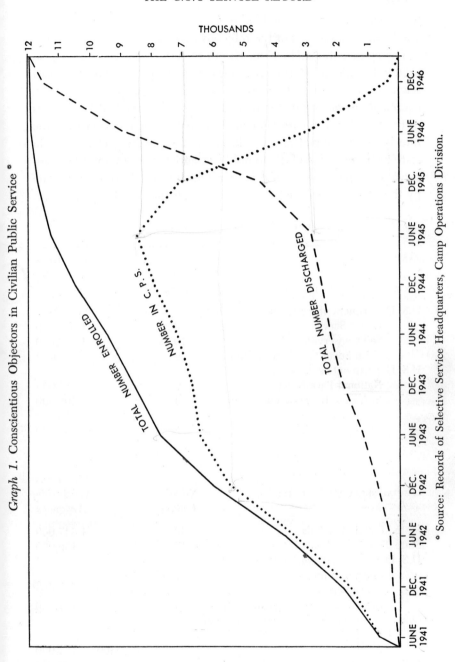

THE C.O.'S SERVICE RECORD

Graph 1. Conscientious Objectors in Civilian Public Service *

THOUSANDS

TOTAL NUMBER ENROLLED

NUMBER IN C.P.S.

TOTAL NUMBER DISCHARGED

JUNE 1941 DEC. 1941 JUNE 1942 DEC. 1942 JUNE 1943 DEC. 1943 JUNE 1944 DEC. 1944 JUNE 1945 DEC. 1945 JUNE 1946 DEC. 1946

* Source: Records of Selective Service Headquarters, Camp Operations Division.

125

their maintenance in church-administered camps and for the C.P.S. administrative services of the religious agencies.[3]

The conscientious objectors' record of service must also be measured in less tangible terms: the long-range values of the medical and scientific discoveries stemming from experiments performed with conscientious objectors; the demonstration of nonviolent techniques of treatment in the care of mental patients; a new concern for the fate of the deranged as c.o.'s brought the appalling conditions in state institutions forcefully to public attention; the continuity of conservation experiments and programs which would have been broken by the war had it not been possible to staff them with c.o.'s.

TABLE VI. CIVILIAN PUBLIC SERVICE PROJECTS *

CAMPS: Technical Agency Supervising Work	No. of Camps	Man-Days Worked by Assignees
U.S. Department of Agriculture		
Forest Service	30	1,213,000
Soil Conservation Service	19	1,112,000
Farm Security Administration	2	122,000
U.S. Department of the Interior		
National Park Service	9	413,000
Bureau of Reclamation	4	208,000
General Land Office	1	79,000
Fish and Wildlife Service	2	47,000
	67	

SPECIAL SERVICE PROJECTS:	No. of Units	Man-Days Worked by Assignees
State Mental Hospitals	40	1,347,000
State Training Schools	17	166,000
U.S. Department of Agriculture		
Dairy farming	34 (counties) ⎫	
Dairy herd testing	14 (states) ⎬	669,000
Agricultural Experiment Stations	9	117,000
Office of Scientific Research & Development; and Surgeon General, U.S. Army	41 (experiments)	151,000
U.S. Veterans Administration Hospitals	3	120,000

U.S. Public Health Service (in co-operation with state boards of health)	4	54,000
Puerto Rican Reconstruction Administration (including Virgin Islands project)	1	51,000
U.S. Department of Commerce		
Weather Bureau	1	31,000
Coast and Geodetic Survey	1	30,000
General Hospitals (private)	3	*
GENERAL OVERHEAD		
Administrative Personnel		1,004,000
Furloughs, Sickness, etc.		1,303,000
		8,237,000

* Man-days of work were computed by Camp Operations Division, Selective Service Headquarters, on the basis of the monthly work reports by the project superintendents. The figures cover the full period of C.P.S. operations, May 15, 1941, to March 31, 1947. A few individual assignments, including those who worked in the relief depots of the religious administrative agencies, have not been listed above.

No figure is cited in the Selective Service summary for man-days worked in the three general hospitals at which C.P.S. units were established (Presbyterian Hospital, New York City; Duke University Hospital, Durham, North Carolina; and Alexian Brothers Hospital, Chicago, Illinois).

Civilizing the Forest Primeval

In the summer of 1944 a ranger in the vast forest wilderness along the western mountain ranges spotted a dark expanse of pine and fir blurred by drifting, billowing smoke. A fire starting near the bottom of a wide gully was reaching for the head.

Three hours later, C.P.S. "smoke jumpers," parachuted into the canyon. As they plunged they manipulated their guide lines, anxious to keep from drifting into the fire or the winding Salmon River which flowed nearby.

After untangling themselves from the trees and sharp snags into which they landed, the jumpers divided and went down opposite sides of the fire, chopping, raking, digging a controlling fire line.

Between six on Sunday afternoon and five the next morning the crews completed their line around the fire.

Then came the breeze. The fire jumped the line. Fighters nearest the break were forced back. Furiously they dug a new line. Fortunately, it held. Twenty-four hours later, weary and sleepless, the c.o.'s were released by the ranger and began the long hike out to the road, carrying their equipment, torn parachutes, tools, and pumps. The fire had been held to fourteen acres. The quick, skilled, air-borne attack, under experienced Forest Service coaching, prevented the serious and irreparable loss that would have resulted from failure to secure prompt control. This Berg Mountain fire was typical of hundreds of blazes suppressed by C.P.S. smoke jumpers from 1944 to 1946.[4]

The prevention and fighting of forest fires under the direction of the United States Forest Service, the National Park Service, and the General Land Office, was the largest work of the c.o.'s, occupying 1,700,000 man-days or about a quarter of all their time.[5] Only a select few were actually chosen for the dramatic role of jumpers. Most were assigned to forestry "base camps," one hundred to two hundred men strong. During fire season a westward migration of C.P.S. men usually occurred to bring the camps to capacity. Most of the men were then scattered in small "spike camps" twenty-five to fifty miles deep in the mountains and placed on constant call. Food and mail, brought in by truck once or twice a week, were their only contacts with the outside world. The cry "Fire on the mountain" therefore was hailed as an exciting break in the monotony, and the crews would tackle enthusiastically the gruelling, and sometimes dangerous, tasks of "suppression." The most important stage of forest conservation, however, was the prevention of fires. This task occupied most of the time of c.o.'s in forestry camps. They constructed trails and built truck roads to inaccessible sections. To open firebreaks, they hewed timber and cleared underbrush.

Some of the early work in Civilian Public Service was clearing debris left by the New England 1937 hurricane—a grave fire hazard. Some men became specialists in telephone maintenance, adept at repairing lines to ranger stations and stretching new lines to improve and strengthen the system. As the war drew persons away from the professional Forest Service, C.P.S. men took their places in the solitude of lookout towers.

Several hundred c.o.'s were assigned to a more positive aspect of the national forestry program—timber stand improvement. Men would "cruise" through woodlots, surveying timber, estimating yields, marking trees for cutting. Others would follow, felling, splitting, piling. To eradicate blister rust, C.P.S. men mapped affected areas, ringed the trees, and sometimes topped them. In large burned-over areas, as in western Oregon, a "sustained yield program" was conducted. Seedlings were planted—one million in one sixteen-hundred-acre "burn." In the forest nursery, C.P.S. labor produced the seedlings—planting the seed, weeding, irrigating, pruning roots, controlling rodents and disease. Every year five hundred million board feet were cut off the "revested" land and sold.

Some men had the opportunity to assist in the experimental work conducted by the United States Forest Service. In the San Dimas National Forest, California, where a fifty-year analysis of the chief watershed for Los Angeles County was under way, c.o.'s checked the rain gauges, the record of precipitation, and runoff. A c.o. in the experimental laboratory analyzed and tabulated the figures. Others checked soil samples. Gradually this work exposed the life history of a drop of water landing on the rocks and scrub pine of the mountain basin, and furnished vital statistics for the search for methods of retaining an adequate water supply. On the opposite side of the country, at Cooperstown, New York, one of the nation's leading cartoonists gave birth to "Joe the Beaver," whose antics and mottoes on posters throughout the country taught farmer and roadside tourist how to care for trees. A minister's son, watching the tedious work of the cruisers as they surveyed and estimated the yield of a stand of timber, invented a gadget by which the total yield could be figured in less than one-fifth of the normal time. He was promptly assigned to the regional office to develop his instrument and explain its use to foresters throughout the northeastern United States. At the same office a young sociologist applied the latest opinion-testing methods to the analysis of public attitudes on forest conservation, as a basis for the development of an effective public educational program by the United States Forest Service.

Least interesting of the forestry projects was maintaining the national parks—"manicuring the trees" or "vista-schnitten," as the c.o's contemptuously called it. Along the Blue Ridge Skyway, crew after crew cleared brush to open views from the road, seeded and graded road banks, built stone and rustic fences. They laboriously hacked at hardwood stumps left by former C.C.C. men in prospective picnic areas. Benches, tables, and signs, neatly fashioned and painted according to the approved National Park Service pattern, testify to the meticulous work of C.P.S. men.

Conserving the Source of Life

One hundred million acres is the sum of the land in Illinois, Ohio, North Carolina, and Maryland. One hundred million acres of the United States have been eroded so completely that the topsoil will not produce food for human life.

One out of every six man-days worked by C.P.S. was devoted to the battle against soil erosion, and the record of accomplishment was substantial. It included, in part: 49 large diversion dams constructed (also 164 reservoirs and 200 permanent check dams); 481,000 rods of fence built; 1,455,000 square yards of bank sloped; 1,650,000 square yards of gullies sodded and seeded; 680,000 linear feet of diversion ditches dug; 1,070,000 trees planted or moved; 2,870 miles of contour furrows dug; 15,790,000 square yards of clearing (in channels, levees, etc.); and 2,670 water control structures built for irrigation.

Much of this work was hard, menial, and tedious. To Objector Smith "soil conservation," whatever its over-all importance, meant only the perpetual digging of four-foot-deep postholes as he fenced in pasture, or the grubbing out of weeds as he hunched over row upon row of experimental grasses in the nursery at Big Flats, New York, or the shoveling of load after load of gravel and muck as he cleaned out ditches and built levees.

Some projects were more impressive. On the eastern shore of Maryland the Pocomoke River had regularly flooded the neighboring flatlands and drowned a substantial portion of the farms. For over two hundred years residents had wanted to straighten out the kinks in the river, allowing it to flow swiftly into Chesapeake Bay rather than backing up onto their farms. The C.C.C. had started to realize the dream. Civilian Public Service, operating under the Soil

Conservation Service, brought it virtually to completion. A crew, knee- or hip-deep in swamp, cut down the trees in the channel. A second crew, armed with grappling hooks, chains, and tractors, drew the logs to the bank of the river and cut away the underbrush. A third group manipulated "drag lines" which reached in and scooped out the mire. Coming behind, the cleanup gang leveled and smoothed the embankment. Months later, flowing fields of corn and thriving truck gardens grew in the place of sodden swamp.

At Coshocton, Ohio, C.P.S. men staffed the Soil Conservation Service's experimental station, investigating the effect of water upon the soil. They checked the mammoth lysimeters, which measured evaporation and transpiration of rainfall, and conducted experiments designed to discover the best types of soil for different conditions of humidity and kinds of crops. Soil samples from all sections of the state were analyzed by C.P.S. men with scientific agricultural training. One of the country's outstanding botanists, drafted into Civilian Public Service, made the most comprehensive study of plant life in the state of Ohio. C.P.S. mathematicians provided the station with the best quality of statistical analysis in its history. Several men used mechanical aptitudes to design and build new technical equipment for the station's studies.

The Mennonite and Brethren committees, particularly interested in agriculture, developed a unique demonstration project in co-operative subsistence farming in Washington County, Maryland. The church agencies bought five run-down farms and, in co-operation with the county conservation agent, C.P.S. units put them on a self-sustaining basis by the application of model conservation practices and efficient farm management. The men built their own domitories, replaced old farm buildings or built new ones, "contour-stripped" the land, and raised livestock or poultry. Meanwhile, they worked a full 51-hour week on general conservation work in the county. These projects set a pattern for similar experiments in other parts of the country.

Farm reclamation and development on a much larger scale was undertaken in North Dakota and Montana, where thousands of farmers had been "dusted out" in the drought of 1935–1937. Under the Farm Security Administration, C.P.S. men, following in the wake of W.P.A. and C.C.C. labor, constructed irrigation dams, canals, and ditches, leveled the land with bulldozers, and constructed family farm units, including home, barn, and poultry house for each 80- to 160-acre tract. These were entrusted to farmers' co-operatives, organized by farmers in the low income brackets, primarily former residents of the area; thereby a permanent addition was made to the food-producing area of the country.

Relieving the Food Emergency

The world food shortage drew c.o.'s into a third major service—agricultural work.

Many men in C.P.S. with farm background demanded to go back to the land when they heard of wheat that could not be harvested, tomatoes rotting on the ground, fruit spoiling on the trees, no hands to till the ground or care for livestock. Meanwhile, farmers called for the help of conscientious objectors to meet their acute labor shortage, and the relief needs of war-devastated countries impelled the Historic Peace Churches likewise to press for the use of C.P.S. men to boost agricultural output.

Selective Service was slow to respond, fearing hostile community reaction if it allowed c.o.'s virtually to replace drafted farm hands. Furthermore, the Comptroller General dampened the enthusiasm of many c.o.'s for a back-to-the-farm movement by ruling that all wages earned would have to be turned over to the United States Treasury.[6] This aroused qualms of conscience, inasmuch as the Treasury's chief current business was to finance total war. But by the spring of 1943 the farm crisis brought pressure from the office of Economic Mobilizer James F. Byrnes, and a plan for five hundred C.P.S. men to work on dairy farms was finally agreed upon.

The War Food Administration designated twenty-five counties as acutely short of necessary dairy-farm labor. The county agents designated the farms where assignees were to work and contracted with the farmers concerning the terms of employment. The farmer paid the prevailing wage—*not* to the c.o. but to the National Service Board. Out of these wages came the expenses of administering the farm service program and maintaining the c.o. The balance was turned over to the United States Treasury, which agreed to freeze all such funds in a special account and not use them until after the war was over.[7] The individual farmers, subject to instructions from

Selective Service, had full charge of the c.o.'s, just as though they were their own hired hands.

The men who went onto the farms were usually employed as general farm hands, handling horses and tractors, farm machinery, and milking machines, cutting hay, cleaning out stables, working from two or three A.M. until evening with just one day off each month. Yet on the whole the men were satisfied, and the farmer usually found the conscientious objector a quiet, steadfast, hard worker, often his best hired man.

About 170 conscientious objectors were assigned to the skilled task of dairy testing. They kept meticulous records of herds of cattle belonging to members of co-operative cow-testing associations. Each day the c.o. traveled to an appointed farm and made the acquaintance of approximately thirty cows, listing each by name or number, weighing its grain and roughage, weighing the milk, and taking a sample from which butterfat tests were made. He left a copy of the record with the farmer for study and at the end of the month prepared a full report for the state office. In this way, the dairy tester helped materially to maintain and improve the general standard of milk production.

A few men performed an even more specialized service as technicians and inseminators for artificial-breeding associations in Delaware and Pennsylvania, in the hope that their experience might later be useful to relief agencies striving to rebuild the dairy herds slaughtered during the war. Traveling out from the headquarters of the breeding association they would care for and manage the bulls, wash and disinfect equipment, take and distribute semen. In this way they were able to make available to all members of the association the service of the best bulls in the association at very low cost.

C.P.S. men also helped state agricultural schools and experimental farms to keep their programs going in the face of the manpower crisis. At Beltsville, Maryland, the unit of twenty-five c.o.'s under the Mennonites had primary responsibility for the experimental herd of five hundred dairy cows. At Lincoln, Nebraska, the men ran experiments on grasses and seeds, planted, cultivated, harvested, and tagged specimens for the next planting. At Ames, Iowa, a fifty-man Friends unit worked on a crop-breeding program. They cultivated small plots of different strains, testing and comparing the results with other plots. The directors of these projects were particularly appreciative of this service, as it made possible the continuation of long-range experiments designed to improve the quality and yield of foodstuffs and livestock. On their part, the c.o.'s felt that their work might help increase the ultimate stocks of food and export to starved Europeans and Asiatics, as well as develop knowledge and techniques that would speed the process of agricultural rehabilitation.

The most controversial phase of the C.P.S. farm program was the use of c.o.'s for emergency farm labor near the camps. The pool of C.P.S. men in a rural area was a great temptation to neighboring farmers, caught with bumper crops which they could not harvest. Community pressure, added to the tremendous demand of the government for increased food production, finally led Selective Service to direct the use of men from C.P.S. camps for farm work within a fifteen-mile radius whenever the county agent decided that they were needed. The c.o.'s and the church agencies were distressed at the peremptory character of these assignments, in which neither the desire and experience of the men nor the welfare of their main project was taken into consideration. Many were disturbed by what they felt to be military implications of farm service under such emergency conditions; the products of their efforts, they feared, would be used to further war production. But the order stood, and one hundred and fifty thousand man-hours of emergency farm labor from the camps were used. Wages (over and above expenses) were transferred to the United States Treasury, as in the case of the men who worked on dairy farms. The grudging efforts of c.o.'s saved crops on the verge of spoiling, but the project narrowly avoided a showdown clash between the men and the churches, on one side, and Selective Service and the hard-pressed farmers, on the other.[8]

Salvaging the Mentally Ill and Deficient

The outstanding contribution of conscientious objectors to the national welfare was probably their service in mental institutions. Responding to desperate pleas for attendants and other help, a cavalcade of over 2,000 C.P.S. men moved into 41 mental hospitals in 20 states and into 17 training schools for mental deficients in 12 states. Shocked by the appalling conditions of human degradation which they found, the c.o.'s threw themselves into the task of improving the lot of the patients. Some went further, pressing for reform and seeking to arouse the nation's conscience to the shame of the asylum. A new awareness of America's No. 1 health problem is in no small measure a result of this C.P.S. experience.[9]

Before the war 800,000 patients, crowded into inadequate quarters, depended for care and treatment upon harried, overworked, and often incompetent attendants. Low wages, long hours, and depressing work could not attract conscientious and considerate assistants to these institutions for lost minds. With the advent of the war, the shortage of help became acute. The pool of unemployed was absorbed into lucrative war jobs, and the more fit and able attendants were drafted for military service. "We are 150 attendants short out of 256," wrote one superintendent. "Our situation is so acute that we shall be forced to close half our main building," declared another. "We have been forced to refuse any new admissions" was the word from a third hospital.

In such situations, the majority of the c.o.'s worked as ward attendants. Some tended the farm, dairy, and orchards. Others stoked the furnaces, peeled potatoes, cooked the meals, helped maintain the grounds. A few in the better-equipped hospitals assisted in recreational and occupational therapy. The work was hard and long. Hours of labor were rarely less than 72 a week and sometimes as much as 100.

What the C.P.S. units accomplished depended greatly upon the character of the institution and the quality of administration. At many hospitals, the main function of the c.o. attendant was to assure effective custody of the patients—in itself no mean task. At Eastern State Hospital, Williamsburg, Virginia, one attendant was solely responsible for 100 to 175 persons in a violent ward, where at any moment a patient might swing a fist or a chair. This required constant watchfulness, quick and resourceful action to prevent or stop belligerency, and occasionally a firm grip upon a patient to escort him to confinement. A broken jaw could well be the price of inattentive or ineffective custody. The most distasteful, yet a major, task of the attendant was to care for bed patients, many of whom were incontinent as well as diseased. Frequent bed-changing, the dressing of irritating pressure sores, special feedings, and the watching of the more disturbed or gravely ill demanded, the c.o.'s found, "limitless patience and a strong stomach." A C.P.S. attendant at a hospital in the state of Washington graphically described some of his problems:

Sometimes a patient must be prompted and urged to eat in spite of the fact that he is firmly convinced that he has no stomach. The job is a little more difficult if he thinks you are trying to poison him. He must be bathed even during the times when he is sure that the attendant is set on drowning him, or that the tub is full of crocodiles. When he is in the most disturbed condition the patient will continue to grow whiskers and when he eyes you from the bathroom wielding a gleaming straight-edge razor it may be fairly difficult to convince him that the razor is to cut the beard and not his throat. But even more trying on the nerves of the average attendant than the patient with delusions and hallucinations which are fairly pronounced, is the one with whom and about whom you seem to be able to do nothing. One can only suppose his trouble and be even more patient than usual. Perhaps he is senile, or getting that way. He can't remember that an hour ago you told him where he is, and why you can't call his wife, so he will ask you again and again at regular or . . . [irregular] intervals. Perhaps he is suffering from the effects of a stroke and is constantly irritable. Nothing you can do will make him happy or put him at ease. Or perhaps he is of the persistent type that insists on telling you his story over and over again, making you wonder more and more why he is in the hospital at all, but on the other hand making you very certain that he is in the right place. The constant small irritation of never knowing what your patients will do next manages to set many an attendant on edge to the extent that civil response to the patient becomes very difficult. Routine becomes set and patterns to keep patients in order rather than to keep them happy become the line of least resistance and the accepted custom.[10]

In some hospitals, the c.o.'s were encouraged by the superintendents to do what they could to raise the quality of care for the masses of patients. "Byberry," the Philadelphia State Hospital, had become notorious for the deplorable state of its inmates. Wartime conditions had virtually stalled the efforts of an able superintendent to make improvements. During two years of war he had suffered a loss of 42 per cent of his 956 employees. The hospital was equipped to accommodate 2,500 patients; actually, it housed 6,100. Only one doctor and one nurse were on duty for every 300 patients, and one attendant for every 100. (The minimum standard set by the Psychiatric Association was one attendant for every 10 patients.)

The superintendent welcomed the offer of ten of the c.o.'s to take over the worst spot in the hospital—where 350 incontinent patients lived virtually without care, naked and filthy. The C.P.S. men scraped, cleaned, and freshly painted the entire building. They installed a new feeding program, calmly encouraging patients to eat slowly, instead of shoving through the line and bolting all food within reach. Each morning the attendants painstakingly helped every individual to dress. Foul and wet bedding was removed promptly. Laundry was carefully counted and a daily tally of destruction was kept. Progress was slow, but the ultimate improvement was substantial. Even the foul aroma of "A" Building almost disappeared under the conscientious attack.

Many of the institutions in which C.P.S. men worked were in much better condition than Byberry, with their buildings and equipment more adequate and their staff more plentiful. For instance, the hospital at Ypsilanti, Michigan, a $7,500,000 institution built since 1931, had well-equipped kitchens, cafeterias, bakery, dairy, orchards, men's and women's gymnasiums, athletic, music, and motion-picture equipment, golf course, tennis courts, and 1,200 acres of farm land. A progressive superintendent provided efficient and considerate management. Under these circumstances the c.o.'s slipped into a more normal routine where their hours were long but their duties regular and prescribed. Their accomplishment was less spectacular and they could not see great changes in the standards of care resulting from their efforts. Yet they were the critical margin of manpower which kept these institutions from sinking to the Byberry level.

Some C.P.S. men were able to take part in experimental and remedial work with the mentally ill. In one sense, they were the most fortunately placed of the conscientious objectors, for they could often see before their eyes, and in part as a result of their work, the transformation of an insane mind into a normal one. At Duke University Hospital and the Highland Hospital in Asheville, North Carolina, C.P.S. men were tremendously challenged by the curative measures attempted—medical, psychiatric, and operative treatment, occupational therapy, individualized care, and delightful surroundings. One group of C.P.S. men were fully responsible for cleaning and preparing the operating equipment at Duke Hospital. Others assisted as technicians in the blood bank, the Department of Experimental

Surgery, the Physiology Department, and the Spastic Clinic. Two men helped to design and build a machine to study motion sickness in the Department of Neuropsychiatry. One part of the C.P.S. unit was assigned full time to the psychiatric ward at Duke and under doctors' supervision administered the most advanced methods of therapy. At Asheville, C.P.S. men undertook a life-and-death responsibility when they assisted in deep-shock insulin treatments. They were often rewarded by a striking change in the behavior and attitude of a treated patient, who might emerge from a sullen, combative, and hallucinated state to become a rational, pleasant personality. "No thrill is comparable," said a c.o. after working on this treatment, "to the restoration of a disintegrating personality to a good level of behavior. . . . Watching a young man improve week by week, I have a sense of personal triumph." [11]

The units assigned to "training schools" for the mentally deficient taught classes adapted to the limited capacities of the inmates and helped the boys learn skills and vocations which enabled some to be paroled to simple occupations. Most C.P.S. men in training schools also acted as housemasters, each in charge of a cottage or unit of boys. Here they tried to create an atmosphere of home and family and arouse interest in extracurricular activities—puppet shows, parties, movies, Bible and craft classes, hikes, and nature walks.

The effectiveness of their work was not as apparent as in the mental hospitals, but those responsible for the institutions insisted that the c.o.'s were filling key positions and that the schools could hardly have continued to function without them.[12]

In his service with mental patients, the c.o. confronted at first hand the issue of "using force." By conviction he was presumably committed to nonviolence in all human relationships, and this was precisely the approach required by law and the psychiatric profession in the handling of mental patients. Yet under the tensions of the average mental hospital a great deal of forceful restraint was practiced by attendants, even to the point of physical violence and injury to the patients; such practices were acknowledged, if not condoned, by the administrative staff. Conscientious objectors were strongly tempted to use force, and some succumbed to the temptation. When a ward was in turmoil with a patient gone berserk, a C.P.S. man as well as a regular attendant might seize the unruly man, sharply crack him with the flat of the hand, and march him off to solitary confinement. Violence would sometimes result from fear that a patient was about to attack the attendant himself, or, after a long and grueling day on ward duty, an attendant irritated with a stubborn patient might beat him or roughly push him about.

With few exceptions, c.o.'s considered outright acts of violence unworthy of their standards and made little attempt to justify such lapses from their commitment to a pacifist, nonviolent way of life. Some felt so guilty at their failure to practice their belief that they asked for release from wards and their assignment to less responsible and more menial duties. Those who felt no remorse and persisted in acts of violence met the full censure of their fellows and were often discharged from the hospital on the initiative either of the unit or of the sponsoring religious committee.

On the other hand, many c.o.'s concluded that they could justify using physical "force of control" to keep destructive patients from harming themselves or others. Sometimes physical pressure was needed in conjunction with sedative measures or other therapeutic treatment. "When experience assures us that the treatment promises ultimate good rather than damage to the patient," a c.o. might conscientiously resort to "force of control," provided it did not involve any insult or physical injury to the patient.

C.o.'s in training schools ran into the same acute problem of forceful restraint as did those in mental hospitals. Some of their charges were confirmed delinquents, surly and belligerent. When one of these boys broke a school rule or rebelled against the housemaster, the c.o. had to decide whether to use corporal punishment. He faced a grave dilemma. In most cases, the institution's rules officially banned the use of physical force against the patients. Yet the employees were expected to maintain discipline, and corporal punishment was widely condoned by staff and supervisors alike as an inescapable necessity under the prevailing conditions of institutional care. The c.o. thus had to choose between faithful adherence to his principles and the prescribed regulations or accepting what he came to believe were the practical requirements of his assignment. Despite such difficulties, the c.o.'s service to the mentally ill and deficient was notable for his personal respect and consideration for the individual—a spirit often lacking among many of the regular employees.

Warm and humane care, buttressed by an intelligent understanding of the nature of the patient's condition, was characteristic of Civilian Public Service in mental institutions. In some places this had little permanent effect and was even resented as a challenge to the accepted ways.[13] Elsewhere the whole tone of an institution would change during the course of the c.o.'s service. Staff doctors, nurses, and even hardened attendants caught the new spirit, discovered that considerate care and human sympathy worked—and worked more effectively than harsh or impersonal supervision—in treating and in restraining those whose minds failed to meet the exacting demands of modern civilization.

Reconstructing America's Social Health

The c.o. yearned to serve "normal people" as well as the mentally deficient. He wanted to remedy social ills and improve the lot of the "common man." Public health projects in Florida and Mississippi and in Puerto Rico and the Virgin Islands particularly met this demand.

The South's Subtle Foe. In five Florida counties where up to 85 per cent of the people were infected with hookworm, C.P.S. units produced and installed inexpensive sanitary privies, built septic tanks, dug deep wells—chief weapons of attack upon this insidious parasite. Because they developed methods of mass production and installation and because their labor was without cost, C.P.S. men brought such sanitary facilities to many people too poor to install their own. State Board of Health officials credited C.P.S. units with devising the best privy-building system in the country and called on them to train their county sanitarians and public-health students at the University of Florida in the science. Thanks to the "system," twenty-seven hundred C.P.S.-built privies dotted Polk County when the last C.P.S. man left, while the unit at Orlando made and installed almost fifteen hundred in Okaloosa County.

C.P.S. men aided Florida's public health program in other ways. They screened homes, painted and repaired Negro and white school buildings, built baby incubators and cribs. One man toured the state in a "dentmobile" and, as dental assistant, cared for the teeth of school children too poor to get private treatment. A thorough sanitary survey was made of twelve thousand of Polk County's eighteen thousand homes, checking on the condition of the houses, the breeding places of mosquitoes and flies, the arrangements for garbage and waste disposal. A two-man survey crew in another area visited about twenty-five houses a day, made recommendations to the tenants for sanitary improvements, and served as "salesmen" for the privies.

A Selective Service officer, returning from an inspection of the C.P.S. work in Florida, could not restrain an unusual burst of enthusiasm, reporting that the "entire hookworm project will stand out as one of the most worthwhile contributions made by c.o.'s in this war." [14]

Misery in America's Back Yard. C.P.S. men plunged into depths of poverty, disease, and misery greater even than in the slums of continental United States when in June, 1942, they opened the Martin G. Brumbaugh Reconstruction Unit in Puerto Rico and, later, set up a similar unit in the Virgin Islands. Population in Puerto Rico— 541.6 per square mile—was twelve times as dense as that in continental United States. Income—four hundred dollars a year or less for 70 per cent of the families—could barely buy enough salt pork, flour, and beans for most people. The Island had the highest tuberculosis rate in the Western Hemisphere, a malaria rate twice that of the United States, widespread hookworm, syphilis, and intestinal diseases. Medical aid—one doctor to five thousand inhabitants in normal times—could not reach out beyond the main urban centers and the well to do. With sugar the basic crop, employment and life itself hung upon United States corporation policies, quota restrictions, and the vagaries of weather and hurricanes. The war profoundly aggravated all these problems. At times the Island was virtually cut off from the mainland, able neither to export nor import the commodities on which its life depended. Slashing of funds almost strangled the efforts of the Puerto Rican Reconstruction Administration (P.R.R.A.), which had been trying since 1935 to remedy some of the major economic and social defects. [15]

The Brethren and, later, the Friends, Mennonites, and Presbyterian Board of National Missions each set up a C.P.S. unit in cooperation with the P.R.R.A. to provide medical aid, public health education, and community social services to the rural population. The Brethren unit built and staffed a twenty-six-bed hospital at the village of Castaner with an operating room, obstetrics room, nursery, laboratory, and X-ray equipment. This hospital, with two rural dispensaries which the unit set up in other villages, became the medical center for twenty thousand people in an area of thirty miles' radius. In addition to caring for a continually full house of bed patients and performing over a hundred operations monthly, ten clinics were held weekly by the unit at the main hospital and six at the dispensaries. The medical staff went out to the schools to give complete physical examinations and to immunize the children against smallpox, typhoid fever, and diphtheria. The Mennonites and the Friends followed suit, the former establishing another hospital (at La Plata) and the Friends a clinic at Zalduondo.

Developing a program of public health education, the c.o.'s taught in the schools, conducted a school health service, and presented films, talks, puppet shows, and other audio-visual programs on health and nutrition problems. A social worker visited individual homes to see that doctors' orders were followed and to check on undesirable home conditions. On one occasion, home visiting uncovered an epidemic of whooping cough among infants, and all preschool children were promptly immunized.

The C.P.S. units attacked the problem of malnutrition. Milk stations provided breakfast for young people whose customary diet was almost milkless. The government supplied the food; C.P.S., the distributors. C.P.S. men also helped Puerto Ricans plan and plant their garden plots, made special efforts to popularize the growing of soy beans to supplement the deficient diet, and sponsored the formation of 4-H clubs.

Each unit stimulated recreational activities in its community and established general community centers with hobby clubs, libraries, and a full schedule of outdoor sports, movies, classes, and home-talent events. A summer boys' camp was jointly sponsored by all three units. These activities were largely attended and in time became an essential part of community life. This same kind of program —especially the development of neighborhood social centers—was later organized in the Virgin Islands.

Despite the degradation and stifled spirit of the people—caused largely by their deplorable physical and economic environment— Civilian Public Service constantly strove to train them to care for themselves. There was no thought of starting an endless cycle of paternalistic philanthropy. At Castaner, for instance, Puerto Ricans assigned by P.R.R.A. worked alongside the C.P.S. men as fellow members of the unit. The Island government showed increasing interest in the work, and in 1945 it appropriated twenty thousand dollars to each of the two hospitals set up by C.P.S. Governor Rexford G. Tugwell asserted that the service of the c.o.'s had touched the heart of Puerto Rico's problems: "Your projects give medical and hospital care; they are educating the people in the sanitation which will destroy hookworm . . . and are showing Puerto Ricans how to help themselves."

Human Guinea Pigs for Medicine and Science

Dubbed "guinea pigs," over five hundred C.P.S. men served as live subjects for medical and scientific experiments sponsored by the Office of Scientific Research and Development or the Surgeon General's Office of the United States Army. These projects, demanding submission to grueling, acutely uncomfortable, and often dangerous tests, challenged the c.o.'s more than any other aspect of Civilian Public Service. They saw here a chance to prove personal, physical courage in service which might help to save life or facilitate recovery from illness and malnutrition. No experiment which C.P.S. men could in good conscience undertake went begging for volunteers—whether it aimed to produce effective means of controlling the spread of typhus, find a cure for malaria, study the transmission of jaundice or atypical pneumonia, analyze the nutritional effects of extreme heat and cold, high altitude, or vitamin deficiency, or discover the best rations for persons shipwrecked and cast adrift at sea.

The Louse Camp. The first taste of guinea-pig life came when two Harvard doctors carefully doled out a quota of lice to thirty C.P.S. men segregated in a side camp in the New Hampshire forests. They were seeking a safe, easy, and cheap method of killing the carrier of wartime's most feared epidemic—typhus.

The men wore the same lice-infested clothes for three weeks, meanwhile continuing their usual nine hours of road building per day. Every day they were inspected and from time to time they were dusted with powders designed to kill the lice. Two safe and effective powders were discovered and recommended for use on soldiers and civilians in typhus-fever areas. Though the lice were both prolific and provocative, the c.o.'s maintained their pacifism throughout the experiment and never took a life intentionally.[16]

Tracing Infectious Hepatitis. In 1944 United States Army doctors announced that, as a result of tests on conscientious objectors, they had partly unraveled the mystery of "infectious hepatitis," or jaundice, the most widespread epidemic disease of the Second World War. At the beginning of the war no one knew the cause of the sickness, how it spread, or the most effective means of treatment and control. The disease, though seldom fatal, was extremely debilitating, often requiring months in bed and the best of care for a full recovery.

A whole battery of experiments was undertaken, first on c.o.'s working in several of the mental hospitals, later on full-time guinea-pig units of thirty to sixty men at the University of Pennsylvania and Yale University. Under controlled conditions, the C.P.S. men were inoculated with suspected blood plasma or yellow-fever vaccine, swallowed nose and throat washings and body wastes of infected patients, or drank varieties of contaminated or presumably purified water. Expectantly they waited to see if they were among the "chosen."

Preliminary reports indicate that an especially elusive virus is responsible for jaundice, that the organism can be effectively transmitted not only by human filth but in plasma or serum, and that the disease can also be acquired from drinking water, even if it is disinfected by commonly used methods of chlorination. Major changes in the methods of purifying water might therefore be necessary in some cities to prevent jaundice epidemics.[17]

How to Get Atypical Pneumonia. Over a hundred C.P.S. men experienced the scientific way to catch a common cold or other varieties of atypical pneumonia. First at C.P.S. Camp Rufus Jones in Gatlinburg, Tennessee, then in two experiments in isolation at Holly Inn, Pinehurst, North Carolina, the c.o.'s successfully caught the disease by inhaling or drinking throat washings taken from soldiers having the disease. The tests proved, according to the physicians of the Surgeon General's Office who were in charge, that this rapidly increasing disease must be caused by a virus; men became sick even when their "drink" had been filtered through glass to remove bacteria.

How to Recover from Malaria. War in the Pacific brought to thousands of United States troops a grim acquaintance with the burning fever, racking chills, and often fatal effects of malaria, common but dread disease of the tropics, reputedly responsible for more morbidity and mortality than any other in the world. Its cause was well known—the sting of an anopheline mosquito carrying the bacteria from an infected person. Its best cure—quinine in heavy doses —lay behind Japanese lines and was virtually unobtainable. Atabrine had proved only a partially effective substitute. Chemists perfected new drugs capable of curing malaria. Tested on animals, they proved nontoxic, but could human beings take them without ill effect? Physicians were especially anxious over the possibility of fatal complications when the drugs were actually given to persons seriously ill.

C.P.S. men agreed to make the trial, in lengthy experiments at the Massachusetts General Hospital, the University of Chicago Medical School, Columbia, Cornell, and Stanford universities, and Goldwater Memorial Hospital in New York City. Some, while healthy and free of any trace of malaria, received injections of the drugs to test their absorption into the blood, the length of time the concentration lasted, and other physiological effects. The critical tests came when a selected group of the guinea pigs allowed themselves to be deliberately bitten by mosquitoes infected with malaria. After three or four days of fever at the peak of the disease, the most promising of the antimalarial drugs were administered. No one died as a result, and some drugs proved far better than atabrine and quinine.[18]

Other experiments, at the University of Minnesota, tested the physiological effects of malaria. Twelve C.P.S. volunteers, normal and healthy, were inoculated with malaria. After 5 to 8 paroxysms and an average of 193 degree-hours of temperature above 101° F., the malaria was terminated with quinine sulphate. With the first 36 to 48 hours after temperature returned to normal, the men resumed the "standard activity" of a previous 6 months' conditioning period —laboratory work plus one hour daily of walking on a motor-driven treadmill at 3.5 miles per hour on a 10 degree grade. A series of tests during the next 3 to 8 weeks determined that a number of bodily functions related to performance capacity had markedly deteriorated, and indicated the amount of time needed for recovery. The effects of malaria on the liver, heart, and blood serum were also studied, furnishing the basic information for a thorough analysis of significant factors in deterioration and rehabilitation.[19]

On Staying Alive—Adrift at Sea. When the ship has sunk, and the life raft floats under a blistering sun, will a drink of salt water poison you, true to maritime prophecy, or can it quench your thirst? Should the lifeboat have been heavily stocked with hardtack and Spam to keep you well nourished until rescue? To save your energy, should you lie as still as possible?

These questions became critically important as the Battle of the Atlantic reached its climax and submarine attacks shipwrecked thousands of seamen and soldiers; they were also basic to the permanent improvement of safety conditions on the high seas.

Experiments to find the real answers again drew on C.P.S. for its guinea pigs. Two men drank ocean water by the pint, sometimes with food and sometimes fasting. Doctors measured their drop in weight and their loss of hydration, mixed the ocean water with varying quantities of fresh, and concluded that one part of sea to four of fresh water would keep a man alive indefinitely. Meanwhile the Navy had discovered how to "freshen" salt water for drinking, so the formula went unused.

The experiments in food rations put several groups of c.o.'s on different diets—from nothing at all for four days (the c.o. had neither food nor water) to the official Navy ration for eight days (hardtack, canned meat, malted milk tablets, chocolate, and 400 cc. of fresh water daily). The man on Navy ration ended up in the emergency ward with a temperature of 101 degrees. A typical test diet consisted of 500 cc. of water and 50 grams of butterscotch daily for six days. Each set of experiments went through a cycle of standardization, followed by the restricted diet, then recuperation. At the end of a year of research, the directors urged the government to eliminate all old emergency rations and substitute on all lifeboats and life rafts a simple ration of candy composed of 80 per cent glucose and 20 per cent fats, with a pint of fresh water per man per day.

Seeking ways to reduce the evaporation of body liquid, five men went out on a raft in Boston's Cotuit Bay. They lay in the sun eight hours a day for two weeks. With clothes on and no breeze they lost thirteen ounces of water an hour instead of one ounce an hour under normal conditions. If there was a breeze and they soaked their clothes, or took them off altogether and hung over the side five minutes of each half hour, the loss of bodily water could be almost entirely prevented.

Nutrition and Starvation. Almost 300 men jumped at the chance to take part in experiments exploring the effects of nutrition under different conditions and seeking ways to utilize limited food resources most effectively in rehabilitation. Some sat for hours in the "cold chamber" of the University of Illinois Research Hospital, watching the effect of their controlled diets at twenty degrees below zero. Others spent their days in "ovens" while the scientists discovered which foods they lost most easily through sweat in the high temperatures and humidity of a tropical climate. The effects of diet on men flying at fifteen thousand feet and at forty-five thousand feet were tested by C.P.S. men in pressure chambers at the Metropolitan Hospital on Welfare Island, New York. In a six months' experiment at a New Hampshire C.P.S. camp, the Harvard Fatigue Laboratory placed men engaged in hard physical labor on restricted diets and periodically tested their extreme physical capacity on an "Iron Maiden" —in this case a sixteen-inch wooden step. Carrying up to sixty-five pounds on his back, the subject stepped up and down the step every two seconds for five minutes, or until he stopped breathing; then he repeated the test after a five-minute rest. Fifty C.P.S. men at Camp Magnolia, Arkansas, ate dehydrated grass tips for three months to see if this might be a relief substitute for fruits and vegetables.

Most dramatic and ambitious of the nutrition experiments was the study of rehabilitation following semistarvation, conceived and conducted by Dr. Ancel Keys and associates at the University of Minnesota Laboratory of Physiological Hygiene. The object of the experiment was to discover how to achieve the most effective food relief for war-devastated areas with fixed and obviously inadequate food resources.[20] Thirty-six C.P.S. men were selected out of many volunteers, on the basis of their health and general physical condition, to go through a three-month period of "standardization" on a normal diet of about 3,200 calories, then a six-month period on 1,800 calories or less of food most commonly available under European famine conditions, and a final three-month period of controlled rehabilitation. During the starvation period, the men's weight was to come down 20 to 50 per cent. Throughout the experiment detailed quantitative measurement of the physiological and psychological effects of starvation was secured through a battery of tests, checking morphological changes, metabolism, blood, respiration, strength and muscle function, speed and co-ordination, capacity for work, sex drive, personality, and intellectual functions. Meanwhile each man tried to pursue at the University a full course of studies related to relief and rehabilitation.

Results were significant—even startling. The men weakened physically, of course. The most dramatic functional change in semistarvation was a reduction of almost 75 per cent in capacity to continue at severe work for brief periods. They would often become dizzy, and some collapsed during a five-minute run on a treadmill set at 7½ miles an hour. They also lost capacity for sustained intellectual effort. The educational program "quietly but decisively collapsed." Day and night the craving for food was overpowering—though only two of the men failed to keep their diets straight through the experiment. A decided tendency toward introversion was noted, a decrease in ambition and a growing lethargy.

Recovery proved much slower and more trying than anyone expected, despite substantially increased diet following semistarvation. Capacity to undertake hard physical work returned most slowly. But psychological effects during rehabilitation struck the experimenters even more forcefully. During starvation, the men drew the praise of the scientists for their co-operativeness, good spirits, and perseverance despite their weakened physical condition. But instead of a rise in spirits with increased food and the approaching end of a long confinement, the opposite took place—a sharp slump in morale, irritability, and a deep feeling of depression. The men could not shake the intense fatigue and sense of physical weakness which had come upon them during starvation. They therefore lost their earlier buoyant confidence that their ordeal would benefit others who had undergone enforced starvation, and this pulled out their major incentive for service. So severe was the total experience that most of the men doubted whether they would have been ready to undertake it if they had foreseen its rigors.

Nevertheless, conclusions of vital importance to relief policies emerged, and in the end the experience of starvation appeared to have left no permanent physical defects. Weight was regained, bodily functions were restored to prestarvation conditions, even endurance and work capacity were recovered. Of course, the scientists cautioned that these results were secured under almost optimum conditions, in regard to the previous health of the men, their youth and vitality, the relatively brief period of food restriction, and the stable and comfortable surroundings of the experiment. There was no assurance that such complete recovery could be expected where people had undergone the full consequences of the war. Yet the experience did offer some hope that rehabilitation could be effective—*if adequate;* noting the geniality and general satisfaction of the men when they ultimately fattened during the high refeeding period, Dr. Keys speculated drily whether a peaceful world would not be "one inhabited by fat people, with all the attendant difficulties of increased diabetes and cardio-vascular disease."

The knowledge and understanding gained from the study materially affected postwar relief policies, increasing the effectiveness of both private and public operations and thereby easing a measure of the world's suffering. The findings were made available to all major groups engaged in relief work and were extensively used by United States government agencies concerned with postwar world food and nutrition problems, including the Departments of State, War, and Agriculture and the Committee on Emergency Food Problems.

Evaluations

With a few exceptions, those immediately responsible for directing and supervising the work of the c.o.'s in C.P.S. were gratified with the accomplishment and considered that the men had rendered a valuable national service. They generally agreed that without the labor of the c.o.'s the various projects would have been severely handicapped or would even have had to shut down. This was particularly true in the case of the services in hospitals and in the experimental and scientific fields.[21]

Evaluations of the personal attitudes and performance of the c.o.'s varied widely, as one might expect considering the great diversity among assignees, work projects, and project supervisors. Some of the latter condemned certain objectors as "eye servants, inclined to shirk their duties," or considered that they "did inferior work, lacked interest and cooperated very poorly." [22] The chief of the United States Forest Service judged the labor of assignees not very efficient as a whole.[23] Project supervisors were particularly unhappy at the deterioration of work following the end of hostilities, and a number urged that more effective discipline should have been maintained, with greater and more uniform control by the directors over the assignees. One official bemoaned the "lack of corrective measures when workers were A.W.O.L. or walked off the jobs, or refused to work" and suggested that "these workers should be handled with the same type of corrective measures as a man who is in the Armed Forces." [24] The most caustic criticism was made by the superintendent of the Eastern State Hospital at Williamsburg, Virginia:

Selective Service would have accomplished more by declaring these so-called conscientious objectors unfit for military service because of mental disorders and let it go at that. It is my further opinion, that they are a group of men who are anarchistic in their thinking and general plan of living, and by and large are the most selfish group of men I have ever had dealings with.[25]

The preponderance of the c.o.'s supervisors, however, did not share these harsh sentiments. On the contrary, they found their charges "sincere, loyal and co-operative," [26] "competent at their work and eager to learn to do an even better job." [27] "This Service," said a Park Service official, "views favorably the work of the individual assignee. In almost every instance he did his work with willingness and to the best of his ability." [28] On farms, c.o.'s were generally reported to have worked earnestly and skillfully. "Guinea pigs" were especially commended for their good nature, perseverance, and steadfastness, while a hospital superintendent expressed the prevailing view toward those who worked in mental institutions when he said:

We have a feeling of deep obligation to these men and their wives who joined them here, for the quiet strength and endurance of their courage to give their best to a very disrupted service in our mental hospitals during World War II. Their serious yet cheerful response to the guidance of nurse and physician teachers, their quick adjustment to an entirely new situation, is an example that we hope will set a standard of service in the future.[29]

The religious administrative agencies held the service of the c.o.'s in high esteem despite the problems caused by the dissident elements. The churches concurred in the evaluation of the American Friends Service Committee, which was convinced,

both of the good faith, and the high ability of the large majority of the men. . . . With few exceptions, usually occasioned by unsatisfactory work or health conditions, the men have worked hard and well at the tasks assigned them. In many cases, the results accomplished have exceeded the expectations of their technical supervisors. This is noteworthy because the men have had neither the incentive of pay, nor the imperative challenge of preparing for battle. As a matter of fact, their work has often appeared futile and lacking in any immediate importance. Nevertheless, the work record of the men has been such as to make the government technical agencies extremely reluctant to have men transferred to other assignments, while a steady stream of requests for C.P.S. assignees has come in from government departments and public institutions throughout the country.[30]

VIII: The Struggle for Social Justice

To some men in Civilian Public Service objection to war was but one consequence of a social conscience which drove them to strike out at human injustice wherever they found it. The "social actionists," though a minority, were so articulate and vigorous that they seized much of the initiative in C.P.S. They startled, sometimes offended, often aroused the many c.o.'s who had come to camp intending merely to abstain from war. At times the passion for social justice swept with such force through C.P.S. that the whole current of life was altered and "service" became incidental to an intense struggle for "reform."

The Impulse to Social Action

Social conscience in C.P.S. stemmed from four roots. For some, it was the direct result of religious insight. Believing in the spiritual dignity of man and the brotherhood of all men, these c.o.'s could no more acquiesce in racial discrimination or the abuse of mental patients than they could in war.

Others engaged in social action because they had traced the roots of war to social injustice.[1] No firm peace could be achieved, they were convinced, unless poverty, starvation, intolerance, and conscription were attacked and removed in the United States and throughout the world.

A third group of c.o.'s was shocked into social consciousness when they witnessed in the course of their personal experiences in C.P.S.

the abuse of man by men—brutal treatment of mental patients, racial discrimination in communities where they worked, the misfortunes of fellow c.o.'s who ran afoul of the Selective Service Act. Injustice, seen first-hand, compelled action.

The isolation of the c.o.'s and the routine character of their work also stirred a social conscience. As men sought more challenging outlets for their energies, they turned with relish to grapple with issues of national import which could lift their vision beyond the camp limits.

The c.o.'s struggle for social justice had a surprisingly wide out-reach, despite the confining environment of C.P.S. and a reproving governmental eye. Neighboring communities served as laboratories for social experimentation. United States mail carried thousands of messages and appeals from C.P.S. to home town and White House. The pungent and iconoclastic *Pacifica Views,* a four-page leaflet of editorials, news items, and letters published weekly by a small group at the Glendora, California, camp under the leadership of a brilliant theosophist, bitingly indicted pacifist timidity and goaded all to do social battle.[2]

When the pressure for social action turned from general agitation to organized group effort, C.P.S. men usually appealed first to the religious administrative agencies to take action. These organizations did not always respond with quick enthusiasm, wondering if too many issues might not upset the C.P.S. applecart. In the end, however, the church committees usually met the demands of the social actionists, at least part way, and thereby became, albeit reluctantly, the most effective instrument in pressing the struggle for social justice.[3]

Some of the men, impatient at delays in Service Committee action, proceeded to act on their own. In the second year of C.P.S., a Conference on Social Action was precipitated at Chicago against the orders of General Hershey and the advice of the church agencies. Under the circumstances, its broader social objectives largely dissolved in the more immediate and striking consequences of a deliberate flouting of Selective Service authority.[4] Later, social action councils, organized in individual camps and units, stimulated anti-conscription campaigns, financial support of progressive and pacifist organizations, and, above all, protests against conditions in C.P.S, and the imprisonment of c.o.'s who had violated the law. A C.P.S. Union formed in 1944 also rallied interest in social problems, though its main function was to lay claim to the principle of collective bargaining on behalf of C.P.S. men.[5]

The c.o.'s attacked a wide variety of issues. Many were eager to help victims of war. The fast became a familiar practice in camps, men voluntarily dropping dinner once a week or substituting soup for meat, so as to save money for relief. Penniless as were many of the men in C.P.S., special collections and fund-raising projects were frequent. During 1945, Mennonite men personally contributed $15,-500 to their church's War Sufferers' Relief Fund; earlier, men from a Friends New England camp raised over $1,000 for Greek relief by fasts, contributions, and a benefit program of music and drama which they presented in Boston; a special Christmas drive by the relief training unit at Ypsilanti State Hospital topped $1,000; several Brethren units organized community-wide relief drives for clothing and money and shipped boxes of food, medical supplies, and clothing to Europe; an Oregon camp printed and distributed five thousand folders explaining relief needs and sold handmade Christmas cards to secure money for the purchase of relief packages.

C.P.S. men were equally devoted to the welfare of their immediate neighbors, offering voluntary service to the communities in which they lived. In their spare time they painted and repaired local schools and churches, assisted social agencies, made toys for needy children, conducted recreational programs, sang for the churches. At one camp, the continued absence at dinner of its leading philosophical anarchist led to the discovery that after work he milked the cow and fed the chickens of an aged farmer, two miles down the road, who had been laid low with rheumatism.

Three issues caused the greatest stir among C.P.S. men: conscription, racial discrimination, and the reform of mental care.

The Campaign against Conscription

All social action forces in C.P.S. were galvanized into fervent and co-ordinated effort in 1944 when Congressmen Andrew J. May, chairman of the House Military Affairs Committee, introduced an Army-backed bill to require a year of military training in peacetime for all males between seventeen and twenty-one. Supported wholeheartedly on this issue by the religious administrative agencies and other pacifist and church groups, C.P.S. men launched a sustained campaign to defeat the measure. Speakers, posters, articles, fliers, and an avalanche of letters poured out of the camps to arouse public sentiment against peacetime conscription and impress congressmen with "grass-roots" opposition.

Within the Brethren Service Committee, staff members themselves undertook to map a grand strategy, issuing "Memos on Action" to the men under their administration. When the propriety of so direct a legislative effort on the part of a tax-exempt institution was questioned, the series became "unofficial," issued by the C.P.S. administrative staff in their "individual capacity." "Anti-Conscription Campaign Goals" directed the line of activity week by week. Men were urged to write letters to congressmen admonishing them to vote "right." Next the staff called for "letters to the editor" and suggested how they should be written. Goal for December 6–12 was letters to personal friends in the armed forces. G.I.'s were urged to communicate their opinions to Congress. Then came the turn of labor and farm organizations to hear from C.P.S. The campaign effort was also well organized at the local camp level.

The Mennonites attempted a more decorous program, planning a "Conscription Institute" early in 1945 to consider the question "What should be the Christian attitude toward peacetime conscription now, and if it comes?" A carefully prepared outline of issues went ahead of time to representatives of the Mennonite units who were delegated to attend.

The campaign passed its peak when Congress recessed in the summer of 1945 without acting on the May Bill or on other proposals for peacetime military training, but C.P.S. watchdogs continued to hound every move in Congress or administration which threatened to revive the issue, ready at a moment's notice to swing their cohorts into a further barrage of mail, wires, and talk. The direct influence was probably minor. Legislators knew they could discount the opinions of confirmed pacifists. But C.P.S. did furnish much of the actual manpower behind the broad fight of religious, educational, labor, and farm groups against the perpetuation of conscription in peacetime, thus indirectly helping to shake off the shackles which they had found so objectionable.

The Testimony of Racial Brotherhood

The unpredictable social dynamic of conscientious objection drove the issue of race relations sharply to the fore in C.P.S., even though few c.o.'s entered camp with a ready-made concern on this question. The passion for racial justice grew as men unexpectedly faced concrete instances of discrimination or segregation, and many of them struggled to determine the action demanded of them by their religious commitment to a brotherhood of man. Once raised, the issue cut deeply. It split the ranks of C.P.S. between those who placed the problem on the periphery of conscience and those who regarded it as fundamental, between those who wanted to grapple headlong and uncompromisingly with injustices and those who sought methods of conciliation that would avoid outright conflict and categorical decisions.

The Color Line in C.P.S. For the most part, C.P.S. was an interracial community which accepted without distinction white and Negro, Japanese-American or Indian. The religious agencies and most assignees assumed that a man's race was quite irrelevant to his service as a c.o. They took it for granted that there would be no segregation or discrimination of any kind in the setting up of the camps and units, the assignments to work, or the conduct of camp life. This came as a surprise and even a shock to a few assignees of southern background, but their uneasiness usually did not last in an environment where racial equality was accepted as a matter of course by the administration and the majority of the camp. Project supervisors or foremen who showed signs of racial prejudice were likewise brought into line by c.o.'s who stoutly resisted any semblance of discriminatory treatment.

The race issue forced a serious dilemma, however, in regard to camps and units established south of the Mason-Dixon Line. Prevailing community sentiment opposed interracial association. Yet barring Negroes from such projects would in effect constitute segregation in C.P.S. and might even involve discrimination if the c.o. were thereby deprived of an equal opportunity to secure a desirable assignment.[6]

Failure of Selective Service to transfer two Negroes along with the rest of the camp, when it was moved from near Baltimore to the eastern shore of Maryland, led to a tense situation. The government officials maintained that community sentiment would not tolerate an interracial camp in the new location. Insisting that they intended no discrimination, they arranged attractive detached service posts for the two men in a school for colored delinquent boys, the first "social service" jobs to be approved for C.P.S. The C.P.S. camp, however, pressed for permission for the men to make their own choice. Selective Service finally yielded, allowing one of the men to stay with the camp, while the other preferred to go to the school.

The most serious crisis arose when C—— L——, a Negro professor at Fisk University, was classified 4-E and deliberately requested assignment to the camp at Gatlinburg, Tennessee. This was the camp to which he would normally have been assigned had he been white, but "unwritten law" tolerated no Negroes in that county overnight. The camp was profoundly agitated. A strong minority, mainly northern in background, demanded that L—— be assigned as he had requested or that the camp be closed. Another group, including most of the southern c.o.'s, insisted for diverse reasons that L—— should go to a camp above the Mason-Dixon Line. The issue was thrashed out in the Friends C.P.S. Committee, which finally decided to request L——'s assignment to Gatlinburg without making note of his race. Selective Service at first agreed to the assignment, but upon discovering L——'s race through its own records firmly refused, and finally sent him to Big Flats, New York, the Friends Reception Camp.[7]

This action prompted a thorough reconsideration by the Friends C.P.S. Committee (which included representatives elected by all Friends camps and units) of the propriety of administering or sponsoring C.P.S. projects which could not be interracial. On no issue was disagreement greater. A subcommittee on race policy proposed a clear-cut declaration that

all camps and special service units shall be operated on the basis of racial equality. In line with the unquestioned position of the Society of Friends, all qualified assignees, without reference to race, color or creed, shall be equally eligible for all units. . . . In any projects where progress toward the achievement of this policy cannot be made, we suggest the withdrawal of the unit.

Agreeing with the general objective, other Committee members were reluctant to adopt so categorical a policy threatening withdrawal of established units which might be rendering useful and important service, though not interracial. No decision was reached other than to study each situation where progress toward the goal of complete racial equality appeared not to be forthcoming, but the net effect of the consideration was to close the door to any new projects under Friends administration which could not be interracial.

Mennonites and Brethren, too, were forced to face the issue of racial discrimination and to clarify their policies. The Mennonite Central Committee was widely criticized for agreeing in 1944 to establish and administer a new public health unit in Mississippi limited to white assignees. The Committee defended its action on the grounds that an interracial camp was impossible in the situation, and that by carrying on a program which served both white and Negro families, and quietly demonstrating a belief in the brotherhood of man, more could be accomplished toward a solution of the race problem in the South than by having no project at all. Mennonite assignees appear generally to have supported this stand; the unit was fully staffed and the project was actually continued beyond the conclusion of the C.P.S. program as a volunteer service of the Committee.[8]

The Brethren Service Committee took much the same position. It avowed the principle of racial equality in its administration of C.P.S. and pledged itself to work toward elimination of racial discrimination in its units, but it would only consider withdrawal of units if it judged that "such action is the wisest method of achieving racial equality."[9]

Testing White Supremacy. Neither Selective Service nor the cooperating religious bodies nor the men themselves had foreseen that C.P.S. might challenge the prevailing pattern of racial attitudes and behavior in the communities where projects were located. But the practice of brotherhood occasionally took forms which violated the accepted color line and brought the C.P.S. unit squarely into conflict with local traditions of white supremacy.

Such a situation arose at Orlando, Florida, when in May, 1944, the C.P.S. unit gave a party in honor of the graduating class of a Negro high school. Within two weeks repercussions became serious, and the county commissioners asked for the withdrawal of the unit. At the request of the officials responsible for the unit's public health project, the commissioners relented to the extent of allowing those to remain who would agree to refrain from all future "interference" in the racial issue.

Under these circumstances, five men of the twenty-five-man unit asked for transfer and the remaining members asked the A.F.S.C. to determine whether to continue the work when it was contingent on observance of race segregation. Those who wanted to withdraw felt the issue of race had become of greater importance than the public health work in which they were engaged, and that the social customs which they were asked to accept "so infringed on the principle of racial equality and restricted individual action in working toward the elimination of segregation . . . that reasonable progress could no longer be made." [10] The others, no less concerned with the race problem, were convinced that effective action toward the betterment of race relations in the South could be taken only by those intimately acquainted with both white and colored attitudes and could come only by the gradual process of education. This would involve observance of the color line while working with white southerners to advance the Negro's physical welfare and offering encouragement to Negro self-help enterprises such as co-operative stores and credit unions. The men who wanted to stay aimed to "bore from within rather than penetrate from without." [11] Some of the men felt that continuing the health project would benefit the colored race more than withdrawal of the unit and that this should be the major interest of the c.o.'s on the unit, as it afforded an opportunity for action without arousing strong emotional reactions in the community.

Louis Schneider, Assistant Executive Director of Friends C.P.S., undertook to interpret to the State Health Department and local government officials the religious belief in the brotherhood of mankind which prompted the concern of many C.P.S. men to overcome racial prejudices and antagonisms. The officials finally agreed to "reaffirm their confidence in the good judgment of the unit concerning inter-racial activities and relationships," to require no rigid agreement by the men or the A.F.S.C. to refrain from interracial action, and to cancel their request for the transfer of specific members of the unit.[12] Four men persisted in their decision to withdraw, but the rest of the unit stayed on following this remarkable concession by southern tradition to the moral imperatives of conscientious objectors. The outcome confirmed the "gradualist" approach of C.P.S. to the racial problem.

Revolution in Mental Care

The experience of C.P.S. men in mental institutions haunted them. Some came close to neurosis. Others lost faith in the worth of man and tried to insulate their personal lives by a wall of deliberate indifference toward the human degradation which they encountered. But many c.o.'s could not stand idle before the plight of those in their care. The evils they discovered—the filth and disease, the inadequate buildings and equipment, the nauseating meals, the incompetent, untrained, overworked, and underpaid attendants, and, above all, the pattern of cruelty and violence which surrounded the daily life of the mentally ill—drove them to challenge the rutted course of institutional administration, the niggardliness of state legislatures, and the ignorance and apathy of a complacent public. They demanded and, in the end, succeeded in instigating radical measures of reform in many of the prevailing practices of mental care.

Bucking Complacent Administration. Usually they sought first the reform of conditions within their own institutions. They turned to the hospital administration, confident that ignorance alone could account for failure to check practices which flaunted official regulations as well as humanity. To their amazement, they found superintendents aware of the situation and generally tolerating it.

Some roughly rebuffed the c.o.'s with a stern warning to tend to their own jobs.[13] Other administrators pleaded that their hands were tied because no replacements were available if they should fire the attendants responsible. The c.o.'s recognized that the fewness of their numbers seriously handicapped efforts to accomplish reform, so they undertook to recruit reinforcements. The source of manpower to which they could most effectively appeal was C.P.S. itself. Through letters and personal visits, men in the hospitals sought to attract men away from the camps, asking them in the name of the desperate need to put aside a natural reluctance to undertake the thankless tasks of an attendant. As the ranks of the C.P.S. units gradually swelled, the shortage of female attendants appeared by contrast the more appalling. C.P.S. attendants, with the encouragement of the institutions, called on their wives to join them. In the summer of 1943 a regular women's service unit was started on an experimental basis at Byberry, including eight recruits from pacifist organizations in addition to the group of C.P.S. wives. These women worked as regular employees of the hospital, receiving the going wage for attendants, but they considered themselves active members of the C.P.S. group. The idea spread, and ultimately such women's units were established at many hospitals, noticeably boosting morale in the C.P.S. groups.

These recruits could at best provide momentary and limited assistance in the struggle for an improvement in mental care. As a matter of fact, some c.o.'s questioned on principle how far they should encourage recruitment of unpaid C.P.S. attendants. They feared that the dependence of institutions on C.P.S. labor might perpetuate or even lower the depressed conditions of work and inadequate pay of the regular attendants, postponing the frank facing of basic causes for degraded standards of attendant care.

A few superintendents sincerely welcomed the criticisms of the c.o.'s and co-operated in efforts at reform, but so ingrown were the abuses that even a joint attack made only a slight dent. The regular staff stood committed to the system in existence, bound by unwritten laws to support each other. The superintendent hesitated to repudiate a principal assistant in a controversy with a c.o. attendant over the handling of a patient, especially if there were dispute over the facts. In the meantime, the c.o.'s exposed themselves to the vicious resentment of the other employees by violating the code of confidence which had shielded acts of an individual from official censure.

Failure to reform the institutions from within led the more determined c.o.'s to challenge publicly the competence of the administrators—especially where the reformers felt that administrative vetoes had been primarily responsible for stalling their efforts. In the case of the Eastern State Hospital at Williamsburg, Virginia, an unusual combination of circumstances enabled the C.P.S. unit to play a significant part in precipitating a dramatic exposé of conditions and a drastic administrative reorganization. On the basis of evidence collected by the C.P.S. unit concerning mistreatment of patients and the incompetence of administration, the Governor of Virginia called upon the State Hospital Board to undertake a full investigation with public hearings. The administration strenuously attempted to deny responsibility, painting the c.o.'s as the chief source of the institution's troubles and ordering dismissal of the more outspoken members of the unit. The Board, however, recommended, and the Governor agreed to, the immediate appointment of another superintendent, the removal of a number of subordinate employees, and sweeping changes in other state mental institutions as a result of the conditions uncovered at Williamsburg.

Tracing the Ultimate Criminal. Most c.o.'s soon recognized that attacks on the institutions's administration failed to solve the problem with which they were basically concerned. The c.o.'s became convinced they would have to look behind the immediate administration, however faulty it might be, for the essential causes of the human tragedy in which they were involved. As they probed, the immensity and complexity of the problem staggered them. Lack of funds obviously hamstrung the best-intentioned administrator. When the average appropriation for mental hospitals in thirty-three states was less than seventy-four cents per patient per day,[14] it set definite limits as to what could be done to better the diet, recruit and train higher-type attendants, build attractive and sanitary housing, or furnish competent medical and psychiatric care.

Finances led directly to politics. Politicians could scarcely expect to arouse the enthusiasm of taxpaying voters by increasing the budgets of state institutions. Nor could superintendents who owed their positions to political appointment afford to initiate bold reforms or challenge legislative complacency.[15]

Outdated laws also stood in the way of needed reform. For instance, some states provided that persons could be committed to a mental institution by any physician regardless of his expert knowledge of mental disorders. This permitted not only errors of judgment but the occasional tragedy of "railroading" by ignorant relatives or vindicative acquaintances. Statutory provisions often made it extremely difficult for a patient to secure release.

Underneath the financial, political, and legal tentacles on mental care, the c.o.'s unearthed what appeared to them to be the taproot of the trouble—public apathy and prejudice. As a result of his own direct experience, the c.o. recognized the misconceptions of a medically illiterate public in regard to mental illness: that once insane, a person is always insane; that the mental deficient is insensitive to

physical pain or personal affronts; that all the deranged are danger-
ously violent and must be isolated and restrained. It became the
supreme aim of many c.o.'s to break through these barriers to intelligent and sensitive concern and to arouse a public conscience that
would support and demand a revolution in mental care. It was at this
point that C.P.S. men made their greatest and most lasting contribution to the betterment of the condition of the mentally ill, setting in
motion the slow but forceful processes of public education.

The Indictment of Cleveland. The strategy of reform through the
agitation of public opinion was most fully successful in Ohio, where
a nucleus of men at the Cleveland State Hospital started a campaign
which ended with the complete reorganization and expansion of the
state's program of mental care.

Finding Dr. Lee, the superintendent, belligerently unco-operative
in their desire for reform, the men quietly approached religious and
professional leaders and editors of the *Cleveland Press* in regard to
conditions at the hospital, and aroused keen interest in pressing for
major changes. Before the men could complete a thorough documented report, Dr. Lee caught wind of the c.o.'s intentions and
promptly asked Selective Service to remove eight of the leaders,
charging them with being troublemakers and ineffective employees.
Selective Service obliged. Under the circumstances, most other members of the unit were unwilling to continue at the hospital, and the
American Friends Service Committee asked that the whole unit be
withdrawn.

Far from quieting the stir, this action precipitated a crescendo
of vehement community criticism, spearheaded by the *Press* and the
Cleveland Federation of Churches. Armed with ammunition furnished by the dismissed c.o.'s, they demanded thorough state investigation. The Governor at last acceded. A grand jury under the
foremanship of Dr. D. R. Sharpe, president of the Federation of
Churches and one of the earliest confidants of the C.P.S. unit, conducted a firsthand three weeks' inquiry and produced a report devastating in its criticism, penetrating in its assessment of guilt, and
trenchant in its recommendations. "It would be a prison for the well.
It is hell for the sick," the report charged. The grand jury urgently
advised remedies ranging from the removal of specified personnel
to the construction of new buildings.

Pressed by state-wide concern over the revelations at Cleveland, the state legislature enacted a comprehensive revision of the mental health program, providing for a well-paid post of Commissioner of Mental Diseases and appropriating substantially larger funds for the improvement, maintenance, and servicing of the state's mental institutions. The organization of an active State Mental Hygiene Association, with one of the C.P.S. instigators as its executive secretary, assured continuity of the process of public education and action beyond the initial stages of legislative and administrative reform.

The role of the c.o. in the accomplishment of these reforms was symbolically indicated when a second C.P.S. unit went to work at Cleveland Hospital on the direct invitation of the new state Commissioner and a new superintendent. Under the judicious direction of the Mennonite Central Committee the unit established satisfactory relations with the hospital staff, including those who had held over from the previous regime.

The Mental Hygiene Program of C.P.S. As they sought to better the lot of the mentally ill, C.P.S. men expressed a need to share common experiences and co-ordinate their efforts to fulfill this function. Regional conferences of hospital unit leaders were arranged by the sponsoring agencies, sometimes including hospital superintendents and Selective Service officials. Of more lasting significance was the Mental Hygiene Program of C.P.S., started by a group of c.o. attendants in the Philadelphia area with the blessing of the National Committee for Mental Hygiene and some initial financial support from the religious agencies administering C.P.S. Ultimately the founders set up a permanent organization, the National Mental Health Foundation, which survived the dissolution of C.P.S.

The genius of "M.H.P." was its effective utilization of the first-hand experience of C.P.S. men in an attack on three critical and largely neglected problems of mental health—attendant training, legal reform, and popular understanding of the nature of mental illness.

A monthly periodical, *The Attendant*, was an innovation, for it dealt directly and exclusively with the problems faced by an attendant in his daily duties. It presented examples of good attendant practice and offered suggestions by leading medical authorities and out of practical ward experience on effective methods of treating and handling patients. Circulation of *The Attendant* extended much beyond the ranks of C.P.S., reaching virtually every mental institution in the country.[16] To help orient employees starting work in a mental hospital, the Mental Hygiene Program prepared and mimeographed a simple, forthright "Handbook for Psychiatric Aides," enlivened with humorous drawings.

An ambitious legal survey was undertaken to form the basis for the preparation of a model state statute governing mental care and institutional commitment. With the help of legally trained men scattered throughout C.P.S., the Program compiled an index and brief of all controlling state and federal laws. This set the stage for recommendations by the Pennsylvania State Bar Association and professional bodies in other states for revisions of the prevailing legislation.

Expansion of the organization's activities into the field of public education was the latest development. After preparing a series of popular pamphlets on mental patients and institutions, the Foundation teamed up with the Public Affairs Committee of New York in a "grass-roots" campaign to inform laymen of the real nature of mental disorders, their treatment, and prevention. One step was to distribute "Toward Mental Health," a Public Affairs pamphlet written by a former C.P.S. man, to state and city mental hygiene departments, social agencies, schools, and citizens' groups. This was followed by the inauguration of a thirteen-week series of transcribed radio plays entitled "The Tenth Man," (based on the general assumption that one person out of ten needs mental help). With Ralph Bellamy as narrator and an outstanding cast, the program had its New York debut over station WNEW on October 17, 1947.

Nothing short of a revolution is under way in the public attitude toward mental disease. Slowly, understanding is replacing prejudice and a sense of remorse is overcoming neglect. This is the most effective guarantee that legislative atonement for the inhumanities of the past will continue until those who lose control of their minds may have a decent chance to recover or at least to receive kindly and considerate care. The struggle of C.P.S. hospital attendants to institute reform, culminating in the ambitious and dynamic program of the National Mental Health Foundation, has been one active force in generating this revolution and pressing it forward.

IX: The Schooling of Peacemakers

Much of the early enthusiasm of pacifists for the program of Civilian Public Service was based on their confidence that it afforded an unprecedented opportunity to develop a superior breed of peacemakers. While soldiers trained to destroy, conscientious objectors could train for tasks of reconstruction, reconciliation, and harmonious communal living. Taking full advantage of compulsory attendance enforced by governmental authority, C.P.S. would nurture a worthy pacifist leadership and citizenry, equipped to practice the good life in the postwar world.

The paramount goals set for pacifist training demanded a social rather than an individualistic pattern of schooling for the c.o. The C.P.S. program was designed, said the Brethren, "to develop and exemplify ways of cooperative, non-violent, democratic and serviceable community living" and "to prepare for service of reconstruction both at home and abroad to alleviate the ill effects of war." [1] C.o.'s, said the Mennonites, would gain experience in the "familistic way of life" on which the church and the social order would both have to rely to survive barbarian force.[2] Such objectives repudiated the archindividualist who claimed in the name of his conscience the right to be free of all corporate responsibilities and to pursue unmolested whatever might be his personal aims. C.P.S. was not intended to become an anarchist hothouse. Its members were to be a brotherhood of "*creative* pioneers" joined together in common commitment to the development of a "New Third Order." They would grow into men of mature social conscience and disciplined spiritual life, who could "see and express the great spiritual values of the ages in the language and idioms of today." [3] A *society* of free men knit by ties of brotherliness was the ideal to be achieved within C.P.S., rather than a "state of nature" where each individual could demonstrate his freedom by his own peculiar forms of self-expression. If C.P.S. were to have a patron saint, it would be St. Francis of Assisi, not John Dewey of Teachers College.

The Assortment of Novices

It was left to the sixty-five hundred local draft boards to select the human material out of which the new community would have to be fashioned. They succeeded in throwing together in C.P.S. a motley crew of candidates, fantastically diverse in occupational, educational, religious, and racial background, sharing only one characteristic in common, namely, their refusal to participate in war, and even in that respect differing fundamentally on the reasons for their stand. Their upbringing and their convictions did not guarantee a co-operative disposition or a benign spirit. If anything, C.P.S. had somewhat more than its share of the tough-minded, the firm-willed, the zealously fanatic, and the sheer ornery, alongside many others whose good will and true friendliness warmed their associations through all the vicissitudes of the service.

Denominational diversity most impressed those in touch with C.P.S. Over two hundred religious sects and denominations were represented and over four hundred men claimed no religious affiliation (see Table VII). The Mennonites taken as a whole had almost 40 per cent of the total C.P.S. enrollment. But differences of doctrine and personal conduct and dress among their seventeen branches were greater than between many of the other denominations. Second in numbers were members of the Church of the Brethren, approximately 11 per cent of the C.P.S. enrollment. This denomination was even less homogeneous than the Mennonites. It included a much larger urban group, and a wide gulf separated their most liberal from their most conservative religious views. The Friends, comprising about 7 per cent of the men in C.P.S., were probably the most diversified religious group of all. Looseness of organization, the heritage of schisms which had rent the Society in the latter half of the nine-

TABLE VII. DENOMINATIONAL AFFILIATIONS OF C.P.S. MEN *

Baptist, Northern	178	Friends, Society of	951
Baptist, Southern	45	German Baptist Brethren	157
Catholic, Roman	149	Jehovah's Witnesses	409
Christadelphians	127	Lutheran (nine synods)	108
Church of the Brethren	1,353	Mennonites	4,665
Church of Christ	199	Methodist	673
Congregational Christian	209	Presbyterian, U.S.A.	192
Disciples of Christ	78	Russian Molokan	76
Episcopal	88	Unitarians	44
Evangelical	50	Other churches and sects	1,695
Evangelical and Reformed	101	Unaffiliated	449
		TOTAL	11,996 †

* *Directory of Civilian Public Service* (Washington, 1947), pp. xviii ff.
† An unexplained discrepancy exists between the total C.P.S. enrollment as computed by Selective Service (11,950) and that computed by N.S.B.R.O. as above).

teenth century, and, above all, the basic assumption of Friends that the perception of truth rests ultimately on the insight of the individual permitted a tremendous range of religious difference within a very small body. Near-humanist and extreme fundamentalist came into C.P.S. under the name of Friend. Many Friends were accustomed to "programmed services" and "pastoral churches" similar to the major Protestant denominations; others were devoted to the more traditional Quaker "meetings for worship" in silence or with spontaneous ministry of the laity. Differences in moral standards ran the gamut from the man who looked on dancing or smoking as carnal sin to the lad who complained that C.P.S. had infringed on his personal belief by discouraging an alcoholic New Year's Eve party in the camp dormitory. Some Friends scorned political and social action as worldly; others condemned any of their coreligionists who did not accept socialism as an inescapable Quaker testimony. The Historic Peace Churches may have furnished the central core of the C.P.S. "brotherhood," but it was hardly a core of firm and assimilable elements.

About 15 per cent of C.P.S. was composed of members of major Protestant denominations, with Methodists furnishing by far the largest segment. These men formed a fairly uniform "middle" group, theologically speaking, between the extreme fundamentalist sects and the "unchurched" c.o.'s who had no creedal basis for their religious views. Many of these men had been leaders in denominational youth organizations, and coupled strong loyalty to the established church with an active sense of the social implications of the Christian religion.

A relatively small number of Roman Catholics were assigned to C.P.S., as the clergy had refrained from condemning the war as unjust and there was no doctrinal support for the position of conscientious objection to all war. Financial difficulties led to the abandonment of a special camp administered by the Association of Catholic Conscientious Objectors; thereafter, Catholics were assigned to other C.P.S. camps with no attempt to group them together apart from other c.o.'s.

C.P.S. mirrored the kaleidoscope of independent religious sects peculiar to the United States. Almost every months's induction lists contained surprising additions to the roster of religious affiliations —Church of the First Born, Church of Jesus Christ, First Divine Association, Four Square Gospel, Walking Jerusalem, Zoroastrian, Vegetarian Pacifist Society. Jehovah's Witnesses were the most numerous of the sects, despite the fact that most Witnesses, insisting on exemption as ministers, had declined to go to C.P.S. and consequently had ended up in prison. The Church of Christ was largely represented. Christadelphians formed one of the most solid and loyal of the sectarian pacifist groups. A characteristic of most of the sects was their tendency to draw apart from the rest of the camp into their own circle, with the object of maintaining the solidarity of their particular habits and beliefs.

As religious training and belief was a legal qualification for assignment to C.P.S., no one expected the large number of men who had no religious affiliation of any kind. These included a group of about fifty War Resisters League members. Most of the men were city-bred and had arrived at their opposition to war as a result of their own thinking or the influence of friends without becoming identified with an established church. There was a prevalent assumption among both Selective Service officials and the Historic Peace Church administrators that these men were the most discordant element in C.P.S. and the chief source of "trouble." Such a conclusion is not warranted by their record of service and co-operation in camp activities or by the attitude toward them of responsible fellow c.o.'s. Some of the nonaffiliated men were among the most eager supporters of the community ideal of C.P.S., and the proportion of "dissidents" among them was not materially larger than among Friends, Methodists, or Brethren. What gave the nonaffiliated their reputation was probably the prominence of several of them in opposing the administration of C.P.S. by the religious agencies.

In education and occupational experience, C.P.S. men were almost as heterogeneous as in religion. Some had barely finished the primary grades of school. As a matter of fact, two assignees from Georgia could neither read nor write when they arrived at camp. Others were already outstanding professional leaders. Twenty-five doctors were in C.P.S.; there were also lawyers, physicists, botanists, and university professors. Skilled artisans slept and worked alongside college students. A large percentage of the men were farmers. C.P.S. assignees averaged considerably more education and professional experience than men drafted into the Army and Navy. This was particularly true of the group under Friends administration, who had an average of over fourteen years' education compared with about nine for enlisted men. Though the educational level of men in Brethren and Mennonite C.P.S. was lower than that in Friends C.P.S., it was still higher than that of military draftees. (See Tables VIII and IX.) The average level of intelligence of men in C.P.S. also appears to have been considerably higher than that of men drafted into the Army.[4]

Conscientious objectors came from all parts of the United States, but the largest number were inducted from Kansas, Pennsylvania, Ohio, and Indiana, the chief centers of population of the Historic Peace Churches. There was a dearth of c.o.'s from New England and the Rocky Mountain states.[5]

Mennonite camps maintained the greatest measure of homogeneity, though they too were affected by the ever-broadening stream of recruits inducted into the program. The Mennonites were so much more numerous than all other groups that they inevitably predominated in every project they administered, sometimes forming as much as 90 per cent of the unit. This made for a cohesion and group solidarity which other camps lacked. Most of the men had a common occupational interest—farming—and the educational level was more even, though lower, than in other units (about a tenth-grade average). This homogeneity the Mennonite Central Committee sought deliberately to preserve. The assignment of "liberals" to Mennonite camps was frankly discouraged to avoid a likely source of criticism of administrative policies and "misunderstanding" with the Mennonite men.[6] The Mennonite directors made plain their determination to prevent disruption of harmony and unity within their camp "families," though they did not seek to force conformity on the part of those who differed from the accepted pattern of life. They tried instead to prevent a concentration of non-Mennonite men at points where friction had arisen. A regional director urged that the more extremely evangelistic men—the Jehovah's Witnesses and the Amish—be transferred out of a camp where others were "getting confused" by the "overly large proportion" of non-Mennonites.

Diversity was most marked in the Friends camps, where Friends themselves rarely constituted as much as one-third of the assignees. Heterogeneity increased as time went on, and extremes were extended by new groups of arrivals. On the other hand, the educational

TABLE VIII. EDUCATIONAL DISTRIBUTION OF MEN IN C.P.S.*

	In Mennonite projects	In Brethren projects	In Friends projects	Army enlisted men	Navy enlisted men
Grammar	41%	16%	4%	29%	26%
1—3 years' high school	14%	14%	7%	33%	39%
High-school graduate	24%	32%	20%	28%	28%
1—3 years' college	15%	21%	28%	8%	5%
College graduate	4%	9%	20%	2% ⎫	
Postgraduate	3%	9%	20%	1% ⎬	2%
Average years of education	10.45	12.22	14.27	9.4	9.3

* Adrian Gory and David McClelland, "Characteristics of Conscientious Objectors in World War II," *Journal of Consulting Psychology*, XI (September–October, 1947), 248. Figures are adjusted to the nearest per cent. Original sources of the data on the education of Army and Navy enlisted personnel were, respectively, War Department, Bureau of Public Relations (as of June 30, 1944), and Navy Department, Bureau of Naval Personnel. (Table reproduced by permission of the American Psychological Association and the *Journal of Consulting Psychology*.)

TABLE IX. PREINDUCTION OCCUPATIONS OF C.P.S. MEN *

	Mennonite C.P.S.	Brethren C.P.S.	Friends C.P.S.
Technical and Professional Work (teachers, social workers, artists, accountants, draftsmen, etc.)	12%	18%	43%
Students	5%	12%	12%
Business Management, Sales and Public Administration (including clerical)	11%	16%	12%
Skilled and Semiskilled Trades (carpenters, painters, electricians, machinists, printers, etc.)	9%	21%	11%
Farming and Other Agricultural Work	59%	29%	11%
Factory Work and Other	5% †	4%	11%

* Adapted from Adrian Gory and David McClelland, "Characteristics of Conscientious Objectors in World War II," *Journal of Consulting Psychology*, XI (September–October, 1947), 248; and Leslie Eisan, *Pathways of Peace*, p. 56. The compilation of occupational background of C.P.S. men was originally made during 1945 by the personnel sections of the religious administrative agencies. (Table reproduced by permission of the American Psychological Association and the *Journal of Consulting Psychology*.)

† Approximate.

level in Friends-administered projects was higher and more uniform than in the other parts of C.P.S., and there was an unusually high proportion of professionally trained men. (See Tables VIII and IX.)

At best, the assortment of novices in C.P.S. was so diverse that many men had to complete a difficult process of social adjustment before they could hope to qualify as full-fledged colleagues in the brotherhood of peacemakers. So sharp were the personal differences, as a matter of fact, and so intense was the spirit of individualism, that the tensions within the C.P.S. community called for the highest qualities of self-restraint and skillful reconciliation as the c.o.'s underwent their ordeal of pacifist training.

The Indoctrinations of Religion

Leaders of Civilian Public Service expected that the intensive cultivation of religious faith would overcome the divisions among the men and construct a firm and common foundation for the pacifist community. As all assignees were presumably committed to belief in a single and universal God as the mentor of their conduct, would they not find unity in the course of spiritual exercise? From the beginning, an active religious program was encouraged both by the administering agencies and by individual efforts of C.P.S. men as the core of the peacemakers' curriculum. The church bodies, indeed, considered their supreme function in C.P.S. to be the religious stimulation of the men under their care.[7]

Yet few phases of C.P.S. were so generally disappointing as the attempt to weld together its diverse elements in a common discipline of the spirit. Even in the pious Mennonite environment, belief and behavior did not uniformly measure up to the prescribed standard, while the atmosphere of many of the other C.P.S. camps became so secular that those accustomed to conventional religious habit were taken aback and retired to nurse their faith in private or with nuclei of like-minded communicants. Something in the context of C.P.S.—the routine and isolated life, the enforced and often aimless labor, the absence of tangible marks of achievement in the struggle for spiritual victories, the successive checks on dedicated service imposed by government decree—dragged upon the incentive to religious endeavor. The longer C.P.S. continued, the more these factors loosened the fibers of faith and moral discipline. A strict, formal, and firmly led religious program undoubtedly kept many men from sinking deep into a mire of spiritual despond, but those who once succumbed to the frustrations of their circumscribed environment were rarely salvaged from their lethargy and laxity by artificial stimuli.

The Mennonites organized the most comprehensive and fully developed religious program in C.P.S. Each director was given primary responsibility for planning the religious life of his camp or unit. He was the "spiritual leader and counselor of the men," vested with the authority of the church over the spiritual nurture of the Mennonites who entered C.P.S.[8] He usually selected a "religious life committee" of seasoned assignees to help plan the organized activities and set the religious pace of the camp. Sunday services were held regularly, preceded by Sunday school. Ministers from neighboring churches were invited to officiate, with members of the camp staff or assignees picked by the director taking part in the music, prayers, or Sunday-school discussions. Everyone in camp was expected to attend, though there was no means of exacting compliance. Sunday evening worship, a midweek prayer meeting, and daily morning devotions were customary. The content of the services was orthodox. "What Sin Is Like," "The Remedy for Sin," and "When the Church Fails" were typical of the subjects treated. Occasionally services were arranged in nearby community churches for C.P.S. men. Bible study was an important part of the week's program in all Mennonite units.

The Mennonite administration strengthened local efforts by assistance from the outside. Each month a "pastoral" and an administrative visit were arranged to most camps and units. "Area pastors" were employed full time to visit the camps and units for extended periods, conducting series of religious meetings and study groups and counseling with the director and individual men. Some directors felt personally inadequate to counsel men in their spiritual problems, so the Committee appointed permanent pastors to devote their entire work to guidance of the religious life in the camps.[9] Intercamp religious conferences drew a good response from some men. Careful planning, centralized responsibility, persistent administrative stimuli, and the constant encouragement of the home churches and the entire Mennonite community were the vital factors in shaping the religious program in Mennonite C.P.S.

The Brethren, like the Mennonites, sought to develop an organized pattern of formal religious activities, but they depended more upon the initiative of the assignees than upon the responsibility of directors to secure results. The program was substantially weaker. To strengthen it, the Brethren ultimately encouraged the selection of religious-life secretaries by the various camps and units from among interested applicants, and usually allowed them three days a week on overhead time to develop religious projects and study programs. The secretaries spent their remaining time on projects, to maintain a close contact with the other assignees.[10] Together with a religious-life committee, the secretary was expected to map a long-term and short-term religious "strategy" of Sunday and midweek worship services, panels, study groups, special speakers, religious movies, book reviews, music programs, and institutes that would enrich the devotional life of the men and promote the "building of the Kingdom of God." The Brethren stressed interdenominational understanding through "My Credo" programs at which various groups presented their faiths. They also emphasized "action projects"—deputation teams to neighboring churches, volunteering for local church leadership, social services to delinquents and the underprivileged, supporting foreign missions. "Progress reports" by the secretaries were expected to chart the accomplishments of organized religion in their respective units and to provide the basis for further revaluation and strategic planning. Toward the end of C.P.S., a pastoral service located trained ministers in camps which desired them, either full or part time, to guide the religious program and counsel with the men.[11]

The Friends units had the least formal and probably the least effective religious life in C.P.S. Initiative was left almost entirely to the men themselves. This was not the result of any lack of concern on the part of the administration but was, rather, a reflection of Friends reliance upon the Inner Light to motivate religious expression. Freedom for individual seeking rather than a directed pattern of religious activities characterized Friends C.P.S. The Friends looked hopefully to daily meetings for meditation and prayer and a camp meeting for worship on Sunday to challenge the men's spiritual life, regardless of their denominational affiliations, though arrangements were made to transport men to churches of their own faith in surrounding communities or to provide opportunities for various forms of religious service at the camp if the men preferred. The more enthusiastic exponents of Friends ways expected that the meditation groups would become "powerhouses" which would "transform conventionalized, ritual-ridden religious programs into living cells of Christian brotherhood.[12] But the increasing poverty of vital spiritual growth drove even the Friends to try special devices of religious stimulation. Able and provocative religious leaders were invited to visit the camps and units to speak and meet with the men individually. Some of these subjected themselves to the daily routine of project work in order to cement personal relations and overcome suspicion of "outsiders'" preachments. When camp and unit educational secretaries were chosen, religious activity was included as one of their responsibilities.

Other denominations evinced an increasing concern for the spiritual welfare of their members in C.P.S. The Methodist Commission on World Peace belatedly appointed a full-time secretary-chaplain for work with Methodist conscientious objectors; he proceeded to enlist Methodist ministers near C.P.S. camps as chaplains to visit and counsel with the men. He wisely cautioned these men against sermonizing or perfunctory visits and urged their respect for a variety of points of view, including those which might be critical or even bitter toward the orthodox church. Several denominations encouraged circuit riding by their leaders among C.P.S. camps, and some arranged special conferences for their members in a particular area. Many C.P.S. men continued active denominational work, serving on church committees and attending their regular denominational gatherings. The Federal Council of Churches undertook a particular responsibility for men outside the Historic Peace Churches, arranging for ministerial visits and, in the case of the government-run camp at Mancos, Colorado, maintaining a camp chaplain for several months.

Those responsible for the religious evolution of C.P.S. were concerned to minimize fanaticism and promote respect for differing beliefs. The diversity of faiths had a certain value in cultivating broader religious horizons and an ecumenical spirit. "The pooling of religious thought," pointed out an assignee in a Brethren camp, "has caused men to rethink their beliefs and church teachings, see them in . . . perspective, sift, readjust and emerge with convictions which contribute to more effective living both personally and for the community. . . . [The men] cannot live, work and play together without having a greater appreciation of the other's view, greater understanding, and added tolerance." [13] Mennonites found that as a result of their intermingling with men of other churches they "were forced to rethink their own positions and to decide what was mere tradition and custom in their practices and beliefs as over against what was basic and biblical. Mennonitism, therefore, was subjected to searching analyses so that its weaknesses and its strong points were brought into clear light." [14]

On the other hand, there were real dangers of fanatical controversy among uncongenial sectarians and of the disintegration of some men's faith before the onslaught of contrary opinions or of sheer cynicism. The price of harmony and mutual fellowship seemed to be a ban on proselytizing joined with an attitude of "let live" toward all views, no matter how rabid or unorthodox they might be. The administering agencies made every effort to facilitate religious observances by every man according to his own faith, even the unique practices of personal hygiene of the two Parsee sun worshipers who entered a Friends camp. On the other hand, they discouraged pressure methods of conversion. Jehovah's Witnesses were usually asked to leave their phonographs and records outside camp. The Mennonites in particular resisted intrusion either by evangelists or enthusiastic recruiters for pacifist organizations. The issue arose pointedly in the case of a representative of the Fellowship of Reconciliation who wanted the director of a Mennonite camp to back his efforts to enlist supporters. In reply to a request for instructions, Orie Miller, the executive secretary of the Mennonite Central Committee, firmly laid down the following policy.

Our M.C.C. attitude to the F.O.R. in this C.P.S. program is exactly what it is to any other denominational group. We want to treat them with the respect that we expect from others. Our camps should be open to F.O.R. representatives getting in touch with their members in the same way that our camps are open to Methodists or Baptists or any other group for the same purpose. We however are not interested in opening our camps for F.O.R. propaganda or F.O.R. enlistment of members under any circumstances whatever. Neither would we expect them to be open to Mennonite propaganda were the tables turned.

A somewhat broader view of what constituted "propaganda" was applied by Friends and Brethren, but they too frowned on belligerent proselytizing either by visitors or by members of the camp. In government-administered camps, there was virtually no limitation upon visitors, either in terms of who was allowed to come or what was said. Pacifist leaders such as A. J. Muste and Frank Olmstead talked freely with the men, expounded their absolutist views, and indirectly encouraged the assignees to resist some of the government's directives or to walk out of C.P.S.

Attendance figures at religious activities were anxiously scanned by C.P.S. leaders. The Mennonites had by far the best quantitative record, but they too were troubled by periodic lapses of the spirit in their camps, and consciously tried to broaden participation by planning the types of programs most appealing to the men (Mennonite men seemed to take to music and Bible study) and by asking large numbers of men to take part in the programs. Individuals who had become apathetic were often directly upbraided. But differing religious views and modes of expression among assignees hampered the Mennonites in developing a program pleasing to all. On the average, 70 to 80 per cent attended church services in Mennonite camps and 50 per cent went to Sunday school. This did not satisfy Mennonite leaders, who expected a better attendance in C.P.S. than in the churches from which the men came. They explained religious "absenteeism" on several grounds: the Amish would sometimes appear only at services where one of their own ministers was preaching, others objected to Mennonite religious doctrine, a few "political" objectors dispensed with all religious instruction, and some who had been reared in strict homes took the opportunity in C.P.S. to rebel against church. Sheer lethargy and indifference took a toll.[15]

In Friends and Brethren units, rarely did as many as half of the men take any part in religious activity. The Friends daily meditation groups would often dwindle to the director and one or two men. Big Flats leaders were gratified with an attendance of 25 to 40 per cent at a Sunday vesper service, which was substituted for Sunday morning worship to broaden the appeal.[16] The chief factors responsible for this limited interest appeared to be a lack of vigorous religious leadership either from the outside or within the camps, a definite reluctance on the part of the C.P.S. administration to "force" religion upon the men, the wide mixture of religions which prevented a uniform approach, and especially the growing disillusionment of men with the practice of the "ideal" under the actual conditions of conscripted service in C.P.S.

Moral standards also troubled those responsible for C.P.S. To the more strait-laced directors, even the customary habits of the "liberal" element appeared questionable. Mennonite directors in keeping with their church principles deliberately tried to discourage smoking, but were often unsuccessful. Card playing was frowned upon in some camps, and drinking was strongly discouraged throughout C.P.S.—with limited effect as far as the personal habits of many men off the camp premises was concerned, though only a few violated the prevailing moral code in regard to liquor while within the church camps. The government, in the camps it administered, did not prescribe ethical standards for the men, and a more worldly atmosphere prevailed.

In some of the camps, the extremists among the liberals cultivated a Bohemian reputation, concentrating their eccentricities in a chosen dormitory. Fancy beards, rough and hard speech, slovenly beds and cupboards, snappy calendars and pin-ups, an unpredictable array of souvenirs and bric-a-brac, ingenious lighting arrangements, a conspicuously placed bottle of rye, and an air of studied individuality characterized the "Tobacco Road" or "Casbah" of C.P.S., shocking the conservatively bred c.o. or the Selective Service inspector but often revealing to the more penetrating observer a touch of play-acting or sophomoric revolt. Occasional instances of serious moral nonconformity, especially homosexuality, did occur, and thoroughly baffled the C.P.S. administration. C.P.S. men, on the other hand, rarely stole, despite their poverty, and were apparently seldom guilty of promiscuous relations with women in the neighborhood. On the whole, lapses in moral behavior were remarkably infrequent, considering the circumstances of frustration and boredom of C.P.S. life, and were certainly far less of a problem than in the armed forces.

Several experiments were undertaken by C.P.S. men on their own initiative to recapture the religious ideals which the C.P.S. program itself had failed to nurture. Some pressed an individual search for the roots of vital spiritual life through a personal discipline of prayer, meditation, and study. By common consent, a group of concerned men at Trenton, North Dakota, declared a "long recess" in organized activity, to "allow individuals to find new directions." [17]

Others felt the need for a corporate quest. At Coshocton seven men met by themselves regularly in meditation. A group statement of "A Way of Life" finally emerged, suggesting a "discipline of achievement," even in C.P.S., by which through "active desire, expectant receptivity and resolute action one's life may be advanced toward that greatest of all goals: making the most of one's potentialities as a son of God." Toward the end of C.P.S. twelve men attempted to deepen their experience of mysticism by securing assignment to a special camp at Cades Cove, Tennessee, where they would be able to seclude themselves in a permanent "retreat" with congenial spirits. The unit worked on a regular Park Service project but devoted their leisure time to religious study. Negotiations for transfers were so prolonged that the unit barely got under way before demobilization began to dissolve C.P.S., but the participants were convinced that the unity of the group had been a valuable asset in seeking the life of the spirit.

Individually, a great many men found that their religious understanding and spiritual devotion had grown deeper and stronger in the course of their experience in C.P.S. In a Mennonite evaluation 76 per cent of the men surveyed felt they had "gained some understanding of the Christian life which the home church needed," and 53 per cent reported an increase in the importance of personal devotions in their own lives.[18] In other parts of C.P.S., also, a large and significant number of c.o.'s experienced a marked spiritual growth. But five years of wartime alternative service did not succeed in binding together the whole body of c.o.'s into a "New Third Order," fired by the dynamic of religious fervor. C.P.S. never became a firm spiritual brotherhood, for the c.o.'s failed to find the bases of a common corporate discipline.

The Nurture of Brain and Brawn

Religion was to furnish the dynamic for the new order of peace-makers, but the training of intellects and practical skills was also considered vital preparation for the mission. "An educational program for the men in the camp will be a responsibility of the camp director," clearly stated the Selective Service Regulations, and no suspicion of governmental censorship restricted the content of such a program. The Historic Peace Churches were left full discretion to use C.P.S. as the pivot of pacifist indoctrination if they wished. Yet accomplishments were far from noteworthy, reflecting confused objectives and a failure to discover educational methods appropriate to C.P.S.

Sharp disagreement arose over the aims of the educational program. Should "education" be a definite course of study and training conducted during the time when men were not at work on projects? Or should the entire C.P.S. experience be considered an educational undertaking? Those who took the former approach conceived of education as a process of intellectual and technical preparation for a specific vocation or service, quite distinct from the performance of the physical jobs in C.P.S. and in a sense competing for time and attention with the work project. The educational program therefore had to be defended against too great an encroachment by project or camp responsibilities. Otherwise the men would not be able to achieve the goals set.

The second conception implied that education was the conditioning of the whole life for selfless and sacrificial service. There could be no conflict with the project or with camp responsibilities, for these were vital instruments of "education for life," providing an opportunity to learn by experience how to integrate body, mind, and spirit in human service. Such activities as were planned during free time should tie in closely with the development of the camp community and with effective performance of the project.

C.P.S. leaders also differed in regard to the basic content of the educational program. "Progressives" insisted that only "self-education" would succeed; hence the expressed interests of C.P.S. men should dictate the range and character of the program. Others said that this would only result in a hodgepodge of miscellaneous activities catering to individual fancies or needs, unrelated to the central objectives of the C.P.S. program, and well-nigh worthless as training for Christian pacifist leadership. They urged the necessity of planning out at least the fundamentals of a program that would help fit every man to make an effective contribution to peace and to the service of his religion.

Hodgepodge won out. The men imposed the final sanction of non-attendance on activities in which they were not interested, and individual interests, especially vocational, so far overshadowed any common interest in the pacification of the world that no educational program could live unless it spread out to meet a great variety of personal needs and desires. The nurture of peacemakers actually became a minor segment of the total educational activity of C.P.S., rather than the all-inclusive and unifying concern of everyone. As a matter of fact, pressures of camp and unit life were such that a great many men took little or no part in any formal educational activity in C.P.S. "The camps were *work* camps and not schools. When men worked a full day at physical labor out in the wind and cold

air, and then sat in a warm classroom, only the most interesting
classes could keep many of them awake. In addition, there were letters to write home and many other activities that competed for the
time of the camper." [19] There was furthermore a group of men who
shunned any educational program, regardless of its character, which
was sponsored by the religious agencies, in order to demonstrate
their scorn for the "administrators of conscription."

The chief impetus for the "whole life" concept of C.P.S. education
came from the Friends. The first director of Friends C.P.S. (who
was the president of Fisk University and a long-time champion of
relating education to practical life) envisaged a three-cornered educational system, with the C.P.S. camp, the Friends college, and the
Friends meeting each contributing to the life of the C.P.S. assignee,
thereby producing the desired unity of "body, mind and spirit." Formal classes could obviously be only an incidental part of a program
designed to accomplish such aims; as a matter of fact, the director
envisaged a "community-centered program, worked out in an in-
verted College House Plan where teacher and students live together,"
which would integrate both project and neighborhood activities into
the C.P.S. assignee's personal educational roster.[20]

This vision of the education of c.o.'s by means of "a Progressive
School workshop, a Harvard House Plan, an Adult Education Forum,
a Manual Arts School and a Missionary training center all rolled up
in one" was too much for the men to digest, even in the most experimental mood of Friends C.P.S. After a three months' attempt to
enroll the men as charter pupils for the New Education, the first
Friends educational secretary (a brilliant, intuitive, provocative
British pacifist mystic) resigned, despairing that under the prevailing conditions any such plan could work.

The Friends were slow to recover an educational initiative after
this demise. Though camp and unit educational secretaries were
later selected and a three-man educational staff was organized at
headquarters, they spent most of their time servicing special interests of C.P.S. men and guiding the orientation of new assignees to
C.P.S. They did not succeed in developing an integrated educational
program aimed directly at preparing C.P.S. men for human service
or specific pacifist leadership.

The Mennonites approached closest to having and carrying out

clear-cut educational objectives. Cautious about indulging in grandiose experimentation, they put major emphasis on four tasks: careful instruction in the Mennonite "heritage and mission in the world,"
understanding the Christian's relation to the state and the community, deepening Christian experience, and promoting personal
growth, especially through the development of skills and aptitudes
that would have occupational value to the men in their camps. The
Mennonite Central Committee did not want to divorce its organized
educational program from the rest of life in C.P.S.; it felt that "the
intimate daily contacts of camp life—working together, worshipping
together, living together, solving common problems together" would
produce "the real educational experiences of C.P.S." But the Mennonites introduced a basic "curriculum," as an integral part of the
camp program, pivoted on a three months' "core course"—"Our Mennonite Heritage"—which every camper was most strongly urged to
take on arrival in C.P.S. This course "unified camp experience around
the central objectives of the Mennonite faith and the Christian peace
principle." The importance attached by the Mennonites to organized
educational activities was also evident in their administrative organization, which included from the start an educational director
in each camp, an educational secretary attached to the headquarters, and an "educational advisor" or "dean" who provided the
counsel of a professional educator in planning the over-all program.[21]

The Brethren educational program was frankly eclectic, but it
catered skillfully to the great variety of interests among the men in
camps and units in addition to initiating the most effective of all
C.P.S. educational techniques—the specialized school, where men
with a common interest were brought together in one camp or unit
for a course carefully planned around the subject of their concern.

Two primary aims for the Brethren program were set forth by
the national education secretary, a dynamic and well-trained assignee with a "feel" for the C.P.S. situation: "(1) growth of each
individual in development and application of his life plans and (2)
peaceful change of our culture and its institutions in the direction
of our ideals." [22] Recognizing the importance of relating the educational activities to the individual choices of the men, the Brethren
made deliberate efforts to encourage the participation of assignees

in both the planning and execution of educational projects and to develop "methods consistent with democratic education." This resulted in a strong emphasis on discussion groups and panels in order to allow maximum expression of the different points of view of the c.o.'s.

In the end, six main phases of education emerged: (1) basic orientation for C.P.S.; (2) training for the work projects; (3) preparation for reconstruction and relief service; (4) vocational and professional training; (5) the study of pacifism; and (6) the fostering of special group interests such as farm and community life, co-operative living, and industrial relations.

Orientation. Induction into C.P.S. was an experience without parallel for most assignees. Unspectacular and almost furtive compared with marching into the Army, it had the same element of poignant uncertainty of what was to follow. Few anticipated the peculiar problems of personal adjustment which faced them in a routine of life so foreign to their accustomed ways. They knew little of the kind of work expected of them and less of the men with whom they would be associated day and night. They were particularly unprepared for the accumulated tension and the gnawing discontent which came to permeate much of C.P.S.

Yet for a long time no deliberate attempt was made to "orient" a new arrival or to assist him in making a quick and congenial adjustment. At camp a member of the staff welcomed the newcomer, checked his medical record, told him the time of the next meal, and directed him to his bunk. If time did not press, the director interviewed the man and explained the nature of the project and administration. Then he was on his own, with the aid of cordial—or taciturn —old-timers to explain the camp routine, expose the current camp "crisis," or brief him on the eccentricities of the project foremen, the camp director, the "Second-Milers," and the fellow who bunked across the barracks.

Where the camp program was largely prescribed by the administration and a full schedule of activities ran through the day, the new assignee could fit into the regular pattern without difficulty—especially when camp morale was high and the group well-knit. But often a man was left "free" to find his own way in the midst of sharp dissensions, a haphazard program, and widespread lethargy. Furthermore, the camp staff and many of the mature and experienced campers felt a certain diffidence about intruding too vigorously and immediately upon the newcomer. They wanted to avoid an impression of pressure or regimentation. All too often, this resulted in leaving the new man without a sense of direction. He drifted uncertainly into the routine of work and camp life, not knowing what was really expected of him or what he could look forward to accomplishing in his C.P.S. service. This aimless initiation quickly sapped away whatever enthusiasm the assignee may have had when he entered upon his wartime vocation.

Into such a vacuum of purpose, the counsels of gripers swiftly flowed—with demoralizing effect, especially upon younger men. One sophisticated and bearded cynic made a profession of solicitously "enlightening" each new arrival as to the folly and sinfulness of performing more than "eight cents worth" of work a day—the equivalent of the cash allowance provided by the administrative agencies.[23] As the crusade of dissent grew in numbers and fervor, efforts to capture the allegiance of the newcomer became systematic, persistent, and effective. The movement was dynamic, though unorganized. It had purpose, though its immediate action was necessarily negative. It had *esprit de corps,* though the incentive was primarily the challenge of opposition rather than a real community of spirit. Whatever the shortcomings, dissent offered a meaningful pattern of life to many a C.P.S. "freshman," confused and perhaps a bit forlorn in a situation where signposts were few and the appointed guides were gracious but uncommunicative.

The failure of automatic orientation became especially apparent and serious in Friends projects because of the extraordinary diversity of the assignees. By the third year of operation, the Friends convinced Selective Service that a "reception center" for new assignees, with a well-defined program of orientation during the first three months of service, was essential. Men entering Friends C.P.S. from locations east of the Mississippi were henceforth sent to the camp at Big Flats, New York. Forty seasoned men were chosen to form a continuing nucleus of pace setters who would demonstrate the methods and the "spirit" of C.P.S. A full-time educational director conducted a course on the background, purposes, and organization of C.P.S. and invited speakers to describe each of the main C.P.S. projects and the philosophy and role of each of the administering agencies. A personnel director interviewed every man on arrival, kept in touch with him during orientation, and conferred with him at the end of the period to determine a suitable future assignment—if possible, in line with the man's own interests and preference. Colonel Kosch usually added fireworks by a scheduled interpretation of Selective Service policies, which never failed to prompt a barrage of indignant rebuttals from the newly oriented.

The Brethren and Mennonites, rather than selecting a particular camp as an orientation center, devised a twelve-day "conditioning" program for new arrivals in any camp where the approval of the work-project superintendent could be secured.[24] In personal counseling with each man the director sought out dependency problems, personal habits, social attitudes, and educational background. An hour's talk gave the assignee a bird's eye view of the neighboring community and of the camp's public relations. The nurse discussed physical and mental health. Along with typhoid injections and instruction in first aid and safety precautions, physical hardening got under way through graduated doses of manual labor. Meanwhile, the nature and the purpose of the work project were outlined by those in charge. Following this intensive period of full-time orientation, the process of indoctrination continued in the general educational program, especially in the three months' "core course" on Mennonite Heritage.[25]

Those who hoped that orientation would act as a sedative for discontent in C.P.S. were disappointed at the results. Because the program started so late, much of the stability and balance gained by new assignees at the reception center was dissipated as they moved into their next assignments and collided with hardened dissidents. As a matter of fact, some additional causes of friction arose as a result of the Friends reception program. Assignees were often reluctant to leave the Big Flats camp at the end of orientation and make way for others, especially when their wives had settled down to income-producing jobs in a neighboring town.

The program did justify itself on other grounds. The assignee knew promptly where he stood in regard to the responsibilities expected of him, the prospects for other types of service in the future, and the policies and character of the agency under which he was serving. He

could make his own particular interests and problems evident at once
to the staff, and the staff could in turn help plan in advance to meet
them. Orientation could not change the character or mood of C.P.S.
so late in the season, but it did make adjustment to an abnormal
situation simpler, swifter, and more satisfactory for the new man,
giving him a larger measure of self-confidence as he came to understand the terms of his new existence.

Project Training. After persistent prodding from the religious agencies, Selective Service officials and project superintendents belatedly
recognized the importance of telling C.P.S. men not only what they
were to do and how, but why. Being neither educators nor skilled
managers of men, the government technical men had failed to understand the necessity of "selling" their projects in order to secure
competent service from their workers. Finally, three years after the
opening of C.P.S., Selective Service Directive No. 17 authorized the
appointment of a full-time project training assistant in each camp
and allotted one hour a week of project time for a training program.
Unfortunately, while the officials were discovering the connection
between work performance and intelligent job training, their conscripted labor was developing a chronic allergy to "Project." Months
under an unimaginative foreman, leveling stumps, clearing brush,
digging postholes, or pulling weeds was enough to kill even robust
work incentive.[26]

Nevertheless, project education did tend to lift the men's morale
and infuse them with a fresh vision of the significance of their work.
Project officials personally explained the wherefore of the work, outlined their plans, listened to criticisms, and attempted to answer
questions thrown at them by the men. Such conferences were supplemented by concrete instruction in the work techniques to be
used. The best training programs were carried on in the hospitals,
where men saw at once the need of skill and information in order to
perform their assignments adequately.

Preparing for Relief and Rehabilitation. Many men in C.P.S. set
as their supreme goal of service a chance to aid victims of war and
to help in the reconstruction of war-devastated countries. The religious agencies administering C.P.S. were particularly responsive
to this interest, as they were themselves actively engaged in foreign
relief operations. Training for relief service consequently became the

most carefully conceived and, on the whole, the most successful of the educational efforts in C.P.S.

From the very start, groups in almost every camp and unit vigorously studied languages, first aid, methods of disaster relief, and the history and social conditions of particular areas. Later, a group of twenty C.P.S. men were selected for a full year of specialized training at Columbia University, alongside sixty Navy and civilian candidates for military government posts. This program was planned and directed by Professors Philip Jessup and Schuyler C. Wallace. It included language and comprehensive area studies related to the countries where the men were expected to serve, in addition to particular training for the C.P.S. assignees in problems of relief and rehabilitation administration. Preparation for relief service reached a climax when 250 men were assigned to a "C.P.S. Training Corps" for three months of intensive specialized instruction at Brethren, Friends, and Mennonite colleges, with the prospect of overseas appointment immediately thereafter. A sharp setback quickly followed when legislative opposition and the timidity of Selective Service caused the plans to be canceled and the men to be returned to regular C.P.S. projects.[27]

Though this cruel frustration dampened the ardor of some, many determined to pursue their training as best they could, hoping for a future break. Several sympathetic hospital superintendents and directors of other special service projects were willing to co-operate with their units and the religious agencies in planning a definite program of reconstruction studies as an integral part of the assigned work, sometimes even reducing the hours of work in favor of study. Men with a persistent interest in relief were gradually grouped in these institutions.

The practical character of the courses in relief and reconstruction strongly appealed to the c.o.'s. Simple technical skills were constantly stressed, such as cooking, truck driving, carpentry, nursing, sanitation, mental hygiene, group leadership, and language facility. Of greater significance to the Committees than professional qualifications were qualities of personality and spiritual development that would make for stability, buoyancy, co-operativeness, and congenial personal relations in tense situations within as well as outside the relief team. These points were driven home by study and by visitors who had carried on relief work and could depict concrete problems which had to be met on the field. The special relief training units each selected a particular area for concentrated study—usually France, Germany, or China. This enabled the group to unify its efforts, especially in learning the language, collecting adequate study materials, and securing the assistance of competent outside leaders.[28]

Problems arose where a relief training group was part of a larger unit which did not share its interest. Yet most of the relief training programs held up remarkably well considering the collapse of plans for actual service, the time-consuming demands of the immediate work assignments, and the general deterioration of morale which beset C.P.S. A large number of men devoted themselves more consistently to such training than to any other educational activity in C.P.S.

Opportunity to put this training to use in overseas service never materialized under C.P.S. because of the "Starnes Rider." [29] But toward the end of the program, the Brethren Service Committee succeeded in working out an arrangement whereby Selective Service transferred 350 men to a "C.P.S. Reserve" to work as cattle attendants on U.N.R.R.A. relief ships. These "seagoing cowboys" were selected from among men nearly eligible for discharge, and received pay from U.N.R.R.A. (the same as regularly employed attendants). This opportunity was immensely popular. Those who were chosen felt that at last they were engaged in actual relief service, even though there was little connection between their preparation and the work which they were called on to do. Men were afforded one other outlet for relief work in C.P.S. when a limited number were assigned to sort, repair, and ship supplies in the relief depots of the three Historic Peace Churches.[30] Ultimately, after discharge, many of the men who had taken the training offered in C.P.S. realized their ambition for direct service in the war-devastated areas through appointments with U.N.R.R.A. or private relief agencies. The Service Committees, particularly, recruited many of their relief workers from among the men who had completed their terms in C.P.S.

Vocational Training. The longer C.P.S. dragged on, the more anxiously men considered what they would do after they were released. This concern assured a ready response for vocational training activities.

A man could secure instruction from qualified fellow assignees in manual skills and trades, livestock breeding, poultry husbandry, farm accounts, bookkeeping, commercial art, principles of co-operative marketing, music, and creative writing—to mention only a random and limited sampling of the classes offered in different camps. Arrangements were made for C.P.S. men to enroll for the correspondence and extension courses of state agricultural colleges, the University of Chicago, and other such institutions.[31] Textbooks, study outlines, visual education aids, and visiting lecturers were rounded up by the educational secretaries to supplement resources within the camps.

Men in special service projects in metropolitan areas enjoyed particular advantages in securing vocational education. Many were able to take regular courses of study during their free time, at outstanding academic institutions and professional schools. Some men secured vocational training as part of their own assigned service. A remarkable instance was the full professional course in nursing offered to members of the unit at the Alexian Brothers Hospital in Chicago, the first of the C.P.S. "special projects." Class time was counted as work, and instruction was given by qualified doctors and Brothers in the structure and function of the body, the treatment of common diseases, public health, the emergency care of wounds and injuries, and the ethics of the nursing profession. Eleven members of the unit graduated from the Alexian Brothers School of Nursing as R.N.'s. Many others attained a practical familiarity with such advanced nursing techniques as intravenous injection, oxygen therapy, and the application of drugs.

For many of those in C.P.S., vocational preparation required completion of an academic or high-school degree. The religious agencies succeeded to a limited extent in securing credit from colleges (mainly those connected with their respective denominations) for satisfactory work completed by men while in C.P.S. This spurred some men to competent intellectual endeavor and shortened the period of schooling they required after the end of their C.P.S. days. During the last two years of C.P.S., a program of vocational counseling and testing supplemented actual training.

A few men had the intellectual and physical stamina to press forward on individual research for advanced degrees. The Pulitzer Prize was awarded in 1945 for Carleton Mabee's biography of S. F. B. Morse, largely completed in C.P.S. as a Ph.D. dissertation. Barriers to creative achievements were usually too great, however, to enable the more highly trained man to pursue his vocation while in C.P.S.

Peace Studies. Only an earnest few in the C.P.S. community carried their zeal for a peaceful world to the extreme of serious and continued study as to how it might be achieved. Pacifism was a major emphasis in the C.P.S. curriculum during the first "honeymoon" years. But by 1943, formal classes dealing with pacifist principles and international affairs were languishing and, except for the Mennonite core course and passing reference in the other orientation programs, these subjects went begging for attention.[32] While fiction circulated from the camp libraries, the best literature on international problems and pacifism lay largely neglected.

Attempts were made to provoke a more positive response by special programs and visits of challenging speakers. The American Friends Service Committee held an Institute of International Relations at Big Flats camp at which the future of Germany was discussed by Norman Thomas, a high official of the former German government under Bruening, and other able lecturers. The Mennonites planned panel discussions on "The Church and Current World Peace Proposals" to center attention on the San Francisco Conference of the United Nations. A group at the Brethren hospital unit at Fort Steilacoom, Washington, organized a "pacifist information center" which collected a library of pacifist writings and published a mature but short-lived pacifist periodical, *Viewpoint.* The Fellowship of Reconciliation strove to maintain active pacifist study groups, supplying them with well-prepared study guides and a steady barrage of suggestions and advice by mail, as well as personal visits of their staff. One "School of Non-Violence" was organized at the Big Flats camp and another at Powellsville to provide an opportunity for intensive study of the philosophy of pacifism and methods of pacifist direct action. The schools lasted two to three months and were built around a series of week-long visits by national pacifist leaders such as A. J. Muste, Douglas Steere, and Richard Gregg. Even this major effort did not succeed as planned. Attendance was smaller than expected —partly because men from other camps and units who wanted to attend the schools could not secure Selective Service permission to transfer. But local interest was also surprisingly meager. Only about 15 of the 150 men already at Powellsville took part.

The conclusion is inescapable that most C.P.S. men deliberately played truant from schooling when it concerned the intelligent application of their beliefs to affairs of state. Alibis of work weariness, unimaginative educational planning, or the enervating effects of conscription do not explain this curious lethargy, because vocational and relief training, we have seen, blossomed despite such handicaps. The sad fate of peace studies in C.P.S. seems rather to reveal a basic trait of American conscientious objection—the shunning of responsibility for public policy. Most men simply had no interest in peacemaking at the national or international level. Pacifism was their code of personal action, not a social force. The c.o.'s cold-shouldered the great problems of organizing the postwar world because they never considered these issues particularly relevant either to what they were doing today or to what they wanted to do tomorrow. They had no personal intention of challenging the judgments or decisions of the world's leaders—hence why bother to study the perplexing course of human events?

Special Schools for Group Interests. Among the most successful educational ventures were specialized "schools" organized to enable a group of men with a particular interest to pursue a systematic study of that subject. The Brethren Service Committee and the Co-operative League jointly sponsored a School of Co-operative Living at Wellston, Michigan. The Mennonites developed an elaborate Farm and Community School in connection with their model rural settlement near Hagerstown, Maryland. One of the earliest efforts was undertaken by a group interested in the arts, who congregated at Waldport, Oregon, during 1943. By the end of 1944, others had followed: a Psychiatry and Christian Service School, an Education Workshop, a School of Industrial Relations, a Latin-American study group, a School of Race Relations (in the South at Gatlinburg, Tennessee).

Selective Service was persuaded to permit men to transfer from various camps to take part in a school of their choice. Thus the group was knit by a serious and common purpose vital to the success of the project. Furthermore, the courses were better planned and co-ordinated than most C.P.S. educational programs. The religious agencies and other concerned organizations made every effort to supply adequate resources and leadership.[33]

The Literary Product of C.P.S. Apart from the formal educational activities, a great variety of intellectual, journalistic, and artistic ventures sprouted from the fertile imaginations of C.P.S. men. These played a significant part in the c.o.'s general "schooling." Though spontaneous and largely unrelated to any specific educational goal, they provided channels for creative self-expression.

A group in almost every camp and in many special service units published a bulletin, paper, or magazine concerning their segment of C.P.S. life and thought. Some were hastily-thrown-together collections of local news items and tidbits of personal interest to the men at a particular camp. A few, such as *The Compass,* were noteworthy accomplishments in the quality of descriptive and editorial writing and in graphic illustration. A number of the C.P.S. groups decided to leave written and pictorial records of their service and prepared and published "yearbooks" or magazines describing their work and accomplishments. *Smoke Jumpers* splendidly portrayed the work of the fire-fighting unit at Missoula, Montana; *Of Human Importance* gave a vivid illustrated account of the service and training of the male nurses' unit at Alexian Brothers Hospital in Chicago; *Service for Peace*—issued by the men of the Fort Collins, Colorado, Camp—included, along with montages of camp scenes and project activities, portraits of each of the assignees for the benefit of posterity; *On Sequoia Trails* similarly enshrined the camp at Three Rivers, California.

C.P.S. also produced "thought-pieces." *Pacifica Views* was the gadfly of C.P.S., but avowed as its chief aim "to stimulate serious thought concerning both the basic and the particular problems confronting the present generation of pacifists." Out of the "arts" camp at Waldport, Oregon, came *The Illiterati,* a periodical of prose, verse, and design, product of the most sophisticated element in C.P.S. The editors proposed "creation, experiment and revolution to build a warless, free society"; suspected "tradition as a standard and eclecticism as a technique"; and rejected "war and any other form of coercion by physical violence in human associations." Their contributions, in addition to a demonstration of skillful craftsmanship in printing, included such distinctive items as "The Mikado in C.P.S." (parody à la Gilbert and Sullivan), "Katharsis at Wyeth" (poetry in the obscure style), and "The Metaphysical in Graphic Art" (expository essay by the publication's chief illustrator).

C.P.S. publications suffered a high casualty rate. Each of these creative efforts had to surmount the constant competition of work projects for time and energy, as well as the continuing dissolution of their editorial personnel through transfers to other camps and units. Nevertheless, the stream of written words flowed with astonishing regularity and volume, as the c.o.'s sought a more productive "education" than they could secure through the formal programs.

The Practice of Self-Government

The exercise of administrative responsibility and group leadership within the framework of C.P.S. completed the apprenticeship of the budding peacemakers. If competence in self-government tests the capacity to govern, the c.o.'s, with some notable exceptions, failed to demonstrate conclusively their fitness to assume the direction of the world into the paths of peace.

They were, to be sure, denied a full and fair chance to try out their managerial hands. The officials of Selective Service—and also the religious agencies—were reluctant to explore the ultimate consequences of pure democracy by entrusting complete discretion to the assignees in the running of C.P.S. affairs. As a matter of fact, Selective Service refused to admit that the men had any right of self-government in C.P.S. Authority stemmed from the President down, not from the camp up.[34] Nevertheless, in practice, many areas of responsibility were open in the daily operation of camp and unit life, and later even in regard to the selection of staff and the determination of policies by the religious committees. But the C.P.S. community as a whole showed an aversion to self-discipline and was often loath to undertake obligations which required a substantial expenditure of voluntary effort.

Camp Government. Each of the religious administrative agencies offered the men a share in the government of their own camp or unit, but self-government meant something quite different under Mennonite auspices than it did under the Friends or Brethren. The Mennonite conception of responsibility, essentially theocratic, called for the choice of a camp council *by the director,* to help him conduct the camp program. At his request, and subject to his approval, it would plan religious services and recreational activities, prepare reports, supervise the "housekeeping," and possibly confer with the project superintendent and foremen regarding work problems which concerned the camp. As confidence in the reliability of the councils grew, the directors tended to place increasing responsibilities upon them and to seek their advice on critical issues. As a matter of fact, a new director, accustomed to centralized "rule," sometimes found the council's increasing self-reliance difficult to understand. In one case, a Mennonite director about-faced after an initial period of tension and humbly admitted that he had not been "wise enough to see sooner" that the men really expected him to delegate responsibility as had his predecessor.[35] Yet there was never any uncertainty as to the final authority in a Mennonite unit. It lay with the man who had his appointment from Akron, Pennsylvania, and not with the men who were conscripted from Washington, D.C.[36]

The Friends and some of the Brethren camps at first attempted to become nutshells of pure democracy, with self-determination carried to the limits possible under Selective Service regulations. Every facet of life in C.P.S.—the time of rising, the daily work assignment, the director's correspondence, the latest statement of Service Committee policy, the discontinuance of the "midnight snack," the disciplining of an assignee for refusal to work, the tidying of the dormitories—was considered the business of the whole camp. Each man should have an equal share in making decisions, said the exponents of c.o. "democracy"; even representation was suspect. The camp or unit "meeting" was the final seat of authority and at first the only acceptable vehicle for collective action. The unwieldiness of this arrangement, particularly when the meeting could confidently be expected to split into irreconcilable elements on every issue, shortly led to the election (*by the camps*) of representative "councils" empowered to transact business but ultimately accountable to the camp as a whole. In a number of camps, "work policy committees" were also elected to represent the men in regard to problems on project; where the technical staff agreed, they actually took on the responsibility of assigning men to their daily jobs.

This pattern was novel. Newcomers to some camps were amazed that there were "no orders or disciplinary machinery." Many defended it as the only administrative system appropriate and feasible among c.o.'s. The Coleville meeting insisted that community government was the "only valid method of organization in social groups if men are to be treated as human beings of ethical integrity . . . men can grow only as they can be entirely responsible in making choices." A convert was convinced that "our morale and accomplishment are naturally dependent on the felt and *freely fulfilled* obligation to give effort." [37]

Unfortunately, the results of self-management by individualists did not always satisfy. The prim tastes of Selective Service inspectors usually suffered rude offense on a tour of a "self-managed" dormitory, with its array of unmade beds, clothes-laden rafters, muddied floors, and unkempt lockers. Even c.o.'s wearied of interminable talkfests without decision in camp council or meeting. The anarchy of freedom when the camp organization attempted to tackle the problems which came before it disillusioned many assignees with the blessings of "democratic discipline," and many called for a surrender of assignee responsibilities and a retreat to authoritarianism. In addition an increasing number of c.o.'s deliberately declined responsibility for camp government because they felt it would involve them in administering conscription.

Control of Staff Appointments. The setbacks to self-government in C.P.S. did not prevent c.o.'s from demanding an ever broader share in its administration. The more audacious advocated that the assignees have final control over all C.P.S. staff appointments both in the camps and in the Service Committee headquarters; generally, C.P.S. opinion was satisfied with an opportunity for consultation or nomination in regard to the appointment of personnel *within* the camps and units.

The Service Committees were at first taken aback by the bold bid of the men to share their authority; gradually they acquiesced; finally they became thoroughly convinced of the value of the assignee's participating hand. At first, the executive directors made all major personnel appointments, including those of camp directors, assistant directors, nurses, dieticians, and their own headquarters staff. As it became evident that a main qualification for success in a C.P.S. appointment was the person's capacity to secure the respect and cooperation of the men, the executive directors increasingly selected for their staffs assignees who had demonstrated competent leadership in their camps and units. The next step was to consult a camp for suggestions prior to making an appointment in that camp; finally, systematic methods were developed for nomination of staff by the assignees.

Representation. Assignees also secured definite recognition in the policy-making organs of the Service Committees. At first the demand of C.P.S. men for representation in policy was countered by regional conferences arranged by the National Service Board, to which the camps and units sent delegates. These were welcomed as a chance to air grievances and exchange views between men and administration, but did not satisfy the desire for a real share in the responsibility for decisions. The shrewd c.o. felt "that the conferences are somewhat dishonest in lending an appearance of democratic-control-from-below to a program where such control does not exist. We have found that the unanimous opinions of camp meetings, as well as the decisions of such conferences, are ignored by the administrators." [38]

To meet the criticisms that C.P.S. was operated by too remote a control and that its top leaders, especially committee members, were insensitive to camp interests because they were not chosen by campers, the Friends C.P.S. Committee invited proposals looking toward a system of assignee representation at the national level. A rotation plan was first tried. Three camps or units in turn selected representatives to attend the monthly C.P.S. executive meetings, with expenses paid and with full right to report, speak, and vote. Through them, concerns from all Friends C.P.S. were to be channeled for presentation. They usually prepared a statement following the meeting which was circulated to all the unrepresented units. This had the obvious disadvantage of limiting a particular unit's actual representation to once or twice a year, and the representatives almost always came to the Committee without previous background or contact with it. To correct these defects, the Committee approved a more elaborate and very much more expensive plan. Each camp, including those in the Far West, could choose a representative who would attend the committee meetings regularly; the special service units were grouped and one representative was chosen by each group. This produced a body of twelve full-fledged assignee members of the Executive Committee, and they became, by virtue of their deep interest and sense of responsibility, the most dynamic element of the Committee. Each month one of their number was designated to stay in Philadelphia as a member of the staff and as co-ordinator of assignee concerns in preparation for the meeting to follow. This was the most advanced stage reached at any point in C.P.S. in granting policy-making power to assignees.

The Brethren confined assignee representation to an Advisory Council, elected by the camps and units, which met twice a year simultaneously with the Brethren Service Committee to discuss problems of concern to the men. After conferring with the administrative staff, the Council presented recommendations for action to the B.S.C., but the Service Committee then made its decision *without* the participation of the men. This system did not satisfy the more self-conscious advocates of representation, and the Advisory Council persistently sought equality in the formulation of policies that determined the direction of C.P.S. The Service Committee insisted, however, that it must retain the voting privilege as a "creature" of the Church of the Brethren, though it conceived of its role as that of a "genuine partner" with the men in mapping the direction of C.P.S.[39]

The Mennonite Central Committee did not adopt a formal system for the representation of C.P.S. assignees in its deliberations. The Committee was strictly, and necessarily, representative of the seventeen co-operating Mennonite bodies, and these in turn considered that they were the appropriate agents to represent and interpret the interests of their members in C.P.S.

The development of an effective system of representation was the most satisfactory of the attempts to school c.o.'s in self-government within the framework of conscription. The results of the gamble went far toward easing the sharpened tensions between assignees and administration, though critical differences of point of view at times still occasioned conflict.[40] The outlook of the religious agencies became steadily more liberal and understanding because of the direct contact established between their executive committees and the opinions of assignees through the careful consideration of the men's concerns in open meeting. An unforeseen consequence was the tempering of radical and extremist opinion among C.P.S. men. At first the representatives elected by the camps were among those who were most outspoken in their criticism of Service Committee policies and of the whole C.P.S. system. These were the men who had most vigorously agitated for a representation scheme, and they came "with blood in their eye" to the first meetings when they could speak with a voice of authority. But these very men mellowed in their association with the Committee as they met not the expected cold front of opposition but a sincere eagerness to meet and solve the problems which they raised. They were especially sobered by the responsibilities of decision as they weighed the full consequences of alternative choices in the light of a fuller knowledge of facts than they had been able to secure in camp. Shortly, also, the awareness of the vital role which the representatives were to play in affecting Service Committee policy led the camps and units to choose the most responsible, rather than the most vocal, of their leaders to represent them. These tendencies dissolved some of the distrust and opposition between the men and the religious agencies which had been growing steadily since the early days of the program. The two sides never completely "made up," but a working partnership was forged, based on mutual respect, if not on a full unity of point of view.

X: The Restraint of Liberty

THOUGH legal provisions for the alternative service of conscientious objectors were conceived in tolerance and tempered by respect for religious liberty, neither the executive nor the legislative branch of government effectively fulfilled its commitment to freedom of conscience.

As applied by rigorous administrators, the law became restrictive and even punitive. Selective Service officials, clothed with virtually unlimited legal authority over the c.o.'s, shackled their personal behavior, curtailed their opportunities for significant service, and denied them pay and other perquisites of drafted men. Congress did nothing during the war to liberate the c.o.; instead, it imposed additional restraints. It excluded foreign service for C.P.S. men, denied financial assistance to their dependents, refused them compensation for injuries or death suffered as a result of their compulsory duties, and stalled their final release from service. As a result, the law-abiding inmate of Civilian Public Service actually had to pay stiff penalties for his conscience—the limitation of his civil liberty, the likely frustration of his incentive to service, and the probable impoverishment of himself and his family.

The Restrictive Arm of Selective Service

The Selective Service System was the chief agency of restraint upon the conscientious objector in C.P.S. It exercised a meticulous and firm custody over the whole of a man's life from the moment of assignment to the date of discharge, devising a network of regulations and directives to assure the responsible discharge of his duties.

His movements and conduct were subject to continual supervision, his infractions to peremptory discipline. The control of Selective Service was all-encompassing and its net effect was sharply restrictive.

The acts of Selective Service had the sanction of law by virtue of an executive order of the President,[1] endowing the Director of Selective Service with full authority to determine the work the c.o.'s were to perform, provide for its civilian direction, maintain general supervision and control, make assignments, and "prescribe such rules and regulations as may be necessary to carry out the provisions of this order." The Director in turn exercised his authority by issuing and publishing in the *Federal Register* detailed "regulations" governing the basic organization and operation of C.P.S. Since these regulations were authorized by law, they too were legally binding on all concerned. From time to time, Selective Service also issued specific "directives" to the religious agencies, technical staffs, and camp and unit directors, setting forth instructions to be followed in their administrative responsibilities. More flexible than the regulations, the directives were in effect just as forceful, for they could, if necessary, have been reissued as an executive order.

Selective Service was at first content to specify a minimum of formal regulation, leaving rather wide discretion to the religious agencies in the evolution of the C.P.S. pattern and the control of the men. But as time went on, the government officials concluded that the agencies were guilty of administrative incompetence and laxity, and the number, length, and detail of regulations and directives increased. This tightening of Selective Service control proved to be an irreversible process. Once an administrative directive was issued, the religious agencies were never able to regain responsibility for the subject covered, though their remonstrances occasionally secured some modification or relaxation of the rule imposed.

The McLean Memorandum. The position of Selective Service was unequivocally set forth in a memorandum issued by Lieutenant Colonel Franklin A. McLean, who asserted the virtually unlimited legal authority of the Director of Selective Service over conscientious objectors drafted for "work of national importance." [2]

All assignees were "required to do any work which the Director of Selective Service declares to be work of national importance as long as it is directed by civilians." Theoretically this could include defense work such as the making of munitions or the erection of fortifications, but Selective Service had no intention, according to Lieutenant Colonel McLean, of exercising its authority to demand services of this kind which were repugnant to the conscientious objectors. Using his discretion to administer the law as he thought wise, the Director of Selective Service would aim to approve projects about which the c.o.'s would have little scruple. Under no conditions, however, did the c.o.'s have a right either individually or in a group to decide whether they would or would not do the work, whether it was or was not defense work, or whether it was or was not "work of national importance." [3]

Lieutenant Colonel McLean stressed that "the program is not being carried on for the education or development of an individual, to train groups for foreign service or future activities in the post-war period, or for the furtherance of any particular movement." The Director was under no obligation to assign a man to work for which he was particularly prepared or which he might wish to do or which he regarded as socially significant. "Assignees can no more expect choice of location or job than can men in the Service, or a great many civilians. Camps are located primarily where the work is to be done."

Selective Service recognized no area in which the individual conscientious objector was free from control.

From the time an assignee reports to camp until he is finally released he is under the control of the Director of Selective Service. He ceases to be a free agent and is accountable for all of his time, in camp and out, 24 hours a day. His movements, actions and conduct are subject to control and regulation. He ceases to have certain rights and is granted privileges instead. These privileges can be restricted or withdrawn without his consent as punishment, during emergency or as a matter of policy. He may be told when and how to work, what to wear and where to sleep. He can be required to submit to medical examinations and treatment, and to practice rules of health and sanitation. He may be moved from place to place and from job to job, even to foreign countries, for the convenience of the government regardless of his personal feelings or desires.

The presence of religious agencies in the administration of the program did not, according to Lieutenant Colonel McLean, modify in any way either the primary purpose of the program, the authority of Selective Service, or the accountability of the conscientious objector.

The Historic Peace Churches had agreed to provide food, clothing, medical attention, heat, and light for all men ordered to camp by Selective Service. In return they could select the camp staffs, recommend the assignment of men to various camps, and carry on religious, educational, and recreational programs. They had no responsibility either for determining the work to be done or for directing the c.o.'s in their work. While on the job, assignees were entirely under the control of the project superintendent and "subject only to his orders." During nonworking hours assignees were under the control of the camp director appointed by the Historic Peace Churches. The camp director was responsible in turn to Selective Service.

This individual serves in a dual capacity being a representative of the church sponsoring the camp and also of Selective Service. As agent of the church he is responsible for the physical and spiritual welfare of the men in the camp. For Selective Service he carries out and enforces certain regulations such as the granting of leaves and furloughs, accounts for the men assigned to the camp and prepares various reports. As far as Selective Service is concerned the camp director is in charge of the camp.

The role of the Historic Peace Churches in Civilian Public Service was thus conceived by Selective Service to be that of an *agent* to carry out and enforce rules and regulations which Selective Service felt necessary to insure adequate performance of the work assigned.[4]

Line of Command. The legal mandates of Selective Service were implemented by a "line of command" stretching from the Director himself through responsible subordinates on his own staff to the staffs of the religious and technical agencies and ultimately to the lowly c.o. who, as "private," was to obey as ordered. The hub of the administrative system was "Camp Operations Division." To its chief, Colonel Lewis F. Kosch, long-time army colleague of General Hershey and former official of the Civilian Conservation Corps, the Director delegated his authority in all matters affecting the service of IV-E assignees, whether they were actually in camps or in other types of projects. General Hershey carefully supported the authority of his subordinates by insisting that theirs was the responsibility for decision except on issues of major policy (such as the opening of government-operated camps or the undertaking of a new type of service). Camp Operations Division was frankly jealous of its prerogative and was at pains to define explicitly its line of authority to each person who held a position of responsibility in the administration of the program. The director of a camp, even if he was appointed by a religious agency, was accountable to Selective Service for the execution of its orders in regard to the c.o.'s under his charge. The superintendent of a work project, though a civil service employee of another government department and responsible to it for the operation of the project, was likewise considered a representative of the Director of Selective Service in handling the assignees. The superintendent or official head of a hospital or special unit was designated as the "responsible official," combining the functions of both camp director and project superintendent, and was held directly accountable for carrying out every Selective Service "administrative instruction." [5] Even the executive directors appointed by the religious agencies were included in the line of command, as the persons finally responsible under Selective Service for the men assigned to their agencies.

Selective Service insisted that its authority to require these officials to carry out its orders *in regard to the conduct and service of the assignees* was complete and final, and superseded any conflicting responsibility. Selective Service would not concede to the religious administrative agencies, to government departments in charge of the technical work, or to the institutions using C.P.S. men the right to step between itself and the c.o.'s and contradict its policies or decisions.

As a matter of courtesy, Selective Service acceded to a request of the religious agencies and forwarded directives and instructions to camp directors through the National Service Board. But this did not alter the "line of command." When the religious agencies balked at passing on an order they felt unreasonable, Selective Service simply dropped the procedural courtesy and rerouted the order directly to the responsible official.

Instruments of Control. In practice, Selective Service depended upon two instruments for the exercise of day-to-day control over C.P.S.: it demanded and reviewed methodically a battery of reports covering the activity of each assignee and the general conditions of his life and work, and it maintained an inspectorate which regularly made an on-the-spot check of each camp and unit. The system of checking was highly effective. Sooner or later the c.o. and his administering agency would hear if their conduct had transgressed the prescribed groove. Explanation and correction were expected. Infraction of the rules rarely escaped ultimate detection, though Selective Service continually complained of the sloppiness and slowness of many of the camps in making their reports.

As a matter of fact, the channels of administration became easily clogged by the volume of reports demanded, for C.P.S. was not spared the bureaucratic passion for paper. From each camp, hospital, and special unit, Selective Service exacted the following:

DSS Form 52.	Quarterly Work Progress Report. (to report work accomplished by C.P.S. assignees).
DSS Form 52-A	Monthly Camp and Personnel Report.
NSB Form No. H105	Monthly Time and Work Report (showing by name the status and work performed by each assignee; illnesses, absences, etc.). Basis of the personal record of each assignee; prepared in quadruplicate, 3 copies for "channels."
NSB Form 112	Report of Furlough Granted. Prepared in quadruplicate, 2 copies for "channels," 1 given to assignee as his pass.
NSB Form 121	Report of A.W.O.L. Quadruplicate, 3 copies for "channels."
DSS Form 51-A	Daily Record of Ill or Injured Assignees.
DSS Form 51-B	Report of Serious Illness or Injury. Submitted if a man is "sick in quarters" for more than 3 consecutive days.

NSB Form 119 and NSB Form 119-A. Receipt, Discharge or Transfer of assignees. Submitted through channels within 24 hours after assignee leaves or arrives at unit.

At intervals of roughly six months, barring some special crisis, a representative of Selective Service appeared personally at each camp and unit to examine the performance of the c.o.'s and of the administration. These inspections were thorough in their review of the physical aspects of C.P.S.—inventory of government equipment, standards of "housekeeping," upkeep of fire-protection equipment, quality of food, quantity of work accomplished, business management, accuracy of records, and so forth. Where conditions fell short of the Selective Service standard of a well-run program—a chronic situation in numerous camps—the inspector bluntly informed the camp director or project superintendent to that effect and turned in to headquarters a caustic report which in turn was forwarded to the administrative agencies with appropriate remarks by Colonel Kosch or Mr. Imirie. Inspectors were quick to detect and criticize:

barracks in poor condition—crowded, lack neatness and order because of large amount of personal belongings each man keeps around his bunk; arranging of bunks at odd angles and the hanging of curtains should be discontinued; center of barracks should be clear with bunks placed against and at right angles to the side walls alternating head and foot; appearance of grounds poor—cans and bottles scattered around near the barracks, trash cans full; latrine and bathhouse poor; dirty towels lying on floor and wash bowls dirty.[6]

On occasion, Selective Service did not hesitate to question the competence of the camp personnel and even to press for their dismissal. The agencies took the criticism seriously, though they were reluctant to let Selective Service wield the hatchet on their staffs. Instead, they struggled to erase their faults through improving administration— a process which often ran afoul of the recalcitrant individualism of the c.o.'s and usually failed to satisfy the passion of Selective Service for swift, decisive action. Nevertheless, the general record improved until the inspectors were rating most camps "good" except for the quality and quantity of their food.

Inspection, however rigorous in regard to the physical operation of C.P.S., was inept in its assessment and appreciation of human relations. The Selective Service visitors, with remarkable consistency, managed to stir fresh trouble wherever they went, leaving behind a turbulent, discontented, and often embittered group of men and a confused, harassed staff. This was not altogether their fault, for some c.o.'s delighted in "scientific needling" until the officials, completely exasperated, were driven to brandish their authority. The inspectors were also handicapped by their inescapable role as representatives of the conscripting authority which the men so deeply resented. But, in addition, the officials were so obsessed with the technical observance of administrative routine—instead of with the accomplishment of constructive service—and were so unresponsive to the personal problems and concerns of the men that they appeared cold, arbitrary, and unfeeling.

"No" Men. The restrictive disposition of Selective Service in regard to the c.o.'s was dictated in part by the wartime pressures of intolerant segments of legislative and public opinion. At several points Congressional action or inaction froze on C.P.S. men restraints which Selective Service would have removed, and complaints from veterans' groups that c.o.'s were being treated too liberally tended to tighten the reins. But external pressures rarely forced the hand of Selective Service when it was not already so inclined. The forbidding administrative countenance of Camp Operations Division reflected above all the personality, habits, prejudices, and ambitions of its staff, and particularly of the most forceful member, A. S. Imirie, who was executive officer to Colonel Kosch, the chief of the Division.

Before the Division was organized, Imirie had already been hired to help organize the C.P.S. program. Privately, he admitted that he was opposed to the participation of the religious agencies in a "dual administration" and firmly intended to see this arrangement to a quick end, after which the government would run the show by itself. In the meantime, he ran his part of the Selective Service System with sufficient efficiency and shrewdness to forestall public criticism and to merit the approbation of responsible government officials.

Imirie persistently criticized the weaknesses and unruliness of the religious groups, and undermined their standing with Colonel Kosch and General Hershey. At the same time, he blocked measures proposed by the religious agencies to facilitate their administration—for instance, in regard to the closing of camps where the project had become unsatisfactory. His objections usually persuaded his superiors; this in turn aggravated their difficulties and reinforced

Imirie's argument that they were incapable of effective administration and should be entrusted with lessened rather than increased responsibility.

Imirie also advocated a firm subjection of the c.o.'s at all times to the controlling hand of Selective Service. This policy, he felt, not only diminished the danger of adverse public relations but enabled Selective Service to fulfill its commitments for manpower to other government departments and opened the way for it to intervene in the administration of the religious agencies whenever they failed to enforce the desired control. Charged with oversight of the records, he insisted on a strict accounting for the time of every C.P.S. man, and made sure that regulations were observed to the letter or that the appropriate penalty was imposed. He was loath to allow exceptions: the desire of a man to take part in one of the C.P.S. special schools was not a satisfactory reason in itself for granting a transfer; the straits of a man's dependents did not mean that he could expect permission to use his spare time to earn money; imminent impairment of a man's mental or physical health did not qualify him for removal from service in a mental hospital.

Imirie's influence was enhanced by his own undoubted capacities among men of lesser ability and by the sense of collective responsibility within the Division. On several occasions representatives of the religious agencies sought to go around Mr. Imirie and negotiate directly with Colonel Kosch. It was even suggested to General Hershey and Colonel Kosch that Mr. Imirie's presence was a serious complication in the administration and that his replacement would be desirable. This never received favorable consideration.

The restrictive policies of Selective Service were, however, far more than the work of one man. Restriction was implicit in the concept of responsibility held by the entire Selective Service organization. The officials understood that their task was to run the program not in the interests of the c.o.'s but in the interests of a nation at war. They considered themselves under a definite obligation to get each c.o. to do his proper duty by his country, and to do it in a way that would satisfy President, Congress, and public.

According to the Selective Service philosophy of administration, to modify or relax regulations to meet recommendations of the c.o.'s or the churches would admit weakness under pressure, invite further demands, and thereby complicate the administrative process. General Hershey, for instance, conceded at the end of the program that he would favor pay for c.o.'s in any future service; nevertheless, he still insisted that to have granted pay *during* the war would have been a mistake, because it would have involved surrender of a fixed position and exposed administration to further importunities. Firmness, not flexibility, was therefore the credo of Selective Service administrative policy.[7]

The C.O.'s Regulated Life

With the Army as a model, Selective Service comprehensively ringed the daily life of the c.o. with its regulations. It saddled him with six main duties. He was required to remain in the camp or unit to which he was assigned at all times except when on duty or on "authorized missions or leave." He was bound to move to another camp or project whenever ordered. He was obliged to perform assigned work "promptly and efficiently." He was responsible for the conservation and protection of government property. It was his further legal duty to keep his person, clothing, equipment, and quarters "neat and clean." Finally, his deportment, both in and outside of camp, was under regulation "to bring no discredit to the individual or the organization."[8]

Hours of work. Selective Service demanded that all c.o.'s in camps work at least as many hours a week as the government required of its civilian employees. The prescribed work week therefore lengthened as the country's war effort intensified and bore no necessary relationship to the amount of work required for the project. From 40 hours in 1941, the week stretched to 44, 48, 51, and ultimately 54. The adjustment was accomplished primarily by adding a part or all of Saturday to the work week.

When there was insufficient work to occupy the full effort of the c.o.'s during the longer hours, some of the men proposed a "piecework" plan to stimulate better and more efficient service; the project supervisors would lay out the amount of work expected for a day and allow the men to return to camp if they finished it in less time than the official workday. Selective Service insisted, however, that assignees put in the full number of hours required, even if it meant "stretching out" the project and excusing some loafing on the job.

V-E Day did not bring an immediate relaxation of the work of
C.P.S. men, although most government departments were dropped
back to a 44-hour week by Congressional action. Selective Service
held that the reduction did not apply to C.P.S. so long as servicemen
and war agencies were unaffected. Not until August 20, 1945, did
the c.o. regain a 44-hour week and the privilege of having his Saturday afternoons free.[9]

A different criterion governed the work requirement for c.o.'s in
hospitals and special units. The men were expected to serve the
same number of hours as the regular civilian employees of the institution to which they were assigned.[10] This meant, in effect, a considerably longer week than in camp—sometimes running 72 hours or
more—because of the heavy work loads in state institutions confronted with manpower shortages.

Leaving Camp. Selective Service permitted no c.o. to leave camp
without official sanction. Six months after C.P.S. began, it set precise conditions for the granting of such permission, taken virtually
intact from the Army manual. Two and a half days of furlough could
be earned by a month of service, and furlough was not permitted
until it was earned. In cases of illness or death in the assignee's family,
emergency furlough could be secured, to be made up by subsequent
service if not yet earned. Specific approval by Selective Service headquarters was needed for all other absences. Not more than 15 per cent
of the camp could have furlough at any one time, and all furloughs
could be restricted by the project superintendent in fire season or
other times of emergency.

The camp or unit director could issue "leaves" to men to go off
the grounds when they were not at work, but a strict record was
required of the time allowed and the place the man was going;
later the number of leaves was restricted (two week ends per month
in camps and a day and a night a week in hospitals). Written authority from the director for an absence from camp was necessary, and
the c.o. had to carry a copy of this authorization with him.

For "administrative reasons," for disciplinary action, or for no
announced reason at all, furloughs could be suspended or revoked by
any responsible authority. Occasional blanket suspensions for all
C.P.S. men on order of Selective Service emphasized the fact that
even "earned" furlough was a privilege. In April, 1943, a ban was

placed on all furloughs for twenty-two days without explanation, though rumors spread that the government feared furloughed c.o.'s would clog the railroad lines and obstruct a large troop movement. Similar concern for the congested transportation system led Colonel Kosch to restrict furloughs during the Christmas season in 1944 to not more than 10 per cent of a camp or unit. The c.o.'s could hardly understand why the movements of their modest numbers should suddenly acquire such national importance.

In the hospital and special units, assignees were entitled to the vacation and off-duty privileges of regular employees, instead of furlough and leave. The superintendent was instructed to control and keep a record of all absences.[11]

Living and Working Off-Grounds. More stringent instructions in regard to hospital "leaves" were issued when Selective Service discovered that superintendents were allowing men to secure employment in their time off-duty and, in several instances, to live with their wives in the neighboring community. In response to protests by veterans' organizations over the "privileged" status of the c.o.'s, Administrative Instruction No. 4 explicitly directed that all assignees "must live on the grounds of the Hospital or other Institution" unless some other arrangement was specifically approved by "headquarters," and also made any outside employment of assignees subject to Selective Service approval. Superintendents could and frequently did request such approval in individual cases on the grounds that men who led a normal life outside of regular duties and were able to relieve financial desperation by some personal earnings would render more effective service. Selective Service stiffly turned down most requests for living with wives, and the superintendents would not risk losing their units by defying categorical instructions. On the other hand, Selective Service was more lenient in regard to jobs when superintendents declared that the assignee's health and project efficiency would not be impaired and the prospective employer gave assurance that other laborers would not be displaced and no public relations problem would result.[12] Each superintendent then had to make a monthly report listing jobs acquired during the month and jobs discontinued, verifying to Selective Service satisfaction the acceptability of each man's job.

Regimental Discipline. In order to exact compliance with its regulations, Selective Service evolved a disciplinary system designed to greet each violation with an appropriate punishment and thereby discourage repetition. The religious agencies had originally been granted major responsibility for discipline.[13] But their peculiar notions of "redemptive" discipline did not satisfy the regimental temper of Colonel Kosch and his associates, who insisted that unless offenders were sharply penalized for breaches of duty all semblance of respect for the obligations of service would evaporate. To stiffen the disciplinary fiber of the religious agencies, the Director of Selective Service demanded a full and immediate report from the camp director whenever an assignee refused to work ("R.T.W."), was absent from camp without leave for a total of ten days ("A.W.O.L."), or in other ways seriously violated the rules.[14] The camp directors were themselves expected to exercise "punitive powers": admonition, reprimand, suspension of "privileges," assignment of extra work on nonworking days, reduction of "rank" of an assignee-foreman, forfeiture of up to half a man's cash allowance, cancellation of up to twenty days of furlough in a year, or imposition of additional service up to forty days in any one year.[15]

Except for the withdrawal of furlough, however, these deceptively impressive powers had little meaning and were hardly used. Of what significance was a fine of half a man's total monthly allowance of $2.50, or what director could be expected to add extra work on top of a fifty-four-hour week? Certain penalties were made mandatory, however, notably a loss of three days of furlough time for each full day of unexcused A.W.O.L. and the making up of all time lost because of A.W.O.L., R.T.W., or other misconduct. (The director was free to handle A.W.O.L. of less than twenty-four hours as he wished.) "This action," Colonel Kosch optimistically predicted, "will tend to discourage the common practice of assignees absenting themselves from camp or work without proper authority with the feeling that nothing will be done about it."[16]

After the establishment of government camps, Selective Service increasingly adopted the practice of transferring c.o.'s out of church camps and placing them directly under its administration as a disciplinary measure.[17] Selective Service threatened to report the most serious offenders to the federal Department of Justice as violators of the Selective Training and Service Act, or, as an alternative, to suggest that their local draft boards reclassify them for military service. On the eleventh day of A.W.O.L. an assignee was deemed a "deserter" subject to prosecution; refusal to work or inciting others to refuse to work always made a man liable either to reclassification or to arrest and conviction for a federal crime.[18]

But the system of "punitive" discipline backfired. Despite a steady stiffening of the dose of punishment, the C.P.S. community became ever more unruly. The ultimate sanction, legal prosecution, was really an abdication of disciplinary authority on the part of Selective Service, for, while it saved face, it didn't save men for "work of national importance." Furthermore, Selective Service could never be sure that the courts would convict. In Oregon, Michigan, and California, violations reached a peak in camps administered directly under Selective Service authority, and officials were consequently eager for the strongest possible judicial support. Yet judges in these states did not relish serving as a coercive arm to buttress the damaged authority and salvage the floundering administration of Selective Service. They imposed sentences with more and more reluctance, took an embarrassing interest in hearing the grievances of the c.o.'s, and finally, to the consternation of government officials, began to hand down suspended sentences or such mild penalties that they seemed to be almost inviting assignees to defy C.P.S. rule. Under the circumstances, the Department of Justice grew coy about undertaking c.o. prosecutions except in extreme cases. It refused, for instance, to take action against ten assignees at Big Flats who had staged a work strike but later returned to work while awaiting discharge.[19]

Attempts to secure reclassification of "troublemakers" into I-A fared no better. Actually, the main significance of such action was its threat value, for if a local board did decide to send the man into the Army, he still retained his original rights of appeal and in the end could refuse to go, electing instead to take the consequences of a civil trial. In other words, reclassification merely introduced an extra procedural step before the c.o. suffered his actual punishment. As a matter of fact, Selective Service pressed few requests for reclassification to a final conclusion, and its efforts in this regard were limited to men in government camps, because the religious agencies vigorously resisted reclassification of men in their units without the assent of the assignee.[20]

Toward the conclusion of the program, General Hershey frankly admitted that punitive discipline had largely failed to produce the desired results, i.e., an effective performance of c.o. duties, although Selective Service had run the gamut of penalties, except for the use of physical force.[21]

Black List. One disciplinary measure was markedly successful: an unpublicized "black list" which C.P.S. men firmly believed prevented the unregenerate from securing transfer to desirable special service projects.

Whenever requests of assignees were denied "for administrative reasons," they suspected their names had been chalked up on the fatal roll. The device was all the more effective for its mystery. Selective Service neither denied nor admitted the existence of the list. No one knew for certain whether he was among the elect, or what actions would merit selection, or what he might do to secure absolution. As transfers to desirable projects became the prize plums in C.P.S., many men decided to play safe and refrain from actions that would excite the seismograph in Selective Service headquarters. Several instances indicate that Selective Service did take a man's record into account in determining action on his behalf, though it is doubtful if any formal "list" was kept of black sheep. While the black list was a potent instrument of control, it encouraged no friendliness for its sponsors and vastly complicated the administrative problems of the religious agencies in trying to strengthen morale and gain constructive co-operation among the assignees.

Redemptive Discipline. The religious agencies attempted to introduce an entirely different approach to discipline. They were convinced that, given a chance, a sensitive and alert conscience could act as its own sanction, impelling men to discipline themselves in the interest of creditable service to mankind.[22] But the churches were caught between a government demanding strict conformity to imposed regulations and c.o.'s whose consciences dictated not compliance with, but resistance to, external authority. To stave off arbitrary action by Selective Service, the religious administrators were driven to adopt a more positive disciplinary initiative than they had intended, but to secure the acquiescence of the c.o.'s they had to develop a disciplinary technique which the majority of the men would accept as fair and reasonable. The result was a practice of discipline which was remedial, rather than punitive. The staffs of the religious agencies sought out the roots of misdemeanor and tried to relieve situations which prompted men to violate regulations. Where a man refused to work, the Brethren Service Committee, for instance, was "committed to discipline only for restoring the man to creditable performance on project." Should his refusal to work on a specific task (woodcutting, emergency farm work, etc.) stem from conscientious reasons, the Committee undertook to urge an assignment which he could conscientiously perform and to protect him against coercion. If he refused because of mental or physical disability, it would seek remedial treatment for him. If there had been misunderstanding between the man and project officials, the B.S.C. encouraged friendly consultation looking toward a solution at the local level. On the other hand, if a man refused *all* work, the B.S.C. assumed he had changed his convictions and was now unwilling to accept alternative service under its administration; it so informed Selective Service, meanwhile counseling the man in his "reorientation" to another alternative (presumably Army, jail, or government camp).[23]

When the offense involved an act directed against its own authority or its camp staff, rather than a Selective Service regulation, the religious agencies were able to try even bolder experiments in redemptive discipline. In a Mennonite camp, when two men tarred and feathered the director, the government technical staff was insistent that they be reported both to Selective Service and to the civil authorities. The Mennonite staff, though deeply shocked, refused and stood on their prerogative, pointing out that discipline was part of their responsibility. Instead, the Executive Camp Director immediately caught a plane from Akron, Pennsylvania, to Idaho. With each of the men he discussed the full seriousness of an act which was "not only a crime against man but a terrible crime against God's moral order and the faith which they had professed." Three alternatives were considered *with the culprits:* turning them over to the civil authorities and Selective Service, transferring them to another camp with full information of their misdeeds, or securing permission for the men to remain in the camp to "redeem themselves in their own eyes, the eyes of the campers, and the eyes of the technical agency." The men chose the latter, apologized to the director, admitted to the technical agency their "terrible misdeed," and asked forgiveness of the whole camp and permission to be received back "into a relationship of trust and fellowship." The director was magnanimous, but the technical men vigorously opposed the penalty as inadequate. They finally yielded only upon Mennonite assurance that the men must make good and not reflect on the technical service. "If this thing works," said one of the most adamant of the technical staff, "we will have learned something new about methods of dealing with people who are caught in serious crimes against human personality and human society." The camp gave its consent unanimously, following a statement by the Executive Director and by each of the men. A number of other campers publicly confessed that they also had not been very constructive and asked to be "forgiven." Presumably a final step of redemption prescribed by the Executive Director was also accomplished, i.e. getting into a "right relationship with their own God." [24]

Not all instances of redemptive discipline succeeded so well. Some c.o.'s scorned redemption, and Selective Service for its part often took matters arbitrarily into its own hands when the religious agencies could not redeem swiftly enough.

Despite such setbacks, the religious agencies did considerably soften the impact of the punitive process upon the men under their administration. Consequently, the full futility of coercive discipline as applied to c.o.'s became apparent only where Selective Service could exercise unmitigated control, namely, in the government-administered camps.[25]

The Denial of Compensation

The conscientious objector was compelled to labor in Civilian Public Service without remuneration. His dependents had to fend for themselves without government aid or benefits of any kind. He was left financially unprotected in case of injury or death during his service, except where he was assigned to work covered by state workmen's compensation laws. These three severe financial penalties were deliberately inflicted on men who allowed their consciences to direct them into civilian rather than military service.

This made a virtual farce of freedom of conscience. In practice, men had to pay for their conscience by the impoverishment not only of themselves but of their families. In principle, the service of the conscientious objector was reduced close to the "slave labor" which many men in C.P.S. considered it. More than any other factor, depriving c.o.'s of reasonable financial compensation impaired their service and violated the just observance of civil liberty. In the opinion of the American Friends Service Committee, such a situation could not "long continue without jeopardy to the health of our democracy. Equal respect and consideration for the welfare of all its citizens should prevail if we are to maintain the foundation principles of our nation." [26]

No Pay. The denial of wages to c.o.'s was primarily the work of General Hershey, who consistently blocked every proposal for pay. He refused to initiate a request for appropriations from Congress for this purpose (though, in Public Law 135, pay comparable to that of a private was authorized). He specifically opposed pay in public testimony before Congressional committees and forestalled the introduction of legislation for pay. He categorically refused to take any administrative action which, without the necessity of appropriations, might have resulted in pay for men working in hospitals, in other institutions, or on farm service.

Considerations of expediency rather than vindictiveness entered into Hershey's adamant stand on this issue. He was convinced that if C.P.S. men were paid "it would destroy the best public relations." [27] Later both Hershey and his staff outspokenly argued that the c.o.'s did not deserve pay. C.o.'s were free of the risks of the G.I., so why should they be compensated for their service? These views could not be shaken by the protests of the c.o.'s or the remonstrance of concerned organizations.

Congress frankly had only slight knowledge of the administration of the C.P.S. program. Selective Service officials usually spared the legislators a review of c.o. problems unless pressed for it. When the veil was lifted, the payless labor of c.o.'s always startled the congressmen, and a few were shocked. "You are treating these fellows worse than the Japs," declared Senator Wallgren (Washington) at one point.[28] But, on the whole, the issue was passed by without real concern, and certainly no one was ready to make a fight to get a change.

The whole matter was further confused by the inability of the religious administrative agencies to agree among themselves to press wholeheartedly for pay. This enabled General Hershey to pass the buck to the c.o.'s and their sponsors, most of whom, he claimed, would not accept any money. The position of the agencies had originally been clear and consistent on the issue.[29] They urged pay for all willing to receive it for service under government administration. They did not want to have the government pay for those in their service. This remained the basic position of the Mennonites and to some extent of the Brethren, even when *all* c.o.'s were assigned to religious agencies. Unfortunately, they were then in a position where a plea for pay could only mean pay for men rendering service under religious administration. When the government camps were set up, the dilemma was removed, and the agencies again joined in asking that all men who wanted pay receive it. But the payless pattern was now deeply grooved, and Selective Service continued to shrug off some of its responsibility by saying that "no pay" was what the c.o.'s sponsors had wanted—and that was what they got.[30]

Whether or not Congress would have appropriated funds to pay c.o.'s if Selective Service had asked for such in its budget, there seems little doubt that arrangements for pay would have been possible *without appropriations* in most of the special service projects if Selective Service had been willing to make them. Most state institutions had funds sufficient to pay c.o.'s the customary rates for the type of work they did. If they could have received the going wage of an attendant—$50 to $65 a month—instead of a $2.50 allowance from the church agency, much of their financial desperation would have been relieved. Selective Service never opened this question, even when in December, 1943, the N.S.B.R.O. formally requested it to seek a ruling from the Comptroller General to determine the legality of such a procedure. It contracted with the institutional officials to furnish "free labor" and to that policy it stuck.

Even when c.o.'s were assigned to farmers and other *private* employers who were required to pay the "going wage" for the work, a series of restrictive rulings by the Comptroller General dictated that the wages be turned over to the United States Treasury (after deducting specified approved expenses connected with the assignment, such as medical bills, maintenance, allowance of $10 a month to cover clothing as well as incidentals and workmen's compensation insurance). Selective Service had originally approved of using funds earned by the detached c.o.'s for rehabilitation in war-torn areas, but the Comptroller General ruled that the law appropriating Selective Service funds for 1943 contained no authority for such a disposition of the funds. "They should be accounted for to the Government and covered into the Treasury as miscellaneous receipts, unless and until Congress provides by law some other disposition.[31] An alternative proposal providing that the funds be used to defray some of the costs of operating the C.P.S. program, subject to a quarterly accounting to the Director of Selective Service, was likewise turned down as without adequate legal authority.[32] The religious agencies and almost all of the c.o.'s affected agreed that under these circumstances they would not co-operate in forwarding plans for work on farms, and the men who had already started on an experimental basis would be withdrawn. At this point the Treasury Department resolved the impasse by its agreement to segregate the amounts received in a frozen fund; disposition of this fund would be determined after the cessation of hostilities.[33]

The Comptroller General categorically denied the right of c.o.'s to retain personally any money they earned. Like soldiers, men in C.P.S. were under obligation to serve the government full time; any earnings, from whatever source, were properly the possession of the United States, to be expended only according to legal authorization.

These rulings, which prevented any mitigation of the no-pay principle by administrative action, reflected a sternness unwarranted by the actual context of the laws. The Comptroller General himself later intimated that a broader interpretation of the relevant legislation would have been amply justified. Unfortunately, the original line of policy was fixed before either Selective Service officials or representatives of the religious agencies had undertaken to confer personally with Mr. Warren and to explain to him the nature and legislative background of the C.P.S. program, and the unique relationships which had been established between the government and private agencies in regard to the maintenance and financial support of the c.o.'s. Consequently, the General Counsel, a man who later was found to be deeply prejudiced against conscientious objectors, drafted the initial rulings and committed the Office to an antagonistic position which the Comptroller General hesitated to reverse despite his own more friendly disposition.[34]

So while C.P.S. assignees became paupers, their "frozen assets" accumulated in the United States Treasury, until an estimated $1,300,000 was in hand by the time the program ended—*after* all deductions for the expenses incidental to their work. Knowing that their labor had produced such riches did not enable the c.o.'s to contemplate their enforced poverty with greater equanimity or their unpaid status with any less resentment.

Women and Children Last. The refusal of Congress to make any provision for assistance to dependents of drafted c.o.'s exposed the wives, children, and aged parents of men in C.P.S. to extreme hardship and insecurity, and put the men themselves under severe psychological strain as they helplessly watched their families struggle to survive without adequate income. A more callous method of disabling conscience could hardly have been devised, for in effect it made a c.o.'s dependents victims of his integrity. The conscientious objector faced the wracking choice of surrendering his ideals by entering the armed forces or sacrificing the security of his dependents, when they might not even share his convictions.

Congress was entirely responsible for this discrimination. Selective Service repeatedly urged and supported measures to grant assistance to c.o. dependents equivalent to that received by the dependents of other draftees, but neither House nor Senate approved the suggestion.[35] Finally, as the problem reached the crisis stage with a large number of fathers being inducted during 1943–1944, Selective Service and the religious agencies agreed to seek legislation permitting release of the "frozen fund" to make allowances to C.P.S. dependents.

Congressman W. Sterling Cole of New York introduced a bill to this effect in the 78th Congress (amending an earlier measure that would have turned the funds over to U.N.R.R.A.). The Bureau of the Budget, the Treasury Department, Selective Service, and the White House approved. After considerable delay, the House Military Affairs Committee reported it favorably. But the objections of three congressmen prevented its passage by unanimous consent and Congress adjourned without a vote.[36]

Actually, Congress had reached the limit of its tolerance. Some important members were quite content to see a c.o. coerced into the Army through pressure upon his dependents, even though they would not go so far as to repeal the alternative-service program outright. Was it not just that they should suffer some privation when other families were suffering the loss of their men?

The snapping of Congressional tolerance at this point, however, produced a train of serious consequences not only for the individuals involved but for the entire C.P.S. program. Over one-third of the men in C.P.S. after 1943 had one or more dependents in need. Some of these persons were in desperate straits. The wife of one man deserted their two children, leaving him to find the means of caring for them. The mother of another assignee, afflicted with bad varicose veins and fainting spells, was utterly incapable of self-support; shortly after his induction, she was evicted from her apartment for nonpayment of rent. The wife of a man assigned to government camp needed an operation, but was too run down to have it and could not work in her condition; yet she had a young child to support. The husband himself was returned home on sick status with a heart condition aggravated by his camp experience. Another C.P.S. wife attempted to support herself and her baby by caring for a ninety-four-year-old man who himself received only forty dollars a month in old-age pension as his sole income.

Men with wives, children, and parents in these circumstances did not work well. Some strove to earn money off-hours to be sent home, and this often interfered with their service. Others bitterly resented the injustice and fought the system which permitted it. Some c.o.'s finally did break down and enter the Army, jettisoning their ideals to secure the allotment for their dependents. In a typical case, a man whose wife and baby were having to stay with the wife's parents wrote:

I have seen lots of trouble and heard lots about me not caring for my family. . . . I was taking my furlough at home and it was a very unpleasant one. I wired the Director that I would go I-A-O but it isn't my desire to do so. . . . But I have got to get my wife a place to stay other than with her parents or no telling what kind of trouble will happen next. My wife's mind has been changed in the last few months until it makes it very hard on me and her also. . . . My wife has said that if I could get support for her that she would go with me. . . . My mother-in-law is the one that has said the most to cause trouble between us.[37]

In the meantime, the National Service Board, the Historic Peace Churches, and other denominations sought to meet the most serious cases which came to their attention by financial and other aid. What Congress actually did was to force upon the already heavily burdened religious agencies an additional responsibility, which by all reason was the obligation of the government which had drafted the income producers.[38]

The C.P.S. Casualty. In the course of their "riskless" occupations, though not always as a result of their work, 30 C.P.S. men were killed, 1,566 were discharged for physical disability, and hundreds more suffered injuries which did not incapacitate them from further service.[39] Most of these men received no public compensation whatever for the injury they received. Some, working on state projects, were covered by workmen's compensation laws, but Selective Service officials by administrative rulings trimmed their return to a minimum usually far short of the amount needed to provide for an adequate recovery.

The C.P.S. man was in a peculiar position. He could qualify for none of the benefits of a soldier—life insurance, predischarge rehabilitation, permanent veterans' medical care, etc.—for he was not a soldier. He could not qualify for compensation as a civilian governmental employee, for he was a drafted man and the federal compensation laws did not apply. Furthermore, if he were eligible for compensation, it would be computed on the basis of his wages, and the c.o. was an unpaid worker!

Attempts to secure special legislation to provide accident compensation for all C.P.S. men failed, even though warmly advocated by Selective Service on the grounds that the government would otherwise be open to damage claims.

One final recourse was tried to secure compensation on behalf of the seriously injured or killed. Against Selective Service opposition, a "private bill" was introduced as a test case to provide payment of five thousand dollars to the estate of Warren Dugan, a C.P.S. guinea-pig worker on infantile paralysis at the Yale University Hospital, who contracted and died of the disease while on his assignment. The bill was dropped when Selective Service and certain congressmen agreed to support a measure to authorize use of the "frozen fund" for compensation. This alternative never materialized.[40]

In assigning men to detached service, Selective Service arranged for some kind of accident and disability insurance, though the circumstances varied. Those on farm work were covered by a commercial policy at a cost of twenty cents per day, deducted from the wages turned over to the National Service Board by the farmers. Men working in state training schools or mental hospitals were supposedly covered by the state compensation acts applicable to other employees in the institution. The Selective Service directives explicitly stated that "hospitals or other institutions desiring the use of conscientious objectors will provide . . . compensation insurance." [41] Nevertheless, a number of c.o.'s assigned to state institutions experienced great difficulty in collecting claims, even for adequate medical treatment, when they were disabled in the course of their duties.

Medical care and expenses were the responsibility of the administrative agencies in the case of the C.P.S. camps, and of the employing institutions for men in special service projects.[42] A special arrangement was made for men assigned to farm work, whereby medical expenses were paid out of the earnings before they were frozen in the Treasury. The adequacy of medical treatment varied greatly. The religious agencies usually secured competent local professional service, but where need arose called upon specialists or paid the bills of a man's own physicians in serious cases. Some of the state institutions were niggardly in the care provided, but others were exceptionally thorough and competent, giving regular and full examinations by staff physicians. Sharpest criticism arose over the treatment afforded men on dairy farms—where theoretically the whole of the accumulated earnings was available to pay medical service if needed. But Selective Service officials were wedded to a "conservative" policy in authorizing disbursements by the N.S.B.R.O. from this fund. They insisted on applying a scale used in determining payments for the care of veterans outside of the veterans' hospitals. Strange results occurred: a man burned with acid after falling down stairs received one thousand dollars *less* than his hospital and medical expenses; a man with tuberculosis received nothing for his expenses in a sanatorium outside the state where he had been working, on the grounds that there was no provision for compensation during a period of convalescence. Yet the frozen fund had by this time passed the million-dollar mark.

By the end of C.P.S., most casualties still stood unrequited. The disabled c.o. was still licking his own wounds, seeking a niche in life without benefit either of counsel or financial recompense from the government during whose service he had been injured. The dead were buried with no governmental provision for those who may have been dependent on them.

The C.P.S. Boondoggle

Many of the personal restraints on the c.o.'s might have lost their sting if challenging service had consistently been demanded and the men had felt that what they were doing qualified as "work of national importance." But much of Civilian Public Service was unworthy either of the caliber of men and convictions placed at its disposal or of the sacrifices of freedom and security which were imposed. Because C.P.S. men were the most easily "expendable" in a war whose scale made impossible a concern for the individual, their manpower was allocated with slight regard for the essential social value of the project, the efficient use of the men's skills and talents, or the competence of technical supervision. Because the labor was unpaid, yet chained to the job assigned, the C.P.S. "management" was under none of the usual compulsions to employ its twelve thousand men wisely and secure the most value from their work. Consequently, much of the labor of C.P.S. men was wasted in fruitless boondoggling which made their penniless and confined state even more unpalatable. "There's a war on. Why don't you take what you've got and be thankful you're not in the army?" foremen and officials would reply when urged to improve their personnel policies and the significance of the projects.

Work Without Value. Selective Service retained full control over the approval of C.P.S. projects and the assignments of men to them.[43] Five factors purportedly governed the approval of new projects by the Director of Selective Service and his cohorts:

1. Is the project important to the government in the emergency considering the manpower available, and is the project the most important thing that can be done at the time, and will it continue to be important with the probable changes in the situation?
2. Will the conscientious objector do it?
3. Will the public tolerate the objectors in the community where the project is located?
4. Will other employable labor be displaced?
5. Will it raise political controversy?[44]

In practice, the selection of projects demonstrated that what Camp Operations Division considered "important to the government" bore little relation to the urgency of the task or its broad social utility. The convenience of government agencies determined the selection of most C.P.S. projects. Federal and later state agencies had first and almost exclusive call upon the services of the c.o.'s. The needs of private institutions were generally dismissed regardless of the character of their work or its comparative value alongside the jobs assigned by government agencies.

As between government agencies, Selective Service parceled out its manpower with due regard for their former co-operation and the pressures which each could exert through legislative or administrative channels. At the beginning of C.P.S., several federal departments were reluctant to use c.o. labor. Later, when the c.o. had proved his worth and his service stood at a premium, Selective Service catered more generously to the requests of those agencies which had co-operated from the start.

On the whole, Selective Service favored doing business with the few "proven" agencies. It resisted innovation, preferring the ease of administration and simplicity of doing business with established contacts. Colonel Kosch believed further that "more can be accomplished by the expansion of the present types of projects rather than by entering new fields of a different character and spreading our efforts too thinly." [45]

Another factor important to Selective Service in the choice of a project was its seclusion from public attention. The officials were eager to ward off hostile criticism, both from veterans' organizations and local groups. The easiest safeguard, they thought, was to place

men on work which excited little interest and which removed the
c.o.'s as much as possible from contact with the population. This
made social service projects appear less attractive than clearing national parks in the mountains.[46]

These criteria led to some strange choices of projects. Colonel
Kosch and Mr. Imirie, with the backing of General Hershey, turned
down requests for C.P.S. men to work at:

A tuberculosis hospital in Rhode Island
A crippled children's hospital
Orthopedic hospital in Los Angeles
Cancer hospitals
The Pittsburgh Settlement Houses
The Nursery and Child Study Home of Maryland
The Chicago Y.M.C.A. (boys' work)
Department of Public Welfare, Richmond, Virginia (in connection with
    juvenile delinquents)
Pennsylvania School for the Deaf

All of these institutions, and hundreds of others, petitioned both
Selective Service and the religious agencies for assistance to meet
acute shortages of personnel in the face of a critical demand for their
services.[47]

Meanwhile, Selective Service insisted that camps be continuously
manned, even though the work might involve mainly the maintenance and development of isolated national parks, the weeding of a
seed nursery, the clearing of timber trails, soil conservation of doubtful future value, or the cutting of firewood to keep the camp warm in
winter. In certain instances, camps were continued when the technical agency was admittedly at a loss to know what to do with the
men, simply because the farmers of the area wanted a labor supply
easily available at harvesttime and were able to express their wants
in the language of political pressure.

The American Friends Service Committee estimated that at least
half of the men in their program had been assigned to "work which
did not affect the wartime social emergencies of the nation and
which could, if necessary, have been largely suspended until the
drastic need for manpower had slackened." It condemned most of
the Park Service work, much of the forestry work—especially where

fire fighting was needed only during a limited season of the year—
and some of the soil conservation programs as "of minor significance
under present conditions and incapable of utilizing effectively the
men which have been placed at their disposal." Meanwhile, it noted,
five million homes stood in need of sanitary privies to prevent the
spread of hookworm, dysentery, and typhoid; five thousand beds in
tuberculosis sanatoria were unused because of lack of attendants,
while active cases of tuberculosis circulated at large; welfare agencies cried for workers, while juvenile delinquency was skyrocketing.[48]

Selective Service consistently contended that the value of all the
projects it approved was beyond question and that criticism misrepresented important work that was being undertaken in the camps.[49] In
the opinion of Camp Operations officials, "no program would be
successful for conscientious objectors which did not provide for some
camps. It was in the camps that a screening procedure became possible and permitted the proper reassignment of men to projects for
which they proved qualified. At the same time too it could be determined whether or not a man was going to cooperate with the program
as a whole." [50]

Selective Service admitted that some of the first camp projects
selected for C.P.S. were not considered of high priority, but they had
to be used to get c.o.'s away from their home communities quickly.
Later, after C.C.C. was abandoned in 1942, "highest type priority
projects were secured." Many of the projects advocated by the religious groups had to be turned down, according to the officials, in
the interest of public relations. "Public opinion and the necessity of
maintaining the war effort prevented the use of conscientious objectors in the fields of education and social welfare work where there
was a possibility that they might spread their philosophies and thus
interfere with the winning of the war." [51]

When Selective Service ultimately began to approve detached
service projects, the struggle for significant work became a struggle
to expand the quota of men allowed in such projects. Rarely would
Selective Service consider closing camps so as to provide more men
for needy special service projects. Technical agencies in charge of
the camps were given a chance to state the minimum number of
men they would require, taking into account the season of the year.[52]
The minimum often became the maximum which the agency could

possibly justify. The figures were sometimes revised downward by Selective Service when it was obvious that they exceeded reason or availability. Special service projects were entitled only to the remainder. Constant pressure from the religious agencies finally secured a commitment to assign a fixed proportion of the total number of men to special service. The proportion was set first at one-third and later boosted to 50 per cent. In the eyes of Selective Service, this represented a great concession to the value of hospital, guinea-pig, and other special work—for these projects were now recognized as of equal importance to the "manicuring of trees" and posthole digging. But when it came to demobilization, the special projects were closed down more rapidly than the camps.

The crushing blow to the hopes of c.o.'s for significant human service was dealt by Congress at the instigation of Representative Joseph Starnes of Alabama. An amendment, inserted by Starnes in the Army Appropriation Bill and passed without debate on June 30, 1943, made it impossible for C.P.S. assignees to engage in relief service outside continental United States or to receive training in colleges for relief service overseas. Plans for such service and training had already progressed far, with Selective Service approval.[53] At first, Congress was really unaware of what it had done, and the religious agencies hoped that careful explanation of the circumstances would lead to prompt retraction. The real implications did not appear on the face of the measure, for Starnes had simply provided that none of the funds appropriated in the Army bill could be used, directly or indirectly, to facilitate the overseas relief service of c.o.'s. This gave the impression that the only objective was to keep the Army funds from being siphoned into support of c.o. relief work. Because the salaries of General Hershey and other Army men in Selective Service were met out of this appropriation, however, the legislation barred them from approving the specified assignments for C.P.S. men. When approached by representatives of the religious agencies, Starnes admitted that he knew full well what he was doing, and would make it his business to see that the prohibition stayed. He had no wish to see c.o.'s glamorized by overseas service.[54]

In a most careful and persistent campaign the religious agencies explained to other key members of Congress that the use of Army funds was never contemplated for any part of the expense of overseas c.o. service, and that such service of c.o.'s was urgently rec-

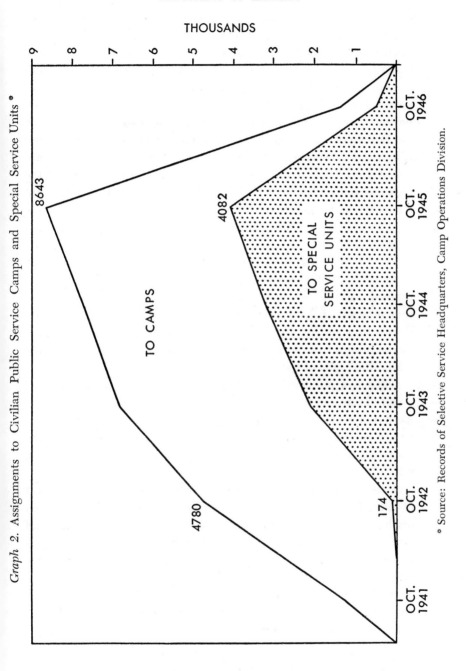

Graph 2. Assignments to Civilian Public Service Camps and Special Service Units *

THOUSANDS

9 8 7 6 5 4 3 2 1

8643

4082

TO CAMPS

TO SPECIAL
SERVICE UNITS

4780

174

OCT.
1941

OCT.
1942

OCT.
1943

OCT.
1944

OCT.
1945

OCT.
1946

* Source: Records of Selective Service Headquarters, Camp Operations Division.

ommended both by United States military authorities and Allied governments. Though astonished at the largely unintended consequences which had flowed from the innocent-looking amendment, a majority of the House Military Affairs Committee, under Starnes's prompting, nevertheless refused to be convinced. Each successive year, the identical provision was carefully inserted in the War Department appropriation, although neither the War Department nor the Bureau of the Budget included it in their proposals, and several congressmen, especially Representative Walter Judd, vigorously protested it. The Senate on three occasions took steps to strike out the measure, but each time a House-Senate Conference Committee put it back in, due to the adamant stand of the House conferees, especially of D. Lane Powers, whose prejudice against c.o.'s surpassed even that of Starnes.[55]

No Skills Wanted. In assigning men to their "work of national importance," Selective Service took little trouble to put their skills or professional training to effective use. Colonel Kosch, perhaps in reminiscence of Army experience, felt no obligation "to provide a man with a job for which he may be especially prepared," though he did profess to a desire to employ special skills "whenever possible within the limits of the various projects."[56]

The bases on which Selective Service determined assignments were: distance of the projects from a man's home, length of his service in C.P.S., the blanket needs of particular projects for raw manpower, personal choice of the men, disciplinary action, and, in some instances, the importance of a particular individual to the project on which he was working.[57]

A new assignee was usually sent to the camp nearest to his point of induction, provided it was at least one hundred miles away from his home. The one-hundred-mile limit was rigidly observed in all further assignments, even to the extent of denying New Yorkers a chance to serve in Philadelphia institutions, ninety-two miles removed.

Men served at least sixty days (later ninety) in a camp before becoming eligible for transfer to special service projects. The period of initiation often lasted much longer, for the number of applicants exceeded the number of vacancies and those with a longer service record were usually favored.

From time to time Selective Service undertook major transfers of men to expand the strength of certain camps and projects (for instance, the western camps during fire season). These were handled on a mass basis, with specified camps ordered to furnish quotas, fixed in terms of Pullman-car loads. The administering agency was free to take personal factors into consideration in choosing the men to go, but government officials often advised them to take a leaf from the Army's book and just pick every fourth or fifth name, regardless of any other factors, including training or other qualifications.

Within these rather narrow limits, Selective Service was usually willing to follow the choice of the men for assignments, though it might refuse to assume the cost of transporting them to a new project if the transfer was not for the "convenience" of the government. Assignments to special service projects were made only when men volunteered for them, and if a man wanted to change camps or move back to camp from special service, approval could usually be secured if a replacement were found, so as not to disturb the quota.

Some men unhappily made themselves so valuable to the project on which they were working that they became "key men." They were frozen to their assignments unless the project superintendent could be persuaded to release them. This was the only recognition which Selective Service gave to individual talent in its assignment policy.

Selective Service did not approve of making individual assignments, though a few exceptions were made in the first year or two of operation, for men with qualifications for jobs of particular importance. As a result of the official policies in regard to the selection of work projects and the assignment of men, a great reservoir of skill was dissipated in largely meaningless manual labor. The waste of training and talent not only was a wartime loss but affected the future contribution of many men whose skills became impaired by lack of use.

A high proportion of men in C.P.S. had had either professional or technical training and experience before induction. Of those under Friends administration or sponsorship, 55 per cent had had professional training or occupations, 5 per cent had done technical work (drafting, laboratory work, etc.), and 30 per cent were skilled workers (carpenters, electricians, machinists, farmers, printers, etc.). Less than ten per cent were unskilled.[58] (See Graph 3.)

Graph 3. Preinduction Training *

| 55.2% | 5.3% | 30.1% | 9.4% |
| PROFESSIONAL | TECHNICAL | SKILLED | UNSKILLED |

* Reprinted from American Friends Service Committee, *Projects and Incentives*, 1946.

In contrast, over half of the jobs to which men were assigned in camp called for unskilled labor. This inevitably meant that great numbers of men technically qualified for skilled work were unable to use their training, and became deeply dissatisfied at the waste of their abilities when they heard of widespread demands for what they had to offer. For instance, of 803 men in Friends camps in the spring and summer of 1945, 506 had advanced training and experience that was not being used (63%). While 40 per cent of these 506 were college students with incomplete professional training, the others included teachers, technicians and laboratory assistants, social service workers, engineers, draftsmen, chemists, accountants, a botanist, and a geologist.[59] The situation in special service units was no better in this regard, even though many of the projects appealed to the men as inherently more worth while than the work in the camps. Of 707 men in special service units under Friends administration in 1945, 471 or 66 per cent were not using their preinduction training and experience in their work. This included a large number of teachers, social service workers, and skilled craftsmen.[60] (See Graph 4.)

Examples of the incongruity and wastefulness of the C.P.S. assignment policy appeared in individual cases.

Case I—20 years of formal education; Ph.D. in political science; college teacher 3½ years; 14 months' European study and travel; two books and articles on international law published; fluent in three languages.

Assignment: unskilled work as attendant in a mental hospital.

Graph 4. Job Assignments in Friends Civilian Public Service for Men
with Professional, Skilled, and Technical Training *

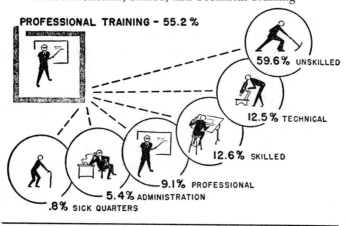

PROFESSIONAL TRAINING - 55.2 %

59.6% UNSKILLED

12.5% TECHNICAL

12.6% SKILLED

9.1% PROFESSIONAL

5.4% ADMINISTRATION

.8% SICK QUARTERS

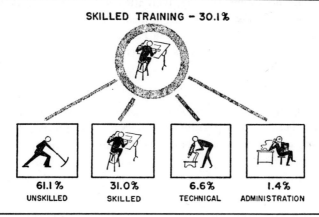

SKILLED TRAINING - 30.1%

| 61.1% | 31.0% | 6.6% | 1.4% |
| UNSKILLED | SKILLED | TECHNICAL | ADMINISTRATION |

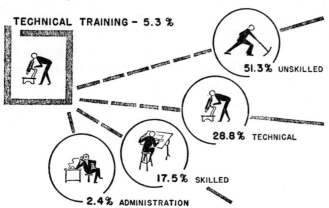

TECHNICAL TRAINING - 5.3 %

51.3% UNSKILLED

28.8% TECHNICAL

17.5% SKILLED

2.4% ADMINISTRATION

* Reproduced from American Friends Service Committee, *Projects and Incentives,* 1946.

233

Case II—18 years of formal education; two years' graduate study in chemical engineering; four years' employment as chemical engineer.

Assignment: pull weeds in a nursery.

Case III—B.S. degree in electrical engineering, experienced as an electrical engineer and draftsman.

Assignment: pull weeds; then cook.

Case IV—one of the nation's leading botanists, employed as associate curator of the New York Botanical Gardens; Fellow of American Association for the Advancement of Science and 9 foreign scientific societies.

Assignment: maintenance work in a mental hospital. (Selective Service refused a request of the Smithsonian Institute to have him assist their staff.)

Case V—leading research physicist in electronics, optics, and the electro-microscope.

Assignment: swamp clearing; then attendant in a mental hospital.

Case VI—biochemist, specializing in penicillin research.

Assignment: maintenance work in Fish and Wildlife Refuge; later sent to prison when he refused work in favor of continuing his research in a camp-made laboratory.[61]

A typical work crew clearing logs and stumps from a drainage canal were a machinist, a mechanical engineer, a research physicist, two YMCA secretaries, a personnel manager, a turpentine distiller, and a piping engineer, as well as an assortment of farmers, lawyers, and students.[62]

Selective Service on occasion attempted to show the other side of the coin—the fact that in camps "many and varied uses are made of men trained along scientific, professional, technical and semi-technical lines . . . men are employed as electrical engineers, civil engineers, agronomists, foresters, draftsmen, engineering aids, mechanics and accountants." In detached service projects, General Hershey informed the Senate Special Committee Investigating the National Defense Program, "a number of chemists or men similarly educated and trained are used." But he complained that a number of qualified men remained in camps and would not volunteer for the detached service projects. Others, according to the official explanation, did not have the co-operative attitude necessary to justify their transfer to projects which did not have the close supervision of the work camps.[63] For the most part, Selective Service officials simply stated that it was no concern of theirs whether a man could use his skill on his C.P.S. assignment. They did not accept as a general principle that a man's greatest value to his country would be rendered in the work he was best fitted to do.

Supervision without Incentive. The service of C.P.S. men, especially in the camps, was often severely handicapped by the quality of supervision they received from the government departments responsible for the work projects. Many of the local staffs, by their "autocratic methods, inadequate project planning and poor personnel policies" destroyed morale and cut the working efficiency of intelligent and imaginative assignees. C.o.'s at Big Flats, for instance, were blamed by the project administration for a poor work record, but a detailed analysis of the technical direction they had been receiving showed that crews were kept waiting for as much as an hour and a half after reporting for work before they were assigned a job, while foremen issued contradictory orders as to how the jobs were to be done and failed to give instructions that would have accelerated production.[64] Such criticisms of poor planning and organization of the work were common throughout C.P.S. Too many project superintendents tended to choose their crews on the spur of the moment from day to day, leaving the c.o.'s with a feeling of insecurity and doubt as to the significance of the work. Frequently work was done by hand when machinery could have been made available by proper project management.[65]

A wide cultural gap often separated the technical staffs from the c.o.'s. Many of the foremen, in particular, had little schooling and were unprepared to "boss" a crew made up of the highly educated. On the other hand, they could hardly appreciate how utterly unprepared many of their charges were for work outdoors, and how much needed to be explained to men reared in a city. Then the c.o.'s were not experienced in the taking of orders as common labor, while their supervisors were bred "overseers," accustomed to giving orders without explanation and having them carried out without question. Some c.o.'s were argumentative, disrespectful, and even antagonistic toward the technical men. Some of the supervisory staff, in turn, treated the c.o.'s with contempt or hostility either on account of their beliefs or because they were unpaid, forced labor.[66] Such attitudes, according to the observant Mennonite Educational Director, impaired the c.o.'s service.

The most serious shortcoming of supervision was its failure to interest the men in the work they were doing by an adequate explanation of its significance and of the proposed plans for accomplishing it. In some instances, government technical personnel did provide challenging leadership, and demonstrated a keen personal sense of the project's importance. All too often, however, the government men regarded the project most casually, simply as a source of income, and their indifference infected those working under them. A typical superintendent was "not inclined to tell the men why they are asked to do a particular job nor how it fits into the Park project. He and the foremen tend to give minute instructions for each bit of work, making little allowance for individual initiative or imagination." The A.F.S.C. reported that in none of its camps was there a carefully planned training and placement program run by the technical staff.

Little thought was given to the incentives necessary in a compulsory-work program with unpaid labor. Work was done and then redone when the foreman decided to do it differently; power equipment often was not used for work when it would have been in private enterprise; work was devised to keep men busy; men were not rotated in the more arduous or monotonous jobs.[67]

Supervision in many hospitals and schools for the mentally deficient was scarcely better than in the camps. Too little attention was given to personnel policies and to the training of C.P.S. men for their assignments. The hospital caste system, with segregated dining rooms for the "untouchable" attendants, created an unfortunate barrier between supervisors and the men.

On the other hand, excellent supervision was characteristic of public-health and agricultural special projects and of the medical research units. The supervisors carefully explained the nature and purposes of the work, and sought to make good use of the men's skills, to meet the men's choice of job assignments as much as possible, and to rotate job assignments when they were monotonous. They often included the assignees in the planning and direction of the work. This incited the men to do superior work and markedly increased their interest and their eagerness to co-operate.

Service without End

The c.o.'s prescribed term of service in C.P.S. was equivalent to that of other draftees—a year according to the Selective Service Act as first enacted, lengthened to the "duration plus six months" after the United States entered the war. But c.o.'s were denied the same opportunity for demobilization on "points" which was granted to men in the armed forces after V-E Day; and they encountered extraordinary difficulty in securing discharge from C.P.S. for medical reasons and on grounds of hardship.

The medical discharge policy of Selective Service not only worked injustice upon individual c.o.'s; it imposed a most serious handicap upon the effective administration of C.P.S. The basic principle governing Selective Service policy appeared reasonable enough: a C.P.S. assignee would not be released unless physical disability were sufficient to have entitled him to discharge from the Army. But the medical staff of Selective Service took such a narrow and technical view of the grounds for discharge that it would often reject recommendations for release by camp physicians and even specialists if the terminology of their diagnoses did not conform exactly to the regulations. This was especially true in cases involving psychiatric problems.

Nor did the policy take into account the much more restricted opportunities for "limited service" for partially disabled men in C.P.S. than in the Army. As a result, men were retained in camp and often assigned to project work for which they were physically unfit. In one case, despite repeated recommendations by the camp physician that a man be released because of high blood pressure which was "entirely incompatible with work even of a mild degree under camp conditions," the Selective Service Medical Officer refused release, discredited the findings of the doctor, and suggested that the assignee might have artificially influenced his heart pressure by drugs. Though another doctor corroborated the first report after thorough checking of the man during a four-day commitment to a hospital, Selective Service still denied discharge and instead transferred the c.o. to a government camp. Nine months later, after transfer to still another government camp and a diagnosis which found that the cardiac condition had been progressive during the previous year and that "total and apparently permanent disability is present now," the man was released.[68] In such situations, Selective Service officials were misled by an exaggerated suspicion of "goldbricking" and their extreme insistence on applying Army standards despite differing circumstances.

Aside from injury to the individuals concerned, the net effect of this shortsighted and inflexible medical policy was to saddle the C.P.S. camps with a large number of chronic "S.Q.'s" (Sick in Quarters). There was virtually no hope of their adjusting to life within C.P.S. Few of them could work. The camps usually had no means of providing them with adequate medical care. They consequently deteriorated physically and emotionally in the situation to which they were confined. They exercised an enormously depressive effect upon the whole camp and were a constant source of irritation to administration and fellow assignees alike. Ultimately the camp directors and staffs of the religious agencies succeeded in securing the discharge of an increasing number of the chronically sick, but only because they were able to get the understanding and co-operation of appropriate specialists in working up the cases in the particular form acceptable to Selective Service.[69]

Selective Service likewise adhered to the Army criteria for discharge in regard to dependency hardship cases, without taking into account the fact that the c.o.'s dependents received no government allotments. Thus an assignee could secure discharge only to prevent or relieve actual destitution caused by the death or disability of a member of his family. Pregnancy of the assignee's wife, marriage of a brother who had supported the assignee's mother prior to his marriage, and so forth were *not* accepted as causes for discharge, even though this deprived the dependent of all means of support.[70] C.o.'s were usually refused release to take over farm work when their parents became physically incapacitated. On the other hand, a growing number of hardship and physical disability discharges were granted, especially toward the end of the program when the Army became more lenient.[71] (See Table X.)

Obvious discrimination, prompted by Congressional action, kept C.P.S. men from being demobilized as rapidly as the armed forces. A "point system" was originally designed by Selective Service to provide for discharge of assignees at a rate approximating that of the military. Eligibility for release was determined by virtually the same factors—length of service and dependency—with a heavier weighting in favor of the latter because of the urgent situation of many C.P.S. dependents without government financial assistance.[72]

Injudicious public announcement without adequate interpretation of the implications of the plan brought strong protests from veterans' groups, some of whom jumped to the conclusion that c.o.'s were getting off more easily and swiftly than the soldiers. Representative Arthur Winstead (Mississippi) forthwith introduced a bill in Congress which would have prevented any discharges from C.P.S. until a large proportion of the Army had been demobilized.[73] Although Selective Service officials explained to the House Military Affairs Committee that the plan they had prepared would not favor the c.o., the Committee reported out favorably a modified version of the Winstead bill [74] providing that no point system should be applied to

TABLE X. DISCHARGES FROM C.P.S.*

Reason	Number	Per cent of total
Physical disability	1,566	13
Death	30	†
Dependency	290	2½
Occupational	184	1½
Entered military service	905	7½
Delinquency	523	4½
Systematic demobilization	8,408	70
Miscellaneous	44	†
	11,950	

* Tabulated by Selective Service Headquarters, Camp Operations Division.
† Less than one-half of 1 per cent.

the release of c.o.'s. The committee declared: "Conscientious objectors . . . should not be permitted release to resume normal life while the armed forces are still engaged in combat with the enemy and members of such forces are denied release. To provide for release of such conscientious objectors under the point system would adversely affect morale in the armed forces." The committee decisively rejected a proposal of Representative Paul J. Kilday (Texas) which would have permitted release of the same percentage of men from

C.P.S. as from the armed forces, and in committee and outside congressmen leveled their sharpest attacks of the war against c.o.'s.[75]

Congress recessed without voting upon the bill, but Selective Service suspended C.P.S. demobilization in deference to the pending legislation. On reconvening, the House almost passed the Winstead bill on the consent calendar; only one congressman objected when the bill was first called up and he did so under misapprehension.[76] Church representatives, thoroughly alarmed, undertook a major effort to interpret the discriminatory implications of the bill to congressmen, and it never again came near passage. The impasse was finally resolved when Paul French and Colonel Kosch, with the cooperation of Representatives Sparkman and Kilday persuaded Representative Winstead to withdraw his bill in favor of a "systematic release" of C.P.S. men without a formal point system. On this basis, demobilization slowly began in October, 1945, first for older men, then for groups picked according to length of service and number of children. The process was still subject to endless administrative delays, so demobilization continually lagged far behind the armed forces. This was the final blow to C.P.S. Prolonged uncertainty in regard to the prospects for discharge made the c.o.'s increasingly restive and prone to disregard regulations, wrecked their incentive to serve, and intensified resentment and resistance against the whole C.P.S. program. In the face of so direct and sharp a demonstration of intolerant discrimination, coming at the very conclusion of their work "of national importance," the Creative Pioneers of C.P.S. could hardly help but feel that their testimony of public service had been in vain.

Taken as a whole, the pattern of C.P.S. administration woven by Selective Service, by Congress, and by the project supervisors restrained liberty and failed to provide adequate incentives to service. This not only thwarted adequate recognition of freedom of conscience; it robbed the nation of the full measure of the c.o.'s potential services. The American Friends Service Committee well summarized the impact of coercive restraint upon the service record of the c.o.:

In addition to the fact that they had been conscripted, were forced to do work not of their own choosing, and could not come and go with adult freedom, the men . . . were not paid and therefore lacked funds for even those things which are regarded as necessities. They faced or saw their friends face serious dependency situations in which the only way to provide minimum food and shelter for wife and child or aged parent was to ask friends or the religious agency for help. They saw their fellows die in project accidents without any compensation available to their dependents. They saw men with unusual talents unable to use them for the common good, and they saw serious social needs going unmet while men pulled weeds. Only rarely did they find project superintendents who could impart enthusiasm for their work, who planned the work program carefully and made the best possible use of the men. The situation . . . represented a miscarriage of the desire of the religious agencies and of the men to render valuable social services at a time when they were so critically needed.[77]

XI: *Government Camps:*

Prescription for "Troublemakers"

GOVERNMENT-ADMINISTERED camps became the ultimate penal colonies of Civilian Public Service—though at first they were advocated and hailed, by many c.o.'s and church leaders, as a highly desirable alternative for men who objected to service under religious administration.

The government ran afoul of a hard core of c.o.'s who were frankly committed to an all-out attack on the system of conscription. These men calculated to nullify all efforts to operate the government camp program and deliberately goaded government officials to ever more repressive actions. Government C.P.S. therefore soon acquired the unsavory reputation of an Alcatraz, with one important difference— in the end, the inmates virtually dictated to the wardens. The experience showed, not necessarily the lesser merit of government as opposed to religious direction of alternative service, but rather the inability of government within the present limits of American constitutional rights to *compel* public service out of men whose conscience or personal embitterment against society blocked their willing cooperation.

The Impetus for Government Camps

Selective Service did not wish on itself the troubles of direct administration of C.P.S. camps. For over two years, General Hershey and his associates put off successive propositions for government-directed service from the radical wing of the pacifist movement, the representatives of major Protestant denominations, and a large body of men within C.P.S., finally acceding only when the religious administering agencies themselves united in requesting such action.

Though the authority of the government to undertake partial or full operation of C.P.S. was never in question,[1] General Hershey felt that two parallel systems—government and private—would cause difficult administrative problems and might not even secure Congressional approval. A specific deficiency appropriation needed to finance government camps might cause Congress to investigate the whole setup, throwing over any continuing operation by the religious agencies or even changing the legislative provisions for alternative service under civilian direction.[2] Furthermore, Selective Service officials did not believe that setting up a separate organization was justified for the small number of assignees who at first indicated their willingness to transfer to a government-operated camp.[3]

These arguments were vigorously disputed, especially by those groups which had shunned administrative responsibility for C.P.S. The War Resisters League—assuming the role of spokesman for the secular wing of the pacifist movement—charged that the C.P.S. system as it stood was unduly sectarian and that some men were distressed at having to go to the religious camps. It urged that the National Service Board ask the government to maintain and direct some projects to provide more than just one type of service alternative.[4] The Federal Council of Churches fully supported this view, insisting that no c.o. should be legally compelled to serve under a private religious agency and made dependent for his maintenance on voluntary contributions.[5]

For over two years, however, the personal opposition of Paul C. French, Executive Secretary of the National Service Board, effectively blocked the consummation of an acceptable arrangement for government-administered and maintained C.P.S. projects. French agreed with General Hershey that a request for government appropriations might precipitate total government control. Consequently, he dissuaded the National Service Board during this lengthy and critical period from actively sponsoring the proposals for government C.P.S., and, what is more, he was chiefly responsible for the misfire of direct negotiations undertaken by the War Resisters League, the Federal Council of Churches, and others to persuade Selective

Service to start such a program. For instance, he informed General Hershey that while "we [N.S.B.R.O.] felt we had no right to inter- fere with Bishop Oxnam (representing the Federal Council of Churches) or any other group presenting any program which seemed right to them . . . our group was of the opinion that the existing system was more satisfactory than a government camp program would be." [6] The General naturally assumed that this constituted outright opposition to any change by the groups to whom he had committed the major responsibility for Civilian Public Service. Yet the National Service Board had actually registered its "approval of the proposed action of the Federal Council in overturing the Selective Service System, looking toward the establishment of one or more such government-operated camps," though it did not itself join in the representation.[7]

French's interposition following a conference of Federal Council leaders with General Hershey on June 8, 1942, was even more dis- astrous. In response to the churchmen's plea for a government- supported camp, General Hershey had agreed to survey the opinion of all men in C.P.S. to discover how many wanted such a camp and would be ready to serve in one. The questionnaire prepared by Selec- tive Service contained a candid statement of the policies that would be followed in a government camp, notably that no distinction would be made between defense and nondefense activities in the work as- signed.[8] This in itself heavily "loaded" the poll against the govern- ment camp, but Paul French made matters worse by adding, on his own initiative, a two-page covering "interpretative" letter to camp and unit directors. A request to Congress for funds for a government camp might threaten the entire legal provision for alternative c.o. service, he argued. French stressed the decision of Selective Service to make no distinction between defense and nondefense work, and expressed his personal opinion that men once in a government camp would have great difficulty getting back into the existing projects or onto detached service, and that men who did not obey regulations would be reported for prosecution to the Department of Justice.[9]

Protests stinging with ecclesiastical indignation poured in upon the National Service Board, out to the camps, and into the Selective Service headquarters. To General Hershey, Bishop Oxnam wired,

"Do not believe a fair vote can be taken in the light of French's unfortunate misstatements to directors." To French, the Bishop's wire regretted "exceedingly that your statements no doubt unintentional misrepresent our presentations to government and raise so many doubts in selectees' minds as to prejudice vote. It would seem you could have conferred with us to ascertain what we did present to General Hershey before sending such a letter." Selective Service promptly disclaimed all responsibility for the "argumentative letter by Mr. French. . . . It was sent without our knowledge and the statements therein concerning what Camp Operations would or would not do are merely Mr. French's opinion and have no official backing." Colonel Kosch agreed to ask assignees to submit another questionnaire in case their previous votes were submitted under false information.[10]

All might yet have been saved had not the battle scene shifted to French's further comment that the church leaders had told Hershey their groups were no longer willing to support their c.o.'s. This, the Federal Council leaders insisted, was a "grave injustice"; they categorically denied that anything said in their interview with General Hershey would have warranted such a conclusion, and intimated that Selective Service officials might have misrepresented them.[11] This nettled Colonel Kosch.

Unfortunately, military and clerical prestige were now hopelessly embroiled and Selective Service virtually washed its hands of the matter, on the grounds that the poll showed an inadequate number of men prepared to transfer to a government camp if one were established.[12] The responsible leadership of the religious administering agencies now saw they could no longer keep neutral in regard to this issue. If they were to regain a measure of good will and respect among the disaffected church leaders and c.o.'s, they would have to prove their good faith by taking the lead themselves in finding a solution acceptable alike to the other churches, the dissatisfied c.o.'s, and Selective Service—no mean task under the circumstances. The directors of the National Service Board took a poll "to end all polls" and the Friends C.P.S. Committee made an intensive study of the problems involved in government administration and definitely decided that "the difficulties and disadvantages of asking for a government camp now are probably less than those of continuing without such a camp." The National Service Board finally took the fateful plunge and on April 16, 1943, unequivocally urged Selective Service to operate one or more camps, with three main provisos: (1) *pay* in addition to maintenance, (2) projects without military significance, (3) opportunities for men to use skills other than manual labor.[13]

General Hershey thereupon agreed in principle that the agencies should not have to maintain men who did not wish to be in a religious-administered camp, but he opposed the request for compensation.[14] Following Hershey's conversion, Selective Service on July 1, 1943, opened a camp at Mancos, Colorado, under its own exclusive direction. Later two other government camps were set up—at Lapine, Oregon, and Germfask, Michigan—and after March, 1946, when the A.F.S.C. ceased its participation in C.P.S., the camps which it had been administering were operated by the government.

All assignees who did not clearly elect to serve under the religious agencies were invited to transfer to a government camp. If they did not deign to choose, their choice was automatically made for them— in favor of the government camp. Yet a total of only eighty-one men were transferred to the first camp on July 1, 1943, many of them dragooned under the "no-choice rule" with protests fully as loud as their earlier insistent demands.

This reluctance to follow through, after the two and a half years of churchly and pacifist clamor for a government administered service, stemmed from four main factors. Many men had sincerely favored a government camp as a good and proper alternative for others, but never intended to move into it themselves. Second, some of the most vociferous advocates of the government camp were apparently seeking merely to further discontent in C.P.S., and this had been a handy issue at the time. Third, a number of assignees were reluctant to pull up stakes from where they were fairly well settled in C.P.S., to move to the new, uncertain, and highly isolated environment of a government camp. But most important of all, the c.o.'s were deeply disappointed that the government continued to deny pay even when the service was under its direct control. It appeared to foreshadow a further restriction of freedom, rather than the hoped-for widening of freedom through an additional type of service.

The Repressive Turn of Government C.P.S.

When Selective Service finally yielded to the importunities of the religious pacifist advocates of government-administered service, it disavowed any intention of setting up concentration camps. It proposed "to provide adequate food, clothing, shelter and medical care and to operate with as few rules and restrictions as possible." [15] Government camps would have the same furlough privileges, camp regulations, and working hours as other C.P.S. camps. "Regardless of a man's record in the past," Colonel Kosch promised, he would enter government camp "with a clean slate. . . . We recognize that some men are going out there with chips on their shoulders. What we want to do is brush them off, if possible without making them mad." [16]

The first c.o.'s at Mancos joyfully reported that Selective Service was as good as its word. *The food*—budgeted at the Army garrison ration of sixty cents per man per day (almost 50 per cent more per man than in the regular C.P.S. camps)—was superior in quality and quantity. *The project*, in comparison with others, was constructive and provided opportunity for the use of a variety of skills, including the operation of machinery. It involved the construction of a dam, the clearing of a reservoir site, and the improvement of irrigation systems so as to release ten thousand acres of farm land. This work, furthermore, had no connection with the war effort, so the fear that Selective Service would assign c.o.'s to defense work proved groundless. *Work standards* were light.[17] *The director*—an experienced engineer—and his staff impressed the men generally as fair and friendly, eager to secure good work on the project, and ready in return to be liberal in the privileges within their power to grant. *Regulations* were more lenient at Mancos than in the church camps, because of the wider discretion allowed the director by Selective Service. No attempt was made to restrict the use of free time. A *"welfare allowance"* —one dollar a month per man for the first one hundred assignees— made possible the purchase of books, movies, athletic equipment, and so forth for the camp, and the men supplemented the library with their own items and contributions from interested organizations. The camp director willingly included some pacifist publications among the camp purchases. The director generally welcomed visitors, especially if they had no axe to grind, and encouraged ministers of the denominations represented among the assignees to come into the camp (though the extreme isolation of Mancos severely restricted contact with the outside world). Selective Service even concerned itself with the *religious life* of the camp, despite the belligerent secularism of some of the assignees. It first agreed to the appointment of a full-time chaplain at Mancos by the Federal Council of Churches, paid by the Federal Council. The man selected, Christian Kehl, was himself a C.P.S. assignee, and Selective Service placed him "on reserve" for this purpose. The arrangement was later modified to provide for visiting chaplains when Kehl was dismissed for taking issue with the camp director in regard to the latter's policy toward assignees. Independent religious services were held freely by any group of assignees who desired them, such as the Jehovah's Witnesses, the Mennonites, and the Disciples of Christ.

This veneer of liberality did not conceal for long the strongly repressive implications inherent in the cardinal principle of Selective Service administration—that full control and determination of policies must rest exclusively with official authorities and must under no circumstances be shared with assignees. Attempts by assignees to challenge this principle, either directly or secretly, immediately stiffened the administrative backbone and led to abrupt, arbitrary, short-tempered, and often ill-advised action by the camp and headquarters staffs as they sought to assert the inviolability of their authority.

The camp officials were further handicapped in their relations with the assignees because many of the men came to camp with a grudge against the government. The director and Selective Service staff had expected a contingent composed primarily of men who deliberately chose to serve under government direction in preference to the religious administration and would therefore be disposed to cooperate in making the program a success.[18] A majority of the men were probably so intentioned, especially those who were transferred at their own request. For instance, one man asked to transfer to Mancos because he had an interest in its project, the construction of earth dams; another desired to be independent of religious administration and financial support; three men declared they were more in sympathy with the "philosophy" of the government camp; one c.o. believed he would receive better medical care and relieve the Brethren of the financial burden of his medical bills; and an assignee actually paid his own travel expense from New Jersey to Colorado because he so disliked being a hospital attendant that he wanted a quick transfer out.

Unfortunately, the government camp also became the dumping ground for C.P.S. "misfits"—chronic "objectors" who wished to obstruct the administration as a means of opposing conscription, men placed under medical examination to determine eligibility for discharge, and men involuntarily transferred to government camp for disciplinary or other "administrative reasons." Some of the reasons for which men were moved into government camps against their will were as follows:

Punishment for insubordination

Unsatisfactory work

Failure to choose service under religious agency

Medical observation

Many men therefore came to government camp with the mental cast of a convict or invalid, and in due course the camps acquired the atmosphere of prison or hospital. The antagonism of the dissidents, and their determined refusal to co-operate, disillusioned and baffled the administrative staff and invited repression upon the whole camp. A harassed Selective Service inspector complained:

Having them [the "problems"] all together makes it tough on us. . . . Looks to me they lay awake all night trying to think up ways to get out of work and make us Government men sick of them. . . . [I]t is one of the hardest tasks we have to be civil to them. . . . They don't trust anyone but themselves, they make it impossible for one like myself to help. They have bad tempers, are disorderly, arrogant, insulting and unreasonable.[19]

Colonel McLean offered a more judicious explanation of the deterioration of relations between assignees and the government camp officials.

Inclined to judge men by their attitude toward the job and the way the work was done rather than by what they said or professed to be[,] they [the administrative staff] could not understand some of the people with whom they had to deal. Unfavorable opinions as to sincerity and motives were formed, which, unfortunately, were extended to persons entirely blameless. Confusion and antagonism were deliberately fostered and spread by certain individuals who claimed to be pacifists but who employed all methods of force and coercion except, possibly, physical violence. Various measures were adopted by the camp administration in an effort to correct the situation. Mistakes were made at times and there were errors in judgment, the result being that in some instances the majority of the assignees, who were sincere and well intentioned, were the ones who really suffered. . . . [T]here still remains as a result of these activities a lack of confidence and a certain amount of distrust between assignees and staff that it will be extremely difficult to overcome.[20]

The belligerency of the c.o.'s in government camps was intensified in many cases by a deep sense of injustice over the refusal of the government to pay for their compulsory labor, to give fair consideration to some cases where men requested discharge on medical grounds, and to permit the same opportunity for assignment to special service projects as was available to men in the religious-directed camps. The major cause of conflict, however, was the heavy concentration in government camps of those whose consuming ambition was to overturn the entire "damnable conscription system." These men set the stage for a fierce trial of the disciplinary powers of Selective Service.

The Debacle of Discipline

Camp officials attempted serious disciplinary action on two major issues: a suspicious sick list and the intentional obstruction of project work.

The Professional Sick. At Mancos, and later in other government camps, c.o.'s had a remarkable tendency to develop semipermanent illness, thus qualifying for assignment to their quarters instead of to work on project. (The sick list reached 15 to 20 per day at Mancos in the fall of 1944 and over 30 per cent of Germfask's camp strength on occasion.) These illnesses were often devoid of outward symptoms which could be easily verified by nonprofessional persons like the camp directors; as a matter of fact, some of the men were surprisingly able to pitch horseshoes, shoot pool, play a rousing game of ball, and generally enjoy all aspects of camp life except work with no apparent handicap.[21]

The directors speculated that a dose of work might provide some surprising cures. They peremptorily ordered some of the chronic invalids onto project, on pains of being prosecuted for refusal to work. The therapy worked in some cases, but mistakes were made and the officials were loudly charged with cruel and abusive treatment of the men under their care. The c.o.'s were quick to point out the number of men who were sent to government camps specifically on the grounds that they were to be under medical observation preparatory to treatment or discharge. They claimed that others were inducted by local boards without proper medical screening. They strongly protested the inadequacy of medical care provided in government camps, especially in the case of men who complained of complex ailments, and condemned the camp director for arbitrarily refusing to press his superiors in Washington for prompt review of pending requests for reclassification.[22] When Selective Service medical examiners finally appeared, their review produced a few discharges, but generally supported the action of the camp director and corroborated his opinion that the men were not really sick at all but were simply avoiding work. These examinations were criticized for being cursory and biased.

At Mancos, the FBI was then called in to get evidence for prosecution, but to the glee of the c.o.'s the FBI agent took their side, challenging the right of the administration to overrule the sick status of men, especially when it was confirmed by a local doctor. The Mancos sick list scored an ultimate moral victory over the camp administration when Colonel McLean arrived on a semiannual inspection trip and discovered that a man for whom the director had prescribed "fresh air and light exercise" (on project) had collapsed several times from heart attack in the high altitude. McLean acted swiftly and arranged for the man to return home with an attendant.

This and similar incidents shook the confidence of the authorities in regard to the use of discipline to prune the sick list, though they remained suspicious that some c.o.'s were professionally invaliding themselves out of their proper duties. After considerable delay, Selective Service improved its provisions for competent and expeditious medical examinations where reclassification might be in order, and with those who were not discharged resigned itself to a policy of "laissez-faire," rather than running the risks of compelling sick men to work. The chronic "S.Q." thus became a familiar figure in government C.P.S., lying idle on his bunk with eyes fixed moodily on the rafters, reclining comfortably with a book in the sun, or meandering into lunch in bathrobe and slippers—the symbol of thwarted government authority and all too often of a conscience and personality sickened and warped by the unhealthy environment of conscription.

Isolating the Unco-operative. Of particular concern to the camp authorities was the demoralizing impact which a small minority were able to exercise by "obstructive tactics" upon the work of the whole camp. Although the projects undertaken at Mancos and later at Lapine, Oregon, were generally admitted to be superior to most C.P.S. camp projects in interest and usefulness, unbiased observers (not attached to the official administration) doubted whether more than 50 per cent of the men turned in a reasonable day's work.[23] This was in large measure the result of deliberate "slowdown." [24]

At first the camp directors labored to discover penalties which might persuade objectors to put forth a full day's work and discourage others from joining the slowdown. But aside from withholding furlough and leave, the officials could do little to make life any more uncomfortable than it was for most of the men in question, and once a man's furlough had been docked for several months in advance, further applications of this penalty had little meaning. Threats to report men for legal prosecution were likewise of little avail. The slowdown virtually immunized men from effective legal action, for they could usually point to a record of perfect compliance with every order issued, from reporting to roll call in the morning to returning their tools at night—*if* orders to this effect were given. Neither Selective Service nor the Department of Justice was eager to undertake wholesale suits when deliberate violation of the regulations could not easily be shown.

The method finally adopted to deal with the "obstructionists" was to isolate them from the "co-operators," first on special "assignments" apart from the main project, and in the end in a separate camp. The third government camp, at Germfask in the far north of Michigan, was admittedly designed as a final repository for C.P.S. troublemakers, where, according to Selective Service, "their activities would not interrupt an orderly program elsewhere in C.P.S." [25]

The nucleus of Germfask, as seen by one of its charter members, was formed by "non-cooperators, men chronically reporting to sick call, men with psychiatric ailments, agitators and general trouble makers" transferred from Mancos and Lapine.[26] This constituency rapidly succeeded in making Germfask the most notorious of C.P.S. camps. A visitor was amazed that "no one was required to do any- thing—and didn't." An assignee truck driver took a bird-and-flower book with him as he drove a crew leisurely to project and stopped occasionally when he saw interesting specimens. "Three loads of dirt were moved in the morning when ten could easily have been moved." [27] Another visitor, highly sympathetic to the c.o.'s, was stunned to find "washrooms the filthiest anywhere, dining habits those of hogs, 75% of the men unshaven, unkempt and dirty, liquor being drunk in the dorms on Sunday morning at church time, almost no project work done." [28] Instead of the harsh, punitive regime of the disciplinary barracks which many of the c.o.'s had expected to find in Germfask, they found a reception "more friendly than at Mancos or Lapine" at the hands of government personnel with "more insight into the plight of c.o.'s under conscription than the Bureau of Reclamation engineers." [29] The director, apparently primed to his situation, decided that the best camp direction would be the least. He rode with easy reins, content to let the Fish and Wildlife Refuge go to weeds, while he wet-nursed his unworkable charges. "Work regulations," remarked one of the assignees, "have been lighter than in probably any other C.P.S. camp. . . . Liberty, leave and furlough provisions are more liberally interpreted than in many church camps. A requirement laid down from Washington that men produce two weeks of work before getting a furlough has been loosely applied. Partially sick men have been given jobs at which they can work until choosing to return to quarters." [30] Segregation did not get the c.o.'s to work, but it did provide a *modus vivendi* for Selective Service with the wayward. A kind of truce prevailed at Germfask, with the c.o.'s acquiescing in their confinement and the administration good- naturedly ignoring their individualistic disregard of regulations.

"*Mutiny*" *of the Conscientious.* The objectors might have continued to grumble peacefully in their self-made Tobacco Road, doing dam- age to none but themselves, had not irate neighbors and the Hearst press conjured up a full-fledged "mutiny" in the camp and forced Selective Service authorities to make a public issue of asserting them- selves. Culminating a series of local incidents which led the camp director under community pressure to declare nearby villages out-of-bounds for the c.o.'s, the *Detroit Times* sensationally reported that the war objectors were in "open revolt," with camp officials "powerless to cope with the conditions." [31]

Time magazine (February 19, 1945) went Hearst one better in a juicy exposé of the "Tobacco Road Gang" and its campaign of "studied defiance." Selective Service officials, according to *Time*, "were at their wit's end," for the troublemakers were mostly "guardhouse lawyers" who stayed carefully within the limits of the "loosely drawn Selective Service Act."

The c.o.'s at Germfask took vehement exception to the story in *Time* magazine, charging that it distorted facts, exaggerated the number of men who were "defiant," ignored the psychological and other factors which made some men unco-operative, and biased its readers against the c.o.'s by the use of emotionally colored expressions such as "Tobacco Road Gang" and "thumbing their noses at all authority."

By the c.o.'s own admission, there was substance to most of the charges made, but they claimed these had been bloated by the publicity into a major upheaval, whereas in reality officials and c.o.'s alike had come to accept such incidents as the normal but not too alarming "explosions" of a frustrated and unruly element, which could be brushed aside as of no vital consequence.[32]

Though this publicity was fortuitous and played journalistic havoc with the truth, Selective Service officials, once plunged into the limelight, acted their assumed parts without faltering. The director dramatically appealed to the FBI for an "immediate investigation." Lieutenant Colonel Simon P. Dunkle of Selective Service headquarters dashed to Germfask and then ruefully admitted there was little that could be done without a new law. Colonel Kosch supported the call for new legislation, declaring that federal courts could not be relied upon to crush the "revolt," for they were inclined to dismiss such cases as "minor infractions." He suggested a "commissioner system" similar to the national park service where an administrator could arrest and jail a violator of regulations without legal process. The Germfask district's congressman, Bradley, jumped to rescue the endangered officials and obligingly introduced a bill incorporating Colonel Kosch's scheme. Pending the outcome of this maneuver, Selective Service undertook to rid its camps of the worst offenders by further attempts at prosecution and by sending their files back to the local boards for reconsideration.

None of these stratagems worked. Congress was not sufficiently moved by the lurid tales of Germfask to pull the Michigan congressman's bill out of committee. The courts were little disposed to see their dockets any more crowded with c.o. disciplinary cases. The attempts to secure reclassification fizzled out, as the conclusion of hostilities ended inductions before the c.o.'s had exhausted their rights of appeal. Selective Service could devise no disciplinary technique with which to make its control effective upon those c.o's determined to practice resistance. It discovered—too late—that the co-operation of consciences could not be secured by coercive threats or action, even when lashed by outraged public opinion.

Instead, conditions worsened as a result of the attempted suppression of the Germfask "mutiny." Open conflict and personal recrimination replaced the truce between men and camp officials. Many of the men in the camp who had not sympathized with the behavior of the extremists, especially with their acts of vandalism, now united in condemning the camp officials for giving out a false impression of the situation based on the isolated acts of five or six individuals. The real trouble, according to Germfask c.o.'s, was the failure of Selective Service to handle opposition by an "improved, enlightened administration with a liberal outlook." [33] They had no fear of further penalties. Indeed, they dared the officials to try their worst. Any situation, said the "action group"—and they were now definitely established as the leaders—would be better than the hypocrisy of Selective Service in running a slave labor system under the guise of recognition of conscience.[34] So the last days of Germfask were unpleasant ones for the government camp administrative staff. It was especially disconcerting when an ex-serviceman resigned within a few weeks after appointment as camp manager, convinced that the treatment of men at Germfask amounted to "the re-establishment of slavery in our nation and the punishment of men whose conscience does not permit their participation in war." [35] Conscience thus not only frustrated discipline but infiltrated the very ranks of the disciplinarians.

Sporadic gestures of "firmness" were made until the men were ultimately discharged. But the show of authority had failed, and Selective Service knew it. At Minersville, California, which fell heir to

Germfask inmates upon the latter's demise, twelve men were arrested and held for grand jury on charges of insubordination (their crime— refusal to tear down partitions around their bunks!). After protracted legal and extralegal formalities, the charges were dropped. A "tough" project superintendent at Minersville aggressively threatened fisticuffs after "scientific needling" by c.o.'s, but was fully as unsuccessful in maintaining control as were his Germfask predecessors.

The experience of Government C.P.S. proved convincingly that authority was not a match for conscience when the two were joined in conflict. Selective Service officials struggled hard and patiently to deal fairly with their difficult charges. Though the government officials could not understand the psychology of many of the objectors and were often thoroughly disgusted with some of them, they were rarely harsh or vindictive in their treatment. They did, however, seek to exact minimum compliance with government regulations, and in this they failed. Selective Service administrators could not cope with the skilled devices of resistance matured by c.o.'s to obstruct the enforced marshaling of their labor under conditions they deemed to be unjust. On the other hand, the experience took a toll of the c.o.'s. A careful observer, visiting Mancos, felt that the assignees had largely lost their vision of protest against war and had come to the point where they merely protested the immediate situation in which they found themselves. Furthermore, he predicted that the antagonism and frustration so clearly present in the camp would continue until the camp was demobilized. This prediction proved accurate not only for Mancos but for the other battlefields in government-administered C.P.S. camps where the objectors were locked in direct combat with the agents of state authority.

XII: The Protests of Conscience

As THE c.o.'s term of duty lengthened and the restraints of government became more onerous, a spirit of protest swept the ranks of the pacific. C.P.S. men, in conscientious indignation or petty peevishness, took up cudgels against the "system" which enmeshed them. Some sought to change it, others forswore it, a minority tried to break it down, and some just griped. In the end, the experiment in tolerance was transformed into an embittered struggle between the authority of government and the will of the objector. Neither won. The protesters failed to secure their demands and lived out their C.P.S. terms in unmitigated restraint. The government was rewarded by a slackening C.P.S. work record, administrative frustrations, and an engraved reputation for abasing religious liberty. The most serious loss was the ideal of service as the distinctive mark of the American conscientious objector. "Inevitably in the prosecution of a program in which 'service' is obtained by threat of penalty or exile, a point is reached," philosophized the *Pacifica Views,* most erudite organ of C.P.S. protest, "where the very term becomes a synonym of canting pretense." [1] With these and similar convictions, some c.o.'s resurrected the traditional role of the "objector." Many others in C.P.S. continued quietly to offer their testimony through service, but the protesters stole the spotlight and stamped "objection" in bold type across the whole face of the alternative service program.

The Objectors' Objections

C.o's were far from united on the basis for their protests. The "gripers" were merely annoyed at the personal inconveniences which beset them. A second group protested against the injustices of C.P.S. and its failure to provide satisfactory conditions for significant service. A third group raised issues of conscience, finding C.P.S. in part or in whole incompatible with their basic convictions.

Gripes. The complaints of the gripers included at one time or another every facet of C.P.S. The food was insufficient and unpalatable, the project was hard, the supervisors were unkind. Each increase in the work week brought a flurry of protests. Each suspension of furloughs was challenged in part on the ground of the unnecessary inconvenience it caused to individual plans. Some men considered themselves abused when an amply stocked larder was not made available for midnight snacks. When first the religious agencies, then Selective Service, frowned upon personal cars being kept at camp, owners complained. Men disliked their isolation and the primitiveness of their quarters. Mass transfers ordered by Selective Service called forth objections from those who had to pull up well-established stakes, which sometimes included wives happily employed in a neighboring community.

These protests against inconvenience, always numerous, sometimes bitter, never agitated C.P.S. very profoundly. They did form an undercurrent of discontent which could veer easily into channels of deeper import.

Injustices. Far more potent was the sense of injustice which grew as men labored under the restrictions and discriminations of C.P.S. The denial of pay, many felt, was an especially raw deal for the c.o. The government had "hit below the belt at an unpopular minority." [2] The C.P.S. man was indignant when he learned that prisoners of war received eighty cents a day and that the United States Army paid Guadalcanal native labor sixteen cents a day, while his own allowance barely topped eight cents. Men vehemently protested public assertions by Selective Service officials that pay was withheld because the c.o.'s did not want it, and showed in a barrage of polls that the great majority would take pay if it were provided.

The injustice of forcing dependents to subsist without government assistance stirred the c.o.'s with equal fervor. There was unanimous agreement that a government which drafted men for income-less service should provide for their dependents; failure to do so in the case of c.o. dependents when the dependents of military men were liberally aided was to the objector a shocking violation of basic human rights.

C.P.S. men became disgusted with the work they were ordered to perform. It was, they exploded, "senseless, routine, without goal. It deadens initiative and makes no use of talent. One comes to feel that every moment spent at work on the project is waste." [3] "How can we be content day after day to manicure mountains," asked a seasoned assignee, "when the world has such crying need for practical real help and help that we want to give." [4] There was less objection to work in special service projects, and c.o.'s kept up constant pressure for more such assignments, particularly where they could contribute to immediate social welfare needs.

Dissatisfaction with the project was intensified by inefficient and arbitrary project management. The men caustically criticized many of the technical staffs for their lack of imagination, poor handling of personnel, waste of labor and equipment, and bad planning.[5] They especially resented unwarranted accusations against them by project officials. On one occasion a crew stopped work when a man suffering from hay fever was rejected by the foreman for "unsatisfactory work" (a penalty offense) simply because the man had asked to be spared the handling of straw.[6]

The restrictive and expanding control of Selective Service over the administration of C.P.S. also deeply disturbed the c.o.'s. To some this control became an actual issue of conscience (see below), but many objected simply because they felt they and their churches were being unjustly deprived of their right to direct the program. "Selective Service is telling us how to run our camps," they complained. "The historic peace churches pay all the bills, accept all the responsibility, and all the trouble, yet they have no actual jurisdiction in the simplest matters." [7] The assignees objected particularly when Selective Service dictated disciplinary action and insisted on the churches' carrying it out; this was an outright violation of the basic agreement to entrust discipline to the discretion and insight of the religious agencies. The adamant refusal of Selective Service to recognize any right of the c.o. to share in the policy making and administration of C.P.S. seemed to many of the men undemocratic. On the other hand, a great many c.o.'s, especially under Mennonite administration, accepted and obeyed Selective Service regulations without protest even when they were considered unfair.

The religious agencies themselves did not escape without criticism. They were constantly attacked for acquiescing in the unsatisfactory features of the program and for failing to act quickly to secure changes and improvements. Some charged that those administering C.P.S. were frankly afraid to raise questions of principle lest privileges be lost, such as their right to operate the camps.[8] Sometimes the c.o.'s objected because they felt the Service Committees were dictatorial and arbitrary in their administration, did not take the men sufficiently into their confidence, and failed to keep them well informed about matters affecting their welfare. "Many men are irked by the 'we know what is best for C.P.S. men' attitude of the administrators,"[9] commented a loyal and co-operative assignee. The assistant director of a hospital unit complained that requests for information from the N.S.B.R.O. on matters of concern to the men received replies of "one or two sentences which really tell us nothing about the actual nature of what is going on." Men at a Mennonite camp were deeply disturbed when they were assigned to emergency farm labor before assurance had been given that the money earned would not be used for defense purposes, yet the answer from N.S.B.R.O. to their urgent plea for information and counsel was, "Negotiations are still in progress." This was too much of a brush-off even for the mild-tempered. Finally, some condemned entirely the participation of the agencies in C.P.S. on the grounds that they were abetting conscription and "directing slave colonies." But this was more than a grievance. It was the staking out of a new and strikingly different stand, rooted in conscience rather than a mere sense of injustice.

Issues of Conscience. Protests on grounds of conscience were the most serious in C.P.S. For where his conscience was involved, the c.o. hovered on the edge of a complete break with C.P.S., no matter how committed to the service ideal he might be or how temperate and co-operative he might have been in the program to date.

Two main issues excited conscientious objection *to* C.P.S.: military implications in the program and the infringement of freedom resulting from conscription. Any development suspected of tying the c.o. into war work or subjecting him to military control was challenged as a threat to integrity of conscience.[10] Most men refused to volunteer for dairy-farm work until they were assured that their earnings would not be siphoned by the government into military expenditures. Large numbers of men objected to emergency farm labor as essentially a war-supporting activity; showdowns were averted only by the willingness of Selective Service and project superintendents to assign to other tasks those who objected. A camp refused to cut wood if the proceeds went into the United States Treasury for military purposes. Men would not construct a fire tower until assured it was not intended for aerial spotting. The Department of Agriculture had to reassure men picking sugar beets that they would not be used to manufacture glycerine. One-third of a camp refused to work on a timber road because it would make lumber available for war shipbuilding. Men at Trenton, North Dakota, asked to be exempted from work on a fifty-acre tract of flax because its chief by-product, linseed oil, was used primarily to make explosives.

Many men found the entire control exercised by Selective Service over C.P.S. repugnant to their consciences because of what appeared to them its essentially military character. The presence of Army officers in the key posts of administration, the payment of their salaries out of military appropriations, the awarding of military honors to some of them for their service in C.P.S. administration (Colonel Kosch received the Distinguished Service Cross), and the military pattern of the regulations prescribed for C.P.S. convinced c.o.'s that the civilian direction assured in the Selective Service Act had been denied in spirit and practice. They were unimpressed by the legal fiction that in Selective Service military officers were acting in their "civilian capacity." So indistinguishable were Selective Service and military control to many men that, if convinced they were irretrievably under the Selective Service thumb rather than the administration of the religious agencies, they were prepared to quit service.[11]

Other men repudiated the entire C.P.S. system rather than its discomforts, injustices, or militaristic features. They were really misplaced absolutists, for they had come to believe that C.P.S. was not a "true alternative of military service" but an evil thing which ought to be completely done away with. They denounced it as "involuntary servitude without pay . . . in violation of the 13th Amendment."

This condemnation was elaborated by a leading c.o. who walked out of C.P.S. after a sojourn of six months:

It encourages hypocrisy, wishful thinking, 'gold bricking,' hypochondria, self-deception, submissiveness, laziness, idle grumbling, selfishness, sheepish citizenship and countless confusions and stupefactions of the mind.

It discourages honesty, forthrightness, responsibility, courage, initiative, independence, constructive thinking, strength of character and mental health in general.

As a factor on the American scene it is making good dupes for some possible future fascism; it is making poor citizens for democracy. . . . It is a polite and gentlemanly version of what we have been hearing of forced labor elsewhere in the world. . . . Acquiescence in it is not consistent with my understanding of pacifism.[12]

The supreme issue to most such objectors had become the "octopus extension" of conscription which threatened personal liberty, democratic society, and Christian principles. C.P.S. mirrored the global trend to totalitarianism—the insidious imposition of authority from the top and the demand of unquestioning obedience to that authority in the name of "national interest," or, as speciously presented to the c.o.'s, the "welfare of society." Both c.o. and church were indulging in fatal collaboration with the "uncontrolled authority" of the state. Conscience should repudiate concessions to dictates of state which curtailed human freedom, and the individual, by whatever means seemed most appropriate to him, should resist its efforts to reduce men to the status of slaves. "Men will not lose their liberty," prophesied one of the ablest yet most reasonable spokesmen for the absolutist objectors, as he wound up a checkered career in Friends and government camps, "if they will refuse to comply when others seek to take liberty from them—and if they, in turn, do not seek to infringe upon the liberty of others." [13]

Complaint through Channels

The men usually brought their grievances first to the persons directly responsible for their administration, the staffs of the religious agencies. The camp directors were, of course, on the front line of the gripe barrage, but Akron, Elgin, and Philadelphia and the N.S.B.R.O. offices were also soon aware of rumblings of discontent wherever they occurred. Periodically, intercamp conferences offered a chance for complaints to be fully aired by representatives of the assignees before the top religious leaders. The system of assignee representation also furnished an important channel through which protests could be brought directly to the committees' attention by spokesmen designated by the men.[14]

The grievances of the assignees usually secured serious and sympathetic consideration from the church staffs, though some of the protests were badly mishandled.[15] The main problem was not the lack of responsiveness of the churches but the difficulty in working out acceptable solutions. Complicated and time-consuming negotiations were necessary to overcome obstacles not easily visible to men in camp, and sometimes obstacles proved insurmountable regardless of the merits of the case and the best efforts of the religious agencies. This severely tried the patience of the protesters and undermined their confidence in the competence or good faith of the agencies.

Unchanneled Protest

The more impatient of the protesters, disgusted with the slowness and apparent ineffectiveness of complaining to the religious agencies, urged independent action to secure satisfaction of their demands.

Some injudicious strategists thought a direct appeal to Selective Service as the seat of authority might bring results, but quickly found that they could not short-circuit administrative channels. Neither mass petitions nor individual pleas secured an official hearing, though Selective Service officials did expose themselves informally to the barbed criticisms of assignees when they were visiting camps. Officialdom, as Colonel McLean carefully explained to the Williamsburg unit when it sought Selective Service attention directly, would recognize no action of assignees or assignee organizations which was not properly communicated through the unit or camp administrations (unless it were a violation of regulations or an incident of "public relations" whereupon recognition was swift and peremptory even before word of the action had traveled the official escalator).[16]

Another technique of independent protest was the fast. Some c.o.'s staged "sympathy fasts" to demonstrate their solidarity with men who had run afoul of Selective Service and the law by walking out of C.P.S. or engaging in work strikes. On the other hand, a group at the Wellston, Michigan, camp went on a seven-day fast to protest the failure of the government to provide dependency allowances. Their action was precipitated when a mass transfer of assignees to the west coast robbed many men with dependents of their opportunity to earn money by spare-time work in the community. The fasters carefully avoided any appearance of a work strike—they continued to put in full time on project. The Brethren Service Committee co-operated in the effort by agreeing to devote to dependency needs the money saved on food.[17]

The Chicago Conference. A decisive test of the strategy of protesting outside of channels came in the ill-fated Chicago Conference on Social Action, called in April, 1943, by an assignee committee independently of the religious agencies and against the express prohibition of Selective Service.

The conference was planned not as a mere protest meeting but to give C.P.S. men a chance to exchange views and consider action in regard to their common problems. Topics on the proposed agenda did not sound rebellious:

What work is possible under conscription?

How can conscientious objectors gain opportunity for greater service?

How can c.o.'s develop an adequate training program?

What should c.o.'s do about conscription?

What should c.o.'s do about winning the peace?

The sponsors admitted that the organization of the conference was "indicative of serious discontent with C.P.S. as a pacifist program during wartime" but insisted that they intended no mutiny against the administration. Indeed, they invited the presence of both religious and governmental administrators and particularly of General Hershey. The conference, in other words, was an attempt to initiate direct negotiations between the assignees and those who exercised authority over them. This was the project's undoing.

Pointedly avoiding a direct reply to his invitation, General Hershey informed the National Service Board that "no assignee in a Civilian Public Service Camp will attend this meeting and no Directors of Civilian Public Service Camps will grant furloughs to assignees for the purpose of attending this meeting." He "directed" that this communication be brought to the attention of each camp director a week before the scheduled opening of the conference and demanded confirmation that "this directive has been complied with." Paul French, after trying unsuccessfully to get the decision changed, reported that Hershey felt

very strongly that such a conference at the present time will only make more difficulties in the whole c.o. problem in Congress and the govern- ment. . . . The whole pattern of General Hershey's thinking is based on a systematic and orderly manner of procedure and he feels that meet- ings such as this should be organized by the administrative agencies as a part of the whole administrative program.[18]

Colonel Kosch was even more belligerent about not tolerating "men in the camps organizing mass meetings and conferences without their [Selective Service] approval." Selective Service was definitely ready for a showdown, quite prepared to have the non-co-operators walk out over this issue.[19]

Within and outside of C.P.S. the ban was vehemently denounced as a denial of civil liberties, specifically of freedom of speech and freedom of assembly. Sixty-three men at the Big Flats camp urged the A.F.S.C. to discontinue its administration if the order was not withdrawn. Sixty-seven out of seventy-two men at the Powellsville camp meeting also pledged individual noncompliance with the order. Throughout C.P.S. men advocated "measures as drastic as may be necessary to secure the removal of General Hershey's order." This attitude was by no means unanimous. Particularly in Mennonite camps there were many who agreed with Selective Service that "no good could come of such a conference" and cautioned their fellow pacifists to "lay aside these small petty issues and take a clear look at the teachings of Christ to restore this world to peace." [20]

From the outside, A. J. Muste of the Fellowship of Reconciliation and Evan Thomas of the War Resisters League questioned the con- stitutionality and legality of the order, challenged C.P.S. men to refuse co-operation "with this totalitarian regime," and urged the Service Committees to oppose the penalization of men who might leave camp or refuse to work in protest. The Service Committees themselves took a very serious view of the crisis, and the A.F.S.C. associated itself with the views of the protesters.[21]

The immediate question was whether to postpone or cancel the conference at least until after a full-dress attempt had been made by the religious agencies to get Hershey to revoke his order. The agencies counseled that to hold the conference in direct defiance of both the General and the specific furlough bans would make effective negotiations virtually impossible and also obscure the civil-liberties issue. Most C.P.S. men apparently agreed that the path of negotiation should be left unobstructed. They were committed to the handling of protest through established channels as long as hope of a solution remained, and were confident that their interests would be "fully and completely protected" by the religious agencies in the conferences with Selective Service.[22]

But the key promoters of the conference insisted that the civil-liberties issue did not permit of "temporizing." To await official sanction for the conference would, they felt, imply that the exercise of their civil rights depended upon Selective Service permission.[23] So the leaders proceeded with their plans.

In the meantime Hershey met with representatives of the religious agencies, who reported enthusiastically that he had been "friendly, understanding, and reasonable" and that prospects were good for "a real improvement in the whole C.P.S. situation." The ban on the holding of the conference was not lifted, however, and the religious agencies declined to divulge particulars of their discussion until Selective Service had had a chance to act officially.

In retrospect, it is difficult to reconcile the grave concerns which prompted the meeting with Hershey with what actually transpired in the discussion. The churches in effect put *their* C.P.S. problems before Hershey, rather than confronting him squarely with the issue of civil liberty raised by the men who protested the banning of the Chicago Conference. They really misled the c.o.'s in regard to the character of the negotiations which they were carrying on behind the screen of confidence.

As it was, the Chicago Conference was convened while the Selective Service ban still stood. The proceedings were innocuous and attendance was small. Many of the original sponsors did not come, preferring to await the outcome of the representations to Selective Service. But forty did attend from C.P.S. (thirteen camps and units) with full knowledge that they were leaving camp without authorization. This raised a new issue which quickly displaced the original problems for which the conference was called, as well as the question of civil liberty to which attention had been diverted by the Selective Service ban. What penalties would the men suffer for their A.W.O.L. and their deliberate disobedience of the Hershey order? And what action should be taken if the penalties imposed were unjustified?

This issue completed the cleavage between the religious agencies and the supporters of the Chicago Conference. The conference itself opposed penalties of any kind and called on its members and others who shared their views to refuse to work if penalties were exacted. The religious agencies, hoping to forestall drastic action by Selective Service, imposed the customary three days' furlough penalty for each day of A.W.O.L. The A.F.S.C., after animated staff discussion, did not accept a suggestion of Paul French to add a penalty of several days' furlough on account of the direct disobedience of Hershey, but the Brethren and Mennonites did. (This affected only a few men, as most of the attenders were from Friends C.P.S.) The action of the agencies keenly disappointed many C.P.S. men, aside from those who attended the conference, and also a number of the leaders of the Historic Peace Churches. They charged that conscience was being sacrificed for expediency, and the principle of civil liberty for the chance to continue the administration of C.P.S. Did the religious agencies have a moral right, they asked, to punish men for an action dictated by conscience, involving the violation of a regulation which the agencies themselves admitted infringed upon civil liberties? [24] Some credited the Service Committee with desiring to protect the men who had left camp and the rest of C.P.S. from the wrath of Selective Service; the men rejected such protection as bought at the cost of compromising important pacifist principles and the very essence of religious freedom. "We are not refugees but citizens," they protested. "We do not want your kindly ministration, but rather wish you as a single unit to set forth a pacifist witness regardless of consequences." [25]

The Service Committees defended their action on the grounds that the men went ahead with the conference without awaiting possible repeal of the ban and thereby left the Committees no alternative but to list them A.W.O.L. and impose the usual penalty. So long as they continued to work in the program, they had to carry out agreements made with Selective Service, one of them being the three-day furlough penalty for A.W.O.L. Its prompt application would, they hoped, put them in a strong position to contest any special punitive action which General Hershey might have in mind.

This theory was soon put to the test. Selective Service ordered all liberty and leave refused to the men who attended the conference and indicated it would not approve of their assignment to any detached service. The N.S.B.R.O. refused to send on the order affecting liberty and leave, explaining that it considered this a type of ex post facto regulation which it did not feel able to enforce, especially as it lay "in a field in which we understood we had freedom to function according to our basic concepts." [26] This stand approximated a showdown. Unaccountably, Selective Service did not force the issue, though for about a year it did consistently turn down the Chicago Conference men for detached service. Protest fizzled out.

The attempt at unchanneled protest had merely confirmed the restrictions under which the c.o. labored in C.P.S. Selective Service had not yielded an inch in its claim to control the entire life of the C.P.S. man and to prescribe his every right. In the face of the religious agencies it did not exact as stringent a penalty as it at first intended for the flouting of its authority, and General Hershey did agree to set up government-directed camps as a result of his meeting with the religious agencies which the protest had in part instigated. But the fundamental issue of civil rights for the c.o. remained unresolved, and the issues over which the Chicago Conference had originally been called lay smothered.

Dyer's Plan. The debacle of the Chicago Conference convinced most C.P.S. men that Selective Service would reject their protests, whether channeled or unchanneled. But one man insisted that c.o.'s should carry an appeal over the head of Selective Service directly to the President, who had the ultimate responsibility for executing the Selective Service Act and determining the conditions of alternative service. Henry Dyer, who had earned the respect of fellow c.o.'s and C.P.S. administration alike for his integrity, critical judgment, yet co-operative and friendly disposition, sponsored a petition requesting the President to "appoint a civilian board to place each man in suitable and useful work in the public welfare at regular wages."

Circulating throughout C.P.S., the petition soon was signed by about eighteen hundred men, a demonstration of unity in protest which far exceeded any other action in C.P.S. (This represented about 20 per cent of the C.P.S. enrollment at the time.) Dyer then pressed for an appointment with President Truman for three "representative conscientious objectors" to present the petition along with a substantiating report which would demonstrate "the serious and unnecessary waste of training and experience in these camps and units" and show "how this waste is being avoided in England and Canada." Dyer deliberately steered clear of the administrative agencies in making his approach so that its "grass-roots" character would be unsullied.

Prospects for such a meeting brightened when Senator Burton K. Wheeler took a hand and asked for the appointment, but the White House finally turned down the request and rejected the petition after consulting Selective Service.[27]

Thus the final and most judicious attempt of the c.o.'s to secure favorable consideration of their grievances by direct appeal to governmental authority was frustrated by Selective Service, which thereby emerged victorious in the battle over "channels."

Collective Bargaining for Conscience

Several of the "left-wing" leaders among the c.o. protesters decided that if their action was to be effective it would have to be collective and continuous. The c.o.'s undoing, they claimed, was their lack of unity, persistence, and organization. So during 1944 a C.P.S. "union" was organized.

The founders stressed that its object was not to *oppose* the administration of C.P.S. but to abolish its "waste and injustice" and secure recognition of the legitimate "rights" of c.o.'s as employees of the government, such as adequate opportunity for service, pay, workmen's compensation, and dependency allotments, "through the orderly processes of a democratic union."[28] Incidentally, the union was to encourage C.P.S. interest in the labor movement and vice versa. The union would use the techniques of "explanation, discussion, persuasion, negotiation" to arouse public support. "Direct nonviolent group pressure" (i.e., strikes) might be undertaken after "full democratic discussion and vote," but only as a last resort. The union leaders advocated and solicited collaboration with the religious agencies in the accomplishment of their objectives and urged union members to emphasize the desire to serve well as the motivation of their efforts to win better conditions. "An honest day's work," asserted one union local, "is one of its best arguments for collective bargaining." [29]

On this basis, about five hundred members were signed up in sixty-four camps and units (initiation fee twenty-five cents and dues twenty-five cents monthly), seventeen full-fledged "locals" were organized, and a "general executive board" was elected.[30] Much of the activity of the union was directed toward publicizing the shortcomings of C.P.S., especially its waste of service, and promoting a "practical alternative achievable under the present statute," i.e. to abolish the "camp and unit system" in favor of individual service assignments with pay. This alternative coincided with the Dyer plan, already mentioned, for which the union furnished the principal documentation and active support.[31]

Though the union never actually sponsored a strike in C.P.S., its organization soon aroused the suspicions of Colonel Kosch, who asked the N.S.B.R.O. to "expedite" him a "complete" report concerning the organization and its activities. The N.S.B.R.O. astutely suggested instead that Kosch talk personally with the union's officers so that he could get firsthand knowledge of its plans.[32] Somewhat reluctantly he agreed, though he declared firmly he had no intention of recognizing the union as a bargaining agent for the men. The conference passed pleasantly, once Kosch had reiterated his determination not to be "pressured" by any groups of assignees and had warned the men that most unions were just out to get what they could for themselves. The Colonel then discussed freely and frankly with the union's representatives the problems that were on their minds. Concrete gains, the men admitted, were small, if any, for the Colonel vigorously defended Selective Service's every act. But he interposed no objection to their further efforts if the union remained "altruistic," and the representatives thought they had an open door to come back "when we've got our specific proposals worked out so we can meet him on his ground when it's reasonable and to insist he meet us on our ground when it is solid." Such an occasion did not materialize, so the union's original primary objective of establishing collective bargaining for C.P.S. men was stillborn.[33]

The Disobedient C.O.

The ineffectiveness of his protests forced the c.o. to make a critical decision. Should he resign himself to conditions as they stood in C.P.S., with whatever minor reforms might come from continued protest and the patient pleading of the religious agencies? Or should he refuse to co-operate with the system and openly declare his resistance to it? In the last analysis, the majority of those who entered C.P.S. chose the first course and performed, however reluctantly, the duties required of them. But a sizable minority, which grew larger through the years, determined to carry their opposition to the point of deliberate disobedience. Such disobedience usually took the form of a walkout, a work strike, or a slowdown, depending on the motivation and immediate objectives of the individual c.o.

The Walkout. The walkout was not intended as an act of resistance. It was a simple, clear, and total act of personal renunciation. The c.o. would no longer "walk the second mile with evil." He condemned C.P.S. and refused to submit himself to its regulation—but he neither hoped nor intended that his act would force a change in the existing conditions of service. He was frankly no longer interested in the improvement of C.P.S. "Improving it and making it more palatable would only encourage people to accept it and I want to see it abolished," firmly declared one man.[34] Walking out thus became the recourse of an honest man who could find no niche for his conscience within the framework of conscription and who considered it "indecent" to accept privileges within the framework of the system against which he would protest.[35]

The Work Strike. The strike and the slowdown, on the contrary, were acts of positive resistance, deliberately designed to force either a basic change of policy in C.P.S. or its complete abandonment by the religious agencies or the government. Unlike the walkout, the strikers and the slowdowners were revolutionists rather than martyrs.

The first strikes were sporadic affairs, prompted by a particular incident on project, an arbitrary transfer order, or individual opposition to a policy. Shortly after his arrival at the Mancos camp, for instance, James Manoukian refused to work until he was paid, charging that to do otherwise was to accept "a theory abhorrent to basic American principles." Twenty-eight men at Mancos joined in a one-day fast when Manoukian was arrested, and fourteen staged a one-day work strike against "forced labor without compensation." Twenty-six assignees at Walhalla, Michigan, refused to do emergency farm work, though they willingly performed regular project work. These actions were usually disposed of with little official flurry, except for the customary penalties and an administrative settlement of the issue which brought the refusal to work.

A far more serious situation was precipitated when, after the end of hostilities, mass strikes broke out in a number of camps in a deliberate attempt to force action upon the c.o.'s accumulated grievances. By May, 1946, seventy men at Glendora and thirty-five at Big Flats (camps at this time under government administration) had completely stopped work. A strike of twelve men at Cascade Locks had ended a few weeks earlier. Other camps were seething. Stated objectives ran the gamut of opposition to the arbitrary transfer of assignees, the imposition of unjust penalties, the lack of dependency allotments, slow demobilization, forced labor without pay, and the system of conscription. But the all-consuming purpose was to throw C.P.S. overboard.

> Whatta yah got to lose, boys,
> Nothin' but your chains, boys

chanted the strikers.

> We labored lo! these many years
> For all those hazy goals;
> The Forest Service got our sweat
> And the Brethren got our souls.

> Break the system down, boys
> Strike the lick that does the trick
> And break the system down.[36]

The refusal of men to perform their work and other C.P.S. duties was the greatest crisis to confront both Selective Service and the religious agencies. The former, as has been seen, was unable to meet the challenge by means of commensurate discipline, and only with the promise of discharge within two weeks were some of the strikers persuaded to return to work.[37] The Service Committees, for their part, sympathized with the complaints of the men, but insisted that the assignees should co-operate as long as they chose to remain in C.P.S. under their administration.

This was the issue which ultimately embittered the relations of the Friends with their camp at Elkton, Oregon. For two years the camp had been a model of harmony between the men, the A.F.S.C. staff, and the project administration. But in late 1944 contingents of veteran protesters arrived from Big Flats and Powellsville and soon the project staff reported organized efforts to impede the work program. Poor judgment on the part of some of the project officials in dealing with the men, the suspected military implications of one of the major work assignments, and the diminishing value of the rest of the work, as well as the antagonistic attitude of the dissident c.o.'s toward the C.P.S. program as a whole, led to a rapid deterioration of the camp's morale and a rising mood of criticism. A sizable group of men openly declared their desire to see Friends C.P.S. fail, and the camp was soon confronted (as other camps had already been) by men who would not work, or who claimed to be sick yet refused the medical treatment prescribed for them. Various expedients to improve the quality of the project relations, to avoid assigning men to work of which they disapproved, and to rebuild a closely knit camp community proved ineffective. The camp staff and A.F.S.C. administration moved progressively, though reluctantly, to the conclusion that there was no basis of co-operation "with men who seek to destroy C.P.S. or who could not assume the responsibilities required in Friends C.P.S." Such men should, the staff felt, be persuaded or obliged to transfer out of Friends C.P.S.

This conclusion was resisted both by the non-co-operators and by many supporters of Friends C.P.S., who maintained that men should not be obliged to leave because they objected to C.P.S. "The responsibility assumed [by the A.F.S.C.] for other people," protested the former educational secretary, "was not to make them make C.P.S. work, but to serve them as individuals . . . it is then well that we serve those who do not agree with us." [38] There was particular opposition to the suggestion that men be forced to leave against their will.

The issue was brought to a head by the point-blank refusal of Americo Chiarito to work and his outspoken determination to resist by every means at his disposal the administration of "enforced involuntary servitude" even though it was "disguised by our own government in the saintly robes of religion." He specifically announced his determination to remain at Elkton in order to persuade others to join him in his resistance. The A.F.S.C. finally decided to ask for his transfer to a government camp. The momentum for protest slowly gathered; almost two months later, after Selective Service had authorized the transfer, about half the camp urged it to be canceled, excusing Chiarito's actions as a "direct outgrowth of his pacifist convictions" and testifying that they considered him a valuable member of the camp community. The A.F.S.C. would not budge. Neither would Chiarito, who refused to obey the transfer order.

The camp thereupon defiantly elected Chiarito its representative to the A.F.S.C.–C.P.S. Committee. The Committee's decision not to seat him, on the grounds that he had removed himself from the program by his refusal to work, was vehemently denounced by many men at Elkton and elsewhere as undemocratic, and two of the assignee representatives on the C.P.S. Committee resigned under instructions from their constituencies. Camp government at Elkton was discontinued in further protest.

Chiarito was eventually arrested. Six disciples thereupon followed his suit and refused to work, either on project or overhead. Soon they too joined him in the clutches of the law.

The disobedient had, however, succeeded in their primary purpose of disrupting the administration of C.P.S. in their camp. Elkton never recovered, despite the most earnest efforts of an able and well-respected camp staff to "put Humpty Dumpty together again." The men were divided and mutually suspicious. The A.F.S.C. was cordially detested by many. The project staff had become definitely hostile toward the men, and the feeling was thoroughly reciprocated. Neither credited the other with good faith, and a chain of incidents culminated in the project officials' charging more men with refusal to work and demanding punitive action from Selective Service. This time the A.F.S.C. took the part of the men because of extenuating circumstances, but the offenders were ordered to a government camp anyway. Only the closing of the camp brought an end to its many trials.

The Slowdown. The slowdown was the most calculated of the

strategies of protest used in C.P.S. It was a product of the government-administered camp and was hailed among the pacifist "left-wingers" as a most important discovery in the methods of nonviolent resistance to authoritarian government and social injustice. The avowed object of its practitioners was to wreck the administration of C.P.S. and show that "forced labor . . . can be made to be the world's most inefficient way of getting work done"—provided it was resisted "with a will." They astutely realized that to do this, they would have to keep their actions within the technical bounds of the law. Whatever value the walkout or the work strike might have as a means of demonstrating protest and clearing one's own conscience, these methods would not dent the system itself, for by committing a clear violation of the law, the protesters exposed themselves to removal behind bars, where neither their voice nor their actions could have any effect. The problem which the true pacifist "resister" set himself to solve was how to "oppose the State and its power to make war without being shuttled completely out of sight." The slow-down was the answer given, after careful thought and preliminary tryout, by a small core of c.o.'s who wanted above all else to rid themselves of the reputation of "passivism" and "attain a significant political relevance" without espousing violence.[39]

The C.P.S. slowdown combined psychological warfare with passive resistance. At every opportunity the accomplished slowdowner sought to demoralize his administrator. He reminded him that the c.o. "was a slave . . . that the foremen are slave overseers . . . that slave driving is morally wrong, but that he personally holds no grudge against the foreman for his part in the slave system." In the meantime, the resister would try "to accomplish as near to nothing on the project as it is possible to do—and this to be done while working at all times!" A disgusted foreman at Germfask told of an encounter with a model slowdowner assigned to hang wire on fence posts:

After a strip of the wire had been installed, I noticed the wire sagging in several places . . . had not been attached to the staples. . . . The assignee said, "You only told me to drive the staple into the post. You didn't tell me to put the wire in the staple." So then I carefully explained that the wire must be put into the staple before the nail is driven into the pole. Later I noticed that the man had remained in almost the same position on the fence line. . . . I found that he had driven many staples into the single post, all of the staples attached to the wire. When I asked him about that, he only shrugged and said that his orders were simply to drive staples with the wire attached into the post and nothing had been said about driving only a single staple into a single post.[40]

The advocates of the slowdown recognized its real shortcomings—the danger of public misunderstanding, the alienation of c.o.'s who believed in the philosophy of service as well as of those who supported more clear-cut non-co-operation, the probability that the slowdowners would be segregated in order to minimize their influence on other men, and, in the last analysis, the possibility that they would be prosecuted for obstructing the law, even though they had not technically violated it. They were confident that these shortcomings were not absolute. As against furnishing ammunition to the American Legion, the slowdowners would arouse the support of the "leftist" sector of public opinion. By appealing for mutual respect of each other's integrity, they could prevent a wide breach from developing between them and the second-miler, the work striker, and the walkout. By persisting in his slowdown, regardless of isolation or the inconsequence of the job assigned, he would nullify the administration's effort to break his will, and in the end prove his case—that the state cannot by duress get work done. Finally, the slowdowner was confident that he was relatively lawproof, and that the government would have real difficulty in securing his conviction. The slowdown, though it involved risk, was a calculated risk which its advocates urged as the best chance of throwing over the detested system.[41]

The slowdowners did go farther than any other of the c.o. protesters toward frustrating the administration of C.P.S. They succeeded in proving that Selective Service, even in its own camps, could not exact satisfactory service from determined resisters by the disciplinary measures within its power. They were also elated by the defection of several of the government's administrative staff under the pressure of the psychological offensive. But they won few converts among their fellow c.o.'s, many of whom were repelled by the coercive implications of the strategy, nonviolent though it might be. Russell Freeman, a c.o. who himself had resigned as director of a Friends C.P.S. camp because he believed pacifists should not administer conscription, observed:

When persons are engaged in exploiting and encouraging attitudes of defiance, rebellion and unrest, they can hardly expect much more than purely destructive results, despite the fact that there is much evil and social injustice apparent in the structure they seek to destroy. There is an organic and direct relationship between aim and methods, vision and means, attitudes and resulting conduct, which cannot be ignored, even by those who would practice "nonviolence," if the highest goal is to be realistically sought. . . . When one concentrates upon the evils and injustices being perpetrated by others, either upon oneself or upon neutral parties, sooner or later one begins to lose perspective and to assimilate, consciously or unconsciously, portions of the adversary's psychology and methods.[42]

The fatal weakness of the slowdown was the strain that it put upon the personalities of those who took part in it. Some of the men were at first exhilarated by "a new sense of freedom" which they experienced as they tossed aside "the confusion and irritating inhibitions which characterized the church sponsorship" and undertook a sharply defined opposition to the system they abhorred.[43] But a number who joined in the strategy, at first, refused to continue because, as one of them concluded, "it was too internally degrading for the small effect it was having in the right direction." [44] Long before they could seriously undermine the C.P.S. program and the structure of its administration, some of the slowdowners demoralized themselves, succumbing to the very embitterment, chronic slothfulness, belligerence, and disintegration of personal integrity which the leaders had foreseen as the danger above all others to be avoided. "The fundamental difficulty," one c.o. discovered, was "that an injurious evil principle cannot be conquered by protest and negative indictment." [45]

Taken all together, the protests of the conscientious objectors— "channeled" and "unchanneled," "obedient" and "disobedient"— were unable to secure the relaxation of restraints upon their liberty in C.P.S. Those who were responsive to the complaints, notably the religious agencies, lacked the power of reform. They could only attempt conciliation. Those who had the authority to act, notably Selective Service, repulsed protest as an affront to that authority. The objections of the c.o.'s broke upon an inflexible administration convinced that in its exercise of the executive responsibility it had done, and could do, no wrong. Only a heretic would oppose its policies, and heresy deserved not greater leniency but sterner suppression.

As protest met repression, the experiment in tolerance turned sour. Negativism engulfed the ranks of the conscientious, and many who had come to serve in Civilian Public Service remained—or left—to object. In the long run, the frustrations of C.P.S. probably did not seriously affect most men, and a considerable number undoubtedly grew in "maturity" and balance as a result of their experience. But many a c.o. became a chronic pessimist, a griper, a ranter, a saboteur, or a law-breaker instead of a buoyant peacemaker, because his protest had been greeted as insubordination rather than as constructive criticism.

XIII: *Reform and Salvage*

Despite the intense struggle between restrictive government authority and protesting conscientious objectors, Civilian Public Service survived. A final convulsive showdown was averted by unceasing effort to win reform, and where this was frustrated—as for the most part it was—stopgap relief sufficiently eased the oppressive impact of conscription upon conscience to forestall revolt. By their personal solicitude, those concerned with religious freedom salvaged the service of c.o.'s from complete disintegration; but without the authority to control or alter fundamental policies they could not cure the basic ills of C.P.S. and undo the damage wrought to the cause of tolerance by governmental discrimination and repression.

The Churches' Administrative Bromides

Over against Selective Service as the chief agency of restraint in Civilian Public Service, the religious administrators championed liberalization and reform. Not only did they try to win basic concessions from government; they sought through their own efforts to resolve crises and soothe the fevered tempers of aggrieved c.o.'s.

The Improvisation of Religious Bureaucracy. None of the religious agencies was really prepared to assume the major administrative responsibilities of C.P.S. They lacked understanding of the problems and procedures of public service, as their experience had been limited to voluntary welfare programs on a small scale. They had no reservoir of personnel trained in public administration. Few of their staff had worked closely with government.

Moreover, the religious agencies had never collaborated; each had its own methods of doing business and each wished to preserve its autonomy. Consequently the agencies did not agree to a unified administration for all C.P.S. units, but undertook independent direction of separate programs. The tangled web of administrative relations which resulted grew more, rather than less, complex as time went on.

For purposes of liaison and negotiation with the government, the religious bodies worked jointly through the National Service Board for Religious Objectors. The Board consisted of responsible executives of the chief religious administrative agencies, of the Fellowship of Reconciliation, and of the Federal Council of Churches.[1] While the members of the Board acted in an individual capacity, the positions they held in their own organizations assured a close representation of the points of view of the major bodies co-operating in the program.

Paul Comly French served continuously as the Board's Executive Secretary until the closing months of C.P.S. Mr. French, a Friend and formerly a journalist and pacifist author, had taken an active part as representative of the Friends War Problems Committee in pressing for legislative provisions for c.o.'s during the Congressional hearings and debate on Selective Service in 1940. French quickly demonstrated in his position with the N.S.B.R.O. that he was not only able to win the confidence and respect of officialdom but that he also had a flair for administration. He built a staff and organization which functioned with high efficiency in the discharge of manifold tasks. Each member of his staff was assigned clear and definite responsibilities. The organization was divided into appropriate sections whose heads reported daily to the Executive Secretary. Close personal liaison was maintained by each staff member with his coordinates in Selective Service and the religious agencies. Somehow, a rule was observed that all correspondence should clear the N.S.B.R.O. desks in twenty-four hours.

Despite the N.S.B.R.O.'s administrative competence, the religious agencies were loath to delegate administrative responsibility to the N.S.B.R.O., such as the power to select and direct camp and unit staffs or to assume commitments to the government without their prior approval. They insisted that because each was held directly accountable by its own constituency, *administration* would have to be separate, though *negotiation* could be joint. Furthermore, the religious agencies distrusted "bureaucracy," especially a Washington bureaucracy, and feared that the N.S.B.R.O. staff would become too susceptible to government influence.

In actual fact, the line between administrative and negotiating functions could not be drawn clearly, and the N.S.B.R.O. gradually assumed an administrative role without the express consent of the agencies. Selective Service and the N.S.B.R.O. staff tacitly teamed together in pressing for unified responsibility and often finessed the reluctant church bodies. Except for the Friends projects, direct channels were opened between N.S.B.R.O. and the camp and unit staffs for the passage of information, directives, and reports. N.S.B.R.O. staff took over from the agencies the promotion and investigation of new work projects and much of the manipulation of assignments and transfers. For the Brethren and Mennonites, the N.S.B.R.O. handled dependency aid to men who did not belong to their own churches, communicating directly with both staff and assignees, though subject to policies laid down by a council representing the agencies. When additional church agencies undertook to sponsor C.P.S. units and had no ready-made administrative organization, they gave the N.S.B.R.O. virtual power of attorney to discharge their responsibilities.[2] This gave the N.S.B.R.O. acknowledged status as an administrative agency in its own right.

The trend toward centralization never ran its course, and administrative relations were therefore left confused and unco-ordinated. The Friends in particular insisted on retaining independence in such matters as the dependency program and the clearing of communications and reports to and from the camps through their headquarters. All the Historic Peace Church agencies categorically turned down a proposal by Paul French to reorganize the administration of C.P.S. so as to concentrate in the hands of the N.S.B.R.O. the day-to-day responsibilities of operation. As a result, the N.S.B.R.O. came to perform certain administrative functions on behalf of all religious agencies (development of special service projects); some functions it undertook for certain of the agencies but not for the others (dependency aid, relations with special service units sponsored by non-administering denominations); for other functions it had no responsibility at all (selection of camp staffs, relations with the project superintendents). This situation prevented clear lines of responsibility between the agencies, their staffs, and the government; it also increased the difficulty of working out common efforts to deal with critical C.P.S. problems and reduced the effectiveness of action to secure reform. Each agency tended to improvise solutions independently according to its own best judgment, often without regard to the effect upon the others.

The religious agencies had to develop bureaucracies of their own to manage C.P.S. Each created a new section in its organization headed by an "executive director" with full responsibility for C.P.S. operations. Lack of administrative experience showed up at once. Learning to delegate functions came hard to the teachers and ministers who formed the early core of the C.P.S. staffs both in camp and headquarters. Executive directors attempted to hold the reins of responsibility in their own hands, interviewing at great length every candidate for their staffs, personally investigating each proposed camp site, attending each meeting with a Selective Service official, barnstorming their constituencies to stir up interest and support, checking publicity, and when possible visiting the projects and talking with the assignees. Meanwhile, administration bogged down for want of prompt decisions and follow-up of commitments. Reorganizations more or less radical brought specialization of various functions among the staff and a delegation of responsibility through an administrative hierarchy whose rigidity was tempered by the usually cordial personal relations and intimate religious fellowship among staff members, regardless of rank. This freed the executive directors to concentrate on matters of major policy and improved the efficiency of routine administration.

The key to successful administration, however, was the camp director or, in the case of special service units, the assistant director. Standing in the "hotbox" of C.P.S., he had to combine managerial competence with ability to enlist the confidence and co-operation of assignees, project supervisors, Selective Service, the religious constituencies, and of course his own administrative superiors. Actually he served two masters. The religious agencies which hired him stressed the importance of the director's leadership and understanding of the c.o.'s in his camp. Selective Service on the other hand stressed the responsibility of the director to enforce observance of its regulations and to co-operate with the technical agency in ensuring that the c.o. fulfilled his obligations of service.[3] These responsibilities often conflicted and subjected the directors to great strain. A number of them reached the conclusion that they could not serve in the dual capacity of "spiritual leaders of the camp and at the same the agents of Selective Service." [4] Others simply failed to meet the essential requirements of administrative competence under such trying conditions. But gradually there emerged, especially from among the ranks of C.P.S. assignees, men who had the necessary qualities for leadership in the program. Steady progress in the discovery of men with these extraordinary talents was the agencies' chief contribution to the administrative reform of C.P.S.[5]

The Pursuit of Responsibility. To retain responsibility for C.P.S. and secure "leverage" to win Selective Service concessions, the religious agencies resorted to increasingly "firm" administration vis-à-vis the assignees. For the Friends and, to some extent, the Brethren, this meant a deliberate and painful decision to abandon their initial commitment to democracy in the camps. A study of "crises" with Selective Service (over transfers, discipline, etc.) convinced the most ardent of the "democrats" on the Friends C.P.S. staff that

it is only possible to demand the right of control . . . when we take the responsibility of exercising that control. When we do not accept the obligation to handle a discipline situation we are not in a position to object when another agency steps in. . . . We need good understanding and management of our own problems in order that we may deal with them without the intervention of Selective Service.[6]

The problem was less difficult for the Mennonites, who had consistently upheld the authority of the church over the men in their program.

The staffs of the religious agencies undertook to discharge faithfully Selective Service instructions in regard to transfers, work assignments, leaves and furloughs, hours of work, and all other camp regulations (unless they believed conscientious scruples were being violated). Increasingly, they applied disciplinary measures satisfactory to Selective Service, though they also tried to exercise their own "redemptive" techniques of discipline.[7] When the churches disagreed with government policy, they enforced it first and argued about it later.[8]

As discontent rose over the conditions in C.P.S., the churches explicitly declared minimum standards of service for men under their administration. An assignee who entered or remained in a Friends project was expected to do an "honest piece of work on any project of national importance assigned by Selective Service, that has no material military significance"; to display "an intelligent, constructive and cooperative spirit toward his work"; to conduct himself so as to "bring credit to the camp and to the principles for which he, as a conscientious objector, stands" (for instance, not to become intoxicated); to maintain his quarters "in a manner that will contribute to the attractiveness of the dormitory, and to the health and comfort of other campers" (specifically, to make his bed neatly and put his personal belongings in order before work call).[9]

The crucial test of responsibility for the religious agencies was the refusal of some men to abide by their standards or to obey instructions transmitted from Selective Service. The churches were obligated to report all major violations of regulations.[10] This for the most part they did. They also had the authority to turn back to Selective Service any man whom they considered unacceptable, and they were pledged before their constituencies to do so. But some of the church administrators, especially among the Friends, shied away from dismissing the irreconcilables, even at the cost of internal friction and the weakening of their administration. Their squeamishness was prompted in part by a deep-seated aversion to compulsion—especially when the fate that would befall the excommunicated was jail or assignment to government camp—in part by the hope of redeeming the wayward, and finally by the difficulty of determining the precise point at which an objector fell so far beneath the standard that he could no longer be tolerated. The churches sometimes strove to secure a separation by mutual consent, camp directors laboring long and hard to convince obstructionists that they really belonged elsewhere. But they rarely appealed to the government to take action against the unpersuaded.[11]

Pacifying the Objectors. Instead of employing the sanction of excommunication, the religious agencies sought means of inspiring voluntary co-operation by the c.o.'s in their administration. By promoting educational and religious development, stressing the values in group living, keeping the camps better informed of national and local C.P.S. and pacifist news, and offering the men a chance to be represented in the administration of C.P.S., the churches tried to divert the c.o.'s attention from his grievances to the constructive opportunities which he could still realize in C.P.S.[12]

The most important safety valve for discontent, the churches recognized, was greater opportunity for the c.o. to render significant service in line with his qualifications and interests. Accordingly, they bent strenuous efforts to expand the number and variety of special service projects, to close camps where the work was relatively worthless or supervision was inadequate, and to place men where they could most effectively utilize their skills and capacities.[13]

An enormous amount of preliminary investigation and negotiation was required before new projects could be opened, especially those which would be most acceptable to the c.o.'s. A section of the N.S.B.R.O. and several of the staff of the religious agencies were constantly exploring possible openings for detached service, explaining to institutions the services which C.P.S. men were capable of rendering, and helping those that were interested to prepare applications which could meet the formidable requirements for Selective Service approval. A considerable amount of the work bore no fruit, either because Selective Service was generally loath to diversify the services of the c.o.'s or because of local or Congressional opposition.[14] But patient persistence ultimately succeeded in making possible the assignment of more than half of the c.o.'s to projects outside the camps, most of which went a long way toward satisfying the craving for a significant and challenging service.

The agencies attempted to select men for such assignments on the basis of their personal qualifications. At first the comments of camp staff weighed heavily in determining the men chosen for detached service. As the number of openings increased, a more objective and systematic review of interests and aptitudes was undertaken. The assignee filled out an extensive questionnaire concerning his educational and work background and indicated his preferences for service among the different types of projects in prospect. This was supplemented by an analysis of the individual's fitness either by a special camp personnel committee, the camp council, the director, the camp personnel secretary, or some combination of these. In the end, selections were made by a personnel secretary in the agencies' headquarters and, of course, confirmed by Selective Service.

General "fitness" was measured by such searching questions as:

Does this man make a good impression? Is he friendly, congenial and well-mannered?

Are his emotions well-balanced?

Has he been sick in quarters excessively?

Does he do his full share of work?

Does he work well with his foreman and fellow workers?

Is he tolerant of persons with backgrounds and attitudes different from his own?

Is he recognized by his associates as a leader?

Does he relate his religion to life?

Can he be depended upon to meet enmity with non-violence?

Does he demonstrate an interest in C.P.S. life?

Is his motive in seeking the assignment one of personal convenience or rendering maximum service? [15]

In addition, a man's technical qualifications for a particular job were noted.

The procedure was criticized as favoring the "co-operator" against the "troublemaker," thus subjecting the c.o. to a kind of blackmail ("be good or you'll be stuck in camp"); also, the evaluation of such qualifications was bound to be partly arbitrary, even when done by a committee. The arrangement seemed fair to most c.o.'s, however, for it substituted the opinions of a man's personal acquaintances for the impersonal judgments of far-removed headquarters staff in the determination of his qualifications.

A fundamental problem complicating the relations of the administrative agencies with their assignees was the agencies' frequent unwillingness to accept certain unsatisfactory conditions as irrevocable, and their consequent failure to give the men in C.P.S. a candid understanding of their true position. This was particularly the case in regard to the degree of control which Selective Service actually exercised over the administration of C.P.S. The religious agencies did not admit to themselves, and hence they could not admit to the men, the stringent limits to their autonomy. The c.o.'s therefore quite naturally held the agencies responsible when "things went wrong," even though in fact Selective Service might really have been responsible.

Resolving Administrative Loggerheads. Friction between the c.o.'s and their project supervisors confronted the churches with an endless series of irritating incidents and crises handicapping the performance of service, intensifying the dissatisfaction of the c.o.'s, and threatening the breakup of important segments of the C.P.S. program. To prevent these irritants from producing an explosion and to patch up relations so that the projects could continue was the outstanding administrative achievement of the religious agencies—a tribute to the patience and skill of their staffs, who persisted in seeking a basis for accommodation in the face of trying circumstances.

The particular issues in dispute were usually complicated by difficult traits of personality, emotional conflict, and deep-rooted misunderstandings. An overbearing project supervisor or hospital superintendent would manage his c.o. workers with a highhanded disregard of their concerns and grievances. The men in turn, nursing resentment, often indulged in rash moves of opposition which put them in the wrong and further hardened the mood of the administrator as he felt his authority challenged. Thus battle lines were frequently bitterly drawn before the churches began their task of mediation.

Three main obstacles handicapped the churches in dealing with such administrative loggerheads. First, Selective Service rarely supported their efforts. More often than not, it thwarted them, especially in relations with the hospitals and special service units. This tempted superintendents to disregard the agencies or even to rebuff their mediation brusquely as unwarranted interference. Second, the local leadership of the units was frequently immature, inefficient, or untactful in relations with the administration. Third, the agencies were slow in coming to grips with incipient problems, often allowing them to reach crisis stage before acting vigorously to meet them.

But the religious agencies were remarkably successful in their mediating role. At Eastern State Hospital, Williamsburg, Virginia, for instance, a crisis arose when the superindentent asked Selective Service to remove an assignee from the hospital on the grounds of improper relations with a woman patient. The unit protested vehemently that the accusation was unfounded, and demanded that the superintendent withdraw his request for the transfer pending "a reasonable attempt to determine the validity of his charge," in consultation with a committee of the assignees. Injudiciously, it threatened to ask the A.F.S.C. to withdraw the unit from the hospital if the superintendent did not oblige. Swiftly the A.F.S.C. made clear to the unit and to the superintendent that it had neither the authority nor the intention to press for the unit's removal, but only a desire to promote a co-operative relationship. Under gentle prodding, the superintendent admitted that there had been misunderstanding and that he ascribed neither an immoral act nor immoral intentions to the assignee. He still believed a transfer was necessary because the man had not exercised good judgment in handling the patient, but he undertook (successfully) to clear the man's name with Selective Service and to facilitate his transfer to another hospital unit rather than back to base camp. Replacement of the unit's assistant director by one of the ablest administrators in Friends C.P.S. eased other tensions which had developed between the superintendent and the unit. Proper administrative procedure on the local level could thus forestall the development of an impasse precipitating arbitrary action. The Mennonites were particularly successful in their administrative relations, being able to secure favorable attention from Selective Service for most of their concerns.

Where the project or institutional administration welcomed the assistance of the churches in ironing out relations with the assignees, a fine harmony was usually attained. Such was the situation at the Philadelphia State Hospital, where a potentially serious conflict over personnel policies was neatly resolved. An assignee refused to obey the order of the supervisor changing his work assignment. He felt the order had been given without proper consideration of the problems as he saw them. The administration declared an order was an order and should be obeyed regardless. The unit backed the assignee and objected to any disciplinary action against him. Full discussion between the unit's leaders and the superintendent brought agreement that the responsible head of an institution must insist upon obedience to his subordinate's orders but that an adequate channel should be provided through the unit's own personnel committee for appealing to a superior officer when the assignee felt the order was wrong. The assignee was not disciplined. There was no further personnel difficulty of any consequence in this unit.[16]

On the other hand, a number of project supervisors disliked the part played by the church organizations in the administration of the program. They objected to "dual control"—by Selective Service and religious agency—as a source of confusion and difficulty which complicated their task. The chief of the United States Forest Service frankly advocated the government's assuming the total cost and the full administrative control of the program. Certain camp project superintendents resented efforts by the religious agencies to promote special service projects as of greater national importance than the camp work. A hospital superintendent accused the religious agency of always seeking its own advantage within the Selective Service regulations and interfering in his administration.[17] Some of the project supervisors felt that the church groups had too much responsibility for the assignees and objected that they obtained "decisions in Washington, not merely without us being consulted but without us being informed of them through official channels." [18] On the other hand, relations between many of the project supervisors and the staffs of the religious agencies were very cordial and cooperative, each considering the other a helpful partner in a common service.

One method of advancing understanding and working out more satisfactory administrative relations was through regional conferences providing for a frank exchange of views between representatives of the religious agencies, Selective Service, and the institutions or government agencies for whom the c.o.'s were working. Such conferences were particularly helpful in the case of hospital units, and often led to a revision of official administrative instructions by Selective Service, as well as a more considerate and understanding approach by the hospital superintendents. Following a meeting in 1943, the hospitals were instructed to furnish adequate food, quarters, and laundry service within the institution, uniforms or a $5.00-a-month clothing allowance, a $10.00-a-month maintenance allowance (instead of the $2.50 previously allowed), medical and dental attention equivalent to that of other employees, and workmen's compensation insurance as provided by state law.[19] The work week came up for discussion the following year, and a national hospital administrative conference was ultimately engineered by the A.F.S.C. hospital supervisor to consider improving the significance of the work in the institutions, raising morale, and handling demobilization so as to avoid inconvenience to the hospitals yet allow the discharge of their assignees in a fair order.

The Losing Struggle with Selective Service

Important as they were in staving off a total breakdown of C.P.S., the administrative reforms achieved by the religious agencies did not touch the crucial issues. On almost every matter of *fundamental* policy, Selective Service vetoed proposals seeking arrangements more satisfactory to the c.o.'s and to their supporting groups. The official attitude appeared so persistently and unreasonably negative that even the most sanguine defenders of C.P.S. ultimately abandoned hope of effecting major reform through the existing administrative channels.

On two questions of basic importance, Selective Service did accept the recommendations of the religious agencies, i.e., the approval of special service projects and the opening of government-directed camps.[20] But on other vital issues the churches were constantly frustrated in their administration by the strong allergy of Selective Service to basic reforms suspected of liberalism. As has been seen, proposals to provide pay for the c.o.'s met short shrift.[21] On seven other issues which the churches considered of critical importance to their administration of C.P.S., in a conference with General Hershey in April, 1943, satisfaction was secured on only one—the opening of government camps. The General rejected, stalled, or, as was his wont, evaded commitment on proposals: (a) to include the churches in the consideration of new projects, the closing of old types, mass transfers and shifts, and proposals for service in new areas; (b) to eliminate the mandatory 3-day furlough penalty for A.W.O.L. and to return the authority for discipline to the religious agencies; (c) to cease prohibiting men to transfer to special service units because of their "inability to adjust to camp life" (i.e., the "black list"); (d) to discuss with the religious agencies contemplated action in regard to future conferences of C.P.S. men before prohibiting them (such as the Chicago Conference); (e) to define the relationship of the churches to all units, including special service units, so that this would be clearly understood by all technical agencies; (f) to clear all orders, memos and directives from Camp Operations through the N.S.B.R.O. *after* mutual consultation.[22] Such recalcitrance on the part of Selective Service seriously complicated the efforts of the religious agencies to deal adequately with many of their basic administrative problems.

Medical Discharges. The churches were eager to secure the discharge and reclassification of men who were medically unfit for service, not only out of consideration for their personal welfare but because they were a heavy administrative and financial burden. For almost two years, in the face of competent medical recommendations secured by the agencies from camp doctors, from the agency's own medical staffs, and even from Selective Service medical advisory boards, Selective Service headquarters refused to expedite medical discharges, largely on the grounds that they could not be justified by Army standards.[23] Ultimately the A.F.S.C. Medical Director succeeded in getting Selective Service to define standards and procedures which permitted discharge of the more serious cases after a detailed medical report to headquarters. The agencies then concentrated on "processing" the disabled men in their camps, building up a thorough and convincing medical history for each. Some camps became veritable "discharge mills" as directors caught on to the semantic and procedural tastes of the Selective Service medical office. Sometimes the camp directors would actually work over the reports of examining physicians and specialists (subject of course to confirmation by the doctors) so that the diagnoses would be presented in the form and language necessary to secure approval for release.

The Questionable Sick. Selective Service likewise blocked the discretion of the religious agencies in regard to the handling of men who were sick but not eligible for discharge. Incensed at men who feigned sickness, Colonel Kosch ordered camp directors to justify every furlough granted to a man who had been listed sick in quarters previous to the furlough, and in the case of one Friends camp (Big Flats) completely forbade the granting of furlough until a man had performed fourteen days' continuous work satisfactory to the project superintendent immediately preceding the furlough. The A.F.S.C. pointed out that the Selective Service regulation would not fully solve the problem, as it would encourage any men so disposed to work only preceding their furlough requests, while some men who could profitably convalesce at home would be unable to do so. Yet Selective Service did not withdraw its restrictions for six months.[24]

Disciplinary Transfer. Selective Service never abandoned its habit of summarily ordering men transferred for disciplinary reasons without consulting the religious agencies. As a result of patient pleading, these actions were sometimes reversed, but in the meantime the agencies were blamed by assignees for failing to prevent injustice, and lost all discretion in dealing with the situations which prompted the transfers. Late in the program, for instance, Colonel Kosch, without warning, ordered two men transferred from a Friends to a government camp because of "their failure to co-operate in what we consider a proper manner." The A.F.S.C. held up the transfer orders, objecting that there were definite extenuating circumstances. Colonel Kosch refused to reconsider and threatened to report the men to the Department of Justice for prosecution if they did not transfer as ordered. Under this pressure, one man transferred and the other left camp suffering from a severe mental collapse. The camp director (one of the ablest and most objective in C.P.S.) bitterly observed:

This action strikes at the heart of C.P.S. administration. I feel pretty deeply about this matter of arbitrary action by Selective Service at the request of the technical service without so much as a by-your-leave from the A.F.S.C. which is paying the bills and supposed to be administering the program. . . . As long as Selective Service takes their word over ours, then our "administration" becomes a farce.[25]

Administration of Detached Service Units. The church agencies could not persuade Selective Service to grant them real administrative responsibility for special service projects—the very projects which they had most keenly promoted and in which they had the greatest interest. The agencies had confidently expected that they would have exactly the same relationship to the men and to the project administration in special service as they had in camp, namely, that of general direction except during actual work. They were amazed to discover in the initial instructions issued by Selective Service covering such projects that no reference at all was made to the religious organizations. What at first seemed an oversight later was confirmed as policy. Selective Service would concede only a sponsoring role to the churches, and Colonel McLean made clear that this excluded any direct responsibility for the control, discipline, and administrative operation of the unit. The superintendent was vested with the prerogatives of camp director as well as project supervisor, and he was under no obligation to deal administratively with the religious agencies, except to forward his reports through them to Selective Service. He had the right to request transfers at any time without obtaining approval from or explaining his actions to anyone except Selective Service. While the sponsoring organization selected an assistant director for the unit, the superintendent's approval was required and the assistant director was administratively responsible to him, not to the agency which selected him. Selective Service did commend the agency to the institution's administration as capable of providing valuable assistance in the adjustment of personnel problems, but did not at all insist that the superintendent avail himself of its service. Colonel McLean specifically and categorically refuted a suggestion of the A.F.S.C. that the hospital superintendent transmit requests for transfers through the religious agency; those must go direct to Selective Service. The agency only entered in if an assignee originated the request for transfer and the superintendent approved; then it could act as a forwarding channel.[26]

Unwelcomed Reformers. Efforts by groups other than the religious agencies to influence Selective Service to revise its administrative policies were equally unavailing. The National Committee on Conscientious Objectors was formed by persons who thought that more forceful representations with bolder proposals for change than those advanced by the Historic Peace Churches might bring results. The Committee shortly amalgamated with the American Civil Liberties Union and then urged General Hershey to make radical changes in the Selective Service administration of C.P.S., ending contractual relations with the Historic Peace Churches, creating an all-civilian C.P.S. Division in the place of the existing Camp Operations Division, and assigning c.o.'s immediately upon induction to special service projects as well as to camps, on the basis of their individual abilities.

General Hershey unhesitatingly rejected the proposals, commenting that "efforts to satisfy objectors may easily be carried to the place where considerable proportions of our citizenry will refuse to tolerate the present methods of supervising public service." [27] Following the wave of strikes in 1946, the A.C.L.U. denounced the punitive attitude of Selective Service and repeated substantially the same recommendations. But they met the same fate.[28]

As a result of its narrow conception of the meaning of tolerance and its fear of public criticism, Selective Service therefore blocked the road to reform and confined the challenging experiment in religious freedom to the limits of its own "safe" policies of rigid control.

Appeals for a New Deal

Failing to secure satisfaction from Selective Service, the partisans of conscience turned to the President and to Congress for an administrative reorganization and for legislative revisions that would assure just treatment of the c.o. and the fullest and most constructive use of his services. Every attempt misfired. The appeals for reform suffered from the inexperience of the reformers in lobbying for governmental action, from the active opposition of Selective Service and of key figures in Congress, and, above all, from the preoccupation of all branches of government in the running of the war.

A.C.L.U. vs. Selective Service. The American Civil Liberties Union made the first attempt to go over the head of Selective Service. It submitted through a delegation to the President a succinct summary of major complaints about the handling of c.o.'s and asked him, among other changes, to remove the responsibility for c.o.'s from Selective Service and place it in the hands of a special civilian commission directly accountable to the President. The presentation was ill prepared. Though the criticisms were essentially valid, the Selective Service staff, to whom President Roosevelt referred the matter for comment, was able to counter with a withering 150-page report attacking the factual accuracy of the A.C.L.U. statement. The President thereupon dismissed without further consideration the basic proposal for a change of administrative organization.

The A.F.S.C. Experience. The foundation for a more elaborate attack was laid when the A.F.S.C. prepared an extensively documented, critical report of its experience in Civilian Public Service, on the basis of which it urged eight recommendations for administrative or legislative action to improve the program:

1. eliminating the test of religious training and belief from the law and permitting c.o.'s opposed to conscripted service to engage voluntarily in socially useful work;

2. establishment of a civilian board to have full responsibility for the classification and assignment of conscientious objectors;

3. assignment of c.o.'s to serve with private as well as government agencies on projects of "unquestioned social value and urgency";

4. assignment of c.o.'s to foreign relief service;

5. placing the work of each man under the direction and control of a single employer or agency (in contrast to the dual or triple control of Selective Service, technical agency and religious agency);

6. federal allowance to dependents;

7. compensation for men injured or killed;

8. government remuneration and maintenance for men serving on government projects.[29]

In due course the other religious administering agencies associated themselves with the A.F.S.C. in exploring and attaining these objectives.

The Experience Report and its recommendations were first given wide circulation among Washington officials, denominational leaders, the religious press, and peace and civil-liberties organizations and were released in summary form to selected newspaper columnists and radio commentators who were thought likely to be sympathetic. Next, arrangements were made for a presentation of the Report to members of Congress by influential constituents in personal interviews or, where this was impossible, for a written plea to the congressman that he give his attention to the problem and the proposed changes. On the basis of replies received from this selective courting of Congressional consideration, representatives of the churches conferred individually with those who expressed sympathy and pointed out the specific legislative steps that would help. The reluctance of Selective Service to make the changes which lay within its authority was tactfully reported, as well as its susceptibility to Congressional opinion. General Hershey and Colonel Kosch wryly remarked that Congress had suddenly become unusually solicitous about the c.o.'s, judging by the phone calls they had to answer.

The Attorney General Sides with Reform. Neither Selective Service nor the legislative machinery budged as a result of these efforts. Finally, the co-operation of Attorney General Francis Biddle was unexpectedly secured. The basic complaints and the substance of the recommendations made by the A.F.S.C. were presented to him and were incorporated in his annual report to Congress.[30] Mr. Biddle officially and publicly declared that the government's treatment of conscientious objectors had been unsatisfactory. He proposed the establishment of a single board to classify all objectors and assign them to "suitable and useful work." He implied that absolutists might have to be given complete exemption if they were not to be a "constant source of difficulty, taxing the resources of firmness and understanding with which the administrative authorities have attempted to deal with them." He specifically advocated the opening up of overseas relief work for c.o.'s and the granting of dependency allotments out of the frozen fund. Mr. Biddle was the first and only high-ranking government official to challenge so boldly the engrained system for dealing with c.o.'s. It was, however, a farewell gesture, as he shortly resigned and was not in a position to press his recommendations influentially either with Congress or within the administration. Selective Service ignored the implied criticism of its activities and made no move to modify its well-established policies.

A last move to secure an administrative reorganization was precipitated by the mass strike at the Glendora camp against Selective Service policies.[31] The Friends Committee on National Legislation and representatives of the strikers conferred with Presidential Secretary David Niles and urged a change of C.P.S. administration from Selective Service to a separate civilian direction. Mr. Niles seemed seriously impressed and at one point appeared ready to recommend such action to President Truman. But he did not press the matter in view of the approaching end of the program.

Preoccupied though it was with the war, Congress did not entirely ignore the problems of the c.o.'s. The net effect of its intervention was to impose even further restrictions upon them.[32] But some members of Congress sought for more constructive solutions, especially in regard to the waste of manpower in the assignments of c.o.'s, the dire straits of c.o. dependents, and the uncompensated risks of the c.o.'s in their service.[33]

The Senate Investigates. The inefficient use of c.o.'s aroused both Senator Pepper, chairman of the Senate Education and Labor Committee, and the Special Senate Committee Investigating the National Defense Program, headed by Senator Mead. Early in 1945, Senator Pepper (prompted by the N.S.B.R.O.) expressed amazement to General Hershey that c.o.'s would be kept at work in national parks and on reforestation when there was such great need for men in public health work, tuberculosis sanatoria, general hospitals, and other services which would contribute to the physical well-being of the people of the country. Noting that many of the 40 per cent of men rejected for military service because of physical defects were victims of disease stemming from lack of sanitary facilities, inadequate health precautions, and lack of medical care, the Senator urged the General to assign one thousand to fifteen hundred c.o.'s to this type of work.

A few weeks later, the Mead Committee challenged General Hershey to account for the service of the c.o.'s, after receiving a report from the American Civil Liberties Union charging that most of the eight thousand objectors were an "unused reservoir of manpower . . . now assigned to trivial tasks." His reply, justifying the projects as approved by Selective Service and blandly professing that the Historic Peace Churches had given no indication that the program was unsatisfactory to them, drew a sharp rejoinder from the A.C.L.U., but the Senate Committee refrained from probing further into C.P.S.[34]

The Frozen Fund. The *cause célèbre* in the campaign for Congressional action on behalf of the c.o.'s was the "frozen fund"—the impounded earnings of the men assigned to work for farmers and other private employers.[35]

After the Comptroller General had ruled that Congress alone could authorize the disposition of this money, legislation was persistently pressed to release the fund in accordance with the desires of the c.o.'s, first for foreign relief, then for the assistance of c.o. dependents, later for the compensation of men injured in C.P.S., and finally for relief again. But each move faltered in the face of a nucleus of sharp and influential opponents.

Strangely, the initiative to pry open the fund was taken by Representative W. Sterling Cole, Republican of New York, whose first interest in c.o.'s was anything but friendly. Representing the upstate milkshed, he was incensed when he heard that c.o.'s were refusing to work on dairy farms in the midst of the acute manpower squeeze. A visit to Big Flats persuaded him, however, that the c.o.'s were for the most part sincere and willing workers, and that they objected to farm service not because they were slackers but because they were honestly concerned lest their earnings contribute to the war effort. He promptly consulted with the N.S.B.R.O. and Selective Service and introduced a bill to turn over the c.o. earnings to the Office of Foreign Relief and Rehabilitation (later to U.N.R.R.A.), believing that this would encourage more C.P.S. men to volunteer for emergency farm work.[36]

In 1944, when efforts to include c.o. dependents in the Servicemen's Dependents Allowance Act had collapsed, Representative Cole agreed to a request of the N.S.B.R.O. that the fund be used to provide dependency aid. The House Military Affairs Committee approved the amended measure, but consideration was blocked in the House itself. At the following session, an almost identical bill was introduced by Representative John Sparkman, Democrat from Alabama, chairman of the House Military Affairs subcommittee concerned with this issue.[37] Despite this important sponsorship and support from the American Public Welfare Association and other impartial organizations, as well as Selective Service and the Historic Peace Churches, action could not be obtained.

At the conclusion of hostilities, the religious agencies, in the light of a poll taken to determine the preference of men still in C.P.S., decided to seek release of the fund, first, to reimburse the Peace Churches for all allowances they had made to dependents and, second, to aid the foreign relief and reconstruction programs of religious and other private agencies. Both proposals would in effect have made the fund available to the Historic Peace Churches for foreign aid, as their financial responsibilities for C.P.S. were rapidly declining.[38]

Behind the scenes in the N.S.B.R.O., this plan met the objection of Paul French, who did not feel that it was feasible or desirable to ask Congress to turn over the funds to the private agencies. Despite the clear decision of the Board, French stalled on the matter for six months, by which time (April, 1946) the strategy on the frozen fund had become tangled with the issue of accident compensation. Congressman Kilday of Texas introduced a bill to this effect. French urged that the religious agencies support legislation authorizing appropriation of the fund to U.N.R.R.A., with the hope that U.N.R.R.A. might then earmark the money for projects which concerned the religious groups.[39] The agencies agreed to this alternative, as did U.N.R.R.A., so the Kilday bill was revised to provide first for the payment of compensation to injured C.P.S. men, with the balance to be made over to U.N.R.R.A. White House support was secured (for the first time, in regard to a c.o. measure), but with Congress in the midst of its June log jam, the legislative leaders were insufficiently interested to give the bill priority.

A post-C.P.S. chapter remained. With U.N.R.R.A. in process of liquidation, the Historic Peace Church agencies all agreed to support allocation of the frozen fund to the United Nations International Children's Emergency Fund on the understanding that U.N.I.C.E.F. would use it for jointly approved relief projects conducted by these agencies. This proposal was reintroduced in the House by Representative Cole in the opening weeks of the 80th Congress, and later a similar bill was introduced in the Senate by Senator Saltonstall. The legislation was ably supported by representatives of both the United Nations and the Historic Peace Churches. Treasury officials were informed of Representative Cole's action on the day the bill was introduced and at that time the N.S.B.R.O. was assured that the fund was still being held as special deposit pending Congressional action.

Six weeks later, however, when the bill actually came before the House Military Affairs Committee for consideration, the Committee was informed that, at the specific request of Selective Service, the money had been transferred out of the special account into the general funds of the Treasury and was no longer available for appropriation. Selective Service had acted without consulting either the N.S.B.R.O. or the concerned members of Congress, disregarding entirely its previous vaunted respect for pending Congressional action.

In view of this action, the bill was revised to authorize the appropriation of an *equivalent* amount, approximately $1,300,000, with the agreement of Treasury and State Department. It was unanimously approved by both House and Senate Military Affairs Committees. The reports accompanying the bills lauded the work of the c.o.'s—a kind of posthumous panegyric. The bill passed the House by unanimous consent but in the Senate encountered the fatal opposition of Senator Vandenberg, preventing its final passage. Later efforts, engineered by Paul French (now executive director of CARE), to secure an appropriation, equivalent to the frozen fund, for the CARE book program were equally futile.

The sad history of the frozen-fund legislation reveals the obstacles which prevented legislative reform of C.P.S. The opposition of key congressmen and the devious policies of Selective Service were abetted by the bungling interpretation of the issues to Congress by the sponsors of reform and, above all, by the failure of those concerned to agree on their objectives and to pursue a common and effective strategy of action.

Succor for the Unliberated

In the absence of basic reforms freeing the C.P.S. system of its abusive and discriminatory features, the religious agencies and other organizations tried as best they could to ease the c.o.'s most pressing personal problems: the care of his dependents and the re-establishment of himself after discharge.

Dependency Aid. Available private resources were totally insufficient to provide security to C.P.S. dependents comparable to that assured the families of G.I.'s by the government. The N.S.B.R.O. estimated that dependency allotments to C.P.S. men at the Army rate would have totaled over two million dollars annually, on top of the expense the churches were already carrying for the C.P.S. program proper.[40]

Consequently, aid had to be furnished only in cases of real need, rather than to all dependents as a matter of established right. This raised two difficult problems. Some men and their families suffered from a "charity" complex and were unusually sensitive about asking and accepting aid from the churches, even though their impoverishment was due to factors over which they had no control. This sensitivity was increased when they had to demonstrate their need to persons whom they did not know. The second problem was to determine a fair test of need, when circumstances and customary living standards varied so greatly and the available resources were so limited.

The attitudes of the religious agencies differed so radically in regard to the proper handling of these problems that four separate dependency programs were created: one administered by the

A.F.S.C. for all men in Friends projects, a second administered by the N.S.B.R.O. Dependency Council for all men except Brethren and Mennonites in the remaining C.P.S. projects and in prison, and two separate assistance programs for Mennonites and Brethren, run directly by their own churches.

The difference in administration was necessitated by an irreconcilable conflict of policy in regard to the proper means of succoring the needy. All three of the Historic Peace Churches had traditionally "taken care of their own." Each local church was expected to minister to its destitute, members feeling a common obligation to help the less fortunate of their number. The aid was not given or taken as charity but as an act of spiritual fellowship, regardless of the personalities involved. At first, all three of the churches inclined to deal with C.P.S. dependency needs on much the same basis, referring them back to the churches or meetings to which the men belonged and creating a small "pool" of aid for those who were unaffiliated with any church. Such an arrangement broke down immediately in the case of men who did not belong to the Historic Peace Churches, for most of their denominations were no more prepared to care for their dependents than to finance their maintenance in C.P.S. The Peace Churches confronted a dilemma: should they abandon completely the idea of depositing dependency needs on local churches and set up a uniform system of aid within the limits of their resources, or should they operate a dual system distinguishing between their own members and others? The Mennonites and Brethren chose the latter course and set up the N.S.B.R.O. Dependency Council to handle the needs of the "others." The Friends, with a majority of their C.P.S. flock not Friends and a number of their staff imbued with the standards and concepts of professional social work, adopted the former alternative.

A second basic disagreement soon emerged. In prescribing the policies of the Dependency Council, the Brethren and Mennonites carried over their highly personal conception of relief. Each case was studied and considered individually. The Council obtained a report from a person in the community whom the agencies trusted (where possible, a Brethren or Mennonite minister) on the dependent's needs. Every effort was made to discover relatives, friends, or churches who would aid the dependents in securing jobs, housing arrangements, or other needed help. Grants from the N.S.B.R.O. were made as a last resort and were limited to the balance needed for minimum subsistence. Need was quite naturally judged in comparison with the austere living standards common among Mennonite and Brethren contributors, mainly rural folk.[41]

In regard to their own members, the Mennonites and Brethren in 1944 adopted a policy of providing uniform allowance payments of $25 a month to a wife or adult dependent and $10 a month for each dependent child, with extra allowances for special and emergency needs. The Mennonite Central Committee continued to make the constituent church groups responsible for meeting these C.P.S. dependency needs, but the Brethren Service Committee itself took on the responsibility of implementing the dependency program and assigned a committee to the task of investigating each application for assistance.[42]

The Friends deliberately tried to minimize the personal element in the consideration of dependency needs, on the ground that it accentuated the "charity-consciousness" of those receiving aid. Modest monthly grants (up to $25 a month for wife and $10 per child) were made available virtually on statement of need by the assignee. Where larger amounts were asked, a fuller explanation of the need was requested, including a budget of expenses; where acceptable to the man and his dependents, an interview was arranged with someone representing the A.F.S.C. in the community (more often a sympathetic social worker than a minister). The A.F.S.C. strongly encouraged C.P.S. dependents to accept established public and private welfare assistance wherever this could be arranged, emphasizing that this was something to which they were really "entitled" as residents of their communities in view of the delinquency of the government in providing special allotments. Local family welfare agencies proved especially helpful in many cases, securing medical and social services and often finding satisfactory employment for the dependents. But where this was insufficient or the aid of welfare agencies was unacceptable to the dependents, the A.F.S.C. furnished monthly allotments on the basis of a reasonable budget considering the locale, personal obligations, and customary living standards of the individual. Recreational expense and keeping up insurance premiums were considered legitimate budget items. The Friends C.P.S. Committee embarked on this trusting and liberal program a little hesitatingly, but was convinced within a few months that there was virtually no gold digging. Men usually requested aid only when it was urgently needed, and on a scale often more modest than the Committee would have considered warranted. They felt under compulsion to keep their demands at a minimum so that they would not impair the chances of others in equal or greater need.[43]

About 5 per cent of the men in C.P.S. secured financial aid for their dependents, though well over one-third of the men had dependents. Financial assistance was furnished to some 600 families (about 1,300 individuals) at a cost of about $250,000. The average amount given by the A.F.S.C. in a typical month at the height of the dependency need was under $60 per family, with half of the allotments $35 or less. The grants of the Dependency Council were considerably lower. The usual composition of the family receiving aid was a wife and one child, but in a number of instances the size was much larger. Frequently the dependents had no other income than the allotment.[44] The bulk of this cost fell upon the Historic Peace Churches, but nineteen other denominations assumed the full cost of their own members, and a number of others paid a portion of the cost, while pacifist organizations such as the Fellowship of Reconciliation also contributed.[45]

Demobilization and Rehabilitation. As the war passed its climax, the tolerant and the sympathetic, unable to reform C.P.S. itself, concentrated on planning for the c.o.'s demobilization. Despite the dissatisfactions of C.P.S., many men found little solace in contemplating their day of discharge. The insecurity of the future appeared as disconcerting as the restraints of the present. Orphaned by the G.I. Bill of Rights just as he was by the Dependents Allowance Act, the c.o. leaving C.P.S. could expect no governmental assistance, either in securing employment, returning to school or college, buying a house, or starting a trade or business. In C.P.S. he at least received maintenance. But after receiving his transportation home, he would be on his own, without even a separation allowance to tide him over the first jobless days of freedom.

So the religious agencies and other groups began (after some fifteen hundred men had already been discharged from C.P.S. for medical and other reasons) to devise schemes—grandiose and otherwise—to facilitate the rehabilitation of c.o.'s released from C.P.S. and from prison. These services were rather better co-ordinated than was customary in C.P.S., by an "inter-agency demobilization committee" operating through the N.S.B.R.O.

The man in C.P.S. who did not know what he wanted to do when he got out could have his vocational interests and aptitudes "scientifically" tested either while in his camp or unit or by a professional testing agency. He would read over a mass of vocational information bulletins sent by the Service Committees to the camps and would consult with the camp's counselors and personnel secretaries. If he wished more extensive guidance, he could talk with vocational experts in various fields who, at the invitation of the religious agencies, either visited the camps or interviewed c.o.'s in their communities.

The c.o. who decided that his next step should be the completion of education but was unable to finance further study was eligible for special scholarships offered by the Historic Peace Church colleges; if he wished to study at other institutions, he could apply for grants-in-aid from the Service Committees to supplement his own earnings and any assistance for which he could qualify at the school he attended. In certain of the Historic Peace Church colleges, credit was granted for special educational accomplishments in C.P.S.[46]

The man who above all else wanted a job when he left C.P.S. and who did not have one already lined up could turn to the religious agencies and to local committees in a number of communities for "placement service." A job file was built up of openings which came to the attention of C.P.S. agencies, and notice of them was sent regularly to the camps and units. The A.F.S.C. put a full-time staff member to exploring employment possibilities for c.o.'s in various vocations. The agencies also organized their personnel records so as to provide adequate and prompt information on the occupational experience and interests of all assignees. But because of the wide differences and changing character of local employment situations, the main effort to provide employment assistance was undertaken by volunteer community or regional demobilization councils that were organized in fifty or more areas, representing all groups concerned in helping the c.o. Though they varied greatly in their methods and efficiency, they generally directed job-seeking c.o.'s to sympathetic employers in various vocations and maintained a local file of jobs known to be available to men discharged from C.P.S. or released from prison. These efforts were severely handicapped by the inability to discover in advance of demobilization where C.P.S. men were likely to settle and what the interests and qualifications of men coming to a particular area might be.

The religious agencies and other groups were particularly eager to enable c.o.'s to enter "service careers" in line with their convictions. The Mennonites developed an extensive plan of rural community resettlement and colonization, setting up ex-C.P.S. men on farms or in small-town business and industry, and helping them establish modest homes so that they might become pivots of wholesome brotherly community living.[47] In northern California and elsewhere groups of service-minded c.o.'s were dedicated to starting new "co-operative communities" on their own initiative, and financial and other support was solicited to help them.[48] (Most of these independent communal-living dreams failed to materialize.) The Historic Peace Churches, U.N.R.R.A., and other organizations accepted several hundred discharged c.o.'s for foreign relief service. The Brethren worked out a plan with U.N.R.R.A. which gave many c.o.'s a period of adventuresome service as "seagoing cowboys," caring for livestock during its shipment to devastated European countries; another contingent went to China as tractor drivers. Other men were employed on the regular staffs of the relief organizations.[49]

The c.o. who wanted to start in business on his own but had no credit could appeal to the religious agencies for a loan. Special funds were created by the A.F.S.C. and B.S.C. out of which C.P.S. men could borrow up to two thousand dollars for business, professional, farming, or other self-sustaining enterprises approved by the Committees. The first loans approved by the A.F.S.C. were to help start a truck garden in Tennessee, a farm in Minnesota, an electrical repair shop in North Dakota, an auto repair shop in Iowa, and the selling of kitchen utensils in California. The different Mennonite branches had their own plans to deal with the financial needs of their released c.o.'s. The usual method was "mutual aid," whereby local congregations or individuals made loans for specific purposes to the c.o.'s from their community who needed help in getting started. A section of the Mennonite Central Committee co-ordinated appeals for financial help from the men with the proper church body or official.[50]

At several points this vast array of proffered aid to the demobilized c.o. actually seemed to exceed demand, once it was fully organized. Few c.o.'s had difficulty getting jobs, as the predicted postwar wave of unemployment did not sweep the country and discrimination against the men for their convictions was not widespread. Yet even if some of the efforts were superfluous, the men were reassured by the wide interest in their welfare, and their morale within C.P.S. rose considerably as they gained confidence that the world outside was not all cold.

XIV: The Erosion of Tolerance

THE frustrations of the Civilian Public Service experiment strikingly demonstrated that Americans during the Second World War did not share a common conception of the meaning of tolerance. The appearance of unity which had characterized the launching of C.P.S. concealed aims that were actually contradictory. Then, as misunderstanding led to mistrust and protest to repression, the mutual tolerance of government, church, c.o., and public disintegrated. The continuance of C.P.S. to the end of the war under these circumstances was therefore not evidence of a well-grounded democratic respect for a minority but rather of the dogged faith of those who continued to stand committed to the scriptural injunction of "walking the second mile."

Tolerance: Defined by Selective Service

The early resignation of Dr. Dykstra as Director of Selective Service, and his replacement by General Hershey, allowed the implicit contradictions between the aims of the government and of the other participants in C.P.S. to come into the open. This change in personalities was not followed by a formal modification of the C.P.S. pattern, but the attitude of Selective Service in regard to the c.o.'s became steadily more arbitrary and restrictive, the limits of official tolerance ever more circumscribed.

Dr. Dykstra was basically an educator. His conception of tolerance began with a deep regard for the worth of an individual. What did the individual believe? What service would the conscientious objector's conscience tolerate? Then, how far could the government

307

permit such action? Tolerance to Dr. Dykstra meant maximum recognition of the freedom of the individual to act in accordance with his belief. The only limits should be those imposed by legislative restraint.[1]

The increasing rigidity and insensitivity of Selective Service after Dr. Dykstra's departure reflected at least in part a different estimate by his successor of the implications of tolerance. General Hershey and his staff, a considerable number of whom were military men, were committed both by position and by personal conviction to the prosecution of the war as their supreme objective. Tolerance for the conscientious objector should never hamper the overriding task of Selective Service—recruitment of manpower for the national defense. Tolerance demanded above all else, according to Selective Service, that the c.o. faithfully perform "work of national importance" in return for the "privilege" of exemption from fighting. The conditions of work should be as nearly equivalent as possible to the conditions of military service, yet meet the legal requirement of civilian direction. General Hershey advocated "that assignees should be neither favored nor punished because of their beliefs, but as far as the law allowed, they should undergo the same inconveniences and receive the same benefits as the men in service." [2]

This point of view of Selective Service was spelled out explicitly in the detailed regulations previously outlined (in Chapter X), and consistently guided its administrative control of the C.P.S. program.

Tolerance: The Churches' Creed

The American churches generally conceived of tolerance in a different light. To them, preserving the integrity of an individual's religious faith was paramount. In a society which accepted war as an essential instrument of its security, a line would inevitably separate the actions of a conscientious objector from the community. The purpose of Civilian Public Service in the eyes of the Historic Peace Churches and other denominations was to draw that line in a way that would enable each c.o. to remain true to his religious convictions.

Of Military Significance? The first requirement of such tolerance was freedom from all military service and training. The Historic Peace Churches were not prepared to accept at any point the prospect of work which could be considered military. Nor were they prepared to leave to Selective Service the ultimate decision as to what service had military implications. It was obvious to them and to most of their conscientious-objector members that work could be military even if the work supervisor or director were wearing civilian clothes. Erecting an airplane spotting tower, building a road as part of a strategic communications system, and cutting wood for use in naval shipbuilding were all projects which entailed a military purpose.

But could either the Historic Peace Churches or the men under their administration define a clear line between military and non-military service when the national organization for war was so complete? Did not each and every human activity in a country undergoing total mobilization involve some contribution to the war effort? The Historic Peace Churches did not attempt to state the area which they considered nonmilitary, but they insisted that the decision be left in the last analysis to the individual conscientious objector. Whatever his decision might be, and however unreasonable and foolish it might appear to even his own friends and church, it should be respected and followed. The only test to be applied should be one of sincerity. Doubt should always be resolved in favor of the conscience of the individual.

Testimony by Work. The vision of tolerance, particularly as seen by the Historic Peace Churches, demanded, however, something far more positive of C.P.S.—namely, an opportunity for an effective testimony of Christian pacifist conviction. The compulsion of conscription, declared the Mennonites, must be transformed "into the free service of a Christian who seeks to establish the Kingdom of God among men by the preaching of the gospel and the practice of Christian discipleship." Tolerance did not imply merely an escape from war. It meant the right for c.o.'s to practice and declare a "way of peace and love administering to human need which they hold to be a divine imperative." [3]

The Historic Peace Churches believed such a testimony would be more effectively expressed through service than through preachments. Work performed in a spirit of friendliness and consideration for human welfare would demonstrate the essential qualities of the "life which takes away the occasion of war." This witness of service would not antagonize but would win respect. It would show what the conscientious objector stood for, as well as what he stood against.

The Strategy of the Second Mile. The Historic Peace Churches were convinced that the testimony of love could be rendered even within the framework of conscription. From Christian experience and teaching, c.o.'s could learn a remarkable strategy for overcoming the restraints of arbitrary governmental authority, the strategy of walking the second mile. As explained by a Mennonite, this strategy,

in place of gaining its point by law . . . operates on the level of love which restores the broken fellowship; in place of using the tactics of pressure to gain its point, it expresses instead its concern on the basis of principles involved; it does not insist on personal rights, but rather gives thought to the obligations and duties that one has when under the Spirit and direction of Christ. When compelled to go one mile, the non-resistant Christian does not resist the compulsion, but rather stands prepared to volunteer the services of the second mile.[4]

Personal liberty did not appear to the Historic Peace Churches as the primary issue in the fight for tolerance. They did not consider restrictions on the travel and the movement of the c.o., on the place and particular nature of his work assignment, and on leaves and furloughs as matters of vital principle.[5] The religious agencies assured their assignees that discomforts and privations, however unjust and unfortunate, did not bar the achievement of a striking pacifist testimony by "audacious voluntary goodwill and love."[6]

One requirement was necessary, however, for this kind of testimony to succeed. While the individual went the first mile under compulsion, he had to go the second voluntarily. The conscientious objector had to give "inner consent" in undertaking Civilian Public Service if his act was to serve as a positive demonstration of faith. The Historic Peace Churches assumed in the beginning that a c.o. who came to C.P.S. wanted to serve and shared to some extent their objective of a second-mile testimony, even though he was drafted. Within the first year of operation many conscientious objectors thoroughly disabused the churches of any such expectation. Under these circumstances the "second-mile testimony" was thwarted not only for the men who had no desire to make such a stand but also for those who did, because some of the former deliberately obstructed the accomplishment of a significant work record.

The churches tried to salvage their vision by pressing the government to undertake direct administration of camps and projects for all persons who did not voluntarily accept service under a religious agency. When the government finally yielded to this petition the Peace Churches explicitly determined to accept in their projects *only* persons who shared some conception of the "second-mile testimony" and gave their consent to serve under conditions as they stood.

The Sacrifice of Pay. An essential principle of "second-mile testimony," according to the Historic Peace Churches, was that men should perform their service without pay. Paul Comly French, executive secretary of the National Service Board, defended Civilian Public Service

as a way of giving the state-community the service which it asked . . . and then going beyond that and paying for the privilege of serving . . . I am satisfied that the fact that people believe in a thing sufficiently to pay for it has worth in making our testimony clear in a society in which material things are predominant and the basis on which values are judged.[7]

While the churches did not propose that c.o.'s should be *compelled* to labor without pay, and urged that the government provide wages for work under *its* administration, they insisted that to pay men serving under their auspices would nullify the "testimony."

The Church's Ministry to the C.O. The Friends, Brethren, and Mennonites insisted that they were not agents of Selective Service in the administration of C.P.S., but were partners with the conscientious objectors.

Thomas E. Jones, first director for Friends Civilian Public Service, continuously pleaded with his constituency to "go to camp with the boys"; if they could not themselves perform the service, they could at least go in spirit or through their pocketbooks or through personal visits. The Mennonites were deeply concerned to identify themselves in a fellowship with their members in Civilian Public Service. The Central Committee considered that "participation in the life of a Christian Brotherhood Community such as it seeks to maintain in C.P.S. projects in the truest sense means sharing by all members, not only in the benefits, but in the creation of these benefits through mutual counsel and the bearing of burdens." The Brethren Service Committee likewise stressed that its role was not one of command over the c.o. but of co-operation with the men in seeking ways of true Christian living.

Obedience to the State. While the three Historic Peace Churches held the same basic conception of religious toleration, differences between their underlying attitudes toward government profoundly affected their respective relations with Selective Service.

The Mennonites had learned to see the state through the eyes of Paul.[8] "It is the Christian's duty," they said, "loyally and faithfully to obey the state in all requirements which do not involve violation of the Christian conscience, that is, a violation of the teachings of the word of God." In following this principle of obedience the Mennonite groups readily co-operated with Selective Service in the administration of Civilian Public Service, accepting without protest the terms and conditions laid down by government, whatever the hardship imposed upon the churches or the individual c.o.'s. The Mennonite Central Committee did reserve "the right of conscience to reject forms of service which contribute to war or coercion in any form or to any other social evil." But it did not feel a "nonresistant church" could appropriately make demands of Selective Service or actively oppose it.

The Friends, on the other hand, did not feel under any scriptural compunction to obey the powers that be. What was right and what was wrong in the body politic was in the last analysis to be discovered by an Inner Light burning within each Friend. If Selective Service acted in a way which contradicted a Friend's inner sense of right, it could confidently expect to hear about it. For the Friends felt a moral obligation to persuade, if they did not combat, the powers of the state when they felt it was in the wrong. At times, when they were unsuccessful in persuasion, they withheld their co-operation. Just as Selective Service could usually count on Mennonite acquiescence, so did they come to count on Quaker recalcitrance.[9]

Between these two, the Brethren Service Committee took a position of conciliation. It was bound by no creedal obligation to obey the commands of the government, but it appreciated the opportunity to carry on a public service and to enjoy the trust of government. The Church of the Brethren affirmed that

Christian citizenship implies full support of the state only insofar as it represents good government and the righteous will of God. We realize that the total rejection of government on the one hand means anarchy, and the unquestioned acceptance of the authority of the state on the other hand means tyranny and totalitarianism. The Christian citizen must take his position somewhere between these two extremes.[10]

The Brethren leaders were convinced that Civilian Public Service struck the proper balance between individual, church, and state in time of war. Consequently, they eagerly sought to compose disagreements which arose between Selective Service and the religious administrative agencies.

Tolerance: A Responsibility of Government

Most Protestant denominations joined the Historic Peace Churches in defending the right of the c.o. to serve as his conscience directed without repression. The Federal Council of Churches and a number of churches by their own independent action attempted to secure a liberalization of government policies in several respects. They urged that the work of c.o.'s be used to maximum social advantage and include service with religious and social welfare organizations and in relief and rehabilitation abroad. They asked that the government meet dependency needs and provide just compensation when c.o.'s were killed or injured in their duties.[11]

On one point, an important segment of religious opinion tended to disagree with the Historic Peace Churches' conception of tolerance for the c.o. Denominational leaders were increasingly convinced that the government should assume full responsibility for the supervision and maintenance of conscientious objectors assigned to C.P.S. They contended that the Brethren, Friends, and Mennonites had really undermined tolerance, as well as the principle of separation of church and state, by relieving the government of a portion of its rightful responsibility. Bishop G. Bromley Oxnam, chairman of the Federal Council of Churches Committee on the Conscientious Objector, battled for provisions that would make it unnecessary for any man to accept service under a religious agency. The opportunity for alternative service should be provided at government expense, with compensation to the c.o. sufficient for his personal needs and the support of his dependents. Civilian Public Service therefore fell short of assuring religious liberty so long as it remained under the exclusive administration of religious agencies.

Many c.o.'s shared Bishop Oxnam's conception of tolerance, especially those who were "absolutists." They insisted that lack of government support for all c.o.'s willing to accept it was a crucial gap in the pattern of Civilian Public Service. Under these conditions alternative service did not assure tolerance but imposed an "involuntary servitude."

Tolerance: C.O. Visions

The c.o.'s came to C.P.S. with widely differing expectations. Some looked for the blissful anarchy of Thoreau's Walden. A good many expected to find a voluntary work camp, a self-disciplined pacifist co-operative, or a pious religious brotherhood. Most, however, anticipated merely an opportunity for nonmilitary service which did not violate their convictions against war. They came prepared to accept the vision of C.P.S. held by the Historic Peace Churches and to co-operate in its fulfillment, though as time wore on the vision paled and many lost their enthusiasm for it.[12]

For one group of c.o.'s real tolerance implied not simply freedom from *military* control but freedom from *all* control. Unless a man could decide his own destiny—his job, his clothes, the length of his beard, the arrangement of his bunk, the hours of his meals, the hours he worked—his conscience was abused. There must be no compulsion either by government or by church. Any regulation, any discipline or penalties, infringed the fundamental conditions of religious tolerance. These men looked to Civilian Public Service to provide, on the one hand, all the essentials of personal security and, on the other, to shield them from any restrictions which they were unwilling to accept voluntarily.

Yet certain of the devotees of freedom recognized that tolerance could not possibly extend so far unless the c.o. was able to substitute for external restraints a sense of social responsibility within himself. Tolerance meant simply that the government should stay its coercive hand while c.o.'s of their own free will worked and behaved in a way the public would accept. In the proving ground of C.P.S., c.o.'s would demonstrate that a self-governing, self-controlled group of men could do far more, impelled by the incentive of their own desire to serve, than the government could exact by rules and the threat of penalties.

By far the majority of the men started their C.P.S. careers committed to substantially the same goals as the Historic Peace Churches under whose administration they came to serve. To them,

Civilian Public Service was an alternative to military conscription rather than a phase of it. They recognized specific injustices as existent within the plan but felt that these might be eliminated without denying the validity of the total program. . . . In more positive terms, many assignees of this persuasion hoped through the work projects to contribute materially to the conservation of both the human and the natural resources of the world. . . . At a time when all the world seemed engaged in a work of destruction they sought to render a positive service of peace. To some of this group such a service was regarded as an opportunity to "witness" for peace, to demonstrate to the world a way superior to that of war. Others felt that . . . Civilian Public Service has a practical means of conserving the peace belief among pacifists themselves. . . . C.P.S. was looked upon as an opportunity for pacifists to meet others of like belief and through study and association together to work toward a common plan of action for building a peaceful world.[13]

Tolerance: The Public View

On the whole, the American public cast a somewhat puzzled but not unfriendly eye on C.P.S. as the channel for conscientious objection in the face of war. Sporadic outbursts of hostility occurred, but the general temper was unfevered and often kindly.

C.P.S. had a good press. The strange phenomenon of the tiny minority whose religion impelled them to "fight without weapons" excited lively news interest in the communities where C.P.S. units were established, in the home towns of the assignees, in religious publications, and even in the national press and on the radio. A flurry of publicity greeted the initiation of C.P.S., and each new camp or project was a local news item. Soon a *Saturday Evening Post* writer caught the scent, to be followed by other major periodicals, almost every one ultimately carrying at least one article on the c.o.'s. When the services grew and c.o.'s started to work in hospitals, and as "guinea pigs" for medical and scientific experimentation, C.P.S. hit the feature pages of the *New York Times, Philadelphia Evening*

Bulletin, Boston Daily Globe, Cleveland Press, Los Angeles Times, and many other metropolitan dailies. Another spark was kindled when Lew Ayres, the movie actor, was assigned to C.P.S. A little uncertain at first, the Hollywood newshounds soon decided the event was not "poison" and proceeded to write up "Dr. Kildare's" new exploits and associates. H. R. Baukhage introduced the C.P.S. men in 1943 to the major radio networks in a dramatic story of the guinea-pig experiments, which he later wrote up for *Cosmopolitan.* Other commentators picked up the lead. Meanwhile, denominational publications gave attention to the work of the c.o.'s of their respective churches. Outstanding stories appeared in Methodist, Baptist, Congregational, and other periodicals.

Most of this press comment was favorably disposed both to the c.o.'s and to their program of service. In the later stages, however, some sharp criticism appeared from two opposite points of view. Sensational attacks on the "rebelliousness" of c.o.'s and the softness of their lot occasionally occurred.[14] Unwillingness of men to engage in emergency farm labor often drew the fire of county newspapers. On the other hand, the *Washington Post* and the *Christian Century* denounced the administration of C.P.S. as unjustifiably harsh, particularly in denying pay to c.o.'s, and condemned the waste of their service on worthless work.[15]

The c.o.'s generally secured respect for their beliefs and approval of the services which they were rendering from the communities in which they worked. After the ice was broken and the men became known, they were usually treated without antagonism or discrimination by their neighbors and were welcome to take part in community organizations and activities. In isolated instances public relations deteriorated, and occasionally a crisis arose. A few c.o.'s were physically attacked—in one case because of resentment over the refusal of some men to engage in emergency farm labor, in another situation because the c.o.'s were too attractive to the local girls. Ill feeling developed in another community because the C.P.S. men made use of the public swimming dock and other recreation facilities. Apparent abuse of privileges by the c.o.'s or evidence of disrespect for their country and the sensibilities of their fellow citizens also aroused local hostility. The director of the National Music Camp at Interlochen, Michigan, protested to his congressman and to Senator Vandenberg that c.o.'s visiting from a nearby camp had behaved objectionably and were disrespectful during the playing of the National Anthem. In another Michigan community, the local prosecutor objected to the c.o.'s coming into town from camp in a government truck for recreational purposes "when local citizens cannot secure five gallons of gasoline to attend the funeral of a deceased relative." The visiting of the local taverns by some c.o.'s often excited unfavorable reaction. But on the whole, the objectors acted with discretion and consideration for the feelings of their neighbors, and the communities in turn accepted their presence and viewed their work and conduct in C.P.S. sympathetically.

Tolerance likewise appears to have been the prevailing attitude of the public at large. In a scientifically conducted national survey of public opinion made in April, 1945, by the Office of Public Opinion Research (Princeton, N.J.) 65 per cent "disapproved" of conscientious objectors, but 75 per cent approved of their being "sent overseas to help in relief work in war areas," 67 per cent approved of their dependents receiving some federal aid, 60 per cent approved of c.o.'s receiving some pay for their work, and 70 per cent felt that they should be "assigned to jobs which make use of their skills and training," rather than to "manual work in labor camps." A more discriminating analysis of American public opinion toward c.o.'s, undertaken by Leo Crespi, showed that nearly one-fifth of the public *approved* of c.o.'s and that disapproval generally did not extend to active discrimination or social rejection. For instance, two-thirds of his sample indicated that Lew Ayres's being a c.o. did not affect their willingness to see his pictures, while a majority declared they would accept c.o.'s as personal friends. More than one-third showed no degree of discrimination toward c.o.'s, even to having them as close relatives by marriage. "Though the amount of public disapproval of c.o. *principles* is considerable," concluded Dr. Crespi, "the present study reveals that the amount of public antagonism toward c.o.'s as *individuals* is relatively small." This underlying disposition was reflected in the public attitude regarding proper wartime treatment for c.o.'s. Four-fifths of the general public, according to this study, approved of providing alternative service for c.o.'s rather than insisting that they be given the choice of fighting or going to jail. Significantly, the remaining fifth were mostly persons whose education was limited to grammar school or less. A considerable proportion of those who approved of alternative service envisaged assignment of c.o.'s to noncombatant service at the front, but a larger proportion favored assignment to jobs not directly related to the war effort. Very few, however, favored allowing c.o.'s to remain at their peacetime jobs. On the issue of economic support for c.o.'s, over three-fourths of the general public answered that the men assigned to camps should receive wages and money for their families from the government. The majority felt that this support should be the same as that received by a private in the Army.[16]

Despite this broad tolerance and lack of discrimination by the general public toward c.o.'s, there were pockets of organized hostility. Veterans' groups, in particular, scored the Civilian Public Service program for coddling c.o.'s The American Legion of Pennsylvania and several other Legion departments urged complete abolishment of the camps and the induction of all c.o.'s into the armed forces. At the national level Selective Service officials succeeded in turning aside resolutions along this line, but veterans' organizations repeatedly demanded the subjection of c.o.'s to more rigorous discipline. The 45th Encampment of the Veterans of Foreign Wars declared that "thousands of young 'men,' who claim conscientious objections to war are being mollycoddled by 'sobsisters' of the Selective Service System and State officials." Regulations should be made "more stringent and drastic so that these young 'men' may endure in a minor measure some of the hardships being imposed upon and cheerfully borne by the men and women who are fighting our common enemies." They should be "disciplined, restricted and visibly identified on or off duty." If "appropriate" action were not taken by the Director of the Selective Service System the law should be amended to compel conscientious objectors "to perform hard manual labor without pay and be subject to the same discipline and regulations enforced upon members of the armed service."

The hard and tough school of thought cast a long shadow over the operation of Civilian Public Service. Selective Service officials, most of whom were themselves members of the Legion or V.F.W., attached great importance to the official edicts of these organizations, even though they personally defended the C.P.S. program before veterans' gatherings and even praised the work of the c.o.'s. A constant fear of public opinion was acknowledged by the Selective Service Administration to guide and temper its decisions in regard to the conscientious objector, and the veterans' groups succeeded in passing off what were evidently minority views as general public opinion. By their influence over Selective Service, these organizations hardened the government's policies toward c.o.'s and braked the broad views of tolerance held by the founders of Civilian Public Service.

Selective Service vs. the C.O.

Because these conceptions of tolerance were so contradictory, conflict among the partners in Civilian Public Service was inescapable. C.o.'s condemned the government for encroaching on their "rights" through the regulations which it presented, and accused Selective Service of pursuing a policy of calculated repression. On the other hand, the protests of the c.o.'s and the methods of resistance adopted by some of them baffled, annoyed, and often disgusted the government men. Officials complained they could not reconcile a conscientious objector's professed belief in friendliness and brotherhood with the viciousness of his attack upon the government as an institution and upon the individuals who represented the government. Was it consistent for a pacifist to denounce a foreman as a liar? Was it tolerant for a pacifist to ridicule a project superintendent as a Hitler? Was it peaceful to break open a storeroom and pour molasses over government food supplies? Selective Service officials usually admitted that these were the acts of individuals and did not represent the majority of c.o.'s. But they became increasingly uncompromising in their decisions to exact full penalties for given misdeeds, and their actions therefore took on an ever more repressive appearance. "No" became its natural response to the recommendations and petitions of c.o.'s and religious agencies.

Pacifist against Pacifist

A major schism also split the pacifist movement as Civilian Public Service unrolled. If anything, the bitterness of pacifist toward pacifist was more acute than that of pacifist toward a conscripting government. Some c.o.'s went so far as to charge that the Historic Peace Churches had "betrayed" the conscientious objector and had become accomplices of the government in maintaining C.P.S. as a penal system—"a System which denied and punished individuals for holding, unqualified, the very ideals which the administrators themselves supposedly maintained in more prudential form." [17] Other critics, while giving the churches credit for good intentions, held them responsible because of their continued administration of C.P.S. for "marking the lives of thousands of men with years of involuntary paupery, of enforced neglect of loved dependents and with the wearing strain of deliberate and calculated injustice." [18]

The dissidents aroused a strong and often equally bitter counter-action among those who feared that the destruction of C.P.S. would lose precious gains in the struggle to recognize conscience. The wedge driven into the pacifist movement by differing views in regard to the merits of C.P.S. was never withdrawn during the war years.

The line of division within C.P.S. did not strictly follow denominational affiliation. Some of the most willing co-operators came from outside the members of the Historic Peace Churches. Some of the severest critics of the religious agencies and the strongest advocates of direct protest action were Friends, Brethren, and even Mennonites. On the other hand, the disunity between C.P.S. men and religious agencies was more pronounced in those camps and projects that were most heterogeneous.

Breakdown of Morale

The disunity within the C.P.S. frustrated the best qualities of many c.o.'s and destroyed the good will that is essential to tolerance. Men who came expecting to find a noble opportunity for service beside their fellow pacifists, and an island of freedom within the sweep of conscription, were shocked by the dissention. Few could avoid a letdown after several months in the combative atmosphere engendered by differing views of tolerance. Disillusioned, sometimes by the government, sometimes by their church, and sometimes by the narrowness or belligerency or bigotry of their own fellow pacifists, men grew sour.

Their frustrations were aggravated by the unskilled work that many of them were required to do, the deprivation of all income in C.P.S., and the other restrictive conditions which surrounded the life of the drafted c.o. A sociologist who was also a C.P.S. assignee attributed the breakdown of personality among c.o.'s largely to the influences of life under conscription.

The C.P.S. camps were characterized by social isolation, routine, and diminished cultural and social stimulation. Stultification easily followed. . . . The results were uniformity of functions, of routine and of experience, and inversion of the group. The first produced monotony and boredom. These, in turn, produced organic and emotional tensions and restlessness. . . . Inversion produced stereotyped thought patterns . . . highly charged with personal and emotional feelings. It further resulted in emotional instability, withdrawal, outcroppings of homosexual tendencies, emotional or social dullness and intellectual sterility—types of responses not uncommon in isolated, monosexual groups.[19]

On the other hand, a survey made of a large Brethren camp by A. T. Boisen, a psychiatrist, concluded that the source of breakdown was chiefly the emotional patterns which the men brought with them to camp in the first place. Those who came well adjusted, with well-grounded beliefs and firm support from their homes, friends, and churches, tended to weather the pressure of C.P.S. without a collapse of morale. The men who had acquired some previous maladjustment or feared social disapproval were the ones who suffered most in the constrictive and tense environment of C.P.S. This opinion was shared by other competent observers.[20]

Some of the c.o.'s surrendered completely their desire either to serve constructively or to express their convictions actively. Without the stimulus of vigorous and united group action, they retreated into a world of routine where they performed without spirit the minimum duties required of them and sought to secure as tolerable a life as possible during the days of their confinement. They abandoned for the duration the hope of constructive personal achievement. They were stirred by neither the campaigns of protest nor the faith of the "Second Milers." For them, C.P.S. lost all meaning as a laboratory for Christian living or pacifist action. It became simply a place to sit out the war with a minimum of inconvenience. Most of these men retained sincere and firm scruples against military service which prevented them from going into the Army. They could not generate, however, any enthusiasm for the service to which they were assigned, for the churches under which they worked, or for the personality and welfare of their fellow c.o.'s.

Defections

The problems and tensions caused by the widely divergent views of the partners in Civilian Public Service led a number to demand that the program be abandoned—if not completely, then at least by the sponsoring religious agencies. Most of the voices which called for its liquidation were pacifist. Even before the program was launched a few had warned that the crucial issue of the time was the imposition of conscription and that in C.P.S. both the church and the conscientious objector would sell out their beliefs to the government. Around this core of moral repudiation gathered the various elements of discontent within the pacifist ranks: the group that disliked a note of conservative religious piety to color their lives; those driven to desperation by the financial insecurity of their unsupported families; men who were irked by insignificant work projects; those who felt the injustice of government regulation; and those who, because of the absence of pay, felt themselves mere objects of charity. All these for their different reasons concluded that the church agencies should withdraw their sponsorship and give up their administrative responsibility.

The chorus of dissidence rose and fell in accordance with the conditions of the moment, with the character of the camp, and with the intensity of the war. Mennonite circles were never as aroused as other denominations, although they, too, faced repeated requests to take no further part in Civilian Public Service. On the other hand, a great majority of men in Friends Civilian Public Service projects were at times ready to see the Quakers withdraw. Each new crisis in the struggle of competing views of tolerance added recruits to these who would abandon ship. When the crisis passed or hope for a solution was offered, the opposition would drop. Nevertheless, the ground swell of opposition always grew a little stronger and broader as it moved along through the repeated tensions and the deepening dilemmas of Civilian Public Service.

Exposed to such a barrage of criticism and disillusionment, some collaborators in Civilian Public Service left the fold. In 1944 the Fellowship of Reconciliation decided by a close vote of its Council and of the general membership to become a "consultative" rather than an "administrative" member of the National Service Board for

Religious Objectors. In October, 1945, the Association of Catholic Conscientious Objectors severed its relations with N.S.B.R.O., convinced that they should never have participated in the program because pacifist leadership had thereby "allied itself with the military in administering conscription, one of the most essential phases of the war effort." Other co-operating church groups, including the American Friends Service Committee, the American Baptist Home Mission Society, and the Methodist Commission on World Peace withdrew from administrative responsibilities after the conclusion of hostilities, their action being dictated by unwillingness to be identified with the administration of "peacetime conscription."

Far more serious was the loss of the many conscientious objectors who walked out of C.P.S. in violation of the law. Many of these men had given strong leadership in the program but came to the point where they could no longer conscientiously serve when their service was legally compulsory. They had to break totally with conscription.[21]

For some, disunity and the conflicts within Civilian Public Service were so devastating and discouraging that they turned from their pacifist alternative and entered military service. Victory was a goal more tangible, more direct, more coherent than tolerance.

The Partnership Continues

The attacks on Civilian Public Service made each of the participants—government, churches, and conscientious objectors—uneasy. Nevertheless, the threefold partnership continued until the conclusion of the war.

Conditions for Continuance. In agreeing to continue, the religious agencies did not intend to acquiesce unconditionally in the status quo of C.P.S. The American Friends Service Committee in particular laid down definite terms whose fulfillment it considered essential if it were to carry on its administration. The Friends concluded that progress toward achieving these conditions was sufficient to justify renewal of their agreement with Selective Service and the continuance of their administration and their financial support.

As a matter of fact, only two fundamental changes in C.P.S. were brought about throughout the duration of the war: the assignment of c.o.'s to "detached service" projects and the establishment of government-administered camps. Though these proved significant and satisfying outlets for many men, they failed to affect the fundamental relationship between the trinity of participants—Selective Service, conscientious objectors, and the Historic Peace Churches. Selective Service yielded up no authority in principle or in practice to the religious agencies, despite the protests of the Friends or the conditions they set for their continued co-operation. This authority actually tightened. The Historic Peace Churches had to relapse more and more into the role of a reluctant but acquiescent agent. Nor did Selective Service at any point relax in principle or in practice the yoke of its control over individual c.o.'s. Nevertheless, those who had assumed major leadership and responsibility for C.P.S. were still convinced that the partnership should not be dissolved, and a major portion of the assignees, as has been seen, agreed with them. A strange imperative drove the experiment in tolerance through all vicissitudes to a settled and deliberate conclusion.

Incentives for Perseverance. Those who urged continuance of C.P.S. placed great value upon the constructive service rendered by the c.o.'s. Whatever charges there might be of wasted labor on some projects, the total record of service never failed to impress. Supporters of C.P.S. were especially gratified at the expansion of opportunities for "detached service." Detached service was a safety valve through which some of the accumulated tension and dissatisfaction could pour, leaving the atmosphere clearer and the sponsoring agencies more determined to go forward.

The churches and those conscientious objectors who continued in C.P.S. were further convinced that the performance of these services was consistent with their fundamental religious convictions. Many conditions were unsatisfactory, but when the question was asked, "Do these conditions actually violate principle?" the answer was constantly "No." The Historic Peace Churches made a sharp distinction between conscientious objection to conscription and conscientious objection to war. Both convictions were held in high esteem, but for the Historic Peace Churches the latter took precedence whenever the issue of continued support of Civilian Public Service arose.

The real test of principle for the Historic Peace Churches was the military quality in C.P.S. So long as the nature of the service did not involve too direct a relationship to the war effort, they were content that the integrity of their faith was not compromised.

Furthermore, many supporters of C.P.S. were convinced that it did afford opportunities for a strong "testimony" for peace. In reviewing the record of C.P.S., a special committee of the Brethren Service Committee, including assignees, firmly concluded that despite defects and disappointments the program had "been a medium through which our witness for peace and brotherhood in the world could be expressed. The movement remains as the most outstanding protest in the United States against military service and against war as a method of adjusting international disputes." [22]

Some advocated continuance of Civilian Public Service because they felt it dammed back at one point the surge of totalitarian state authority. Far from surrendering the independence of the church to the state, Civilian Public Service thrust the church forward in the struggle to resist encroachments on personal liberties and religious freedom. In this struggle, according to Mr. Mould and many others, Civilian Public Service staked out the claim of the church to maintain unharassed the sanctity of conscience. They could speak not as outsiders but as parties with responsibility. The supporting church leaders would constantly assert that only as they adequately discharged their responsibilities in C.P.S. could they expect Selective Service to respect their intercession for the rights of c.o.'s.[23]

Another extremely important factor in persuading the churches to continue with Civilian Public Service was concern for the welfare of those c.o.'s who wanted to work under church rather than under government direction. When a substantial majority of the men indicated that they had no desire to transfer to government projects, the churches did not want to force this choice by withdrawing from C.P.S. The Mennonite churches were especially eager to continue with C.P.S. because they felt "the church could follow its drafted men and minister unto them." This ministry could not take place effectively, they argued, unless the church itself kept its administrative responsibility. All of the Historic Peace Churches came to feel, as did many of the c.o.'s in both their camps and in the government camps, that the personal services and the educational and religious programs available in the church projects contributed greatly to the welfare and to the convictions of the men. Some asked if an equally effective program of personal services could not go on if the government took over, but supporters of C.P.S. were sure that this would not be possible. Furthermore, a sense of mutual regard arose between the three Historic Peace Churches and restrained each from unilateral action. They disagreed widely on many issues in the administration of C.P.S., but none of the churches wished to jeopardize the aims and accomplishments of the others.

Finally, a strain of optimism affected the Historic Peace Churches as they confronted the problems of their C.P.S. program. In keeping with their faith in the potential goodness of every man, they expected the best both of the c.o.'s and of the government officials with whom they worked. Any straw in the wind from Selective Service which could possibly be interpreted as a promise of concession or an evidence of good will was seized upon as the herald of a new and better day. The disaffections of conscientious objectors were usually interpreted as temporary, a response to some particular local or individual tension that would pass, either if the condition were corrected or if time were allowed to heal. It was extremely hard for the Historic Peace Churches to accept as fact the intention of some c.o.'s deliberately to wreck the effort to build in C.P.S. a "peaceable community."

Conscience Money. In the spirit of the "second mile," the Historic Peace Churches undertook to raise the necessary funds for the support of c.o.'s in Civilian Public Service. They appealed for contributions—in money, canned goods, clothing, and other supplies—to their own members, to denominations with c.o.'s assigned to C.P.S., to concerned individuals, and even to the men in C.P.S. and their families. As the program continued and involved increasing numbers, the costs mushroomed and at times threatened to exceed the resources which the churches, especially the Friends, could muster. Yet in the end, accounts balanced. All together, the churches and the c.o.'s raised over $7,000,000 to pay the expenses of C.P.S.[24]

The constituencies of the Historic Peace Churches were the major source of support for C.P.S. The Mennonites gave by far the most —in total amount and in proportion to their membership—and were more solidly united in their support. A church of about 120,000 members contributed over $3,000,000 during a period of six years. The

Mennonite Central Committee was authorized to allocate quotas to the different branches of the church, distributing the budget of C.P.S. evenly among the membership, regardless of the number of men which each branch had in camp. The amount of the per capita assessment ranged from 50 cents for six months in the beginning to 50 cents a month at the peak load and amounted in the end to a levy of $21.45 per member. An extra contribution was asked and received from the Amish churches in view of the very much larger proportion of their men in C.P.S., and some of the branches with relatively few assignees were unable to raise their quotas. Nevertheless, the financial burden was shared on a remarkably equitable basis. In addition to cash, the Mennonites contributed a vast quantity of foodstuffs to their camps. The food was canned or dried at home or by local church organizations and then assembled at collection centers, where it was picked up by trucks from nearby camps or shipped in carload lots to the more remote ones. The project assumed major proportions in the life of the average Mennonite community, tying it closely to the C.P.S. program. In a Pacific coast district one year, sewing circles representing some three hundred families canned forty-five hundred jars and dried sixteen hundred pounds of food. These donations not only reduced costs but provided for C.P.S. men a more adequate diet than was possible with rationed goods.[25]

Brethren support for C.P.S. came principally through the organized channels of the church, and was raised as an integral part of the general church budget for service activities by its regular promotional machinery. A section of the church paper, the *Gospel Messenger*, was devoted to the C.P.S. program; the church's promotional secretary included C.P.S. among his responsibilities; regional, district, and local representatives of the Brethren Service Committee carried the appeal directly to local congregations. The response varied greatly. In some places, it was wholehearted; elsewhere, support was weak or entirely lacking. Rural churches gave stronger backing to C.P.S. than did urban, and the churches which had a large number of their young men in C.P.S. were, as might be expected, the most generous in their contributions. All together, the Brethren constituency contributed over $2,000,000 for wartime service work, of which $1,328,000 was spent for C.P.S. Large amounts of clothing and food were also given. Church groups and individuals cultivated "God's acres" for the camps, canned tons of fruits and vegetables, prepared meats and lard, made blankets and comforters, knitted sweaters, and sewed clothing. As C.P.S. needs lessened, the program of food collection was expanded to include contributions for foreign relief.[26]

The Friends faced three difficult problems in securing support for C.P.S. First, they lacked a united organization, authorized to raise funds from their twenty-four autonomous Yearly Meetings (and numerous independent local meetings) for a common project. Thus separate arrangements had to be made with each meeting in regard to the method and amount of its support for C.P.S., and delicate planning was necessary to avoid competition with the meeting's regular budget, which was often no larger than the amount needed for C.P.S. Second, the Friends were deeply divided in their attitudes toward the war. Only a minority in most meetings were pacifists, and many actually denounced the c.o.'s and opposed any action on their behalf. Third, the Friends had to raise more than double the amount necessary for the expenses of their own members in order to care for men from outside their denomination. While the Brethren and Mennonites contributed approximately the same sum for this purpose (for several years the three churches agreed to divide the "deficit" for nonmembers evenly among themselves), the amount loomed proportionately larger to the Friends, who had a smaller number of their own members in C.P.S. (Though the Historic Peace Churches had obligated themselves to support C.P.S. regardless of the affiliations of the c.o.'s in it, they all found that the response of their constituencies depended to a very large extent upon the number of their own members who were involved.)

Because of these factors, the Friends were forced to adopt a much more individualistic approach in soliciting financial support for C.P.S. At first, they appealed to the assignee and his family to contribute (as loyal "second milers"); then they turned to the meeting of which he was a member and asked it to meet the balance of his expenses, which were calculated to be thirty-five dollars a month including administrative costs. This plan proved increasingly unsatisfactory. Though the contributions were supposed to be purely voluntary, many c.o.'s felt under strong moral pressure to "pay for their own keep," and some who were unable to do so considered them-

selves "charity cases." Instances occurred where men decided to go
into the Army so as to avoid subjecting their families to privation or
a sense of obligation on their behalf. Less than a year after the opening of C.P.S., this approach was dropped and each Yearly Meeting
was asked to undertake a general effort throughout its membership
to secure an agreed amount, which it felt was reasonable in view of
its size, other financial commitments, and the number of its members assigned to C.P.S. Many c.o.'s and their families continued to
give, far out of proportion to most other Friends, but gradually the
sense of *personal* responsibility gave way to a recognition of the
Meeting's responsibility. Nevertheless, none of the meetings felt
they could assess their members for C.P.S., and their efforts were
confined to encouraging voluntary contributions given out of individual concern. Throughout the program, Friends also depended
heavily upon individual donors who were willing to make sizable
contributions directly to the American Friends Service Committee
for this purpose. All together, members of the Society of Friends
gave about $1,200,000 out of $2,300,000 contributed for the support
of Friends-administered C.P.S.

Support for C.P.S. from groups other than the Historic Peace
Churches was more limited and far harder to secure. The Christadelphians and a few smaller churches met the expenses of their own
c.o.'s in full as they were incurred. Most of the major Protestant denominations, in due course, accepted official responsibility for the
maintenance of their c.o.'s in line with their professed recognition
of the right of conscientious objection. But some of their leaders were
antagonistic because they felt the Historic Peace Churches had gone
ahead without consulting them in incurring financial obligations on
behalf of their c.o.'s. They therefore stoutly denied any debt to the
Peace Churches, legal or "honorable." Furthermore, the denominations were unwilling to include the cost of c.o.'s as a part either of
their regular budgets or of the funds which they raised for wartime
services, fearing that an appeal for the c.o. would stigmatize their
other programs. Consequently, separate solicitations had to be undertaken either by an authorized organ of the church (such as the
Methodist Commission on World Peace) or by a special committee
set up for the purpose (for instance, the committee established by the
General Assembly of the Presbyterian Church). Despite vigorous and

devoted efforts, those responsible were usually unable to enlist substantial support outside the small minority of sympathizers in each church, and this was insufficient to cover the costs of the men assigned. As a matter of fact, the contributions of the c.o.'s and their immediate families constituted a very large proportion of the amount raised. Ultimately, representatives of the National Service Board joined with the denominational commitees to contact personally the churches' district leaders and bishops and to appeal for official action by the various regional bodies of the church. A growing number of these did rally to the support of C.P.S. and by the end of the program ten denominations had raised the full cost of maintenance for their c.o.'s (the Assemblies of God, Christadelphian, Disciples of Christ, Episcopal, Evangelical and Reformed, Faith Tabernacle, United Lutheran, Seventh Day Adventist, Church of Jesus Christ, and Dunkard). The Congregational, Evangelical, Presbyterian, Methodist, Unitarian, and a few other churches succeeded in raising over half the cost for their men in C.P.S. The amount contributed by all groups other than the Historic Peace Churches was about $1,300,000, which left about $1,250,000 paid by the Peace Churches for the expenses of men who were not their members, including a large number of men unaffiliated with any church.

Until 1944 the three churches shared this cost evenly between them, regardless of the number of nonmembers which each had in its camps. This meant in effect that the Mennonites, with the fewest nonmembers, subsidized the Brethren and especially the Friends, who had the largest group of unsupported assignees. The Mennonites decided they would not continue the arrangement because the cost of maintenance of a man in Friends camps was higher than in their own and because their constituency was reluctant to pay out a large sum for the support of men outside their own program. The decision caused the Friends some anxious moments, as their resources were already strained to the limit, but the reduction of their costs through the assignment of increasing numbers of men to the self-sustaining special service units saved the day.

Despite a crescendo of dissension, a stern and restrictive governmental policy, an increasingly resentful body of conscientious objectors, and at points a hostile and intolerant public, the uneasy partnership of c.o., government, and church in the pursuit of tolerance continued until the end of the war. To a large extent, Civilian Public Service contained the ingredients out of which tolerance is made. On the other hand, it also contained the seeds of intense prejudice and intolerance. It demonstrated that even the highest ideals could be undermined by the pressure of conscription, of war, of arbitrary governmental authority, of the personal egotism and self-centeredness of even dedicated conscientious objectors, and of the inexperience and often blind optimism of church groups attempting to administer a complex and intricate pattern of public service.

XV: *Prosecuting the Objector*

MANY of those who supported the conscientious-objector section of the Selective Training and Service Act of 1940 hoped that the seemingly liberal provisions for conscience would minimize the necessity for prosecution of objectors. This, however, was not to be. Both because of the provisions of the act itself and because of the nature of its administration and interpretation, relatively large numbers of individuals claiming to be objectors began to be prosecuted after the law had been in effect only two years. Actually, about nine times as many objectors were sent to prison during the Second World War as were incarcerated during the First World War; even in proportion to the total numbers conscripted, there were between two and three times as many. The prosecution, trials, and sentencing of conscientious objectors provide an important chapter in the whole study of the subject. How objectors clashed with the law and why they did so casts a significant light not only on the objectors but also on the agencies of the law which were called upon to deal with them.

The Legal Offenses

According to the Department of Justice, there were 5,516 prosecutions of persons claiming to be conscientious objectors down to a month before the conclusion of hostilities with Japan. Table XI indicates the offenses charged and the total number of prosecutions for the years 1940 to June 30, 1945. Individuals claiming objection continued to be prosecuted until well into 1947, when the Selective Training and Service Act expired (on March 31). All together, more than 6,000 objectors, including the Jehovah's Witnesses, were prosecuted down to the expiration of the Act.[1] This represents 37.5 per

TABLE XI. PROSECUTIONS OF CONSCIENTIOUS OBJECTORS *

	Oct. 16, 1940 to June 30, 1942	July 1, 1942 to June 30, 1943	July 1, 1943 to June 30, 1944	July 1, 1944 to June 30, 1945	Total
Failure to register	112	133	13	8	266
Failure to return questionnaire	26	14	9	1	49
Failure to report for preliminary physical examination	18	32	19	1	70
Failure to report for induction	128	916	1,551	735	3,331
Failure to report to C.O. camp	99	519	618	303	1,539
Failure to comply with C.O. assignment—walkouts, refusals to work, etc.	1	49	79	104	233
Counseling and aiding evasion	2	22	3	1	28
TOTAL	386	1,685	2,292	1,153	5,516

* Adapted from figures of the Department of Justice. See *The Reporter*, Nov. 1, 1945, p. 3.

cent of the total of approximately 16,000 persons prosecuted for violations of the Selective Training and Service Act.[2] More than one person out of every three prosecuted under the Act was, therefore, a conscientious objector. It is possible that the percentage was even higher, as many of those not classified by the Department of Justice as "objectors" could probably have been placed in that category without straining the term too much, for the line between conscientious objector and "draft evader" was often a fine one. Sometimes the so-called evader had genuine objections but was not articulate about them.

The Explanation for Law Violations

The Nonregistrants. There is, of course, but little difficulty in explaining the nonregistrants. For the great bulk of them, their refusal to register under the law was deliberate and not the result of misinformation or of any obviously low intelligence (as might have been true of some nonregistrants who were not conscientious objectors). It is true that it is a bit surprising to find that the largest religious group of nonregistrants was composed of the Negro Moslems. But the Moslems themselves (more than 100 out of the 300 nonregistrants) seemed to have had no doubt about their duty not to comply with the law. They could fight only in a holy war called in the name of Islam, and even the act of registration would constitute a violation of Allah's will.

As for the remaining nonregistrants, they had dramatized their case for nonregistration from the very beginning of the Selective Training and Service Act. As early as October 16, 1940, the first registration day, 8 students at Union Theological Seminary had publicly announced their refusal to register and were later sentenced to prison. The 8 were followed by others, the greatest incidence of conscientious nonregistration occurring in the year July 1, 1942, to July 1, 1943, when 133 objectors (including Negro Moslems) announced their intention of refusing to comply even with the first requirements of the act. On the other hand, the number of conscientious nonregistrants during the last year of hostilities was only 8.[3]

Nonregistrants usually made some public announcement of their action, often by means of a letter to the federal district attorney or to the local Selective Service Board. This, it was felt, would differentiate them from mere "draft evaders." Conscientious nonregistration was primarily an open protest not only against war but also against the principle of conscription.

The number of prosecutions for nonregistration would have been larger had the Department of Justice chosen to prosecute those men above forty-five who refused to register—about twenty of this group took the nonregistrant position, including A. J. Muste, Evan Thomas, Richard Gregg (author of the pacifist classic, *The Power of Non-Violence*), Julius Eichel, Walter Longstreth (well-known Philadelphia attorney), and others.[4] But the Department took the position that since persons in this age group were above the age of service it would regard their letters informing the Department of their attitude as adequate for registration purposes. One exception alone was made: Julius Eichel was prosecuted, for some curious reason.

It should be emphasized that nonregistrants in this older group did not request favored treatment. Indeed, several of them expected to go to jail along with their younger fellow pacifists. And many argued that it was unfair to send younger nonregistrants to jail for a deliberate breach in the law while allowing the older men, who had committed precisely the same offense, to go free. The Department of Justice, nevertheless, had spoken.

The Denial of IV-D. The denial of classification IV-D to Jehovah's Witnesses was the explanation for the great bulk of failures to report to the Army or to Civilian Public Service. As has been shown before,[5] many local boards refused to consider Jehovah's Witnesses for either IV-D (ministerial exemption) or IV-E (conscientious objector to both combatant and noncombatant military service) classification. In such cases the devout Witness could only refuse to report to the Army and thus subject himself to civil prosecution. On the other hand, most Witnesses were equally opposed to Civilian Public Service; when local boards were willing to give IV-E classifications to them, they declined to report to Civilian Public Service camps. All together, about 75 per cent of all conscientious objectors prosecuted during the war were Jehovah's Witnesses, and in the overwhelming majority of these cases the technical offense charged was failure to report to the Army or to Civilian Public Service, as ordered.

The Denial of IV-E. Next to the denial of IV-D, the refusal of the Selective Service System to classify the objector, as requested, in

IV-E constituted the most important explanation for clashes with the law. An objector would be denied IV-E by his local board; he would go through the hierarchy of appeals and the decision of the local board would be sustained. That exhausted his administrative remedies. He had now to decide whether to surrender his conscientious objection to service in the Army or subject himself to prosecution. The Department of Justice, on the other hand, was obliged to prosecute those who failed to obey the orders of the Selective Service System. Occasionally, confronted by prosecution, the objector would agree belatedly to obey the orders of the local board, in which event the Justice Department would drop its proceedings. Such examples, however, were rare. It was usual, as in the case of nonregistrants, for the defaulter to give notice to the local board and to the federal district attorney of his intention to ignore the summons to report to the Army. Again, as in the case of nonregistrants, the objector was trying to differentiate himself from those who evaded Army service for "unconscientious" reasons; again, the dividing line between a "conscientious" and an "unconscientious" objector was at certain points rather hard to discern.

Objection to Alternative Civilian Service. Some objectors received the classifications they requested but refused at various points to comply with other requirements of the law. Thus they might receive a tentative classification of IV-E and refuse to report for physical examinations. That, of course, violated the law, as they were well aware. Their explanation was that they wished to take this means to protest conscription or, in some cases, the type of alternative civilian service set up under the Act. Similarly, others might obey the law up to the point where they were required to report to Civilian Public Service and at that point announce their disobedience. Sometimes the point of "absolutism" would be at the stage of returning the questionnaire. But whatever the point and however the precise explanation was stated, prosecution would follow.

Walkouts and Refusals to Work. As restrictions in Civilian Public Service increased during the course of the war and dissatisfaction with the structure and administration of alternative service became more widespread, many of those who had received IV-E classifications and had actually worked in the system became restive and sought to give expression to their profound dissatisfaction by act as well as word. Some of them carried on "slowdowns" in Civilian Public Service or refused to perform their assigned tasks.[6] Sometimes slowdowns and refusals to work led to prosecution. In other cases, objectors walked out of Civilian Public Service camps to evidence their opposition or disgust. After 1942, slowdowns, refusals to work, and walkouts constituted a gradually increasing proportion of all those objectors prosecuted. Thus in 1942–1943, 2.9 per cent of all the objectors prosecuted were in the category "walk-outs," refusals to work, and slowdowns; in 1943–1944, 3.4 per cent; and in 1944–1945, 9 per cent.

With the end of the war, or at least of the large-scale fighting, dissatisfaction in C.P.S. camps mounted, and it became more and more difficult for Selective Service to justify its continued detention of men. The protest against unpaid labor grew until it became a reverberating and defiant roar. Larger and larger numbers of the obstreperous were transferred to Selective Service's camp at Minersville, California, which became something of a punitive detention barracks.

Slowdowns, refusals to work, and walkouts, particularly in government camps, were accentuated. Would the Department of Justice prosecute vigorously in cases of this kind or would it be lenient? The question took on an added importance in view of the well-known feeling in Selective Service that the Department had been too lenient throughout the war in prosecuting c.o.'s.

The problem was best illustrated, perhaps, in the long drawn-out case of the Glendora government C.P.S. camp strikers. On May 17, 1946, six assignees at Glendora were arrested. Two of them were charged with refusal to transfer to another camp when ordered to do so by Selective Service, and four were accused of refusal to carry out assigned duties. Placed in the county jail originally, they were released on bail and their trial was expected to take place in June, 1946—nearly one year after the conclusion of hostilities.[7] A picket line of 30 other strikers, together with wives and children of the men and ministers of the gospel, kept incessant vigil at the jail before they were released pending trial.

But when the June date for trial arrived, the hearing was postponed. By this time a total of 47 men at the Glendora camp had been arrested and were awaiting trial. Since almost all the other men in the camp were also striking, the government was confronted with what was virtually a mass refusal to work. The American Civil Liberties Union had taken up the cause of the strikers, both those who had been arrested and those who had not yet been formally charged with an offense.[8]

Another month passed by and the protests at Glendora had increased. The general work strike had now lasted one hundred days. The few assignees still working at the camp had been transferred to a side camp. Although the strikers continued to refuse to perform their assigned duties and constantly iterated their protests at lack of pay, boondoggling nature of the work, discrimination in discharges, and other grievances, they were busily engaged in packaging food for European relief. Meanwhile, the trial date for the men who had refused to transfer had been pushed forward to September 17, 1946.[9] A motion for dismissal of the remaining cases was to be heard August 5.

But the September 17 trial date, too, was postponed, while the demand for dismissal of the cases increased in volume. All over the country, groups of objectors and nonobjectors alike were asking that the prosecutions stop. A new trial date was now fixed for October 7, and the defendants had increased to 62. A number of the strikers were attending polio patients at a Los Angeles hospital while their cases were pending in the courts. The Department of Justice and the Selective Service System had in the meantime tried to induce the men to return to work, promising them early discharge if they would do so. The overwhelming majority of the men refused to consider this offer.[10] A Glendora Strikers' Defense Committee was organized and preparations were made for a long legal battle. By September 1, the Glendora legal struggle had won even more attention and sympathy throughout the nation.

It was obvious that by now the Department of Justice was in a quandary. If it pushed the prosecution of the men and insisted on stiff penalties, it would incur the hostility of civil-liberties organizations and many churches. If, on the other hand, it failed to push the case with vigor, it might appear to be encouraging wholesale disregard of the Selective Service Act, which, after all, was still on the statute books. The Department chose to temporize. It had the trial postponed again—this time to March 11, 1947. The number of those under indictment had now been slightly reduced, to 58.[11]

In the meantime, the date for expiration of the Selective Service Act, March 31, was approaching. The Department of Justice now recommended that charges against 36 of the 58 men be dropped. Charges remained against only the 22 supposed "ringleaders." The 36 men who were released protested vigorously, arguing that either all or none of the cases should be dismissed. The Department of Justice, however, refused to countenance such a move, but insisted on bringing only the 22 to trial—this time on the postponed date of March 24 (one week before the expiration of the Selective Training and Service Act).

On March 24, then, came the anticlimax. The 2 men who were considered ringleaders by the Department of Justice (Behre and Atherton) were sentenced to two years and were immediately placed on probation. Their parents were to be their probation custodians! A few days later, just before the Act expired, the remaining 20 men were sentenced to ten months for "failure to work according to regulation" and to one month each for "failure to report for roll call on a specific day." All the sentences were suspended and two years' probation was decreed.[12]

The Glendora case had dragged out for nearly a year, and the mighty machinery of prosecution, which had originally planned a mass trial and conviction, ended rather lamely by placing the leaders of the strike in the hands of their parents. The protests of the Strikers' Committee had undoubtedly proven effective when considered in connection with the fact that the general postwar reaction against the war was now in full swing and that the Department of Justice itself had no real enthusiasm for its task.

Counseling and Aiding Evasion. One of the most interesting phenomena with respect to prosecutions was that there were only twenty-eight cases of "counseling and aiding evasion" down to the end of hostilities. This may indicate any number of things, but it surely demonstrates again that there was relatively little "political" opposition to the war. It may also show that the Department of Justice was somewhat careful about charging persons with this offense. Certainly there was no tendency, such as that noticeable in the First World

War, to bring charges against every person who might give out public utterances against the war. But on the other hand there were in World War II very few public utterances to prosecute. There was no prosecution during the Second World War comparable to the Debs case during the first conflict.

The Trials of Objectors

The offenses of conscientious objectors, being violations of national law, were tried in the several federal district courts. The objector, after arrest (and it was usually not difficult to find him, since he made it a point to inform the district attorney of his whereabouts), would often be lodged in jail for a time and then be released on bail. Bail ranged in amount from $250 to (in one case) $25,000. Most common bail bonds were $1,000 to $2,000. And some objectors were released on their own recognizance, without bail.

On the day appointed for trial the accused objector would appear with his attorney in the district court. Often a considerable number of friends would accompany him, and in many instances special representatives of defense organizations for conscientious objectors were present. Ministers and sometimes representatives of such organizations as the American Friends Service Committee would give moral support to the objector in court. Girl friends and wives not infrequently were present. And the tenseness of the hearing was in a few cases accentuated by the quiet weeping of sympathizers, as, for example, when the original eight Union Theological nonregistrants were sentenced.

Once in court, the objector could plead "guilty," "not guilty," or "nolo contendere." If he pleaded guilty, he would be sentenced by the judge immediately, although the judge often allowed time for a statement by the objector, his attorney, and the United States district attorney. If the plea were "not guilty" (and in most cases it was not), there would be a trial, either by the judge or by a jury. Most trials of objectors were not jury trials. Many objectors preferred the plea of "nolo contendere," which meant that the charge, while not being contested, was not being admitted with any sense of "guilt." In such an event, the district judge would usually afford ample opportunity for comment by all the parties involved.

It is obvious in going through court records that many judges were puzzled by the problem of conscientious objectors. On the one hand, the judges were under an obligation to apply the law of the land to the particular instance; on the other, the offender, in demeanor and attitude, quite frequently reminded one of George Fox, William Penn, or another of the seventeenth-century Quakers. In at least one instance the judge himself was a member of the Society of Friends; this particular magistrate, Judge George Welsh of Philadelphia, frequently gave expression to the problem which he, a Friend, confronted in sentencing young Friends who claimed to be acting in response to the voice of conscience.

The case of Frederick H. Richards will serve to illustrate one type of objector and the attitude of one kind of judge. Richards was a nonregistrant who had voluntarily returned from Mexico (where he had been working on an American Friends Service Committee reconstruction project) in 1941 to announce his refusal to register. His case came up before the district court on November 26, 1941. He was allowed to make a statement giving his reasons for refusing to register. He said:

I stand before you today, your Honor, for two reasons. The first is conscription. The second is war. . . .

If our draft law contained a clause exempting men who, like myself, cannot conscientiously accept any compulsory service demanded by the State, I would be glad to volunteer for dangerous constructive service for my fellow men. . . . But to perform such service as a slave, under compulsion, and as a conscript, is contrary to both Quaker and American principles. Conscription is the denial of the personal responsibility of a man to live up to the right as he sees it. . . .

As a Quaker, I cannot but oppose this war. I do not believe that the butchery of another twenty or thirty million people will further the Christian religion. . . .[13]

After the Richards statement, there was a cross-examination by the district attorney:

Q. Just one question, Mr. Richards. Would you take up arms to defend this country in the event of actual military invasion?

A. No, sir.

The Court: Doesn't a religion that teaches love of your country require obedience to constituted authority? Don't you embrace obedience to constituted authority as one of the requisites of love of country?

A. I do until it conflicts with my conscience.

The Court: Then you put your conscience above love of country, wouldn't that follow logically?

A. Yes, it would.[14]

The Richards hearing concluded with the following interchange:

Counsel for Richards. Fred's deliberate and voluntary return to the United States from Mexico, when he did not have to do so, for the specific purpose of making a maximum protest against what he considers the greatest of all evils, war and conscription, called to mind the story of the journey and protest of another man in history.

In the year A.D. 404, the custom was to hold gladiatorial fights for public amusement in Rome—A Christian monk, Telemachus, reached the conviction that it was his duty to make an open protest. Leaving Syria, he made the journey all the way to Rome for the specific purpose of protesting against the gladiatorial fights. In the midst of such a fight he ran into the arena, calling upon the Emperor to stop the cruel performance. When his purpose was realized, he was stoned to death before the watching multitude. Losing his life, Telemachus apparently failed to accomplish his purpose. In reality, however, his vicarious sacrifice succeeded, for that gladiatorial fight was the last one ever held in Rome. . . .

District Attorney. If your Honor pleases, there cannot possibly be any comparison between the gladiatorial story and the case before the court today. No one is trying to force that man from becoming a gladiator.

However, what I do not like most about this defendant is that which he apparently brags about, and has repeated several times on the stand, that he was not in the country and he deliberately came back here to become a law violator. He was in Mexico where he says he had sufficient money to stay, and could have stayed there, but he took upon himself and thought that it was his duty to add to the trouble we already have here and become a conscientious objector, and give statements to the press, and so forth, as to what his feelings were. . . .

The Court. It is . . . an unpleasant and difficult task for me to perform, Mr. Richards, but you have admitted violating the law of the land, and as I said, if you had chosen to register and have yourself classified as a conscientious objector, there would be no question or no necessity for you to bear arms, as apparently your ancestors for many generations did. . . .

The sentence of the Court is that you . . . undergo imprisonment . . . for a period of one year and one day.[15]

Other district judges showed similar attitudes toward conscientious objectors who came before them. Some were apparently genuinely disturbed by the prospect of sentencing objectors to the penitentiary. They tried to draw out every possible reason for a light sentence. Thus one Los Angeles judge expended his own funds to find out what effect probation for four C.P.S walkouts would have on other conscientious objectors in Civilian Public Service camps. He reached the conclusion that for him to put the four boys on probation would tend to encourage others to walk out.[16]

On the other hand, some judges seemed to take delight in lecturing objectors on their lack of patriotism. Federal Judge Michael L. Igoe, of Chicago, ordered one conscientious objector under indictment, Robert Chino, from his courtroom while he pronounced sentence on another objector. In the process of ejecting Chino from the courtroom, Judge Igoe attacked the War Resisters League as "that bunch out on the south side that thinks it is greater than the laws of the United States." Then the Judge turned to Lauren Wispe, graduate student in philosophy at Northwestern University, whose case was at bar. Wispe had refused to register, allegedly at the instigation of Chino, who was of Japanese descent. Judge Igoe shouted at Wispe: "You are a slacker of the worst type, letting yourself be influenced by an alien. When even your own mother wants you to join the army." Wispe's attorney at this point tried to protest that his client was not a "slacker." But the judge would brook no interruption, and continued: "All I can see is that he is unwilling to obey the laws of the United States."

Sentence of three years was imposed on Wispe and a deputy sheriff led him away. Then Judge Igoe remarked: "I hope those smart young people on the south side of Chicago will take that as a lesson." He called for Wispe's friends to come before him before he adjourned court. One of these friends was Georgia Lloyd, of the well-known publishing family. She had provided bail for a number of objectors. Judge Igoe now lectured the little group before him. "Get out of here," he shouted as a final word of warning, "and don't ever let me see you in my court again." [17]

On another occasion a district judge was called upon to hear arguments on a writ of habeas corpus involving a conscientious objector allegedly sent into the Army through wrong classification by a local board. After hearing the pleas of counsel, the judge ordered the objector removed to an adjoining courtroom used for naturalization purposes. Mounting the bench, he heard the oath of allegiance of several hundred new citizens and delivered himself of the following:

There is a person in the rear of the room whom I want to hear what I am going to say. You new citizens have taken an oath which obligates you to defend this country with your lives. There is a man in the rear who is willing to let you do this for him though he was born in this country and you were not. If you violate your oath to defend the country, the government may cancel your citizenship, but it may not revoke the citizenship of a person born here who refuses to carry out his obligations in that regard.[18]

In all fairness to the judges, it should be pointed out that certain cases of conscientious objectors were ample cause for wonder. In some courts, the presiding judge was confronted by defendants whose language and climate of thought were so much at variance with usual modes of reacting that it was not surprising that the judge often found himself angry and at a loss. When Jehovah's Witnesses spoke of Armageddon, members of Mankind United debated the World Conspiracy, and other objectors talked about the mysterious operations of Divine Providence, it is not surprising that rather prosaic judges should become impatient. John Andrew Schubin, a Molokan, had been given a IV-E by his local board but had refused to report to C.P.S. Brought before a federal district judge in Los Angeles, he was asked by the magistrate why he could not chop wood under civilian control. He replied: "Well, it is the foreign cause of the war activity." The judge persisted and the answer now was, "Well, the Holy Ghost forbids me to accept anything." At another point he was asked whether he had not accepted the protection of the government all his life. To this he answered: "No, God is the only protector, Jesus Christ and the Holy Ghost. . . . That is all I need." Finally the judge exploded: "Well, all right. The Holy Ghost won't forbid you to accept a sentence in jail. It is the judgment of the court for the offense for which you stand convicted that you shall be sentenced to an institution of the county jail type for a period of six months. . . . All right, you fight it out with the Holy Ghost. I say that with all due reverence, gentlemen." [19]

This sampling of hearings and trials should not be taken to mean that every conscientious objector received individual treatment and an individual ceremony, nor does it imply that the judge in many, if not most, cases honored him with either a denunciation or with appreciative words. Indeed, as the war became more and more bitter and all-embracing and the number of Selective Service cases mounted, many judges found it convenient to allow the numerous hearings involving conscientious objectors, particularly Jehovah's Witnesses, to accumulate. When the number became sufficiently large, the judge would hold mass hearings and settle the cases in batches of thirty and forty at a time. This practice was more common in some judicial districts than in others, but was sufficiently common in any event to deserve emphatic notice.

Mass hearings were made practicable partly by reason of legal rulings which denied to the objector the right to raise the question of misclassification (by local or appellate board) in the trial court.[20] The courts ruled right down to the end of hostilities that the question of classification could not be raised in the courts at the point where the objector refused to obey a local-board order. The objector must first obey the order and complete the administrative process (by reporting to the Army or Civilian Public Service, as the case might be) and then petition for a writ of habeas corpus. At that point the problem of classification could be raised, but not before. Since many objectors, and practically all Jehovah's Witnesses, could not in conscience "complete the administrative process," they were limited to a hearing on the simple question of disobedience of a local board. In the hearing or trial for failure to obey a local-board order, the sole question at issue was whether the objector did in fact disobey the order. Since the objector would usually not deny that disobedience— and would sometimes, indeed, proclaim it in stentorian tones—the disposal of his case was relatively simple; many cases, especially of Jehovah's Witnesses (which were usually very similar to one another), could be passed upon at a single judicial sitting. Thus the dockets of the courts, filled to overflowing with the extra burden of Selective Service cases during the latter half of the war, could be cleared in some instances with relative rapidity. Whether this was a wise expedient is, of course, another matter.

Sentences and Probation

What sentences conscientious objectors received depended largely upon the discretion of the individual judge, subject to the statutory (Selective Training and Service Act) maximum of 5 years and a $10,000 fine. In the latter years of the war, judges within a given geographical area (for example, Philadelphia) would sometimes reach an agreement for standard and uniform sentences for given categories. But by and large, and taking the period of the war as a whole, sentences varied widely in a geographical sense. Thus the average sentence of all Selective Service violators in Vermont up to the middle of 1943 was 1.1 months, while in South Dakota it was 55.7 months.[21] And it should be remembered that a large proportion of Selective Service violators were classified at that time as conscientious objectors.

Down to the middle of 1943, the average sentence of all Selective Service violators was 30.6 months. For violators of the narcotics law, the average was 20.8 months; of the liquor laws, 10.6; of the postal laws, 27.3; of the white-slave laws, 28.3.[22] The philosophical observer of men and affairs, reflecting on these figures, could draw interesting conclusions as to the relative heinousness of the several violations of national law.

Looking at the matter from a different perspective, the average sentence of Jehovah's Witnesses for the year ending June 30, 1944, was 42 months; for other conscientious objectors, it was 34; for those violators of the Selective Training and Service Act who did not claim conscientious objection, it was only 28. By 1945 the averages had been altered only slightly, being, respectively, 45, 37, and 28 months.[23] Rather consistently throughout the course of the war, Jehovah's Witnesses were more harshly treated in terms of sentences than other conscientious objectors, while conscientious objectors as a class received higher sentences than those violators of the Selective Service act who did not claim to be conscientious objectors. In order of increasing severity of sentences we thus have violators of liquor laws, violators of narcotics laws, defiers of the postal laws, white slavers, Selective Service Act violators who did not claim to be conscientious objectors, conscientious objectors, and Jehovah's Witnesses.

But averages do not reveal the whole story, for they do not indicate anything about highest and lowest sentences, relative proportion of high to low sentences, and the differences, if any, in lengths of sentences imposed as between years. The figures in Table XII more nearly reveal the complete story. An examination of the tabulated figures discloses that 64 per cent of all objectors sentenced between 1940 and 1942 received sentences of a year and a day or above; between July 1, 1942, and July 1, 1944, the percentage rose sharply to 90; after the cessation of European hostilities—between July 1, 1944, and July 1, 1945—the proportion dropped to 85. After the surrender of Japan, six-month sentences were increasingly common. After Pearl Harbor, then, there was a sharp increase in length of sentences imposed, and after August, 1945, there tended to be a sharp decrease, even though objectors continued to be sent to prison for more than a year after the surrender of Japan. It may be inferred that courts seemed to feel that so long as a "shooting" war was in progress sentences should be relatively stiff, but that when hostilities ceased district attorneys and judges agreed that penalties might well be lightened.

One problem that always arises in connection with the types of offenses committed by conscientious objectors is the question of resentencing for what may be considered to be the same offense but which is technically a separate one. The case of James Ball is typical. Ball refused to register for the draft and was sentenced to a year and a day. He served his sentence, the government registered for him while he was in jail, and his case was reopened by his local board. He was classified a conscientious objector, refused on conscientious grounds to report to Civilian Public Service, and was sentenced for his refusal to five years.[24] Arnold Satterthwait found himself in a similar position: his original sentence had been a year and a day for nonregistration; his registration was completed by the warden of the prison (in accordance with Selective Service regulations); when, after his release from prison, his case had been reopened by his local board, he refused to report for his medical examination. He was given a second prison term of three years, the judge arguing that as a second offender the more severe sentence should be imposed not as punishment but to deter others.[25]

Similar cases of what was called "cat-and-mouse" treatment occurred all together about one hundred times during the course of

TABLE XII. SENTENCES OF CONSCIENTIOUS OBJECTORS *

	Oct. 16, 1940 to June 30, 1942	July 1, 1942 to June 30, 1943	July 1, 1943 to June 30, 1944	July 1, 1944 to June 30, 1945	Total
Fine only	2			2	4
Probation	30	56	77	55	218
1 month or less	5	5	7	3	20
1 month through 6 months	18	18	12	6	54
6 months through 1 year, 1 day	83	87	130	106	406
1 year, 1 day–2 years	112	246	391	268	1,017
2 through 3 years	68	675	713	265	1,721
3 through 4 years	39	191	224	127	581
4 through 5 years	29	405	738	321	1,493
Over 5 years, 2 or more counts		2			2
TOTAL	386	1,685	2,292	1,153	5,516

* Department of Justice figures. See *The Reporter*, Nov. 1, 1945, p. 3.

the war. It was felt by many objectors and defenders of civil liberties that second sentences of this kind for what was essentially the same offense were unfair, and some argued that they violated the spirit, even though not the letter, of the Fifth Amendment's double-jeopardy clause.

Some objectors who were sentenced did not, of course, actually go to prison; they were placed on probation. About 225 objectors were thus enabled to avoid the problem of prison, even though they had committed breaches of the law. Probation as a technique for handling conscientious objectors was most widespread in the Los Angeles area, where federal judges early decided that it was generally more intelligent than an outright prison sentence. In the early part of 1943, Federal Judge Ralph E. Jenney of Los Angeles made public an announcement that he would send no more objectors to jail but would place all of them on probation.[26] And by 1945 an Oregon federal judge was stating the same general policy.[27] While eastern judges generally lagged behind those in Los Angeles, by the end of 1943 even a New York City judge had placed his first objector on probation.[28] Despite all this, however, and the genuine sympathy of many judges, fewer than 4 per cent of all the conscientious objectors coming before the courts were placed on probation. The remaining 96 per cent went to prison or were fined, or both.

There are several explanations for the relatively small numbers placed on probation. In the first place, the Selective Service System in many jurisdictions did all it could to discourage probation, apparently feeling that it was in duty bound to see that violators of the Selective Service law served their time in jail. Also, it was objected that allowing men to go on probation subjected them to different standards from other objectors; men on probation were often paid, for example, and their movements were restricted only by the court and not by Selective Service.

A second reason for the small number of probationers was the pressure exerted by various groups, like the American Legion, who believed that it was particularly heinous to place violators of the Selective Training and Service Act on probation, whatever might be desirable with respect to other types of offenders.

Finally, many objectors could not conscientiously subscribe to the conditions usually required. Each recipient of probation had to promise to "obey all laws, live morally and ethically right." To many objectors, the promise to obey all laws was one which they could not make; after their period of probation had expired, or even during it, they might feel called upon by conscience to violate the law again.

Those who were placed on probation were assigned to a wide variety of work. Some were sent to Civilian Public Service camps, where, of course, they continued (as elsewhere on probation) to be under the general jurisdiction of the court. Others were sent to hospitals, both general and mental, where they might be given nominal wages. One judge in placing a nonregistrant on probation laid it down as a condition of his probation that he not mingle with the "bohemian colony" which had presumably influenced him to violate the law.[29] One probationer was assigned for three years to a seminary, and there was at least one instance of a nonregistrant being sent on probation back to his own farm.[30] Others were directed to work in the Forestry Service of the Department of Agriculture, in the conscientious-objector advisory work of the American Friends Service Committee, and in the National Foundation for Infantile Paralysis.

The case of one probationer will serve to illustrate the pressures and conditions which might affect the working out of the system. Richard Petherbridge had been denied a IV-E by his local board. When it came time to sentence him, he was sent on probation to the C.P.S. camp at Glendora, California. Then the conditions of his probation were changed, on his request, to permit him to work for the California Institute of Technology, which was providing research assistance for the National Foundation for Infantile Paralysis. Petherbridge's task was to care for animals used for experimental purposes. He was at first given $50.00 a month; later this was raised to $75.00. When his services were ended here, the court allowed him to do research for another professor who was interested in a guayule project having for its objective the resettling of Japanese-Americans in northwest Arizona. A little later, however, certain members of the Biology Division of California Institute of Technology apparently objected to any conscientious objector working on any project having anything to do with Japanese-Americans. The result was that later he left this position for yet another.[31] He felt, however, that the real cause for his dismissal was his activity, along with that of several other conscientious objectors, in the interests of racial equality. He and several of his Negro and Japanese-American friends had attempted to attend a dance in the Pasadena Civic Auditorium. They were denied admittance; later on, the manager of the Auditorium, learning that Petherbridge was an objector, called the city manager, a prominent member of the American Legion. That official, in turn, called the secretary to the head of the California Institute of Technology, who then sent out memos to the members of the department for which Petherbridge was working. The memos stated that he was a conscientious objector, a fact of which many of his colleagues were apparently ignorant. The result was that he was transferred.

On the whole, it was extremely unfortunate that probation was not used much more widely, as it seems fairly evident that it was a principle eminently suitable for application to the cases of conscientious objectors. One curious fact does, however, stand out when considering the problem of probation in relation to the whole question of conscientious objection: many objectors on probation were paid, whereas objectors in regular C.P.S. camps were not. Here were men who had violated the law being assigned to service (in many cases) with salary, however small, while those sent to regular C.P.S. camps and who had violated no law were denied any wages. It illustrates again the curious quirks and paradoxes which characterized American treatment of the conscientious objector during World War II.

XVI: The Objector in the Prison Community

A SUMMARY of the experiences of the nearly six thousand conscientious objectors who served "time" in prison is important, not only for the interest one has in relationships between the group and prison administration, but also because the observations of objectors on prison life in general provide comments of relatively highly educated persons. Conscientious objectors, in many instances, were often close observers of the impact of prison on men and frequently tried to analyze their own experiences in writing.

The County Jail

Immediately after arrest and before his release on bond, the conscientious objector might be lodged in a county jail as a federal prisoner. In some cases—where the sentence was below a year—the entire sentence would be served in a jail, and the objector often thus had an opportunity to observe closely the penal practices of this, the lowest rung of the prison ladder.

The experiences of conscientious objectors in county jails seem to confirm the judgment of the Federal Bureau of Prisons that county jails were for the most part dirty, badly managed, and dominated by graft and corruption.[1] Yet it should be remembered that objectors were housed only in the comparatively few jails (about one-quarter of the entire number) which were designated "approved for the housing of federal prisoners" or "approved for emergency use only." The picture one gets of jails through the experiences of conscientious

352

objectors is thus an impression of the relatively few supposedly "good" jails.

The reports even on these "good" jails are virtually unanimous, however. "The cell block where I spent most of my time was kept pretty clean by the inmates," wrote one objector, describing his experiences in the Cuyahoga County (Cleveland, Ohio) jail. "But the mattresses were filthy and ridden with bed bugs . . . and other vermin. . . . The food was inadequate and terrible. We had no greens of any kind and almost no vegetables." [2] In the San Francisco county jail another objector "was given a set of dirty, smelly blankets. . . . The second time I had clean blankets, but was in a cell inhabited also by numerous bed-bugs, which left great welts on me that itched for two weeks and left scars." [3] And another inmate spoke thus of the Indianapolis jail: "No toilet paper, no sheet, no towel, no toothbrush, no toothpaste, no pillow, one very filthy straw tick and blanket, not enough food, and very little fresh vegetables or fruits." [4]

Initiation into Prison Life

Since 90 per cent of the conscientious objectors after 1942 were receiving sentences of more than a year, and hence were lodged in federal institutions to serve their sentences, main interest must naturally be directed to federal penitentiaries, reformatories, and correctional institutions. At the height of the movement of conscientious objectors into federal prisons, twenty-two institutions in nineteen states housed the objectors. (See Appendix J for the list.)

Assignment to "maximum custody institutions" (penitentiaries) was usually a matter of location or convenience, since objectors to war were not considered dangerous persons. Therefore, at such institutions they were generally assigned to the relatively light custody of the farm camp, apart from the main prison. Men refusing cooperation, however, might be returned to the main institution.

When he entered a federal prison, the objector, like all others, was asked to turn over most of his personal things to an attendant. Often he might be allowed to keep his glasses and sometimes such items as his Bible, or, in the case of Catholics, his crucifix. He was examined rather cursorily by the prison physician, given prison clothes, and fingerprinted.

Then he was usually sent to Quarantine, where such rules as those applying to discipline, making the beds, the "count," and other varied aspects of prison life were explained to him. For about thirty days, as a rule, the objector remained in Quarantine and was given a thorough physical examination, intelligence tests, and all types of interviews. He became acquainted with the chaplain, classification committee, and other officials, who would have much to do with his weal and woe while a prisoner.

Leaving Quarantine, he was assigned to work—in a machine shop, laundry, library, kitchen, farm, or other division of the labor program. All labor was strictly supervised, and refusal to work almost always brought that lowest circle of the inferno—solitary confinement.

Life in all prisons was operated in accordance with a strict routine which admitted few, if any, exceptions. While that routine differed widely from prison to prison—in prison camps, for example, individual freedom was relatively great—one summer schedule in a fairly strict institution follows: 6:10 A.M., get up; 6:15, count (at bedside); 6:15–6:45, dress, clean cell, make bed, and so on; 7:00–7:30, breakfast; 7:30–11:30, work; 11:40, count; 12:00, lunch; 12:30–4:00, work; 4:15, count; 4:30, reception of mail; 5:00, supper; 5:30–7:00, yard period; 7:00, count; 7:00–9:00, library and school; 9:30, count; and 10:00, lights.

The "count," or check on the presence of the prisoner at a particular place from two to five times a day, was one feature of prison life which constantly called the objector's attention to the fact that he was living in prison. No escape was possible—there he stood to be "checked off."

Religious Affiliations

How objectors reacted to prison life was to some extent influenced by their religious affiliations or absence of religious ties. Only 5.4 per cent of all those sentenced were classified as philosophical or political objectors; all the rest, with the exception of the 1.5 per cent who were unclassified, were presumably "religious" objectors—a total of 93.1 per cent. The second fact which should be emphasized is that most of those sent to prison were Jehovah's Witnesses. As a matter of fact, of the nearly 6,000 objectors sent to prison, placed on probation, or fined during the entire war and immediate postwar period, 4,500, or 75 per cent, were Witnesses.[5] In other words, roughly three out of every four objectors in prison belonged to a group whom many, including Selective Service, did not regard as objectors at all.

Jehovah's Witnesses in Prison

Because of their numbers and general peculiarities it is most convenient to treat Jehovah's Witnesses separately from other objectors in prison. The Witnesses were peculiar, in the first place, with respect to their theological opinions. These have been discussed in the abstract elsewhere.[6] But to show with what intensity and vividness they were held in concrete form by many Witnesses in prison, one might cite the case of a twenty-two-year-old man in prison who remarked rather casually that he supposed he might as well postpone marriage to his fiancée until the battle of Armageddon and the coming of the Kingdom.[7] A non-Witness might well have spoken in those terms and have meant that his engagement had been broken, or he might have spoken in sarcasm. Not so the Jehovah's Witness, however; for him the Kingdom was apparently as near at hand in time as the prison guard was in terms of space.

On the whole, the Witnesses had been to school for shorter terms than their non-Witness fellow prisoners. Department of Justice figures indicated that fewer than 1 per cent of the Witnesses were college graduates and that about 15 per cent had not completed grammar school. A random sample of twenty-seven imprisoned Witnesses showed that only three had ever attended college. Of the remaining twenty-four, eight had completed high school, two had gone through the eleventh grade, four through the tenth, four through the ninth, five through the eighth, and one through the sixth.[8]

It is not surprising to learn, then, that very few of the Witnesses in prison were members of the so-called learned professions. In a chance sample of some twenty cases, the occupations represented were farmer, general laborer, coal miner, timber cutter, mason, fireman, truck driver, stenographer, machinist, welder, patternmaker, automotive mechanic, biologist, carpenter, and electrician. Like most first-century Christians, Jehovah's Witnesses in prison came from humble walks of life and made no great pretense to the learning of "this world." Secure in the sense of their divine vocation, it was to that calling that they usually referred, and not to their secular occupation.

Generally speaking, the Witnesses possessed a high sense of group solidarity. They tended in each prison to act as a group under the direction of a chosen leader.[9] Disciplined from above as well as through a common intensely believed doctrine, they could usually be persuaded (by the prison administration, for example) to act as a unit, once their leader had decided on a given course of action. Thus it seemed to be a common practice in many prisons, when the authorities felt that an individual Witness was in need of discipline, for the warden first to speak to the prison leader of the Witness group and thus make it possible to apply prison discipline indirectly through the Jehovah's Witness leader himself.[10] This method was usually successful in attaining its ends; if in a minority of cases it did not succeed, the warden and other officials could then, of course, resort to direct action. It was this sense of group responsibility which, among other things, so sharply separated Jehovah's Witnesses from most other conscientious objectors in prison, for while the latter might form *ad hoc* groups to gain particular ends, the degree of individualism, with a few exceptions, was much greater than among the Witnesses.

In general, and with certain limitations, it was the policy of the Bureau of Prisons to allow the Witnesses to hold their religious meetings within the prison; non-Witnesses were generally excluded from such assemblies—supposedly in order to prevent "friction." However, the exact interpretation of this policy varied from institution to institution, and in a few places Witness meetings were open to other inmates.

Constantly in the minds of the prison authorities was another problem relating to the Witnesses: what to do with their literature. In general, the answer was that they were permitted to receive some Witness literature, but not all, and that a man might not have more than two copies of magazines in his cell at the same time. Witness literature barred included all that which was likely, according to the authorities, to stir up strife with other religious groups. In some prison libraries, Witnesses' constant demand for publications of the

Watchtower Bible and Tract Society [11] was to a degree satisfied by keeping complete files of such publications as *The Watchtower* and *Consolation*.

On the whole, most Jehovah's Witnesses seem to have co-operated with the great bulk of prison regulations and to have worked steadily and well. At times, it is true, they engaged in work "slowdowns," but such activities were almost always traceable to prison policy with respect to literature and meetings,[12] and seem to have declined after 1944. Where such frictions did not develop, the Witnesses were more assiduous in their work than other inmates. Though in prison they could not "witness" even as freely as in a Civilian Public Service camp, C.P.S. seemed to the Witness a voluntary acquiescence in the restrictions which governed the camps, while prison was interpreted as an involuntary servitude which they must suffer for the Lord's sake.

While there were always individual exceptions, the Witnesses in prison were no more popular, either with inmates in general or with other conscientious objectors, than they were outside the walls of penal institutions. Not that there were not personal friendships built up between Witnesses and other conscientious objectors; not that the Witnesses were not admired for what one non-Witness termed the "totalitarian" grip of religion upon their lives; not even that Witnesses and other objectors did not co-operate at times in matters of common interest—but rather that even in instances of co-operation between Witnesses and non-Witnesses the sense of different assumptions and widely varying objectives served to obscure to a certain extent these temporary agreements.

Jehovah's Witnesses—with several notable exceptions—did not share the reformist enthusiasm so prevalent among non-Witness objectors. Such issues as race relationships, prison censorship (with the exception of their own publications), general opposition to conscription (except with reference to their vocational emphasis), and prison "abuses" did not, on the whole, interest them. For them, the Kingdom's imminent coming was to put an end to all terrestrial tribulations, and the social consciousness so often revealed in the relationships and acts of other objectors was largely absent among them. The "socially conscious" conscientious objectors differed from the Witnesses not so much in the consistency with which they carried their beliefs into practice as in the assumptions with which they began.

Non-Witness Objectors

As for non-Witness objectors, they fitted into prison routine far less readily and participated far more frequently than the Witnesses in dramatic acts of opposition to prison administration. Methodists, Friends, and Catholics, among the better-known denominations, were among the leading groups in terms of numbers, but many, of course, belonged to such exotic groups as the Negro Moslems and the Molokans.

But besides these groups there remained a group almost as large, the members of which either professed no religious affiliations, yet claimed religious objections, or frankly disavowed religious objections and called themselves "political," "philosophical," or "rational" objectors. The 237 who up to June 30, 1944, had been classified in the "philosophical" objector group were often the leaders in prison strikes and other activities disapproved of by the prison authorities. According to the Bureau of Prisons itself, the "philosophical" and "political" objectors constituted "the most difficult group of conscientious objectors." [13] And the Bureau went on to contend that the political and philosophical objector "is primarily the reformer with a zeal for changing the social, political, economic, and cultural order. Objection to war frequently is only one element in his program. He objects to many things, including the present military system." [14] It should be clearly pointed out, of course, that the nonreligious objector was not alone in acting in this manner—many of the most active participants in prison strikes, for example, were deeply religious men (in the traditional sense of the term "religious").

And denomination-affiliated and non-denomination-affiliated religious men, as well as so-called "political" and "philosophical" objectors, were more articulate with reference to their experiences than Jehovah's Witnesses. Like Eugene V. Debs in the First World War,[15] many of them saw the impact of prison on themselves as one of the most significant aspects of their lives, whether for good or for ill. They believed, in not a few instances, that their activities and vocations in the postwar world would be affected profoundly by what they underwent in prison.

The "Respectable" Background of Objectors

As the Bureau of Prisons itself recognized, "many members of this group [non-Witness objectors] come from respectable families and communities unaccustomed to the restrictions of prison life or the associations which go with it." [16] When men of this type were suddenly thrown into prison—which, by its nature and however well conducted, spells restriction of freedom—it is not surprising that they often did not "adjust" themselves to prison life.

For example, one was a young man with a B.S. degree from the University of Illinois, a member of several honorary societies and a graduate with honors. He had done well in his chosen profession, but when his attitude toward war became known he was dismissed from his position and found it impossible to obtain another professional post. When arrested, he was working as a manual laborer with a trucking concern. Another prisoner was a college graduate with one year of graduate work in botany. His father had been a college professor and he himself was an excellent student.

One objector had been a student at Oberlin and was a musician and composer. Another was a graduate of Rollins College and a student of dramatics. A twenty-nine-year-old Methodist minister, graduate of Boston University School of Theology, and father of two children, also found himself in prison. Another prisoner was the able son of an Army officer. Another was a competent student of art. Yet another was a very capable graduate in ceramic engineering whose Jewish parents were very much perturbed by his attitude, which reflected in their minds on the "respectability" of their middle-class cultured home. Not all, it is true, came from social strata of these levels, but none, with few exceptions, had ever before clashed with the law in a serious way.

The Impact of Prison

How prison affected objectors—and here reference is primarily to non-Witnesses, although many of the observations made would be applicable to certain Witnesses as well—varied from individual to individual; and nothing is more dangerous than to take too literally general statements made about the impact of prison. Degrees of reaction on the part of objectors varied all the way from passive acceptance of prison routine to almost continuous and active opposition. In this wide variability, one notes a close approximation to the reactions of objectors to Civilian Public Service. In some respects the resemblance of prison to C.P.S. experience is indeed astonishing.

It should be remembered that perhaps the majority of written expressions concerning prison experiences—including both Witness and non-Witness writers—were concerned only secondarily, if at all, with a critical evaluation of prison experiences. A very large percentage of prison correspondence discussed personal problems, including individual religious development.

The atmosphere of prison—even "minimum custody" institutions —affected objectors in devious and subtle ways. There was the absence of customary sights and sounds. The absence of women affected objectors, as well as other prisoners. Although generally federal penal institutions were spotlessly clean and physically often attractive, the casual observer frequently could not comprehend the climate of repression. As one highly sensitive objector put it: "Punishment is subtle, psychological—guards hovering about you . . . locked doors; bars; high walls . . ." [17] And Earl Kepler, another objector, captured something of the atmosphere in verse:

> The screw [guard] comes by to take the last count
> Through the corridor dim-lit and drear—
> When the big door clangs and lights go out
> While about you creeps coldness and fear.

Apparently many objectors who had served in C.P.S. and had walked out found prison much more satisfying psychologically than alternative service. It had at least more of the "involuntary" character so desirable to some men—one was not weighed down by the thought or feeling that one was "co-operating" with evil. In Civilian Public Service one was constantly forced to make decisions which implied an acceptance of the principle of conscription and yet gave the government a plausible basis for maintaining that it was in reality recognizing the rights of conscience. As a competent observer noted, C.P.S. men tended to be much happier in prison than in Civilian Public Service camps because, aside from entering the Army, there was nothing more they could do. [18] Prison was hardly ever a pleasant experience, however. At best, it might be less unsatisfying physically or psychologically, or both, than the Army or C.P.S.

Food and Prison Psychology

Not only was there a wide difference in setting and amount of restraint between a prison of the road-camp variety, like Tucson, and a maximum-custody institution, like Lewisburg, but the quality of the food differed from place to place.

In prison, food assumed an importance disproportionately great when compared with its position in the world outside prison walls; even the slightest supposed improvement which might come about from week to week, or, in case prisoners were transferred, from prison to prison, would be greeted with enthusiasm.[19]

Some objectors were vegetarians; since the diets of prisons all included meat or foods cooked in animal fats, the conscientious vegetarians had no alternative except to refrain from eating most types of food until a wholly vegetarian diet could be provided. In practically every case such a diet was provided by prison administrators, although the result was not always entirely satisfactory to the vegetarian involved. In at least one case the objector not only insisted upon vegetable dishes but also held that he could eat only raw vegetables from dishes which he had cleaned himself.[20] Another objector, in Ashland, could not reconcile his vegetarianism with the wearing of leather shoes and so went about his work barefooted, until his foot became infected and he had to be hospitalized. In the meantime, it was reported among other conscientious objectors that he had been placed in the "blue room"—that is, had been placed in isolation as psychotic or insane. Thereupon, several other conscientious objectors went on "barefoot strike" themselves. The issue was settled when the prison authorities provided the original protester with "sneakers," and he was released from the hospital well and content.[21]

Relations with Other Inmates

In their relations with nonobjectors, all types of attitudes, from warm friendship to coldness and hostility, were to be met. Initial antagonism not infrequently gave way to respect and even close attachment, although in a great many other instances the nature of prison routine was such as to maintain, on the part of nonobjectors, an attitude of indifference. Then, too, the personalities of some objectors were more conducive than those of others to the establishment of confidence and affection—argumentative objectors, whether Witnesses or non-Witnesses, on some occasions clashed with strong and emphatic personalities among the other inmates. Where nonobjector inmates, for example, sought to demonstrate by words and action their patriotism and support of the war effort, they sometimes could not refrain from verbal attacks on the supposed cowardice of the objector group. This was especially the case where the prison was a reformatory housing young offenders—an institution such as that in Chillicothe, Ohio, for example.[22] In a few instances the verbal attacks on objectors gave way to physical assaults, although this development was relatively rare and was, of course, severely punished by prison authorities. To many inmates, the difference between a conscientious objector and a "shirker" or "draft dodger" was extremely tenuous, if not entirely lacking.

In most institutions, nonobjectors tended to be very suspicious, at least in the beginning, of the attitude of prison administrators to objector groups; this suspicion was fostered by the apparent ease with which some members of the war-resisting groups were assigned "soft spots" in prison work. Many inmates failed to reflect that the objector group on the whole was better educated than the average nonobjector and hence supposedly entitled to claim, under a system of adaptation to individual capacity, the so-called "attractive" positions. Where the prison administration made clear to nonobjector inmates its desire to deal with all on the basis of individual capacity and adaptability, whether the individual happened to be a conscientious objector or not, it was often found that the suspicions of "regular" inmates were modified.

In those cases—and they clearly represent a minority—where objectors were able to serve nonobjectors directly or to build up friendships with them, the relationship often became close. For, regardless of the physical and administrative excellence of a prison system and the humanitarian intentions of its directors, most inmates are essentially lonely and feel crushed by the world; if one can gain their confidence and show them that someone regards them as human beings, they usually repay one with a profound gratitude. That some conscientious objectors were able to demonstrate to other prisoners their integrity and unselfishness, despite many handicaps, is not to be doubted by anyone who has read the prison correspondence of objectors and the comments of prison visitors. Thus the inmate of one institution, speaking of a certain conscientious objector in the same prison, remarked: "He is a different person from anyone I ever knew. I've known many who were Christians part of the time. He is the first person I've known who is a Christian all of the time." [23]

A thoughtful summary of the problem of conscientious-objector relationships with other inmates will be found in the analysis of a pacifist prisoner writing from Lewisburg:

> Our relations with other inmates are, on the group basis, about what might be expected. As a group, COs are regarded by the few patriots as cowards or traitors. By the many military prisoners they are regarded variously with envy, with contempt, with sympathy, with respect. (Envy because COs have shorter sentences without having had the troubles of army life.) Other Selective Service violators either consider COs as people whose pretensions are the only thing that differentiate them from the SS violators, or as just another form of draft dodger. . . . Men who have been in and out of prison all of their lives think COs are just stupid. "You could just as easily get some soft spot in the army, and you wouldn't have to go to jail." And so on. Among a small minority some of these reactions naturally lead to an intense hostility. And the hostility probably exists in some degree in almost all inmates. . . . So far I have been speaking of COs as a group. As a group they are subject to the prejudices which any group—the Jews or the Negroes, for instance—are subject to.
>
> As individuals our score may be a little higher, though it's hard to say. . . . To the extent that COs regard themselves as just another prisoner, not too different from the rest, their personal relations with other inmates are good. But to the extent that they (even unconsciously—or especially unconsciously) set themselves apart, their relations deteriorate.[24]

Work and Education in Prison

What types of work were done and what educational activities were carried on by conscientious objectors? In general, they were like those done by other prisoners, taking into account individual characteristics. There was one exception to this rule: conscientious objectors were usually not assigned to work having a direct connection with the war effort, as that would have created "trouble"— and did, in several cases—for prison administrators.[25] Objectors worked on prison farms (milking cows, cleaning out barns, and assisting with other farm chores), blasted rock formations in order to construct roads five thousand feet above sea level (as in Tucson, Arizona, prison camp), designed murals for prison dining rooms and stained-glass windows for the chapel in Alcatraz penitentiary, produced fine leatherwork, worked as assistants in prison parole offices, cleared woodlots, labored on wood crews, carved out wooden toys, nursed in prison hospitals, served in wardens' residences, harvested lumber, acted as secretaries to chaplains and other prison officials, produced furniture in prison factories, constructed "tamped-earth" buildings,[26] drove trucks, and in certain prisons provided practically the only inmate teachers.

Non-Witness conscientious objectors were particularly active in educational and library work, and often they were allowed considerable freedom and initiative in the performance of their duties. In some instances, for example, an objector would be given virtually a free hand in recommending new books for the library, subject, of course, to the usual veto of the chief prison librarian in Washington. In Danbury at one time there were fifteen inmate teachers, all of them conscientious objectors. In Lewisburg the work of one conscientious objector included teaching four high-school classes: European History, American History, Physical Geography, and Economic Geography.[27] Other objectors were engaged in teaching illiterates, and many looked upon this type of work as particularly "constructive."

But interest in educational activities among both conscientious objectors and other inmates was spotty. In those cases where men had to work hard out of doors all day, they often returned to their cells or dormitories in the evening with little desire for formal instruction. Then again, shortage of regular educational staff, due to depletion on account of war, made it almost impossible in some institutions to carry on an "adequate" educational program, either for regular inmates or for conscientious objectors. While library facilities in some institutions were decidedly good, in others they were meager. Finally, from the viewpoint of educating "political" prisoners like the conscientious objectors, plans were almost everywhere entirely inadequate. While some supervisors of education were intensely interested in inaugurating a program that would be suitable to the advanced educational status of most non-Witness objectors, others were indifferent or did not even see the need. Even where the educational director was sympathetic, the problem of obtaining adequate instructors and necessary facilities was a large one.[28]

Despite these difficulties, conscientious-objector groups in several prisons went ahead with their own self-education and attempted to stimulate the interest of other inmates. With the permission of prison officials, classes in Spanish, German, French, and co-operatives were inaugurated. Others met together for the study of art and drama. At Tucson a "literary" society was begun, and similar groups were set on foot elsewhere. At Ashland, conscientious objectors once went in for drama and staged an objector-written play whose major theme was a criticism of American prisons.[29]

Most articulate objectors seemed to feel, however, that their major educational progress lay in their prison experience itself, and not in any formal educational efforts conducted by themselves or by the prison educational system.

Prison Administration and Discipline

It is when one attempts to describe the relations between conscientious objectors and the prison system and administration that difficulties become greatest. In the first place, the usual warning regarding variations from prison to prison must be issued. Lewisburg was not Danbury, and Danbury was not Tucson. Despite certain general directives from the Bureau of Prisons in Washington, there seemed to be considerable autonomy at the local prison level. Instructions were to be carried out, but *how* they were carried out, whether strictly or loosely, depended in considerable degree on the warden and associate warden (who usually handled discipline) involved. Then, too, reports of incidents involving discipline varied even as between objectors and more so as between prison administrators and objectors. Often an incident involving supposed mistreatment of a conscientious objector would be witnessed only by the objector himself and by a nonobjector inmate. In such cases, it was the word of the objector against that of the other inmate. Similarly, when the only witnesses were a guard and the objector who supposedly had been mistreated, there was really no way of determining what actually happened except by cross-examining both objector and guard; and this procedure was not always followed. It has generally been observed that a higher prison administrator tended to accept the word of the guard in cases where versions of guard and prisoner differed substantially; hence the guard's version often became the official prison version. To discover the truth in cases of tension thus becomes an extremely difficult problem.

Refusal to work (and for various reasons to be explained later, conscientious objectors carried on work strikes) usually resulted in some form of solitary confinement. "Solitary" might be incarceration in a normal-type cell where contact with other prisoners was cut off, while in some cases it meant the "dark hole"—really, a room in which the quantity of light entering from outside was reduced. Theoretically, the "dark hole" had been abolished by central prison regulations, but it still actually existed in some institutions.[30] On the other hand, some institutions, especially prison camps, had no system of solitary confinement whatsoever.

In addition to "solitary," one might be deprived of the normal prison diet and placed on what was officially called a "monotonous" diet. This was a round of meals in which the food was cooked in such a way as to make it practically tasteless, although theoretically it was nutritionally adequate. A monotonous diet, objectors observed, was not particularly "cruel" in any physical sense, but under the circumstances in which it was usually administered it could prove rather irritating.

Other irritating punishments which accentuated the frustrations of prison life included deprivation of the right to attend movies, to use the yard (with its exercise in the open air), or to share in the recreational program of the prison. Sometimes prisoners were transferred to "tougher" prisons if their conduct did not satisfy the officials. The transfer of nine objectors in the early morning of May 9, 1944, from the "minimum custody" institution of Danbury to Lewisburg penitentiary is a good example.[31] For minor offenses against discipline, such devices as "the bench" were used, at least in one institution. To be sent to "the bench" meant that one would have to sit perfectly still for several hours while other inmates were engaging in recreation or going about their normal tasks. Some objectors were punished in this manner for refusal to eat all the food on their plates, the food-eating rule being a requirement in all federal prisons. One objector with a reputation as a careful observer thus described his "bench" experiences: "Just back from my 2nd nite on the bench. The bench is where one sits for 2 hours perfectly quiet as punishment for refusing to finish eating one's potato salad. In this case I would have eaten the stuff if I had been left alone, but as soon as the guard made a point of it, that was that." [32]

Many reported cases of seemingly disproportionate punishment of objectors are on record. For these examples it was not possible to get adequate confirmation, but neither could the Bureau of Prisons offer substantial disproof. The cases mentioned here are noted because, whether exaggerated or not, they illustrate the difficulty of obtaining corroborative evidence in disciplinary cases. It should also be observed that the offense alleged by the prison administrator was often not the real reason for the imposition of punishment, but only the occasion; a prisoner's general attitude, especially any "arrogance" which he might manifest, was sometimes the determining factor in punishment. Thus one objector, it is reported, was sent to "solitary" for disobeying the rule which required all prisoners to keep their hands out of their pockets while standing in line for food.[33] Another objector (a Jehovah's Witness) was sent to the "dark hole" because he would not help with the butchering (on the ground that it made him violently sick).[34] A Molokan absolutist, because he refused to work, was thrown into solitary confinement and remained there for 111 days on a diet of corn flakes and milk.[35] Other reports had it that men were "holed" (placed in solitary) for not cleaning their cells properly, for smiling while in line, or for taking food from the kitchen.

What is extremely difficult to discover is the amount and type of force, definitely outside the rules, which was used by guards and other custodial officials. Prison officials were certainly under definite instructions not to permit guards to use physical force against prisoners except in clear cases of defense. That there were times when guards did use force is fairly obvious to anyone familiar with prison conditions, but it is always difficult to prove such incidents. Officials involved would deny that force had been used; and in the end, it became the word of the official against the testimony of the objector and (rarely) any other witnesses who might have been present. Another question which is almost impossible to answer satisfactorily is the degree to which objectors were favored or discriminated against with respect to the use of physical force.

The case of Lester Lermond, a conscientious objector imprisoned in Lewisburg, will serve to illustrate the problem of illegal use of physical force. From the viewpoint of substantiating the objector's charges against custodial officials, this is one of the better-documented cases. Yet the prison administration flatly denied his version.

In the fall of 1945, according to the facts as stated by two witnesses, Lermond was suffering acute pain on account of an infected tooth. He asked for dental treatment and did not receive it. After several days, he decided that the only solution was to walk to the prison dentist's office, sit down on the bench outside the office door, and wait until the dentist arrived. This Lermond did one morning, seating himself some minutes before the dentist's scheduled arrival. Shortly after he had established himself on the bench, an officer requested him to move. He refused, saying that he preferred to remain there until the dentist arrived. Thereupon the officer seized him, "dragged him by the hair the length of the hall, and deposited him in an elevator which took him to the floor on which he is housed." [36] In the process of removing him, the guard twisted his arms severely and pummeled him.

This version was vouched for by two observers who happened to be in or near the hall down which Lermond was dragged. Larry Gara, a rather level-headed objector who was imprisoned in Lewisburg at the same time, said that there could be no doubt about the essential correctness of Lermond's story.[37] Yet this story of physical mistreatment was termed false by the warden of Lewisburg and by Director of Prisons James V. Bennett. The latter wrote that Lermond "appears to be one of those individuals who refuse to abide by institutional regulations" and that "there is no evidence that he was mistreated." [38]

Which version should be accepted in casting up the account? In this case, at least, the weight of evidence in the form of specific detail vouched for by at least two separate sources seems to lie clearly in favor of the objector's account. Yet the official story given out to the press was that of Mr. Bennett and of the warden.

That there were times when guards did use force, sometimes with very painful effect, is fairly certain, though difficult to prove. The difficulties of proof were obvious enough even in the above case, where documentation was relatively full. But what could one say about such reports as that of John Shubin, who charged through a friend that he had been so abused by guards that he lapsed into a state of "semi-consciousness"? [39] Confirmation could come only from fellow prisoners, who probably were not present, or from guards, who would usually deny the contention.

The probability is that all cases of reported physical violence against objectors cannot be untrue—even prison authorities would sometimes admit that guards had been a little "rough." In saying this, however, one should keep in mind the position of the guard. He was usually underpaid and often had family worries. The independent and seemingly "stubborn" conscientious objector belonged to what was virtually a new prison species to the custodial official. A murderer he could handle; a bootlegger was understandable. But a non-co-operating conscientious objector disrespectful of prison authority and traditions was something else again.

It ought also to be remembered that prison guards, like most other Americans, had relatives or friends in the fighting line. To expect men in this position to be always dispassionate and rule-observing in their relations with those who refused to support the war would have been to expect the improbable. Also, it might be remembered that the use of physical force against inmates, while rigorously forbidden by the federal prison system, is undoubtedly a factor in all prison relations, whether with objectors or nonobjectors, whether in war or in peace. Then, too, it should be constantly emphasized that the demands of the Selective Service System for the military services of guards resulted in the substitution, all too often, of inexperienced personnel. All these factors played their parts in the use of physical force against objectors.

Psychiatry and Objectors

One important question with which many objectors in prison were concerned was the nature of the use to which psychiatry was put. There was undoubtedly a place for psychiatric examinations in the federal prison system, for if rightly used, it might be argued, they might be valuable aids in proper classification and treatment of prisoners. The question before some conscientious objectors in prison, however, was whether psychiatry *was* being properly utilized. Some felt, for example, that prejudice of medical officers against conscientious objectors was often simply rationalized by psychiatric jargon: that objectors and other prisoners were first judged by officials to be "psychotic" (insane) and "queer" and then, after this prejudgment, were arbitrarily placed in a classification which would seem to confirm the original bias. It was frankly alleged by objectors that the medical officer at one institution, to cite a single example, was thus abusing psychiatry in cases of the more unconventional objectors; [40] and this charge may have been a factor in the officer's subsequent transfer to another institution.

Professor Donald Taft, a well-known criminologist, was very emphatic in expressing orally his opinions regarding psychiatry in prisons. After a systematic survey of conscientious objectors in many federal prisons, he reached the conclusion that the objectors' complaints against the use of "psychiatry" were well founded. He thought there was ground for the allegation that prisoners, whether conscientious objectors or others, were in some instances "threatened with Springfield" (a prison hospital where many medical and mental cases were sent) unless their behavior should become (from the viewpoint of the psychiatrist) less "erratic." He thought that there was need for a thorough investigation from all angles of the use of psychiatry in federal prisons.[41]

Dr. M. R. King, who had been warden of the Springfield, Missouri, federal prison hospital and medical director of the Bureau of Prisons, told the writer in the summer of 1945 that the psychiatric analysis of prisoners was still often a hit-or-miss proposition. Men were "bugged" (declared mentally ill) sometimes without sufficient evidence. In the beginning of prison experience with conscientious objectors, Dr. King indicated, there was a tendency in some institutions for psychiatrists to classify a large proportion of conscientious objectors as "psychoneurotic," although by the summer of 1945 the number of "psychoneurotics" among objectors had greatly declined. The diminution in supposed mental "abnormality" among objectors Dr. King attributed to a more careful use of terms by prison psychiatrists and a better acquaintance with the objectors' general outlook.[42] One can only comment that prison psychiatry must have been an inexact "science" indeed to have varied its standards of judgment as greatly as Dr. King indicated.

The kind of psychiatric-psychological view to which many objectors took exception is illustrated in Dr. Robert M. Lindner's book, *Stone Walls and Men,* which was published shortly after the conclusion of hostilities.[43] Although Lindner was not a psychiatrist, he was a psychologist and psychotherapist of considerable experience; he had studied conscientious objectors in Lewisburg prison, and his explanation of objectors' conduct agreed in many respects with that of some prison psychiatrists. In general, he saw most prisoners as victims of environmental circumstances and treated their problems sympathetically. Conscientious objectors he divided into two categories—religious and philosophical. Religious objectors could be subdivided into two classes—those who objected simply because they were conforming to the traditions and practices of their sect (like Mennonites) and the newcomers to religious sects, who were attempting to satisfy needs for security, companionship, and status. In some of the latter, according to Lindner, there was a strong homosexual urge. Philosophical objectors also could be divided into, on the one hand, a few who took their position because of home training and habit and, on the other hand, a larger number who "present a series of highly interesting psychological motivants." [44]

Lindner then proceeded to analyze these "interesting psychological motivants." He agreed that some objectors resisted service from "the most noble of convictions." He cited Debs as an example. Others, however, objected to service under such circumstances as to demonstrate a type of "reaction formation": that is, they had homosexual tendencies and sought to deny the fact by withdrawing into conscientious objection; or they had sadistic trends and "overdetermined" their denial of sadism by extreme objection to war service. The consistent picture of the latent homosexual type Lindner saw as a "somewhat effeminate, well-mannered, college-bred, artistically inclined, highly-intelligenced, unmarried youth who has ambitions either in the arts or in social service as a sublimation." [45]

The fact that so many of the group overtly professed a "love for all humanity" Lindner saw as a demonstration of homosexuality. Many conscientious objectors sublimated their homosexual and sadistic tendencies—the homosexual by actions that were supposed to demonstrate their love for all humanity, the sadistic by becoming violent against whatever system they attacked "by brush or pen or chisel." [46]

This type of behavior might, according to Lindner, express a "psychoneurosis." Some objectors yearned profoundly for punishment and actually welcomed the stringencies of a prison regime. They were often victims of a mother fixation and had not resolved the "oedipus conflict." They spurned society as they had spurned their fathers. Other objectors were "obsessional" types, "anxious and insecure" neurotics, and "dependent" characters.[47] While Lindner thought that very few objectors were "cowards," he implied that the "reasons" for their bravery were somehow "abnormal" and hence to be treated as a mental illness.

It is easy to see how views like those expressed by Lindner might cause tension and conflict between prison psychologists and psychiatrists, on the one hand, and objectors on the other. However sound such classifications might be from the viewpoint of psychiatric or psychological analysis, they said nothing whatever about the ethical validity or invalidity of the objector's actions. What is more, they might easily be used to rationalize whatever prejudices some psychiatrists might have against conscientious objectors in general.

Prison Strikes

Prison atmosphere, elusive and difficult to describe, was not conducive to conformity in the case of men who had gone to prison from what they regarded as conscientious motives. Nonconformists outside prison, objectors could not see why they should suddenly put on the mantle of conformity once they became part of the prison community. Throughout the six years in which objectors were imprisoned, individual conscientious objectors carried on personal campaigns of non-co-operation centering on various issues, and groups of objectors organized collective acts of passive resistance. Here we are not concerned primarily with the non-co-operation of individual objectors,[48] but rather with the collective "strikes."

Explanations of strikes differed. Some saw in collective refusals to work an exemplification of "abnormal" personality. Others thought that work and hunger strikes were "normal" reactions to an "abnormal" situation.

To the Bureau of Prisons, those conscientious objectors who were active in the major prison strikes were primarily reformers "with a zeal for changing the social, political, economic, and cultural order." [49] Some strikers, according to the same source, were "bewildered and frustrated in their efforts to find a constructive answer to the complex problems of a world in conflict, and finding none, satisfy some inner need through protest and escape from reality." [50] Frequently, the Bureau thought (following its psychiatric and psychological experts), the motivation of the strike leader stemmed from an "overprotective" home or from mother fixation or from a general rebelliousness against the overprotection of home. [51]

Many pacifist sources looked upon prison strike leaders as among the most able, conscientious, and "normal" of all those men who had been attracted to the pacifist movement. There was, of course, no unity of opinion among pacifists and conscientious objectors as to the merits of specific strikes or of the technique of striking itself. Groups like the War Resisters League tended to encourage prison strikers and to see in the militancy of strike leaders a pattern to be emulated. Many members of the Historic Peace Churches, however, questioned the necessity and desirability of refusals to work and eat. Indeed, some objectors (most Mennonites, for example) saw the whole strike technique as being essentially immoral in that it supposedly smacked too much of the "political" methods of "the world." It was too much like war.

Very shortly after the first conscientious objectors were sent to prison, the initial prison "strike" occurred. The strikes continued into the period far beyond the end of hostilities with Japan, in August, 1945. Indeed, the cessation of hostilities seemed to stimulate the general restlessness of objectors in prison, as was perhaps to be expected. Here we are concerned primarily with sampling a few of the leading strikes. The examples selected will serve to illustrate the major issues involved in all the prison strikes and will also reveal the rather unique problems which confronted prison administrators.

First Danbury Strike. This, one of the earliest of prison strikes, presumably arose because the warden of Danbury Correctional Institution had withdrawn his promise to allow sixteen conscientious objectors to abstain from lunch on April 23, 1941, in order to hold a "strike against war" meeting. When the sixteen (all of whom had been sentenced for refusal to register in the original draft) heard of the warden's action, they refused to report for work on the morning of April 23. Moreover, they would not eat or observe any of the routine prescribed for inmates. Their punishment was solitary confinement for two days and confinement to cells for another thirty. There was one report that the strikers had previously made demands for abolition of racial segregation in the prison, and some maintained that they had planned all along to refuse to work. But it appears that they entered into the strike only because they believed the warden had withdrawn his permission for the original demonstration.[52]

Racial Segregation at Danbury. On August 11, 1943, nineteen conscientious objectors initiated a "work strike" in protest against the policy of racial segregation at meals. They were immediately confined to their cells (which in Danbury were fairly comfortable in a physical sense), and, with forty minutes a day for exercise and the official "monotonous" diet for food, they remained there for 133 days, or until December 23, 1943. Their visiting time was cut from one hour to thirty minutes a month. After the warden had promised to institute a cafeteria system for the dining room—a scheme that was to be introduced only gradually—the strikers returned to work in the hope that the policy of segregation in the dining room would be permanently eliminated.[53] By the end of January, 1944, segregation was no longer required at any meals, and there would seem to be no question that the strike was in part, at least, responsible for this result.

Segregation at Lewisburg. Sometimes a strike which began with one issue in the center shifted to other questions as it progressed. This was true of the demonstration which began at Lewisburg on May 31, 1943.

A colored prisoner had been assigned to the farm dormitory of the prison—the only Negro in that section of buildings. Despite the fact that there were no other Negroes, he was compelled to take his meals in a separate room. Immediately, eight conscientious objectors in that section declined to eat in their "white" dining room and tried to subsist on food which they purchased from the prison commissary. They hoped to protest in this way until prison authorities should see fit to grant the right of free association regardless of race.

With such a limited diet—only certain types of food could be obtained at the commissary—it was not surprising that after two or three days the men should feel so weak that they could not work. Reporting this fact to the proper prison authorities, they were thrown into the "hole" for refusal to work. In the "hole" they decided that their consciences would permit them to eat the usual "monotonous" diet. A little later they were placed together in one room but separated from the remaining prison population—"administrative segregation," as it was called; their writing privileges were limited to one letter a week. The prison authorities apparently hoped that this treatment would lead the strikers to accept the policy of racial segregation.

In the meantime, five other objectors, this time from the main prison, had gone on hunger strike in sympathy with their fellows of the farm dormitory. They also were sent to the "hole," where they accepted the "monotonous" diet and were then transferred to "administrative segregation" with the other eight. The thirteen were reduced to eleven when two decided to return to work, one as a result of pressure from his family.[54] For a few days the original thirteen had gone on hunger strike, after sending a letter demanding abolition of racial segregation in prisons to Director Bennett and Attorney General Biddle. This hunger strike did not last long, however.

Prison Censorship at Lewisburg. By August 11, 1943,[55] the so-called "work strike" of the original conscientious objectors had been transformed for some of them into a strike against the prison system in general. The number of strikers had also been reduced to seven. On September 28, five of the objectors transformed the major emphasis of the Lewisburg strikers to a protest against prison censorship practices and changed their tactics to those of a hunger strike. Paton Price, Jack Dixon, Thomas Woodman, David Dellinger, and William Lovett in thus refusing to eat wished to produce a change in what they termed the "cruel, unnecessary and discriminatory" system whereby prison officials denied inmates certain types of literature and censored their letters in a way which the strikers termed "arbitrary."

In their letter to James Bennett, Director of the Bureau of Prisons, the five fasters asked that two "basic rights" of all prison inmates be recognized. The first was the right of every prisoner to free correspondence with the outside world, even if the prisoner happened to be in "punishment" status. "The second," the fasters went on, "is the right of every prisoner to access to uncensored materials for reading and writing, at all times, regardless of his prison status." [56] The objectors agreed that it was legitimate for prison censors to open letters in order to detect plots and discover drug smuggling, as well as to exclude pornographic materials. But censors should not exclude, they said, expressions of social or religious opinions or descriptions of conditions in prisons. Letters had been repeatedly censored for these reasons, not only at Lewisburg but also at other institutions.

Late in October, 1943, the condition of the hunger strikers had become so weakened as a result of their self-imposed discipline that officials began to feed them through the nose.

On November 6, 1943, Director Bennett wrote to the warden of Lewisburg suggesting certain modifications in prison rules on censorship, and he expressed the hope that the proposed changes would be acceptable to the strikers.[57] In their reply the strikers asked that certain clarifications in the Director's original letter be made, and on November 30 Bennett answered their request. The result was that on December 1 the strikers concluded their fast in the belief that Bennett's modifications, while they did not "embody all the objectives of our original concern," represented "a substantial clarification and improvement." [58]

It seems clear that the settlement of the strike was a compromise. The Bureau of Prisons, for example, refused to promise that library, correspondence, and reading and writing privileges would be allowed to those in punishment status ("the hole" or other forms of restriction). Wide administrative discretion here was to be given to the warden. On the other hand, there was a definite promise that "inspection" of mail should not be interpreted to include the right of censorship of religious or political opinions. The strikers did not gain all they had asked, but it seems equally clear that the prison authorities *did* modify inspection and literature regulations considerably.[59]

Other Strikes. To detail all the other conflicts in prison which could be called "strikes" would involve far more space than is available. In June, 1944, three conscientious objectors in Petersburg went on work strike against racial segregation and the war-connected prison industry. They were placed in "the hole" on June 11, 1944. In the meantime, a large group in Danbury had begun a strike against the parole system. The prison authorities replied by transferring a number of the strikers from Danbury to Lewisburg, where seven of those transferred then began a hunger strike against being deprived of "good time" (statutory remission of part of the sentence as a reward for good conduct in prison) for failure to work. This continued until October 14, 1944, when one of the group was released, with the restoration of part of the "good time" formerly denied. Another was paroled. Those remaining were joined by five others in a "rotation" strike, whereby five men would refuse to eat for a definite period, their places to be taken by another five for a similar (unstated) term. A hunger strike of sympathy was begun in Danbury on October 4, 1944, and ended on October 8, 1944.[60]

In the Ashland federal penitentiary a group began, in the fall of 1944, to protest racial segregation by a program of non-co-operation. In August, 1945, new difficulties at Lewisburg were precipitated by the reduction of "good time" of two nonobjector inmates. Ten conscientious objectors protested to the warden and later refused to work, whereupon they also were deprived of thirty days' "good time" and placed in segregation.[61]

Events of similar nature continued to take place in federal prisons far beyond the surrender of Japan in August, 1945. Moreover, individual protests added their weight to the collective efforts of objectors. Hunger strikes and work strikes throughout 1946 were not uncommon—more than a year after the conclusion of hostilities.[62] As the first postwar months dragged on, objectors still in prison became more and more impatient at their confinement, and individual and collective strikes were the result.

The importance of prison strikes lay not in the numbers involved (a small minority of all conscientious objectors in prison) nor yet in any dramatic results supposedly achieved. The significance was rather that a few hundred [63] prisoners during wartime were willing and able, often in startling fashion, to challenge many of the accepted practices of prison organizations at vital points. Public interest in the general state of prisons, moreover, was on several occasions aroused. It is doubtful whether any other group than conscientious objectors would have been equipped by temperament and background to do these things.

On the other hand, one should guard against any tendency to overemphasize the importance of the strikes and particularly against the tendency of some objectors to make every striker a hero. After all, the overwhelming majority of all imprisoned objectors never engaged in strikes and by and large did what the prison system expected them to do; and some strikers were no more heroic than some conformists.

XVII: *Release from Durance Vile: Parole and the Struggle for Amnesty*

To THOSE concerned about the fate of conscientious objectors sentenced to prison, one of the most difficult, complicated, and, at times, frustrating problems was that of securing the release of objectors and their restoration to ordinary life. Release, of course, could be accomplished through completion of sentence, but the concern of civil-liberties and pacifist organizations during and after the war was to secure freedom before sentences had been completed. Even if the sentence was completed, the objector might be reclassified by his local board or be arrested for a technical infraction of the law (such as refusal to carry a draft card), which in turn might lead once more to prison.[1]

Release of objectors before completion of sentence took several forms. In the first place, the objector might be set free on "good time" or "conditional release"—that is, the statute provided for deduction of a certain percentage of the sentence for good behavior in prison. This form of discharge, often somewhat routine in the cases of ordinary prisoners, created many controversies where objectors were concerned. In the second place, two types of parole were available for the objector that might provide a method whereby the prisons could be relieved of their unwanted guests with rapidity and the objectors themselves returned to productive labor in the outside world.[2] The parole machinery was slow, it was often unadapted to the needs of objectors, and the conditions of parole were such that frequently objectors could not accept it once it was offered. Although the general character of the objectors and their usual lack of previous law violations made them the type of prisoners ordinarily most eligible for parole, they neither felt that their past course had been mistaken nor could they conscientiously undertake to obey in future the law which they had broken. Yet the promise to obey all laws in the future was one of the most important conditions attached to parole. Because of these and other restrictions, many men refused even to consider the acceptance of paroles; conscience would prevent one from avoiding prison and, once there, keep one from getting out.

At the time of Japan's surrender, in August, 1945, there were still 3,000 objectors serving terms in American prisons, despite the release of many on parole and "good time." In addition, about 2,500 objectors had been released but in many cases were still serving under the parole restrictions of the Department of Justice. Thus nearly 6,000 conscientious draft violators were either in prison or out. And most of them would be subject to civic disabilities, such as inability to hold office or to vote. It was on behalf of this whole group that demands for general amnesty began to be made shortly after the Japanese surrender. Only a general amnesty would have the effect of restoring political rights that had been lost. But the amnesty struggle, like that for parole, was to prove disillusioning, for while much effort was put into the fight by objectors, and elaborate machinery was set up by the government, the result seemed to many very much like that of an elephant's laboring and bringing forth a mouse.

Conditional Release

Conditional release was established by national law and applied to all prisoners. The federal statute provided that specified numbers of days per month, depending upon the length of the prisoner's sentence, were to be deducted from time to be served.[3] But this so-called "good time" allowance could be limited or canceled by prison officials if the inmate failed to observe the rules and conform to prison routine. Once released on an allowance of "good time," the prisoner had to conform, until the expiration of his sentence, to certain conditions laid down at the time of release: he had to report regularly to a parole advisor, remain within the geographical limits fixed by the Board of Parole, change his residence and employment only with the consent of the probation officer, refrain from imbibing intoxicating liquor, avoid associating with persons of bad reputation, and promise not to marry without the consent of the Supervisor of Parole. If the prisoner violated these conditions in any way, he could be sent back to prison immediately.

With respect to conscientious objectors, a major issue involving conditional release was whether deprivation of "good time" ought to be used as punishment for non-co-operation in prison. The viewpoint of disciplinary officers was that the law made deprivation in such cases mandatory, for non-co-operation always involved disobedience of the rules, and disobedience, according to the law, canceled "good time." [4] On the other hand, many objectors argued that deprivation was unfair, especially insofar as the "good time" canceled had been accumulated while the objector was co-operating.

A problem of conscience was sometimes involved in "good time" release, since it was necessary to sign "conditional release" papers. A number of objectors felt it impossible to agree to the conditions required, among them William Richards [5] and George R. Kingsley.[6]

Some conscientious objectors who refused to sign conditional release papers were released nevertheless. One of them, Larry Gara, was subsequently arrested and returned to prison for failure to make the required reports, even though he had not agreed to do so.[7] The case of Gara was complicated, however, by the fact that the Bureau of Prisons ordered his return to prison to prevent his further harassment by his local board in Reading, Pennsylvania, which had insisted on trying to reopen his case! In this case, then, the Bureau of Prisons was battling one branch of the Selective Service System; even "absolutist" objectors, who usually thought the Bureau of Prisons very high-handed, arbitrary, and unjust, praised this act of the Bureau as "a very decent thing to do." [8]

The Parole of Objectors

Parole was of two types: regular, which was provided for all prisoners by federal statutes, and special, established for the peculiar conditions arising out of violations of the Selective Training and Service Act.

Regular parole, which could be applied for by any federal prisoner serving a sentence of more than a year, on completion of one-third of his term, was administered under the Federal Parole Act of 1910 by a board of three in the Department of Justice assisted by parole officers in the several judicial districts. Favorable action on a parole application depended not only on a man's prison record but also upon the availability of suitable employment and of a sponsor in the outside community. The parolee had to agree to observe several restrictive rules very much like the ones enforced against those on conditional release: to remain within the geographical limits fixed by his parole; to report once a month to his parole advisor; to abstain from the use of intoxicating liquors or narcotic drugs; to associate only with persons of good reputation; to work at a lawful occupation and support his dependents; to answer truthfully all questions put to him by his parole advisor; to remain at liberty without violating the law; to refrain from marriage, unless with the permission of the probation officer. For conscientious objectors the parole board generally would approve a geographical location at some distance from the objector's home community and employment of hospital or similar type, at a rate of pay not exceeding that of a private in the Army.

Special parole was provided for violators of the Selective Training and Service Act under Executive Order 8641, signed in 1941. It was admittedly designed to hasten the process for release of prisoners to the Army or Navy; it could also be used to parole conscientious objectors to the Medical Corps, Civilian Public Service, or to public service institutions. To be eligible for 8641 parole, the prisoner had to serve at least sixty days of his sentence; the consent of both the Director of Selective Service and the Director of the Bureau of Prisons was required before any release.[9] The order was revised in April, 1944, to provide for the setting up of local Selective Service boards at all federal prisons where violators of the Selective Training and Service Act were confined. These boards were to classify such violators in preparation for possible parole to the Army as I-A, to the Army as I-A-O, or to C.P.S. camps or special civilian public service (such as hospitals) as IV-E. Board members were provided with copies of the Phillips and Kauten decisions dealing with the meaning of religion,[10] and it was hoped that men who had been denied IV-E classification through narrow interpretations of "religious training and belief" might now be permitted, through parole, to engage in the type of civilian service which the law provided for recognized objectors. Those willing to accept the classification of the prison panel boards were given regular physical examinations; those who failed to pass were classified IV-F and could apply for something corresponding to general parole, with similar restrictions. Those classified IV-E who went out to public service employment could receive no more than $15 a month, the amount granted to C.P.S. men on special service. Actual parole, however, did not necessarily result from classification, since each recommendation had to be passed upon by the director of Selective Service and the Department of Justice,[11] and final action awaited the decision of the parole committee established to administer 8641 releases. Conditions attached to 8641 paroles were similar to those established for regular paroles except that there was no specific provision forbidding marriage without the consent of the parole officer.

A study of regular paroles granted to conscientious objectors, as compared with other violators of the Selective Service Act, shows that down to March 1, 1945, a total of 310 regular paroles had been granted to conscientious objectors (including Jehovah's Witnesses). Table XIII shows the figures with respect to regular paroles for the period down to April 30, 1944—the most intensive and extensive of the war.

TABLE XIII. REGULAR PAROLES *

	Paroles granted	Paroles denied	Total	Per cent granted
Jehovah's Witnesses	50	183	233	21.5
Other conscientious objectors	125	123	248	50.4
Total objectors	175	306	481	36.4
Other Selective Service violators	143	368	511	28.0
	318	674	992	32.1

* Figures of the National Service Board for Religious Objectors.

Conscientious objectors found themselves relatively well treated when compared with other Selective Service violators; within the objector category, the startling contrast between the Witnesses and non-Witnesses reminds one of the great disparity in prison sentences meted out to the two groups. One explanation, of course, lies in the very widespread refusal by the Witnesses to accept any conditions which might restrict their preaching activities in any way.

As for special parole, up to May 1, 1944, excluding applications withdrawn and those of men otherwise released, 158 of 307 applications—more than half, it will be noted—were rejected. During the following year a larger proportion of 8641 applications were granted; by May 1, 1945, the totals had grown to 66 for Plan 2 (parole to I-A-O), 132 for Plan 3 (to Civilian Public Service), and 151 for Plan 4 (to public service institutions such as hospitals, without supervision by Selective Service or Civilian Public Service)—a total increase of 200 for these groups.[12]

Before the April, 1944, revised procedure under Executive Order 8641, a number of interpretations had greatly limited the liberal tendencies which had been expected from 8641 parole. For one thing, General Hershey had said that Plan 4 ought to be reserved solely for conscientious objectors who had passed the age of 38 (the upper limit for Army drafting) and for very unusual cases; as a result, up to November, 1943, only six such paroles had been granted,[13] and up to May, 1944, only sixteen, although Plan 4 was obviously the only one, other than "regular" parole, which could be accepted by many conscientious objectors. General Hershey had also maintained that only those who could legitimately be reclassified IV-E under the statute ought to be paroled to Civilian Public Service camps,[14] thus excluding most philosophical objectors even where they were willing to accept parole.

The figures in Table XIV indicate the progress of Executive Order paroles during two significant periods of the war.

It is interesting to note that the Bureau of Prisons rejected nearly four times as many applications for parole as Selective Service during the first year. This is particularly significant in view of the fact that Bureau of Prison officials often said informally that they should like to rid themselves of the responsibility for objectors. Actually, high officials of the Bureau of Prisons acted on the principle that they would keep men in prison as long as they thought the home communities would want to have the men punished; the officials admitted that their judgment in this respect often had no relation to "home" sentiment, but was rather the Bureau's estimate as to how

TABLE XIV. EXECUTIVE ORDER PAROLES *

	Beginning to April 30, 1944	May 1, 1944 to April 30, 1945	Total
Rejected by Bureau of Prisons	126	106	232
Rejected by Selective Service	32	—	32
Withdrawn by applicants	63	20	83
Other forms of release	81	34	115
Parole to noncombatant Army service	35	31	66
Parole to Civilian Public Service	98	34	132
Parole to special public service	16	135	151
Total	451	360	811

* Figures of the National Committee for Conscientious Objectors, Washington, D.C., and the Bureau of Prisons.

long punishment should continue.[15] This attitude undoubtedly played a part in the large number of parole rejections by the Bureau.

Under the revised plan of 8641 parole, the Selective Service System apparently dropped its objection to special service parole under Plan 4, thus making it possible for larger numbers to be released from prison direct to public service. In August, 1944, for example, out of 24 objectors paroled under the revised Executive Order, 20 were given assignments to special public service—more than the total number given such paroles in the three-year period between June, 1941, and May, 1944. But through 1944–1945, many more men were being sent to prison than were being released by means of parole, both regular and special. As of July 1, 1945, approximately one-eighth of all those sentenced had been granted parole (700 out of approximately 5,600).

The conditions attached to parole seemed to many to violate the very principles which had led them to prison. A number felt unable to accept the discriminatory limitations of residence, wages, and project. The Board of Parole, however, feared public anger if parolees were allowed to return to their home communities and to resume their normal activities while other young men were under the restrictions of military service. The Board also appeared to have a rigid policy of not granting paroles to Jehovah's Witnesses unless they were willing to promise not to engage in their preaching activities—a promise which most of them, of course, were unwilling to make. This Jehovah's Witness policy was frequently criticized by objector and civil-liberties organizations on the ground that it constituted a clear violation of the principle of religious freedom.

Prisoners who had gone to jail as absolutists or who had become absolutists in prison found it difficult, if not impossible, to accept or even to apply for parole to I-A-O or to Civilian Public Service. Sometimes they reluctantly accepted parole to Civilian Public Service, only to discover that their consciences would not permit them to remain a part of what they regarded as a "slave labor" system. The case of Arthur A. Dole is illustrative. Dole had originally been willing to accept a IV-E classification, but was denied one by his local board. Sentenced to five years in the penitentiary for refusal to report to the Army, he gradually came to accept while in prison a more nearly "absolutist" position. However, he wished to give Civilian Public Service a trial and agreed to parole to C.P.S. He entered camp in 1943, serving in several units. In the fall of 1945, however, he decided that his acceptance of parole to Civilian Public Service had been a mistake. In order to provide a cause for return to prison, Dole deliberately walked out of camp, thus violating his parole conditions. He went to work for the American Friends Service Committee, where he was eventually arrested for breaking his parole. He was sent to the Lewisburg penitentiary to complete his five-year sentence. Had he remained in Civilian Public Service camp it is likely that his release would have come sooner, but since it was a matter of principle that he should not serve in a "conscript labor" system, he returned cheerfully to prison.[16]

Even parole under Plan 4 seemed to many objectors too much of a compromise, especially because they were expected to work for what they regarded as the substandard wage of maintenance and $15.00 a month. Jehovah's Witnesses objected to all types of parole under Executive Order 8641 for the same reasons which led them to refuse induction into the Army or Civilian Public Service. While the percentage willing to apply may have increased slightly after that date, it was clearly evident that many objectors thought they could not conform to the requirements even of the revised Executive Order.

The revised procedure, for example, required the objector to apply for parole under the classification offered by the prison Selective Service Board previous to going for the physical examination which might give him a IV-F (physical or mental disability) and hence make him clearly eligible for parole under Plan 4. But many objectors refused to accept the classification given, as it might be I-A-O when they had asked for IV-E, or I-A when they had requested I-A-O. Some objectors thought that the whole scheme under the revised 8641 was a device of Selective Service to give the appearance of parole liberality while denying its substance through the local prison Selective Service Boards.

The only ways in which large numbers could hope to be released from prison (during the course of hostilities and for many months thereafter) were for their sentences to end, for presidential pardon to be granted, or for the regulations and policies governing parole to be substantially changed.

By the summer of 1945, however, the various objector and civil-liberties organizations were pressing even more vigorously than at the height of the war for a liberalization of parole conditions. They urged liberalization of Plan 4 paroles under Executive Order 8641. They suggested the elimination of location, job, and salary conditions attached to paroles. They pressed for the elimination of the parole board rule which denied conscientious objectors, although not other parolees, the right even to visit their homes except in case of serious illness.[17] This latter ruling was particularly obnoxious to the objectors, for while the Board encouraged nonobjector parolees to visit their homes, presumably to build up morale, it decreed that visits by objectors might arouse hostile opinion. An organ of the conscientious objectors called the rule "discrimination of the nastiest, most evil sort." [18]

The end of hostilities with Japan gave impetus to the campaign for liberalization of parole, and the parole authorities began very gradually to modify their policies. Thus in the early part of 1946, the Board of Parole announced that it would consider granting paroles to men twenty-six years of age and over (and fathers below twenty-six) without any limitations of location, job, or salary; the Bureau of Prisons and Selective Service announced the same policy for those men who had completed one-third of their sentences.[19] Twenty-six years was now, of course, the maximum age at which men were being drafted.

But it was a slow process and the authorities were reluctant to make sweeping changes, still largely because of a fear of public opinion. Thus, while there were approximately 3,000 objectors in prison at the time of Japan's surrender, nearly one year later—July 1, 1946—there still remained about 2,000 incarcerated.[20] But paroles were speeded up; from November, 1945, to June, 1946, 882 paroles of all kinds were granted to violators of the Selective Service Act, and during the month preceding June 20, 1946, paroles were granted to 74 and denied to 29 [21] (a sharp change, it will be noted, from the 1943–1944 period). By the end of 1946 the number of objectors yet remaining in prison stood at 502, including 455 Jehovah's Witnesses; while the number of nonobjector violators of the Selective Service Act was 985.[22]

Not only were men being released at a snail's pace, but once released they were, if on parole, still subject to all kinds of obnoxious restrictions. Even if released by expiration of sentence, they were by the laws of most states deprived of such rights as the suffrage and officeholding. This problem, dual in nature, provided the occasion for one of the most dramatic stories in the immediate postwar story of conscientious objection—the campaign for amnesty.

The Struggle for Amnesty

The amnesty struggle began soon after Japan surrendered. Beginning as a request for release of all conscientious objectors then in prison and for restoration of civic and political rights [23] to all (whether released or not), it broadened eventually into an insistence on amnesty for all violators of the Selective Training and Service Act, whether objectors or ordinary violators.

The so-called absolutist group among the objectors—centering around the War Resisters League and the publication *The Absolutist*, which was issued by the Absolutist War Objectors Association and edited by Julius Eichel—was perhaps the first to ask for the organization of an amnesty movement. But the absolutists were soon joined by many other pacifist and conscientious-objector organizations, even some of the more conservative.

On October 15, 1945, the Families and Friends of Imprisoned Conscientious Objectors—an organization established during the war—was joined by others in a dramatic picketing of the White House; this demonstration may be said to have initiated the amnesty campaign before the bar of public opinion. The picketing, said its sponsors, was directed against "militarism and war" and for "freedom of all war objectors." [24] On October 31 two of the pickets were arrested for not carrying draft cards. They were held in jail for two days and were then released.[25] But the general outlines of the amnesty campaign had been formulated and were to follow the pattern of picketing, arrests, petitions, and fasts for two full years.

On November 24, the American Civil Liberties Union celebrated its twenty-fifth anniversary, and among the high lights of its program was a round-table discussion on amnesty. The conference debated and approved a vigorous campaign for release of conscientious objectors. But it was soon evident that pacifists and conscientious objectors were split among themselves as to procedures. The bulk of those who had been to prison advocated a public amnesty campaign that would use all the publicity devices so familiar to American organizations and would emphasize general release and restoration of civic rights, rather than a mere liberalization of parole. This viewpoint was also supported by many others who had not been imprisoned during the war. The contrary view, supported not only by some of the older pacifist leaders but also by some among the younger group, questioned the value of an amnesty campaign and advocated a more quiet, "individual" approach to secure the liberalization of parole. This group apparently feared that an amnesty campaign might create unnecessary hostility and not be effective in the end.[26]

In the meantime, the group advocating a public and vigorous amnesty campaign began to organize. A Committee for Amnesty was established in December, 1945. Rev. A. J. Muste, the well-known Fellowship of Reconciliation leader, was made chairman of its executive committee and Dr. Evan Thomas, of the War Resisters League, was elected treasurer.

While the Committee for Amnesty was taking shape, President Truman was preparing an amnesty proclamation of his own. Issued on Christmas Eve, 1945, his proclamation granted full amnesty to all those ex-prisoners who had served honorably in the Army and

Navy for at least a year. "Such convicted persons," the President said, "ought to have restored to them the political, civil, and other rights of which they were deprived by reason of such conviction and which may not be restored to them unless they are pardoned." [27] Objectors carefully noted, however, that the President said nothing about conscientious objectors.

After the organization of the Committee for Amnesty, dramatic incidents in the campaign multiplied. At Danbury Federal Correctional Institution, for example, inmates emerged from Christmas dinner to find a huge "Freedom Now" sign placed on the Christmas tree in front of the mess hall. All around the courtyard of the institution were scattered signs reading "Free All Selective Service Men" and "Free the Political Prisoners." Prisoners were apparently enthusiastic, for they lustily booed the guard who had been instructed to take down the signs. The signs had been erected, while most prisoners were having their dinner, by sixteen conscientious objectors on strike.[28] Walter W. Van Kirk, executive secretary of the Federal Council of Churches of Christ in America, wrote to President Truman indicating the concern of the churches about amnesty. "I am sure," he said, "that you have no desire to see these men suffer for their religious beliefs beyond that suffering which they have already endured." [29] On Lincoln's birthday, Danbury Correctional Institution was picketed simultaneously from inside and outside. Friends and relatives of imprisoned objectors carried placards on the sidewalk in front of the institution, while objectors themselves circled the jail yard within.[30] On May 11 more than one hundred relatives of conscientious objectors, together with former prisoners and war veterans, picketed the White House. Five persons from the group took the plea for amnesty to a presidential secretary. At about the same time, the Council of the Episcopal Diocese of the State of Virginia asked the President for an amnesty proclamation; a district meeting of the American Legion, in response, requested the President not to grant pardon.[31]

In the meantime, the Committee for Amnesty itself had split. The National Service Board for Religious Objectors withdrew because several supporting organizations, notably the Mennonites, objected to the use of picketing. The two N.S.B.R.O. representatives continued to sit on the amnesty committee, however, as independent members.

This withdrawal of the N.S.B.R.O. from the amnesty committee served as an occasion for new criticism of that organization by the "absolutist" group. The National Service Board's defense was that it was simply the agency for its constituent groups and that when the largest of those groups found itself unable to endorse the tactics of the Committee, the only course left for the Board was to withdraw. Without judging the merits of the case, it might be observed that here again was an example of the precarious ties which held pacifist and objector organizations together in co-operative effort.

The withdrawal of the N.S.B.R.O., however, did not seem to impair the efforts of the Committee. It continued to be the center of the campaign, although it should not be thought that all the local efforts were under its direction. Amnesty hunger strikes in federal prisons, for example, were initiated and managed by the objector inmates themselves. Beginning on May 11, the hunger strikes spread to several prisons. And by the middle of 1946, pleas to President Truman for amnesty were coming from many diverse organizations and leaders.[32]

In the meantime, President Truman had replied to the amnesty letter left with him by those picketing the White House on May 11. He remarked that the whole problem was being considered by the Attorney General and commented that he shared the concern of the Committee "for the preservation of our traditions of individual liberty and freedom of conscience. . . ." A. J. Muste, chairman of the Committee for Amnesty, replied to the President's letter, gently pointing out that the matter had been before the Attorney General already for about nine months and that "under the circumstances it is not unreasonable for us to ask for a definite report at an early date." [33]

With fifteen hundred objectors still in prison, the autumn amnesty campaign was accelerated. On September 20, three pacifists, Ashton Jones, Charles Wellman, and Roger Axford (who had just been released from federal prison after twenty-seven months of non-co-operative effort there), attempted to see the Attorney General on behalf of amnesty. They were not only unsuccessful but were forcibly ejected from that official's office, Wellman offering full-fledged non-co-operation in the affair, with the result that he had to be carried out of the office. Axford and Jones thereupon took up stations on the steps of the Department of Justice building, where they remained all night. They stood near an entrance frequently used by Attorney General Clark, in the hope that they might be able to buttonhole him on his way to work the following morning; the Attorney General, however, evaded them. Axford decided to make his residence on the steps semipermanent. His friends brought him a sleeping bag, which enabled him to turn the steps into a dormitory at night, while during the day he picketed the Department of Justice, sometimes with the assistance of friends. Visitors were often struck by the earnestness of the clean-cut young man; while some were simply amused and others put him down as a fanatic, many were genuinely interested.

At midnight on October 3, Axford and Charles Wellman, who had joined him in his vigil, were attacked by two marines who were apparently under the influence of alcohol. Their placards were destroyed and many of their belongings scattered. Meanwhile, the building guards steadily denied them admittance to the building on the ground that they did not have admission cards; when they applied for the required cards they were refused.[34] Axford, an ordained Methodist minister, hoped by these tactics to dramatize the struggle for amnesty, to secure the release from prison of fasting conscientious objectors, and to emphasize what he regarded as the autocratic and arbitrary character of the Department of Justice and the Bureau of Prisons.

The Jehovah's Witnesses had organized their own independent amnesty campaign, as they had acted independently of other conscientious objectors so often during the war. The Witnesses now secured an interview with President Truman to present their concern. According to their official organ, the committee included a friend of President Truman and an officer who had served under Truman during the first World War. President Truman told the Committee, according to the Witnesses, "that he had been a soldier, was a 'fighting man' and did not have any use for a man who would not fight for and protect his country." In spite of this, however, he promised "that he would see that those convicted got a fair consideration and just decision."

Organized public opinion by the end of 1946 appeared to be overwhelmingly on the side of amnesty, and it would seem reasonable to infer that this was not without influence on the White House. The National Convention of the CIO, meeting in Atlantic City, adopted unanimously a resolution which, "reaffirming a high tradition of the American labor movement," urged the President to proclaim an immediate amnesty for all objectors. The American Veterans Committee sent a delegation to ask for amnesty. A retired brigadier general, H. C. Holdridge, speaking from the steps of the Department of Justice building in Washington, referred to the fact that thousands of German prisoners' in the American zone of occupation had been granted pardon and commented, "If we can do it for the Germans we can do it for our own citizens." [35] At the same time, Roger Axford was continuing his night-and-day vigil on the steps of the building from which General Holdridge spoke. He had been there two months.

The press, insofar as it commented at all, seemed to be favorable. A leading editorial in the *Saturday Evening Post* [36] pointed out that General MacArthur had released almost 1,000,000 political prisoners in Japan, including conscientious objectors, that General Clay had proclaimed amnesty for an equal number of Germans, and that Canada had restored rights to more than 14,000 deserters. It concluded that "to extend an amnesty now to conscientious objectors could do no possible harm, and would follow a sound American tradition recognized by such widely different Presidents as Washington, Lincoln, and Coolidge." And the *New York Times* in an editorial of November 24 strongly advocated a "Christmas Amnesty."

Some sections of the press, it is true, did not look with favor on the campaign. Thus the *Kansas City Star* said editorially:

For every conscientious objector behind bars there are thousands of well-remembered graves of American youths who died defending their country, and other thousands of disabled men. . . . The men who were entirely willing to sacrifice our freedom in the name of conscience have a doubtful claim on the nation's mercy.[37]

And the *Cadillac* (Michigan) *News* commented unfavorably on ministerial picketing for amnesty. But sentiments of this kind seemed to represent a minority viewpoint in the press of the United States.

On December 22, 1946, there was a nationwide amnesty demonstration. The reply of the White House came on December 23. There was to be no general amnesty for conscientious objectors. Instead, President Truman announced the appointment of an Amnesty Board of three members which was charged with the task of making recommendations for executive clemency regarding those who had been convicted of violating the Selective Training and Service Act. Members of the Board were to be former Supreme Court Justice Owen J. Roberts; James F. O'Neill, police chief of Manchester, New Hampshire, and vice-chairman of the Americanism commission of the American Legion; and Willis Smith, former president of the American Bar Association. Appointment of the Board indicated that some effort was to be made to review cases on an individual basis rather than grant any general amnesty, as the Committee for Amnesty had asked.[38]

The appointment of the Amnesty Board was received with mixed feeling by pacifist and conscientious-objector organizations. On the one hand, it was felt that something had been gained: the White House was at least in a measure concerned; on the other hand, it was feared by many that the appointment of the Board, and especially the nature of its personnel, indicated that nothing substantial would be done. Some charged that designation of the Board was merely a nice method of evading responsibility. At the time of its appointment there still remained some 300 conscientious objectors, including Jehovah's Witnesses, in prison; there were also, of course, the more than 5,000 men whose sentences had expired or who were out on parole and whose future civic and political rights would be impaired in the absence of amnesty. Curiously enough, the establishment of the Board coincided almost exactly with a Gallup public opinion poll which showed 69 per cent of the American people favoring release of conscientious objectors, 23 per cent against such action, and 8 per cent who expressed no opinion.[39]

It was to be a full year, however, before the Board reached any conclusion whatsoever. While it was deliberating and holding hearings, pacifist and civil-liberties organizations carried on the struggle. Countless organizations—civic, religious, fraternal, and veterans—and hundreds of individuals continued to petition the President and Amnesty Board.[40]

Meanwhile, the case of Thomas J. Leonard dramatized for many advocates of amnesty what they regarded as an unfortunate and, in some respects, ludicrous situation. Leonard had worked in Civilian Public Service during the war. He had been an attendant and "guinea pig" at the Pennsylvania State Hospital. Only after the Japanese sur-

RELEASE FROM DURANCE VILE 395

render did he walk out of C.P.S. He was, of course, arrested and sentenced to six months in prison but, pending his appeal, was released and taught social sciences at Dillard University, New Orleans. After the Supreme Court refused to hear his appeal, he was ordered to begin his sentence in Danbury on April 18, 1947—eighteen days after expiration of the Selective Service Act. In Danbury he immediately began a hunger strike for general amnesty, specifically stating: "I am not out for any personal clemency, pardon, or suspension of sentence. I do not wish to leave until the end of my sentence or until amnesty is granted." [41] By the first of June, Leonard's physical condition was reported to be "deteriorating."

While Leonard continued to fast, a unique kind of demonstration was carried out on June 22 before the White House. Under the auspices of the Committee for Amnesty, forty mourners carrying a coffin labeled "Justice" paraded back and forth. Signs carried included one which said "22 months since V-J Day—No Amnesty"; other placards called for the release of Leonard, who by this time had entered the third month of his hunger strike.[42]

As late fall moved into winter and the first anniversary of the appointment of the Amnesty Board drew near, pleas for a Christmas amnesty once more were heard. The *Christian Century*, in an editorial of December 3, made such an appeal; 545 prominent persons, including Mrs. Dorothy Canfield Fisher, Pearl Buck, Rexford Guy Tugwell, Harper Sibley, Walter Reuther, William Phillips, and Reinhold Niebuhr, in a joint petition, remarked that "It is a matter of deep disappointment to us that more than two years after the end of the war and seven months after the expiration of the Selective Training and Service Act of 1940, no amnesty has been granted conscientious objectors, Jehovah's witnesses, and other persons convicted of violating the law." Harold L. Ickes, former Secretary of the Interior and now a newspaper columnist, added his sharp voice to the refrain.[43]

When finally the long-looked-for amnesty proclamation was issued on December 23, 1947, it came as a distinct blow to most of those who had fought in the crusade. President Truman embodied in his proclamation all the conclusions of the Amnesty Board's report, which was annexed to the proclamation. What the President proclaimed was not an amnesty of all Selective Service violators (which had been the constant objective of the Committee for Amnesty), nor even of all conscientious objectors, but rather a so-called "selective amnesty" which pardoned only 1,523 of the 15,805 who had been convicted under the Selective Service Act. An additional 1,500 had already been pardoned or were eligible for pardon under the presidential proclamation of 1945.[44]

The report of the Board divided the 15,805 convicted under the Selective Service Act into two categories: (1) "wilful violators" (10,000 in number) and (2) those who had violated the law because of religious training or "other convictions." In the first category, the Board found a great many cases which indicated previous criminal records and remarked that of course these could not be considered for amnesty. Similarly, it did not touch the mental cases—those who were in institutions with every chance of remaining there for a long time, said the report, would find deprivation of civil rights no hardship. And again, there were some 1,500 who had already been pardoned or were eligible for pardon under the President's proclamation of 1945 granting amnesty to prisoners who entered the Army. Out of the remaining cases in the first category, the Board selected a few for pardon, but only an infinitesimal proportion of the 10,000.

As for the second group—the objectors—the Board concluded that in general it would recommend for pardon only those objectors who were "religious"—those, that is, who presumably qualified under Selective Service for alternative service but whose local boards had failed to grant them objector classifications. Not all "religious" objectors, however, were worthy of pardon. For example, if a man had refused to go to C.P.S. or walked out of C.P.S. for "religious" reasons, he was usually not considered for amnesty, for, said the report, he had "refused to submit to the provisions of the Selective Service Act" and was convicted for his "intentional violation of the law." As for those who were motivated in their objection by "intellectual, political, or sociological convictions," the Board did not feel itself justified in recommending pardon for them because they had "set themselves up as wiser and more competent than society to determine their duty to come to the defense of the nation." Jehovah's Witnesses the Board generally refused to pardon except in a few cases where it thought local boards had been inconsistent in refusing to grant ministerial status. In its attitude to the Witnesses, the Board generally took the position that one could not be a "minister" unless one had no other vocation; hence, for the Witnesses to claim ministerial status when most of them labored at other trades was to assume a "superiority" to the law and to society.

The President's proclamation provoked widely different reactions. Some journals of opinion seemed to approve the logic whereby the Board made distinctions between "religious" and "political" objectors and between objectors and nonobjectors. Representative of this section of public opinion was the *New York Times,* which interestingly enough had itself published amnesty editorials during the campaign.

On the other hand, civil-liberties, religious, and amnesty organizations and leaders almost without exception denounced the proclamation and report. "The report of the President's Amnesty Board," said A. J. Muste, chairman of the Committee for Amnesty, "is entirely devoid of statesmanship, justice, consistency, and vision." [45] One well-known journal commented: "There was a zealous regard for justice. . . . But there was not much mercy." [46] And Oswald Garrison Villard, the well-known journalist, speaking for the Workers Defense League, argued: "It is particularly reprehensible to deny pardons to those who refused to submit to forced labor without pay in the Civilian Public Service camps." The walk-outs, he went on, had made "a signal contribution to the cause of free labor." [47]

More systematically examined, the objections of the critics seem to have been five: [48]

(1) The distinction between "political" and "religious" objectors was criticized as arbitrary and unwarranted.

(2) The exclusion of Jehovah's Witnesses was condemned.

(3) The Board was so inconsistent that it did not even observe its own system of classification. While it argued that those who refused to accept Civilian Public Service or who walked out of camp "set themselves above the law" and hence were unworthy of pardon, it proceeded to list such men as Gordon Hirabayashi, who refused C.P.S., James Manoukian, who refused to work in C.P.S., and Bruce Miller, a "walkout," among the pardoned.

(4) The critics saw no merit in the Board's statement that it could not recommend for pardon those nonobjectors or "wilful violators"

who had had previous criminal records. After all, civil-liberties organizations contended, the problem of amnesty was concerned with
violations of the Selective Service Law; if a man at some time in the
past had committed a rape, that was a different question altogether.

(5) Finally, and perhaps most fundamental of all, the critics
argued that the Board did not understand the meaning of amnesty.
Amnesty was pardon and restoration of rights to whole groups of
offenders suffering because of a common offense. The only true
amnesty would be a collective pardon to all those who for whatever
reason had violated the Selective Service Act.

The President, nevertheless, had acted, and in such a way as to
make certain that four-fifths of all Selective-Service violators and
about five-sixths of all conscientious objectors would be deprived of
many of their civic rights and privileges, perhaps for many years.
The conscientious objectors, at least, had admittedly violated the
law because of conscience, and the effect of the President's proclamation, whether rightly or wrongly, was to penalize most of them indefinitely because they had dared appeal from the law to what Chief
Justice Hughes in a famous opinion [49] had once called the "higher
forum of conscience."

Like those who had been convicted of political offenses during
the First World War, most objectors of the Second World War might
have to wait fifteen years before any general amnesty would be extended. Until then, they could wait, and agitate, and pray.

XVIII: *Certain Absolutists*

THE story of conscientious objectors during World War II is incomplete without a treatment of what was known as "absolutism." During World War I the basic pattern and temper of absolutism had been in some degree fixed by the activities and attitudes of hunger strikers like Evan Thomas. In World War II, the pattern was adapted to the exigencies of alternative service and prison. We have already met the absolutists in C.P.S. and in penal institutions, but thus far our discussion of them has been general and incidental. Here we look at them more specifically and with different focus.

Who were the absolutists? The term is not easy to define. In general, those wearing the mantle of absolutism were objectors who at some point breached law and regulations as a matter of principle, although some who were forced to violate the law for principle did not consider themselves, and were not considered, absolutists. Those who accepted alternative service and who worked within Civilian Public Service without too much difficulty were definitely excluded from the ranks of the absolutists, as were those objectors who, because they refused Army classifications, were sentenced to prison. Likewise excluded were the overwhelming majority of Jehovah's Witnesses, whether in Civilian Public Service or in prison.

Broadly speaking, the absolutists included nonregistrants under the Selective Service Act, those who because of conscientious scruples refused to take physical examinations or report to Civilian Public Service, those who discovered after trial that they could not conscientiously accept C.P.S., and those who, reaching prison, tended to break prison regulations for conscientious reasons. Degrees of absolutism varied. A nonregistrant might go to prison cheerfully and one might not hear from him again until his discharge. On the other hand, one who registered might eventually walk out of Civilian Public Service and clash at many points with prison regulations. Yet to both the designation "absolutist" was applied.

As a system of thought and a theory of action, absolutism was in part a sincere and sometimes desperate attempt to make action square with profession—to eliminate the seemingly inevitable compromises involved in translating creed into deed. If war was wrong, then the conscription bound up with the war system was wrong and co-operation with conscription was wrong. But if co-operation with conscription was wrong, then co-operation to assist in imposing penalties for refusal to co-operate with conscription was also wrong. In the end, the absolutist who searched for consistency was driven to the hunger strike in prison and to utter passivity with respect to the satisfaction of his own physical needs. If he lifted food to his mouth in prison, he was assisting the penal system to punish him for opposing conscription and war and, indeed, was strengthening conscription and war. Thus suicide was never far away in the absolutist mentality. Yet suicide was deliberate taking of life, which was one of the acts against which all absolutists and, indeed, all objectors were presumably protesting. This was one of the problems always in the background of the absolutist temper. Absolutism pushed to extremes itself constituted a serious compromise, even when it was argued (as some contended) that refusal to co-operate in taking food placed the onus of responsibility, not on the individual involved, but rather on the system which forced him to take the action in order to preserve consistency and integrity. This is said, not in criticism of absolutism (many of the men themselves saw the issue clearly), but rather to make clear the kinds of dilemmas with which it was confronted.

Absolutism became something of a sect within the ranks of pacifists and conscientious objectors. A mimeographed sheet, *The Absolutist*, was published to aid those who were imprisoned and those who at any point challenged the system of alternative service. Some absolutists tended to look upon other conscientious objectors as less pure than themselves, while it is also true that nonabsolutist objectors frequently misunderstood the objectives and motives of the absolutists and sometimes thought of the latter as cranks and fanatics. Always a minority in the ranks of conscientious objectors, the absolutists were nevertheless one of the most important of pacifist schools; among them were some of the most extraordinary, albeit controversial, figures thrown up during the course of the whole conscription experience.

Absolutism was essentially a matter of biographies. Its heroes could not be fitted into neat categories which ignored the personal equation. Here the stories of Corbett Bishop and Don DeVault are told, not only because of their intrinsic interest but also because they are representative of the absolutist temper. Moreover, many of their experiences were not unlike those through which other conscientious objectors went.

Corbett Bishop: the Prophetic Absolutist

Bishop was probably the most dramatic of the absolutists, as well as the one about whose merits and activities men differed most widely. Born in Corinth, Mississippi, in 1906, he was educated in the public schools and at Alabama Polytechnic Institute. He studied chemical engineering and from 1931 to 1932 was a graduate fellow at the University of Wisconsin. A fellow student later reported that at Alabama Bishop was "known for his peculiar ideas," [1] but it is also evident from his scholastic career that he was a person of considerable intelligence and industry.

When he registered under the Selective Service Act, Bishop was a retail bookseller in West New York, New Jersey. According to most accounts he had an excellent collection of books and was apparently making a fair livelihood. On the form which he returned to the National Service Board for Religious Objectors, after receiving a IV-E classification, he indicated that he was a member of the Disciples Church. In reply to the question "Name of the official head of your denomination" he answered "Jesus Christ," and where the form asked for the official headquarters of his denomination, he replied "Heaven—no earthly one." [2]

He was inducted into the Patapsco, Maryland, Friends C.P.S. camp on March 19, 1942, and three months later began his first controversy with Civilian Public Service and Selective Service authorities. The occasion for the dispute was the precarious situation of his bookstore. He argued that he had not received notice of induction far enough in advance to enable him to wind up his business affairs. Hence he was in danger of foreclosure and asked Selective Service to grant him a furlough for the purpose of rescuing the store.

Selective Service declined to act on his appeal for a furlough, whereupon Bishop decided to begin his first fast on June 26. He declined to take any food and announced that the objective of his act was not only to secure a furlough for winding up his business affairs but also to protest the injustice of forcing men to work without pay and workmen's compensation. Day after day the fast dragged on, Bishop continuing to work on the camp kitchen crew for three weeks, despite increasing physical weakness. At length he was admitted to the infirmary or listed as "Sick in Quarters." Five weeks of fasting had now elapsed.

By this time Bishop was, according to the camp newspaper, a "tall, thin, bearded figure with strained features, and penetrating eyes." [3] Fellow campers, camp officials, and doctors alike were amazed at his physical endurance—the fact that he could continue a fast for five weeks and still not become bedridden.

Suddenly, on August 3, Selective Service ordered Bishop to report for work on the camp project. This he did, but it was obvious that the labor could only be nominal, and on August 7 the crew leader sent him back to camp as unfit for work. Two days later he was persuaded to end his hunger strike, which had continued forty-four days. Concluding that the time was not yet ripe for a final stand, he was taken by the camp director to a Baltimore hospital where it was hoped he would regain his health.

Upon his recovery, he was transferred to the C.P.S. camp at West Campton, New Hampshire, on August 31, 1942. He did not engage in any immediate fasting protest (although still avowing his former objectives), but rather began the practice of attacking at mealtimes the "slavery" of Civilian Public Service. Combing the Bible and other sources for appropriate quotations, he rose while other campers were eating and denounced the Selective Service System and the American Friends Service Committee for maintaining a system of payless labor. In a strong voice, he shouted out: "Futile work is blasphemy." His piercing eyes looking directly at assignees, he proclaimed: "A man had better starve than compromise for bread." Or he quoted from religious leaders like E. Stanley Jones: "Let any one be saturated with the thought of the Sermon on the Mount and he will not only not try to argue a man into slavery, but he will not rest until every man is free, including himself."

These tactics won sympathizers. Although a majority of the campers were never his ardent supporters, a strong minority associated themselves with his views. Some, indeed, held that he was largely trying to dramatize himself and to seek publicity, but these became fewer as his sincerity became more and more obvious.

On February 11, 1943, Bishop announced that he was beginning a fast in sympathy with Mahatma Gandhi, who at that time was initiating one of his own familiar campaigns. Bishop's intention was proclaimed in a letter which he addressed "To the Citizens of the World," and in which he said:

> If Mr. Gandhi's terms are met, I shall drop my fast. Otherwise, in sympathy with his fast, which is not unto death, I shall fast for twenty-one days.
>
> By this fast, I desire to contribute . . . toward securing the recognition of the independence of the peoples of India; and toward the Freedom of all those who may be restrained, interned or imprisoned because of "race, creed, color, or national origin." [4]

He sent copies of the missive to Gandhi, the King of England, Adolf Hitler, Emperor Hirohito, Mussolini, Toyohiko Kagawa, Joseph Stalin, and many others, including prominent leaders of pacifists and conscientious objectors. The letters to Hitler, Hirohito, and Mussolini were returned by the post office as "undeliverable."

By June of 1943 Bishop had reached the conclusion that a more direct onslaught on conscription, payless labor, and church and government agencies administering conscription was in order. With Myron Marks, another assignee, he issued on June 19 a statement which said:

> The American Friends Service Committee, represented by the National Service Board for Religious Objectors, is guilty, in our opinion, of conspiracy with the Selective Service System of the United States Government. It has introduced and maintained peonage and involuntary servitude for a period of more than two years through the establishment of "Labor Camps." Assignees are required to work for the United States

Government, without compensation, in violation of their constitutional and moral rights as citizens and free men.[5]

The statement went on to say that its signers had been assigned "under duress" to Civilian Public Service. They would continue to do a fair day's work under compulsion, but would protest the whole system "by a total fast (taking water only)." [6]

In the meantime, the American Friends Service Committee had been attempting to obtain the discharge of Bishop from Civilian Public Service. As early as the time of his Patapsco hunger strike, the Committee, through its Civilian Public Service officials, had had him examined by a psychiatrist, who had recommended release. But the Selective Service System had employed its own psychiatrist, who had stated that there was no ground for release.[7] It was apparently the feeling of many camp and Service Committee leaders, as well as of some assignees, that Bishop could not "adjust" to camp conditions under any circumstances.[8] Bishop's reply was, of course, to admit that he could never "adjust" to what he regarded as slavery.

He continued his fast in the summer of 1943. On June 28 he was so weak physically that he could no longer perform his tasks. Thereafter he was carried A.W.O.L. until he broke his fast on July 8. He had in the meantime been admitted to the hospital and even there was carried on the books as A.W.O.L. In breaking his fast after eighteen days, he remarked that he still felt deeply about the "injustices of conscription without compensation" and thought that the hunger strike had dramatized the plight of conscientious objectors and of the liberties which they were being denied.[9]

While the fast was at its height, the Service Committee continued to press for Bishop's release. Paul Furnas of the C.P.S. section of the Committee stated its position in a letter to Bishop:

The American Friends Service Committee has notified Selective Service that we do not wish to retain you in a camp over which we have responsibility, and we have also told them that we do not believe you should go to a government camp but should be discharged. Of course, if Selective Service decided to transfer you to a government camp, they can do so without consideration of our recommendation.[10]

In effect, then, the Committee washed its hands of him, turning him over to the secular power, for it could be fairly certain that the government would not discharge him.

Selective Service transferred him on July 7 to the government camp at Mancos, Colorado. There he again became a notable, if controversial, figure in camp life. He resumed his dinner quotations and admonitions, attacking Selective Service in no polite terms. The camp newspaper remarked: "A noisy minority invariably applauds him, and sometimes the whole dining room claps and cheers." [11]

Bishop by now had become even more vigorous in his criticisms of conscription, and when the new government camp at Germfask, Michigan, was established to care for the "troublemakers" at Mancos, he was among those transferred. He was not long at Germfask before he decided that he could no longer conscientiously remain in any kind of camp, government or church. He felt that the increasing number of walkouts from C.P.S. was due in part to his agitation and that he would be less than honest if he were to fail to make a "complete break" himself.

Hence, in August, 1944, he took a furlough on days which he had accumulated, fully resolving at the time that he would not return to Germfask. He spent his time visiting various C.P.S. units and stopped off in Washington itself, where he lectured the National Service Board for the nefarious system it was administering. His furlough expiring, he continued to broadcast his views, stating openly that he regarded his self-appointed task of agitation against conscription as of far greater importance than anything he could do in Civilian Public Service.

There was no doubt that he had definitely broken the law now. When on September 9 he was arrested, he announced that his spirit was free and that if the arresting officers desired his body, they would have to take it without any resistance on his part. Transferred to the Milan, Michigan, federal prison to await trial, he refused to eat, stand up, or dress himself. The slightest degree of "servility" or seeming acquiescence in his captivity would, he maintained, compromise his case.

He continued to maintain this adamant stand, and by the latter part of October officials were beginning to feed him forcibly. A tiny tube was pushed up his nose and through the tube nourishment was forced—hardly a pleasant process for the patient. The gaunt and bearded 160-pound figure of C.P.S. days was by the end of November a pencillike form who had lost a quarter of his weight. [12]

On December 6, after eighty-six days of non-co-operation, he was brought to trial in Grand Rapids, Michigan, on a "walkout" charge. He did not deny that he had "deserted" camp, but pleaded that the whole system of alternative service was unconstitutional. Judge Fred M. Raymond promised to take the plea under advisement and told Bishop that he was at liberty without bond until some decision could be reached.[13]

Thus Bishop was once more free to travel and carry on his propaganda. He appeared before Fellowship of Reconciliation and other religious groups, spreading the message of absolutism and resistance to conscription. When January 17, 1945, arrived—the day on which he was to have reappeared in Michigan for sentencing—he made no move to return, and when on January 25 he was again asked to show up in court he reiterated his refusal.[14]

On February 20, three FBI agents appeared at the rooming house where Bishop was staying in Philadelphia and announced that they had been instructed to arrest him.

"Okay, let's go," one of the agents is reported to have said.

The angular Bishop remained immobile. Then: "I am," he said, "offering passive resistance."

After a brief pause, the agents seized him, dragged him from the house, and deposited him in their waiting car. They drove him to the Philadelphia Federal Court House. Because he continued his passive resistance, they had to carry his limp form into the building, deposit it in the elevator, and carry it into the hearing room of the United States Commissioner.

The Commissioner was reading off the names of other defendants and asking them to respond "Present" to their names. There was no difficulty until Bishop's name was called. When the Commissioner said "Bishop" there was at first no response. Then, from the six-foot figure:

"I am here—in body only."

The Commissioner replied:

"I can understand that any one might have scruples against war. But why make it hard for yourself and everyone else?"

Immediately Bishop answered:

"I can maintain my stand. I am not going to co-operate in any way, shape or form. I was carried in here. If you hold me, you'll have to carry me out. War is wrong. I don't want any part of it."

At this point an assistant district attorney interjected:

"Then why did you remain in the conscientious objectors' camp two years before you left, if you felt that way?"

"I suddenly woke up," Bishop answered, "and I felt just like an American soldier would who fell asleep only to wake up in the German Army."

Bail was fixed at fifteen hundred dollars. He announced that he was continuing his passive resistance and no-eating campaign. Thereupon deputy marshals pushed him in his chair, which was equipped with casters, out into the corridors. The casters hit an obstacle in the corridor and Bishop was thrown to the floor. There he remained inert, refusing to move an inch. Finally curious spectators lifted him back into the chair, in which he was then rolled to the marshal's cell room.

Philadelphia police arrived and, because Bishop continued his nonviolent resistance, were forced to carry his limp frame out into the street. There the little party was confronted by a noontime crowd, eager, naturally, to learn what was going on. One of the women in the crowd shouted out: "Somebody was shot. That's him."

"This guy ain't dead," came the reply from a policeman. "And he ain't hurt. He just refuses to go into the Army."

"Serves him right," several women answered.

At Moyamensing prison, where he was taken, Bishop continued his passive resistance.[15] When it became quite evident to prison officials that he would not eat under any circumstances, forced feeding was resorted to.

On February 26 he was arraigned before Federal Judge George A. Welsh in Philadelphia. Again his limp body had to be carried into the courtroom and he sat with eyes closed during the proceedings. When the judge asked whether he opposed his removal to Michigan for trial, he opened his eyes and replied: "What you do with me is your own responsibility." [16]

Before he was returned to Michigan, several conscientious objectors visited him in his Philadelphia prison. To them, he explained his actions: "The basis for my stand is expressed pretty well in the Bible—'And be not conformed to this world, but be ye transformed by the renewing of your mind, that ye may prove what is that good, and acceptable, and perfect will of God.'" [17]

On March 15 he was returned to Grand Rapids, still maintaining his passive resistance and still being forcibly fed. He was sentenced to four years in prison and fined one thousand dollars. Returned to prison as a sentenced offender, he continued his strike and complete non-co-operation, and the prison officials in turn persisted in their tube feeding. It was evident, however, that he was not gaining in strength—indeed, that he was probably becoming weaker. There were even those who thought he would not survive very long.

Perhaps this fear for his life was a leading factor in inducing federal officials to grant a parole on July 13. Technically, he was paroled under the Special Parole Plan of Executive Order 8641,[18] the parole condition being that he work on the Morris Mitchell co-operative farm in Macedonia, Georgia. Actually, however, Bishop signed no papers, made no promises, and regarded himself as absolutely free. Upon release, he brought to an end his passive resistance, which had lasted for the almost incredible period of 144 days. During that time he had done nothing to assist prison officials, even to the extent of walking or rising from his cot. It is true that he had received some nourishment through tube feeding, but it was wholly inadequate for health.[19]

Since he had signed no papers and made no promises, Bishop felt under no obligation to remain in Georgia. In August he made a trip to New York, and FBI agents began to search for him as a parole violator. Two of them discovered him on August 30 in front of the 24th Street Co-operative House in New York City. They questioned him about his activities—he had, of course, been attending pacifist meetings and conferring with pacifist leaders—and then departed. Soon afterwards the redoubtable absolutist himself left.

On September 1, eight FBI men appeared before the home of Ashton Jones—another absolutist leader—in Berea, Ohio. There they discovered Bishop and put the usual question as to whether he was ready to come along with them. He gave what by now was the expected reply—that he would never co-operate in any way with the government's restraint of his body. Hearing this, the agents picked up his suddenly limp body and carried him off in an automobile. He was taken once more to the Milan prison.[20]

The old story was now repeated. Technically in prison again to serve out the remainder of his four-year term, he considered his arrest the signal for resumption of his fasting and non-co-operation.

Once more the authorities seemed to be at a loss as to how he should be treated. They fed him forcibly, of course, but again he offered no assistance and again he lost weight. His case was given considerable publicity in the press, which added, no doubt, to the difficulties of the prison administrators. Then, too, Japan had already surrendered, the war was over, and to those who protested his continued incarceration his imprisonment seemed to be a needless and futile gesture.

The Department of Justice evidently came to the same conclusion, for on March 12, 1946, he was released on parole to his home in Hamilton, Alabama. This ended 193 days of continuous and complete non-co-operation. There were no conditions attached to the parole and again Bishop signed no promises.[21] He was not arrested thereafter.

Thus a remarkable career of individual passive resistance was brought to an end. Altogether, Bishop had fasted 426 days since entering prison. He had regarded himself as a prophet whose role it was to denounce all forms of conscription, and while he had not convinced a majority of objectors that his was the most efficacious method of achieving the end, yet by the time of his final release he had made a deep impression on many.

The Bishop who was finally released from prison was not the personality of C.P.S. days. Gone were the sometimes harsh tones of the West Campton period. The new Bishop, as many of those who visited him testified, was no longer intolerant of those who differed with him. Somehow his experiences had made him a gentle soul. While some continued to think of him as a "psychopathic" personality, many more agreed with the estimate of James Mullin, who was himself intimately acquainted with both Civilian Public Service and prison experiences of conscientious objectors:

He has followed, to its logical conclusion, the proposition that man should not, in any way, cooperate with the State in the waging of war, and that persons who by reason of religious training and belief are opposed thereto should not be imprisoned therefor. . . . What appeals to me most of all is the rare ability which he had developed to endure the consequences of his actions without bearing any ill will and without manifesting any belligerency toward anyone.[22]

Don DeVault: Vocational Absolutist

DeVault became the symbol of all those who regarded their vocation as of prime significance and who therefore based whatever degrees of absolutism they developed on their call to labor at a particular task. If the "system" refused to permit the practice of their vocation, they ignored the system.

DeVault was a young chemist who down to 1942 was deferred by his Selective Service Board for teaching and research activities. In that year, however, his local board declined to continue his deferment. He asked for IV-E but was granted only I-A-O. Refusing induction, he was sentenced to one and one-half years in prison, where he was assigned to work on the prison farm.

In December, 1943, he was paroled to the government camp at Mancos. There, as was true of so many, he was assigned to work which had no connection with his professional interests. A Ph.D. and already at the age of twenty-six the author of several scientific articles, with an intensive interest in penicillin research, DeVault spent his days in Mancos digging ditches and clearing the ground of rocks. After a full day of physical work he and another C.P.S. parolee began chemical experimentation at night. Friends outside C.P.S. sent them laboratory equipment, others in camp assisted in the construction of apparatus near their bunks, and progress in penicillin investigation proceeded despite all the handicaps imposed by the rigidities and stupidities of camp life.

Although they did all the camp work required of them—long, grueling hours of it—their insistence on laboring during the night hours on their own research subjected them to all kinds of annoyances. The camp director, Charles E. Thomas, would sometimes order all the lights turned out if he thought the scientists were working "too late." He would direct transfer of their equipment from one place to another, which would naturally impede their investigations. In the end, he ordered DeVault to the government camp in Germfask, Michigan, thus bringing to a conclusion the fruitful Mancos co-operation.

At Germfask, Dr. DeVault found similar conditions. Other C.P.S. men were willing to help, but at no point was he encouraged by C.P.S. administration. He managed to get an old player piano and from its bellows constructed a device for stirring the mold cultures so essential for penicillin research. He preserved his specimens in a hole in the ground. His "wages" of $5.00 a month he devoted to the purchase of the essential chemicals, and he spent not only his nights but also his furlough periods on his research.

His officially assigned labor was to assist in the digging of duck ponds, the general work of the camp being devoted to the development of a game refuge. DeVault finally reached the conclusion that he must either find a laboratory within the C.P.S. system where he could do full-time research or break with the system itself. He wrote to the parole authorities in the Department of Justice:

There is much that I would at least like to try to do, but instead, I am forced to spend 51 hours a week doing jobs in which I have no interest. . . . The best that I have been able to do so far is to seize all the spare moments that I can to carry on feeble projects with crude equipment. . . . My case is not different from thousands of others in CPS. . . . It is not that we object to making sacrifices, because we do not. It is the uselessness of the particular sacrifices that the authorities designate for us.

The replies of parole authorities and Selective Service were negative and DeVault thereupon repudiated the "system." He refused to report for work projects, laboring instead on his penicillin research. This continued for a month, when he was arrested and sentenced to three and one-half years in prison. Sent to the Springfield federal prison, he was finally assigned to chemical work he could accept and thus began co-operation, on his own terms, with the prison system. He was released from federal prison in 1946, long after the conclusion of the war.[23]

DeVault's position illustrates that of many others who found their vocational interests impeded by Civilian Public Service and prison alike. Instructed to do a particular type of work under restrictive conditions, many of them rebelled inwardly and others, like DeVault, gave their revolt an external form as well. Something within their personalities was injured, argued the absolutists—and violently injured—when they, trained chemists, were ordered to pick up rocks all day; or, expert teachers, were forced on pain of prison to plant trees; or, skilled mathematicians, were compelled to dig ditches. It is true that the personalities of countless thousands in Army and

Navy were likewise violated, but the fact that the offense was wide-spread, contended the absolutists, did not make it right or justify it.

Murphy and Taylor: Absolutist Cause Célèbre

The affair of Stanley Murphy and Louis Taylor became the center of one of the most controversial phases of conscientious objection during the war. Objectors were divided regarding the merits of the men involved and the tactics which they pursued; and the affair was complicated by charges directed against the Director of Prisons himself.

Stanley Murphy and Louis Taylor walked out of the C.P.S. camp at Big Flats, New York, on the second anniversary of the Selective Service Act—October 16, 1942. They had been highly respected by their fellow campers, and the project superintendent (a "government" man, of course) had remarked: "I don't agree with them, but my hat's off to those fellows." [24] Both men left camp because they felt they could no longer do under compulsion work that seemed insignificant.

On February 12, 1943, they began serving a sentence of two and a half years in Danbury Federal Correctional Institution. On the same day began their "fast unto death" against the conscription system. It is thus clear that their non-co-operation in prison was merely a continuation of the act which brought them to prison in the first place. Tube-fed for the first time on the seventeenth day, their fast continued for 82 days, when it was broken on the understanding that Selective Service would liberalize paroles and provide more significant work. According to the Bureau of Prisons, both Murphy and Taylor promised early in June to accept parole to charitable institutions in return for maintenance and $2.50 a month. The men, however, alleged that they had been misinformed of the conditions, and when they were asked to approve arrangements under these terms, they both declined to do so, on the ground that the service would constitute a form of slavery. It is probable that there was a misunderstanding on both sides as to the precise nature of the terms which were originally offered. At any rate, Selective Service refused to modify the terms to suit the men.

The Bureau of Prisons now ordered Murphy and Taylor transferred from Danbury to the Prison Medical Center in Springfield,

Missouri (where psychoneurotics and psychotics, as well as other unusual cases, were often sent). Explaining the transfer as a necessity in view of the physical condition of the men after their prolonged fast, the Bureau also noted that they remained "defiant" and that facilities for their care would be better at Springfield. It was emphatically denied that Murphy and Taylor were being sent to Springfield, as some had suggested, because they had been pronounced "psychotic" (insane).[25]

In the meantime, rumors began to circulate that there were "padded" cells in Springfield, in which at least one conscientious objector, after being stripped of all clothing, had been confined. "Strip" or "padded" cells were supposed to be free of all furniture and to have only a hole in the floor for a toilet. These rumors were immediately denied by Director of Prisons James V. Bennett. "There may be no fear that these boys, Murphy and Taylor, will be placed in a padded cell," he said, "because there are no padded cells in Springfield." [26] A little later the assistant to Mr. Bennett also denied explicitly that there was "solitary confinement" at Springfield, as that term is generally used in prisons.[27]

On entering the Medical Center, Murphy and Taylor announced that they did not regard themselves as bound by the rules of the prison. While they did not enter upon a new hunger strike, they did refuse to work.

Murphy's mother, meanwhile, had journeyed to Springfield and began to send back alarming reports which repeated the charges about "strip" cells, into which men were thrown, unclothed, and sometimes beaten.[28] On July 31 Mrs. Murphy telegraphed a pacifist leader that her son was confined to a "strip" cell and that Louis Taylor was housed in the "insane" ward.[29]

Agitation and concern among conscientious objectors and their friends now increased to such a degree that on August 3 Director Bennett issued a statement completely reversing his former assertions. "Strip" cells, he admitted, did exist in Springfield, and for a short time the Springfield authorities had confined Murphy and Taylor in them, "believing this to be the best method of therapy." [30] Bennett went on to say, however, that Murphy and Taylor had requested such treatment in order to gain publicity.[31] The second part of Bennett's explanation thus seemed to contradict the first. A few days later, the unusual "request" of the objectors to be placed in padded cells was explained by Bennett's assistant. Murphy and Taylor, he said, had announced their refusal to work and after being asked if they knew what such refusal would mean, they had replied in the affirmative. Thus the "request" of the objectors had been merely inferred, in this indirect way, by the prison authorities! [32]

Pressure by civil liberties groups and conscientious objectors now led Director Bennett to appoint an investigating commission, consisting of Austin H. MacCormick, a well-known expert on prisons, Charles W. Palmer, of the American Friends Service Committee, and Dr. M. R. King, Medical Director of the Bureau of Prisons. The commission was asked to inquire into the treatment of Murphy and Taylor as well as their charges that other prisoners were being abused.

In their reports the investigators were somewhat divided. Dr. King found that psychiatrists at Springfield had decided to keep Murphy and Taylor segregated from others "under psychiatric observation." While there was no major mental illness, the doctor thought that there was "suggestive evidence of minor mental disability." Dr. King suggested that their confinement in "strip" cells was a mistake "since such action appears to have been unnecessary and therefore can be interpreted as a form of punishment." But he thought that allegations about beatings were false and misleading.[33]

Charles Palmer's report generally agreed with that of Dr. King and by many pacifists was looked upon as a "whitewash" which ignored relevant facts. Subsequent developments were to show that the critics of Palmer were partly right in this evaluation.[34]

Austin MacCormick's comments were severely critical of the Springfield administration. Without questioning the good intentions of higher administrators, he did think that several errors of judgment had been made by subordinate personnel. Neither Murphy nor Taylor should have been placed in strip cells, he maintained, as that tended to "stiffen their resistance." Use of such cells was "sound medical procedure" for persons who might damage themselves, but at Springfield "had gradually deteriorated into an unsound punitive procedure." As for the charges of beatings, MacCormick concluded that he was "inclined to believe their [Murphy and Taylor's] statements." [35]

Whether as a result of the investigation or not, the warden at Springfield (Dr. Cox) was later removed and a new warden (Dr. Pescor) installed. The treatment of Murphy and Taylor apparently improved greatly.

In one form or another, however, the Murphy-Taylor affair remained before the public until the summer of 1945, when the principals were released on the expiration of their terms. It is impossible to detail here all the incidents that developed. Charges of kickings and beatings of inmates continued to be made by both Murphy and Taylor and were given wide publicity in the New York *World-Telegram* on February 9, 1944. Documents smuggled out of the prison alleged, among other things, severe beating of a Negro prisoner, James White, who died a few days after the asserted mistreatment; withholding of food from some prisoners as a method of punishment; and torture of a Jehovah's Witness by burning his ears with a lighted cigarette.[36]

These charges impressed Norman Thomas, the Socialist leader, and he requested Attorney General Francis Biddle to initiate another investigation.[37] This the Attorney General did, naming as the investigators Director Bennett; Dr. Lawrence Kolb, Medical Director of the Bureau of Prisons; Federal Judge George H. Moore; Julius Klein, of the St. Louis *Star-Times;* and John R. Bell, of the St. Louis *Post-Dispatch.*

After conversations with inmates and guards at Springfield, Bennett, Moore, Kolb, and Bell thought that, on the whole, charges of brutality had not been substantiated, although they admitted that there were undoubtedly some cases of mistreatment. The testimony of inmate witnesses was often contradictory, they pointed out, due partly to the fact that many were psychotics or psychopaths.[38] Where more force than necessary had been used on difficult inmates, it could be attributed to the inexperience of attendants—guards and nurses who had replaced regular employees taken by Selective Service for the war effort.[39]

Julius Klein was much more critical. He thought the charges of brutality sufficiently grave and well enough supported, even though sometimes with contradictions, to warrant a long, thorough, formal investigation, where witnesses could be placed under oath. Moreover, he called attention to the fact that twenty-five inmates "had testified to personal knowledge of brutal treatment of themselves or other inmates. . . ." He was particularly impressed by the statements of the Catholic and Protestant chaplains and of Dr. Hulsey Cason, psychophysiological investigator at the institution, who believed that there had been brutality.[40]

Several prominent pacifists were inclined to agree with the conclusions of Klein and to question those of the other investigators, especially with respect to the necessity for further investigation. Thus, Evan Thomas, Chairman of the War Resisters League, argued that the report summarizing the majority views "glosses over the overwhelming weight of supporting testimony of a prison psychologist, the Catholic and Protestant chaplains, and twenty-three inmates, which establishes that these charges were well-founded." [41] Nevertheless, no further investigation was held.

When all the charges and countercharges in the Murphy-Taylor affair are weighed and exaggerations taken into account, it would seem evident that both Murphy and Taylor suffered physical mistreatment at the hands of prison attendants; that the central prison administration itself was amazingly ignorant, at first, of conditions obtaining at Springfield; and that Murphy and Taylor were responsible for making the Bureau of Prisons and the general public aware of some "mishandling" of prisoners. True, the violence revealed was contrary to the general instructions issued by Director Bennett and by the warden at Springfield. But the fact that the Bureau of Prisons at first denied the use of the strip cell and then made a complete about-face, as well as the fact that so reputable a criminologist as Austin MacCormick believed that unnecessary force had been used, did not speak too favorably of the honesty or administrative capacity of the staff of the Bureau of Prisons. In dramatizing these facts, many pacifists argued, Murphy and Taylor rendered the same kind of service to the community as those objectors who, with different tactics, exposed the conditions surrounding treatment of patients in mental hospitals.

Absolutism: Negation or Construction

This is not the place to enter into a long theoretical treatment and evaluation of absolutism, but a few concluding observations seem to be in order. Running through the whole phenomenon like a golden thread was the influence of Mohandas Gandhi: an influence evident not only in the theoretical justifications of "direct action" which the absolutists developed but also in the personal lives of the absolutists themselves. Thus Corbett Bishop, who began his C.P.S. career as a rather self-righteous and sometimes arrogant protester, came in the end to resemble in many of his qualities the Hindu mystic and politician. This is not to say that Bishop's later attributes were due wholly to his increasingly great admiration for Gandhi—his own experiences in C.P.S. and prison were undoubtedly important—but it does seem reasonable to assume that there was some connection.

One critic has commented privately that the absolutists dramatized "nothing but the stupidity of the government." That they undoubtedly did, in the sense that they revealed and pointed up an amazing lack of imagination and cleverness on the part of government officials. But surely the stories of Bishop, DeVault, and others represented something more. They emphasized the gullibility and lack of understanding of some church officials, the presence of considerable courage among the absolutists themselves, and, by contrast, the tendency of the overwhelming mass of conscientious objectors to adopt patterns of conformity within the scheme of forced labor. On the whole, conscientious objectors were neither "saints," as the "service" concept of objection would have them be, nor vigorous nonconformists, as the absolutists became.

Finally, a word should be said regarding the frequent criticism that absolutism was purely "negative" rather than "constructive" in nature. The absolutists, of course, denied that their actions were mere negations. To them, an act of resistance in certain contexts was as constructive a service as helping the mentally sick. To call the attention of the public to abuse of disciplinary power at Springfield was more constructive than much of the relatively useless work carried on in C.P.S. And the lives of many of the absolutists seemed to show that their dramatic acts of resistance during the war were not ends in themselves. DeVault abandoned his resistance, even within the prison system, when given work compatible with his vocation (after having vainly sought it in C.P.S.); and Bishop, once free, worked first on a co-operative farm and then began what he regarded as his real life work—preaching the necessity for spiritual regeneration and pacifism. The very intensity of belief which led absolutists to resist in the first place caused many of them later to engage in vocations requiring a high degree of devotion and offering but relatively little remuneration.

XIX: The Law of
Conscientious Objection

The legal framework within which the conscientious objector acted was built up slowly and with many seeming contradictions. Ambiguous at some points and all too clear at others, the law of conscientious objection was the occasion for much agitation on the part of objector and civil-liberties groups and the excuse for several long and weighty opinions by the higher courts. The law did not remain the same in all respects during the course of the war; while in some respects it seemed to whittle away at what many thought were the legitimate rights of objectors, in others it extended them beyond previously recognized limitations. While some objector groups appeared to think of the law as being always against the claimed rights of objectors, a candid and careful survey of its development would seem to show that it had no such consistency. Like law in general, it grew in response to particular problems raised at given moments; and the frequent initial confusion with respect to the law of conscientious objection was probably no greater than the beginning stages of any branch of the law. After all, the problems to be considered were occasionally unique; and the absence of clear precedents in some instances provided opportunity for judges and administrators to break new ground.

The law of conscientious objection divides itself quite naturally into two parts: first, a consideration of the legal structure built up to define the position of the conscripted conscientious objector, and, second, the effect of the status of conscientious objector on the rights of objectors in ordinary civil society. In the first division the law had to do mainly with the position of the conscientious objector vis-à-vis the Selective Training and Service Act; the second aspect chiefly answered questions raised about the vocational rights of objectors not in the Army, C.P.S., or prison.

The Conscripted Conscientious Objector

LEGAL MEANING OF REGISTRATION

Down through the point of registration under the Selective Training and Service Act, the legal status of an objector differed in no wise from that of the nonobjector. Both objector and nonobjector were required to register, and the act of registration was regarded by many authorities as separable from the conscriptive features of the law. However much nonregistrants and others may have seen the processes of registration and conscription as inseparable, there was strong legal authority for holding that the act of registration in itself was merely to provide information; it was analogous to the power of Congress to obtain information for legislative purposes through questionnaires and the summoning of witnesses before legislative committees.[1] Under this theory, then, one who refused to register was not protesting against war and conscription but was merely attacking the power of Congress to elicit information. Military and civilian conscription might or might not be unconstitutional; but, said the courts, one could not doubt the constitutionality of compulsory registration.

CONSTITUTIONALITY OF WARTIME AND PEACETIME
MILITARY CONSCRIPTION

Wartime Conscription for Military Service. If registration was separable from the conscriptive process, what about conscription itself? The power of Congress to conscript in wartime for military service had been sustained during the First World War by the United States Supreme Court.[2] Then the Court had denied that conscription in wartime for military service was an involuntary servitude under the Thirteenth Amendment or that it violated the due-process clause of the Fifth Amendment. The power of Congress (under Article I of the Constitution) to raise armies and navies was plenary: there were no constitutional implications that armies and navies had to be raised only by voluntary methods. Congress was at liberty, said the court, to use any methods it chose.

In important cases between the wars, the Court had reaffirmed this principle, adding that the duty of citizens to defend the government against all enemies whenever necessity arises is "a fundamental principle of the Constitution." [3]

During the Second World War, this power of Congress to conscript in wartime was reaffirmed by all the courts. And novel doctrines urging the unconstitutionality of wartime conscription were stricken down without long consideration.

Peacetime Conscription for Military Service. But to argue that Congress had the power to conscript for military service in time of war did not deal specifically with the problem of its authority in time of peace. It was argued that the power to conscript, aside from limited militia duty, came into effect, if at all, during a period of actual war; until war was declared, Congress was limited to voluntary methods for raising armies and navies. This issue assumed major importance because for more than a year—from the passage of the Selective Training and Service Act until Pearl Harbor—Congress asserted the power to conscript in time of peace. The argument against the constitutionality of peacetime conscription was urged effectively months before Pearl Harbor by five conscientious objectors who contended that the act of registration was inseparable from the power to conscript and that the latter power was beyond the Constitution in time of peace. The court, however, was not willing to sustain their very plausible argument.[4] It replied that, although there might be no formal war, the emergency was only less serious than war; that to prevent war or to be prepared for war if it should arrive might require the use of conscription before any formal declaration; and that the power to raise armies and navies was sufficiently broad to justify its use in peacetime emergencies, when war was possible, as well as in a period of actual war. And the court took account of the fact that in the modern age it is often difficult, if not impossible, to say precisely just when a war begins.

Despite what seemed to be the decisive opinion of the Circuit Court of Appeals, some conscientious objectors and lawyers continued to urge the unconstitutionality of peacetime conscription, especially in view of the imminence of peacetime conscription follow-ing the Second World War.[5] The Supreme Court was never called upon to answer the question directly.

JUDICIAL REVIEW OF CLASSIFICATIONS

On the level of administrative law, the leading problem involving conscientious objectors became the question of judicial review of Selective Service Board decisions. The issue hinged on answers to two questions: "What should the scope be of judicial review of Board classifications?" and "At what point in the administrative process could review take place?" Generally speaking, organizations in-terested in defining liberally the rights of conscientious objectors were dissatisfied with the answers which tribunals gave to both questions. Eventually, after hostilities had ceased, the Supreme Court came around to the position for which conscientious-objector lawyers had argued during the war.

Under the Selective Service Act decisions of local boards with re-spect to classification were to be final "except where an appeal is authorized in accordance with such rules and regulations as the President may prescribe." [6] On the face of it, then, the Act seemed to say that, once the objector had utilized the administrative appel-late system described elsewhere (see Chapter IV), his classification was final and could not be challenged by any other authority. There was no express statutory provision for appeal to the courts once ad-ministrative appeals had been taken.

Nevertheless, legal counsel for objectors argued from the be-ginning that the absence of specific statutory authorization did not mean that the courts could not review the orders of Selective Service agencies. Basing his argument on what he thought were analogous cases in other areas of the law, one objector argued that the scope of judicial review extended to all board decisions which abridged due process, were made without a fair hearing, were unsupported by evidence, were arbitrary or capricious, or violated law.[7]

Generally speaking, the courts agreed that, at some stage of the administrative-judicial process, review on these grounds was possible. The courts could not retry a classification issue, remarked Judge John J. Parker, but could declare null and void any classification order which was "found to lack foundation in law, or to be unsupported by substantial evidence, or to be so arbitrary and unreasonable as to amount to a denial of due process." [8] And this provision for judicial review was imperative, despite absence of any statutory authorization, because American constitutional and legal theory had always recognized the power of the courts to pass on jurisdictional and due-process questions.

The courts did differ, however, throughout most of the war period, as to how much evidence was necessary to support a classification. There seem to have been three theories developed in connection with Selective Service Board cases.[9] One, the least liberal from the viewpoint of the Selective Service System and most liberal from that of the objector, held that there must be "substantial evidence" in the board record before judicial pronouncement against the validity of the order would be barred.[10] Another view—far more lenient from the standpoint of the Selective Service System—thought that any evidence at all was sufficient to sustain a local board's findings.[11] Yet a third view held that the court need merely inquire whether the board had considered all the evidence presented to it, without regard to what its final conclusions might be.[12] The United States Supreme Court clearly gave its own view after hostilities had ceased. It accepted the second conception, hence providing for a relatively narrow range of inquiry by the courts.[13] Thus the final pronouncement by the Supreme Court would seem to have left Selective Service boards somewhat freer from judicial control with respect to scope of judicial review than administrative authorities in certain other areas.

Point and Procedures of Review. But the most ticklish question with respect to judicial review had to do with the point in the administrative-judicial process at which such review could take place and the procedures through which the objector would have to go to obtain the review. Here the predominant judicial opinion down to the end of hostilities was that no objector could plead the illegality of a board order as a defense in court for violating the order.[14]

The courts enunciated the doctrine that while in general an objector could not plead the illegality of an order when defending himself against a prosecution for violation of that order, the objector could, by obeying the order to report to the Army (or C.P.S.), put himself in a position where he could then ask for release on a writ of habeas corpus. At that time he could raise such issues as illegal classification, arbitrary action, lack of due process, and disregard of evidence. Review of a board's action, according to this doctrine, could come only when the objector, by completing the "administrative process," had obeyed the order of the local board. Since there was no provision in the Act for review at an earlier stage of the process, the nature of the Act and the context in which it was passed had to act as guides to the courts when they were called upon to decide the point at which judicial review would accord with the spirit of the law. The law was passed to raise armies, the courts argued; and the purpose of the statute would be thwarted if the courts should allow judicial review at any point where an administrative order had been disobeyed. The objector must first obey the questioned order, even if it took him into the Army or C.P.S. against his conscience; after that, habeas corpus might effect his release, and at that time he could attempt to show the illegality of the board's decree.[15]

Obviously, this legal doctrine was unsatisfactory to objectors, for it meant that their only alternatives seemed to be to report to the Army (or C.P.S.) against their consciences or to go to jail without having the right to challenge a board's order on the way. Even if the objectors could swallow their consciences by reporting to the Army, the difficulties of obtaining a sympathetic hearing in a habeas-corpus case remained: they might be far from home, family, friends, and legal counsel, and the hearing would take place not in the home judicial area but in the district where the military camp was located. This legal theory was particularly onerous with respect to Jehovah's Witnesses, whose cases involving classification as ministers were crowding the courts. (See Chapter XV.)

It was difficult to get the Supreme Court to pronounce on the issue. In one case, it neatly side-stepped the matter.[16] In the early part of 1944, however, the court sustained, in the Falbo case,[17] the predominant opinion of the lower courts. The doctrine set forth in the Falbo opinion confirmed and restated circuit court rulings and became the leading case on the subject down to the end of hostilities.

But Justice Frank Murphy wrote a strong dissenting opinion in the Falbo case. He contended that nothing in the statute or in the context of its passage through Congress warranted the conviction of any

objector "without benefit of full hearing." As for depriving the Army
of recruits and impeding the administrative process—both of which
the government said would follow on acceptance of judicial review
prior to induction—Murphy observed:

In the rare case where the accused person can prove the arbitrary and
illegal nature of the administrative action, the induction order should never
have been issued and the armed forces are deprived of no one who should
have been inducted. And where the defendant is unable to prove such a
defense . . . the prison rather than the army or navy is the recipient of
his presence.

But however sound such reasoning might seem to objectors and their
friends, the court had adopted the contrary position.

The courts were next called upon to decide in more precise terms
just where the "administrative process" was completed. Did the end
come when one had reported to the Army? Or must one actually be
inducted into and become a part of the Army? In either event many
tender consciences would rebel, more perhaps if the latter were to
be the final ruling.

A case raising the issue eventually reached the Supreme Court.
Arthur Billings had registered with his local board in Kansas. In
January, 1942, he was placed in I-A despite his claim of conscientious
objection. The classification was confirmed by the appellate board.
Billings decided to obey the order to report, but when he arrived
at Fort Leavenworth he announced that he would not take the oath,
submit to fingerprinting, or regard himself as in any sense a part of
the Army. The Army, however, looked upon him in every way as a
part of the military forces and proceeded to bring charges against
him under military law.

In the meantime, he had petitioned for a writ of habeas corpus.
He raised the question of jurisdiction and alleged that if he had violated the law he was subject to civil and not to military jurisdiction.
This plea was denied by the District Court and by the Circuit Court
of Appeals. The Supreme Court reversed the lower tribunals, however, deciding that submission to the ceremony of induction was a
prerequisite for induction and that until such submission took place
the offender had not been inducted into the Army and, hence, was
subject to civil rather than military law. To decide otherwise, said

Justice Douglas, would be to say that the objector must report to the military to exhaust his administrative remedies "and then say that if he does so report he may be forcibly inducted against his will. That would indeed make a trap of the Falbo case. . . ." [18] The Billings opinion seemed to make more clear what was meant by completion of the administrative process and satisfied many who had feared that the Falbo statement meant that, to secure court review of administrative decisions, one had to submit to Army induction.

But while the "end of the administrative process" was thus seemingly determined, the courts apparently still held that the Falbo doctrine excluded as a defense in criminal trials an alleged illegal or arbitrary classification. Only on hearing for a writ of habeas corpus apparently, could such issues be raised. Even after an exhaustion of administrative remedies, questions of illegal classification could not be raised at a criminal trial.

It therefore came as something of a surprise when the Court, in the Estep and Smith cases decided in 1946, denied that a habeas-corpus proceeding was the only way in which a review of board decisions could come about. The Court finally stated clearly that review *was* available at the stage of criminal prosecution. Both Estep and Smith had been convicted of refusing to submit to induction into the armed forces. The Supreme Court agreed that they had come to the end of the "administrative process" in reporting for service while declining to be inducted. Hence the question was whether the trial court should have admitted evidence that the local board had acted arbitrarily in giving the two Jehovah's Witnesses I-A classifications rather than IV-D's, for which they had pleaded. Justice Douglas, speaking for the Court, decided that the evidence should have been admitted:

We cannot believe that Congress intended that criminal sanctions were to be applied to orders issued by local boards no matter how flagrantly they violated the rules and regulations which define their jurisdiction. . . . We are loath to believe that Congress reduced criminal trials under the Act to proceedings so barren of the customary safeguards which the law has designed for the protection of the accused.[19]

Justice Murphy in a concurring opinion went even further. He argued eloquently that a habeas-corpus proceeding was never an adequate remedy; in many cases it was "illusory." The objector seeking a writ would find himself among strangers and there was little assurance "that the military will treat his efforts to obtain the writ with sympathetic understanding."

Justice Frankfurter concurred in the result of the Estep and Smith cases, but only because he felt that appeals from the local board had been denied to Estep; Smith, he felt, had labored under the handicap of a trial court's ambiguous charge to the jury. He could not agree with the majority opinion, which he felt was against all the major precedents established during the war. Forty judges, protested Frankfurter, had during the war repudiated the majority opinion which now became the law's definitive interpretation. Both Frankfurter and the justices who dissented completely—Burton and Chief Justice Stone—thought that the doctrine of the majority would provide too large a scope for "litigious interruption" of the Selective Service process, would impede the waging of the war, and was clearly against the intent of Congress.

The Estep and Smith cases had involved objectors who had been ordered to report to the Army. In the Dodez and Gibson cases, the court was called upon to answer similar questions with respect to objectors instructed to report to C.P.S.[20] Gibson had walked out of Civilian Public Service after five days in camp and during his trial had asserted the right to claim arbitrary classification as a defense. The Supreme Court sustained his claim by analogy with the Estep and Smith opinion. Dodez had not even reported to camp, yet it was ruled that he had completed the administrative process and could utilize any defense open to Gibson. This reversed the opinion of the trial court, which, using the Falbo case as a guide, had ruled that the only question before the jury was whether Dodez had in fact reported to camp.

Thus, after much travail and soul-searching, the Supreme Court finally developed a doctrine of judicial review similar to that for which conscientious-objector lawyers had been pleading from the beginning of the war. But the court reached this position more than a year after hostilities with Japan had ended. During the war itself, the doctrine of judicial review of administrative decisions in its several facets either had remained ambiguous or was weighted against the claims of objectors.

Ultimately, however, the critic would probably point his finger not at the courts, which were trying to interpret the hazy mind of Congress in the light of American constitutional and legal theory, but at Congress itself. The legislative body should and could have been clearer in its definition of the relationship between Selective Service boards and the courts. As it was, Congress had simply provided that decisions of the boards should be "final," without stating what it meant by finality. Constitutional lawyers in Congress ought to have been aware that such language would raise more issues than it clarified, as indeed it did. The eventual statement of the Supreme Court's position in 1946 could do but little for the rights of those many objectors whose claims had been repeatedly denied by the courts down to the end of hostilities. "Too little and too late" is an apt description.

THE COURTS GET RELIGION

The Selective Training and Service Act had exempted from combatant military service or both combatant and noncombatant military service, as the case might be, all those who "by reason of religious training and belief" were "conscientiously opposed to participation in war in any form." We have already seen what difficulties this language gave local boards, appellate authorities, and the Director of Selective Service (see Chapter IV). How did the courts construe the provision, and what was the relation of their construction to the law of conscientious objection?

Here again the Supreme Court never gave its opinion. Hence we are forced to rely upon circuit court constructions, one line of which accepted one position while the other took a contradictory point of view. The Supreme Court, by refusing to grant certiorari, presumably accepted the second position, but never explicitly; it should always be remembered that in strict legal theory refusal to grant certiorari can never be taken officially to indicate that the court supports the interpretation of the lower tribunal.[21] The first line of opinions came from the Second Circuit, while the second series arose in the Ninth.

The Second Circuit interpretation began with the Kauten decision in 1943. Mathias Kauten had been classified I-A by local and appeals boards and had asked the courts to review his classification during the course of his prosecution. The Circuit Court, in accordance with the rule discussed in the previous section, denied that it could review board classifications. But it went on to state its own definition of religion and to observe that Kauten would not have fallen within it, since he professed no "religious" faith. "Religious beliefs," said the court,

arise from a sense of the inadequacy of reason as a means of relating the individual to his fellowmen and to his universe—a sense common to men in the most primitive and in the most highly civilized societies. It is belief finding expression in a conscience which categorically requires the believer to disregard elementary self-interest and to accept martyrdom in preference to transgressing its tenets.

The court went on to distinguish between "political" objection, which was a conviction that a particular war was inexpedient or disastrous, and a "conscientious objection to participating in any war under any circumstances. The latter, and not the former, may be the basis of exemption under the Act." The latter "may justly be regarded as a response of the individual to an inward mentor, call it conscience or God, that is for many persons at the present time the equivalent of what has always been thought religious impulse." [22]

Again, in a habeas-corpus proceeding coming up from the Army and decided May 7, 1943,[23] the court had before it the case of a registrant who had admitted that he was an agnostic but who contended, nevertheless, that his opposition to war was "deep-rooted, based not on political considerations but on a general humanitarian concept which is essentially religious in character." In the Kauten case, the court had said that the defendant was not entitled to classification as a conscientious objector "by reason of religious training and belief." But now the defendant, although an admitted agnostic, was held to deserve objector classification. "Here the opposition to war was a deep-rooted one applying to war in general and was not based upon political objections to this particular war." And the court went on to observe that if a stricter rule than that laid down in the Kauten case were to be observed, the legal interpretation of "religion" would revert to the principles of the Selective Service Act of 1917, which had associated the term with membership in specific sects whose creeds forbade their members to participate in war. The court could thus discover no middle ground between the 1917 conception and its own Kauten rule.

In yet another case, decided January 7, 1944,[24] the court decided that a registrant who did not "believe in God or in any divine power" was nevertheless to be regarded as a religious conscientious objector because he believed that war was morally wrong and a denial of brotherhood. Similarly, a little later the tribunal ruled that an objector who denied any belief in a deity "except so far as there may be a moral force in the universe" could be looked upon as "religious." [25]

The Second Circuit Court of Appeals was thus consistent in holding that "religion" within the meaning of the Act had no necessary connection with belief in a transcendent deity or, indeed, with belief in any deity at all.

But from the Ninth Circuit came a decision in 1946 which explicitly repudiated the doctrines of the Kauten and subsequent opinions. In the Berman case,[26] the Court held that belief in a deity was essential to meet the "religious training and belief" terms of the Act:

It is our opinion that the expression "by reason of religious training and belief" is plain language, and was written into the statute for the specific purpose of distinguishing between a conscientious social belief, or a high moralistic philosophy, and one based upon an individual's belief in his responsibility to an authority higher and beyond any worldly one.

Berman as a Socialist and humanitarian was strongly opposed to all war, the court admitted; but since "religion" as commonly understood included acceptance of the idea of God, the tribunal contended that Congress must have intended its terms of exemption to require belief in a divine being, and that Berman could not show.

There are those who have a philosophy in life, and who live up to it. There is evidence that this is so in regard to appellant. However, no matter how pure and admirable this standard may be, and no matter how devotedly he adheres to it, his philosophy and morals and social policy without the concept of deity cannot be said to be religion in the sense of that term as it is used in the statute.

Despite an elaborate plea for certiorari by Berman's attorneys, the Supreme Court refused to review this opinion.[27]

The conflict between the broad conception of religion outlined in the Second Circuit and the narrower view of the Ninth was thus clearly stated. Both views were subjected to searching criticism. Conscientious objectors generally looked upon the Kauten interpretation with favor.[28] But some jurists and lawyers criticized the Second Circuit approach unfavorably, even before the Berman decision. Edward F. Waite, for example, argued [29] that the Second Circuit Court had in effect usurped legislative power by its interpretation of "religion." By all rules of judicial construction, he contended, the language of a statute should be construed in such a manner as to give words their ordinary sense and popular definition.[30] The jurist should not take minority conceptions and apply them to his statutory interpretations. Now religion, Waite continued, implies belief in a God or gods; he quoted the minority opinion of Chief Justice Hughes in the Macintosh case as representative of virtually all judicial opinion hitherto: "The essence of religion is belief in a relation to God involving duties superior to those arising from any human relationship." The Second Circuit Court of Appeals had gone far beyond any previous judicial definition of religion. It had virtually abolished the distinction between "conscientious objector" and "conscientious objector by reason of religious training and belief." However desirable it might have been to exempt all objectors, the jurist concluded, the fact was that Congress had not chosen to do so, and the court had thus in effect circumvented the will of the highest legislative body.

The question turns, of course, on what Congress intended "religion" to mean. The legislative history of the Act would seem to sustain Waite's criticism (see Chapter III of this study) and hence to uphold the Ninth Circuit's interpretation. Congressmen had declined explicitly to exempt conscientious objectors whose objections were not "religious"; and the context of the discussion shows that the legislators meant something more than general conscientious objection to all wars. If the question was one of interpreting the intent of Congress, the Berman opinion was clearly more soundly based than the Second Circuit decisions.[31]

THE CONSTITUTIONALITY OF C.P.S.

In a constitutional and legal sense, the problem of Civilian Public Service was somewhat unique. At no previous period in American history had a system been created which conscripted men for civilian work over a period of nearly seven years, which made no provision or only slight provision for pay (Chapters VI and VII), and which provided for such a close working agreement between church and state. Dependents were entitled to no dependency benefits, and many were thrown on private charity for relief. Surely, many conscientious objectors argued, there were provisions in the Constitution which could be used to strike down such a system.

Argument from the First Amendment. It was urged, in the first place, that the First Amendment to the Constitution barred such alternative civilian service in that it forbade Congress to pass any law restricting the free exercise of religion. Conscription for alternative civilian work was unconstitutional because it assumed that it was within the discretion of Congress to grant exemption from military service as Congress saw fit. Actually, however, conscientious objection was a constitutional right clearly implied in the religious freedom amendment, and for Congress to condition the exercise of a constitutional right was to purport to destroy the right itself. Hence, the argument concluded, the Civilian Public Service system as established by law was unconstitutional under the First Amendment.

The argument which based the right of conscientious objection on the First Amendment was a familiar one to students of conscription legislation. It had been urged during the First World War. Color was given to it by virtue of the fact that many state constitutions specifically exempted conscientious objectors from militia duty. Moreover, the tradition of the United States had spoken so uniformly in favor of conscientious objectors that some assumed the tradition had become definitive in interpreting the First Amendment. The argument was certainly not fantastic. If the provisions of the First Amendment, as read into the Fourteenth, protected the right of a child, on conscientious grounds, to refuse to give a compulsory flag salute in school,[32] if the right to picket peacefully could be derived from the right of free speech,[33] and if freedom of religion was incompatible with imposition of license fees for the distribution of religious literature,[34] it would seem at least plausible, if not finally persuasive, to argue that religious conscientious objection is a constitutional right which neither Congress nor administrative regulations can restrict or condition.

But the courts held otherwise. Already, during the First World War, the Supreme Court had ruled that conscientious objection was not a right protected by the First Amendment,[35] and the Court's statement between wars in the Macintosh case [36] had confirmed the earlier opinion: "Whether any citizen shall be exempt from serving in the armed forces of the nation in time of war is dependent upon the will of Congress and not upon the scruples of the individual, except as Congress provides."

While the issue was not squarely raised before the United States Supreme Court, the decisions of circuit courts of appeals were implicitly sustained when the Supreme Court refused certiorari in the Roodenko [37] and Kramer [38] cases. In the former, the Court said that it knew of no cases ruling contrary to the principle that there was no constitutional right of exemption from service in the armed forces. The Kramer case involved six walkouts from Civilian Public Service Camp 23, who also pleaded the First Amendment in defense of their action. But again the Court ruled against them, citing *Jacobsen* v. *Massachusetts,* wherein the court, in sustaining the principle of compulsory vaccination, had pronounced that a person may be forced even against "his religious or political convictions, to take his place in the ranks of the army of his country and risk the chance of being shot down in its defense." [39]

The writer has been unable, in his survey of World War II cases, to find any court support whatsoever for the theory that protection for conscientious objection may be derived from the First Amendment. Conscientious objection was thus emphatically confirmed as a privilege granted by Congress and a grant which Congress could constitutionally condition or withdraw at any time. Sometimes objectors argued that, even if conscientious objection was not directly a First Amendment right, Congress and administrative authorities still could not impose an unconstitutional condition (C.P.S.) on the exercise of a privilege once granted. But the courts saw no merit in this form of the argument, either.

Conscription for Civilian Service. But, it was argued, Civilian Public Service was unconstitutional because nowhere in the Constitution is Congress given the power to conscript for civilian service. Article I confers on it the power to provide for the common defense and to raise and support armies and navies. Admitting that the legislative body can select the means by which to raise armies and navies, nothing in the Constitution justifies the contention that these provisions, even when coupled with the "necessary and proper" clause, provide the power to conscript for nondefense purposes. Men in Civilian Public Service camps were performing services which had no direct connection with the war effort and hence Congress was going beyond its constitutional prerogatives in conscripting them for a service which had no relevance for the common defense.

But the courts uniformly took the ground that the absence of a direct connection between work done in a Civilian Public Service camp and the defense "effort" did not justify a claim of unconstitutionality. Because Congress had power to conscript for military service and the authority to grant or refuse to grant exemptions, it could make any exemptions conditional on the performance of other types of service, even though the latter had no direct connection with the waging of war.[40] Again, this issue was not passed upon directly by the Supreme Court except insofar as it denied certiorari in circuit cases where the issue was put.

Argument from the Fifth Amendment. Another constitutional argument centered on the Fifth Amendment. Objectors sent to Civilian Public Service, it said, were deprived of their liberty and property without due process of law. Civilian Public Service discriminated against conscientious objectors as over against soldiers and sailors in that the objectors received no pay and were thus forcibly deprived of their ability to earn a livelihood and at the same time thrown on the charity of others. But where the issue was raised directly, the courts saw no merit in this argument. As in the example of the Japanese evacuation cases,[41] the judiciary interpreted the war power very broadly, and the Fifth Amendment stood as no bar.[42] The Supreme Court did not pass on the issue.

The Thirteenth Amendment. Many were the pleas against the constitutionality of C.P.S. on the ground that it was incompatible with the Thirteenth Amendment. Critical conscientious objectors were fond of terming C.P.S. a "slave labor" system (see Chapters

XI and XII); [43] those who were legally minded quoted Black's *Law Dictionary* definition of involuntary servitude as "the condition of one who is compelled by force, coercion, or imprisonment and against his will to labor for another whether he is paid or not," and asked whether any description of C.P.S. could be more accurate. The characteristics of Civilian Public Service which were often cited as putting it within the category "slave labor" under the Thirteenth Amendment included direction of the objector to work by orders to which the objector did not give consent; employment fixed without the approval of the objector; hours of labor determined without assent of the objector or without other alternative being offered him; no liberty outside working hours without consent of the camp authorities; subjection to discipline administered by the camp director under general instructions of Selective Service; inability to leave work without incurring criminal penalties; virtual imprisonment of the objector in a camp having many of the characteristics of prison, yet without conviction of crime; and absence of compensation.

The interpretation of the Thirteenth Amendment had given some difficulty to American courts, yet in the twentieth century cases involving its construction had been comparatively rare. According to the Supreme Court, the Amendment had reproduced the words of the Northwest Ordinance of 1787, thus giving the language of the ordinance general application to the whole territory of the United States.[44] The general purpose of the Amendment, the Court had later averred, was "liberty under the protection of effective government, not the destruction of the latter by depriving it of essential powers." [45] The Amendment itself had excluded "punishment for crime whereof the person shall have been duly convicted" from its general prohibition.

Judicial interpretation of the amendment had outlawed peonage and anything which smacked of imprisonment for debt. But the courts had not applied the amendment to the contracts of seamen.[46] Later the Court had announced that the amendment was not intended to introduce any novel doctrine "and certainly was not intended to interdict enforcement of those duties which individuals owe the State, such as services in the Army, militia, on the jury, etc." [47] The Court had said explicitly that the state had inherent power to compel labor on the public roads for a reasonable period of time and without compensation.[48] And the Selective Draft Law cases of the First World War, as has been already pointed out, established that compulsory military service in time of war was no violation of the Thirteenth Amendment.

In general, one of the tests used by the Court in distinguishing between legitimate and illegitimate forced work was whether the labor was being performed for a public body or for private profit. Compulsory public labor was sustained, while that for private persons was outlawed. Historically, the Court seems not to have regarded absence of pay as in itself a mark of "involuntary servitude" within the meaning of the Thirteenth Amendment. Some conscientious objectors spoke as though they believed that absence of pay in itself made C.P.S., as established, unconstitutional, but there was little in previous decisions of the Supreme Court which would justify this position.

It was argued by objector lawyers that Civilian Public Service was different in kind from compulsory service on roads, which had always been sustained by the Supreme Court. Service on roads, said this argument, was for a few days in the year only and was usually performed, moreover, in the region of the worker's own home. C.P.S., by contrast, was for the duration of the war and six months thereafter, and Selective Service regulations provided that no assignee should be sent to a camp within one hundred miles of his own home. Road service was sporadic and limited; Civilian Public Service was for an indefinite period of time and the worker's movements were restricted even after his hours of labor were over. Hence cases which had sustained road service were useless as precedents for C.P.S.

To arguments of this kind, the courts turned a deaf ear. In the Roodenko case, the court overruled the pleas of four C.P.S. non-co-operators that their detention in Mancos C.P.S. camp constituted involuntary servitude. The United States Supreme Court denied petitions for certiorari on three separate occasions.[49] Substantially the same result was obtained in the Kramer case. C.P.S. may have been eminently undesirable socially, economically, and politically, but so far as the Thirteenth Amendment was concerned it held an impregnable constitutional position.

Unconstitutional Delegation of Legislative Power. A last important issue of constitutionality was raised when it was charged that Congress had unconstitutionally delegated legislative power in that it failed to establish standards and definite limitations on the power of administrative agencies. Thus when Selective Service set up the system of payless C.P.S. camps it was acting contrary to Article I of the Constitution, which confined all "legislative" power to Congress. The Act, insofar as it purported, without becoming explicit, to grant authority to negotiate with churches, provide for conscription without pay, and establish the elaborate set of regulations which governed the objector, was unconstitutional.

The courts found this argument, too, without merit; the sweeping powers given the Director of Selective Service were thus held to be a constitutional delegation of power by Congress.[50] Once more, however, the Supreme Court never passed directly on the problem.

Despite five different lines of attack, then, the statute and regulations under which Civilian Public Service was established were held to be within the terms of the Constitution.

THE PROBLEM OF MILITARY DIRECTION

Even if Civilian Public Service was not unconstitutional, it was urged, the manner of its administration violated the statute under which it was created. The Act provided that objectors should be assigned to "work of national importance under civilian direction." "Civilian direction," it was argued by objectors, meant *administration* by civilians as well as *civilian work*. But the chief officials of Camp Operations Division of Selective Service were military men throughout the war. Colonel Kosch, head of the Division, signed his orders—all of which had to do with Civilian Public Service—"Colonel, Field Artillery." As a matter of fact, A. S. Imirie was the only leading civilian in Camp Operations Division (see Chapter X). The head of Selective Service himself, who often assumed active direction of Camp Operations Division, was a brigadier general at the time of his appointment and during the course of his "tour of duty" as Director of Selective Service was promoted to major general. There were no retired Army officers among the chief executive officials—all retained their commissions in the regular Army and were subject to duty in the regular Army.

As has been pointed out fully elsewhere (Chapter X), the Selective Service System regulated and directed Civilian Public Service in greater and greater detail as the war progressed. While its orders were transmitted through the N.S.B.R.O. as a general rule, the Camp Operations Division could, and on occasion did, by-pass the National Service Board and the religious administrative agencies and send its orders directly to camp directors. Thus it might, and sometimes did, come about that regular Army colonels would be issuing instructions to ex-Y.M.C.A. secretaries who happened to be camp directors—certainly a direct connection. In terms of disbursements and finance, the relationship of Selective Service to the Army was even closer, for the Chief of Finance of the Army was also the fiscal disbursing and accounting agent of the Director of Selective Service.

All this indicated to many objectors that C.P.S. was actually under military direction, not "civilian direction" as required by statute. Selective Service was thus violating the statute in wholesale fashion.

But authoritative decisions of the courts disagreed. In cases which the Supreme Court refused to review, circuit courts of appeals laid it down that since the Director of Selective Service had been detached from the War Department by a special order (No. 231), he was not acting in a military capacity but rather as a civilian. Other military officers had in the past been similarly detached from the War Department and thus had also served as civilians, even though they had signed their names with military titles. On the authority of *Southern Pacific Co.* v. *United States*,[51] which had held that Army engineers assigned to rivers and harbors work were engaged in nonmilitary activities, the Tenth Circuit Court of Appeals held that General Hershey and Colonel Kosch, together with other assorted colonels in the Camp Operations Division, were in an analogous position.[52] There were no dissents in the two leading cases passing on this question, and no other circuit court questioned the "civilian direction" and hence the legality of Civilian Public Service.

What the courts apparently meant by "work of national importance under civilian direction" was stated by the usually "liberal" Supreme Court Justice Rutledge in cases which had no direct connection with the problem of military direction but which involved a dictum by the court on what the justices conceived to be the character of Civilian Public Service. This discussion by the Supreme Court is the most explicit examination which that tribunal ever made of the meaning of "civilian direction," and generally confirms the opinions of circuit courts of appeals. The conscientious objector ordered to serve in Civilian Public Service, said Justice Rutledge,

remains a civilian; his duties are not military in character; he is not subject to military discipline or authority; and for violation of his duties or orders he cannot be tried by court martial or military tribunal. . . . He is in fact farther removed from military status or jurisdiction after he is finally assigned to civilian public service of national importance . . . than he was before that time.[53]

All of which seems to indicate that the judicial interpretation of "work of national importance under civilian direction" meant simply that the objctor was not to be given military duties under formal military discipline. So long as he was not in the Army or Navy he could be directed by regular Army officers accustomed to military conceptions of discipline, for in the eyes of the law those officers were "civilians." Nothing in judicial opinions touching on the subject would lead one to believe that the legal rights of Selective Service over the conscripted objector in camp were less sweeping than those stated by Colonel Franklin McLean in his famous 1942 memorandum. (See Chapter X.)

The courts seemed to say that the legal status of an objector in C.P.S. was that of a soldier or sailor minus courts-martial, uniforms, and formal control of the War or Navy Departments. Subject to no formal military law, he could yet be directed in his civilian activities for twenty-four hours a day by Army generals. He was suspended in a precarious position between full-time control by generals under military law, on the one hand, and ordinary control by civil statutes administered by civilians, on the other. Legally, his movements could be directed as completely as those of any soldier, but if he violated this control at any point he could be tried, unlike the soldier, only by the civil courts. Yet apparently there was nothing in the statute which even required that Selective Service assign him to nonmilitary work; where he was assigned to civilian work it was a matter of grace on the part of Selective Service. Thus the quasi-military, quasi-civil character of the C.P.S. conscientious objector's legal status seems to have been relatively clear; while that status was challenged at many points as being violative of the statute, the courts confirmed it both implicitly and explicitly.

But the problem of military direction of C.P.S. should be seen in the perspective of other legal developments during the war. By executive order, seventy thousand American citizens of Japanese ancestry were forcibly uprooted from their homes by the military and incarcerated against their will in relocation centers. Despite pleas that the Fifth Amendment was being violated, the Supreme Court sustained the major elements of the program.[54]

And the executive order under which Japanese-Americans were ordered removed was couched in such terms as to make it legally possible for the President or a general to order any citizen or non-citizen from his home, without trial, simply because an executive official deemed him inimical to the "war effort"—all presumably under the war power and under the probable administration of generals. While objectors were legally under the control of Army officers for twenty-four hours a day, ordinary civilians could legally be ordered by Army area commanders to give up homes and friends and, on a moment's notice, be escorted by Army officers hundreds of miles from their former residences. Direction of Civilian Public Service by Army officers and the legal right of those officers to control objectors in working and nonworking hours alike was only part of a general war pattern. The irony of the whole situation lay in the fact that conscientious objectors, above all others, objected to military control, yet, outside soldiers and sailors themselves, objectors were legally the class of citizens most continuously subjected to Armylike methods of control. This is said with full awareness of the judicial fiction under which objectors were held to be under "civilian direction."

OTHER ALLEGED ULTRA VIRES REGULATIONS

Aside from the narrow but important question of military direction, objectors attacked the legality of other Selective Service regulations having to do with Civilian Public Service. It was alleged that General Regulations 652.2(a), 652.1(a), and 653.12 of the Director of Selective Service were beyond his statutory powers. These rules required every conscientious objector so classified to remain in the C.P.S. camp to which he was assigned, created a system of work camps in which objectors were to be set aside from the rest of the community, provided no pay for the compulsory work, and required that objectors keep their persons, clothing, equipment, and quarters clean and neat. On these grounds alone, aside from the issue of military direction, it was urged, the whole system was *ultra vires*. "Where is the authority to compel a citizen to work without pay, and to require his family to shift for themselves?" asked John A. Chamberlain, attorney for six objectors.[55] And he went on:

> If it is answered that soldiers are so regulated, we reply that this may be a necessary part of Army discipline and is so provided by law, but [as for] C.O.'s, as act of Congress itself shows, there is no more reason for treating them as criminals than for treating all the rest of the population outside the military in the same way. If it is suggested that young men are to be discouraged from claiming to be conscientious objectors, I ask where is the authority found in the Selective Service Act for so doing?

But the courts uniformly rejected pleas of this kind, maintaining that Section 5(g), while not saying so in specific terms, actually delegated sufficient power to the Director to support his restrictive regulations. With respect to scope of administrative power, the Act was to be construed liberally and in light of the fact that its major purpose was to raise armies; the courts with this principle in mind could not hold that there was any *ultra vires* act in the regulations which the Director had promulgated.[56] Not only, then, would the delegation of such power not be unconstitutional, but the Act actually delegated the power.

Thus, as in the question of military direction, the Selective Service System was victorious when challenged on the score of *ultra vires* regulations.

LEGAL STATUS IN THE ARMY, PRISON, PROBATION, PAROLE

No serious legal problems arose with respect to the legal position of the conscripted objector outside Civilian Public Service. In the Army and in prison, his status was precisely that of the nonobjector except insofar as the Selective Service Act could be held to protect the Army objector in his refusal to bear arms. As for the objector on probation or parole, it was generally held that the former continued to be under the legal control of the court, rather than Selective Service, while the latter, so long as he remained on parole, was subject to regulation by the Board of Parole. Parole could, of course, turn the objector over to Civilian Public Service, where his position would be substantially the same as that of an objector assigned to C.P.S.

Rights of Objectors in Civil Society

The law and custom involving the position of objectors in ordinary society—that is, outside Army, C.P.S., prison, probationary status, and parole—developed in spotty fashion. There was certainly but little uniformity: in some communities practice and legal rulings were relatively liberal; in others, restrictive. In only two cases did the Supreme Court of the United States pass directly on constitutional and legal questions concerning the position of objectors in civil society, but these two decisions were to have wide repercussions.

OBJECTORS AND THE PRACTICE OF LAW

On at least two occasions during the war the question arose as to whether the status of conscientious objector was incompatible with a man's entrance into the legal profession.

The Summers Affair. In the first case, Clyde W. Summers, a Methodist conscientious objector whose objections had been recognized by his local board but who had not been called to service, was denied admission to the Illinois bar by the bar's Committee on Character and Fitness. The Committee admitted his intellectual qualifications. His rejection was solely because he was deemed "morally unfit" and his moral unfitness was held to root in his objection to war. The Committee contended that his objection to war conflicted with the oath which he would have to take to "support" the Constitution; "support" meant "defend" and "defend" meant "defense by force," to which Summers objected. Therefore, while Summers offered to take the oath, the Committee held that he could not take it in good faith. Hence he was morally unfit.

The Committee also claimed that Summers' beliefs were contrary to the militia clause of the state constitution, which gave the General Assembly power to conscript male citizens for militia service in time of war.[57] There was to be no exemption for objectors under such circumstances.

Finally, it was charged that pacifist beliefs made it impossible for Summers to perform the work of a lawyer, since law might necessitate force and objectors did not sanction force.

It should be observed here that Summers did not disavow the use of all types of force. He thought that police force used for restraint and correction was legitimate. But he made a distinction between legitimate police force and the violence of war. He was also conscientiously opposed to the personal use of violence to protect himself. He objected to the death penalty. As a lawyer, he said that he would try to settle most cases out of court, since litigation always created antagonism.[58]

On September 20, 1943, the Supreme Court of Illinois sustained the judgment of the Committee on Character and Fitness that Summers was morally unfit to practice law. The case then went to the Supreme Court of the United States on writ of certiorari.

In the Supreme Court Summers contended that the action of Illinois denying him admission to the bar was a limitation on the free exercise of religion and hence a violation of the due-process clause of the Fourteenth Amendment. The *amicus curiae* brief submitted to the court by Professor Zechariah Chafee and Harold Evans on behalf of the American Friends Service Committee argued the case at length. Religious freedom was unconstitutionally infringed "when an applicant for admission to the bar of a state is rejected solely because he is a conscientious objector to war." Exclusion from the bar under such circumstances was an "invalid interference with the purpose of Congress as embodied in the Selective Service Act of 1940."[59] Conscientious objection to war had about as much relevance to fitness for the practice of law as it did to capacity for barbering and electric work;[60] there was, moreover, no overriding public purpose to be served by the denial to an objector of the right to practice law. Summers was refused admission solely because of religious belief; religious belief is protected from interference or penalty as against the national government by the First Amendment and, under its terms, through the Fourteenth Amendment as against state action. Religious freedom under the Fourteenth Amendment also includes the prohibition against test oaths embodied in Article VI of the Constitution of the United States,[61] and the Illinois interpretation of the lawyer's oath under which Summers was excluded was clearly a "religious test . . . as a qualification." Finally, Congress had made provision for conscientious objectors; Summers had obeyed the law; yet state action was attempting to penalize him for conforming to the higher federal law—clearly an illegal action on the part of a state agency.[62]

But the Supreme Court denied these contentions. By a 5 to 4 vote it held that the Supreme Court of Illinois and the bar's Committee on Character and Fitness could not be held to have violated the Fourteenth Amendment in excluding Summers from the bar. The opinion of the Court, written by Justice Reed, refused to regard the Illinois decision as discrimination on the ground of religious faith. The Court held that the issue turned on the possibility of Summers' swearing in good faith to "support" the constitution of Illinois, which envisioned the possibility of the legislature's enacting compulsory military service for all men within specified age groups during time of war. It was not unreasonable, asserted the opinion, for the Illinois Court and the Committee on Fitness to rule that an applicant for admission to the bar who was also a conscientious objector could not in good faith take the oath.[63]

On the other hand, Justice Black, dissenting for the four minority justices, maintained that the only possible reason for the rejection of Summers was his religious beliefs. The act of rejection was therefore a violation of the Fourteenth Amendment. Justice Black went on to observe that it seemed to him "inescapable that if Illinois can bar this petitioner from the practice of law it can bar every person from every public occupation solely because he believes in non-resistance rather than in force." It was highly improbable, moreover, that Illinois would ever in the future draft conscientious objectors for service, even in time of war; the question of good faith in taking the oath of office was for this as well as other reasons irrelevant and academic. Generalizing, Justice Black summed up his opinion: "I cannot agree that a State can lawfully bar from a semi-public position, a well-qualified man of good character solely because he entertains a religious belief which might prompt him at some time in the future to violate a law which has not yet been and may never be enacted."

The Etter Affair. Elsewhere, however, admission committees were not always as strict as the Illinois authorities. In California, although Orval Etter, secretary of the Northern California Fellowship of Reconciliation, was at first denied admission to the California bar by the Northern Subcommittee of Bar Examiners (one year after the end of hostilities with Japan),[64] the full Committee of Bar Examiners later overruled the Subcommittee and admitted him. He was admitted despite the fact that he had testified he would not report to Civilian Public Service if ordered to do so by his local board.[65] There was, however, no Illinoislike compulsory service militia clause in the constitution of California.

Significance of the Problem. Despite Etter's case and similar ones in which objectors managed to secure admission to the bar, the significance of the Summers litigation and Supreme Court decision remains. The majority opinion established very wide allowable limits for discrimination against objectors. The seal of approval of the United States Supreme Court was affixed to the proposition that states could refuse to admit objectors to the bar because of their religious opinions. If this wide latitude was to be given to the states with reference to bar admissions, there was little reason to assume that it would not be extended to other vocational areas. The Summers decision, indeed, was to be influential in defining the rights of teachers who happened to be objectors (see below).

To the critics, the significance of the Summers opinion, in the context of the whole issue of objector rights in civil society, was obvious. As the *Tuscaloosa* (Alabama) *News* put it in the middle of 1945:

We seem to be leaving behind some of the fundamental freedoms of conscience guaranteed by the founding fathers of our country. . . . The Supreme Court of the United States . . . , it seems to us, turns its back on a basic and urgently necessary freedom when it upholds a minor court in a decision denying a conscientious objector the right to be admitted to the bar.[66]

OBJECTORS AND EDUCATION

How did the conscientious-objector teacher and student fare during the war? Practice and legal rulings varied considerably from community to community, from institution to institution.

Colleges and Universities. Most universities put conscientious-objector and nonobjector students on substantially the same footing with respect to special rules for obtaining degrees in wartime. At the University of Illinois, for example, a rule provided that students called to service during their last semester in school should be entitled to receive their degrees despite their inability to finish their course of work; this rule was applicable to those called to C.P.S. as well as those summoned to the Army. At Tulane University a similar rule was in effect.[67]

The University of Illinois was only one among many institutions which adopted regulations prescribing automatic reinstatement in their teaching positions of those called to military service. The formal rules of the University of Illinois made no provision for conscientious objectors on the staff, but as a matter of practice all teaching assistants who went to C.P.S. were reinstated in their positions if they had not yet obtained their degrees.[68]

A generally wide degree of tolerance was shown by colleges. While there were occasions where promotions of college teachers were held up because of antiwar positions, there were few outright dismissals. This frequent college tolerance is illustrated by the experience of J. Benjamin Stalvey. Stalvey was drafted from his teaching assistantship at the University of Illinois, served in Big Flats and Trenton C.P.S. camps, and on his discharge was appointed an instructor in political science at Duke University. When he arrived at Duke he was interviewed by the chairman of the department, who during the course of the conversation commented on Stalvey's views: "I suppose you do not regret the decision you made." Stalvey indicated he did not. The chairman then said: "I want to let you know that you will not find any difficulty here over the position you have taken. We want in this department men who have demonstrated that they have strong convictions." [69] Later Stalvey was reappointed to his teaching assistantship at the University of Illinois and eventually received his Ph.D. degree.

Sometimes, of course, this general college and university tolerance was strained. The writer knows of one instance, for example, where an objector was scheduled to teach a course in international relations at a large university; at the last moment the chairman of the department informed him that he was not to teach the course, "for the obvious reason that it would be undesirable to have an objector teaching international relations in wartime." The same instructor was warned by his college dean that he should not teach pacifism in his classes. And when a well-known pacifist teaching philosophy at Northwestern University remarked, on the morrow of Franklin Roosevelt's death, that the late President might well be regarded

later as the "Judas Iscariot of his generation," he received a telephone call from the head of his department saying, "Schilpp, you
are through." The professor took this to mean that his contract would
not be renewed. Later, however, he discovered that the chairman
was announcing a policy of personal ostracism and that the university did not intend to force his resignation.[70]

There were, however, examples of refusals to renew contracts of
college teachers. In one fairly prominent case, Dr. Janet Aiken was
told that her antiwar views were responsible for Brooklyn College's
refusal to renew her contract to teach in the night school, where she
had instructed for twelve years. The action which presumably precipitated this decision was Dr. Aiken's refusal to become an air-raid
warden; [71] and William and Mary College declined to renew the
contract of Harrop Freeman, a well-known teacher of law, presumably because of the pronounced antiwar views which he had expressed. In Freeman's case, however, the dismissal was but the
prelude to promotion, for he soon became a professor of law at
Cornell University.

Elementary and Secondary Schools. The position of the teacher
in elementary and secondary schools seemed to be more precarious
than that of his college and university colleague. Subject as always
to the direct pressures of the local community, he was hardy indeed
if he successfully defied in public the war sentiment of the times.
Some teachers did, however, openly refuse for conscientious reasons
to sell war-savings stamps and bonds and to engage in other work
having direct connection with the war. The writer, for example,
knows personally of one high-school teacher of English who frankly
expressed her views before her classes. An extraordinarily courageous
woman in every respect, she asked the principal of her school to
excuse her from participation in sale of war-savings stamps—a task
which she, along with other public-school teachers, was supposed to
perform. The principal granted her request. Needless to say, she
was not popular with the school authorities, although they never
moved to dismiss her.

It has been impossible to obtain a complete record of all high-
and elementary-school teachers dismissed because of their antiwar
positions. The number getting into difficulties seems to have been
relatively large, although official reasons given for dismissal or sus-

pension often concealed the real reason. Even in peacetime, American school boards customarily exercise rigorous control over the morals, manners, and speech of their teachers.

The school board of a southern Illinois community refused to renew the contract of a young teacher of English who had just been classified IV-E. It was fairly definite that the school board's action turned on the teacher's war views. The dismissed instructor later joined the staff of the Fellowship of Reconciliation.[72]

On February 8, 1944, Frank A. Knutsen of Clairsville, Ohio, was classified IV-E by his local board. On February 9, 1944, he was suspended from his teaching position on the ground that his known status as a conscientious objector "might create a disturbance."[73]

In 1942, Ronald Chinn, a Sacramento, California, High School teacher, was temporarily suspended from his position by the school board after officials of his local Selective Service board had asked school officials if "it was good policy to employ a conscientious objector" as a teacher of history and civics. The local draft board, having achieved success in its local school board relations, now asked the State Board of Education whether Chinn had violated his teacher's oath by becoming a conscientious objector and whether he could, under California law, be barred forever from his teaching position. The State Board of Education answered in the negative on both counts. Nevertheless, the local school board apparently decided that it was not "good policy" to employ an objector as a teacher of history, for the suspended Chinn was now assigned to a nonteaching position. Later he served in Civilian Public Service. Upon his discharge he was re-employed by the school board, which, however, carefully assigned him to English rather than history and civics classes.[74]

The educational case involving most court litigation was that of Edward Schweitzer. Schweitzer was Dean of Boys at a junior high school in Miami, Florida, and had been teaching there for some ten years. Active in the Y.M.C.A. and as a Sunday-school teacher, he was apparently popular with students and townspeople alike. In May, 1943, he was classified I-A by his local board, which later changed the classification to I-A-O after his protest. But he had asked for IV-E and hence appealed. Meanwhile, an anonymous telephone call to the school board informed officials that Schweitzer was a conscientious objector and asked that the board act immediately.

Schweitzer was summoned to a preliminary hearing, where he stated his beliefs. Thereupon the school board preferred charges of incompetence, maintaining that it was impossible for him as a conscientious objector to teach patriotism and defense of country as required by school regulations. A formal hearing on the charges was set for August. Just before the formal hearing, Schweitzer was informed that his local board had reopened his case and classified him IV-E.

After the formal school-board hearing in August, Schweitzer was discharged from his position, the school authorities ruling that his conduct and attitude were "wholly inimical to the ideals of citizenship" and that he had become "and now is incapable and incompetent longer to perform his full duty as a teacher or dean." [75] Some time after this final ruling of the school board, Schweitzer reported for his Selective Service physical examination and was rejected as physically unfit.

He now took his case to the courts and the Florida Circuit Court ordered the school board to reinstate him. [76] But when it appealed, the board was sustained by the Florida Supreme Court, which held that "the true test of patriotism can accurately be measured by the willingness of the citizen to bear arms and fight in defense of his country" and that therefore the board was within its rights in dismissing a teacher under the Florida statute which provided that instructors must inculcate "by precept and example the principles of truth, honesty, patriotism, and the practice of Christian virtue." [77]

While preparations were being made to appeal the decision of the Florida court to the United States Supreme Court, the Summers opinion was handed down. Since Schweitzer's appeal to the high federal court raised Fourteenth Amendment issues similar to those posed unsuccessfully in the Summers case, and for certain technical reasons, it was decided by American Civil Liberties Union lawyers not to perfect the appeal. [78] It would seem to have been unfortunate that the Union attorneys did not press for a writ of certiorari; in that event the Supreme Court would at least have been forced to reject the plea. But whether right or not, this decision of the Civil Liberties Union thus indicated that some lawyers at least believed that the

Summers opinion controlled not only with respect to practice of law but to schoolteaching as well. It is difficult to say that these lawyers were wrong, especially when we remember that the *amicus curiae* brief in the Summers case had argued that a decision like that eventually rendered would undoubtedly apply to schoolteachers and other professional persons licensed by the state. In the end, the legal position of the schoolteacher vis-à-vis the Fourteenth Amendment seems to have been similar to that of the lawyer.

OBJECTORS AND THE CIVIL SERVICE

Closely connected with the problem of objectors in educational positions was that of public employes occupying noneducational offices. Here, as in the practice of law, some argued that the conscientious objector should not be employed since he refused to fight for the government whose employe he was or sought to be. The seemingly perennial question of his ability to take the oath of office in good faith was also raised.

Only one state actually barred conscientious objectors from all public offices, including, apparently, educational positions. In 1942 Louisiana passed an act forbidding the state government or any subdivision of the state to employ enemy aliens and "any persons who refuse to serve in the armed forces of the nation on the ground of being a conscientious objector." Any official who violated the law by hiring an enemy alien or an objector was subject to imprisonment of six months or a fine of one thousand dollars.[79]

In at least two other states legislation specifically barring objectors from public office was seriously considered. In one of them, Tennessee, the legislature defeated a sweeping proposal to that effect, but only after some members had expressed a fear that should the law be passed it would give rise to another Scopes "monkey trial." [80]

The attempt to bar objectors in California, spurred on by the American Legion and other groups suspicious of the objector, came very close to success. When the bill reached the Assembly, however, the legislative counsel gave a formal opinion that it would be unconstitutional. A new bill abandoned outright prohibition and instead required that every applicant for a public position answer in writing the question, "If necessary, are you willing to take up arms in defense of the United States of America?" A negative answer to this question would not automatically bar an objector from office but, by placing his views on record, would probably discourage him from applying in the first place or lead to his withdrawal after the application had been submitted.[81] The substitute measure passed both houses of the legislature.

It was vetoed, however, by Governor Earl Warren. In his veto message of May 15, 1945, the Governor, after arguing that the proposed law violated the spirit of the religious-liberty clauses of the California and the United States constitutions, asked, "Shall persons who thus exercise their constitutional and statutory rights in connection with their religion be held up to public scorn merely for doing so?" He also observed that the proposed civil service question would penalize only the sincere objector, for the "faker" would lie to achieve his ends. Finally, he contended that the legislation would impair the unity of the war effort in that it would open the floodgates for all other types of questions bearing on religious belief.[82] The legislature sustained the veto.

Governor Warren's attitude undoubtedly played a part in the defeat of efforts to restrict conscientious objectors' rights to public employment in Los Angeles. In 1945, an attack on conscientious objectors in public employment was made in the Los Angeles County Board of Supervisors. There an ordinance was introduced to bar objectors from taking county civil service examinations, apparently partly on the assumption that the Summers interpretation of the Fourteenth Amendment would permit such action. Before the Board voted on this proposal, however, it submitted the matter to the county counsel, who thereupon held that the Board had no authority under the county charter to bar civil service applicants on account of religious beliefs. Only an amendment of the charter, he argued, might make possible the proposed action, and even then the legislation might violate the religious-liberty clauses of state and national constitutions. The counsel relied heavily on Justice Black's minority opinion in the Summers case and on Governor Warren's veto of the proposed state legislation. The County Board gave up the proposal entirely.[83]

The defeat of most state and local legislation barring conscientious objectors from public employment was matched by the refusal of Congress to consider like proposals. A bill of Representative Carter

Manasco of Alabama which would have denied employment to conscientious objectors "and persons refusing to subscribe to an oath
to uphold and defend the Constitution of the United States" was
referred to the Civil Service Committee [84] but was never reported out.

This generally favorable legislative attitude did not mean, of
course, that objectors were not discharged from public service in
some instances or that the legal rulings of Civil Service Commissions
were necessarily nondiscriminatory. It has been impossible to discover how many public employes lost their positions because of their
objection to war, or how many suffered with respect to promotions or
in other ways. There are on record, however, cases like that of the
Boston fireman who was singled out for dismissal because he had
been classified IV-E and had gone to C.P.S. camp.[85] Instances of this
kind should be carefully distinguished, of course, from those cases
where the individual requested objector status and for various reasons
was never called upon to serve. In this latter category discharge
seems to have been rare.

But with reference to those objectors who were classified as IV-E
and called upon to serve, the United States Civil Service Commission
ruled that the Selective Service Act did not protect them in their
positions as it did Army conscripts. They might reapply for civil
service positions after their term in C.P.S., but without veterans'
preference or any guarantee that they would secure employment.
They lost their Civil Service status and, unlike Army men, were not
given automatic leaves of absence.[86] There was, however, to be
no prejudice against them if they should later reapply. Objectors who
served in I-A-O apparently received the same Civil Service protection accorded to regular Army personnel.

Similar interpretations seem to have prevailed in most Civil Service Commissions. San Diego County, California, denied to C.P.S.
objectors the leaves of absence extended automatically to Army
inductees,[87] and the Attorney General of New York ruled likewise
with reference to the New York Civil Service.[88]

On only one occasion did a higher federal court pronounce on
the relationship between opposition to war and the capacity to hold
a federal position. In that instance, a lawyer employed by the Department of Labor in the opinion section of the Solicitor's office had
been held to be "insincere" by the Selective Service System, presum-

ably because it was assumed that his oath of office implied a promise to bear arms. Also, part of his work in the Department consisted of checking the conformity of war contractors to the Fair Labor Standards Act and the Public Contracts Act; Selective Service alleged that this constituted "participation" in the war effort, thus belying the objector's profession of opposition to war.

In granting a writ of habeas corpus releasing the objector from the Navy (into which the Labor Department lawyer had been inducted following the rejection of his claim for IV-E), the Circuit Court of Appeals denied both allegations and in the course of its opinion made remarks relevant to the meaning of the oath of office. The oath to "support and defend the Constitution," said the court, should not be read to mean that the official necessarily promises to bear arms in all future contingencies. The court pointed out that, while the government "disclaims any intent to hold that federal service automatically forecloses the employe from exemption as a conscientious objector," any interpretation which makes of the oath a promise to bear arms must necessarily have that result. If so, conscientious objectors would be barred not only from federal office but from many state, local, and public-school positions as well. From interpretations of this kind the court drew back, concluding that Congress could not have intended any such result. Oaths to "support and defend" could, therefore, be taken in good faith by objectors, and Congress had not intended, by means of the oath, to exclude objectors from public office.[89] The Supreme Court, however, never passed explicitly on the issue.

As for conscientious objectors who had served terms in prison, there was no blanket ruling of the United States Civil Service Commission against their employment. Question 28 of Civil Service Form 57 did ask the applicant for his record of arrests and convictions, but the Commission did not regard a criminal record in itself as a bar to employment or to taking the examination. The Commission would be governed, with respect to objectors and nonobjectors alike, by the specific facts, "the recency of the offense, and whether the person has rehabilitated himself in his community."[90] Despite this apparently liberal ruling, however, there could be but little doubt that the status of the objector who had gone to prison would be substantially lower vis-à-vis the Civil Service than that of his C.P.S. comrade and vastly lower than that of the objector who had served in the Army.

Congress had long required applicants for naturalization to subscribe to an oath renouncing allegiance to all foreign powers and promising to "support and defend" the Constitution and laws. The Immigration and Naturalization Service, which administered the naturalization law, had for years included a question on the application form which asked the applicant whether he would "bear arms" for the United States in future wars. This question presumably was included to test the applicant's sincerity in taking the oath and was apparently a specific application of the oath. Congress had not specified the question but it had provided the oath.

Long before the Second World War, the problem arose as to whether the question on arms-bearing, especially in relation to conscientious objectors, was a legitimate interpretation of the intent of Congress. In two famous cases, the Supreme Court answered in the affirmative. In the Schwimmer case, a woman applicant for naturalization had stated that she was a pacifist and could participate in no future wars, but argued that Congress had not provided that a promise to bear arms was to be a test of allegiance. The Court decided, however, that it was not illegal for the Naturalization Service to include the question and to require an affirmative answer.[91] Later the Court applied the same ruling to Macintosh, an alien who was not an "absolute" pacifist but rather one who wished to reserve the right to decide whether he would support any given future war.[92]

The Schwimmer and Macintosh opinions were cited in many legal cases involving conscientious objectors during the Second World War. But they were strictly applicable, of course, only to naturalization issues. Even here, however, courts differed widely in applying them. Some district courts continued to deny naturalization to objectors, as in the case of Verner Nielsen, whom the District of Columbia federal court refused to admit.[93] On the other hand, there were cases on record during the war where courts admitted objectors, as with William R. Kinlock and William McKillop.[94] It is not surprising that the absence of a uniform rule of action caused some confusion.

The issue was not clarified until the Supreme Court in the Girouard case explicitly overruled the Schwimmer and Macintosh opinions, six months after the end of hostilities. Girouard was a Canadian Seventh-Day Adventist who was willing to enter the Army in a noncombatant capacity but naturally could not promise to bear arms. Justice Douglas, in rendering the opinion of the court, said explicitly that the precedents (Schwimmer and Macintosh) "do not state the correct rule of law." Three justices, including Chief Justice Stone (who had been in the minority in the Macintosh decision), dissented, on the ground that Congress had not chosen since the Macintosh case to exclude the arms-bearing interpretation of the oath; therefore, argued the minority, Congress must have given its approval to the Schwimmer and Macintosh constructions of the statute.[95]

The Girouard opinion represented a genuine extension of the rights of objectors. Seemingly, moreover, it ought to have cast light on the meaning of oaths in other areas of the law of conscientious objection. Nevertheless, the Court only a few months before the Girouard case had denied a rehearing to Summers, thus appearing to confirm its judgment on application of the oath to the practice of law. The relationship of the Supreme Court to oaths and conscientious objectors constitutes a curious chapter in legal history.

OTHER ASPECTS

A variety of miscellaneous legislative proposals and legal interpretations affected the position of the objector in civil society during the Second World War. Although they are in no sense treated exhaustively, a few are noted here as illustrations.

The Montana Resolution. The legislature of Montana passed a lengthy resolution in the form of a memorial to Congress suggesting that Congress pass legislation which would provide that any objector who refused to go into the Army or do work of national importance be deprived of the right "to own or acquire any real property within the confines of the United States, beyond a limited amount"; that no group holding conscientious objection as a principle "be permitted to acquire any further tracts of land in this country"; and that income tax exemptions extended to pacifist groups that were also religious groups be repealed.[96] The Montana resolution never became a concrete legislative proposal in Washington.

Massachusetts Soldier's Bonus Law. The Massachusetts Soldier's

Bonus Law was seemingly so interpreted that the one-hundred-dollar payment given to returning servicemen was to be withheld from men who had served in the Army but who had been so unwise as to have begun their Selective Service careers in C.P.S.[97]

Passport Oath. On the other hand, the State Department reaffirmed the so-called "qualified" oath for passport purposes which it had first recognized in 1926. According to a 1945 interpretation of the chief of the Passport Division of the State Department, the phrase "support and defend the Constitution" did not necessarily imply a willingness to bear arms. The objector who affirmed that he would support the Constitution and, "so far as my conscience will allow," would defend it, would be given a passport.[98]

Objectors and Relief Work. There is on record at least one clear-cut case where a well-known economist from a large university was not accepted for relief work solely because of his conscientious objection and his membership in the War Resisters' League. He had been placed in Class III-A by his local board because he had a family. Eminently qualified for relief work, according to the Relief Commission headed by ex-Governor Herbert H. Lehman, his services were eventually rejected by the State Department because of his War Resisters' connections.[99] But U.N.R.R.A. did not bar objectors.[100]

Law of Taxation. Government departments involved seemed to be very lenient indeed in cases like that of Ammon Hennacy, a well-known anarchist pacifist, who not only refused to register for the draft but, during the latter part of the war, announced openly that he would not pay income taxes. He was not prosecuted.[101]

Freedom of the Press. As for the pacifist press, it was by and large left free. Such publications as *Fellowship, The Conscientious Objector,* and *Pacifica Views,* which represented generally a "leftward" approach, were published without interruption during the height of war tension. It was thought, with good reason, that the FBI had dossiers on leading pacifist personalities, including editors, but except insofar as the men were involved in the draft machinery itself they were unmolested. The only exception to the rule that the press remained free occurred when the *Boise Valley Herald* was denied second-class mailing privileges in 1942. Published in Idaho, the paper had taken a vigorous stand against conscription and its comments on war and government had been forceful and pungent. Action against this paper was taken under the Espionage Act of 1917 and over the protest of the American Civil Liberties Union, which denied that the "clear and present danger" doctrine could be invoked. Early in 1944, however, the *Herald's* mailing privileges were restored.[102]

LAW AND CUSTOM IN SUMMARY

When all the details of the law and custom of conscientious objection have been noted, certain elements assume primary significance. With respect to the position of the conscripted objector, they were: (1) the ambiguity of the statute with respect to judicial review of administrative action and the slowness and lack of clarity characteristic of the courts in the development of their interpretation; (2) the unfortunate circumstance that "religious training and belief" was never defined by the Supreme Court; (3) the constitutional impregnability of alternative service as developed during the course of the war: while the Supreme Court never passed directly on the issue, by refusing in a number of cases to grant certiorari it virtually did so; (4) the near certainty that the Supreme Court would uphold the constitutionality of peacetime conscription; and (5) the legal position of the objector in C.P.S. as halfway between that of a soldier and that of an ordinary civilian: subject to the civil courts only, he was yet legally under the control of Army officers for twenty-four hours a day, and no court seriously challenged this statement of the law.

Outstanding in the law and custom of objection in civil society were (1) conflicting interpretations of the oath of office: in education and the practice of law, the courts thought that an implicit promise to bear arms might be discovered, while in civil service, and, eventually, in naturalization, no such promise could be found; (2) the sweeping implications of the Summers opinion: consistently applied, the decision would seem to mean that the Fourteenth Amendment afforded no protection whatsoever if a state wished to make practice of a trade or profession contingent on the practitioner's not being an objector; (3) general failure to pass special laws restrictive of the rights of objectors in civil society; (4) the precarious position of the high- and elementary-school teacher who happened to be an objector: he was subject in many cases not only to the usual pressures of school board and public opinion but also to several adverse legal opinions; and (5) relatively great freedom enjoyed by pacifist and objector press, despite statutes which might have been invoked against it.

The law and custom of conscientious objection was thus in large part a tapestry of conflicting patterns woven together without general plan or design.

XX: *Conscience and Conscription in the American Nation*

A<small>N</small> E<small>VALUATION</small> of American experience with conscientious objectors in World War II raises five key questions: (1) Did the American nation tolerate freedom of conscience during the war? (2) How much conscience was there? (3) Did the churches betray religious liberty by collaborating with Selective Service in the administration of alternative service? (4) Was compulsion effective in securing the compliance of conscience with the demands of the state? (5) Can conscience be more adequately recognized, assuming continued conscription?

Did the American Nation Tolerate Freedom of Conscience during the War?

The struggle for tolerance of conscience within the United States was not conclusively settled when unconditional surrender brought an end to the war. The boundaries of freedom for conscientious objection, which had at first been staked (in original church and civil-liberties proposals) far beyond the limits set in World War I, were contracted, yet their defenders on the whole had not been pressed back into the original narrow confines.

The American nation through its government had sized up its pacifist minority and divided them into sheep and goats, "co-operators" and "non-co-operators." To the former they granted substantial freedom to express their convictions, by word and by deed. The latter, whose ranks grew steadily during the course of the war, were firmly and coldly restricted in the exercise of conscience. Both groups were obliged to pay a large price for their refusal to join the war effort. By law, administrative practice, and some public demand, they were denied the privileges and consideration accorded those who took up arms. The nation prescribed that the conscientious objector should accept a "second-class citizenship," and that in return for tolerance he should perform an acceptable national service.

American conscientious objectors could voice their convictions with little interference either by government or public, so long as they were content to express themselves individually. They could speak their minds in C.P.S. camp, hospital unit, church service, home community, and even in prison without much suppression. They could publish their views in writing. A prolific and diversified pacifist press circulated without restraint through the mails into the most remote corners of the country. Occasionally, outbursts of hostile opinion, accompanied in a few instances by a barrage of rotten eggs, met the objectors in their community contacts, and in a few cases Jehovah's Witnesses in prison were kept from meeting together or receiving their religious literature. Whenever personal expression of belief turned into organized public protest, however, it ran head on into the adamant opposition of Selective Service, as in the ill-fated Chicago Conference on Social Action called by men in Civilian Public Service. Appeal to the bar of public opinion was not the prerogative of conscience in the Selective Service rulebook, and any concerted transgression of "channels" by vociferous objectors was rudely resisted. Yet, on the whole, the objector's proclivity to talk was virtually unhampered, even to the "scientific needling" of government officials or religious administrators. A running bedlam of argument and discussion consequently distinguished the aggregations of objectors which were collected under the Selective Training and Service Act.

When the objector turned to reconcile his actions with his professions, he was allowed—as he had not been until the very end of World War I—to engage in civilian service. This important concession to conscience was sturdily maintained against sporadic attacks throughout the war and represented an advance in the level of American tolerance. Within the framework of this alternative a large proportion of the objectors were able to preserve the integrity of their beliefs and to accomplish a noteworthy service. The conservation of natural resources, the care of the mentally ill, the maintenance of agricultural production, and the advancement of scientific and medical knowledge depended during the war years at vital points upon the labors of the conscientious objectors.

The channels of service were too rigidly prescribed by Selective Service, however, to allow the objectors an adequate choice of the means for expressing their convictions. The men were restricted to locations where the government felt they would be unlikely to arouse public criticism or to sway easily influenced groups with their pacifist views. Similar considerations limited the opportunities for parole of imprisoned objectors. Selective Service was particularly reluctant to approve social welfare projects and continually favored work administered by government as contrasted with private agencies. In assigning men, relatively minor consideration was given to the effective use of their individual skills and capacities. The result was not only a heavy wastage of valuable manpower on worthless or inappropriate projects, but often the frustration of the objector's "testimony through service." Many men thoroughly committed to the advancement of the well-being of their fellow men as an integral part of their belief could not find satisfaction within the limits of Civilian Public Service set by the government.

In addition, three groups of objectors fell completely outside the scope of American tolerance. These outcasts were the Jehovah's Witnesses, the nonreligious objectors, and the "absolutists" who not only opposed military service but all conscripted service as well. Legally, no alternative was provided for the man whose conscientious objection was not based on "religious training and belief"; legally, no objector could secure exemption from compulsory service, even if his conscience clearly dictated repudiation of compulsion; and administratively, most Jehovah's Witnesses were not permitted to pursue a self-chosen vocation as ministers. Consequently, the proportion of the conscientious who populated prisons swelled to approximately three times that in World War I.

The inadequacy of American tolerance was still further expressed in deliberately discriminatory treatment of conscientious objectors. The Civilian Public Service draftee received no pay (by contrast with World War I, when objectors given "farm furloughs" were paid), no compensation for injury or death, no allowance for his dependents, and none of the demobilization benefits accorded to the G.I. His demobilization was longer delayed. These penalties did not apply to the man willing to do noncombatant service in the Army, and there were many who justified such a distinction between the "degrees" of conscience on the grounds that it would test the sincerity of the more extreme objector and also encourage him to relax his belief sufficiently to join the Army. These pressures sometimes did succeed in inducing an objector to change his status, presumably to the benefit of the war effort, but often at the sacrifice of his personal integrity and to the discredit of the national profession of tolerance and religious freedom.

Discrimination likewise appeared in the operation of the draft machinery; local boards often denied objectors a deserved occupational or medical deferment, erroneously classified them as eligible for military service, or pushed them, contrary to their requests, into noncombatant military service as against civilian service. Such mistakes were frequently corrected on appeal, but, by the subsequent admission of Selective Service Headquarters itself, many were upheld. Much of the difficulty arose because the same agency responsible for manning an army was charged with determining whether a man's conscience should exempt him from the Army—a rather stern challenge to objectivity in ascertaining the quality and nature of individual belief. The fact that the highest rung in the appeals system —the Presidential Appeals Board—was composed entirely of military officers was hardly calculated to offset this liability to discrimination; indeed, this arrangement probably violated the letter and spirit of the original law, though later, at Selective Service insistence, the law was modified to permit military composition of the Appeals Board.

Under rulings which prevailed until the conclusion of hostilities, discrimination resulting from such administrative miscarriage was not subject to judicial correction unless the objector first carried out the order given him—which really meant that he had to be prepared to violate his conscience by entering the Army before he could gain legal recognition of the validity of his claim. The Supreme Court ultimately amended this proceeding to permit prior review, but by then it was too late for most of the objectors affected. In general, the courts upheld the discriminatory interpretations of the Selective Service Act.

Objectors who violated the law under these conditions met with discrimination as well as incarceration. On the average, their sentences were considerably longer than those of other Selective Service Act violators and, indeed, longer than those imposed on white slavers and car thieves. For the most part, moreover, they were denied amnesty, while criminals who agreed to enter the Army received a full pardon for their offenses, whatever they might be.

Conscientious objectors outside the draft fared better at the hands of their communities and employers than during World War I. Though two states forbade them certain types of public employment and though in isolated instances they were discharged from private employment because of their stand, there was no general witch-hunt. The record of tolerance notably improved in colleges and universities, and objectors generally escaped public ridicule and pressure.

One disquieting legal decision, however, cast its dark shadow over objectors outside the draft. The implications of the Supreme Court opinion in the Summers case were far-reaching and disturbing to those who wished to prevent occupational discrimination.

The limits to tolerance of conscience in the United States were fixed not so much by general public mandate as by pockets of influential opinion predisposed to view the objector as an unpatriotic slacker and resenting the fact that he was spared the risks of combat. Some studies of public opinion (those, for example, of Leo Crespi) revealed astonishing liberality toward conscience in the nation as a whole, with wide acceptance of the objector's sincerity and loyalty, and willingness to treat him without discrimination. Veterans' groups, however, funneling the various elements of hostility, forcefully demanded a rule of iron for the objector. Their spokesmen in Congress effectively prevented any relaxation of legislative restraints and discrimination, while Selective Service responded to the pressures—actual, anticipated, and imagined—by progressively hardening its administrative regulations.

In the battle over conscience, the objectors and their supporters among religious and civil-liberties groups achieved a victory by implanting the principle of alternative civilian service in the American democratic tradition. But they did not win equality of treatment for the conscientious objector, and they failed completely to persuade the nation to concede freedom to the man who could not conscientiously perform any conscripted service in time of war emergency.

How Much Conscience Was There?

It is evident on the record that the number of conscientious objectors in the United States during World War II was very small, in both absolute and relative terms. All together, probably not more than 50,000 were actually conscripted or sent to prison—out of some 13,000,000 called up under the Selective Training and Service Act. If one adds to this total the number deferred for various reasons, the total number of objectors was not more than 100,000. However, the number had undoubtedly grown, both absolutely and relatively, since World War I.

What of "conscience" qualitatively? Here it is important to point out certain characteristics which stand out in the whole story, whether before draft boards, in the Army, in Civilian Public Service, or in prison. In the first place, many objectors were inexperienced in the ways of the world and in the problems of human relations. In part, this was simply due to the fact of youth; in part, however, the religious background of most objectors had sheltered them from many of life's unlovely but real relations. Sometimes they exhibited an astonishing ignorance even of their rights under the law.

In the second place, when acting collectively they often reflected a rather glaring absence of agreement among themselves and a lack of clarity about their objectives, and these disagreements were accentuated during the course of the war.

A third underlying characteristic was the tendency for emphasis on individual conscience to create a kind of self-centeredness which frequently affected profoundly the perspective from which the objector viewed the world. The psychological pattern inherent in this egotism is relatively clear: that is, when emphasis was placed on individual conscience and upon its rights against the practices of a warmaking and conscripting society, the individual objector sometimes tended to build a wall about himself and to view all problems solely from the perspective of his individual salvation. It was but a

short step from this position to the conclusion in thought and action
that "I am right and society is totally wrong." The formula might,
and did in some instances, easily become "I am right and my fellow
objector is totally wrong." Thus the very tendency to see all things
from the perspective of an individual salvation individually attained
led in certain cases to a kind of intolerance, not only of those who
were deemed to be wrong in making war but also with reference to
those other objectors whose consciences dictated different courses
of action. Among some "absolutists" there grew up, for example, a
kind of moral hierarchy which saw the I-A-O at the bottom of the
heap, the conformist C.P.S. man close to the bottom, the non-co-
operating C.P.S. man third, and the walkout or nonregistrant at the
moral pinnacle. Many Jehovah's Witnesses tended to look down
upon "heathen" objectors who could not accept the tenets of the
Watchtower Society. And some conformist C.P.S. men and church
administrators thought of nonconformist objectors as simply stubborn
"obstructionists."

This is not to say, of course, that the emphasis on conscience always, or even in most cases, degenerated into intolerable egotism.
But it was a sufficiently common thread in the whole pattern to
deserve comment. This is simply another way of pointing out that a
very large proportion of conscientious objectors were not saints,
whether they happened to be in the Army, in Civilian Public Service,
in church and National Service Board administration, or in prison.

On the other hand, it is clear that most objectors, once they had
elected the pacifist position, retained it throughout the course of the
war. The number who began as objectors and later transferred into
combatant military service was small, despite all the pressures of
Selective Service and the other serious handicaps under which conscience labored. In some cases, experiences in Civilian Public Service
and prison greatly strengthened objectors in their original convictions. In other instances, initial attitudes of intolerance gave way to
much deeper spiritual experiences which changed the attitudes of
individuals involved, made them more tolerant, and led them to
see new implications of pacifism.

The terrific pressures of war and conscription had both obvious
and subtle effects. The many objectors who tended to be somewhat

naïve about things of the world often began the war period with high hopes of what pacifism and objection could accomplish. Some thought of new techniques of community relations; others, in terms of the development of higher ideals of service. Great was the disillusionment of many when war and Selective Service taught them differently; how many "cynics" were produced we shall probably never know. So frustrated were some that they surrendered their original convictions. Others managed to salvage something of their earlier high hopes through participation in some of the more constructive projects of alternative service.

But increasingly, as the pressures of conscription tightened and disillusionment grew, many objectors reached the conclusion that they could preserve the integrity of their consciences only by various types of "resistance" tactics: slowdowns, strikes, or walkouts in Civilian Public Service and in prison. As a matter of fact, there is discernible among objectors as a whole a marked shift in emphasis from "service" as the key word of conscientious objection to "resistance" as the motif. Some, indeed, looked upon "resistance" as a most important kind of service to society, but it is sufficiently clear that in saying this they did not have in mind the same kind of service as those who talked in more orthodox terms of "service" to the community. The shift from orthodox service conceptions to resistance ideas was particularly reflected in government camps and in prison, but it was also evident in Friends, Brethren, and even Mennonite camps. This change in emphasis among conscripted and imprisoned objectors was encouraged by important pacifist organizations, notably the Fellowship of Reconciliation, the War Resisters League, and the Absolutist War Objectors Association.

What was the effect of the "resistance" approach on the objectors themselves and on their conceptions and actions? Here one enters a highly controversial realm.

On the one hand, it was argued by leaders of the "resistance" that the tactics were necessary if pacifists and objectors were to retain their integrity in light of the encroachments of war and conscription. It was also contended that "resistance" experience was valuable in that it was essentially nonviolent and yet provided an effective weapon against tyranny. "Resistance" techniques, it was maintained, could make of pacifism and conscientious objection a truly political movement, whereas they were now largely individual and nonpolitical. Resisters saw themselves as emulating Gandhi.

The opponents of resistance, on the other hand, thought that they discerned a tendency within resistance groups to become violent and intolerant of others. "Resistance," they said, found it difficult, if not impossible, to distinguish between principle and personality; hence it was inevitable that the "resisting" objector, while professing hostility to an idea only, tended in the course of his resistance to identify the idea with a person. Thus he sometimes came to hate the camp foreman, the prison guard, or the Army officer who might be administering the scheme to which he took exception. It was also argued that "resistance" was, after all, negative and not positive in its approach, and hence incompatible with conceptions which should be implicit in the ideals for which objectors stood.

What are we to say about this controversy in the light of World War II experience? On the whole, it would seem that the experience of the war was inconclusive. Despite widespread resistance tactics in camp and prison, the numbers involved were after all very small and the planning and training of the resisters necessarily often inadequate. Moreover, it is difficult to make definite statements with respect to the effect of resistance on the men themselves. These observations, however, do seem to be in order: (1) Care should be taken to differentiate between types of resistance—the slowdown was not the same as a strike, for example, and statements made about the former might not necessarily be applicable to the latter. (2) Many of the leaders of the resistance were young men of great intellectual and moral capacity, and for them the tactics served clearly to cut through the complex of Selective Service and prison authoritarianism and to resolve the inner contradictions created by the conflict between their ideals and forcible submission to systems antagonistic to those ideals. (3) The effect of resistance tactics on others as well as on those using them depends in considerable degree on the social context in which they are used and, above all, on the training and self-discipline of those who use them. This was recognized by Gandhi again and again, particularly when he would call off civil disobedience and non-co-operation campaigns that had degenerated into violence. And it is true that some objectors in their resistance during World War II adopted tactics which violated human freedom and dignity. A few tended to become enslaved by the fight to get rid of the system they called slavery. As in any social struggle, truth was sometimes eclipsed by the fascination of action.

Did the Churches Betray Religious Liberty by Collaborating with Selective Service in the Administration of Alternative Service?

This was one of the most important questions to emerge during the whole course of the experience. Much bitterness was exhibited by some who answered "yes," while those who replied in the negative were often equally stinging in their remarks.

The answer depends partly on the meaning of such expressions as "betray," "religious liberty," and "freedom of conscience." Generally speaking, there seemed to be two implications. It was maintained by those who gave an affirmative answer, first, that the churches had a peculiar obligation to defend the rights of conscience, and above all the rights of the objector, and that somehow they impaired their effectiveness in this role by administration of Civilian Public Service; and, second, that the churches, and particularly the so-called Historic Peace Churches, were peculiarly obligated to defend the principle of separation of church and state and failed to do so by the very act of consenting to administer alternative service.

How, then, shall we analyze these charges? It would seem well, first of all, to cast up a balance sheet of church administration and, secondly, to evaluate that sheet in terms of the problem of "betrayal."

On the favorable side of the ledger there are a number of items. Before enumerating them, however, the basic position of the Historic Peace Churches in relation to Selective Service and the government should be kept in mind. The churches had little, if any, independent authority in the administration of Civilian Public Service, as we have shown in this study. Particularly after the earlier years of administration were the church Committees rather strictly accountable to Selective Service, either through the formal medium of the National Service Board or directly. The churches, in return for what they had hoped might be a measure of autonomy in administration, were expected to act as enforcement agents of Selective Service, to become policemen in disciplining objectors according to the rigid ideas of an agency headed by a major general. In the end, the churches were denied their administrative autonomy but were not relieved of their theoretical responsibility for discipline. This was, to say the least, a difficult and frustrating situation.

Within the rather narrow limits granted them by a Selective Service increasingly jealous of its prerogatives and sensitive to its version of "public opinion," the churches did accomplish something.

In the first place, they did defend, sometimes quite vigorously, the objector's integrity of conscience. This was particularly true with respect to such problems as arbitrary transfers from camp to camp. It was also well illustrated in the strong stand the Committees took on work which objectors might regard as military; here the churches were quite certain of their position and defended the objector as against the demands of authorities who might ask him to do war work.

In the second place, it seems to be true that church-administered camps in general provided a more congenial and freer atmosphere within which to work than government-administered camps. There was on the whole greater opportunity for self-expression, and the tendency, so marked in government camps, to treat every act of protest as insubordination was less evident. In many cases, directors of church-administered camps actually ignored Selective Service regulations and refused in some instances to report violations or to impose penalties—a polite form of administrative "sabotage." Moreover, by the end of the war there were functioning institutions of representative government in Brethren and Friends camps and advisory councils in Mennonite camps. Severely criticized as church camp administrators often were—sometimes with full justification —they gave greater weight, on the whole, to the opinions of men in camp than did government camp administrators.

Third, the religious administrative agencies and the National Service Board for Religious Objectors constituted an important spearhead in the campaign for greater service opportunities. It was the insistence of the Service Committees and the National Service Board which was often decisive. This is not to minimize the role of other organizations striving for the same objective but rather to emphasize the key position in which the churches were placed.

Fourth, many men undoubtedly felt more at home in camps managed by churchmen or church-trained individuals than in the government camps more impersonally administered. Most Mennonites, for example, probably would not have felt at ease in camps like Mancos or Germfask, however much they might experience the serious tensions and frustrations which permeated even the best-administered church camps.

On the other hand, it is equally clear that church administration is rightly subject to a severe indictment. In the first place, the Peace Churches never really achieved any large measure of unity of outlook and practice in their dealings with Selective Service; thus their effectiveness in standing between the conscripted objector and Selective Service was greatly impaired. This lack of unity was in some degree due to the difference in philosophical assumptions which separated the Friends from Mennonites and Brethren. The Mennonites, for example, had definite scruples against any methods of action which might be termed "resistance," whereas Friends were constantly confronted by those within their own circle who urged more independent action. In part, the lack of unity was due to clashes of personalities; administrative co-operation was novel, and it is hardly surprising that it was constantly tending to fall apart. But its failure often meant that the objector was the victim.

Second, the churches and church administrators were extraordinarily gullible and naïve with respect to certain of the most important matters. Their very readiness to accept responsibility for camp administration in the absence of any written agreement with Selective Service is an excellent example of gullibility. This absence of a definite written contract left them, and the conscientious objectors entrusted to their care, at the mercy of an ever-encroaching Selective Service. They began their administrative relationship in an atmosphere of vagueness and uncertainty, and, once having begun it under such auspices, they found it increasingly difficult to overcome this enormous handicap, even when, later on, they realized their mistake.

But they seemed unable to learn from experience, for they repeatedly illustrated their gullibility. Thus, in the case of the "frozen fund" controversy, they trusted Selective Service to make all necessary arrangements to have the wages earned by objectors on farm service made available for reconstruction or Civilian Public Service expenses; they therefore neglected until too late a direct approach to the Comptroller General, which might have forestalled his unfavorable ruling as to the legality of such use of the fund. Or, again, with respect to the setting up of detached units, they trusted Selective Service and found that in the end they were denuded of administrative power, much to the dismay of many objectors in the units, who had begun their work under the assumption that they were to work in church-administered units. The Service Committees and many of their administrators seemed not to understand the nature of Selective Service, but proceeded blandly on the assumption that, despite previous disappointments to the contrary, things would get better and better. The result was that a relationship which, from the church point of view, had begun as a partnership, rapidly degenerated into something substantially like that of a cat yoked to a mouse. Some church administators seemed not even to realize that they were in the position of the mouse. It is small wonder that many objectors, particularly after 1942, began to doubt the perspicacity of church administrators.

Third, church administrators were frequently less than candid in dealing with objectors. In most cases they were not deliberately dishonest, but they seemed all too frequently unable to convey to the objectors in camps and detached service units any feeling of oneness with themselves. Multiplied examples of this lack of candor led even mild-mannered and tolerant objectors to become bitter; while the less mild filled the air with epithets of opprobrium.

Fourth, some church officials were administratively incompetent. These were gradually displaced during the course of the war and, after about 1942, capable assignees were increasingly added to the staffs, raising the level of administrative competence. Nevertheless, the churches had not entirely overcome their deficiencies in this respect when Civilian Public Service came to an end.

So much for the balance sheet of church administration. The larger issue remains: should the churches have refused to administer alternative service in the first place or have withdrawn when they discovered the narrow limits of their authority?

The authors differ sharply in their answers to this question.

Mr. Sibley's View. Admitting that the wisdom of hindsight always has an advantage over that of foresight, and without questioning the motives of those involved, I believe emphatically that the long-run interests of religious and civil liberty would have been better served had the churches refused to administer alternative service in the first place, and particularly alternative service without provision for pay and under the other conditions actually obtaining. The nature of the system was certainly sufficiently clear by the end of 1942. Even if the churches up to then had hoped for greater autonomy, the evidence by that time should have convinced them that their autonomy was being whittled away steadily and that they were becoming mere arms of a military machine which cared little for the principle of liberty. They ought at that time, if not before, to have withdrawn from administrative responsibility.

Freed of their responsibility to a major general, they might then have served the interests of objectors more forcefully. They could really have pressed for pay, compensation, and dependency allowances, whereas, in actual fact, with administrative responsibility, they were constantly concerned lest they offend Selective Service and thus lose still more of their narrow autonomy. They were put in a false position—trying simultaneously to be churches and agents of a military state bent primarily on warmaking. As a result, they became something less than churches and were yet uneasy in their position as agents and taskmasters of Selective Service. The nonpacifist churches supplied chaplains for the Army and Navy, thus falling in with the demands of a military machine. The pacifist churches, by their mere presence as administators for a military agency, lent an air of religious sanction to a quasi-military treatment of conscientious objectors. It is difficult to imagine the great leaders of seventeenth-century Quakerism consenting to such an arrangement.

Withdrawal would have emphasized the responsibility of the government for objectors—it could no longer have used the churches as a shield, an arrangement which General Hershey and his colonels found very convenient indeed. While the *principle* of alternative civilian service was a valuable addition to the American tradition, it was so perverted and distorted in practice as to make one wonder whether there had really been much progress in the actual recognition of conscience.

This is not to deny that the churches performed many services for objectors, even within the system. Nor need their sincerity be called in question. All that need be maintained is that they were unwise in consenting to the arrangement in the first place, unwise in continuing it, and wrong in allowing the principle of church-state separation to be so greatly impaired. By continuing to administer conscription, they established a precedent which might well bolster the arguments of Erastians and militarists in the future. By assuming an enormous financial burden, they not only enabled the state to evade its responsibility for the support of objectors but also depleted their own limited resources, which were so desperately needed for relief. By continuing for so long to co-operate with a compulsory system of payless work, they served poorly the cause of social justice and helped set a precedent for future exploitation of labor. The courts, as was to be expected, certified the legality and constitutionality of the whole system; it was unfortunate that the churches felt called upon to certify, by implication, the system's social ethics.

The churches ought to have issued a declaration of independence against the warmaking state. Instead, while gaining incidental benefits for objectors in the process, they allowed themselves to be manipulated by the state for its own ends. It was a tragedy of World War II that, while the churches strove to protect liberty within the narrow limits prescribed by military officers, they did not see that their unique role ought to have been to stand outside the system and judge it from the perspective of religious absolutes. In so doing, they would have served better the cause of conscientious objectors and of liberty in general.

Mr. Jacob's View. Although the higher ideals of service which were espoused in Civilian Public Service were grievously frustrated, the churches which financed and administered the program won a new and significant place for the religious-pacifist minority in American society. First, they persuaded most of the c.o.'s to persist in a demonstration of good will and of constructive concern for human welfare, instead of merely rejecting governmental authority, despite the arbitrary and often unjust acts of the government. Second, the dogged determination of the religious agencies succeeded in opening to c.o.'s publicly acclaimed opportunities for service, notably the work in mental hospitals and training schools, medical research, public health, and agricultural work. Third, the churches' administrative responsibilities enabled them to resist at many points the impairment of the c.o.'s service by senseless and inept governmental restraints. Finally, by assuming the role of sponsor rather than critic of Civilian Public Service, the religious bodies were able more effectively to interpret and defend the c.o.'s actions before public and government and thereby convince a great portion of the nation not only of his sincerity but of his worthy and upright citizenship.

From the standpoint of the c.o., most of those assigned to C.P.S. deliberately chose to serve under religious administration, even when they had the option of service directly under the government. Though some made their decision for reasons of personal inconvenience, a sizable number, including most members of the Historic Peace Churches and others, believed that the sympathetic support of the church administrators made the conditions of service far more congenial to the maintenance and strengthening of their faith. Under such circumstances, if the churches had decided to withdraw from C.P.S. they would arbitrarily have forced all c.o.'s under government administration, closing the channel of service which most preferred as the means of expressing their beliefs.

The heavy financial responsibilities of religious administration of C.P.S. strengthened the recognition of the right of conscientious objection within the churches. Most Protestant denominations were impelled to go beyond nominal profession of belief in the sanctity of individual conscience and to support their c.o.'s materially, even though their members were overwhelmingly committed to the war. As a result, the legitimacy of the position of the c.o. was vindicated "under fire." The Historic Peace Churches which bore the major responsibility were not weakened by the call of C.P.S. upon their resources; instead, the divisions which had thwarted real unity of action heretofore among their varying branches were overcome in the course of their ordeal on behalf of the c.o. Their members gave more generously and more completely to support the C.P.S. program than any of their previous church enterprises—*without* detracting from the other aspects of their church work. As a matter of fact, the habit of giving to C.P.S. carried over to the benefit of the relief programs of the churches, which were looked upon as an essential outgrowth of the same spiritual convictions upon which the service of the c.o.'s was grounded.

In the long run, church administration of C.P.S. may have made its most significant contribution to the cause of religious freedom in the United States by exploring the means of assuring independence of religious thought and action from state control, even under conditions of war which appear to dictate the absorption of all of life by the state. The traditional separation of church and state has been distorted by the growth of nationalism to the point where, at least in time of war, the church has joined forces with the state in the prosecution of avowedly common ends. Even in the United States, churches during the last war tended to treat their independence as essentially an *organizational* matter, not one of principle. The Historic Peace Churches sought to reverse this relationship. By accepting organizational and administrative responsibility under government authority, they undertook to defend the separation of religious *principle* from state control. In this attempt, they achieved notable results. They suffered increasing encroachments upon their administrative autonomy, but they vigorously resisted the dictates of the government when clear issues of conscience or religious belief were at stake; Selective Service almost uniformly yielded at these points (for instance, assignment to work of military significance). In contrast to the respect accorded religious administrative agencies, the government customarily brushed aside as of little consequence the representations of the churches "outside."

Three alternatives confront the church in its relation to the modern state. The identification of church and state is implied by the unquestioning support of war by the church, even though the state refrains from direct control of church activity. The complete separation of church and state suspends the church in a lofty but ineffectual judgment seat surveying the acts of the state. The third alternative is that which was piloted by the churches administering C.P.S. They paid the price of subservience to government authority in assuming *public* responsibilities, but in return they secured a substantial measure of freedom for *individual* religious thought and expression on the part of the c.o.'s whose convictions they upheld. In so doing, they in effect reinterpreted for the days of World War II the persistent Christian enigma of "Render unto Caesar the things that are Caesar's and unto God the things that are God's."

Was Compulsion Effective in Securing the Compliance of Conscience with the Demands of the State?

Efforts to extract obedience and service from the conscientious objector by means of compulsion met resounding defeat. The discipline, morale, and physical work product of conscientious objectors

—in camp, prison, and armed services alike—deteriorated markedly as the government invoked its coercive powers.

Despite liberal use of the devices of restraint and punishment permissible under the law, Selective Service could not prevent a sizable minority in Civilian Public Service from transgressing its directives. The withholding of privileges such as furlough, segregation of "troublemakers" in isolated camps, and the threat of prosecution or reclassification failed to overcome the resistance of objectors to regulations considered arbitrary, unfair, or in violation of conscience. The government was unable, for instance, to compel men to work on a project which they considered of military significance. Compulsion was particularly ineffective against those who came to oppose the whole alternative-service system as an evil compromise with conscription. Whether these men refused to register, resisted induction, walked out, or sought to sabotage the program from within by work strikes or slowdowns, they withstood most attempts to force their compliance. The stringent penalties imposed for violation of the Selective Service Act appear to have had little if any effect in dissuading these men from stepping outside the law. Indeed, the amount of resistance actually increased as sentences meted out by the courts lengthened during the course of hostilities; the dockets of the courts which were most stringent (Pennsylvania, Iowa) were as well filled with cases as those of the most lenient (California, Oregon).

Even the application of physical force and solitary confinement in Army and prison could but rarely compel an objector to cease "recalcitrance" dictated by conscience, and in prisons, at least, the authorities finally abandoned the more extreme measures of enforcement against objectors.

The ineffective results of coercion applied to conscience led to sharp disagreement among those responsible for the administration of conscription with respect to the ultimate recourse which should have been adopted. Selective Service, uncompromisingly committed to compulsory discipline as the means of controlling conscience, urged that additional powers of coercion should be entrusted to the administrative authorities. It argued that the limits of Constitution and law should be stretched to allow officials to take peremptory action outside of judicial process whenever their directives were infringed. In other words, Selective Service concluded that if civil authorities could have the scope of punitive power enjoyed by military authority—including detention, forced labor, and even physical force—they could haul conscience into line with the demands of government.

The Department of Justice reached no general conclusion with respect to the most effective method of handling conscientious violators of the law, but a substantial segment of those responsible became more and more skeptical of the efficacy of compulsion in such cases. In several situations, especially after the end of hostilities, district attorneys were reluctant to prosecute objectors reported to them by Selective Service and were sustained by their superiors in this inaction on the ground that the courts should not have to serve as the disciplinary arm of the administrator. Generally, however, the Department of Justice did not shrink from its assigned task of arresting all those who broke the law and demanding that they be put behind bars.

In prison, objectors continually prodded their jailers to raise prison practice to the standards of modern "reformist" penology ostensibly already in effect; though some of the objectors, especially absolutists and Jehovah's Witnesses, were harshly treated, the net effect of the objectors' protests was a marked advancement of "progressive" penal policies. The men increasingly secured individual consideration with respect to privileges granted in the prison system. Certain significant concessions were made on account of conscience, notably special provisions for the parole of objectors under Executive Order 8641 and, in the end, unconditional release of absolutists like Corbett Bishop who conscientiously resisted all compulsion. But it was a long and involved struggle, some phases of which, like the Murphy–Taylor controversy, cast but little credit on the Bureau of Prisons.

The problems of enforcing law against the imperatives of conscience finally convinced the Attorney General who had been most continuously responsible (Francis Biddle) that, rather than increasing the dose of compulsion to secure compliance of objectors, over-all administrative policies should be changed to afford wider outlets for their diverse convictions and thus minimize the occasions for use of coercion. In reaching this conclusion, the Attorney General was, of course, simply going back to church and civil-liberties-group proposals made in 1940.

The churches agreed heartily with the conclusion of the Attorney General. Self-discipline, they insisted, was the effective method of regulating the conduct of objectors. The voluntary consent of conscience must be won to assure satisfactory fulfillment of responsibilities to society. But the religious administrative agencies never really proved their case. Selective Service constantly demanded that they assume a firmer disciplinary role and, when dissatisfied with their slowness or laxity in enforcing regulations, deprived them of discretion to use what they regarded as their "redemptive" methods.

The extraordinary frustrations of many objectors under the pressures of war and conscription, their lack of clarity and unity in regard to the ends they were seeking, and their failure to achieve agreement among themselves as to the nature of their social responsibilities presented great obstacles to the maturing of an effective alternative to external compulsion as a means of reconciling the conflicts of conscience with a government at war. However futile and pernicious constraint from without proved to be, its existence was not unrelated to the fundamental weakness of objectors and their organizations— a division of purposes so profound as to prevent attainment of a united, closely knit, and self-ordered pacifist community, capable of acting collectively (at least on major issues) within the broader society of which it was a part.

Experience with American conscientious objectors in World War II proved that government cannot "handle" conscience by compulsion within the constitutional limits of American democracy. On the other hand, it also seemed to demonstrate the incapacity of American objectors to reach agreement on objectives and types of action to be adopted by the group as a whole.

Under the circumstances, then, the conflict between conscience and the state can be minimized only if objectors are allowed, as suggested by the former Attorney General, to fill niches individually appropriate and acceptable to them, while the upholders of conscientious objection to war strive to clarify their over-all social objectives and discover a basis for greater unity among themselves in regard to the role which they can properly fulfill as a small minority in a country overwhelmingly committed to conscription and war.

Can Conscience Be More Adequately Recognized, Assuming Continued Conscription?

Even under the most favorable circumstances, complete freedom of conscience can hardly be reconciled with a system of conscription, and conscription would seem to be an inevitable accompaniment of modern war or threat of war. The real "solution" to the problem of conscientious objection to war would be the elimination of war itself; war and the preservation of democratic values are incompatible with each other.

Short of the abolition of war, further progress toward recognition of the rights of conscience within the framework of a would-be democratic society would seem to call for the following *minimal* conditions:

(1) There should be legal recognition of the validity of conscientious conviction, regardless of the source of that belief, whether religious or nonreligious, philosophical or political.

(2) As a corollary of the first principle, the sole test of conscience should be sincerity. It should be recognized, however, that any external judgment on the sincerity of belief of an individual is highly dubious and difficult, at best.

(3) Determination of individual claims of conscientious objection and assignment of objectors to alternative service should be made by tribunals wholly independent of the regular draft machinery.

(4) Provision should be made for at least the following alternatives: (a) Noncombatant service in the armed forces; (b) alternative civilian service, both governmental (conservation, public health, mental institutions, slum clearance, institutions for juvenile delinquency and mental defectives, etc.) and nongovernmental (religious and relief agencies, social welfare institutions, hospitals, schools, etc.); and (c) complete exemption of those having conscientious scruples against any and all types of service under conscription.

(5) The agency or institution to which the objector is assigned under alternative civilian service should have full administrative responsibility, with the responsibility and types of agencies to be clearly defined by presidential executive order. Neither public nor private agencies using objectors would have any connection, direct or indirect, with the draft machinery.

(6) Provision should be made for pay equal to going rates for

the type of work involved, allowing the objector to retain for his own use only that part equivalent to remuneration provided in the armed services for comparable work. The objector would contribute the difference between going wages and what he receives to a philanthropy of his own choice.

(7) Dependency allowances and compensation for casualties should be provided on a scale comparable to that prevailing in the armed services.

(8) Automatic re-examination should be effected after three months' imprisonment of the claims of those pleading conscientious objection when imprisoned. This would apply to both military and civil prisoners, would enable tribunals to rectify their errors, and would keep the number of imprisoned objectors at a very low minimum.

Provisions similar to these were actually embodied in the British law of conscientious objection and put into effective practice during World War II. But it would probably be no easy task to persuade Congress to adopt them for the United States. On the whole, there is much greater respect for eccentricity and individual liberty in the British tradition than in the American. British society is less subject to pressures of the mass mind and of social conformity. Moreover, pacifist opinion is much more widespread in Great Britain than in the United States, with pacifists in Parliament and well-known conscientious objectors in the fields of literature and the arts. Consequently, more liberal legislation respecting conscientious objectors will probably come hard to the Congress of the United States.

In one sense, the Selective Training and Service Act of 1948 was an advance in that it deferred (without any requirement of alternative service) all religious conscientious objectors to military service. But in another sense it was a retrogression, since it defined religion very narrowly (by contrast with the Act of 1940, which had left the term undefined, thus leaving a fairly substantial latitude for administrative interpretation). Moreover, the Act made no advance whatsoever toward recognition of nonreligious objection or objection to conscription as such, which, as the war demonstrated, can also be conscientious.

We can only hope—on evidence of things not seen—that the

American nation has not fully exhausted its potentialities of tolerance for the conscientious scruples of its pacifist minority, and that it may yet respond to the imperatives of a democratic faith by its consideration for the liberties of those who cannot join in its military defense.

Appendix

A. *Chronology of American C.O.'s.*

January 10, 1940	Memorandum of Brethren, Friends and Mennonites suggesting to President Roosevelt a scheme for alternative civilian service and exemption for "absolutists" in the event of war.
July 22, 1940	Friends War Problems Committee suggests broad and liberal provision for objectors in the pending Selective Training and Service Bill.
August 28, 1940	Senate passes bill including provision for objectors opposed by "religious training and belief" to all military service, to perform "work of national importance under civilian direction."
September 16, 1940	President signs Selective Training and Service Act.
October 5, 1940	National Service Board for Religious Objectors is organized to represent the Historic Peace Churches and other concerned groups in discussions with the government relating to c.o.'s.
October 24, 1940	Churches propose to the President's Advisory Committee on Selective Service programs for service by c.o.'s under both government and private civilian administration, with provision for pay to those electing government service.
November 29, 1940	President objects to liberality of initial proposals for alternative service.
December 6, 1940	Executive Order 8606 provides for assignment and defines duties of c.o.'s able to accept noncombatant service.

483

December 20, 1940	President approves alternative service without pay for c.o.'s, administered and financed by religious agencies under Selective Service supervision.
January 18, 1941	Executive Order 8641 makes special provision for parole of Selective Service Act violators.
May 15, 1941	First Civilian Public Service camp opens.
March 5, 1942	First C.P.S. "detached service" unit starts.
April 19–25, 1943	Forty C.P.S. assignees attend Chicago Conference on Social Action, violating order by General Hershey.
June 13, 1943	Stanley Murphy and Louis Taylor transferred to Federal Prison Medical Center, Springfield, Missouri.
June 30, 1943	Congress passes amendment by Representative Starnes preventing C.P.S. assignees from serving in foreign countries.
July 1, 1943	Selective Service undertakes full administration of C.P.S. camp at Mancos, Colorado.
December 5, 1943	Congress legalizes action of Selective Service in creating presidential review committees composed of military officers.
June 11, 1945	Supreme Court in Summers case decides that state action denying qualified person the right to practice law because of his conscientious objection to war is not a violation of religious liberty under the Constitution.
October, 1945	Systematic demobilization of C.P.S. begins after four-month delay by Congressional opposition.
March 2, 1946	American Friends Service Committee ceases administration of C.P.S. and Selective Service assumes direction of Friends camps.
April 22, 1946	Supreme Court in Girouard decision declares that a conscientious objector can take a qualified oath of allegiance under naturalization law, thus permitting naturalization of c.o.'s.
March 29, 1947	C.P.S. program closes.
December 24, 1947	President Truman in an "amnesty" proclamation declines to pardon most conscientious objectors convicted of violating the law.

B. *Appeal of the Historic Peace Churches to President Roosevelt regarding provisions for c.o.'s in the event of conscription, January 10, 1940.*

The Honorable Franklin D. Roosevelt   January 10, 1940
The President of the United States
The White House
Washington, D.C.

Dear Mr. President:

On February 12, 1937, you graciously received representatives of the Society of Friends, the Mennonite Church, and the Church of the Brethren, who presented to you statements expressing the historic and unbroken convictions of these groups against war, and their devotion to peace and good will. These attitudes grew out of deep religious convictions, based on the spirit and teachings of Jesus, and are a part of a way of life which we believe cherishes the highest values for all men. Today we again submit to you our concerns in view of present world conditions.

We desire, first of all, to express our deep appreciation for your repeated effort to prevent the European war, our warm support of your confident insistence that the United States shall not be drawn into this conflict, and our hope that opportunity will arise for our nation to co-operate with other neutral nations in offering mediation or other peace-promoting techniques toward the earliest possible establishment of peace. We have also warmly appreciated your personal interest in the large number of political and racial refugees whose relief and resettlement are so urgent a present obligation for all men of good will. Your recent challenging appeal for humanitarian relief to European war sufferers has likewise won the hearty response of our groups. Our own organizations are definitely planning to contribute to such projects in the future, as in the past, not only with the desire to minister to human need, but also to keep vivid the vision of a better way of life than that of intolerance, persecution, and war.

Opportunities and responsibilities of relief and rehabilitation for the war sufferers in Spain and elsewhere have come to us recently through the American Friends Service Committee and the service agencies of the Mennonite Church and Church of the Brethren. Our Spanish relief program, after more than two years, is probably drawing to a close, but relief responsibilities in China continue. Refugee colonies in Paraguay and Brazil still require our care and support. Just now we are being asked by interested American groups to assume important new responsibilities for the many tragic Polish war sufferers, and our representatives are now in Europe to investigate and, if possible, to inaugurate this project.

If, in spite of all efforts to maintain neutrality, the tragic day should come when our beloved nation is drawn into war, we should expect to continue our work for suffering humanity, and to increase its scope because of the greater need at home and abroad. Such service would permit those whose conscientious convictions forbid participation in war in any form to render constructive service to their country and to the world. We appear today chiefly to discuss with you plans to provide for this alternative service as it may relate to possible conscription, reserving the privilege to offer at a later date a supplementary memorandum dealing with other types of conscientious objectors.

As you know, in the last war the United States Government finally authorized such nonmilitary humanitarian service to be substituted for military service, and furloughed conscientious objectors to this relief work or to farm labor. But this arrangement was provided only after months of confusion and distress, and only after repeated conferences between our representatives and officials of the War Department, because of the lack of any previously established policy. Since we understand that plans are now being formulated for mobilization of the nation's man power if war should come, and since the need for dealing with conscientious objectors would again emerge to confront Government agencies, we venture to suggest the advantage of advance discussion of the problem with the appropriate officials. We should much appreciate the opportunity for such discussion and are prepared to make concrete proposals to such officials regarding procedures for handling conscientious objectors and types of service which might be provided. In this connection we also venture to suggest the desirability of again setting up a civilian agency for dealing with this problem. There is a precedent for this in the action of President Wilson in 1918.

We have come to you, Mr. President, with these requests, because our previous conversations with you have persuaded us that you both understand and appreciate the position of the historic peace churches. Our desire is to co-operate in finding the best solution to the problem of the conscientious objector, and it is even more to render as loyal citizens the highest type of constructive service we can to our country and to the world.

Faithfully yours,

FOR THE SOCIETY OF FRIENDS
Rufus Jones
Walter C. Woodward

FOR THE MENNONITE CHURCH
P. C. Hiebert
Harold S. Bender
E. L. Harshbarger

FOR THE CHURCH OF THE BRETHREN
Rufus D. Bowman
Paul H. Bowman

C. *Selective Training and Service Act of 1940, Section 5(g).* (Pub. L. No. 783, 76th Congress, 2d Sess.)

Nothing contained in this act shall be construed to require any person to be subject to combatant training and service in the land or naval forces of the United States who, by reason of religious training and belief, is conscientiously opposed to participation in war in any form. Any such person claiming such exemption from combatant training and service because of such conscientious objections whose claim is sustained by the local board shall, if he is inducted into the land or naval forces under this act, be assigned to noncombatant service as defined by the President, or shall, if he is found to be conscientiously opposed to participation in such noncombatant service, in lieu of such induction, be assigned to work of national importance under civilian direction. Any such person claiming such exemption from combatant training and service because of such conscientious objections shall, if such claim is not sustained by the local board, be entitled to an appeal to the appropriate appeal board provided for in section 10(a)(2). Upon the filing of such appeal with the appeal board, the appeal board shall forthwith refer the matter to the Department of Justice for inquiry and hearing by the Department or the proper agency thereof. After appropriate inquiry by such agency, a hearing shall be held by the Department of Justice with respect to the character and good faith of objections of the person concerned, and such person shall be notified of the time and place of such hearing. The Department shall, after such hearing, if the objections are found to be sustained, recommend to the appeal board (1) that if the objector is inducted into the land or naval forces under this act, he shall be assigned to noncombatant service as defined by the President, or (2) that if the objector is found to be conscientiously opposed to participation in such noncombatant service, he shall in lieu of such induction be assigned to work of national importance under civilian direction. If after such hearing the Department finds that his objections are not sustained, it shall recommend to the appeal board that such objections be not sustained. The appeal board shall give consideration to but shall not be bound to follow the recommendation of the Department of Justice together with the record on appeal from the local board in making its decision. Each person whose claim for exemption from combatant training and service because of conscientious objections is sustained shall be listed by the local board on a register of conscientious objectors.

D. *D.S.S. Form 47, Special Form for Conscientious Objector.**

* Most of the space under the questions has been deleted.

SPECIAL FORM FOR CONSCIENTIOUS OBJECTOR

Order No. _____

Name _____
         (First)   (Middle)   (Last)

Address _____
         (Number and street or R. F. D. route)

_____
(City, town, or village)   (County)   (State)

_____
(STAMP OF LOCAL BOARD)

This form must be returned on or before _____
                                        (Five days after date of mailing or issue)

INSTRUCTIONS

A registrant who claims to be a conscientious objector shall offer information in substantiation of his claim on this special form, which when filed shall become a part of his Questionnaire.

The questions in Series II through V in this form are intended to obtain evidence of the genuineness of the claim made in Series I, and the answers given by the registrant shall be for the information only of the officials duly authorized under the regulations to examine them.

In the case of any registrant who claims to be a conscientious objector, the Local Board shall proceed in the ordinary course to classify him upon all other grounds of deferment, and shall consider and pass upon his claim as a conscientious objector only if, but for such claim, he would have been placed in Class I. The procedure for appeal from a decision of the Local Board on a claim for conscientious objection is provided for in the Selective Service Regulations.

Failure by the registrant to file this special form on or before the date indicated above may be regarded as a waiver by the registrant of his claim as a conscientious objector: *Provided, however,* That the Local Board, in its discretion, and for good cause shown by the registrant, may grant a reasonable extension of time for filing this special form.

D. S. S. Form 47

488

Series I—CLAIM FOR EXEMPTION

INSTRUCTIONS.—The registrant must sign his name to either Statement **A** or Statement **B** in this series but not to both of them. The registrant should strike out the statement in this series which he does not sign.

A. I claim the exemption provided by the Selective Training and Service Act of 1940 for conscientious objectors, because I am conscientiously opposed by reason of my religious training and belief to participation in war in any form and to participation in combatant military service or training therefor; but I am willing to participate in noncombatant service or training therefor under the direction of military authorities.

....
(Signature of registrant)

B. I claim the exemption provided by the Selective Training and Service Act of 1940 for conscientious objectors, because I am conscientiously opposed by reason of my religious training and belief to participation in war in any form and to participation in any service which is under the direction of military authorities.

....
(Signature of registrant)

Series II—RELIGIOUS TRAINING AND BELIEFS

INSTRUCTIONS.—Every question in this series must be fully answered. If more space is necessary, attach extra sheets of paper to this page.

1. Describe the nature of your belief which is the basis of your claim made in Series I above.

----

2. Explain how, when, and from whom or from what source you received the training and acquired the belief which is the basis of your claim made in Series I above.

----

3. Give the name and present address of the individual upon whom you rely most for religious guidance.

----

4. Under what circumstances, if any, do you believe in the use of force?

----

5. Describe the actions and behavior in your life which in your opinion most conspicuously demonstrate the consistency and depth of your religious convictions.

SPECIAL FORM FOR CONSCIENTIOUS OBJECTOR (continued)

6. Have you ever given public expression, written or oral, to the views herein expressed as the basis for your claim made in Series I above? If so, specify when and where.

Series III.—GENERAL BACKGROUND

INSTRUCTIONS.—Every question in this series must be fully answered. If more space is necessary, attach extra sheets of paper to this page.

1. Give the name and address of each school and college which you have attended, together with the dates of your attendance; and state in each instance the type of school (public, private, church, military, commercial, etc.).

2. Give a chronological list of all occupations, positions, jobs, or types of work, other than as a student in school or college, in which you have at any time been engaged, whether for monetary compensation or not, giving the facts indicated below with regard to each position or job held, or type of work in which engaged:

----

3. Give all addresses and dates of residence where you have formerly lived:

----

4. Give the name, address, and country of birth of your parents and indicate whether they are living or not.

Series IV.—PARTICIPATION IN ORGANIZATIONS

INSTRUCTIONS.—Questions 1, 2, and 3 in this series must be fully answered. If more space is necessary, attach extra sheets of paper to this page.

1. Have you ever been a member of any military organization or establishment? If so, state the name and address of same and give reasons why you became a member.

490

2. Are you a member of a religious sect or organization?_____ If your answer to question 2 is yes, answer questions (a) through (e).

(Yes or no)

- -

(a) State the name of the sect, and the name and location of its governing body or head if known to you:

- -

(b) When, where, and how did you become a member of said sect or organization?

- -

(c) State the name and location of the church, congregation, or meeting where you customarily attend:

- -

(d) Give the name and present address of the pastor or leader of such church, congregation, or meeting:

- -

(e) Describe carefully the creed or official statements of said religious sect or organization in relation to participation in war:

- -

3. Describe your relationships with and activities in all organizations with which you are or have been affiliated, other than religious or military:

- -

Series V.—REFERENCES

Give here the names and other information indicated concerning persons who could supply information as to the sincerity of your professed convictions against participation in war:

- -

SPECIAL FORM FOR CONSCIENTIOUS OBJECTOR (continued)

REGISTRANT'S AFFIDAVIT

INSTRUCTIONS.—The claim made on this form will not be considered unless it is supported by the following affidavit. (If the registrant cannot read, the questions and his answers thereto shall be read to him by the officer who administers the oath.)

STATE OF _____, COUNTY OF _____, ss:

I, _____, do solemnly swear (or affirm) that I am the registrant described in the foregoing questions and answers, that I know the contents of my said answers, and that each and every statement of fact in my answers to said questions is true, to the best of my knowledge and belief.

_____
(Registrant sign here)

_____
(Signature or mark of registrant)

Subscribed and sworn to (or affirmed) before me this _____ day of _____, 19____

_____
(Signature of officer administering oath)

_____
(Designation of officer)

If the registrant has received assistance from an advisor, the advisor shall sign the following statement:

I have assisted the registrant herein named in the preparation of this form.

_____
(Signature of advisor)

_____
(Address of advisor)

492

E. *Memorandum submitted to the President's Advisory Committee on Selective Service, October 24, 1940, by Paul Comly French on behalf of the National Council for Religious Conscientious Objectors.*

Suggestions for handling the problem of the Conscientious Objector under the National Training and Service Act of 1940. General Policy.

1. Appointment of one person as the responsible person to handle the problem in the Selective Service system under the direct supervision of the National Director.

2. All local Selective Service Boards, or Appeal Boards, to certify all persons found to be sincere to the conscientious objector officer in the national office of the Selective Service System with a notation of the type of work the individual was best qualified to perform.

3. Establishment of a list of general types of work, both within and without the governmental service, which conscientious objectors might study in suggesting the type of work they are qualified to perform.

4. Establishment of an advisory board to the conscientious objector officer consisting of representatives from the groups concerned with the whole problem. This Advisory Board might consist of a Friend, a Mennonite, a Brethren, a Methodist (because they will likely have the largest number of conscientious objectors among the non-historic peace sects), a representative of the Federal Council of the Churches of Christ in America, a representative of the Fellowship of Reconciliation and one other person representing whatever organization has a large number of conscientious objectors in its membership.

5. The national conscientious objector officer would be charged with the responsibility of arranging for assignment of boys to the several governmental agencies willing and able to use them. (It should be understood that any work so assigned would not be part of the military establishment).

6. The national conscientious objector officer would have the responsibility of arranging for maintenance for boys so assigned, although the question of pay (which should not in any case exceed army rates) should be left to the individual. Many conscientious objectors may be unwilling to accept government pay, but will accept maintenance.

7. Many boys will feel unwilling to accept governmental work, but will be willing to perform work of national importance under civilian direction with such agencies as the American Friends Service Committee, the Brethren Service Committee, the Methodist Peace Commission or the Mennonite Central Committee. Work performed under this section would be financed by the agencies involved without governmental aid.

8. The national conscientious objector officer should establish the types and standards of work under which these agencies should function and

make the assignment of boys either through a Central Board located in Washington, representing all of them, or directly to them individually. It would be the government responsibility of checking that standards were maintained in the units operated by these groups.

9. Representatives of the groups concerned about the problem have informally discussed types of work with various governmental agencies and would be glad to continue this work, if it would be helpful to the Selective Service officials, or to withdraw from such discussions if that proved the best policy.

F. *Memorandum to President Roosevelt, December 20, 1940, from C. A. Dykstra, Director of Selective Service* (initialed "O.K., C.A.D., F.D.R.").

Memorandum to The President.

From: The Director of Selective Service

Re: Conscientious Objectors

The Problem: The Selective Service law provides that conscientious objectors who object to noncombatant military training "shall in lieu of such induction be assigned to work of national importance under civilian direction." There is at present no specific appropriation for this purpose.

During the World War conscientious objectors presented difficulties to both the armed forces and the law enforcement agencies far out of proportion to the numbers involved. To avoid so far as possible a recurrence of such difficulties, a temporary and experimental solution along the following lines is believed desirable.

All conscientious objectors willing to accept noncombatant military service will be inducted in the Army for such service. It is estimated that approximately half of the conscientious objectors will fall in this category.

It is recommended that the remaining conscientious objectors, estimated at about 5,000 of the current quota of 800,000 men, be assigned to civilian camps for soil conservation and reforestation work.

In the absence of specific appropriations the Secretary of War, the Secretary of Agriculture, the Secretary of the Interior, and the Director of Selective Service have informally agreed as follows, subject to your approval:

1. The War Department will furnish or loan cots, bedding, and other items of camp equipment so far as feasible and necessary.

2. The Departments of Agriculture and The Interior will provide technical supervision for soil conservation and other similar projects for these men, as well as tools and other necessary equipment to the extent practicable. The Department has many projects of national importance for which man power has not heretofore been available, which can be undertaken if this plan is approved.

3. The Federal Security Agency has agreed to co-operate, and may be able to make available certain abandoned C.C.C. Camp sites, and perhaps certain tools and equipment.

4. Selective Service will furnish general administrative and policy supervision and inspection, and will pay the men's transportation costs to the camps, as permitted under the Selective Service appropriation.

5. The National Council for Conscientious Objectors, representing those church groups which include in their membership a large proportion of the conscientious objectors, has agreed for a temporary period to undertake the task of financing and furnishing all other necessary parts of the program, including actual day-to-day supervision and control of the camps (under such rules and regulations and administrative supervision as is laid down by Selective Service), to supply subsistence, necessary buildings, hospital care, and generally all things necessary for the care and maintenance of the men. Admittance to these camps will not be dependent on membership in the particular church groups undertaking this work. These church groups recognize the special problem created by the conscientious objector. Although generally opposed to the institution of war, they wish to serve their country in a manner compatible with their point of view by undertaking this voluntary obligation.

It is believed that a more intelligent and understanding handling of the problem of the conscientious objector will be possible in the type of co-operative program herein outlined than would be possible under entire governmental auspices. It is further believed that the voluntary assumption of financial and supervisory responsibility by those who have taken part in the religious training leading to conscientious objection will meet with general public approval, if properly administered.

There is precedent in the successful furloughing of conscientious objectors to the Society of Friends during the World War.

Should it develop that the church groups cannot permanently meet the considerable financial outlay, or that difficulties develop in the program here outlined, the Government could at any time modify the program or take it over in its entirety.

Due to the absence of specific appropriations and possible legal limitations in the co-operating departments to the use of personnel and material, it may be necessary to request a comparatively small amount from the President's special defense funds or an appropriation by Congress to implement the program herein outlined.

The Director of the Budget and the Advisory Committee on Selective Service concur in this recommendation.

C. K. DYKSTRA
Director of Selective Service

G. *Executive Order of President Roosevelt, February 6, 1941, establishing alternative service under civilian direction for conscientious objectors.* (No. 8675, 6 F.R. 831.)

EXECUTIVE ORDER

Authorizing the Director of Selective Service to Establish or Designate Work of National Importance Under Civilian Direction for Persons Conscientiously Opposed to Combatant and Noncombatant Service in the Land or Naval Forces of the United States.

By virtue of the authority vested in me by the Selective Training and Service Act of 1940 (Pub. No. 783, 76th Congress), it is hereby ordered as follows:

1. The Director of Selective Service, hereinafter called the Director, is authorized to establish, designate, or determine work of national importance under civilian direction to which may be assigned persons found under section 5(g) of the Selective Training and Service Act of 1940 to be conscientiously opposed to participation in combatant and noncombatant training and service in the land or naval forces of the United States.

2. The Director shall make the necessary assignments to such work, shall determine the agencies, organizations, or individuals that may provide civilian direction thereof, and shall have general supervision and control over such work.

3. To the extent that he may deem necessary to carry out the provisions of this order, the Director may utilize the services of the Departments, officers, and agents of the United States; accept the services of officers and agents of the several states, territories, and the District of Columbia, and the subdivisions thereof; and accept voluntary services of private organizations and individuals; and may obtain, by purchase, loan or gift, equipment and supplies from Federal and other public agencies and private organizations and individuals, with or without advertising or formal contract.

4. The Director is authorized to prescribe such rules and regulations as may be necessary to carry out the provisions of this order.

FRANKLIN D. ROOSEVELT

THE WHITE HOUSE
February 6, 1941

H. *Religious administrative agencies authorized to provide direction for Civilian Public Service projects:*

American Friends Service Committee
American Baptist Home Mission Society
Association of Catholic Conscientious Objectors
Brethren Service Committee
Disciples of Christ, Conscientious Objector Committee

Evangelical and Reformed Church, Commission on Christian Social Action

Mennonite Central Committee

Methodist Commission on World Peace

I. *United States governmental agencies authorized to provide technical supervision for Civilian Public Service projects:*

Department of Agriculture—Forest Service, Soil Conservation Service, Farm Security Administration

Department of Commerce—Coast and Geodetic Survey, Weather Bureau

Department of Interior—Bureau of Reclamation, Fish and Wildlife Service, General Land Office, National Park Service

Office of Scientific Research and Development

Public Health Service (in co-operation with state boards of health)

Puerto Rican Reconstruction Administration

Surgeon General, United States Army

Veterans Administration

(Fifty-seven state mental hospitals and training schools in twenty states were authorized to provide both technical supervision and administrative direction for the work of conscientious objectors assigned to C.P.S.)

J. *Conscientious violators of the Selective Training and Service Act, 1941–1947.* (From *Federal Prisons,* 1947, p. 19.) (See table, p. 498.)

NOTE TO TABLE: Conscientious objectors served their sentences in penitentiaries at Atlanta, Georgia, Leavenworth, Kansas, Lewisburg, Pennsylvania, McNeil Island, Washington, and Terre Haute, Indiana; in "correctional institutions" at Ashland, Kentucky, Danbury, Connecticut, La Tuna, Texas, Milan, Michigan, Sandstone, Minnesota, Tallahassee, Florida, and Texarkana, Texas; in reformatories at Chillicothe, Ohio, El Reno, Oklahoma, Englewood, Colorado, and Petersburg, Virginia; in "prison camps" at Columbia, Washington, McNeil Island, Washington, Mill Point, West Virginia, Montgomery, Alabama, and Tucson, Arizona; and in the prison hospital at Springfield, Missouri.

K. *Presidential Executive Order, January 18, 1941, authorizing parole for conscientious objectors.* (No. 8641, 6 F.R. 563 [1941].) Relevant parts:

By virtue of the authority vested in me by the Selective Training and Service Act of 1940 (Pub. No. 783, 76th Congress), I hereby amend Section VIII, Volume One of the Selective Service Regulations, by adding thereto the following paragraph:

176. Parole. a. Any person who has heretofore or may hereafter be convicted of a violation of any of the provisions of the Selective Training and Service Act of 1940 . . . shall at any time after such conviction be

SELECTIVE SERVICE ACT VIOLATORS: COMMITMENTS, MEDIAN AGES, AVERAGE LENGTHS OF SENTENCE, END-OF-YEAR POPULATIONS, AND PAROLES, FISCAL YEARS ENDED JUNE 30, 1941 TO 1947

	TOTAL	1941	1942	1943	1944	1945	1946	1947
RECEIVED FROM THE COURTS INTO FEDERAL								
INSTITUTIONS	11,879	196	806	2,764	3,585	2,477	1,312	739
Conscientious objectors	(a)1,216	(a)139	(b)	(a)495	251	214	106	11
Jehovah's Witnesses	(a)4,120	(a)106	(b)	(a)901	1,735	899	409	70
Others	(a)6,543	(a)757	(b)	(a)1,368	1,599	1,364	797	658
Median age (years)	(b)	(b)	28.5	29.9	27.4	27.0	26.5	26.9
Average length of sentence (months)	31.0	(a)12.0	21.0	32.4	35.2	32.7	22.5	16.3
Conscientious objectors	(b)	(b)	(b)	(b)	34.0	30.9	20.7	15.9
Jehovah's Witnesses	(b)	(b)	(b)	(b)	42.0	40.1	25.9	24.0
Others	(b)	(b)	(b)	(b)	28.1	28.0	23.0	19.0
SERVING SENTENCES IN FEDERAL								
INSTITUTIONS—JUNE 30	—	161	706	2,650	4,679	4,703	2,797	829
Conscientious objectors	—	(b)	(b)	588	694	475	204	13
Jehovah's Witnesses	—	(b)	(b)	981	2,530	2,724	1,339	63
Others	—	(b)	(b)	1,081	1,455	1,504	1,254	753
PAROLES GRANTED—U.S. BOARD OF PAROLE	3,700	—	9	140	428	400	1,338	1,385
Conscientious objectors	(b)	—	(b)	(b)	(b)	(b)	148	57
Jehovah's Witnesses	(b)	—	(b)	(b)	(b)	(b)	881	1,059
Others	(b)	—	(b)	(b)	(b)	(b)	309	269
PAROLES GRANTED—EXECUTIVE								
ORDER NO. 8641.(c)	1,825	12	70	(d)265	(d)500	712	112	154

(a) Estimated. (b) Date not available. (c) By the Attorney General upon the recommendation of the Selective Service System. (d) The proportion for each year of the 765 paroles granted in 1943 and 1944 eligible for release from custody on parole for service in the land or naval forces of the United States, or for work of national importance under civilian direction, or for any other special service established pursuant to said Act, in the manner and under the conditions hereinafter set out.

b. The parole provided for in subparagraph *a* hereof may be granted by the Attorney General to any person required to register under the provisions of the Selective Training and Service Act of 1940 and any provisions of the Selective Training and Service Act of 1940 and any proclamation of the President thereunder, if in the judgment of the Attorney General it is compatible with the public interest and the enforcement of the Selective Training and Service Act of 1940, upon the recommendation of the Director of Selective Service. Before recommending the parole of any such person, the Director of Selective Service shall determine, and include in his recommendation, whether such person should be paroled for (1) induction into the land or naval forces of the United States; or (2) induction into the land or naval forces of the United States for noncombatant service which has been or may hereafter be defined; or (3) assignment to work of national importance under civilian direction in lieu of induction into the land or naval forces of the United States; or (4) assignment to such other special service as may be established pursuant to the Selective Training and Service Act of 1940. If the parole is granted it shall conform to such recommendation. . . .

d. Any person who is paroled for service in the land or naval forces of the United States but is not actually inducted into said forces, or who after induction and before completion of the service specified in the order granting the parole is discharged from such forces, may, upon recommendation of the Director of Selective Service, then be assigned by the Attorney General to work of national importance under civilian direction or to any special service established pursuant to the Selective Training and Service Act of 1940, or may be returned to a penal or correctional institution to complete the sentence originally imposed with or without deduction for the time spent on parole as the Attorney General may determine.

e. If in the opinion of the Director of Selective Service any person paroled for assignment to work of national importance under civilian direction or other special service established pursuant to the Selective Training and Service Act of 1940 fails or refuses to perform such work or service or abide by the rules of conduct established in connection therewith, the Director of Selective Service shall so notify the Attorney General, who may revoke the parole of such person and return him to the penal or correctional institution to complete the sentence originally imposed with or without deduction for the time spent on parole as the Attorney General may determine.

f. The Attorney General shall impose such terms and conditions as he may deem proper upon any person released on parole, and shall supervise the parolee to see that he abides by the terms and conditions of the parole; provided, however, that such power of supervision shall be suspended while the parolee is in the active land or naval forces of the United States.

g. The parole herein authorized may be revoked at any time in the discretion of the Attorney General or his authorized agent; provided, however, that such revocation shall be suspended while the parolee is in the active land or naval forces of the United States. Upon revocation of the parole, the parolee shall thereupon be returned to the proper penal or correctional institution to complete the sentence originally imposed with or without deduction for the time spent on parole as the Attorney General may determine, or until reparole.

h. The Attorney General and Director of Selective Service are authorized to prescribe such rules and regulations not inconsistent herewith as may be necessary for the proper administration of their respective functions and duties set forth in this paragraph. . . .

FRANKLIN D. ROOSEVELT

January 18, 1941

L. *President Truman's amnesty proclamation of December 23, 1947, and Report of the President's amnesty board.*

Proclamation No. 2762 (12 Federal Register 8731,
Dec. 24, 1947)

Granting Pardon to Certain Persons Convicted of Violating the Selective Training and Service Act of 1940 as Amended by the President of the United States of America.

A PROCLAMATION

Whereas by Executive Order No. 9814 of Dec. 23, 1946, there was established the President's amnesty board, the functions and duties of which were set out in Paragraph 2 of the said executive order as follows:

"The board, under such regulations as it may prescribe, shall examine and consider the cases of all persons convicted of violation of the Selective Training and Service Act of 1940, as amended (50 U.S.C. App. 301 FF), or of any rule or regulation prescribed under or pursuant to that act, or convicted of a conspiracy to violate that act or any rule or regulation prescribed under or pursuant thereto.

"In any case in which it deems it desirable to do so, the board shall make a report to the Attorney General which shall include its findings and its recommendations as to whether clemency should be granted or denied, and, in any case in which it recommends that executive clemency be granted, its recommendations with respect to the form that such clemency should take. The Attorney General shall report the findings and recommendations of the board to the President, with such further recommendations as he may desire to make"; and

Whereas the board, after considering all cases coming within the scope of Paragraph 2 of the said executive order, has made a report to the Attorney General, which includes the findings of the board and its recommendation that executive clemency be granted in certain of such cases; and

Whereas the Attorney General has submitted such report to me with his approval of the recommendation made by the board with respect to executive celemency; and

Whereas upon consideration of the report and recommendation of the board and the recommendation of the Attorney General, it appears that certain persons convicted of violating the Selective Training and Service Act of 1940 as amended, ought to have restored to them the political, civil, and other rights of which they were deprived by reason of such conviction and which may not be restored to them unless they are pardoned;

Now, therefore, I, Harry S. Truman, President of the United States of America, under and by virtue of the authority vested in me by Article II of the Constitution of the United States, do hereby grant a full pardon to those persons convicted of violating the Selective Training and Service of 1940 as amended, whose names are included in the list of names attached hereto and hereby made a part of the proclamation.

In witness whereof, I have hereunto set my hand and caused the seal of the United States of America to be affixed.

Done at the City of Washington this twenty-third day of December in the year of our Lord Nineteen Hundred and Forty-seven, and of the independence of the United States of America the one hundred and seventy-second.

HARRY S. TRUMAN

By the President:

Robert A. Lovett
Acting Secretary of State

REPORT OF THE PRESIDENT'S AMNESTY BOARD

The President's Amnesty Board, established by executive order of Dec. 23, 1946, to review convictions under the Selective Training and Service Act of 1940, as amended, and to make recommendations for executive clemency, has completed its task and submits this, its first and final report.

Before adopting any general policies, the board heard representatives of interested parties and groups. It heard representatives of historic peace churches, of the Federal Council of Churches of Christ in America, leaders of the Watchtower Bible and Tract Society (whose followers are known as Jehovah's Witnesses), officials of the United States Army and Navy, and the national headquarters of Selective Service, representatives of citizens' groups, veterans' organizations and pacifist organizations. Some of the violators themselves, formerly inmates of penal institutions, appeared, either in person or by representatives, and were heard.

Their recommendations varied from that of a general amnesty to all violators, regardless of the circumstances, to a refusal of amnesty to anyone. To grant a general amnesty would have restored full civil status to a large number of men who neither were, nor claimed to be, religious conscientious objectors.

In perhaps one-half of the cases considered, the files reflected a prior record of one or more serious criminal offenses. The board would have failed in its duty to society, and to the memory of the men who fought and died to protect it, had amnesty been recommended in these cases. Nor could the board have justified its existence, had a policy been adopted of refusing pardon to all.

In establishing policies, therefore, we were called upon to reconcile divergencies, and to adopt a course which would, on the one hand, be humane and in accordance with the traditions of the United States, and yet, on the other hand, would uphold the spirit of the law.

Cases Reviewed Individually

Examination of a large number of cases at the outset convinced us that, to do justice to each individual as well as to the nation, it would be necessary to review each case upon its merits with the view of recommending individual pardons, and that no group should be granted amnesty as such.

Adequate review of the 15,805 cases brought to our attention would have been impossible had it not been for the co-operation of government departments and agencies, such as the office of the Attorney General, the Federal Bureau of Investigation, the Bureau of Prisons, the Criminal Division of the Department of Justice, the United States probation officers, the Administrative Office of the United States Courts, United States attorneys throughout the country, the armed forces of the United States and the headquarters of Selective Service. The records of these officers were made available, and those in charge furnished requested information.

The information derived from all sources was briefed by a corps of trained reviewers. It included such essential data as family history, school and work records, prior criminal record, if any, religious affiliations and practices, Selective Service history, nature and circumstances of offenses, punishment imposed, time actually served in confinement, custodial records, probation reports and conduct in society after release. In addition, the board had in most instances psychiatric reports and one or more voluntary statements by the offender concerning the circumstances of the offense.

When the board organized in January, 1947, about 1,200 of the 15,805 violators of Selective Service were in penal institutions. The number diminished daily. At the present time there are 626 in custody; 550 of these have been committed since the constitution of this board. The work of the board was directed chiefly to examining the propriety of recommending restoration of civil rights to those who have been returned to their homes.

Two Classes of Cases

In analyzing the cases we found that they fell into classes, but that in each class there were exceptional cases which took the offender out of the class and entitled him to special consideration. The main divisions into which the cases fell were (1) those of violation due to a wilful intent to evade service, and (2) those resulting from beliefs derived from religious training or other convictions.

At least two-thirds of the cases considered were those of wilful violation, not based on religious scruples. These varied greatly in the light of all the relevant facts disclosed in each case. It became necessary to consider not only the circumstances leading up to the offense, but the subject's background, education and environment. In some instances what appeared a wilful violation was in fact due to ignorance, illiteracy, honest misunderstanding or carelessness not rising to the level of criminal negligence. In other cases the record showed a desire to remedy the fault by enlistment in the armed forces.

Many of the wilful violators were men with criminal records; men whose records included murder, rape, burglary, larceny, robbery, larceny of government property, fraudulent enlistment, conspiracy to rob, arson, violations of the narcotics law, violations of the immigration laws, counterfeiting, desertion from the United States armed forces, embezzlement, breaking and entering, bigamy, drinking benzedrine to deceive medical examiners, felonious assault, violations of National Motor Vehicle Theft Act, extortion, blackmail, impersonation, insurance frauds, bribery, black market operations and other offenses of equally serious nature; men who were seeking to escape detection for crimes committed; fugitives from justice; wife deserters; and others who had ulterior motives for escaping the draft. Those who for these or similar reasons exhibited a deliberate evasion of the law, indicating no respect for the law or the civil rights to which they might have been restored, are not, in our judgment, deserving of a restoration of their civil rights, and we have not recommended them for pardon.

Many Mental Cases

Among the violators, quite a number are now mental cases. We have made no attempt to deal with them, since most of them remain in mental institutions with little or no chance of recovery. Until they recover mental health their loss of civil rights impose no undue burden.

The board has made no recommendation respecting another class of violators. These are the men who qualify for automatic pardon pursuant to Presidential Proclamation No. 2,676, dated Dec. 24, 1945. They are the violators who, after conviction, volunteered for service in the armed forces prior to Dec. 24, 1945, and received honorable discharges following one year or more of duty. Most of those who, prior to the last-mentioned date and subsequent to that date, entered the Army and received honorable discharges with less than a year of service have been recommended for pardon. These men have brought themselves within the equity of the President's Proclamation, No. 2,676.

The second main class of violators consists of those who refused to comply with the law because of their religious training, or their religious, political or sociological beliefs. We have classified them, generally, as conscientious objectors. It is of interest that less than 6 per cent of those convicted of violating the act asserted conscientious convictions as the basis of their action. This percentage excludes Jehovah's Witnesses, whose cases are dealt with hereafter. Although the percentage was small, these cases presented difficult problems.

The Selective Service Boards faced a very difficult task in administering the provisions concerning religious, conscientious objection. Generally speaking, they construed the exemption liberally. Naturally, however, boards in different localities differed somewhat in their application of the exemption. In recommending pardons, we have been conscious of hardships resulting from the factor of error.

Many of the Selective Service Boards did not consider membership in an historic peace church as a condition to exemption of those asserting religious, conscientious objection to military service. Nor have our recommendations of pardons been so strictly limited. We have recommended individuals who were members of no sect or religious group, if the subject's record and all the circumstances indicated that he was motivated by a sincere religious belief. We have found some violators who acted upon an essentially religious belief, but were unable properly to present their claims for exemption. We have recommended them for pardon.

Non-Religious Not Freed

We found that some who sought exemption as conscientious objectors were not such within the purview of the act. These were men who asserted no religious training or belief but founded their objections on intellectual, political, or sociological convictions resulting from the individual's reasoning and personal economic or political philosophy. We have not felt justified in recommending those who thus have set themselves up as wiser and more competent than society to determine their duty to come to the defense of the nation.

Some of those who asserted conscientious objections were found to have been moved in fact by fear, the desire to evade military service, or the wish to remain as long as possible in highly paid employment.

Under the law, a man who received a IV-E classification as a conscientious objector, instead of being inducted into the armed forces, was assigned to a civilian public service camp. The national headquarters of Selective Service estimates that about 12,000 men received this classification, entered camps and performed the duties assigned them.

Certain conscientious objectors refused to go to such camps on being awarded a IV-E classification, or, after arriving at the camps, refused to comply with regulations and violated the rules of the camps in various ways as a protest against what they thought unconstitutional or unfair administration of the camps. Some deserted the camps for similar reasons. We may concede their good faith. But they refused to submit to the provisions of the Selective Service Act, and were convicted for their intentional violation of the law.

There was a method to test the legality of their detention in the courts. A few of them resorted to that method. Where other circumstances warranted we have recommended them for pardon. But most of them simply asserted their superiority to the law and determined to follow their own wish and defy the law. We think that this attitude should not be condoned, and we have refrained from recommending such persons for favorable consideration, unless there were extenuating circumstances.

Pardons for Japanese

Closely analogous to conscientious objectors, and yet not within the fair interpretation of the phrase, were a smaller, though not inconsequential number of American citizens of Japanese ancestry, who were removed in the early stages of the war under military authority, from their homes in defense coastal areas and placed in SAR relocation centers. Although we recognized the urgent necessities of military defense, we fully appreciate the nature of their feelings and their reactions to orders from local Selective Service Boards.

Prior to their removal from their homes they had been law-abiding and loyal citizens. They deeply resented classification as undesirables. Most of them remained loyal to the United States and indicated a desire to remain in this country and to fight in its defense, provided their rights of citizenship were recognized. For these we have recommended pardons, in the belief that they will justify our confidence in their loyalty.

Some 4,300 cases were those of Jehovah's Witnesses, whose difficulties arose over their insistence that each of them should be accorded a ministerial status and consequent complete exemption from military service, or civilian public service camp duty. The organization of the sect is dissimilar to that of the ordinary denomination.

It is difficult to find a standard by which to classify a member of the sect as a minister in the usual meaning of that term. It is interesting to note that no representations were made to Congress when the Selective Service Act was under consideration with respect to the ministerial status of the members of this group. Some time after the Selective Service Act became law, and after many had been accorded the conscientious objector status, the leaders of the sect asserted that all of its members were ministers. Many Selective Service Boards classified Jehovah's Witnesses as conscientious objectors, and consequently assigned them to civilian public service camps.

A few at first accepted this classification, but after the policy of claiming ministerial status had been adopted, they changed their claims and they and other members of the sect insisted upon complete exemption as ministers. The Headquarters of the Selective Service, after some consideration ruled that those who devoted practically their entire time to "witnessing," should be classified as ministers. The Watchtower Society made lists available to Selective Service. It is claimed that these lists were incomplete.

The Selective Service Boards' problem was a difficult one. We have found that the action of the boards was not wholly consistent in attributing ministerial status to Jehovah's Witnesses, and we have endeavored to correct any discrepancy by recommending pardons to those we think should have been classified.

Ruling on Secular Workers

The sect has many classes of persons who appear to be awarded their official titles by its headquarters, such as company servants, company publishers, advertising servants, etc. In the case of almost all these persons, the member is employed full time in a gainful occupation in the secular world.

He "witnesses," as it is said, by distributing leaflets, playing phonographs, calling at houses, selling literature, conducting meetings, etc., in his spare time, and on Sundays and holidays. He may devote a number of hours per month to these activities, but he is in no sense a "minister" as the phrase is commonly understood. We have not recommended for pardon any of these secular workers who have witnessed in their spare or non-working time. Many of them perhaps would have been granted classifications other than I-A had they applied for them. They persistently refused to accept any classification except that of IV-D, representing ministerial, and, therefore, complete exemption.

Most of their offenses embraced refusal to register, refusal to submit to physical examination, and refusal to report for induction. They went to jail because of these refusals. Many, however, were awarded a IV-E classification as conscientious objectors, notwithstanding their protestation that they did not want it. These, when ordered to report to civilian public service camps, refused to do so and suffered conviction and imprisonment rather than comply.

While few of these offenders had theretofore been violators of the law, we cannot condone their selective service offenses, nor recommend them for pardons. To do so would be to sanction an assertion by a citizen that he is above the law; that he makes his own law; and that he refused to yield his opinion to that of organized society on the question of his country's need for service.

10,000 Willful Violators

In summary we may state that there were 15,805 Selective Service violation cases considered. In this total there were approximately 10,000 willful violators, 4,300 Jehovah's Witnesses, 1,000 religious conscientious objectors and 500 other types. Of this total 618 were granted Presidential pardons because of a year or more service with honorable discharges from the armed forces. An additional approximate 900 entered the armed forces and may become eligible for pardon upon the completion of their service.

When the board was created there were 1,200 offenders in custody. Since that date an additional 550 have been institutionalized. At the present time there are 626 in confinement, only seventy-six of whom were in custody on Jan. 6, 1947.

Tabulation of Violations

Convictions under Selective Service Act considered	15,805
Willful violators (non-conscientious objectors)	*10,000
Jehovah's Witnesses	*4,300
Conscientious objectors	*1,000
Other types of violators	*500

Tabulation of Pardons

Pardoned by Presidential proclamation in 1945 . . . .   *618
Members of armed forces who may receive pardons *900
Recommended by board   1,523

Total   3,041

* Approximately.

The board recommends that executive clemency be extended to the 1,523 individuals whose names appear on the attached list, attested as to its correctness by the executive secretary of the board, and that each person named receive a pardon for his violation of the Selective Training and Service Act of 1940, as amended.

M. *Statement of Policy, Camp Operations Division of the Selective Service System* (the "McLean Statement"). Released, 1942.

"In order to remove certain misunderstandings which seem to exist among assignees relative to the reason for their assignment and their status while in Civilian Public Service Camps, the following outline has been prepared.

"Under the Constitution of the United States the citizens of this country have certain rights, these are counterbalanced by duties of equal weight. One duty is service to their country. In time of need it may be necessary that this service take the form of military duty. The Supreme Court has held in several decisions that this is an obligation resting on all citizens but that Congress may grant the privilege of exemption or deferment to certain individuals or groups. At present such exemptions or deferments are based on sex, age, physical condition and to some extent on dependents and occupation. Recognizing that certain individuals had religious beliefs which forbade them to take part in war or to perform military service it was provided in the Selective Training and Service Act of 1940 that those persons who, by reason of religious training and belief were conscientiously opposed to both combatant and noncombatant service should, in lieu thereof, perform work of national importance under civilian direction.

"There are two things to be remembered when considering the above provision: First, it is limited to those who are opposed to military service because of religious beliefs and does not include political or economic objectors. Second, the selection of work of national importance, its direction, as long as it is by civilians, and the conditions under which it will be performed are left to the President. He, in turn, by Executive Order delegated these powers to the Director of Selective Service.

"It should be clearly understood that under the law there is no distinction between defense and nondefense work. That all assignees, regardless of the type of camp they are in, can now, or in the future, be required to do any work which the Director of Selective Service declares to be work of national importance as long as it is directed by civilians. This, conceivably, can include the making of munitions, construction of airfields, or the erection of fortifications. Civilians are all persons not subject to Military Law and can include civilian employees of the War or Navy Departments as well as those of Selective Service, Agriculture or other nonmilitary departments and agencies of the Federal Government.

"Realizing that many conscientious objectors are as strongly opposed to engaging in what is commonly called defense work as to military service it is the policy of Selective Service to choose projects as unrelated to the war effort as possible and to operate them through those agencies that are distinctly civilian in character. But, since the determination of what constitutes defense is a matter of opinion, and since there is no distinction under the law, it is impossible to promise an assignee, officially or otherwise, that he will not be obliged to do defense work. As previously stated, it has been, and still is the policy of Selective Service to approve projects about which there can be little question but leave the determination of what is defense or nondefense to assignees, either individually or as groups, or to allow them to decide whether they will do the work or not, cannot be considered. These decisions are powers of the Director of Selective Service and must remain in his hands.

"The work being done is mainly a continuation of projects originated by the CCC. These are known to be, and have generally been accepted by the public, as work of national importance. Additional projects, such as service in hospitals or dairy farm labor have been added, as well as a small amount of work on a detached service basis. Such work calls for men with certain types of training or ability. There is every indication that the bulk of the work and the majority of the men will continue to be handled through the camp system. The program is not being carried on for the education or development of individuals, to train groups for foreign service or future activities in the post-war period, or for the furtherance of any particular movement. Its purpose is to do work of national importance as selected by the Director. There is no obligation to provide an assignee with work for which he has been particularly prepared, wished to do, or regards as socially significant. Neither is there any intention of engaging in what is generally called the social welfare field except as it may enter into the regular projects. Assignees can no more expect choice of location or job than can men in the service or a great many civilians. Camps are located primarily where the work is to be done, recreation and other considerations are secondary.

"All Civilian Public Service Camps are under control of Selective Service and are being operated according to the regulations promulgated by the Director. Those now in existence are being operated under a dual system in which the work on the project is carried on under the Camp Superintendent who is an employee of a governmental agency or department, while the camp life is under the supervision of an employee of a private organization. This system was developed as the result of an agreement between the Director of Selective Service and representatives of various religious groups who had united in a volunteer organization called the National Service Board for Religious Objectors. Under the agreement certain churches, among them the Mennonites, Friends, and Brethren, frequently called the "Historic Peace Churches," agreed to provide food, clothing, medical attention, heat and light for all men classified as IV-E and ordered to camp by Selective Service. In return, through the National Service Board, they select the camp staffs, recommend the assignment of men to the various camps and carry on the religious, educational and recreational programs. Selective Service provides the personnel and equipment for the work project, certain items of camp equipment such as cots and blankets, and, in most cases, the buildings. It also pays transportation to the camp and for those who are transferred for the benefit of the government.

"Under this system the Project Superintendent is completely in charge of the work project and the equipment. He works under the rules and regulations of the technical service employing him plus such additional regulations as may be issued by Selective Service. He may, and should be, open to suggestions but will carry on the work according to his judgment and the regulations. While on the job assignees are entirely under his control and subject only to his orders.

"During nonworking hours assignees are under the control of the Camp Director. This individual serves in a dual capacity being the representative of the church sponsoring the camp and also of Selective Service. As agent of the church he is responsible for the physical and spiritual welfare of the men in the camp. For Selective Service he carries out and enforces certain regulations such as the granting of leave and furlough, accounts for the men assigned to the camp and prepares various reports. As far as Selective Service is concerned the Camp Director is in charge of the camp. The impression that camps are democracies to be run by the assignees is entirely erroneous. They may suggest or recommend but only the decisions and orders of the Director will be recognized by Selective Service.

"At present the camps are operated by the various church organizations but any or all of them could be operated by the government. On the whole, the present system has proved satisfactory to the majority of those concerned. Selective Service is willing but not anxious to organize government camps. Such camps would be in addition to those operated by the churches and would, in no way, be a reflection upon the work they are doing. Assignees would have an initial choice of the type of camp they preferred and transfers, with the approval of Selective Service, could be made. There would be the same opportunities for special work and detached service and the same policies would be followed in the selection of work projects, which would be carried on under the same technical agencies. However, those serving in church camps cannot expect subsistence, pay or other financial assistance beyond that now furnished by the government. The Director of Selective Service has definitely stated that this will be done if the camp is operated by the government.

"The contention of some individuals that they are being forced to accept charity or that their service amounts to involuntary servitude is not correct. No one is forced to accept IV-E classification. In most cases each man voluntarily requests that he be placed in this class and usually is required to prove his right to be so considered. Neither is anyone compelled to remain classified as IV-E for he can and will be reclassified as I-A or I-A-O upon request. Having accepted IV-E classification he must take the conditions that go with it. Every man receives pay consisting of his food, clothing, shelter and a certain cash allowance. The fact that this is supplied by private religious organizations instead of the government is entirely legal under the law since the Director of Selective Service is authorized to make such arrangements and to accept such services. In return for these funds the churches acquire operation of the camps. Neither are they compelled to continue the arrangement, being free to withdraw at any time. They agreed to provide for all men assigned to the camps and so far as is known have scrupulously kept their word. It is true that they request assignees of the churches from which they come to contribute to the support of the camps. These solicitations have the same standing as any request for the contribution of money, they can be recognized or rejected at the will of the individual.

"Since men classified as IV-E and assigned to CPS Camps are not called upon to assume the responsibilities or risks of the men in the service it is to be expected that they were not extended the privileges and benefits. This applies to pay, the benefits of the Soldiers and Sailors Relief Act. The National Life Insurance Act and the Servicemen's Dependents Allowance Act all of which are extended only to those in the armed services. It has also been ruled that service in a CPS Camp does not entitle one to Veterans Preference or to reemployment rights. Neither are assignees eligible for Civilian Employees Compensation at the present time.

"From the time an assignee reports to camp until he is finally released he is under control of the Director of Selective Service. He ceases to be a free agent and is accountable for all of his time, in camp and out, twenty-four hours a day. His movements, actions and conduct are subject to control and regulation. He ceases to have certain rights and is granted privileges instead. These privileges can be restricted or withdrawn without his approval or consent as punishment, during emergencies or as a matter of policy. He may be told when and how to work, what to wear and where to sleep. He can be required to submit to medical examinations and treatment and to practice rules of health and sanitation. He may be moved from place to place and from job to job, even to foreign countries, for the convenience of the government regardless of his personal feelings or desires.

"In obtaining compliance with its regulations Selective Service does not authorize or have any intention of using physical force. Those who fail to conform to the requirements will be turned over to the Department of Justice for prosecution under the civil laws of the United States for failure to comply with the Selective Service and Training Act. Or, should the assignee's actions and conduct indicate that he is not a true conscientious objector, his case may be referred back to his Local Board for reconsideration as one improperly classified.

"It is realized that many will dislike and disagree with the foregoing statements. They have not been prepared for discussion or debate nor to threaten or frighten anyone, but for the purpose of removing certain misunderstandings existing among assignees. They are a factual presentation of what the law can and does imply. There is no more intention of arbitrary application in the future than there has been in the past. Assignees are not regarded as criminals or persons to be punished for their opinions. Neither are they considered as "slackers." The cheerful, co-operative manner in which they have adjusted themselves to camp life and performed their work refutes that view. It is believed that they have a sincere desire to render nonmilitary service to their country and the administration of CPS camps will continue on that assumption. Through consultation and discussion differences of opinion have been reconciled and a workable system developed which it is hoped may be continued."

In February of 1945, when asked if the "McLean Statement" was still considered to be a statement of the policy of the Camp Operations Division, Col. Lewis F. Kosch replied in a letter to Paul Comly French:

"While it is impossible to make a statement covering administrative plans and procedure that would not be subject to change to meet changing conditions, the general policy and views of Selective Service with respect to projects and status of assignees remain the same.

"The basic consideration in selecting a project is, primarily, its importance to the Government coupled with public reaction, availability of other labor and the attitude of the religious organizations and the assignees toward the work. As in the past, it is expected that there will be discussion with your office and the various religious organizations concerning new projects but the final decision must continue to rest with the Director of Selective Service. In general, it is believed that more can be accomplished by the expansion of the present types of projects rather than by entering new fields of a different character and spreading our efforts too thinly.

"It is felt that the CPS program is being carried on to do work of value to the nation, not for the education or training of assignees, for the furtherance of any particular movement or to provide a man with a job for which he may be especially prepared or wants to do. On the other hand, it is desired that the special skills or training of various individuals be employed whenever possible within the limit of the various projects. Individual assignments are not favored and it is expected to continue the present controls over transfers, furloughs, and other assignee activities. Congressional action to provide compensation for disabilities incurred in line of duty is considered desirable and provision for dependents would be approved."

✿ ✿ ✿ ✿ ✿ ✿ ✿ ✿ ✿ ✿

N. *Private Organizations Advising Conscientious Objectors.*

Organization	Nature and function
American Civil Liberties Union	Born during the First World War, the American Civil Liberties Union, with headquarters in New York, was active in defending and advising objectors during World War II. Not "pacifist" itself, it was interested in the problem from the viewpoint of protecting civil liberties in general.
American Friends Service Committee	Co-operative organization of Friends (Quakers) for philanthropic and relief activities. The Committee was also interested in peace education and helped administer alternative civilian service during the war.
Association of Catholic Conscientious Objectors	Organized to educate Roman Catholics in Catholic bases for conscientious objection. During part of the war the Association helped administer alternative civilian service.

Brethren Service Committee .... Organized by the Church of the Brethren for philanthropic and peace education work. The Committee helped administer alternative civilian service throughout the war and down to the death of C.P.S. in 1947. Headquarters: Elgin, Illinois.

Committee on Conscientious Objectors, Federal Council of the Churches of Christ in America The Federal Council, co-operative organization of most major Protestant bodies, proclaimed its concern about the rights of objectors, although not itself pacifist.

Committee on Conscientious Objectors, Socialist Party .... The Committee published a periodical mimeographed bulletin, the *Socialist C.O.*

Fellowship of Reconciliation .... The Fellowship was founded in Great Britain during World War I. A religious pacifist society, it included in its membership many prominent Protestant ministers. Teachers and college students were also numerous.

Los Angeles Branch, American Civil Liberties Union .... One of the most active branches of the American Civil Liberties Union.

Los Angeles County Committee for Conscientious Objectors ... Many groups and individuals co-operated in the organization. It performed the usual advisory functions.

Mennonite Central Committee .. The co-operative organization of Mennonite churches for philanthropic activities. Administration of Mennonite alternative civilian service was in charge of the Committee. Its headquarters were in Akron, Pennsylvania.

Methodist Commission on World Peace .... The "peace arm" of the Methodist Church. It was concerned with peace education throughout the denomination and published a *Bulletin* which kept its constituents informed about peace work activities. The Secretary and several members of the Commission were outright pacifists, although pacifists were but a small minority in the Church as a whole. The Commission's headquarters were in Chicago.

Metropolitan Board for Conscientious Objectors .... The great New York City organization which was very active in advising objectors throughout the metropolitan area. Lawyers and others donated their services to the Board. Many of the consultations took place at night.

National Committee for Conscientious Objectors .... Set up by the American Civil Liberties Union, the National Committee later became independent of the union. Supporters of the Committee believed that it could be more aggressive in protecting objectors' rights than could the National Service Board for Religious Objectors since, unlike the Board, it was in no sense a governmental agency and was not involved in the administration of alternative civilian service.

National Service Board for Religious Objectors .... Established by Mennonites, Brethren, Friends, and other religious groups to represent them in their dealings with the government, the Board set up an elaborate advisory service with a staff in its Washington headquarters and representatives in many communities throughout the country. Correspondence with individual objectors, other advisory services, and governmental agencies was enormous. In addition, of course, the N.S.B.R.O. was the agency through which Selective Service transmitted its orders involving administration of alternative civilian service.

Northern California Service Board for Conscientious Objectors ... With headquarters in San Francisco, the Northern California Service Board performed valuable advisory functions on the west coast.

Philadelphia Committee for Conscientious Objectors .... Very much like the Metropolitan Service Board in New York City.

San Francisco Branch, American Civil Liberties Union .... Like the Los Angeles Branch, one of the most active A.C.L.U. branches.

Seventh-Day Adventist Church .. With headquarters in Tacoma Park, Maryland. Particularly important for the large number of Adventists serving as conscientious objectors in the armed forces.

War Resisters League .... The League tended to represent those objectors dissatisfied with Peace Church leadership and also many "non-religious" pacifists. Jewish objectors also joined the League, some because they could not accept the Christian religious ideology of certain other objector organizations. The League was particularly concerned about the rights of objectors who violated the law. Generally speaking, it was thought of as a "left-wing" group.

Watchtower Bible and Tract Society .... The publishing, educational, and advisory organization of Jehovah's Witnesses. The Witnesses tended to remain aloof from other organizations.

Notes

Chapter I

1. See John W. Graham, *Conscription and Conscience* (London, 1922), and *Towards a Christian International: The Story of the International Fellowship of Reconciliation* (London and New York, 1941).

2. *The C. O. and the National Service Acts* (London, 1943), p. 16, and other publications of the Central Board for Conscientious Objectors.

3. Ernest Bevin, Minister of Labour and National Service, in the House of Commons. *Hansard*, Vol. 387, House of Commons Debates. 5th Series. (Feb. 25, 1943).

4. Figures of the Central Board for Conscientious Objectors.

5. *Ibid.* See Denis Hayes, *Challenge of Conscience* (London, 1949), for a full account of conscientious objection in Great Britain during World War II.

6. *Cat and Mouse* (London, 1942), pp. 21–22; Central Board for Conscientious Objectors, *Catalogue of Conviction: The Case of George Elphick* (London, 1944); and the Bulletins of the Central Board for Conscientious Objectors.

7. Note, for example, the vigorous appeals of the Duke of Bedford in the House of Lords: *The Conscientious Objector*, March 2, 1943; and *Conscientious Objectors* (Second Speech), Jan. 18, 1944 (Glasgow, 1943, 1944).

8. See Lincoln Efford, *Penalties on Conscience* (Christchurch, 1945).

9. *Ibid.*, p. 38.

10. Edith F. Fowke in *Reconciliation* (official organ of the Canadian Fellowship of Reconciliation), June–July, 1945. The discussion in the text is based largely on this account. Miss Fowke's article was reprinted in *The Reporter*, Sept. 1, 1945.

11. See Edward N. Wright, *Conscientious Objectors in the Civil War* (Philadelphia: 1931).

12. *Ibid.*

13. J. S. Easby-Smith, *Statement concerning the Treatment of Conscientious Objectors in the Army*, published by the War Department, June 18, 1919.

14. For other examples, read the sympathetic account of Norman Thomas, *Is Conscience a Crime?* (New York, 1927). See also W. G. Kellogg, *The Conscientious Objector* (New York, 1919).

Chapter II

1. For general works on the theoretical positions of the several groups, see, on the Mennonites, Guy F. Hershberger, *War, Peace, and Nonresistance* (Scottdale, Pa., 1944); on the Brethren, Rufus D. Bowman, *The Church of the Brethren and War* (Elgin, Ill., 1944); on the Quakers, Howard H. Brinton, *Sources of the Quaker Peace Testimony* (Wallingford, Pa., 1942); on Protestants outside the Peace Churches, Walter W. Van Kirk, *Religion Renounces War* (Chicago, 1934); on Roman Catholics, John J. Hugo, *Weapons of the Spirit* (New York, 1943), and George B. O'Toole, *War and Conscription at the Bar of Christian Morals* (New York; 1941); on Jehovah's Witnesses, a pamphlet, *Peace: Can it Last* (Brooklyn, 1942), and the other publications of the Watchtower Society, particularly *Consolation* and the *Watchtower*, both periodicals. Philosophical and political conscientious objection is represented in many scattered writings.

2. On the sixteenth-century Anabaptists, see E. Belfort Bax, *The Rise and Fall of the Anabaptists* (London, 1903).

3. On the history of the Mennonites, see the Bibliography.

4. See Hershberger, *War, Peace, and Nonresistance*, chaps. xi, xii, and xiii, where the author discusses the Mennonite position with reference to modern theories of "nonviolent" resistance and the relation of Mennonite doctrine to industrial conflict.

5. The relevant passages in the thirteenth chapter of Romans (American Standard version) read: "Let every soul be in subjection to the higher powers: for there is no power but of God; and the powers that be are ordained of God. Therefore he that resisteth the power, withstandeth the ordinance of God: and they that withstand shall receive to themselves judgment. For rulers are not a terror to the good work, but to the evil."

I Pet. 2:13–17, reads: "Be subject to every ordinance of men for the Lord's sake: whether to the king, as supreme; or unto governors, as sent by him for vengeance on evil-doers and for praise to them that do well. For so is the will of God, that by well-doing ye should put to silence the ignorance of foolish men: as free, and not using your freedom for a cloak of wickedness, but as bondservants of God. Honor all men. Love the Brotherhood. Fear God. Honor the king."

6. "Ye have heard it said by them of old time 'an eye for an eye and a tooth for a tooth'; but I say unto you 'Resist not evil, but if a man smite thee on one cheek turn to him also the other and if a man taketh thy cloak give him thy coat also . . .'" (Matt. 5:38–40).

7. Hershberger, *op. cit.*, chaps. xi, xii.

8. *Ibid.*, chaps. xiii, xiv, xv.

9. Bowman, *Church of the Brethren*, p. 67.

10. *Ibid.*, p. 315. See also Rufus Bowman, *Seventy Times Seven* (Elgin, Ill., 1945).

11. Brinton, *op. cit.*, p. 16.

12. See Robert Barclay, *The Anarchy of the Ranters and Other Libertines* (1676).

13. For a discussion of seventeenth-century controversies about individualistic and corperate interpretations of the Inner Light, see William C. Braithwaite, *The Second Period of Quakerism* (London, 1919), chaps. xi, xii.

14. The exact proportions of Friends and Brethren who accepted noncombat-

ant and combatant Army service are difficult to determine. However, Harold Chance of the Peace Section of the American Friends Service Committee has estimated that 75 to 80 per cent of all Friends of draft age went into the Army and Navy as combatants. Thus three out of four Friends were *not* conscientious objectors.

15. See Isaac Sharpless, *A Quaker Experiment in Government* (Philadelphia, 1898).

16. William Penn, *An Essay towards the Present and Future Peace of Europe* (1693).

17. Richard Gregg, *The Power of Non-Violence* (New York, 1944).

18. On the Social Gospel, see Walter Rauschenbusch, *A Theology for the Social Gospel* (New York, 1917) and Dores R. Sharpe, *Walter Rauschenbusch* (New York, 1942).

19. The Oxford Oath was originally formulated in the famous Oxford Union debating society at Oxford University. There it took the form of a pledge that one would never again support "King and Country" in war. Many American college students adapted the "oath" to American student perspectives.

20. *Discipline of the Methodist Episcopal Church*, 1928, No. 598.

21. *Discipline of the Methodist Church*, 1940, pp. 777–778.

22. Walter W. Van Kirk, "The Churches and World Peace," *International Conciliation*, No. 304 (Nov., 1934). For a more elaborate treatment of the theme, see Van Kirk, *Religion Renounces War*.

23. On Roman Catholic pacifism and conscientious objection in general, see George B. O'Toole, *War and Conscription at the Bar of Christian Morals;* John J. Hugo, *Weapons of the Spirit; The Catholic Worker*, a periodical; and *The Catholic C.O.*, a paper published by and in the interests of Catholic conscientious objectors during the Second World War.

24. For an elaboration of this doctrine, see Gerald Vann, *Morality and War* (London, 1939), and John K. Ryan, *Modern War and Basic Ethics* (Milwaukee, 1940).

25. For a sociological analysis of the Witnesses, see Herbert H. Stroup, *The Jehovah's Witnesses* (New York, 1945).

26. See Gen. 6:2–4.

27. Watchtower Society, *The New World* (Brooklyn, 1942), p. 64.

28. At this point the Witnesses cited Dan. 4:16, 23, 25, 32; Lev. 26:18, 21, 24, 28; and Luke 21:24.

29. Matt. 24:14.

30. See "The Theocratic Alignment Today," *The Watchtower*, Nov. 1, 1944, p. 330.

31. *The New World*, ch. xi.

32. *The New World*, p. 333.

33. Dan. 11:40.

34. Dan. 11:44.

35. Among the many cases involving the rights of Jehovah's Witnesses, one might mention *Schneider* v. *State*, 308 U.S. 147 (1939); *Cantwell* v. *Connecticut*, 310 U.S. 296 (1940); *Jones* v. *City of Opelika*, 316 U.S. 584 (1942); *W. Virginia* v. *Barnette*, 319 U.S. 624 (1943); and *Prince* v. *Commonwealth of Massachusetts*, 64 Sup. Ct. 438 (1944). See C. C. McCown, "Conscience v. the State," *California Law Review*, 32 (March, 1944), 1–30.

36. See the group's exposition of its doctrine, *Mankind United: a Challenge to "Mad Ambition" and "The Money Changers" Accompanied by an Invitation to the World's "Sane" Men and Women* (International Registration Bureau, Pacific Coast Division of North America, 1940).

37. These observations are based on correspondence with Genevieve Walther, who visited the Hopi during the course of this study and interviewed several leaders. See also Laura Thompson and Alice Joseph, *The Hopi Way* (Chicago, 1944).

38. This statement is based upon information supplied to the authors by a member of the Party who was at the time serving in the Air Corps and therefore had had to leave the Party.

39. See *The Call*, official organ of the Socialist Party, June 12, 1942, pp. 1, 7.

40. See Mulford Sibley, *The Political Theories of Modern Pacifism* (Philadelphia, 1944), and Theodore Paullin, *Introduction to Non-Violence* (Philadelphia, 1944).

41. See Chapters XII, XVI, and XVIII.

42. Krishnalal Shridharani, *War without Violence; A Study of Gandhi's Method and Its Accomplishments* (New York, 1939).

43. See Chapter XII for a full account of the first Social Action Conference.

Chapter III

1. Letter of Rufus Jones and Walter C. Woodward, for the Society of Friends; P. C. Hiebert, Harold S. Bender, and E. L. Harshbarger for the Mennonites; and Rufus D. Bowman and Paul H. Bowman for the Church of the Brethren.

2. N.S.B.R.O., *Congress Looks at the Conscientious Objector* (Washington, 1943), reprints most of the relevant testimony not only of those who proposed more liberal provisions but also of those, like General Hershey, who commented on the bill in general. The questions and comments of the members of the two Committes are also given.

The discussion in the text of this chapter is based partly on *Congress Looks at the Conscientious Objector* and partly on E. Raymond Wilson, "Some Notes on the Evolution of the Provisions for Conscientious Objectors in the Selective Training and Service Act of 1940" (typewritten), Memorandum No. 14, Friends War Problems Committee, Jan. 27, 1943.

3. Wilson, "Some Notes on the Evolution of the Provisions for Conscientious Objectors," pp. 9–10.

4. *Ibid.*, pp. 10–11.

5. *Ibid.*, p. 12.

6. *Congressional Record*, House, Sept. 6, 1940, p. 11689.

7. For the full text of Section 5(g), see Appendix C.

Chapter IV

1. See Appendix D for Form 47.

2. See Chapter II for a more extended discussion of the social philosophy of Jehovah's Witnesses.

3. Selective Training and Service Act, Section 10(a)(2).

4. *Selective Service in Wartime: Second Report of the Director of Selective Service, 1941–42* (Washington, 1943), p. 27.

5. *Selective Service in Peacetime: First Report of the Director of Selective Service*, 1940–41 (Washington, 1942), p. 223.

6. The question was: "Type of men on your Local Board (Occupation, Religion, Social Status). Did you know any or all of your Local Board members?"

7. The experience of one registrant, R——— V——— is well known to the writer. There were other I-A registrants having what amounted to conscientious scruples who were placed in IV-F via the psychiatric route.

8. *Selective Service Regulations*, 625.1(b).

9. J. Lloyd Spaulding to Mulford Q. Sibley, Sept. 24, 1945.

10. The questions are based upon replies of about four hundred objectors to the following queries: "Were you given an oral hearing? Under what circumstances and what types of questions were asked?" Fewer than one hundred of those who replied had had oral hearings, and hence the range of sampling is somewhat narrow and its representative character is in doubt. It is felt, however, that even a much larger sampling would not have altered substantially the general impression of questions asked by local boards. The questionnaire was sent to every C.P.S. camp (although not directly to individual C.P.S. men) and to about one thousand I-A-O's and ex-prisoners whose addresses were available. Thus the replies in no sense represent a "scientific" sampling. However, hardly any evidence is available which would run counter to the general impression left by the replies.

11. Roger K. Johnson to Mulford Q. Sibley. The board was in Seattle.

12. Frederick B. Tolles to Mulford Q. Sibley. The board was in Cambridge, Massachusetts.

13. Old Testament texts were therefore very useful. On the other hand, Biblical literalists among the objectors almost always turned to the New Testament for support.

14. Matt. 10:34–37.

15. Matt. 6:34.

16. The objector in this case was known personally by the writer.

17. Report of Claude Shotts, June 5, 1944. The account of Mr. Shotts, who was sent by the N.S.B.R.O. to investigate the Washita County situation, included a similar report of James H. Elrod, another investigator. The information in the text is based upon these two reports, which, on the whole, agree in their conclusions.

18. Statement of R. Wylie Smith, 1942.

19. *The Varieties of Religious Experience* (Modern Library ed.), pp. 28, 29, 38, 39.

20. See *The Conscientious Objector under the Selective Training and Service Act of 1940* (Washington, 1944), pp. 2–3.

21. *Ibid.*, p. 3.

22. 133 F. 2d 703 (1943).

23. 135 F. 2d 521 (1943).

24. The great doctors of the Roman Catholic Church had elaborated the distinction between a "just" and an "unjust" war. See Chapter II.

25. See Chapter II.

26. Interview with Joe Bonacorse, July 31, 1946.

27. *Selective Service Opinions*, III: 14.

28. Incontrovertible documentation is lacking to support the claim of bias

against Jehovah's Witnesses by Roman Catholic members of local boards. Nevertheless, J—— E—— C——, a Jehovah's Witness, made such a claim to the author with respect to his own case, and other Witnesses and objectors maintained the same with reference to their communities.

29. *Selective Service in Wartime*, p. 27, states the number of board of appeals in 1942 as 274, with 42 co-ordinate boards. The co-ordinate boards were appointed in areas where the volume of appeals was too great for one board to handle. The number of appeals boards remained approximately the same throughout the remainder of the war.

30. *Selective Service in Peacetime*, pp. 224–225.

31. Case of Harvey Corcoran—Hearing Officer's Report, March 8, 1943.

32. See Memorandum of the Metropolitan Board for Conscientious Objectors. Oct. 30, 1942.

33. *Ibid.*, which cites Linton Collins, Special Assistant to the Attorney General.

34. This officer handled a great many cases in the Middle West and had been a Cabinet officer under President Coolidge.

35. Case of A—— T——, Jan. 6, 1943. Before Monroe Goldwater, Hearing Officer.

36. *Report* of Hearing Officer Jackson A. Dykman in case of E—— R——, June 4, 1943.

37. *Report* of Hearing Office Monroe Goldwater in case of J—— P——, Sept., 1942.

38. An officer on the Pacific coast. According to a competent observer, the hearings of this officer were "adequate" only when the registrant brought along several friends as witnesses. In other cases, the officer was usually blunt and harsh and gave only a few minutes to the applicant. Allen Barr to Frank Olmstead (n.d.; about 1943).

39. See *Selective Service in Peacetime*, pp. 226–227.

40. *Federal Register*, March 27, 1941.

41. *Selective Service Regulations* 605.32.

42. The files of the New York City Metropolitan Board for Conscientious Objectors are replete with examples.

43. Selective Training and Service Act of 1940, Section 10(a)(2).

44. Public Law 197, approved December 5, 1943. See also *Selective Service As the Tide of War Turns: The 3rd Report of the Director of Selective Service, 1943–1944* (Washington, 1945), p. 145.

45. Memorandum to All United States Attorneys and All Special Assistants to the Attorney General Designated as Hearing Officers under the Selective Training and Service Act of 1940, Feb. 27, 1942.

46. Case of J—— W—— H——, Oct. 7, 1941.

47. Case of D—— W—— B——, Jan. 19, 1942.

48. The case histories cited in the text are based upon records of the N.S.B.R.O., which in turn compiled them from the accounts of c.o.'s themselves, records of other advisory agencies, and Selective Service records.

49. These statements are made on the basis of lengthy personal interviews with General Hershey and with the statisticians of the Selective Service System.

50. Office of Selective Service Records (formerly Selective Service System) figures.

51. *Ibid.* Official estimates are summarized in the report of the President's Advisory Commission on Universal Training, *A Program for National Security* (Washington, 1947), pp. 255–257.

52. Winslowe Ames, for example, who made a study of I-A-O's for the N.S.B.R.O. during the war, reached this conclusion, although he cited no specific documentation other than his correspondence with objectors in the Army and the general impressions of others. See *The Reporter*, Oct. 1, 1944.

53. Selective Service System, *Conscientious Objection*, Special Monograph No. 11, 2 vols. (Washington, 1950), Vol. 1, p. 315. The whole of ch. xvi, beginning at p. 313, should be read for the complete official statistics.

54. For more detailed statistics and discussions of the backgrounds and varieties of c.o.'s, see particularly Chapters V, IX, XV, XVI.

Chapter V

1. Estimate of Carlyle B. Haynes, General Secretary, Seventh-Day Adventist War Service Commission, in a letter to Mulford Sibley, Aug. 18, 1949.

2. Estimate of Gordon Shull of the B.S.C. as of March, 1945. A letter from Ruth Holsopple of the B.S.C. to Mulford Sibley, Aug. 17, 1949, indicates that this estimate is conservative.

3. Selective Service System, *Conscientious Objection*, Vol. 1, p. 315.

4. See the various Year-books of the Seventh-Day Adventists.

5. Chris P. Sorenson, Seventh-Day Adventist War Service Commission, to Winslowe Ames, May 3, 1944.

6. S. L. Van Akin, Chairman-Secretary of the Christadelphian Service Committee, to Winslowe Ames, Feb. 16, 1944.

7. War Department circular, Jan. 21, 1943. See also *The Reporter*, March 15, 1943.

8. All together, about 1,200 objectors were reclassified from C.P.S. camps to the Army and Navy during the course of the war. Of these, approximately one-half went into straight combatant service and the other half into I-A-O.

9. C—— M—— to Winslowe Ames, April 28, 1944.

10. E—— H—— B—— to Winslowe Ames, Aug. 3, 1944.

11. Testimony before Subcommittee of House Committee on Appropriations, Hearings, Dec. 11, 1941. The testimony is reprinted in *Congress Looks at the Conscientious Objector* (Washington, 1944), p. 34.

12. Business manager of Medaryville C.P.S. camp to Allen Barr, Nov. 16, 1943.

13. Director of Waldport C.P.S. camp to Allen Barr, April 13, 1943.

14. See the several reports of the Selective Service System.

15. This represented the theory of objector training, according to Col. Russell B. Reynolds, director of the War Department's Personnel Division. See *The Reporter*, March 15, 1943. Of course, cases were not wanting where individual commanders disregarded these regulations.

16. T/4 B—— T—— to Winslowe Ames, Aug. 8, 1944.

17. This theme recurs again and again in the letters which objectors in the Army wrote to Winslowe Ames.

18. T/s M—— H—— S—— to Winslowe Ames, Sept. 2, 1944.

19. Private E—— T—— S—— to A.F.S.C., Dec. 10, 1945.

20. T/5 J—— B—— to Winslowe Ames, Aug. 15, 1944.

21. See *The Reporter*, July 15, 1945.

22. *The Reporter*, Feb. 15, 1943.

23. *True Comics*, April, 1946.

24. United Press dispatch in *Philadelphia Record*, Oct. 8, 1945, p. 1. See also *Time*, Oct. 22, 1945.

25. J. A. Ulio, adjutant general, to Winslow H. Osborne, May 8, 1945.

26. See, for example, *The Reporter*, May 1, 1495.

27. Chapter II, Article 7, of U.S. Treaty Series No. 847: "Convention of Geneva on Amelioration of the Condition of Wounded and Sick of Armies in the Field." July 27, 1929. Published in U.S. Senate, 75th Congress, 3d Session, Senate Document No. 134, *Treaties, Conventions, International Acts, Protocols, and Agreements between the United States of America and other Powers.* (Washington: Government Printing Office, 1938).

28. The Geneva Convention permission to use arms in "self-defense" will be found in Chapter II, Article 8, *op. cit.* For a discussion of the Army's view on arming the Medical Corps, see *The Reporter*, May 15, 1945.

29. The official Statement of the Adjutant General was: "It is not believed to be contrary to either the letter or spirit of the mentioned statute and Executive Order to require such personnel to carry clubs while doing guard duty." See *The Reporter*, March 15, 1945.

30. Winslow Osborne to Private Ben Werner, Nov. 29, 1944.

31. Lt. C—— S—— W—— to Winslow H. Osborne, June 10, 1945. See also *The Reporter*, May 1, 1945, and July 1, 1945.

32. From a memorandum of Winslow H. Osborne, June 26, 1944.

33. From a memorandum of the N.S.B.R.O., May 31, 1944.

34. Official Record of Court Martial of Private J—— A——, Jan. 25, 1945, pp. 12–16.

35. *The Reporter*, Feb. 15, 1945.

36. As quoted in *The Reporter*, March 1, 1945.

37. On the development of the Weber case, see particularly *The Reporter*, Feb. 15, 1945, and March 1, 1945. See also the *Conscientious Objector*, Sept., 1945, and *Time*, Feb. 19, 1945.

38. Mrs. Donald E. Bell to LeRoy Dakin, May 30, 1945.

39. Robert A. Bower to Paul C. French, April 2, 1944.

40. Winslow Osborne to Austin MacCormick, March 27, 1946.

41. Navy Department, Circular Letter No. 316-44-44-1224—*Conscientious Objector, Disposition of. RESTRICTED.* (Oct. 20, 1944.)

42. See pp. 425, 426.

43. *Army Regulations*, 615-365, 1-e, July 20, 1944.

44. *Ibid.*, 615–369, 1-i, July 20, 1944.

45. *Ibid.*, 615–368, 1-h, July 20, 1944.

46. One such case occurred in 1943, when, after a seven-month struggle, Private G—— L—— was discharged (over the protests of his commanding officer). See the account in the *Conscientious Objector*, July, 1943.

47. *Selective Service Regulations*, Sections 622.51, 622.52, 652.2, and 652.11 were amended in 1942 to provide specifically for such requests by the Director of Selective Service. The grounds were to be unadaptability of the objectors for military service.

48. This procedure, as formalized by 1944 after a struggle by objector groups to obtain a clear statement of War Department policy, was outlined in a letter from Robert P. Patterson, Under Secretary of War, to Maj. Gen. Lewis B. Hershey, Director of Selective Service, May 17, 1944.

49. The relevant portion of *Selective Service Regulations* at the time these procedures for release were made definite was Part 622.51(b).

50. The N.S.B.R.O. was constantly warning that release procedures should not be made a matter of general knowledge lest it be cut off by the War Department from future sources of "semi-confidential" information.

51. See the *Conscientious Objector,* April, 1945.

52. See the *Washington Post,* June 18, 1945.

53. See the *Conscientious Objector,* Sept. 1945.

54. Ellwood W. Sargent, Colonel, Chief, Military Justice Division, Judge Advocate General's Department, to Mulford Q. Sibley, Jan. 7, 1948.

55. For a general discussion of the court-martial system, see James Barclay Smith, "Federal Procedure—What of the Court-Martial system—A Comparison with Civil Criminal Procedure," *Minnesota Law Review,* 30 (Jan., 1946).

56. On court-martial sentences during the First World War, see Norman Thomas, *Is Conscience a Crime?* (New York, 1927). On civil court sentences during the Second World War, see Chapter XV of the present work.

57. See the *Conscientious Objector,* June, 1943. See also George Reeves to Evan Thomas, June 19, 1943.

58. See the *Conscientious Objector,* March, 1946. These observations on disciplinary practices in military prisons are based primarily upon interviews and written comments of Winslow H. Osborne, Frank Olmstead, and Arthur Billings.

Chapter VI

1. See Appendix H for the church agencies which were given and which assumed administrative responsibilities.

2. Melvin Gingerich, *Service for Peace* (Akron, Pa., 1949), gives in detail the history of Mennonite policy and action in regard to alternative service.

3. See Chapter I.

4. Kenneth Holland and Frank Ernest Hill, *Youth in the CCC* (Washington, 1942).

5. An account of the negotiations between Selective Service and other government officials leading to the use of C.C.C. projects as the basis for the C.P.S. program is given by Lt. Col. Neal Wherry in *Conscientious Objection* (Washington, 1950).

6. See Chapter III.

7. The view of the pacifist critic is presented by Henry Geiger and Gordon Clough, "Origins of C.P.S.—Another View," *Fellowship,* Sept. 1946. See also *Survey Graphic,* Sept. 1946 and Selective Service monograph, *op. cit.*

8. Minutes of the National Council for Religious Objectors and of the Service Committees of the Historic Peace Churches, memoranda, and letters by participants in the discussions provide a clear and accurate documentation of the sequence of events connected with the origins of C.P.S. Several of the relevant documents have been printed in *The Origins of Civilian Public Service* (Washington, D.C., 1946).

9. Organization of the N.S.B.R.O. (originally the National Council for Religious Objectors) was approved at a conference of representatives of the Historic Peace Churches and other demonimations at Chicago on October 5, 1940. See Minutes of the National Council, Oct. 11, 1940, and of the N.S.B.R.O., Nov. 26, 1940, and Paul Comly French, *Three Years of Civilian Public Service* (Washington, Aug. 15, 1944). See pp. 279–282 for the responsibilities of N.S.B.R.O. in connection with the administration of C.P.S.

10. See Appendix E for the text of this proposal. See also Gingerich, *Service for Peace*, pp. 56 ff., and Leslie Eisan, *Pathways of Peace* (Elgin, Ill., 1948), pp. 42 ff.

11. See Minutes of the Board of Directors of the A.F.S.C., Nov. 18, 1940; of the B.S.C., Oct. 21, 1940; of the N.S.B.R.O, Nov. 25, 1940.

12. Paul C. French to Clarence E. Pickett, Dec. 3, 1940. Talking to representatives of the Historic Peace Churches and others on January 22, 1941, Dr. Dykstra summed up the negotiations as follows: "I put this whole matter to the President as experimental. It was a bit of a shock to him. He had assumed that if we are going to have camps for the so-called conscientious objectors, certainly they would be run by the U.S. and he, perhaps thinking in an older pattern, assumed they would be under Army officers and perhaps there would be just a little drill around the corners! But he thinks now that maybe this is a good thing to try out. He is experimentally minded anyway. So there wasn't any difficulty about it."

13. Diaries and personal reports of Clarence E. Pickett and Paul C. French, both of whom were present at the meeting.

14. Cf. N.S.B.R.O. Minutes, Dec. 10, 1940. The Historic Peace Churches, the Association of Catholic Conscientious Objectors, and the Fellowship of Reconciliation undertook direct administrative and financial responsibility. The other participants in the N.S.B.R.O. could not make a definite commitment, but agreed to support the program in every way possible.

15. On December 20, 1940, President Roosevelt initialed a memorandum from Dr. Dykstra, Director of Selective Service, setting forth the agreed provisions for the administration of "work of national importance under civilian direction." An immediate exchange of letters between Dr. Dykstra and Paul French, representing the N.S.B.R.O., confirmed the arrangement. See Appendix F for the text of the Dykstra Memorandum.

Reports differ in regard to what transpired during these critical negotiations between Dr. Dykstra, the President, and the church representatives. In 1946, Dr. Dykstra recollected that the President's opposition to the plan which he first submitted was a casual objection to the apparent liberality of the church-administration aspect of the proposed program. There was, as Dr. Dykstra recalled, no reference to the issue of pay for c.o.'s, and an *all-government* camp program with pay for the men was never proposed to the President. Dr. Dykstra felt that in proposing the second plan, which was finally approved, he was asking for exactly what the Peace Churches wanted. See Geiger and Clough, *op. cit.*

This account would indicate that a serious misunderstanding of the facts and of mutual intentions prevailed between the churches and the government even prior to the inception of the C.P.S. program. For whatever Dr. Dykstra's later impressions were of what happened, this was not what the Peace Church representatives understood at the time, as recorded in the minutes of their respective organizations.

16. Executive Order No. 8675 (6 F.R. 831), Feb. 6, 1941. See Appendix G for text.

17. The N.S.B.R.O. also furnished a bond of $500,000 to cover their responsibility for government property transferred to them for use in C.P.S. Selective Service assumed loss through wear and tear.

18. *The Conscientious Objector,* Vol. 4, No. 5 (May, 1942).

19. Olmstead, "The Power of Service and Good Will," *The American Friend,* 1942. It is only fair to say that Mr. Olmstead later became one of the sharpest critics of the program.

20. Gingerich, *Service for Peace,* p. 396.

21. Cf. statement by Walter W. Van Kirk, secretary of the Federal Council's Committee on the C.O., to N.S.B.R.O.

22. A survey of forty-two denominations made just before the opening of the first C.P.S. camp on May 15, 1941, concluded that most of these denominations wanted the Peace Churches to administer camps for their c.o.'s and would provide the necessary financial support.

23. Memorandum, C. A. Dykstra to President Roosevelt, Dec. 20, 1940. Cf. talk on Jan. 22, 1941.

24. *The Reporter,* Feb. 15, 1943.

25. Senate Committee on Military Affairs, 78th Congress, 1st session, Feb. 17, 1943. Note also Col. Lewis Kosch before Sub-Committee of the Senate Committee on Military Affairs, 77th Congress, 2d session, Hearings on Amendment to the Selective Training and Service Act of 1940, Aug. 19, 1942.

Chapter VII

1. Selective Service System, Camp Operations Division, tabulations of assignments to C.P.S. and distribution of man-days.

2. One hundred and fifty-one C.P.S. camps and units were formally approved by Selective Service. Several of these, however, were "blanket" units which grouped together, for purposes of administrative convenience, a number of different projects of a similar nature. For instance, all "guinea-pig" experiments were considered one "unit." See Table VI, p. 126.

3. The estimate of the saving to the federal government was calculated on the basis of the c.o.'s being paid the going wage of an Army private during their term of service. See M.C.P.S. *Bulletin,* July 11, 1946. The services of the c.o.'s were also a substantial boon to state governments. Lt. Col. Neal Wherry, in *Conscientious Objection,* p. 226, estimated that the states saved $4,000,000 by using c.o.'s in state hospitals alone, not counting the work done in other state institutions. This was the difference between the average monthly wage of hospital attendants in the states where the c.o.'s worked and the actual expenditures of the states on account of the C.P.S. men. For analysis of the contributions of the c.o.'s and their churches, see pp. 326–330.

4. Taken from *Smoke Jumper,* published by C.P.S. Camp No. 103 at Missoula, Mont.

5. This does not include the time of those who worked on camp overhead and maintenance, or who were on furlough or sick. See Table VI, p. 126.

6. See Chapter XI.

7. See Chapter XIII for discussion of the "frozen fund" and its disposition.

8. See Chapter XII for fuller discussion of the protests of C.P.S. men against forced emergency farm labor.

9. The efforts of c.o.'s to secure fundamental reforms in the practices and administration of mental care are discussed in Chapter VIII.

10. Al Benglen, "Custodial Care," *Viewpoint*, Dec. 1, 1943 (published by the C.P.S. unit at Fort Steilacoom, Wash).

11. Lewis Swanson, "Insulin Shock Therapy," *Service*, April, 1944 (published by the C.P.S. unit at Duke University Hospital, Durham, N.C.).

12. See correspondence in the *Christian Century*, Dec. 22, 1943, from a trustee of a state training school.

13. See p. 160.

14. Report of Maj. Lindstrom to Col. Kosch, Nov. 20, 1944.

15. Cf. Earl S. Garver and Ernest B. Fincher, *Puerto Rico, Unsolved Problem* (Elgin, Ill., 1945).

16. Doctors William A. Davis and Charles M. Wheeler report this experiment in the *American Journal of Hygiene*, March, 1944.

17. See the *Journal of Clinical Investigation*, Sept. 1944; the *Journal of the American Medical Association*, July, 1945; and Delisle Crawford, *A Civilian Public Service through Medical Research* (Philadelphia, 1945, mimeographed).

18. Dr. Alf S. Alving, Associate Professor of Medicine, University of Chicago, quoted in C.P.S. Memo. No. 318, B.S.C.

19. Ancel Keys *et al.*, "Factors in Deterioration and Rehabilitation," Final Report to Office of Scientific Research and Development, Feb. 15, 1946.

20. The scientific findings of the experiment were presented in reports from the Laboratory of Physiological Hygiene, University of Minnesota, by Doctors Ancel Keys, Henry Longstreet Taylor, Olaf Mickelsen, Austin Henschel, and Joseph Brozek. These were: "Rehabilitation Following Experimental Starvation in Man" and "Later Stages of Rehabilitation Following Experimental Starvation in Man." A handbook for relief workers summarizing important conclusions from the experiment was written by Harold Guetzkow and Paul Bowman (*Men and Hunger, a Psychological Manual for Relief Workers* [Elgin, Ill., 1947]). A pamphlet, "Research for Relief," was also prepared for popular distribution by the religious agencies supporting the project.

21. Cf. Wherry, *op. cit.*, p. 227.

22. Comments respectively by superintendents of Exeter School, Lafayette, R.I., and of Staunton, Va., State Hospital.

23. Evaluation submitted to Col. Kosch.

24. Evaluation submitted to Col. Kosch by an assistant farm adviser in California. However, see pp. 211 ff., 214 ff., and 250 ff. for discussion of the problem of discipline.

25. Evaluation submitted to Col. Kosch by Dr. Joseph Barrett. See pp. 161 and 287 for analysis of the long and unfortunate relationships between the unit and the administration at Williamsburg, for which Dr. Barrett himself bore considerable responsibility.

26. Evaluation submitted to Col. Kosch by the superintendent of Kalamazoo State Hospital, Mich.

27. Evaluation by the superintendent of Utah State Training School, American Fork, Utah.

28. Evaluation by the superintendent of Glacier National Park.

29. Evaluation by the superintendent of Wernersville State Hospital, Pa.

30. *The Experience of the American Friends Service Committee in Civilian Public Service* . . . (Philadelphia, 1945), p. 10.

Chapter VIII

1. The majority of the c.o.'s, however, held orthodox theological doctrines and found the source of war in personal sin.

2. C.P.S. produced considerable "social action" literature. In addition to *Pacifica Views*, it included the sophisticated *Illiterati* published at Waldport, Ore.; the blunt *Germfask Newsletter* from the "Siberia" of C.P.S., the government camp in Michigan; *Social Action*, from Big Flats, N.Y.; and a number of other camp periodicals which came under the editorial inspiration of the actionists.

3. See Chapter XIII.

4. See Chapter XII for a description of the Chicago Conference incident.

5. See Chapter XII.

6. The race issue also arose in the case of George Yamada, an American citizen of Japanese parentage who was ordered to leave his camp in Oregon for a relocation center because of the wartime Japanese evacuation regulations. See *The Reporter*, Aug., 1942, and the *Conscientious Objector*, Aug., 1942.

7. *Information*, May 25, 1944.

8. Melvin Gingerich, *Service for Peace* (Akron, Pa., 1949), pp. 259 ff.

9. Adopted by B.S.C., March 5, 1945, after agreement between local units, Advisory Council, directors, and Elgin office.

10. Statement, June 4, 1944, of Orlando C.P.S. Unit, "The Race Problem and the Orlando Unit."

11. Samuel Snipes to Louis Schneider, July 1, 1944.

12. Report of Louis Schneider, A.F.S.C. Memo. No. 452, July 6, 1944.

13. Report of Robert Beach, assistant director of the Williamsburg, Va., State Hospital Unit, to A.F.S.C., 1943.

14. See Leonard Edelstein, *We Are Accountable: A View of Mental Institutions* (Wallingford, Pa., 1945), p. 10.

15. *Ibid.*

16. *The Attendant* is now published under the title of *The Psychiatric Aide* by the National Mental Health Foundation.

Chapter IX

1. B.C.P.S. *Directors Memo.*, Dec. 28, 1942.

2. Guy F. Hershberger, *Mennonites and Their Heritage*, No. V, "Christian Relationships to State and Community" (Akron, Pa., 1942).

3. Paul Comly French, *Civilian Public Service* (Washington, 1943), p. 13. Thomas E. Jones, first director of Friends C.P.S., coined the phrase "Creative Pioneers" in his first statement of the aims of the program, and the term hung on despite derisive comments by the disillusioned.

4. Adrian Gory and David McClelland analyzed the intelligence scores of men in Friends and Brethren C.P.S. on tests comparable to those given to the Army. After allowing for various discrepancies in the data, they concluded that the average intelligence of these conscientious objectors was considerably higher than that of men in the Army and probably fell within Army Grade I. (Over 70

per cent of the c.o. sample taking either the GA-1 or the GCT-1a tests scored in the Army Grade I, in contrast to 9 per cent of enlisted men.)

5. Melvin Gingerich, *Service for Peace* (Akron, Pa., 1949), ch. viii; Leslie Eisan, *Pathways of Peace* (Elgin, Ill., 1948), pp. 54 ff.

6. Gingerich, *op. cit.*, ch. viii.

7. See *ibid.*, ch. xviii.

8. *Ibid.*

9. *Ibid.*

10. B.C.P.S. *Memos.* No. 480 and No. 535, Nov. 1 and 28, 1944.

11. B.C.P.S. *Directors' Memo.* No. 199, May 21, 1945; B.C.P.S. *Religious Life Bulletin* No. 24. See also Eisan, *op. cit.*, pp. 169 ff., for a review of the religious program in Brethren camps.

12. Thomas E. Jones, *Testimony by Work* (Philadelphia, 1942), p. 33.

13. Quoted in Eisan, *op. cit.*, p. 170.

14. Gingerich, *op. cit.*, p. 292.

15. *Ibid.*, pp. 282 ff.

16. A.F.S.C.–C.P.S. *Camp Educational Reports,* Aug. 16, 1944.

17. *Information,* Vol. II, No. 26 (Jan. 5, 1945).

18. Gingerich, *op. cit.*, p. 285.

19. *Ibid.*, ch. xix.

20. Thomas E. Jones, *op. cit.*, p. 28.

21. M.C.C. *Manual for Educational Directors,* Oct. 1942; see also Gingerich, *op. cit.*, p. 301 f.

22. Morris T. Keeton, *Report to Regional Men on Current Status and Emphases in B.C.P.S. Education,* May 8, 1945 (Brethren Service Committee, mimeographed).

23. See p. 402.

24. Cf. M.C.C. *Educational Memo.* No. 187, Sept. 19, 1944.

25. See Gingerich, *op. cit.*, p. 297 f.

26. See pp. 230 ff. for analysis of incentives on projects.

27. See pp. 228 and 235 f.

28. The presidents and faculties of Mennonite, Brethren, and Quaker colleges took substantial responsibility in guiding the reconstruction training in the camps and units, and in setting up the ill-fated college courses in the summer of 1943.

29. See p. 228.

30. Cf. Eisan, *op. cit.*, pp. 324 ff.

31. M.C.C. covered half of the tuition for completed correspondence courses at recommended schools. Some courses could be taken free.

32. Cf. Eisan, *op. cit.*, p. 124.

33. See Eisan, *op. cit.*, pp. 139 ff., and Gingerich, *op. cit.*, pp. 311 ff.

34. See Chapters X and XI.

35. Director of the Grottoes camp to Orie Miller, M.C.C. executive secretary, Feb. 26, 1944.

36. Many Mennonite assignees were skeptical of the effectiveness of these camp councils in solving camp problems. Cf. Gingerich, *op. cit.*, ch. xxi.

37. Abe Goldstein to Norman Whitney, Dec. 5, 1941, from C.P.S. Camp No. 12, Cooperstown, N.Y.

38. Crane Rosenbaum to Allen Barr, May 27, 1943.

39. B.C.P.S., *Advisory Council Report,* May 10, 1945.

40. See pp. 273 f. for a major instance of conflict between A.F.S.C. and assignees at Elkton, Ore.

Chapter X

1. Executive Order No. 8675 (6 F.R. 831), Feb. 6, 1941.

2. Lt. Col. Franklin A. McLean, *Memorandum to the Executive Camp Directors,* 1942. See Appendix M.

3. Col. Kosch had previously reserved full discretion in regard to designating the work to be performed. Writing to the Friends Executive Camp Director on February 16, 1942, he stated he could "find nothing in either the Act or the Executive Order which states that this work of national importance shall have no military or naval significance. It merely states that men classified as IV-E will perform work of national importance under civilian direction, and under the Act the Director has authority to designate what is work of national importance."

4. Contrast the view held by the A.F.S.C. when it undertook administrative responsibility for C.P.S. See p. 119.

5. See Selective Service System, Camp Operations Division, *Administrative Instructions No. 4* (mimeographed), to superintendents and assignee group leaders of hospital and special units.

6. Reports by Lt. Col. Franklin McLean on Wellston, Mich., Nov. 16, 1944, and Sept. 6, 1948.

7. Authors' conversation with Gen. Hershey, Feb., 1949. In testimony before the Senate Military Affairs Committee in regard to the extension of the draft in 1948, Selective Service officials made plain that they did not object to provision for pay for c.o.'s in future alternative service; this was in marked contrast to their consistent opposition to pay during the war years. See below, p. 217 f.

8. *Selective Service Regulations,* Amendment No. 265, Dec. 28, 1944.

9. Cf. Selective Service System, Camp Operations Division, *Administrative Directive* No. 27, Aug. 17, 1945.

10. Selective Service System, Camp Operations Division, *Administrative Instructions* No. 1, Jan. 15, 1943, and No. 4, Feb. 1, 1945.

11. Selective Service System, Camp Operations Division, *Administrative Instructions* Nos. 1 and 4 (Note 14).

12. *Information,* March 2, 1945.

13. See p. 119.

14. Later regulation knocked out the 10-day period of "grace" before A.W.O.L. had to be reported. Cf. *Selective Service Regulations,* as amended April, 1945, Sec. 691.17e.

15. *Selective Service Regulations,* Sec. 691.17, *Federal Register,* Jan. 24, 1942, p. 507.

16. Col. Kosch to Paul C. French, Dec. 8, 1941. The director was not permitted to "excuse" A.W.O.L. for "personal reasons," which included the breakdown of private means of transportation back to camp.

17. See pp. 249 and 292.

18. *Selective Service Regulations,* Sec. 691.17, *Federal Register,* Jan. 24, 1942, p. 507.

19. See Chapter XV for trials and prosecutions of c.o.'s.

20. See pp. 252 ff. and 292.

21. Authors' conversation with Gen. Hershey, July 26, 1946.

22. See pp. 309–311.

23. B.C.P.S. *Memo.* No. 185, May 14, 1945.

24. Report to M.C.C. by Henry Fast, Executive Camp Director, July, 1943.

25. See Chapter XI.

26. *The Experience of the American Friends Service Committee in Civilian Public Service* (Philadelphia, 1945), p. 17.

27. Senate Military Affairs Committee, 78th Congress, 1st session, Hearings on S.315 and S.675, Feb. 17, 1943. Col. Kosch before the Committee on August 12, 1942, had said, ". . . the very fact that a man does not get paid is one means of sorting the conscientious objector from the slacker." Testimony concerning legislation affecting c.o.'s is given in *Congress Looks at the Conscientious Objector* (Washington, 1944).

28. *Ibid.* Prisoners of war, under terms of the Geneva Convention, received an allowance of approximately eighty cents a day.

29. See pp. 116 f.

30. See Senate Military Affairs Committee, 78th Congress, 1st session, Hearings on S.315 and S.675, Feb. 17, 1943.

31. Comptroller General Lindsay Warren to Gen. Lewis B. Hershey, July 13, 1942.

32. Warren to Hershey, Dec. 8, 1942.

33. See pp. 132 and 297 ff.

34. Reported by Edwin Brown, Quaker businessman from Murfreesboro, N.C., who conferred with Lindsay Warren about the problem.

35. *The Reporter,* July 1, 1942; also N.S.B.R.O., *Attempts to Secure Compensatory Aid.*

36. See H.R. 3199, 78th Congress, 1st session.

37. Letter to N.S.B.R.O. from an anonymous assignee.

38. See p. 300 re the dependency program of the religious agencies.

39. This was proportionately as high a casualty rate as that of the armed forces.

40. Rep. James P. Geelan (Conn.) in the House and Senator Brien McMahon (Conn.) in the Senate introduced the bill for Dugan. Selective Service opposed such private bills as tending to muddy the case for a general measure covering all c.o.'s.

41. See, for instance, Selective Service *Administrative Directive* No. 18, Oct. 1, 1943.

42. Selective Service *Administrative Directive* No. 18.

43. See Executive Order No. 8675 (6 F.R. 831), Feb. 6, 1941.

44. *Selective Service in Peacetime: First Report of the Director of Selective Service, 1940–41* (Washington, 1942), pp. 200 ff.

45. Quoted in N.S.B.R.O. *Memo.* No. 462 to Board of Directors, Feb. 26, 1945.

46. See *Projects and Incentives in Civilian Public Service* (Philadelphia, 1945), pp. 7–8.

47. See A.F.S.C. *Experience in C.P.S.*, pp. 31 ff., which lists 103 public and private social welfare agencies which requested and were denied assignments of men in C.P.S. as of the date of publication, April, 1945. This list was not complete, for it included only requests made through or in consultation with the A.F.S.C.

48. A.F.S.C. *Experience in C.P.S.*, pp. 12–13.

49. See Gen. Lewis B. Hershey to Robert L. Irvin, acting executive assistant

to the Chairman, U.S. Senate Special Committee Investigating the National Defense Program, March, 1946.

50. Lt. Col. Neal Wherry, in *Conscientious Objection,* p. 171.

51. *Ibid.,* p. 168.

52. In the winter, the camp quotas were substantially reduced.

53. See Chapters VIII and X.

54. Apparently his ire had been roused by a favorable comment on the plans in Eleanor Roosevelt's column.

55. See *The Reporter,* July 1 and 15, 1945; the *Conscientious Objector,* Jan., 1944; Friends Committee on National Legislation, *Washington Letter* No. 9, June 27, 1944.

56. Col. Kosch to Paul French, quoted in N.S.B.R.O. *Memo.* No. 462.

57. See p. 214 for the "black list" and p. 292 re disciplinary assignments.

58. *Projects and Incentives,* p. 6.

59. *Ibid.,* pp. 15 ff.

60. *Ibid.,* pp. 18 ff.

61. Cases I to V are taken from *ibid.,* pp. 21–22; Case VI was an assignee in a government camp.

62. *A.F.S.C. Experience in C.P.S.,* p. 14.

63. See *Conscientious Objection,* ch. xii.

64. Report from C.P.S. Camp No. 46, Big Flats, N.Y. to A.F.S.C., Oct. 16, 1944; also Louis W. Schneider, assistant executive director of Friends C.P.S., to Paul C. French, Oct. 18, 1944.

65. Report to M.C.C. by Regional Supervisor Franz, Aug. 1, 1944, re C.P.S. Camp at Belden, Calif., and memorandum of Ercell Lynn to N.S.B.R.O., September, 1942, re C.P.S. camp at Lyndhurst, Va.

66. *A.F.S.C. Experience in C.P.S.,* pp. 15 ff.; *Projects and Incentives,* pp. 13 ff.

67. *Projects and Incentives,* pp. 14–15.

68. N.S.B.R.O. file for anonymous assignee. See also pp. 250 f.

69. See pp. 291 ff.

70. A.F.S.C. *Memo.* No. 515, to Camp Directors, April 18, 1945.

71. B.C.P.S. *Memo.* No. 69, to Directors and Men, March 21, 1946.

72. N.S.B.R.O. *Demobilization Bulletin* No. 15, "The C.P.S. Demobilization System," June 6, 1945.

73. H.R. 3597, 79th Congress, 2d session.

74. H.R. 3772, 79th Congress, 2d session.

75. *The Reporter,* July 15 and Aug. 1, 1945.

76. *The Reporter,* Oct. 1, 1945.

77. *Projects and Incentives,* pp. 22–23.

Chapter XI

1. Cf. *Selective Service Regulations,* 653.2(b) and 653.3(e), *Federal Register,* Jan. 14, 1942, p. 248.

2. Cf. *The Reporter,* Aug., 1942. The Appropriation Acts for Selective Service's own budget did provide general *authorization* of funds for such a purpose. See, for instance, the budget for the fiscal year 1942–1943, House Document 528, 77th Congress, 2d session.

3. Statement by Col. Franklin McLean in *The Reporter,* Supplement, Nov. 1, 1944.

4. Frank Olmstead to A. J. Muste for presentation to N.S.B.R.O., Feb. 12, 1941.

5. See p. 313.

6. Paul French to M. R. Ziegler, Orie Miller, and Paul Furnas, March 12, 1942.

7. N.S.B.R.O., Board of Directors, Minutes, March 10, 1942.

8. See p. 202.

9. Paul C. French to Camp Directors, June 12, 1942.

10. Col. Lewis Kosch to Paul French, June 22, 1942.

11. Bishop G. Bromley Oxnam to Paul French, June 22, 1942.

12. Cf. A.F.S.C.–C.P.S. Executive Committee, Minutes, July 24, 1942.

13. Cf. A.F.S.C.–C.P.S. Exec. Com., Minutes, March 26, 1943

14. A.F.S.C.–C.P.S. Exec. Com., Minutes, April 23, 1943.

15. *The Reporter,* Nov. 1, 1944.

16. *The Reporter,* Aug. 1, 1943.

17. According to Purnell Benson, one of the first to transfer voluntarily to Mancos from Friends C.P.S. See his article in *The Reporter,* Supplement, Nov. 1, 1944.

18. Cf. *The Reporter,* Supplement, Nov. 1, 1944.

19. Victor Olson to Paul French, Feb. 17, 1944.

20. Lt. Col. Franklin McLean, in *The Reporter,* Supplement, Nov. 1, 1944.

21. Cf. McLean, *The Reporter,* Supplement, Nov. 1, 1944.

22. Cf. Benson, *The Reporter,* Supplement, Nov. 1 1944.

23. Cf. Osborne, report to N.S.B.R.O., May 21, 1944.

24. See pp. 274 ff.

25. Cf. *The Reporter,* Supplement, Nov. 1, 1944.

26. Benson, *The Reporter,* Supplement, Nov. 1, 1944.

27. Douglas Steere as told to Winslow Osborne, Sept. 9, 1944.

28. Robert Horton to Winslow Osborne, Aug. 18, 1944.

29. Benson, *The Reporter,* Supplement, Nov. 1, 1944.

30. *Ibid.*

31. *Detroit Times,* Feb. 5 and 6, 1945.

32. See statement by Roy Kepler and others, "A Reply to *Time,*" issued by the Fellowship of Reconciliation, 1945.

33. Cf. Kepler *et al., op. cit.,* p. 4.

34. Report of James Stanley to Paul French.

35. Paul G. Voelker to Clarence S. Johnson, Superintendent, Seney Migratory Bird Refuge, March 17, 1945.

Chapter XII

1. *Pacifica Views,* May 4, 1945, p. 1.

2. *Ibid.*

3. Richard Sterne, writing from Big Flats, N.Y., camp to Providence Friends Meeting, Wallingford, Pa., May 22, 1943.

4. Stephen G. Cary to A.F.S.C., July 29, 1942.

5. See p. 235.

6. Report, Big Flats, N.Y., camp to A.F.S.C., Oct. 16, 1944.

7. Sterne to Providence Friends Meeting.

8. Cf. *Pacific Views*, Nov. 9, 1945.

9. John E. Baer to M. R. Ziegler, chairman of N.S.B.R.O., Dec. 16, 1942.

10. Cf. Leslie Eisan, *Pathways of Peace* (Elgin, Ill., 1948), pp. 92 ff.

11. See pp. 271, 322.

12. Statement by David Metcalf, upon walking out of C.P.S. Camp No. 46, Big Flats, N.Y., Dec. 28, 1943.

13. Roy Kepler, "Recapitulation," *Germfask Newsletter*, Feb., 1946; see also his "open letter" in the same publication, March, 1944.

14. See p. 197.

15. For instance, the early demands for government-administered C.P.S. camps. See Chapter XI.

16. See p. 292. Lt. Col. Franklin McLean to Col. Lewis Kosch, Dec. 26, 1944.

17. *The Reporter*, May 1, 1945; B.C.P.S. *Bulletin*, May 4, 1945.

18. Paul French to Rex Corfman, April 3, 1943. Corfman was the assignee who had invited Gen. Hershey to the conference.

19. Paul French to N.S.B.R.O. Board of Directors, *Memo.* No. 160, April 5, 1943.

20. Letter from seven assignees at C.P.S. Camp No. 67, Downey, Idaho.

21. Statement by A. J. Muste and Evan W. Thomas to administering agencies, N.S.B.R.O., and C.P.S. men, April 7, 1943; letter from Paul Furnas, Executive Director, Friends C.P.S., to C.P.S. Camp, Oakland, Md., April 9, 1943.

22. Statement of 53 assignees at Powellsville to Paul Furnas, April 15, 1943.

23. Rex Corfman *et al.* to all camps, April 12, 1943.

24. Lloyd T. Cadbury, C.P.S. Camp, Coshocton, Ohio, to Paul Furnas, May 4, 1943.

25. Carne Rosenbaum, C.P.S. Camp, Coleville, Calif., to Mary Newman, A.F.S.C. staff, May 1, 1943.

26. French to Hershey, May 21, 1943.

27. Matthew Connelly to Lewis Hill, director of the National Council of Conscientious Objectors, as quoted in the *Conscientious Objector*, Dec., 1945.

28. "Outline of Objectives and Methods of C.P.S. Union," issued by the organizing committee, April 17, 1944.

29. *Ibid.*; also statement of aims drawn up by "Local 52," Powellsville, Md., Sept. 24, 1944.

30. Secretary's report to the general executive board of the C.P.S. Union, May 6, 1944.

31. See p. 268.

32. See *Information*, Dec. 1, 1944.

33. Ralph Rudd, president of the C.P.S. Union, to the Union's general executive board, Dec. 9, 1944.

34. Statement of David Metcalf, Dec. 28, 1943.

35. See pp. 261 f.

36. Strike song at C.P.S. Camp, Cascade Locks, Ore., sung to the tune of *Pistol Packin' Mama*.

37. See pp. 213, 250–256.

38. Statement by Sam Hays, assignee at C.P.S. Camp, Elkton, Ore.

39. See J. Lewis, *Toward an Understanding of the C.P.S. Slowdown* (mimeographed at C.P.S. Camp No. 128, Lapine, Ore.), p. 6.

40. Harvey Saunders, as reported by the *Escanaba Daily Press*, Feb. 4, 1945.

41. J. Lewis, *op. cit.*, p. 14 ff.

42. Russ Freeman, "Weaknesses of the Slowdown," *Fellowship,* Sept. 1946.

43. Roy Kepler, *op. cit.*

44. George Baird, "Experiment in Conscription," *Fellowship,* March, 1945.

45. Russ Freeman, *op. cit.*

Chapter XIII

1. See p. 526, note 9.

2. See Appendix H.

3. See p. 204.

4. Melvin Gingerich, *Service for Peace* (Akron, Pa.: 1949), ch. xxi.

5. Cf. Earl Garver, *The Director as Administrator,* B.S.C. (mimeographed).

6. Mary Newman to Paul Furnas, A.F.S.C. office memo.

7. See p. 214.

8. See the action taken in connection with the Chicago Conference, pp. 264 ff.

9. From the *Memorandum to Men Considering Application for C.P.S. Camps Administered by the A.F.S.C.* Similar standards were set by the other religious agencies.

10. See p. 205.

11. See p. 308 for statement of the basic policies of the Historic Peace Churches in this regard.

12. See Chapter IX.

13. Efforts to open new projects and close worthless ones are discussed on pp. 226–230.

14. See p. 225. See exhibits in *The Experience of the American Friends Service Committee in Civilian Public Service* (Philadelphia: 1945).

15. Questions selected from among those on the B.S.C. Evaluation Report, Personnel Form 4.

16. Report of R. S. Blanc, assistant director of the Philadelphia Hospital unit, to George Mohlenhoff, A.F.S.C. staff, Oct. 1, 1945.

17. Evaluation by superintendent of Mt. Pleasant State Hospital, Iowa.

18. Evaluation by Professor of Animal Husbandry, University of Nebraska, who was director of the C.P.S. unit at the agricultural experiment station.

19. *The Reporter,* July 15, 1943.

20. See p. 228 and Chapter X.

21. See Chapter X.

22. Paul C. French to Gen. Hershey, April 26, 1943, summarizing an evening conference between Selective Service officials and the directors of the N.S.B.R.O., April 16, 1943.

23. See p. 237.

24. N.S.B.R.O. *Camp Directors Bulletin* No. 154; Paul Furnas to J. N. Weaver, N.S.B.R.O., Mar. 21, 1945; Dr. Alex M. Burgess, medical director of A.F.S.C., to Stephen G. Cary, director of C.P.S. Camp No. 46 (Big Flats), Aug. 10, 1945.

25. Stephen G. Cary to Louis W. Schneider, A.F.S.C., Dec. 12, 1945. See p. 212.

26. Lt. Col. Franklin A. McLean to Col. Lewis F. Kosch, Dec. 20, 1944.

27. *Conscientious Objector,* Nov., 1943, and Jan., 1944. The recommendations of the A.C.L.U. were published in a pamphlet, *Conscience and War* (New York, 1943); they were presented to Gen. Hershey and Attorney General Francis

Biddle in a plea "for fairer treatment of conscientious objectors" signed by 19 prominent nonpacifists. Cf. *New York Times*, Sept. 26, 1943.

28. Ernest Angell, chairman of the A.C.L.U., to Gen. Hershey, May 24, 1946.

29. *A.F.S.C. Experience in C.P.S.*, p. 26. See also B.S.C. Minutes, May 9, 1945, wherein the B.S.C. reaffirmed its position that the government should provide pay, dependency allotments, and compensation provisions for C.P.S. men comparable to those for men in the armed forces, and instructed its staff to work with other administrative agencies in achieving these ends.

30. Cf. Attorney General of the United States, *Report for the Fiscal Year Ending June 30, 1944.*

31. See p. 272.

32. Such as the Starnes "rider" and the Winstead bill. See pp. 228, 239.

33. See p. 220. The case for the c.o.'s was forcefully presented to the House by Rep. John M. Coffee of Washington, Feb. 9, 1944, 78th Congress, 2nd Session.

34. Congressional Record, Vol. 94, part 6, pp. 7303 ff.

35. See p. 132.

36. *The Reporter*, Oct. 1, 1943.

37. H.R. 1343, 79th Congress, 1st Session; introduced Jan. 10, 1945. See Chapter X.

38. See *The Reporter*, Nov. 15, 1945.

39. Paul French to N.S.B.R.O. Board of Directors, April 2, 1946.

40. N.S.B.R.O. to Gen. Hershey, July 2, 1945.

41. N.S.B.R.O., *C.O. Dependency* (pamphlet).

42. M.C.C., *Meeting C.P.S. Dependency Needs;* Eisan, *Pathways to Peace* (Elgin, Ill., 1948), p. 399.

43. See *A.F.S.C.–C.P.S. Dependency Program* (A.F.S.C. [mimeographed]); and H. Stanton Baily, A.F.S.C. staff, to Herbert Huffman, May 24, 1945.

44. Baily to Huffman, May 24, 1945.

45. N.S.B.R.O. to Gen. Hershey, July 2, 1945.

46. See p. 190.

47. Gingerich, *Service for Peace*, ch. xx.

48. Cf. *Will We Prevent the Next War?* by Robert McLane (mimeographed).

49. See p. 189.

50. Gingerich, *op. cit.;* M.C.P.S. *Bulletin*, Feb. 8 and 22, 1946.

Chapter XIV

1. Cf. remarks of Dr. Dykstra quoted above, p. 122.

2. *Selective Service in Peacetime: First Report of the Director of Selective Service, 1940–41* (Washington, 1942), p. 200.

3. Mennonite Civilian Public Service, *Statement of Policy*, Sept. 16, 1943.

4. Albert Gaeddert, executive director of Mennonite C.P.S., quoted in Melvin Gingerich, *Service for Peace* (Akron, Pa., 1949), ch. xxiii.

5. *An Introduction to Friends Civilian Public Service* (Philadelphia, 1945), p. 31.

6. Edward Yoder and Don E. Smucker, *The Christian and Conscription* (Akron, Pa., 1945), p. 55.

7. Paul Comly French, *Civilian Public Service* (Washington, May, 1943),

pp. 3 ff. See also Leslie Eisan, *Pathways of Peace*, p. 366; Thomas E. Jones, *Creative Pioneering* (Philadelphia, 1941); Yoder and Smucker, *op. cit.*, ch. v.

8. See p. 19.

9. See Chapter XIII.

10. Annual Conference of the Church of the Brethren, June 14, 1946.

11. See "Resolution on Conscientious Objectors," adopted by the Executive Committee of the Federal Council of the Churches of Christ in America, March 20, 1945.

12. See below, pp. 320 ff., and Chapter XIII.

13. Eisan, *op. cit.*, pp. 65 ff.

14. See p. 253 for the Germfask fracas; pp. 337 ff. discuss the crisis at Glendora.

15. See, for instance, editorials in the *Washington Post*, Nov. 22, 1944, and Jan. 2, 1945, based on the story of Dr. Don DeVault. See the *Christian Century*, Dec. 8, 1943, p. 1432.

16. Leo P. Crespi, "Public Opinion toward Conscientious Objectors," *Journal of Psychology*, 19 (1945), 209–310. These studies also appear as supplements to *The Reporter*, Jan. 15, Feb. 1 and 15, 1945.

17. *Pacifica Views*, May 18, 1945.

18. *Ibid.*, Jan. 19, 1945.

19. H. Otto Dahlke, "Values and Group Behavior in Two Camps for Conscientious Objectors," *American Journal of Sociology* 51 (July, 1945), 22–33. For a shrewd autobiographical description of life in C.P.S. by a c.o. of the "progressive" wing, see Lloyd Frankenberg, "Conscience Free," *Harper's*, Nov., 1947, pp. 466–475.

20. A. T. Boisen, "Conscientious Objectors: Their Morale in Church-Operated Service Units," *Psychiatry* 7 (1944), 215–244. See also McClelland and Gory, *op. cit.* Under the somewhat parallel conditions of enforced segregation in Japanese relocation centers, the deterioration of morale and personality was apparently strikingly similar to C.P.S. See Alexander H. Leighton, *The Governing of Men; General Principles and Recommendations Based on Experience at a Japanese Relocation Camp* (Princeton, N.J., 1945).

21. See pp. 260 ff. for a fuller account of the views of those who walked out.

22. Report of the B.S.C., accepted March 15, 1946.

23. Ralph Norman Mould, "Why C.P.S. Must Go On," *Christian Century*, Dec. 1, 1943, pp. 1397–1399.

24. The cost of C.P.S. to the main administrative agencies was:

M.C.C.	$3,188,578
A.F.S.C.	2,332,176
B.S.C.	1,681,495
	$7,202,249

Cf. *The Reporter*, Aug.–Sept., 1947.

25. Gingerich, *op. cit.*, p. 345 f.

26. Eisan, *op. cit.*, ch. xiv.

Chapter XV

1. *A Program for National Security: Report of the President's Advisory Commission on Universal Training* (Washington, 1947), 256–257. Total prosecutions down to Nov. 1, 1945, were 5,652. *The Reporter*, Nov. 1, 1945.

2. *A Program for National Security,* pp. 256–257.

3. See *The Reporter,* Nov. 1, 1945.

4. See R. Alfred Hassler, *Conscripts of Conscience, the Story of Sixteen Objectors to Conscription* (New York, 1942).

5. See Chapter IV.

6. See Chapter XIII for a more complete treatment.

7. *The Reporter,* May 31, 1946.

8. *The Reporter,* June 21, 1946.

9. *The Reporter,* Aug. 2, 1946.

10. *The Reporter,* Sept. 1, 1946.

11. *The Reporter,* Feb., 1947.

12. *The Reporter,* April, 1947.

13. *Federal Convicts Numbers 1128 and 1129; College to Prison* (Philadelphia, 1942).

14. *Ibid.*

15. *Ibid.*

16. *U.S.* v. *Philip Curtis Dolve, Gerald P. Darrow, Charles Vincent Worley, Lloyd Scaff,* Reporter's Transcript of Proceedings, before Hon. Ralph E. Jenney, Los Angeles, Calif., June 23, 1943, p. 14.

17. See the *Conscientious Objector,* June, 1942.

18. Judge Matthew T. Abruzzo, in Brooklyn, N.Y., in the case of Randolph Phillips. *New York Times,* March 19, 1943. See also the *Conscientious Objector,* April, 1943.

19. *U.S.* v. *John Andrew Schubin,* Reporter's Transcript, Jan. 25, 1943. The presiding judge was Leon Yankwich.

20. See Chapter XIX for a more elaborate treatment of this problem.

21. *Federal Prisons* (published annually) (El Reno, Okla., 1943), pp. 59–60.

22. *Ibid.,* p. 58.

23. Based upon figures of the N.S.B.R.O. and the Department of Justice.

24. Critical comments on the case will be found in Constance Rumbaugh to A. J. Muste, Aug. 6, 1943, and Mrs. Matilda Ball to Evan Thomas, Aug. 22, 1943.

25. *U.S.* v. *Arnold Chase Satterthwait,* Reporter's Transcript, Sept. 8, 1943 (Eastern District of Pennsylvania).

26. *New York Sun,* April 14, 1943.

27. Judge Claude McColloch. See the *Conscientious Objector,* April, 1945.

28. Federal Judge John C. Knox. See the *Conscientious Objector,* Jan., 1944.

29. Case of David R. Nyvall, III. See the *Chicago Herald-American,* March 9, 1942. The *Herald-American* carried on a public agitation against several nonregistrants, including Nyvall.

30. *Memorandum on Probation for C.O. Violators of the Selective Service Act,* Fellowship of Reconciliation, March 8, 1944.

31. Memorandum of conversation with Petherbridge and records of Los Angeles Committee for Conscientious Objectors.

Chapter XVI

1. See *Federal Prisons* (published annually) (El Reno, Okla., 1943), pp. 87, 27. For a wartime corroborative analysis, see L. N. Robinson, *Jails: Care and Treatment of Misdemeanant Prisoners in the United States* (Philadelphia, 1944).

2. Earl Alexander Welch to George Houser, 1944.

3. Don DeVault to George Houser, Sept. 3, 1944.

4. Ralph Galt to Bureau of Prisons, Feb. 1, 1943. See also the objector Roger Axford's description of the Cook County, Ill., county jail, "This Happened to Me in Prison," *Christian Century*, March 22, 1944, pp. 367–368.

5. See *A Program for National Security: Report of the President's Advisory Commission on Universal Training* (Washington, 1947), 256–257.

6. See pp. 31–35.

7. From an interview by Professor Donald Taft.

8. From information supplied by Professor Donald R. Taft, after his investigation of conscientious objectors in prison.

9. This statement, as well as the subsequent observations, are based upon conversations with Witnesses, letters of observant non-Witness objectors in prison, and various prison visitors. Winslow Osborne, prison visitor for the N.S.B.R.O., for example, was very helpful.

10. A number of prison letters written by objectors speak of this phenomenon.

11. The official administrative and publishing organization for Jehovah's Witnesses throughout the world. The headquarters of the society were in Brooklyn, N.Y.

12. This is the view of Professor Donald R. Taft, of the University of Illinois Department of Sociology, who spent the summer of 1943 studying at first hand conscientious objectors in prison.

13. *Federal Prisons* (1943), p. 11.

14. *Ibid.*

15. See his *Walls and Bars* (Chicago, 1927).

16. *Federal Prisons* (1943), p. 13.

17. Donald Royer to Ernest Lefever, April 23, 1944.

18. Many of these observations agree with those of Miss Lucille Day, a social worker, who had much experience with both C.P.S. assignees and imprisoned objectors.

19. John Mecartney, in a letter to Frances Ransom, May 14, 1944, praises the change in diet after his transfer from Danbury to Lewisburg.

20. *Federal Prisons* (1943), p. 11.

21. *Conscientious Objector*, Aug., 1943. See also *Federal Prisons* (1943), p. 11. Accounts of the incident vary.

22. See the *Report on Visit to the Federal Reformatory at Chillicothe, Ohio, August 6–9, 1943*, by Charles Palmer, a prison visitor for the A.F.S.C. Palmer's report was mimeographed.

23. Quoted in a letter from Charles W. Palmer to Mrs. Caroline B. Lovett, Aug. 23, 1943.

24. William H. Kuenning to Harrop Freeman, June 10, 1944.

25. *Federal Prisons* (1943), p. 12, states that it was the deliberate policy of the Bureau of Prisons not to assign "sincere conscientious objectors to industries producing war products in violation of the inmate's convictions."

26. One conscientious objector, Mathias Kauten, was an authority on rammed-earth houses and published an article on the subject. His interest in the problem was partially due to his belief that such buildings would considerably reduce the cost of residential construction.

27. Donald Royer to Ernest Lefever, April 23, 1944.

28. These observations are based on the report of Donald R. Taft, *General Report on C.O. and J.W. Policy* (manuscript), which was submitted (after a visit to nine federal prisons) about the middle of the war. There seems to have been no substantial change during the last two years of the war.

29. Joe Felmet to Vivian Roodenko, May 1, 1944.

30. Regarding "dark holes," Professor Donald Taft said in his *General Report on C.O. and J.W. Policy*, Aug. 30, 1943; "I understand the use of the dark dungeon type of isolation has been forbidden by the Bureau but is continued on occasion nevertheless. I have discovered this to be true in at least one or two institutions."

31. For comments by an objector, the account of W. Edward Dyson, "About Our American Penal System" (typewritten, and originally sent to George Houser, 1944), is helpful.

32. Mathias Kauten to Marie Nelson, May 9, 1944.

33. The incident was reported from Ashland, in a letter from Arthur Dole to George Houser, 1944. Another Ashland objector told the writer that the incident had actually occurred.

34. Carolyn B. Lovett to the War Resisters League, March 23, 1944. The incident supposedly took place in the Chillicothe reformatory.

35. So reported the *Conscientious Objector*, Sept. 1943. The Bureau of Prisons was unable to offer conclusive evidence either supporting or denying the allegation.

36. James E. Bristol to Warden William H. Hiatt, Nov. 16, 1946.

37. Mulford Sibley talked at length with Gara. The latter was a quiet young man, very careful in his choice of language, and from all appearances a close observer.

38. James V. Bennett to James E. Bristol, Nov. 26, 1945.

39. *Conscientious Objector*, Sept. 1943, p. 1.

40. Oliver Ellis Stone to Dr. Evan Thomas, Aug. 28, 1943.

41. Professor Taft's observations on psychiatry, of course, reflect the frequent conflict between "sociological" and "psychiatric" approaches to the problem of human personality.

42. Interview with Dr. M. R. King, July 28, 1945.

43. (New York: 1946).

44. Lindner, *Stone Walls and Men*, p. 302.

45. *Ibid.*, p. 305.

46. *Ibid.*, p. 307.

47. *Ibid.*, p. 308.

48. See Chapter XVIII for accounts of four dramatic individual "strikes."

49. *Federal Prisons* (1943), p. 11.

50. *Ibid.*, p. 10.

51. *Ibid.*, p. 11.

52. See the account in the *Conscientious Objector*, June–July, 1941.

53. See A. J. Muste, Memo. on Danbury strike (manuscript), Dec. 23, 1943.

54. Memorandum of Frances Ransome (manuscript) to Evan Thomas and A. J. Muste, June 29, 1943.

55. *The Reporter*, Aug. 15, 1943.

56. Quoted from the letter to Bennett in a communication from William Lovett to his mother, Oct. 27, 1943.

57. James V. Bennett to Warden Hiatt, Nov. 6, 1943.

58. The Strikers to James V. Bennett, Dec. 1, 1943.

59. Manual Bulletin No. 96, Bureau of Prisons, Feb. 23, 1944, gives the revisions in mimeographed form. Apparently several of the provisions had been proposed by the Bureau of Prisons a number of years before, but they had never actually been put into effect at Lewisburg.

60. See the *Conscientious Objector,* Nov., 1944.

61. From memoranda of James Mullin, prison visitor of the American Friends Service Committee, following three visits to these prisons.

62. See Chapter XVIII for dramatic examples.

63. Estimates of the total number of strikers vary. Much depends on one's definition of "strike"—whether, for example, one includes individual actions as well as concerted refusals to eat or work. But the maximum number of strikers, construing the term liberally, was probably not more than two hundred.

Chapter XVII

1. See Chapter XV. All together, about 150 objectors were sentenced at least twice to prison (some three times) for what were technically but not actually separate offenses.

2. On parole in general, consult Donald R. Taft, *Criminology, An Attempt at a Synthetic Interpretation with a Cultural Emphasis* (New York, 1942), pp. 537–555, and Harry Elmer Barnes and Negley K. Teeters, *New Horizons in Criminology; the American Crime Problem* (New York, 1943), ch. xxxiv.

3. 18 U.S. Code, Sec. 170.

4. Letter of James V. Bennett, Director of Prisons, Oct. 30, 1944. (mimeographed).

5. See the account in Edward C. M. Richards, *They Refuse to be Criminals; Parole and the Conscientious Objector* (West Chester, Pa.), 1946), pp. 33–36.

6. See the description of his case in the combined issue of *World Peace Car Bulletin,* III, 7, and *The Absolutist,* July 12, 1945.

7. Report of James Mullin, prison visitor for the A.F.S.C., after a visit to Lewisburg, July 12, 1945. See also Richards, *They Refuse to Be Criminals,* p. 30.

8. Richards, *op. cit.,* p. 30.

9. The original version of the Executive Order will be found in *Selective Service Regulations,* No. 643, p. 2.

10. See Chapter XIX for a discussion of these cases.

11. See James V. Bennett, *Executive Order 8641: Revised Procedure: Memorandum for Wardens and Superintendents,* April 15, 1944.

12. Figures of the N.S.B.R.O., based on Department of Justice figures.

13. *The Reporter,* Nov. 14, 1943.

14. *Federal Prisons* (published annually) (El Reno, Okla.: 1943), p. 33.

15. Memorandum of Robert A. Fangmeir to Paul Comly French, April 20, 1945, regarding conversation with Donald Clemmeer of the Bureau of Prisons.

16. Dole's case is recounted in Richards, *op. cit.,* pp. 31–33.

17. See the *Conscientious Objector,* Feb., 1945.

18. *Conscientious Objector,* Feb., 1945.

19. See comments of Winslow H. Osborne, Advisory Section of the N.S.B.R.O., in *Camp Directors' Bulletin No. 171,* Jan. 29, 1946.

20. *The Reporter,* July 12, 1946.

21. *Ibid.*

22. *Ibid.,* Dec., 1946.

23. The laws of the several states differed with respect to deprivation of rights and privileges for those who committeed felonies. Deprivation of the privileges of voting and holding office was common. In some states, disabilities would follow on federal conviction of felony only if the offense was also a violation of state law.

24. *The Absolutist,* Nov. 20, 1945.

25. *Ibid.,* Nov. 6, 1945.

26. See the *Conscientious Objector,* Dec., 1945, and *The Absolutist,* Dec. 4, 1945.

27. 10 *Federal Register* 15409, Proclamation 2676, Dec. 24, 1945.

28. *Amnesty Bulletin,* Jan. 4, 1946; *The Call,* Jan. 7, 1946.

29. *The Reporter,* Feb. 15, 1946, p. 2.

30. *Conscientious Objector,* March, 1946.

31. *The Reporter,* May 31, 1946.

32. See *Amnesty Bulletin,* May 29, 1946, and June 12, 1946.

33. *The Absolutist,* June, 1946, p. 2.

34. The story is detailed in *The Reporter,* Oct., 1946.

35. *Amnesty Bulletin,* Nov. 27, 1946.

36. Nov. 23, 1946.

37. Quoted in *The Reporter,* Dec., 1946, p. 4.

38. See *The Reporter,* Jan. 1947, and *Amnesty Bulletin,* Dec. 25, 1946.

39. *The Reporter,* Jan. 1947.

40. See *Amnesty Bulletin,* Feb. 26, 1947, and March 12, 1947.

41. See *Amnesty Bulletin,* June 2, 1947, p. 2.

42. *Amnesty Bulletin,* June 24, 1947.

43. *Amnesty Bulletin,* Dec. 5, 1947, p. 2.

44. The complete texts of the President's proclamation and the report of the Board were printed in the *New York Times,* Dec. 24, 1947, p. 8.

45. Mimeographed statement, Dec. 24, 1947.

46. *Washington Post,* Dec. 25, 1947.

47. *Amnesty Bulletin,* Jan. 3, 1948.

48. See *Still No Amnesty* (New York, 1948), for the Amnesty Committee's criticisms.

49. *U.S.* v. *Macintosh,* 283 U.S. 605 (1931).

Chapter XVIII

1. Grover Dunn to Arthur Gamble, Aug. 9, 1942.

2. NSB Form 101—Corbett Bishop—Order No. 1026.

3. *Patapsco Peacemaker,* Aug. 13, 1942.

4. Letter of Feb. 11, 1943, copies of which Bishop also sent to American pacifist groups and individuals.

5. *We Protest the Loss of Liberty* (mimeographed), June 19, 1943.

6. *Ibid.*

7. Kenneth Morgan, Director, West Campton C.P.S. camp, to Dr. Simon Stone, Dec. 21, 1942.

8. Arthur Gamble in his letter to Kenneth Morgan, Sept. 14, 1942, tends to agree with this position.

9. *Conscientious Objector*, Aug. 1943.

10. Paul Furnas to Corbett Bishop, June 28, 1943.

11. *C.P.S. G.I.*, Dec., 1943, p. 6.

12. *The Reporter*, Nov. 15, 1944.

13 *The Reporter*, Dec. 15, 1944.

14. See *Philadelphia Evening Bulletin*, March 16, 1945; see also undated letter on the Bishop case addressed to the Philadelphia papers by Roy McCorkel, James Bristol, and J. Passmore Elkinton.

15. See the *Philadelphia Record*, Feb. 21, 1945. The account given here is inaccurate to the extent that it states the F.B.I. had been searching for Bishop for six months. Actually, his whereabouts were known and he had been a "fugitive" for only a month. He did refuse to co-operate, but in this he was consistent throughout.

16. See *Philadelphia Evening Bulletin*, March 16, 1945.

17. *Information*, March 2, 1945, p. 2.

18. See Chapter XVII.

19. See *The Reporter*, Aug. 1, 1945, and the *Conscientious Objector*, Aug., 1945.

20. *Conscientious Objector*, Sept. 1945; *The Reporter*, Sept. 15, 1945.

21. *The Reporter*, March 29, 1946; *Conscientious Objector*, April, 1946.

22. James P. Mullin to Jack Petherbridge, May 28, 1945.

23. This account is based on a memorandum of Purnell Benson. Benson was a C.S.P. assignee in Mancos and Germfask, and observed the activities of Dr. DeVault at first hand.

24. Winslow H. Osborne to James Townsend, Jr., April 15, 1943.

25. Howard Gill, Assistant to the Director, to Evan Thomas, June 14, 1943.

26. James V. Bennett to Evan Thomas, June 26, 1943.

27. Howard Gill to Evan Thomas, July 30, 1943.

28. Mrs. Elizabeth Murphy to Evan Thomas, July 26, 1943.

29. Mrs. Elizabeth Murphy to Julius Eichel, July 31, 1943.

30. James V. Bennett to Evan Thomas, August 3, 1943.

31. *Ibid.*

32. R. B. Brooks to Evan Thomas, August 11, 1943.

33. Dr. M. R. King, *Comments on the Attitude and Conduct of Extreme Conscientious Objectors* . . . (mimeographed), August 9, 1943.

34. See Charles W. Palmer, *Report on Visit to Springfield* (mimeographed), August 13, 1943.

35. Austin MacCormick, *Memorandum for Mr. Bennett* (mimeographed), August 21, 1943. On October 11, 1943, in a letter to Clarence Pickett, Executive Secretary of the American Friends Service Committee, MacCormick was even more emphatic in his criticisms.

36. Louis Taylor to Evan Thomas, January 28, 1944, notes some of the allegations.

37. Norman Thomas to Francis Biddle, February 8, 1944.

38. About one-half of all the inmates at Springfield, according to the testimony, were psychotic (insane) or psychopathic (mentally unstable or borderline).

39. Bennett's *Report*. Moore's report is February 29, 1944; Bell's, February 22; and Kolb's, March 4.

40. Julius M. Klein, *Investigation of Brutality Charges at U.S. Medical Center for Federal Prisoners*, February 22, 1944.

41. Circular Letter of Evan Thomas, March 24, 1944.

Chapter XIX

1. *U.S.* v. *Rappeport*, 36 F. Supp. 915 (1941), sustained in *U.S.* v. *Herling*, 120 F. 2d 236 (1941). On the general power of Congress to compel persons to furnish information, see *Electric Bond and Share Co.* v. *Securities and Exchange Commission*, 303 U.S. 419 (1938).

2. *Arver* v. *U.S.* (Selective Draft Law cases), 245 U.S. 366 (1918); also *Jones* v. *Perkins*, 245 U.S. 390 (1918) and *Angelus* v. *Sullivan*, a circuit court opinion, 246 Fed. Rep. 54 (1917).

3. *U.S.* v. *Schwimmer*, 279 U.S. 644 (1929); *U.S.* v. *Macintosh*, 283 U.S. 605 (1931),

4. *U.S.* v. *Herling* and four other cases, 120 F 2d 236 (1941).

5. For an able argument against the constitutionality of peacetime conscription by a constitutional lawyer and conscientious objector, see Harrop Freeman, "The Constitutionality of Peacetime Conscription," *Virginia Law Review*, 40 (Dec., 1944).

6. No. 10(a) (2).

7. *Edwards* v. *U.S.*, Appellant's Opening Brief (1943), on appeal in 145 F. 2d 678 (1944).

8. *Baxley* v. *U.S.*, 134 F. 2d 998 (1943), at 999. See also *Goff* v. *U.S.*, 135 F. 2d 610 (1943).

9. *U.S. ex rel. Trainin* v. *Cain*, 144 F. 2d 944 (1944).

10. *Rase* v. *U.S.*, 129 F. 2d 204 (1942); *Graf* v. *Mallon*, 138 F. 2d 230 (1943); *Seele* v. *U.S.*, 133 F. 2d 1015 (1943); *U.S.* v. *Messersmith*, 138 F 2d 599 (1943).

11. *Checinski* v. *U.S.*, 129 F. 2d 461 (1942); *U.S.* v. *Buttecali*, 46 F. Supp. 39 (1942), affirmed in *Buttecali* v. *U.S.*, 130 F. 2d 172 (1942); and *U.S.* v. *Pace*, 46 F. Supp. 316 (1942).

12. *Ex parte Stansiale*, 138 F. 2d 312 (1943), certiorari denied, *Stansiale* v. *Paullin*, 320 U.S. 797 (1943); and *Crutchfield* v. *U.S.*, 142 F. 2d 170 (1943).

13. *Estep* v. *U.S.* and *Smith* v. *U.S.*, 327 U.S. 114 (1946).

14. But see *Goff* v. *U.S.*, 135 F. 2d 610 (1943), for a minority view. Here the Circuit Court of Appeals maintained that the "total invalidity" of an order could be used as a defense in a criminal action based on the disobedience of the order.

15. *U.S.* v. *Grieme*, 128 F. 2d 811 (1942); *U.S.* v. *Mroz*, 136 F. 2d 211 (1943); *Harper* v. *U.S.*, 138 F. 2d 536 (1943); *Bronemann* v. *U.S.*, 138 F. 2d 333 (1943); *U.S.* v. *Daily*, 139 F. 2d (1943); *U.S.* v. *Sauler*, 139 F. 2d 173 (1943); and *U.S.* v. *Van Den Berg*, 139 F. 2d 654 (1944).

16. *Bowles* v. *U.S.*, 319 U.S. 33 (1943).

17. *Falbo* v. *U.S.*, 320 U.S. 549 (1943).

18. *Billings* v. *Truesdell*, 321 U.S. 542 (1944).

19. *Estep* v. *U.S.* and *Smith* v. *U.S.*, 327 U.S. 114 (1946).

20. *Gibson* v. *U.S.* and *Dodez* v. *U.S.*, 329 U.S. 338 (1946).

21. Certiorari is an extraordinary writ whose function is "to bring the true

record of an inferior judicial or quasi judicial tribunal, properly extended so as to show the principles of its decision, before a superior court for examination as to material mistakes of law apparent on the face of such record." *Bradley* v. *Board of Zoning Adjustment,* 255 Mass. 160 (1926). Refusal to grant certiorari means that the lower-court interpretation stands but does not necessarily show that the higher tribunal approves the ruling.

22. *U.S.* v. *Kauten,* 133 F. 2d 703 (1943).

23. *U.S. ex rel. Phillips* v. *Downer,* 135 F. 2d 521 (1943).

24. *U.S. ex rel. Brandon* v. *Downer,* 139 F. 2d 761 (1944).

25. *U.S. ex rel. Reel* v. *Badt,* 141 F. 2d 845 (1944).

26. *Berman* v. *U.S.,* 156 F. 2d 377 (1946).

27. For a discussion of the Berman case, see *The Reporter,* Jan., 1947.

28. For a favorable view by a conscientious objector who was also a lawyer, see Julien Cornell, *The Conscientious Objector and the Law* (New York, 1943), and *Conscience and the State* (New York, 1944).

29. "Section 5(g) of the Selective Service Act, as amended by the Court," 29 *Minnesota Law Review* 22, Dec., 1944.

30. Cf. Henry C. Black, *Handbook on the Construction and Interpretation of the Laws* (2d ed., St. Paul, Minn., 1911), p. 141.

31. Cf. "The term 'religion' has reference to one's views of his relations to his Creator, and to the obligations they impose of reverence for his being and character, and of obedience to his will. . . ." *Davis* v. *Beason,* 133 U.S. 333 (1890), at 342. It is interesting to note that Congress, in making provision for conscientious objectors under the Selective Training and Service Act of 1948, extended exemption to "religious" conscientious objectors only and defined "religion" along lines accepted by the majority in the Berman case. The statute reads: "Religious training and belief in this connection means an individual's belief in a relation to a Supreme Being involving duties superior to those arising from any human relation, but does not include essentially political, sociological, or philosophical views or a merely personal moral code." 62 U.S.C.A. 604. There would seem to be a strong case for the argument that Congress thereby repudiated the series of decisions beginning with the Kauten opinion.

32. *West Virginia State Board of Education* v. *Barnette,* 319 U.S. 624 (1943).

33. *Thornhill* v. *Alabama,* 310 U.S. 88 (1940).

34. *Murdock* v. *Pennsylvania,* 319 U.S. 105 (1940); see also *Lovell* v. *Griffin,* 303 U.S. 444 (1938).

35. *Arver* v. *U.S.* (Selective Draft Law cases), 245 U.S. 366 (1918).

36. *U.S.* v. *Macintosh,* 283 U.S. 605 (1931), at 622.

37. *Roodenko et al.* v. *U.S.,* 147 F. 2d 752 (1944).

38. *Kramer et al.* v. *U.S.,* 147 F. 2d 756 (1945). See also *Brooks* v. *U.S.,* 147 F. 2d 134 (1945). Various other cases also raised the issue.

39. *Jacobsen* v. *Massachusetts,* 197 U.S. 11 (1905), at 29.

40. See the Roodenko and Kramer cases cited above.

41. Cf. *Korematsu* v. *U.S.,* 323 U.S. 214 (1944).

42. *Roodenko et al.* v. *U.S., supra.*

43 Cf. Ruth MacAdam, *Civilian Public Service: A System of Slave Labor,* unpublished Master's thesis, New School for Social Research, New York City.

44. *Bailey* v. *Alabama,* 219 U.S. 219 (1911), at 240.

45. *Butler* v. *Perry,* 240 U.S. 328 (1916), at 333.

46. *Robertson* v. *Baldwin,* 165 U.S. 275 (1897), at 282.

47. *Butler* v. *Perry, supra.*

48. Cf. *Adair* v. *U.S.,* 208 U.S. 161 (1908).

49. *Roodenko* v. *U.S., supra.*

50. Roodenko and Kramer cases, *supra.* In the Kramer opinion, the delegation of power was justified on the authority of *Currin* v. *Wallace,* 306 U.S. 1 (1939); *Panama Refining Co.* v. *Ryan,* 293 U.S. 388 (1935); and *McKinley* v. *U.S.,* 249 U.S. 397 (1919).

51. 285 U.S. 240 (1932).

52. *Roodenko, Rockwell, Hutchinson,* and *White* v. *U.S., supra.* The Kramer decision of the 6th Circuit, *supra,* was the second case referred to in the text.

53. *Gibson* v. *U.S.* and *Dodez* v. *U.S.,* 329 U.S. 338 (1946), at 357.

54. For a critical discussion see Harrop Freeman, "Genesis, Exodus, and Leviticus: Genealogy, Evacuation, and Law," 28 *Cornell Law Quarterly* 414.

55. *Brief of Defendants in Support of their Application for Rehearing of Motion for a New Trial,* Cr. No. 18027, Northern District of Ohio, Feb. 25, 1944.

56. *Brooks* v. *U.S.,* 147 F. 2d 134 (1945); *Kramer et al.* v. *U.S.,* 147 F. 2d 756 (1945); *Roodenko* v. *U.S.,* 147 F. 2d 134 (1945). In all three cases, certiorari was denied by the Supreme Court.

57. Constitution of Illinois, Article XII, Sec. 1.

58. Summers' views on the use of force are discussed in Zechariah Chafee, Jr., and Harold Evans, *Brief in Behalf of The American Friends Service Committee as Friends of the Court,* submitted to the Supreme Court of the United States, October Term, 1944, pp. 40–43.

59. Chaffee and Evans, *Brief,* pp. i, ii.

60. *Ibid.,* p. 40.

61. *Ibid.,* p. 64.

62. *Ibid.,* pp. 72 ff.

63. *In re Summers,* 325 U.S. 561 (1945).

64. *American Civil Liberties Union News,* Nov., 1946.

65. *Ibid.,* Jan., 1947.

66. As quoted in *The Reporter,* July, 1945.

67. See the story on Tulane in the *Conscientious Objector,* July, 1943.

68. According to Mulford Sibley, who was on the staff of the University of Illinois.

69. *The Reporter,* Jan. 15, 1946, p. 4.

70. *Chicago Daily News,* April 17, 1945. The incident created a stir throughout the Chicago area.

71. See one account of the affair in the *Conscientious Objector,* July, 1942.

72. Personal knowledge of the writer.

73. *The Reporter,* March 15, 1944.

74. *Sacramento* (Calif.) *Bee,* as cited by *The Reporter,* Feb. 15, 1946.

75. See *The Reporter,* Nov. 1, 1943.

76. For an account, see the *Conscientious Objector,* Feb., 1944.

77. *State of Florida ex rel. Edward O. Schweitzer* v. *Charles G. Turner et al.* 155 Fla. 270 (1944).

78. *The Reporter,* July 1, 1945.

79. Louisiana Rev. Stat., 1950, v. 4, Title 42, Sec. 32, p. 938. See *The Reporter,* May 15, 1945.

80. *The Reporter,* March 15, 1945.

81. *The Reporter,* May 15, 1945; also *American Civil Liberties Union News,* June, 1945.

82. The full text of the Governor's veto message is printed in *American Civil Liberties Union News,* June, 1945.

83. *The Reporter,* Aug. 1, 1945, and Sept. 1, 1945; also *Conscientious Objector,* Sept., 1945.

84. See the *Conscientious Objector,* April, 1945.

85. See *Boston Herald,* June 25, 1942.

86. *Memorandum* of Robert A. Fangmeir, N.S.B.R.O. to Gordon Foster, A.F.S.C. (1945?) summarizes Commission rulings and interpretations.

87. *The Reporter,* Aug. 1, 1945.

88. Minutes of Legal Committee of NCCO, Aug. 4, 1943, NSB files.

89. *U.S. ex rel. Reel* v. *Badt,* 152 F. 2d 627 (1945). In support of its position, the Court quoted Judge Schwellenbach in *In re Losey,* D.C.E.D. Wash. 39 F. Supp. 37 (1944) at 38: "I have taken the oath to perform the duties of two very important offices in this country and nobody asked me whether I would bear arms."

90. Civil Service Commissioner Arthur S. Flemming to Paul C. French, June 14, 1946.

91. *U.S.* v. *Schwimmer,* 279 U.S. 644 (1929).

92. *U.S.* v. *Macintosh,* 283 U.S. 605 (1931).

93. *The Reporter,* May 15, 1945. Nielsen had served in the Army as a I-A-O.

94. Western District of Washington, 1944. Paul French to Earl G. Harrison, July 24, 1944, discusses the case.

95. *Girouard* v. *U.S.,* 328 U.S. 61 (1946).

96. The resolution is reprinted in *The Reporter,* May 1, 1945.

97. The ruling is noticed in *The Reporter,* Sept. 15, 1945.

98. *American Civil Liberties Union News,* Sept., 1945; *The Reporter,* Oct. 1, 1945; *Conscientious Objector,* Sept., 1945.

99. Personal knowledge of the writer, who knows the professor. See also the *Conscientious Objector,* March, 1943.

100. *The Reporter,* Nov. 1, 1944.

101. Correspondence with Hennacy. See also the *Conscientious Objector,* Feb., 1945.

102. The *Conscientious Objector,* Feb., 1944, comments on the *Herald* case.

Selected and Annotated
Bibliography

THIS bibliography does not purport to include everything published on pacifism and conscientious objection. It does hope, however, to provide a substantial introduction to the literature of the subject, particularly with reference to modern theory and to the experience of the United States during World War II.

Historical and Comparative
BOOKS AND PAMPHLETS

Beaton, Grace M. *Four Years of War*. Enfield: War Resisters' International, 1943.

A 32-page survey of conscientious objectors throughout the world during the Second World War down to 1943.

——. *Twenty Years' Work in the War Resisters' International*. London: War Resisters' International, 1945.

Bedford, Duke of. *The Conscientious Objector*. Glasgow: Strickland Press, 1943.

——. *Conscientious Objectors*. Glasgow: Strickland Press, 1944.

Speeches delivered in the House of Lords in defense of the rights of objectors.

Brooks, Arle, and Leach, Robert J. *Help Wanted: The Experiences of Some Quaker Conscientious Objectors*. Philadelphia: American *Friends Service Committee*, 1940.

Deals with the World War I period in the United States.

Central Board for Conscientious Objectors. *Troublesome People*. London, 1940.

A 63-page reprint of the No-Conscription Fellowship Souvenir describing work and experiences of members of the No-Conscription Fellowship in Great Britain during World War I.

——. *Cat and Mouse*. London, 1942.

Repeated prosecutions of conscientious objectors in Great Britain during World War II.

——. *The Case for Stanley Hilton*. London, 1943.

An account of a famous court-martial "cat-and-mouse" case in Great Britain during World War II.

——. *The C.O. and the National Service Acts*. London, periodically throughout the war.

A rather complete "guide for men and women conscientious objectors and their advisers" in Great Britain.

——. *The C.O.'s Hansard*. London, periodically throughout the war.

Valuable because here were brought together all the references made to c.o.'s in Parliament, with citations to *Hansard* itself.

Efford, Lincoln. *Penalties on Conscience*. Christchurch: Author, 1945.

An account of New Zealand conscientious objection and the relation of objectors to the government, with particular reference to the Second World War.

Freeman, Ruth (aided by Robert and Etta Vogle). *Quakers and Peace*. Ithaca, N.Y.: Pacifist Research Bureau, 1947.

The discussion of Quakers in Great Britain and the United States since World War I is particularly helpful, although the pamphlet deals also with earlier history.

French, Paul C. *We Won't Murder: Being the Story of Men Who Followed Their Conscientious Scruples and Helped Give Life to Democracy*. New York: Hastings House, 1940.

A popular account of conscientious objection and pacifism concentrating on World War I and the subsequent years.

Graham, John W. *Conscription and Conscience: A History, 1916–1919*. London: Allen and Unwin, 1922.

The story of British conscientious objection during the First World War.

Gray, Harold S. *Character "Bad": The Story of a Conscientious Objector*. New York: Harpers, 1934.

Experiences of an American conscientious objector during the First World War.

Hartzler, J. S. *Mennonites in the World War*. Scottsdale, Pa.: Mennonite Publishing House, 1922.

Story of the Mennonites during World War I.

Hayes, Denis. *Challenge of Conscience: The Story of the Conscientious Objectors of 1939–1949.* London: George Allen and Unwin, 1949.

A detailed and interesting account of British conscientious objection during World War II written by a lawyer active in the defense of objectors.

Hirst, Margaret. *The Quakers in Peace and War.* New York: Doubleday, Doran, 1923.

A 525-page volume which gives an excellent account of the subject to World War I.

Jonassen, Hagbard. *Resistance in Denmark.* London: War Resisters' International, 1945.

A sketchy statement on the activities of Danish conscientious objectors under the German occupation.

Kellogg, Walter Guest. *The Conscientious Objector.* New York: Boni and Liveright, 1919.

An analysis of American conscientious objection during World War I as viewed by a member of the Board of Inquiry appointed to investigate conditions.

Lund, Diderich. *Resistance in Norway.* New York: War Resisters League, 1945.

A sketchy and incomplete account of experiences and attitudes of Norwegian conscientious objectors under the German occupation in World War II.

Smith, C. Henry. *The Story of the Mennonites.* Berne, Ind.: Mennonite Book Concern, 1941.

A general history, which is particularly valuable for its account of Mennonites in Czarist Russia.

Snyder, William T. *Mennonite Refugees—1947.* Akron, Pa.: Mennonite Central Committee, 1947.

Stevenson, Lillian. *Towards a Christian International.* London: International Fellowship of Reconciliation, 1941.

An account of the development of the Fellowship of Reconciliation from its foundation in 1919 to the opening years of the Second World War. Some discussion of legal rights of objectors in various countries.

Thomas, Norman. *Is Conscience a Crime?* New York: Vanguard Press, 1927.

The best account of American conscientious objection during World War I. By an able writer and sympathetic observer.

Wright, Edward Needles. *Conscientious Objectors in the Civil War.* Philadelphia: University of Pennsylvania Press, 1931.

ARTICLES AND PERIODICALS

Attwater, D. "War, Law and Conscience in England," *Catholic World,* 152 (Oct., 1940), 53–57.

"British Democracy Respects Anti-War Scruples," *Life,* 8 (March 11, 1940), 34–36.

Brockway, Fenner. "Cat and Mouse," *New Statesman and Nation,* 24 (Oct. 3, 1942), 221.

Central Board for Conscientious Objectors. *Bulletin,* published monthly during World War II and one of the best sources for information concerning British conscientious objectors.

Fowke, Edith F. "Canadian C.O.s," *The Reporter,* Sept. 1, 1945.

Krahn, Cornelius. "Public Service in Russia," *The Mennonite,* June 8, June 22, Aug. 31, and Sept. 21, 1943.

> Valuable discussion of alternative service in Czarist Russia—a service which offered such a striking parallel to the Civilian Public Service established in the United States during World War II.

——. "Historiography of the Mennonites in the Netherlands and Parts of Germany: A Guide to Sources," *Church History,* 13 (Sept., 1944), 182–209.

Milner, L. G., and Conklin, G. "Conscience in Wartime: American Treatment of Conscientious Objectors in 1917–1918," *Harpers,* 179 (Oct., 1939), 503–509.

Pickard, Bertram. "English Friends and Civilian Defense," *The Friend,* Jan. 8, 1942, and other numbers of *The Friend.*

Sudermann, Jacob. "The Origin of Mennonite State Service in Russia," *Mennonite Quarterly Review,* Jan., 1943.

The War Resister, quarterly periodical of the War Resisters' International, often having valuable information about relationships of objectors to the state throughout the world.

Theory, Mainly Modern

BOOKS AND PAMPHLETS

Bowman, Rufus D. *The Church of the Brethren and War.* Elgin, Ill.: Brethren Publishing House, 1944.

> A prominent leader of the church discusses historical and World War II attitude of the Church of the Brethren to war. There is also some discussion of Brethren Civilian Public Service experience during World War II.

Brinton, Howard H. *Sources of the Quaker Peace Testimony.* Wallingford, Pa.: Pendle Hill Historical Studies, 1942.

A useful discussion of the historical and ideological background of the Quaker attitude toward war.

Cadoux, C. J. *The Early Christian Attitude to War.* London: George Allen and Unwin, 1940.

——. *Christian Pacifism Re-examined.* London: George Allen and Unwin, 1940.

Case, Clarence Marsh. *Non-Violent Coercion: A Study in Methods of Social Pressure.* New York: The Century Co., 1923.

This is one of the best studies available on the theory and practice of nonviolent coercion. Case studies the problem from the viewpoint of doctrine and examines the historical forms through which the doctrine has been implemented.

Catholic Pacifists' Association. *Blessed Are the Peacemakers.* Catholic Pacifists Association of Canada [n.d., but c. 1941].

Cronbach, Abraham. *The Quest for Peace.* Cincinnati, Ohio: Sinai Press, 1937.

An excellent statement of a Jewish pacifist point of view.

Field, G. C. *Pacifism and Conscientious Objection.* Cambridge, Eng.: University Press, 1945.

An English philosopher who served on a conscientious objectors' tribunal during World War II comments unfavorably on the arguments advanced by objectors.

Gregg, Richard. *The Power of Non-Violence.* Philadelphia: J. B. Lippincott, 1934.

One of the "classics" of the pacifist movement in the United States. By a Quaker lawyer who had studied nonviolent resistance in India.

Hershberger, Guy F. *War, Peace, and Nonresistance.* Scottdale, Pa.: Herald Press, 1944.

The most complete treatment of Mennonite theory.

Holmes, John Haynes, Niebuhr, Reinhold, and others. *If America Enters the War What Shall I Do?* Chicago: Christian Century, 1941.

Articles which originally appeared in the *Christian Century,* leading nondenominational Protestant weekly, from December 4, 1940, to February 5, 1941. Other contributors: John C. Bennett, Albert E. Day, Charles P. Taft, Albert W. Palmer, Francis J. McConnell, Harry Emerson Fosdick, Henry P. Van Dusen, and Ernest Fremont Tittle. A sampling of Protestant, largely clerical, opinion a year before the United States formally entered the war.

Horsch, John. *The Principle of Nonresistance as Held by the Mennonite Church.* Scottdale, Pa.: Mennonite Publishing House, 1940.

A statement of the Mennonite principle of "nonresistance" as contrasted with other pacifist principles of "nonviolent resistance."

Hugo, John J. *Weapons of the Spirit.* New York: Catholic Worker Press, 1943.

Catholic principles of conscientious objection.

Hunter, Allan A. *White Corpuscles in Europe.* Chicago: Willett, Clark and Company, 1939.

Biographical sketches of leading prewar European pacifists, including the British Labor leader George Lansbury.

Huxley, Aldous. *Ends and Means.* New York: Harpers, 1937.

An influential book among pacifists and conscientious objectors, written by the eminent British novelist.

——. *An Encyclopaedia of Pacifism.* New York: Harpers, 1937.

Definitions of terms and answers to the arguments of nonpacifists.

Lewis, John. *The Case against Pacifism.* London: George Allen and Unwin, 1940.

A closely reasoned argument against pacifism and conscientious objection, by one having a Marxist outlook.

Ligt, Barthelemy de. *The Conquest of Violence.* New York: Dutton, 1938.

A careful statement by a Dutch anarchist of the possibility and efficacy of a "strike against war."

MacGregor, G. H. C. *The New Testament Basis of Pacifism.* New York: Fellowship of Reconciliation, 1941.

——. *The Relevance of an Impossible Ideal.* New York: Fellowship of Reconciliation, 1941.

A well-reasoned answer to the views of Reinhold Niebuhr, one of the sharpest critics of pacifism and conscientious objection.

Muste, A. J. *Non-Violence in an Aggressive World.* New York: Harpers, 1940.

O'Toole, George Barry. *War and Conscription at the Bar of Christian Morals.* New York: Catholic Worker Press, 1941.

An excellent presentation of Catholic arguments in favor of conscientious objection.

Paullin, Theodore. *Introduction to Non-Violence.* Philadelphia: Pacifist Research Bureau, 1944.

An analysis of types of "nonviolent" action by the Assistant Director of the Pacifist Research Bureau. Well organized.

Richards, Leyton. *Realistic Pacifism: The Ethics of War and the Politics of Peace.* Chicago: Willett, Clark and Co., 1935.

A careful and critical analysis by a pacifist.

Shridharani, Krishnalal. *War without Violence*. New York: Harcourt, Brace and Co., 1939.

An analysis of the late M. K. Gandhi's techniques by one who participated in the Indian nonviolent resistance of the thirties.

Sibley, Mulford. *The Political Theories of Modern Pacifism*. Philadelphia: Pacifist Research Bureau, 1944.

An analysis and criticism of the major propositions of modern pacifism. Generally favorable to the pacifist case, but highly critical of its ambiguities and evasions.

Thomas, Evan. *The Positive Faith of Pacifism*. New York: War Resisters League, 1942.

By a leader of those conscientious objectors taking a "radical" or "absolutist" stand during World War II. Thomas himself had engaged in hunger strikes during World War I and refused to register in World War II. He was a well-known physician and teacher of medicine and brother of Norman Thomas, the Socialist leader.

Van Kirk, Walter. *Religion Renounces War*. Chicago: Willett, Clark and Co., 1934.

A compilation of statements issued by church bodies. A remarkable testimony to the shift of church opinion on war and conscientious objection between the two world wars.

Watchtower Bible and Tract Society. *Fighting for Liberty on the Home Front*. New York, 1943.

——. *The New World*. New York, 1942.

——. *The Truth Shall Make You Free*. New York, 1943.

The Watchtower Bible and Tract Society—the corporate representative of Jehovah's Witnesses—was a prolific publisher. The three items listed above can give but a faint impression of the literature issued under its imprint, but they will exhibit in sufficient detail the social and political outlook of Jehovah's Witnesses.

Yoder, Edward. *Compromise with War*. Akron, Pa.: Mennonite Central Committee, 1944.

An answer to the views of Charles Clayton Morrison, editor of the *Christian Century*, who had argued in a series of editorials that support of World War II was an "unnecessary necessity."

ARTICLES

Benda, Julien. "Pacifism and Democracy," *Foreign Affairs*, 19 (July, 1941), 693–701.

Bentley, E. R. "Pacifist Defense; Reply to Reinhold Niebuhr," *Nation*, 150 (Feb. 17, 1940), 263.

"Christian and the War, The," editorial, *Christian Century,* 69 (Jan. 28, 1942), 102–104.

An important editorial, written from the viewpoint of the nonpacifist Protestant Christian.

Flournay, F. R. "The Protestant Churches and the War," *South Atlantic Quarterly,* 42 (April, 1943), 113–125.

Furgeson, E. A. "Conscience and the State," *Christian Century,* 59 (July 15, 1942), 881–882.

Hugo, John J. "The Immorality of Conscription," supplement to the *Catholic Worker,* March, 1945.

Joad, C. E. M. "Duty of a Pacifist," *Atlantic,* 164 (Nov., 1939), 689–694.

McCowley, J. "War Versus Conscience," *Catholic World,* 150 (Jan., 1940), 396–401.

Mayer, Milton. "I Think I'll Sit This One Out," *Saturday Evening Post,* 212 (Oct. 7, 1939), 23.

An article that had considerable influence on objectors in the United States, particularly on those of the less traditional type. Mayer did not profess to be a "pacifist" in what he considered to be the ordinary meaning of the term.

Newton, J. T. "The State and the Individual Conscience," *London Quarterly Review,* 166 (April, 1941), 204–208.

Niebuhr, Reinhold. "Idealists as Cynics: Pacifists and Socialists Believe Nothing Is at Stake in the European Struggle," *Nation,* 150 (Jan. 29, 1940), 72–74.

A critique of conscientious objectors and of the groups trying in 1940 to keep the United States entirely clear of the European War.

Oldham, G. A. "Is Pacifism Enough?" *Atlantic,* 165 (June, 1940), 780–785.

By the very highly respected British Protestant leader and critic of pacifism.

Parsons, Wilfrid. "Conscientious Objector: Can a Catholic Find Doctrinal Justification for Conscientious Objection?" *Commonweal,* 34 (June 27, 1941), 224–226.

By the American Jesuit moral philosopher.

Russell, Bertrand. "The Future of Pacifism," *American Scholar,* 13 (Jan., 1944, 7–13.

Smith, B. E. "A Pacifist Student Soldier Looks at the War," *Personalist,* 24 (Jan., 1943), 32–39.

Trueblood, D. E. "The Quaker Way," *Atlantic,* 166 (Dec., 1940), 740–746.

An important statement of "conservative" Quaker pacifism by an influential member of the Society of Friends.

Whitridge, A. "Where Do You Stand? Open Letter to American Under-graduates," *Atlantic*, 166 (Aug., 1940), 133–137.

A critique of American college students' antiwar views.

Wright, C. J. "War and Human History; or, Scepticism and Pacifism," *London Quarterly Review*, 168 (April, 1943), 97–103.

In addition, the periodicals listed in the following section are indispensable for an understanding of theories of pacifism and conscientious objection developed during World War II.

American Conscientious Objection in World War II

OFFICIAL PUBLICATIONS

Annual Reports of the Attorney General of the United States.

Collins, Linton. *Report to the Attorney General on Conscientious Objectors.* July, 1944. (Mimeographed.)

Congressional Record.

Department of Justice. *Memorandum to all United States Attorneys and All Special Assistants to the Attorney General Designated as Hearing Officers under the Selective Training and Service Act of 1940.* February 27, 1942. (Mimeographed.)

Federal Prisons, reports of the Bureau of Prisons for 1941, 1943, 1944, 1945, and 1947.

Federal Register.

House of Representatives, Committee on Military Affairs. *Hearings on the Selective Training and Service Bill.* Washington: Government Printing Office, 1940.

President's Advisory Commission on Universal Training. *A Program for National Security.* Washington: Government Printing Office, 1947.

Selective Service as the Tide of War Turns. Washington: Government Printing Office, 1945.

Third official report of the Selective Service System.

Selective Service in Peacetime. Washington: Government Printing Office, 1942.

Official report of the Selective Service System, covering the period from the establishment of the System to December 7, 1941.

Selective Service in Wartime. Washington: Government Printing Office, 1943.

Second official report of the Selective Service System.

Selective Service Opinions.

Selective Service Regulations.

Selective Service System. *Conscientious Objection.* Special Monograph No. 11. 2 vols. Washington: Government Printing Office, 1950.

> The official report of Selective Service on conscientious objectors, written largely by Col. Neal Wherry. Good historical account of the problem and valuable statistics.

Special Committee Appointed to Study Letter to the President from the National Committee on Conscientious Objectors of the American Civil Liberties Union. *Memorandum to the Director of Selective Service,* May 5, 1944. (Mimeographed.)

> This document represented Selective Service's reply to its critics in civil liberties and church organizations.

United States Senate, Committee on Military Affairs. *Hearings on the Selective Training and Service Bill.* Washington: Government Printing Office, 1940.

PUBLICATIONS OF THE NATIONAL SERVICE BOARD FOR RELIGIOUS OBJECTORS
AND THE SERVICE COMMITTEES

(AMERICAN FRIENDS SERVICE COMMITTEE)

Friends' Experience with Civilian Public Service. 1944.

> A carefully prepared statement evaluating Friends C.P.S. and analyzing criticisms.

Information.

> A newssheet published (in mimeographed form) every two weeks. It attempted to keep assignees and outsiders informed of developments in Friends Civilian Public Service. It also contained general items of interest to objectors and their friends.

Introduction to Friends Civilian Public Service. 1943.

Memoranda of Executive Camp Director.

> Numbered serially and usually sent to Camp Directors and to Assistant Directors of special service units. The *Memoranda* contained information, instructions, statements of policy as adopted by the Service Committee, and general advice.

Projects and Incentives in Civilian Public Service. 1945.

> An examination of the problem of service opportunities in Civilian Public Service.

Testimony by Work. 1941.

> The first report of the Executive Camp Director, then Thomas E. Jones.

(BRETHREN SERVICE COMMITTEE)

BCPS Bulletin.

The official newssheet (mimeographed) of the Brethren Service Committee for Civilian Public Service. Assignees in camp were kept informed of C.P.S. developments. When demobilization set in, the *Bulletin* provided information about job and educational opportunities.

Memoranda of Executive Camp Director.

These were similar in form and purpose to the *Memoranda* of the Friends Service Committee.

(MENNONITE CENTRAL COMMITTEE)

Memoranda of Executive Camp Director.

Similar in form and purpose to the *Memoranda* of the Friends and Brethren.

MCPS Bulletin.

The official C.P.S. news bulletin of the Mennonite Central Committee.

(NATIONAL SERVICE BOARD FOR RELIGIOUS OBJECTORS)

C.P.S. Directory. 1947.

A classified list of all men who served in C.P.S., together with their camps or units.

Congress Looks at the Conscientious Objector. 1943.

A well-edited compilation of debates in Congress and hearings before congressional committees on the problems of conscientious objection in World War II.

The Conscientious Objector under the Selective Training and Service Act of 1940.

This introduction to administrative and judicial procedures under the act of 1940 was designed to help the conscientious objector understand his rights and obligations. It was revised and reprinted several times during the course of the war.

Memoranda of the Executive Secretary to the Board of Directors.

In the *Memoranda,* Paul Comly French, Executive Secretary of the National Service Board, kept the Board of Directors of the National Service Board informed regarding the whole scope of Service Board activities. Dealt with were not only the administrative problems of C.P.S. but also the advisory services which the Board provided. A perusal of the *Memoranda* gives one a good running account of the almost unbelievable complexities arising out of the experiences of objectors.

The Reporter.

The well-edited and informative semimonthly periodical of the National Service Board. One of the most important contributions of the Service Board, the *Reporter* is indispensable for any study of American conscientious objection during World War II. It was managed and edited largely by conscripted conscientious objectors assigned to the National Service Board, and it provided information not only about American conscientious objectors but also on European and Asiatic pacifist movements.

BOOKS AND PAMPHLETS

Alexian Brothers Unit. *Of Human Importance.* Elgin, Ill.: Brethren Publishing House, 1946.
Story of the Alexian Brothers Hospital unit. Large photoengravings of assignees in action, with descriptions.
American Civil Liberties Union. *Conscience and the War.* New York, 1943.
Boisen, Anton T. *The Morale of the Conscientious Objectors in Church-Operated Service Units.* Elgin, Ill.: Brethren Publishing House, 1946.
Bowman, Rufus D. *Seventy Times Seven.* Elgin, Ill.: Brethren Publishing House, 1944.
Cantine, Holley, and Rainer, Dachine (eds.). *Prison Etiquette.* Bearsville, N.Y.: Retort Press, 1949.
A useful collection of the wartime writings of imprisoned conscientious objectors.
C.P.S. Unit 93 (Harrisburg). *Anniversary Review.* Harrisburg, Pa.: 1945.
An account of the mental hospital unit in Harrisburg, Pennsylvania, by the men themselves. Discussions of psychiatric care.
Cornell, Julien. *The Conscientious Objector and the Law.* New York: John Day, 1943.
——. *Conscience and the State.* New York: John Day, 1943.
These two short books by Cornell, a New York attorney active in the American Civil Liberties Union, are helpful in any study of legal relations.
Eisan, Leslie. *Pathways of Peace.* Elgin, Ill.: Brethren Pub. House, 1948.
The official account of Brethren C.P.S.
French, Paul C. *Civilian Public Service.* Washington: National Service Board for Religious Objectors, 1943.
Written from the perspective of the National Service Board's Executive Secretary.
Garver, Earl S., and Fincher, Ernest B. *Puerto Rico: Unsolved Problem.* Elgin, Ill.: Brethren Publishing House, 1945.

The Puerto Rican C.P.S. experiment and a discussion of Puerto Rican poverty and disease.

Gingerich, Melvin. *Service for Peace.* Akron, Pa.: Mennonite Central Committee, 1949.

An elaborate and detailed study of Mennonite C.P.S. which may be taken to represent, in general, the view of the Mennonite Central Committee.

Guetzkow, Harold S., and Bowman, Paul H. *Men and Hunger.* Elgin, Ill.: Brethren Publishing House, 1947.

The story of the "semistarvation" C.P.S. experiment at the University of Minnesota, in which 32 objectors participated, Guetzkow among them.

Hassler, R. Alfred. *Conscripts of Conscience: The Story of Sixteen Objectors to Conscription.* New York: Fellowship of Reconciliation, 1942.

Biographies of sixteen older objectors (including such men as A. J. Muste and Evan Thomas) who refused to register for the draft. With one exception, they were unmolested by the government.

Jacob, Philip E. *The Origins of Civilian Public Service.* Washington: National Service Board for Religious Objectors, 1946.

An examination of the circumstances under which the Civilian Public Service system was organized in 1940–1941.

Jones, Thomas E. *Creative Pioneering.* Philadelphia: American Friends Service Committee, 1941.

By the first Executive Director of Friends C.P.S. It reflects Jones's "service and work" philosophy.

Lindner, Robert M. *Stone Walls and Men.* New York: Odyssey Press, 1946.

A psychologist discusses life in prison. Lindner actually lived and worked with federal prisoners during the war and came to know many imprisoned objectors. Chapter 14, "Crime and Ideological Conflict," deals with the objectors, but in a way which pacifists generally thought rather unsympathetic and unfair.

Mennonites and Their Heritage. A Series of Six Studies Designed for Use in Civilian Public Service Camps. Ed. Harold S. Bender. Akron, Pa.: Mennonite Central Committee, 1942. 2d ed., 1944–1945.

The six studies (all very helpful) follow: Harold S. Bender, *Mennonite Origins in Europe;* C. Henry Smith, *Mennonites in America;* Edward Yoder, *Our Mennonite Heritage;* E. G. Kaufman, *Our Mission As a Church of Christ;* Guy F. Hershberger, *Christian Relationships to State and Community;* P. C. Hiebert, *Life and Service in the Kingdom of God.*

Naeve, Lowell, in collaboration with David Wieck. *A Field of Broken Stones*. Glen Gardner, N.J.: Libertarian Press, 1950.

A conscientious objector's 231-page account of his experiences in prison. Naeve provides the accompanying illustrations.

New Jersey State Hospital Unit. *PRN*. 1946.

Work in a mental hospital from the viewpoint of objectors.

Nunnally, Joe. *I Was a Conscientious Objector; In Camp—in Prison—on Parole. A Very Personal Story of Difficulties, of Experiences, of One Who Believes War Is Now Obsolete*. Berkeley, Calif.: Sooner Publishing Co., 1949.

Olmstead, Frank. *They Asked for a Hard Job*. New York: Plowshare Press, 1944.

A sympathetic and incisive account of objectors' work in mental hospitals. By a leader of the War Resisters League.

Reeves, George B. *Men against the State*. Washington: Human Events, 1946.

A pamphlet evaluating the activities of conscientious objectors from the viewpoint of the "resister" type. While not denying the significance of the services performed by objectors in C.P.S., and particularly in hospital units, Reeves nevertheless feels that those objectors who refused to register, walked out of C.P.S., or otherwise refused to cooperate made the most important contributions. They protested the drift toward totalitarianism and slavery. Reeves himself had been associated with the Advisory Section of the National Service Board and with the National Committee for Conscientious Objectors.

Richards, Edward C. M. *They Refuse to Be Criminals*. West Chester, Pa.: Author, 1946.

A discussion of sentencing and imprisonment of objectors, with considerable space given to an analysis of parole methods. The author is highly critical of the whole prison and parole system.

Rohrer, Mary E., and Rohrer, Peter L. (eds.). *The Story of Lancaster County Conference Men in C.P.S.* Smoketown, Pa.: Editors, 1946.

Story of Experiences of Lancaster Mennonite men in C.P.S. Thirty-two chapters contributed by the men themselves.

Sibley, Mulford, and Wardlaw, Ada. *Conscientious Objectors in Prison*. Philadelphia: Pacifist Research Bureau, 1945.

An analysis of the imprisonment of objectors down to the conclusion of hostilities with Japan.

Stafford, William E. *Down in My Heart*. Elgin, Ill.: Brethren Publishing House, 1947.

On C.P.S.

Wagler, David, and Haber, Roman (ed.). *The Story of the Amish in Civilian Public Service.* Boonsboro, Md.: 1945.

Story of the Amish in C.P.S. down to January 1, 1945.

ARTICLES

Albrecht, Paul. "The C.P.S. Evaluation Questionnaire," *Mennonite Quarterly Review,* Jan., 1948.

A discussion of the questionnaire sent to C.P.S. men in Mennonite camps.

Baldwin, R. N. "Conscience under the Draft," *Nation,* 153 (Aug. 9, 1941), 114–116.

By the veteran leader of the American Civil Liberties Union. Some conscientious objectors and their friends charged that Mr. Baldwin was not sufficiently aggressive and critical with respect to protection of objectors' rights.

Bowie, W. R. "Some Choose Jail Rather Than Register; Eight Students of Union Theological Seminary," *Living Age,* 359 (Dec., 1940), 330–333.

Chamberlin, W. H. "American Conscientious Objectors: Wartime Handling of the Small Minority Who Refuse to Fight, a Test of Belief in Freedom of Conscience," *Survey Graphic,* 32 (Nov., 1943), 436–440.

One of the better popular accounts, by the well-known correspondent.

Clyde, W. R. "C.O.'s in the Caribbean," *Christian Century,* Aug. 29, 1945, 978–980.

Crespi, L. P. "Attitudes toward Conscientious Objectors and Some of their Psychological Correlates," *Journal of Psychology,* 18 (July, 1944), 81–117.

A study of public opinion in relation to conscientious objection during World War II. One of the most helpful studies made during the war period. The article includes tables and bibliography.

Dahlke, H. O. "Values and Group Behavior in Two Camps for Conscientious Objectors," *American Journal of Sociology,* 51 (July, 1945), 22–33.

An interesting study by a social psychologist. A bibliography is included.

"Do Ministers Want Exemption?" (editorial). *Christian Century,* 57 (Dec. 4, 1940), 1503–1505.

An attack by the most influential nondenominational Protestant journal on the principle of draft exemption for ministers of religion.

Fifield, W. "Report from a Conscientious Objector," *Harpers,* 190 (Jan., 1945), 189–192.

Geiger, Henry, and Clough, Gordon. "Origins of C.P.S.: Another View," *Fellowship,* Sept., 1946.

Gory, Adrian, and McClelland, David C. "Characteristics of Conscientious Objectors in World War II," *Journal of Consulting Psychology*, XI, No. 5 (1947), 247.

Gristle, M. "Construction of a Scale for Measuring Attitudes toward Militarism and Pacifism," *Journal of Social Psychology*, 11 (May, 1940), 383–391.

The article includes a bibliography.

Hartmann, George W. "The Strength and Weakness of the Pacifist Position as Seen by American Philosophers," *Philosophical Review*, March, 1944.

An educational psychologist who is also a pacifist tries to understand how 75 eminent philosophers evaluate the pacifist position.

High, Stanley. "Church Unmilitant," *New Republic*, 106 (June 22, 1942), 850–852.

A minister's attack on what he considers the churches' failure to support the war with crusading ardor.

Maechtle, L. E., and Gerth, H. H. "Conscientious Objectors as Mental Hospital Attendants," *Sociology and Social Research*, 29 (Sept., 1944), 11–24.

Written by two sociologists, the article includes a bibliography.

Masland, J. W. "Treatment of the Conscientious Objector under the Selective Service Act of 1940," *American Political Science Review*, 36 (Aug., 1942), 697–701.

"Men Starve in Minnesota: Conscientious Objectors Volunteer for Strict Hunger Tests to Study Europe's Food Problem," *Life*, July 30, 1945, pp. 43–46.

A popular treatment.

Thompson, R. E. S. "Onward Christian Soldiers! Nation's Conscientious Objectors Work Out Their Convictions," *Saturday Evening Post*, Aug. 16, 1941, p. 27.

This article is important chiefly because it describes C.P.S. before the major tensions and conflicts had developed. Looking back on it, both supporters and antagonists of C.P.S. would see it as somewhat naïve in its presentation. Illustrated.

Wilcher, Denny. "Shall the C.P.S. Camps Continue? Relationship between the State and the Peace Churches Inherent in the Program," *Christian Century*, 59 (Dec. 16, 1942), 1556–1559.

An early attack on continuance of Church administration.

——. "Conscientious Objectors in Prison," *Christian Century*, 61 (March 8, 1944), 302–304.

PERIODICALS

Periodical literature written by or concerning pacifists and conscientious objectors was enormous in bulk. Many periodicals mentioned but rarely in the above list dealt with problems of conscientious objection, and the large numbers of articulate objectors themselves were forever mimeographing statements, publishing papers, issuing manifestoes. The following list will supplement the more specific bibliography of periodical articles noted above:

The American Friend.
> A journal of Quaker opinion and information.

The Call.
> Official organ of the Socialist Party, U.S.A.

Camp Newspapers.
> Almost every C.P.S. camp published a mimeographed newspaper at one time or another, and several of them were published over a relatively long period of time. They varied greatly in quality and in outlook, but perusing any one of them will give the reader some idea of what went on in the camp involved. Their names were often intriguing—*The Smoke Jumper, Sage 'Pinion, The Olive Branch,* etc.

The Compass.
> Art and literary periodical published by a group of C.P.S. men. The aesthetic and literary quality of *The Compass* was astonishingly high.

The Conscientious Objector.
> Monthly. A journalistic leader of the "left wing."

Consolation.
> A publication of Jehovah's Witnesses. Later called *Awake!*

Fellowship.
> Official organ of the Fellowship of Reconciliation, published monthly.

The Friend.

Friends Intelligencer.

Gospel Messenger.
> An organ of the Church of the Brethren.

The Grapevine.
> A mimeographed periodical devoted to problems of the conscientious objector in prison. Writers in *The Grapevine* exchanged comments and gossip about prison experiences and discussed prison reform.

Mennonite Life.
> An illustrated periodical devoted to discussions of Mennonite culture.

Mennonite Quarterly Review.

Pacifica Views.

Weekly publication issued by a group of "left-wing" objectors on the west coast. Well edited. Hostile to Civilian Public Service, it stirred many a controversy among and about conscientious objectors.

Socialist C.O.

Mimeographed sheet published sporadically during the war by the Socialist Party's Committee on Conscientious Objectors.

World Peace News Letter.

Organ of the Methodist Church's Commission on World Peace.

TABLE OF CASES

Index